Progress in Zoology

Volume 33

Fortschritte der Zoologie
Progress in Zoology

Herausgegeben im Auftrag
der Deutschen Zoologischen Gesellschaft
von Martin Lindauer

Volume 33

Membrane Control of Cellular Activity

International Symposium of the Akademie der Wissenschaften und der Literatur, Mainz
November 14th–16th 1985

Edited by H. Ch. Lüttgau

205 figures and 12 tables

SEMPER BONIS ARTIBUS

Gustav Fischer Verlag · Stuttgart · New York · 1986

The Symposium "Membrane Control of Cellular Activity" held at and supported by the Akademie der Wissenschaften und der Literatur, Mainz
was sponsored by

Bundesministerium für Forschung und Technologie, Bonn;
Bayerisches Staatsministerium für Unterricht und Kultus, München;
Ruhr-Universität, Bochum;
Stiftung Volkswagenwerk, Hannover.

CIP-Kurztitelaufnahme der Deutschen Bibliothek

Membrane control of cellular activity : internat. symposium of the Akad. d. Wiss. u.d. Literatur, Mainz, November 14th – 16th 1985 / ed. by H. Ch. Lüttgau. – Stuttgart ; New York : Fischer, 1986.
(Progress in zoology ; Vol. 33)
ISBN 3-437-30525-5
NE: Lüttgau, Hans Christoph [Hrsg.]; Akademie der Wissenschaften und der Literatur ‹Mainz›; Fortschritte der Zoologie

All business correspondence should be made with:
Gustav Fischer Verlag GmbH & Co KG, Wollgrasweg 49, D-7000 Stuttgart 70
For USA and Canada:
Verlag Chemie International Inc., 303 N.W. 12th Avenue, Deerfield Beach, Florida 33441

Printed by: Laupp & Göbel, Tübingen 3
Printed in Germany

ISBN 3-437-3o525-5
ISBN 0-89574-229-2 NY
ISSN 0071-7991

Preface

Volume 33 of Progress in Zoology includes 35 contributions presented at an International Symposium on «Membrane Control of Cellular Activity», held at the Akademie der Wissenschaften und der Literatur (Mainz) from November 14th to November 16th, 1985. This symposium was organized to discuss interdisciplinarily the great progress achieved in the field of cell activation during recent years. It was prompted by the development of ingenious methods which allowed a new approach to hitherto unsolved problems (in particular: patch-clamp techniques and methods of modern molecular biology and genetic engineering). The volume includes, among others, articles on the structure and function of Na and Ca channels, the modulation of Ca channels by phosphorylation, the application of *Xenopus* oocytes as a tool for molecular cloning of the genes coding for membrane receptors and channels, electro-effector coupling in skeletal muscle and cilia, the role of protein kinase C in exocytosis, cellular processes in vision, in particular the role of cyclic GMP and Ca in these events, and on Na and Ca transport and Na-Ca exchange in nerve, muscle, and red blood cells. The articles by leading scientists from Europe and the United States are written in a comprehensive style. About two thirds of them are review-like contributions, well suited also for non-specialists and for postgraduate seminars, while the remaining articles supplement the major contributions with short reports on recent and partly unpublished results.

My thanks are due to Prof. M. Lindauer, chief editor of Progress in Zoology, for suggesting this symposium and for much helpful advice, to the president and staff of the Akademie der Wissenschaften und der Literatur at Mainz for financial support, generous hospitality and organizing help, and to Profs. H. Reuter (Bern), H. Stieve (Aachen), and my colleagues from Bochum, Prof. G. Boheim and Prof. H. G. Glitsch, for valuable suggestions concerning participants and topics.

H. Ch. Lüttgau

Contents

I. Session
Structure and function of Na^+ and Ca^{2+}-channels

II. Session
Cellular control of channel incorporation and activation

III. Session
Electro-effector coupling

IV. Session
Cellular processes in vision

V. Session
Active Na and Ca transport and Na-Ca exchange in nerve and muscle

List of Participants

Prof. W. ALMERS: Department of Physiology and Biophysics, G414 Health Sciences Building, University of Washington, Seattle, Washington 98195 USA

Prof. P. F. BAKER, F.R.S.: Department of Physiology, King's College London, Strand, London WC2R 2LS, England

Dr. E. BAMBERG: Max-Planck-Institut für Biophysik, Heinrich-Hoffmann-Str. 7, D-6000 Frankfurt 71 (FRG)

Dr. M. BECHEM: Bayer AG, Postfach 101709, D-5600 Wuppertal 1 (FRG)

Prof. G. BOHEIM: Arbeitsgruppe Biophysikalische Chemie von Membranen, Ruhr-Universität Bochum, D-4630 Bochum (FRG)

Prof. J. E. BROWN: Department of Ophthalmology, Washington University School of Medicine, 660 S. Euclid Avenue, St. Louis, MO 63110, USA

Prof. F. R. BÜHLER: Abteilung für Kardiologie, Department Innere Medizin, Kantonsspital Basel, CH-4031 Basel, Schweiz

Prof. W. A. CATTERALL: Department of Pharmacology, SJ-30, School of Medicine, University of Washington, Seattle, Washington 98195, USA

Priv.-Doz. Dr. J. DAUT: Physiologisches Institut Technische Universität München, Biedersteiner Str. 29, D-8000 München 40 (FRG)

Priv.-Doz. Dr. J. W. DEITMER: Institut für Zoologie I, Universität Düsseldorf, D-4000 Düsseldorf (FRG)

Prof. J. DUDEL: Physiologisches Institut der Technischen Universität München, Biedersteiner Str. 29, D-8000 München 40 (FRG)

Dr. D. A. EISNER: Department of Physiology, University College London, Gower Street, London WC1E, 6BT (UK), England

Prof. H. G. GLITSCH: Arbeitsgruppe Muskelphysiologie, Ruhr-Universität Bochum, D-4630 Bochum (FRG)

Dr. H. H. GRÜNHAGEN: BASF, D-6700 Ludwigshafen (FRG)

Prof. K. HAMDORF: Arbeitsgruppe Sehphysiologie, Ruhr-Universität Bochum, D-4630 Bochum (FRG)

Dr. W. HANKE: Lehrstuhl Zellphysiologie, Ruhr-Universität Bochum, D-4630 Bochum (FRG)

Prof. W. HASSELBACH: Max-Planck-Institut für Medizinische Forschung, Postfach 103820, D-6900 Heidelberg (FRG)

Dr. P. HOCHSTRATE: Lehrstuhl Tierphysiologie, Ruhr-Universität Bochum, D-4630 Bochum (FRG)

Prof. F. HOFMANN: Fachr. 3.3 – Physiologische Chemie, Universität des Saarlandes, D-6650 Homburg/Saar (FRG)

Priv.-Doz. Dr. H.-A. KOLB: Fakultät für Biologie, Universität Konstanz, Universitätsstr. 10, D-7750 Konstanz (FRG)

Priv.-Doz. Dr. H. KÜHN: Institut für Neurobiologie der Kernforschungsanlage Jülich GmbH, Postfach 1913, D-5170 Jülich (FRG)

Prof. P. LÄUGER: Abteilung für Biologie der Universität Konstanz, D-7750 Konstanz (FRG)

Prof. M. LINDAUER: Institut für Zoologie, Universität Würzburg, Röntgenring 10, D-8700 Würzburg (FRG)

Prof. H. CH. LÜTTGAU: Lehrstuhl für Zellphysiologie, Ruhr-Universität Bochum, D-4630 Bochum (FRG)

Prof. H. MACHEMER: Arbeitsgruppe Primärprozesse an Rezeptoren, Ruhr-Universität Bochum, D-4630 Bochum (FRG)

Dr. P. A. McNaughton: Physiological Laboratory, Downing Street, Cambridge CB2 3EG, England
Dr. W. Melzer: Lehrstuhl für Zellphysiologie, Ruhr-Universität Bochum, D-4630 Bochum (FRG)
Dr. Ch. Methfessel: Max-Planck-Institut für Biophysikalische Chemie, Postfach 2841, D-3400 Göttingen (FRG)
Prof. H. Meves: I. Physiologisches Institut der Universität des Saarlandes, D-6650 Homburg/Saar (FRG)
Priv.-Doz. Dr. E. Neher: Abteilung für Membranbiophysik, Max-Planck-Institut für Biophysikalische Chemie, Postfach 2841, D-3400 Göttingen (FRG)
Dipl.-Biol. R. Neuhaus: Lehrstuhl für Zellphysiologie, Ruhr-Universität Bochum, D-4630 Bochum (FRG)
Prof. B. Neumcke: I. Physiologisches Institut der Universität des Saarlandes, D-6650 Homburg/Saar (FRG)
Priv.-Doz. Dr. B. Nilius: Julius-Bernstein-Institut für Physiologie, Martin-Luther-Universität, Halle-Wittenberg, DDR-4020 Halle/Saale
Prof. H. Passow: Max-Planck-Institut für Biophysik, Heinrich-Hoffmann-Str. 7, D-6000 Frankfurt a. M. 71 (FRG)
Prof. R. Paulsen: Abteilung Allg. Zoologie, Universität Ulm, Oberer Eselsberg, D-7900 Ulm (FRG)
Dr. D. Pelzer: II. Physiologisches Institut der Universität des Saarlandes, D-6650 Homburg/Saar (FRG)
Dr. L. Pott: Lehrstuhl Zellphysiologie, Arbeitsgruppe Muskelphysiologie, Ruhr-Universität Bochum, D-4630 Bochum (FRG)
Dr. H. Pusch: Lehrstuhl Zellphysiologie, Ruhr-Universität Bochum, D-4630 Bochum (FRG)
Prof. W. Rathmayer: Fakultät Biologie der Universität Konstanz, Postfach 7733, D-7750 Konstanz (FRG)
Prof. H. Reuter: Pharmakologisches Institut der Universität Bern, Friedbühlstr. 49, CH-3012 Bern, Schweiz
Prof. H. Ringsdorf: Institut für Organische Chemie, Universität Mainz, Postfach 3980, D-6500 Mainz (FRG)
Prof. R. Rüdel: Abteilung Allgem. Physiologie, Universität Ulm, Oberer Eselsberg, D-7900 Ulm (FRG)
Priv.-Doz. Dr. B. Sakmann: Max-Planck-Institut für Biophysikalische Chemie, Postfach 2841, D-3400 Göttingen (FRG)
Prof. H. J. Schatzmann: Veterinär-Pharmakologisches Institut der Universität Bern, Länggass-Str. 124, CH-3000 Bern, Schweiz
Prof. M. Schneider: Dept. Biological Chemistry, University of Maryland, School of Medicine, 660 West Redwood Street, Baltimore, Maryland 21201, USA
Prof. I. Schulze: Max-Planck-Institut für Biophysik, Kennedy-Allee 70, D-6000 Frankfurt a. M. (FRG)
Priv.-Doz. Dr. W. Schwarz: Max-Planck-Institut für Biophysik, Heinrich-Hoffmann-Str. 7, D-6000 Frankfurt a. M. 71 (FRG)
Dr. U. Stein: Knoll AG, Postfach 210805, D-6700 Ludwigshafen (FRG)
Prof. Ch. F. Stevens: Section of Molecular Neurobiology, Yale University School of Medicine, 333 Cedar Street, New Haven, Connecticut 06510, USA
Prof. H. Stieve: Institut für Biologie II, RWTH Aachen, Kopernikusstr. 16, D-5100 Aachen (FRG)

Dr. W. Stühmer: Abteilung für Membranbiophysik, Max-Planck-Institut für Biophysikalische Chemie, Postfach 2841, D-3400 Göttingen (FRG)
Dr. Katumi Sumikawa: Lab. of Cellular and Molecular Neurobiology, Dept. of Psychobiology, University of California, Irvine, Irvine, CA 92717, USA
Dr. M. Traut: Knoll AG, Postfach 210805, D-6700 Ludwigshafen (FRG)
Prof. W. Trautwein: II. Physiologisches Institut der Universität des Saarlandes, D-6650 Homburg/Saar (FRG)
Prof. R. W. Tsien: Department of Physiology, Yale University School of Medicine, 333 Cedar Street, New Haven, Connecticut 06510, USA
Prof. W. Ulbricht: Physiologisches Institut der Universität Kiel, Olshausenstr. 40–60, D-2300 Kiel (FRG)
Dr. B. Wagner: Gödecke Aktiengesellschaft, Forschung und Entwicklung, Postfach 569, D-7800 Freiburg (FRG)
Prof. P. De Weer: Department of Physiology and Biophysics, Washington University School of Medicine, St. Louis, Missouri 6110, USA
Dr. E. Wettwer: Pharmakologisches Institut, Klinikum der Gesamthochschule Essen, Hufelandstr. 55, D-4300 Essen (FRG)
Dr. King-Wai Yau: Department of Physiology and Biophysics, University of Texas, Medical Branche, Galveston, TX 77550, USA

I. Session
Structure and function of Na^{+} and Ca^{2+}-channels

Fortschritte der Zoologie, Band 33 · Lüttgau (Hrsg.): Membrane Control
Gustav Fischer Verlag · Stuttgart · New York · 1986

Structure of voltage-sensitive sodium and calcium channels

WILLIAM A. CATTERALL

Department of Pharmacology, SJ-30, University of Washington, Seattle, WA 98195, USA

Nerve and muscle cells are electrically excitable because of the presence in their surface membranes of voltage-sensitive ion channels that are selective for Na^+, K^+, or Ca^{2+}. One class of Na^+ channels and multiple classes of Ca^{2+} and K^+ channels have been described. These channels open and close as a function of membrane voltage allowing rapid movement of the appropriate ions down their concentration gradient carrying ionic current into or out of the cell and thereby depolarizing or hyperpolarizing the membrane potential. The electrical excitability of cells is influenced by the nature and functional properties of their ion channels, the density of ion channels in their surface membrane, and the location of ion channels in different functional compartments. Voltage-sensitive Na^+, K^+, and Ca^{2+} channels each contribute in a specific way to signal processing and transmission. Knowledge of the molecular properties of these critical components of excitable cells will allow new approaches to studies of cell function. In this article, I review the strategy that has been developed to identify the protein components of voltage-sensitive Na^+ and Ca^{2+} channels, purify them, and analyze their functional properties and physiological regulation.

Voltage-sensitive sodium channels

Electrophysiological experiments using the voltage clamp technique have shown that the initial rapid depolarization during an action potential in nerve, skeletal muscle and heart muscle results from rapid voltage-dependent increases in membrane permeability to sodium ions. Many different lines of evidence indicate that a selective transmembrane sodium channel is responsible for the rapid sodium permeability increase during the action potential. Selective ion permeation is mediated by a hydrophilic pore containing a sodium-selective ion coordination site designated the ion selectivity filter (HILLE, 1971, 1972). Ion conductance through the sodium channel is regulated or ‹gated› by two separate processes: activation, which controls the rate and voltage-dependence of the sodium permeability increase following depolarization, and inactivation, which controls the rate and voltage-dependence of the subsequent return of sodium permeability to the resting level during a maintained depolarization (HODGKIN and HUXLEY, 1952). Membrane charge movements associated with voltage-dependent activation of sodium channels have been detected as gating currents and are considered to represent movement of charged components of the sodium channel protein during the conformational changes leading to channel activation (ARMSTRONG and BEZANILLA, 1974). Sodium channel inactivation is thought to be a sequential, relatively voltage-insensitive process which is initiated by the voltage-dependent conformational changes which lead to channel activation (ARMSTRONG and BEZANILLA, 1977; ALDRICH et al., 1983).

Analysis of sodium channel properties by voltage clamp methods has provided a detailed description of the three essential functional properties of sodium channels: voltage-dependent activation, voltage-dependent inactivation, and selective ion transport. However, an understanding of the molecular basis of electrical excitability requires identification of the membrane macromolecules that comprise the ionic channels, solubilization and purification of these channel components, and correlation of their structural features with the known functional properties of sodium channels. This task has required the development of new approaches.

Neurotoxins as molecular probes of sodium channels

Neurotoxins which bind with high affinity and specificity to voltage-sensitive sodium channels and modify their properties have provided the essential tools for identification and purification of sodium channels. Four different groups of neurotoxins which act at four different neurotoxin receptor sites on the sodium channel have been useful in these studies (Table 1). Neurotoxin receptor site 1 binds the water-soluble, heterocyclic guanidines, tetrodotoxin and saxitoxin. These toxins inhibit sodium channel ion transport by binding to a common receptor site which is thought to be located near the extracellular opening of the ion-conducting pore of the sodium channel (reviewed by NARAHASHI, 1974; RITCHIE and ROGART, 1977; CATTERALL, 1980).

Table 1: Neurotoxin Receptor Sites on the Sodium Channel

Site	Neurotoxin	Physiological Effect
1	Tetrodotoxin	Inhibit ion transport
2	Veratridine Batrachotoxin Grayanotoxin Aconitine	Cause persistent activation
3	North African α-scorpion toxins Sea anemone toxins	Slow inactivation
4	American β-scorpion toxins	Enhance activation

Neurotoxin receptor site 2 binds several lipid-soluble toxins including grayanotoxin and the alkaloids veratridine, aconitine and batrachotoxin (reviewed by CATTERALL, 1980; ALBUQUERQUE and DALY, 1976). The competitive interactions among these four toxins at neurotoxin receptor site 2 have been confirmed by direct measurement of specific binding of [^{3}H]batrachotoxin in A 20-α-benzoate to sodium channels (CATTERALL et al., 1981). These toxins cause persistent activation of sodium channels at the resting membrane potential by blocking sodium channel inactivation and shifting the voltage dependence of sodium channel activation to more negative membrane potentials (reviewed by CATTERALL, 1980). Therefore, neurotoxin receptor site 2 is likely to be localized on a region of the sodium channel involved in voltage-dependent activation and inactivation.

Neurotoxin receptor site 3 binds polypeptide toxins purified from North African scorpion venoms or sea anemone nematocysts. These toxins slow or block sodium channel inactivation. They also markedly enhance persistent activation of sodium channels by the lipid-soluble toxins acting at neurotoxin receptor site 2 (reviewed in CATTERALL, 1980). The affinity for binding of [^{125}I] labeled derivatives of the polypeptide toxins to neurotoxin receptor site 3 is reduced by depolarization. The voltage dependence of scorpion toxin binding is closely correlated with the voltage dependence of sodium channel activation. These experiments indicate that neurotoxin receptor site 3 is located on part of the sodium channel which undergoes a conformational change during voltage-dependent channel activation leading to markedly reduced affinity for scorpion toxin. Therefore, scorpion toxin and sea anemone toxin bind to voltage sensing or gating structures of sodium channels.

Neurotoxin receptor site 4 binds a new class of scorpion toxins that has also proved valuable in studies of sodium channels. CAHALAN (1975) showed that the venom of the American scorpion *Centruroides sculpturatus* modifies sodium channel activation rather than inactivation. Pure toxins from several American scorpions have a similar action (WANG and STRICHARTZ, 1982; MEVES et al., 1982; COURAUD et al., 1982). These toxins bind to a new receptor site on the sodium channel (JOVER et al., 1980; BARHANIN et al., 1982) and have therefore been designated β-scorpion toxins.

These several neurotoxins provide specific high affinity probes for distinct regions of the sodium channel structure. They have been used to detect and localize sodium channels in neuronal cells as well as to identify and purify the protein components of sodium channels that bind these toxins and to analyze their structural and functional properties.

Identification of protein components of sodium channels in neurons

Measurements of the distribution and density of sodium channels indicate that, with the exception of the very small amount of specialized membrane at the node of Ranvier, sodium channels are a minor component of excitable membranes. These results emphasize the need for highly specific probes to identify the macromolecules that comprise the sodium channel. The neurotoxins that bind to sodium channels with high affinity and specificity have provided the tools needed in such experiments. Direct chemical identification of sodium channel components *in situ* was first achieved by specific covalent labeling of neurotoxin receptor site 3 with a photoreactive azidonitrobenzoyl derivative of the α-scorpion toxin from *Leiurus quinquestriatus* (BENESKI and CATTERALL, 1980). Analysis of covalently labeled synaptosomes by polyacylamide gel electrophoresis under denaturing conditions in sodium dodecylsulfate (SDS) to separate synaptosomal proteins by size reveals specific covalent labeling of two polypeptides which have subsequently been designated the α and $\beta1$ subunits of the sodium channel. These proteins, as assessed by polyacrylamide gel electrophoresis in SDS, have molecular weights of 270,000 and 36,000 respectively. The covalent labeling of these two polypeptides in synaptosomes was shown to be specific by inhibition by competition with excess unlabeled scorpion toxin or by block of voltage-dependent binding of scorpion toxin by membrane depolarization.

The β-scorpion toxins derived from American scorpion venoms have also been used to label neurotoxin receptor site 4 on the sodium channel (BARHANIN et al., 1983; DARBON et al., 1983). Toxin γ from *Tityus serrulatus* was covalently attached to its receptor site by crosslinking with disuccinimidyl suberate. A single polypeptide of 270,000 daltons was labeled in rat brain synaptosomes. Photoreactive derivatives of Toxin II from *Centruroides suffusus* covalently label polypeptides of 255,000 and 35,000 daltons in rat brain synaptosomes that are likely to be the α and $\beta1$ subunits of the sodium channel. Taken together, these covalent labeling results indicate that neurotoxin receptor sites 3 and 4 are both located near the contact regions of the α and $\beta 1$ subunits of the sodium channel.

The Molecular Size of the Sodium Channel

The first indications of the molecular size of the neuronal sodium channel *in situ* were derived from radiation inactivation studies (LEVINSON and ELLORY, 1973). In these experiments, membrane preparations from pig brain were irradiated with x-rays and the decrease in the number of functional tetrodotoxin binding sites was measured as a function of radiation dose. From these data, the size of the membrane target can be determined since larger targets are more likely to be hit and are therefore inactivated at a lower radiation dose. Applying target theory, LEVINSON and ELLORY (1973) concluded that a structure of 230,000 daltons was required for toxin binding. These experiments have recently been repeated by BARHANIN et al. (1983) who compared the target size of the sodium channel assessed by either tetrodotoxin binding or *Tityus serrulatus* toxin binding. In each case, the target size was approximately 270,000 daltons in reasonable agreement with the earlier work. This size estimate might correspond to the molecular weight of the entire sodium channel or to the molecular weight of a protein subunit that is essential for binding these neurotoxins.

The molecular size of the intact sodium channel protein has been measured by hydrodynamic studies of the detergent-solubilized channel. The STX and TTX binding component of sodium channels was first solubilized with retention of high affinity and specificity of toxin binding from garfish olfactory nerve membrane using nonionic detergents (BENZER and RAFTERY, 1973; HENDERSON and WANG, 1972). Similar techniques have now been applied to sodium channels in mammalian brain and skeletal muscle (KRUEGER et al., 1979; CATTERALL et al., 1979; BARCHI et al., 1980). In contrast to the ease of solubilization of the sodium channel with retention of STX and TTX binding activity at neurotoxin receptor site 1, neurotoxin receptor site 3 loses high affinity neurotoxin binding activity on solubilization. The molecular weight of the solubilized sodium channel from rat brain and skeletal muscle has been estimated by hydrodynamic studies to be 601,000 (HARTSHORNE et al., 1980; BARCHI and MURPHY, 1981). Since the detergent/channel complex contains 0.9 g Triton X-100 and phosphatidyl choline per gram of protein, the molecular weight of the sodium channel protein solubilized from rat brain is 316,000 (32). This represents the size of the entire sodium channel as solubilized in detergents and corresponds to a complex of three nonidentical protein subunits as described below. If the channel protein is spherical in shape, the diameter indicated by these results is 118 A. Thus, the channel protein is much larger than the postulated transmembrane pore through which Na^+ moves which is proposed to be 3 A × 5 A at its narrowest point, the ion selectivity filter.

Purification of the solubilized saxitoxin/tetrodotoxin receptor of the sodium channel

Although the saxitoxin receptor of the sodium channel was successfully solubilized several years ago, the marked instability of the toxin binding activity prevented progress on the purification of the sodium channel until the discovery by AGNEW et al. (1978) that addition of phospholipid markedly stabilized the saxitoxin receptor from electroplax. These investigators were able to achieve substantial purification of the saxitoxin receptor by ion exchange chromatography and gel filtration resulting in a preparation that was approximately 50 % pure (AGNEW et al., 1980). The only protein component of this partially purified preparation which was clearly correlated with toxin binding activity was a 260,000 dalton polypeptide. This protein is likely to be analogous to the α subunit of the sodium channel from mammalian brain that was identified in intact membranes by covalent labeling with a photoreactive scorpion toxin derivative (Beneski and Catterall, 1980).

Application of similar procedures to sodium channels solubilized from mammalian skeletal muscle and brain also gives substantial purification (Barchi et al., 1980; Hartshorne and Catterall, 1981). In addition, affinity chromatography on wheat germ lectin/Sepharose columns provides a further enrichment of the saxitoxin binding activity from these tissues. The specific adsorbtion and elution of the saxitoxin receptor from this lectin affinity column indicates that it is a glycoprotein containing N-acetylglucosamine and/or sialic acid residues. Saxitoxin receptor preparations that are highly purified can now be obtained from either rat skeletal muscle or rat brain using a combination of these procedures as assessed by the specific activity for binding of saxitoxin and the number of protein bands identified on polyacrylamide gels of the purified protein.

Subunit composition of the purified mammalian sodium channel

The subunit composition of these highly purified sodium channel preparations from eel electroplax, rat brain, and rat skeletal muscle differs somewhat and therefore each is considered individually. Analysis of highly purified preparations of sodium channels from rat brain by polyacrylamide gel electrophoresis in the presence of sodium dodecylsulfate (SDS) without reduction of protein disulfide bonds reveals two protein components of $M_r \sim$ 300,000 and $M_r \sim$ 36,000 that are associated with the saxitoxin binding activity (Hartshorne and Catterall, 1981, 1984; Hartshorne et al., 1982). These two polypeptide bands account for 90 % of the protein stain intensity in silver-stained gels. Reduction of protein disulfide bonds by treatment with β-mercaptoethanol cleaves the protein of $M_r \sim$ 300,000 into two polypeptides of $M_r \sim$ 260,000 and $M_r \sim$ 33,000 (Hartshorne et al., 1982). In previous experiments, the gel electrophoresis conditions used did not allow clear resolution of the polypeptides of $M_r \sim$ 36,000 and Mr ~ 33,000. Therefore, it was necessary to first separate the disulfide-linked complex of polypeptides of $M_r \sim$ 260,000 and $M_r \sim$ 33,000 from the polypeptide of $M_r \sim$ by gel filtration in SDS without reduction and then to demonstrate the presence of the polypeptide of $M_r \sim$ 33,000 by reduction of the complex followed by gel electrophoresis. We have now devised new conditions of gel electrophoresis which allow consistent resolution of these two polypeptides (Messner and Catterall, 1985). Electrophoresis in polyacrylamide gels with reduced crosslinking ([acrylamide]/[methlyene bisacrylamide] = 30/0.20) resolves three polypeptides of $M_r \sim$ 260,000, 36,000, and 33,000 (Figure 1). They are designated the α, $\beta 1$, and $\beta 2$ subunits of the sodium channel (Hartshorne et al., 1982; Hartshorne and Catterall, 1984). As illustrated in Figure 1, the α and $\beta 2$ subunits are covalently linked by one or more disulfide bonds whereas the $\beta 1$ subunit is associated with the complex by noncovalent forces. The total molecular weight of the subunits is 329,000 in close agreement with the estimated molecular weight of the entire sodium channel complex of 316,000. The ratio of stain intensities of the individual subunits also is in agreement with a molar ratio of subunits of 1:1:1. Thus, the data available at present are in best agreement with α subunit stoichiometry of α_1, $(\beta)_1$, $(\beta 2)_1$ for the sodium channel from rat brain.

The initial analyses of the sodium channel purified from mammalian skeletal muscle (Barchi et al., 1980) revealed polypeptides with molecular weights of 64,000, 60,000 and 53,000, but more recent work has shown that these were not components of the sodium channel. Barchi (1983) subsequently reported that the purified saxitoxin receptor from skeletal muscle contains three major polypeptide components with molecular weights of 125,000 to 250,000, 48,000 and a doublet at 38,000. However, it now appears that only

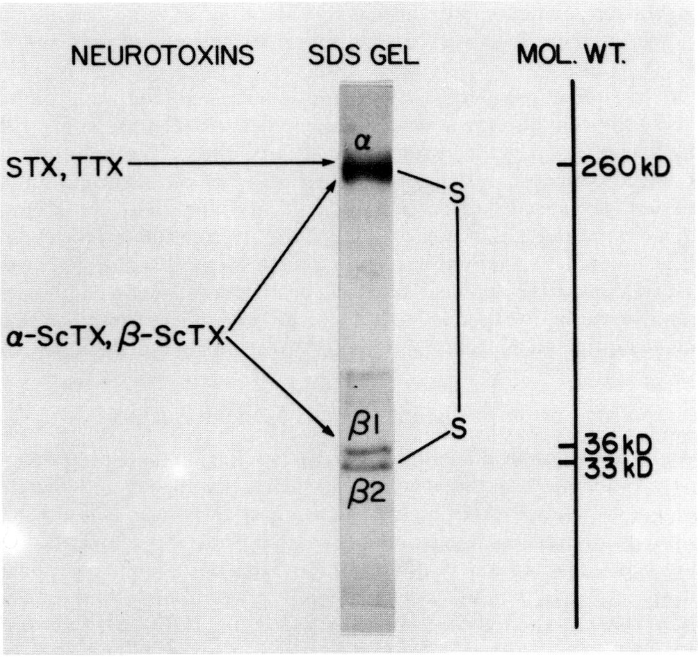

Fig. 1: Properties of the sodium channel subunits. A purified preparation of sodium channel was dissociated by incubation at 100 °C in SDS and β-mercaptoethanol and analyzed by electrophoresis in polyacrylamide gels with a low ratio of cross linking ([acrylamide]/[bisacrylamide] = 30/0.2) as described by MESSNER and CATTERALL (1985). The α, β1, and β2 subunits, as visualized by silver staining, are indicted along with the sites of covalent attachment of photoreactive neurotoxin derivatives, the intersubunit disulfide bonds, and the subunit molecular weights.

polypeptides with molecular weights of 260,000 and 38,000 are components of the sodium channel (KRANER et al., 1985). Thus, it appears that the sodium channels from both rat brain and skeletal muscle have one large and two small subunits.

In contrast to these results with sodium channels from mammalian nerve and muscle, highly purified preparations of the tetrodotoxin binding component of the sodium channel from electric eel electroplax appear to consist of a single polypeptide with a molecular weight of 260,000 (MILLER et al., 1983; NAKAYAMA et al., 1982; NORMAN et al., 1983b). Apparently, the β subunits of the mammalian sodium channel are not present in the electroplax or are not required for tetrodotoxin binding and are lost in the purification procedures. The subunit composition of sodium channels purified from these three sources is summarized in Table 2.

Reconstitution of sodium channel function from purified components

The purified channel binds [^{3}H] saxitoxin and tetrodotoxin with the same affinity as the native sodium channel and therefore contains neurotoxin receptor site 1 of the sodium channel in an active form. The purified channel also contains the α and β1 subunits that

Table 2: Molecular Properties of the Sodium Channel Purified from Different Tissues

Tissue	Molecular Weight	Subunits
Electroplax	–	260,000
Brain	316,000	α: 260,000 β1: 36,000 β2: 33,000
Skeletal Muscle	314,000	250,000 38,000

were identified as components of neurotoxin receptor site 3 by photoaffinity labeling with scorpion toxin, although after solubilization the binding activity for scorpion toxin is lost. However, the purified channel does not have binding activity for neurotoxins at receptor site 2 and cannot transport sodium in the detergent-solubilized state. Reconstitution of these sodium channel functions from purified components is the only rigorous proof that the proteins identified and purified on the basis of their neurotoxin binding activity are indeed sufficient to form a functional voltage-sensitive ion channel. In addition, successful reconstitution will provide a valuable experimental preparation for biochemical analysis of the structure and function of sodium channels.

Several groups have successfully restored aspects of sodium channel function from detergent solubilized brain membranes showing that detergent solubilization does not irreversibly destroy channel function. More recently, sodium channel ion transport has been successfully reconstituted from sodium channels substantially purified from electric eel, rat brain and skeletal muscle (TALVENHEIMO et al., 1982; WEIGELE and BARCHI, 1982; TANAKA et al., 1983; ROSENBERG et al., 1984). We have now applied these methods to essentially homogeneous preparations of sodium channels from rat brain (TAMKUN et al., 1984). Purified sodium channels in Triton X-100 are mixed with phosphatidylcholine in Triton X-100 and the detergent is removed by adsorbtion to polystyrene beads. As the detergent is removed, phosphatidylcholine vesicles with a mean diameter of 1800 A are formed containing an average of 0.75 to 2 sodium channels per vesicle. The functional activities of the sodium channel can then be assessed in neurotoxin binding and ion flux experiments.

Figure 2 illustrates the time course of $^{22}Na^+$ influx into phosphatidylcholine vesicles containing purified sodium channels. In these experiments, the vesicle preparation was incubated for 2 min with veratridine to activate sodium channels and then diluted into medium containing $^{22}Na^+$ to initiate influx into vesicles. Influx into vesicles under control conditions is slow. Incubation with veratridine increases the initial rate of influx 10 to 15 fold. When tetrodotoxin is present in both the intravesicular and extravesicular phases, the veratridine-dependent increase in initial rate of $^{22}Na^+$ influx is nearly completely blocked. Half-maximal activation is observed with 29 μM veratridine and half-maximal inhibition with 14 nM tetrodotoxin in close agreement with the corresponding values for the action of these toxins on native sodium channels. These results show that the purified sodium channel regains the ability to mediate neurotoxin-stimulated ion flux after incorporation into phosphatidylcholine vesicles. Evidently, the purified channel retains neurotoxin receptor site 2 and the ion conducting pore of the sodium channel.

Ion transport by neurotoxin-activated sodium channels in neural membranes is selective, although the rate of transport of large cations such as Rb^+ and Cs^+ relative to the rate of transport of Na^+ is significantly greater than when channels are activated by membrane

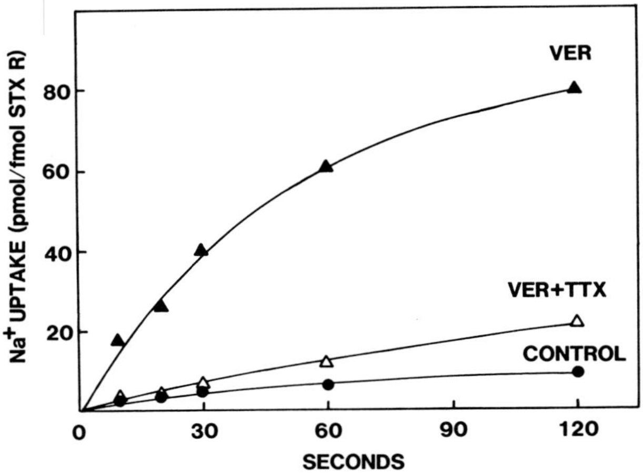

Fig. 2: Neurotoxin-activated ^{22}Na influx mediated by purified and reconstituted sodium channels. Sodium channels were purified as described by HARTSHORNE and CATTERALL (1984) and incorporated into phosphatidylcholine vesicles as described by TAMKUN et al. (1984). The rate of $^{22}Na^+$ influx was measured for the indicated times in the presence of no additions (●), 100 μ veratridine (VER, ▲) or 100 veratridine plus 1 μM tetrodotoxin (TTX, △) added to both sides of the membrane.

depolarization. The ion selectivity of the purified and reconstituted sodium channels has been determined by measuring the initial rate of influx of various radiolabeled cations through channels activated by veratridine or batrachotoxin (TANAKA et al., 1983; TAMKUN et al., 1984). The purified and reconstituted sodium channels from mammalian brain and skeletal muscle retain ion selectivity with permeability ratios relative to Na^+ that compare favorably to those of native sodium channels activated by neurotoxins as summarized in Table 3.

The results of Figure 2 show that at least a fraction of the sodium channels in the most highly purified preparations from rat brain can mediate selective neurotoxin-activated ion transport after incorporation into phospholipid vesicles. Two approaches have been taken to estimating how many of the reconstituted sodium channels contribute to our ion flux measurements. First, we have compared the ion transport rates measured in purified and reconstituted sodium channel preparations to those measured for veratridine-activated

Table 3: Selectivity of Native or Purified and Reconstituted Sodium Channels Activated by Neurotoxins

Ion	Permeability Ratios			
	Native Na^+ Channels		Purified Na^+ Channels	
	Neuro-blastoma	Node of Ranvier	Brain	Skeletal Muscle
Na^+	1.0	1.0	1.0	1.0
K^+	0.17	0.45	–	0.15
Rb^+	0.08	0.27	0.25	0.02
Cs^+	0.04	0.15	0.12	0.01

sodium channels in neuroblastoma cells and synaptosomes. This comparison shows that the transport rate measured in ions/min/STX receptor site is 33% to 70% of that in native membranes suggesting that at least 33% to 70% of the reconstituted sodium channels are active. In a second approach, we have compared the fraction of vesicles that contain sodium channels to the fraction of vesicles whose internal volume is accessible to veratridine-activated sodium channels. Assuming that sodium channels are distributed among vesicles according to a Poisson distribution, this comparison leads to a range of 30% to 70% for the fraction of active channels depending upon whether active vesicles containing more than 1 channel are assumed to have 1 active channel or all active channels. Both of these estimates indicate that a minimum of 30% of the reconstituted sodium channels are active. Since the sodium channel preparation from rat brain is 90% pure and no single contaminant comprises as much as 1% of the protein, we conclude that the purified complex of the α, $\beta 1$, and $\beta 2$ subunits are sufficient to mediate selective neurotoxin-activated ion flux.

While sodium channels reconstituted into phosphatidylcholine vesicles can transport sodium, these channels do not bind α-scorpion toxin at neurotoxin receptor site 3. In contrast, if purified sodium channels from rat brain are incorporated into vesicles composed of a mixture of phosphatidylcholine and brain lipids, scorpion toxin binding is recovered. The toxin binding reaction is of high affinity (K_D = 43 nM) and a mean of 0.76 $\pm$ 0.08 mol scorpion toxin is bound per mol of purified sodium channel (Tamkun et al., 1984). The phospholipid components of the brain lipid mixture that are required for efficient restoration of scorpion toxin binding have been determined by reconstitution of sodium channels in defined lipid mixtures. Addition of either phosphatidylethanolamine or phosphatidylserine from brain to the reconstitution mixture as 35% to 60% of the lipid mass restores high affinity scorpion toxin binding as efficiently as the rat brain lipid mixture (Table 4). Other brain lipid components do not have a marked effect. Evidently, an appropriate mixture of brain phospholipids is necessary to restore the normal function of neurotoxin receptor site 3 on the sodium channel.

Table 4: Effect of Vesicle Phospholipid Composition on Recovery of Scorpion Toxin Binding

Phospholipid$^{\Sigma}$	Ratio (%)	Scorpion Toxin Binding (fmol)
PC/BL	40/60	1.10
PC	100	0.24
PC/PE	65/35	1.25
PC/PS	65/35	0.71
PC/PE/PS	50/35/15	1.20

$^{\Sigma}$ The abbreviations are: PC, phosphatidylcholine; BL, brain lipid; PE, phosphatidylethanolamine; PS, phosphatidylserine.

The results of these reconstitution experiments show that the purified sodium channel preparation from rat brain consisting of a stoichiometric complex of the α, $\beta 1$, and $\beta 2$ subunits is sufficient to mediate most of the functions of the sodium channel that can be measured using biochemical methods. These include neurotoxin binding and action at neurotoxin receptor sites 1 through 3 and selective neurotoxin-activated ion flux. However, in excitable membranes sodium channels are normally activated and inactivated by changes in membrane potential. In order to examine this aspect of the function of purified and reconstituted sodium channels, it is necessary to record their activity electrically on the millisecond time scale. As a first step in that direction, we have employed the methods of MONTAL (1974) and KRUEGER et al. (1983) to fuse reconstituted phospholipid vesicles to preformed planar phospholipid bilayers in a bath equipped for voltage clamp recording. Treatment of bilayers with batrachotoxin causes the appearance of single channel events of the type illustrated in Figure 3. These channels are characterized by a single channel conductance of 23 pS at 20 °C and 0.5 M NaCl (HARTSHORNE et al., 1984) in close agreement with values for native sodium channels activated by batrachotoxin (KRUEGER et al., 1983). The channels are reproducibly blocked by tetrodotoxin with a K_I of 10 nM at −60 mV. The fraction of time an individual channel spends in the open state is strongly voltage-dependent between −130 mV and −60 mV with a 50% open probability at −98 mV (HARTSHORNE et al., 1984). These values are also in close agreement with those for batrachotoxin-activated native sodium channels (KRUEGER et al., 1983; HUANG et al., 1984). Evidently, the purified and reconstituted sodium channel retains the high ionic conductance and voltage-sensitivity of native sodium channels. Recording of voltage-activated sodium currents in the absence of neurotoxins requires more rapid time response than is possible with the current recording apparatus. Experiments are in progress to assess this final aspect of sodium channel function.

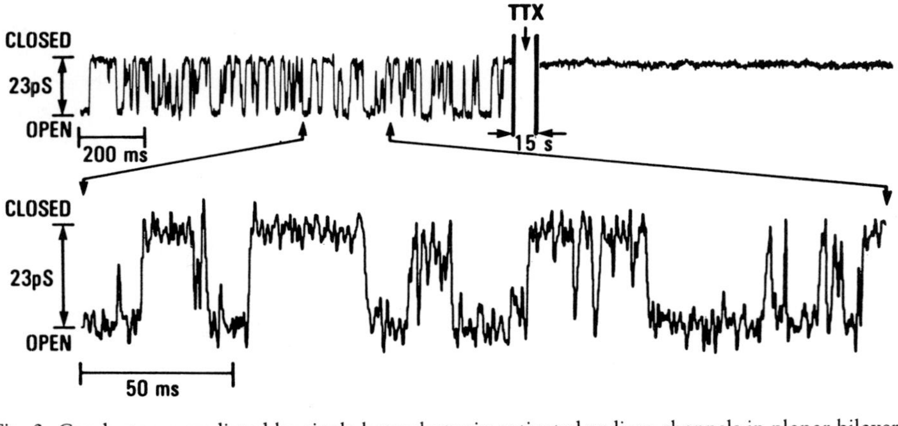

Fig. 3: Conductance mediated by single batrachotoxin-activated sodium channels in planar bilayers. Sodium channels were purified as described by HARTSHORNE and CATTERALL (1984) and incorporated into phospholipid vesicles composed of 65 % phosphatidylethanolamine and 35 % phosphatidylcholine as described by FELLER et al., (1985). The reconstituted vesicles were placed in the cis compartment of planar bilayer chamber (MONTAL, 1974) and vesicles allowed to fuse to the planar bilayer at 22 °C (KRUEGER et al., 1983; HARTSHORNE et al., 1984). Batrachotoxin was added to the trans chamber to activate sodium channels. No activity was observed without toxin treatment as expected for native sodium channels. Addition of tetrodotoxin (3 μM final concentration) to the cis chamber rapidly blocked the observed single channel currents.

Functional roles of sodium channel subunits

A number of lines of evidence indicate that the α subunit of the sodium channel is exposed to the extracellular environment: it is glycosylated (MILLER et al., 1983; BARCHI,

1983; MESSNER and CATTERALL, 1985) and it is covalently labeled by α- and -scorpion toxins (BENESKI and CATTERALL, 1980; BARHANIN et al., 1983; DARBON et al., 1983) and by tetrodotoxin derivatives (LOMBET et al., 1983) which act only on the extracellular side of the channel. The α subunit is also exposed on the intracellular side of the membrane since it is phosphorylated on 4 sites by cAMP-dependent protein kinase within intact synaptosomes (COSTA and CATTERALL, 1984a) and intact brain neurons in cell culture[1]. Thus, the α subunit is a transmembrane polypeptide. Its size allows numerous membrane-spanning segments and could easily form a transmembrane pore as illustrated in Figure 4.

Both the $\beta 1$ and $\beta 2$ subunits of the sodium channel appear to be exposed at the extracellular surface. Each is heavily glycosylated with more than 30% of the apparent mass due to carbohydrate (MESSNER and CATTERALL, 1985). The $\beta 1$ subunit is covalently labeled by α- and β-scorpion toxins which act on the extracellular surface of the sodium channel (BENESKI and CATTERALL, 1980; DARBON et al., 1983). These two subunits have not been shown to be exposed at the intracellular surface. Since their protein mass is small (23,000 and 21,000, respectively) and much of their mass must be extracellular to accomodate attachment of carbohydrate, they may not have regions which protrude from the cytoplasmic surface of the membrane (Figure 4).

The functional role of individual sodium channel subunits has been examined by several approaches. The sites of neurotoxin binding have been identified by covalent labeling as described above. Neurotoxin receptor sites 1 and 3 are located on or near the α and $\beta 1$ subunits, but not the $\beta 2$ subunits. The functional saxitoxin/tetrodotoxin receptor purified from electroplax is composed of only a single glycoprotein of 260,000 analogous to the α subunit of the sodium channel from mammalian sources (NORMAN et al., 1983b; AGNEW

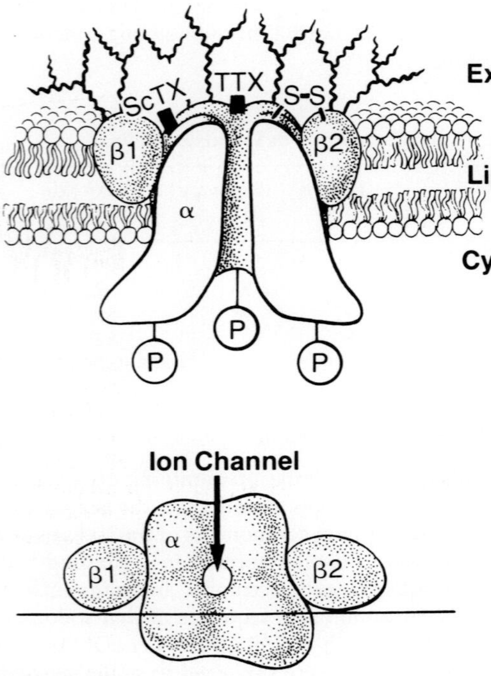

Fig. 4: A structural model of the sodium channel.

et al., 1980; MILLER et al., 1983; NAKAYAMA et al., 1982). Thus, in electroplax, this polypeptide is autonomous in saxitoxin and tetrodotoxin binding in solubilized form. In addition, purified preparations can be incorporated into phospholipid vesicles (ROSENBERG et al., 1984a) or planar bilayers (ROSENBERG et al., 1984b) with recovery of normal ion transport properties. These results are consistent with the hypothesis that this single polypeptide is sufficient for physiological function, but the low rates of ion flux measured and the small number of functional single channels observed do not yet allow a definitive conclusion to be drawn from these data.

Selective removal of the $\beta1$ and $\beta2$ subunits from the purified mammalian sodium channel complex under mild conditions provides a useful approach to assessment of their functional role. The $\beta1$ subunit can be removed by treatment at high ionic strength (1.0 M $MgCl_2$) followed by sucrose gradient sedimentation (MESSNER and CATTERALL, 1986). Dissociation of $\beta1$ is accompanied by stoichiometric loss of saxitoxin binding (Table 5). Both dissociation of $\beta1$ and loss of saxitoxin binding are prevented in the presence of tetrodotoxin. Thus, the binding energy of tetrodotoxin is sufficient to stabilize the $\alpha\beta1$ complex against dissociation. This thermodynamic linkage between binding of tetrodotoxin and binding of the $\beta1$ subunit by the α subunit indicates that the conformation of the α subunit of the rat brain sodium channel having high affinity for saxitoxin and tetrodotoxin requires association with the $\beta1$ subunit, at least in detergent-solubilized form. In contrast to these results which suggest an intimate association between the α and $\beta1$ subunits in maintaining a functional state of the channel, the disulfide-linked $\beta2$ subunit can be selectively removed by reduction of disulfide bonds in the presence of tetrodotoxin with no loss of saxitoxin binding (MESSNER and CATTERALL, 1986). Moreover, the $\alpha\beta1$ complex is sufficient to mediate neurotoxin-activated ion flux and voltage-dependent scorpion toxin binding when incorporated into phospholipid vesicles. Thus, these experiments indicate a requirement for $\beta1$, but not $\beta2$, in maintaining function of the purified and reconstituted sodium channel.

Table 5: Role of $\beta1$ and $\beta2$ Subunits in Saxitoxin Binding

Treatment	Percent $\beta1$	Recovery $\beta2$	Saxitoxin Binding
None	100	100	100
1.0M $MgCl_2$	8	96	2
1.0M $MgCl_2$ + 10μM TTX	92	98	89
1.65mM DTT + μM TTX	89	12	82

A structural model of sodium channel function

The availability of highly purified, functional preparations of sodium channels from various tissues has provided the necessary tools to undertake the isolation of cDNA clones encoding the primary structure of the protein components of the sodium channel. NODA et al. (1984) screened cDNA expression libraries formed in a plasmid vector with both antisera against the sodium channel from eel electroplax and oligonucleotide probes encoding known short segments of the amino acid sequence of that sodium channel which, as purified, consists of a single glycoprotein of 260,000. Short cDNAs were isolated and used to identify long cDNA clones which were subjected to sequence analysis to deduce the complete amino acid sequence of the protein. The inferred sequence consists of 1820 residues with a total size of 208.321 daltons in reasonable agreement with the size of the purified, deglycosylated protein from electroplax (180,000, AGNEW et al., 1983) and the deglycosylated α subunit of the sodium channel from rat brain (220,000, MESSNER and CATTERALL, 1985). In a parallel series of experiments, AULD et al. (1985) used antisera directed against the α subunit of the rat brain sodium channel to identify cDNA clones in a bacteriophage expression library, determined their nucleotide sequence, and deduced the corresponding amino acid sequence of the α subunit of the mammalian brain sodium channel. The average homology between the two polypeptides is 60 %.

Homology matrix comparison of the deduced sequence reveals the presence of four internally repeated domains of approximately 250 amino acid residues having greater than 50 % homology in both the sequences from electroplax (106) and rat brain (107). This high degree of sequence homology is strong evidence that these four domains arose from a common ancestor by gene duplication, and that they adopt similar secondary structures in pseudosymmetric orientations in the channel structure. The amino acid sequence of the α subunit also supports the view that it is a transmembrane polypeptide with multiple membrane-spanning segments. Analysis of each domain for hydropathy and probable secondary structure led NODA et al. (1984) to propose that each adopts a similar configuration across the membrane. Each repeated domain contains four to six regions of predicted α helix which are sufficiently hydrophobic to be assigned as transmembrane segments. All of the predicted transmembrane segments are in these four homologous domains.

The structures of two high conductance ionic channels are known in more detail than the sodium channel and thus provide useful models for the sodium channel. Gap junction channels consist of symmetrical hexagonal arrays of six identical subunits in the surface membrane of each cell. The subunits of each hexameric connexon are approximately cylindrical and are oriented perpendicular to the plane of the membrane (UNWIN and ZAMPIGHI, 1980). Electron diffraction and image reconstruction show that a transmembrane channel is formed at the center of each hexagonal array of subunits. The nicotinic acetylcholine receptor consists of a pseudosymmetric pentagonal array of 5 homologous subunits (reviewed by POPOT and CHANGEUX, 1984). As in the gap junction channel, a transmembrane channel is formed in the center of this symmetrical array of subunits with their long axes perpendicular to the membrane (KISTLER et al., 1982). These two examples suggest the generalization that high conductance ionic channels will form their transmembrane pore at the center of symmetrical arrays of homologous structural units.

The amino acid sequence of the α subunit of the sodium channel contains four internally homologous transmembrane domains as discussed above (NODA et al., 1984; AULD et al., 1985). In light of the structure of the ionic channels of gap junctions and nicotinic acetylcholine receptors, NODA et al. (1984) proposed that the transmembrane pore of the sodium channel is formed at the center of a square array of the four transmembrane domains. The suggestion that this polypeptide can form a functional ion channel by itself is supported by reconstitution studies on the purified sodium channel from electroplax and the suggestion that this is the only transmembrane subunit of the channel. Thus, the sodium channel may accomplish with homologous domains of a single polypeptide what the gap junction channel and the nicotinic acetylcholine receptor do with arrays of homologous subunits. This proposal is illustrated in Figure 4.

Activation of the sodium channel is considered to be a voltage-driven conformational change in which the equivalent of approximately six positive charges in the channel structure move outward across the membrane permeability barrier or a larger number of charges move a shorter distance across the membrane (ARMSTRONG, 1981). The movement of protein bound charge gives rise to gating current and provides the driving force for conformational change. The requirement for such large charge movements within the sodium channel protein focuses attention on the regions of concentrated positive and negative charge in the sodium channel structure. Each homologous domain contains a unique segment of concentrated positive charge in which there are 5 or 6 repeats of lysine or arginine followed by two hydrophobic residues. NODA et al. (1984) suggested that these regions might be involved in channel gating. However, their topological model placed these segments on the cytoplasmic side of the membrane where they would be little affected by the membrane electrical field and no specific suggestions of gating mechanism were made. I have previously proposed a specific mechanism whereby these charged elements might interact to mediate voltage-dependent gating: the *Sliding Helix Model* (CATTERALL, 1986).

In considering how gating charge might be transfered across the membrane, ARMSTRONG (1981) suggested a model in which each gating element contains a row of paired positive and negative charges that extends across the membrane and acts as a charge transfer mechanism. Changes in electric field cause translocation of the negative charges relative to the positive charges resulting in loss of a positive charge on the intracellular side of the protein and appearance of a positive charge on the extracellular side. Thus, full

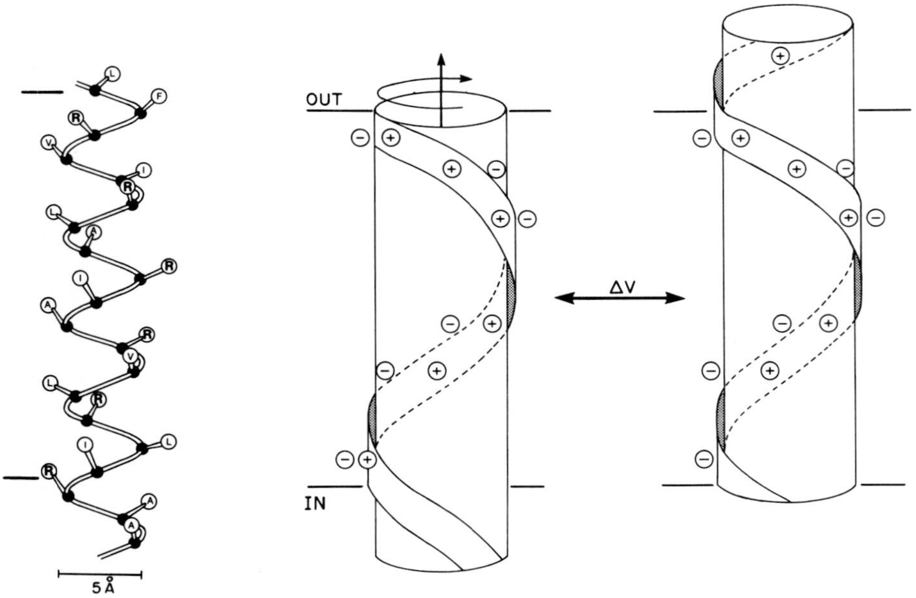

Fig. 5: The Sliding Helix model of voltage-dependent gating. The proposed transmembrane S4 helix is illustrated as a cylinder with a spiral ribbon of positive charge. At the resting membrane potential (left), all positively charged residues are paired with fixed negative charges on other transmembrane segments of the channel and the transmembrane segment is held in that position by the negative internal membrane potential. Depolarization reduces the force holding the positive charges in their inward position. The S4 helix is then proposed to undergo a screw-like motion through a rotation of approximately 60 and an outward displacement of approximately 5.4 Å. This movement leaves an unpaired negative charge on the inward surface of the membrane and reveals an unpaired positive charge on the outward surface to give a net charge transfer (ΔQ) of +1. Note that all intramembranous positive charges are paired in both conformations.

charge translocation is achieved without movement of individual charged species fully across the bilayer. The amphipathic α-helices formed by the positively charged segments of the sodium channel are ideally suited for mediating such charge transfer. If they are postulated to span the membrane, this helix forms a rigid structural element placing positive charges at regular intervals across the permeability barrier. Negative charges are then postulated to form ion pairs with each of the positive charges of the helices.

Figure 5 illustrates such a hypothetical voltage-sensing element. All charges are neutralized in ion pair interactions. Depolarization applies a force to the intramembranous charges causing negative charges to move inward and positive charges to move outward. A spiral movement of the α-helix one turn (5.4°A) with respect to the array of negative charges, creates an unneutralized positive charge in the extracellular compartment and an unneutralized negative charge in the intracellular compartment for a gating charge movement of +1. Movement of amino acid residues over similar distances have been observed in studies of conformational changes in much smaller proteins and, therefore, seem plausible. This movement of the sliding α-helix then initiates a conformational change in its domain as one step in channel activation.

Activation of the sodium channel follows a sigmoidal time course indicating that the channel protein must pass through multiple (at least 3) nonconducting states before channel activation. Analysis of gating current data suggests there are 5 transitions before activation occurs and the last requires movement of twice as much gating charge. If each of the four homologous domains contains a voltage-sensing element analogous to that in Figure 6 and undergoes an independent voltage-driven conformational change, a sequence of 4 changes of state is expected before activation. The sliding helix model of voltage-

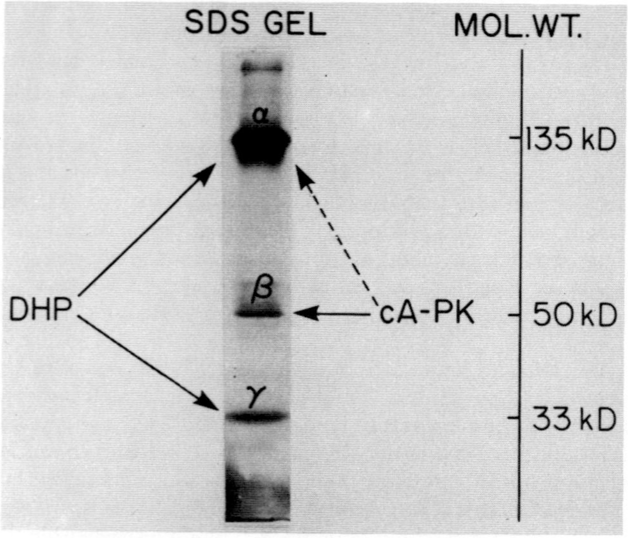

Fig. 6: Subunit composition of the calcium antagonist receptor. The calcium antagonist receptor was solubilized and purified from skeletal muscle transverse tubule membranes as previously described (Curtis and Catterall, 1984). The peak fraction from the final sucrose gradient was denatured in SDS and β-mercaptoethanol and analyzed by polyacrylamide gel electrophoresis. The migration positions of the α (M_r = 135,000), β (M_r = 50,000), and γ (M_r = 33,000) subunits are indicated.

sensing therefore provides a mechanism to connect the sigmoid time course of channel activation with the presence of four homologous domains.

Movement of 6 positive charges outward through the membrane permeability barrier accompanies activation of the sodium channel (ARMSTRONG, 1981). The voltage-sensing element depicted in Figure 6 mediates a movement of gating charge of +1. In fact, the S4 segments of domains I and II contain only 5 positive charges while those in domains II and IV contain 6 that would be membrane associated (NODA et al., 1984; AULD et al., 1985). The total gating charge of +6 may arise from progressive voltage-driven transitions of the four domains yielding +1, +1, +2 and +2 charges transferred if domains III and IV undergo 2 cycles of ion pair exchange.

The sliding helix model attempts to define a workable structure for the voltage-sensing elements of the sodium channel. Each of these elements is proposed to initiate a conformational change in its own domain. The structure of each individual domain defines the energetic barrier to its voltage-driven conformational change and, therefore, the sequence of conformational transitions that occur during the sigmoid time course of activation. Additional structural information is needed to construct a mechanism for coupling of the conformational changes in each domain to opening of a high conductance transmembrane pore.

Voltage-sensitive calcium channels

Voltage-sensitive calcium channels in brain produce action potentials in dendrites (SCHWARZKROIN and SLAWSKY, 1977; LLINAS et al., 1981) and couple changes in membrane potential at nerve terminals to the release of neurotransmitter (KATZ and MILEDI, 1969; BLAUSTEIN, 1975). In muscle tissues, they mediate calcium influx during cellular depolarization and play an important role in excitation-contraction coupling (reviewed by REUTER, 1979; HAGIWARA and BYERLY, 1981). Calcium channels are nonconducting at the resting membrane potential. They are activated by membrane depolarization with half-maximal probability of activation at −20 to +10 mV in various tissues (reviewed by TSIEN, 1983). Calcium channels in some tissues are slowly inactivated upon prolonged membrane depolarization, whereas in others inactivation is partial or absent. Inactivation results from a decrease in the probability of channel activation. Two different mechanisms have been described: inactivation produced by membrane depolarization *per se* and inactivation due to increased intracellular calcium concentration (reviewed by TSIEN, 1983). Calcium channels in secretory cells and skeletal muscle seem not to inactivate significantly while those in cardiac muscle exhibit both voltage- and calcium-dependent inactivation mechanisms.

Under physiological conditions, calcium channels are highly selective yet transport up to 3×10^6 ions/sec (TSIEN, 1983). Ca^{++} and Ba^{++} are efficiently transported while other divalent cations are poor permeants and block Ca^{++} and Ba^{++} conductance (HAGIWARA and BYERLY, 1981). Surprisingly, in the absence of Ca^{++}, calcium channels are much less selective and will transport a variety of monovalent cations effectively (HESS and TSIEN, 1984; ALMERS and MCCLESKY, 1984; ALMERS et al., 1984). Thus, Ca^{++} regulates channel selectivity. A model involving two high affinity Ca^{++} binding sites within the ion conducting pore located close enough for strong intersite repulsive interactions accommodates these findings. When neither site is occupied by Ca^{++}, monovalent cations are bound weakly and transported. When one site is occupied by Ca^{++}, the channel is blocked. When both sites are occupied, transport of Ca^{++} is efficient and selective. Monovalent cations are excluded.

The functional properties of calcium channels are being rapidly elucidated by electrophysiological methods. Although study of the molecular properties of this physiologically important ion channel is of interest, only recently have high affinity chemical probes for the calcium channel become available.

Organic calcium antagonists as probes of calcium channel structure and function

Calcium channels are inhibited by three different classes of organic antagonists: the dihydropyridines including nifedipine and nitrendipine, the phenylalkylamines and diphenylalkylamines including verapamil, and the thiobenzazepine diltiazem (TRIGGLE, 1982). ^{3}H-labeled derivatives of nitrendipine and other dihydropyridines have been prepared and their binding to high affinity receptor sites in homogenates and membrane preparations from excitable tissues has been extensively examined (JANIS and SCRIABINE, 1983). A single class of high affinity binding sites is observed with a K_D for nitrendipine in the range of 0.1 to 1.0 nM. The structure-activity relationships for occupancy of these high affinity binding sites correlate closely with the concentrations of various dihydropyridines required to block contraction of smooth muscle over a wide range of K_D values (BOLGER et al., 1982). Similar relative structure-activity relationships are observed in other tissues but the absolute concentration required to block calcium currents often is substantially greater than required to occupy the high affinity nitrendipine binding sites (LEE and TSIEN, 1983; ALMERS et al., 1981). This apparent discrepancy has now been resolved by the finding that dihydropyridine binding and block of calcium channels is highly voltage-sensitive (BEAN, 1984). In cardiac cells, half-maximal block of calcium currents at the resting membrane potential requires 700 nM nitrendipine. In contrast, when cells are depolarized to -20 mV to inactivate 70% of the calcium current, only 0.8 nM nitrendipine is required for half-maximal block. This value is in close agreement with K_D values for high affinity binding sites in cardiac membrane preparations which are depolarized by tissue homogenization and cell disruption (JANIS and SCRIABINE, 1983). These results resolve an important discrepancy between previous biochemical and physiological measurements and provide additional strong support for the view that measurements of specific binding of nitrendipine and other dihydropyridines represent drug interaction with calcium channels or a closely associated regulatory component.

The binding of nitrendipine to its receptor site is modulated via an allosteric mechanism by diltiazem and various mono- and diphenylalkylamines such as verapamil which interact with separate receptor sites (MURPHY et al., 1983). Verapamil decreases nitrendipine binding and enhances the rate of dissociation of the nitrendipine-receptor complex whereas diltiazem increases binding and slows the rate of dissociation of the nitrendipine-receptor complex. Thus, the calcium antagonist receptor of the calcium channel contains two or three drug binding sites, one specific for dihydropyridines and one or two for diltiazem and phenylalkylamines, which interact allosterically in modulating calcium channel-function.

The development of the calcium antagonists has been important for the therapy of hypertension, atrial arrhythmia, and angina. They have allowed clearer definition of the role of calcium channels in various physiological pathways. In addition, the development of radioactively labeled derivatives of high affinity and specificity now allows the use of these drugs as probes to identify and isolate the protein components of calcium channels and understand their molecular properties.

Molecular size of the calcium antagonist receptor of the calcium channel

The first estimates of the molecular size of the component(s) of the calcium channel that bind dihydropyridines have been derived from radiation inactivation measurements. Estimates of the target size for inactivation of [^{3}H] nitrendipine binding to receptor sites are 180,000 or 210,000 for skeletal muscle (NORMAN et al., 1983; FERRY et al., 1983a), 210,000 for brain (NORMAN et al., 1983), and 280,000 for guinea pig ileum (VENTER et al., 1983). The apparent molecular weight derived from radiation inactivation studies depends upon the radiolabeled calcium antagonist used in the receptor binding assay and on the assay and irradiation conditions suggesting that the calcium antagonist receptor is a complex oligomeric structure (FERRY et al., 1983b).

Identification of protein components of the calcium antagonist receptor by covalent labeling

The dihydropyridines are amenable to structural modification at several positions and therefore are potentially valuable tools for affinity chromatography and covalent labeling. An isothiocyanate analog of nitrendipine covalently labels a protease-sensitive polypeptide with an apparent molecular weight of 45,000 in guinea pig ileum membrane preparations (VENTER et al., 1983). Nitrendipine itself is photolabile and can be covalently incorporated into a polypeptide with apparent molecular weight of 32,000 in cardiac sarcolemma by high intensity irradiation (CAMPBELL et al., 1984). A photoreactive azidobenzoy1 analog of nitrendipine has been prepared by FERRY et al. (1984). This compound labels a polypeptide with an apparent molecular weight of 145,000 in skeletal muscle transverse tubule membranes. In each case, the covalent labeling reactions described were prevented by incubation with excess unlabeled calcium antagonist suggesting that the polypeptides labeled are components of the calcium antagonist receptor in these different tissues. Either the calcium antagonist receptor from these different tissues has different polypeptide components or, as argued below, the receptor is an oligomer of subunits of different molecular weight which are differentially labeled by the probes used.

Characterization of the detergent-solubilized calcium antagonist receptor

Since it is likely to be an intrinsic membrane protein, the first essential step in purification and biochemical characterization of the calcium antagonist receptor is solubilization from an appropriate membrane source and characterization of the solubilized protein. After a survey of several detergents, we concluded that digitonin is the most effective detergent for solubilization of a specific [^{3}H] nitrendipine-receptor complex from brain and skeletal muscle transverse tubule membranes (CURTIS and CATTERALL, 1983, 1984). Up to 40% of the receptor-ligand complex is solubilized. The dissociation of bound [^{3}H]-nitrendipine from the complex is accelerated by verapamil and slowed by diltiazem through allosteric interactions between the nitrendipine binding site and the binding site for those ligands as observed in intact membranes. These results provide further support for the conclusion that a specific [^{3}H] nitrendipine-receptor complex has been solubilized under conditions which allow retention of the functional allosteric regulation of dihydropyridine binding.

Sedimentation of the solubilized [^{3}H] nitrendipine-receptor-digitonin complex through sucrose gradients gives a single peak of specifically bound nitrendipine with a sedimentation coefficient of 19 to 20 S (CURTIS and CATTERALL, 1983). Comparison of the sedimentation behavior of the solubilized complex from brain, heart, and skeletal muscle indicates that they have identical size. These results provide support for the view that the calcium antagonist receptor in different tissues is quite similar.

Many plasma membrane proteins are glycosylated during their synthesis and transport to the cell surface. The solubilized calcium antagonist receptor from brain or skeletal muscle is specifically adsorbed to and eluted from affinity columns with immobilized wheat germ agglutinin or other lectins (CURTIS and CATTERALL, 1983, 1984; GLOSSMANN and FERRY, 1983). Evidently, one or more of the subunits of the calcium antagonist receptor are glycoproteins.

Skeletal muscle transverse tubules as a model system for examination of the biochemical properties of calcium channels

Skeletal muscle fibers have substantial voltage-activated calcium currents that have been measured under voltage clamp (SANCHEZ and STEFANI, 1976). These currents originate almost entirely in the transverse tubular system and are blocked by dihydropyridine calcium antagonists (ALMERS et al., 1981). They have been presumed to play a role in excitation-contraction coupling although direct evidence for such a role has not been obtained. Transverse tubule membranes can be extensively purified from skeletal muscle by a combination of differential and density gradient centrifugation (ROSEMBLATT et al., 1981). Antibodies prepared against the most highly purified fractions of T-tubule membranes stain only T-tubules and not sarcolemma or sarcoplasmic reticulum of intact muscle indicating a high degree of purity of this preparation (ROSEMBLATT et al., 1981). Analysis of [^{3}H] nitrendipine binding to membrane fractions from skeletal muscle reveals a specific localization of the calcium antagonist receptor in the T-tubule fraction (FOSSET et al., 1983; GLOSSMANN et al., 1983). These membranes contain a 10-fold greater concentration of calcium antagonist receptor (10 to 50 pmol/mg) than any other membrane preparation described to date (JANIS and SCRIABINE, 1983). Since T-tubule membranes are the most enriched source of calcium antagonist receptors and they have a substantial voltage-activated calcium current that is blocked by dihydropyridines, they provide a favorable experimental preparation for examination of the molecular properties of the calcium antagonist receptor and its relationship to voltage-sensitive calcium channels. It is anticipated that the T-tubule calcium channel will resemble those of other tissues which are blocked by dihydropyridines and, therefore, that information on the molecular properties of this calcium channel will give insight into others.

Purification and characterization of the calcium antagonist receptor from skeletal muscle transverse tubules

If the calcium antagonist receptor has a molecular weight of 210,000 (NORMAN et al., 1983a) and has one dihydropyridine binding site per mole, the pure protein would have a specific binding capacity of 4760 pmol/mg. The specific binding capacity of purified T-tubule membranes is 10 to 50 pmol/mg (FOSSET et al., 1983; GLOSSMAN et al., 1983; CURTIS and CATTERALL, 1984). Thus, only 100 to 500 fold purification is required to achieve a homogeneous preparation. This degree of purification can usually be obtained by conventional procedures.

We have purified the calcium antagonist receptor solubilized from T-tubule membranes by digitonin 330 fold by affinity chromatography on wheat germ agglutinin-Sepharose, ion exchange chromatography on DEAE-Sephadex, and velocity sedimentation through sucrose gradients (CURTIS and CATTERALL, 1984). The purified preparation contained 1950 pmol calcium antagonist receptor per mg protein implying a purity of at least 42 %.

Analysis of the purified preparation by polyacrylamide gel electrophoresis after denaturation in sodium dodecyl sulfate (SDS) revealed three major protein bands (Fig. 6). Their molecular weights are: α, 135,000; β, 50,000; and γ, 33,000. All three of these polypeptides quantitatively comigrate with the [^{3}H] nitrendipine-receptor complex during velocity sedimentation in sucrose gradients (CURTIS and CATTERALL, 1984) and, therefore, are likely to be subunits of the calcium antagonist receptor. The concentration of the β subunit varies among preparations. This seems to result from both dissociation of the α subunit and high protease sensitivity. BORSOTTO et al. (1984) developed a similar purification procedure and identified polypeptide subunits analogous to the α and γ polypeptides.

It is of interest to compare the apparent molecular weights of the subunits of the purified calcium antagonist receptor from T-tubules with those of the polypeptides covalently labeled by dihydropyridine derivatives. The polypeptide with apparent molecular weight of 145,000 labeled by azidopine (FERRY et al., 1984) has similar size as the α subunit of the purified preparation. The polypeptide with apparent molecular weight of 32,000 covalently labeled by nitrendipine itself (CAMPBELL et al., 1984) has the same size as the γ subunit of the purified preparation. The polypeptide with apparent molecular weight of 45,000 covalently labeled with the isothiocyanate derivative of nitrendipine is somewhat smaller than the β subunit of the purified preparation, but their protease sensitivity suggests that they may be related. Thus, the disparate results of covalent labeling experiments in different tissues may be reconciled by the hypothesis that the dihydropyridine binding site of the calcium antagonist receptor is located near the contact regions of the α, β, and γ subunits such that different dihydropyridine ligands preferentially label different subunits. These results provide further evidence that these subunits are components of the calcium antagonist receptor in intact membranes.

The next steps in development of a molecular picture of the voltage-sensitive calcium channel will be reconstitution of calcium channel function from purified components in order to demonstrate that the calcium antagonist receptor can mediate selective, voltage-activated calcium conductance and determination of the amino acid sequence of the subunits by cDNA cloning and sequencing methods.

Conclusion

The results reviewed here show that the molecular components of two voltage -sensitive ion channels can be identified and isolated using specific radioligand binding assays. The isolated proteins from mammalian sources are large glycoprotein complexes of three nonidentical subunits. In the case of the sodium channel, evidence for specific functional roles of the isolated subunits has been developed from reconstitution and subunit separation studies, the amino acid sequence of the major subunit has been determined, and specific models for the structural basis of voltage-dependent gating and selective ion transport have been developed. It is anticipated that further investigations along these lines will define the relationships between ion channel structure and function and eventually lead to an understanding of the molecular basis of electrical excitability.

References

Agnew, W. S., Levinson, S. R., Brabson, J. S. and Raftery, M. A. (1978): Purification of the tetrodotoxin-binding component associated with the voltage-sensitive sodium channel from *Electrophorus electricus* electroplax membranes. Proc. Natl. Acad. Sci. USA 75, 2606–2610.

Agnew, W. S., Miller, J. A., Ellisman, M. H., Rosenberg, R. L., Tomiko, S. A., and Levinson, S. R. (1983): The voltage-regulated sodium channel from the electroplax of *Electrophorus electricus*. Cold Spring Harbor Symposia on Quantitative Biology. **XLVIII**, 165–179.

Agnew, W. S., Moore, A. C., Levinson, S. R. and Raftery, M. A. (1980): Identification of a large molecular weight peptide associated with a tetrodotoxin binding protein from the electroplax of *Electrophorus electricus*. Biochem. Biophys. Res. Commun. **92**, 860–866.

Albuquerque, E. X., and Daly, J. W. (1976): Batrachotoxin, a selective probe for channels modulating sodium conductance in electrogenic membranes. In: The Specificity and Action of Animal Bacterial and Plant Toxins (Receptors and Recognition, Series B, Volume 1). (P. Cuatrecasas, ed.), pp. 299–338. Chapman and Hall, London.

Aldrich, R. W., Corey, D. P., and Stevens, C. F. (1983): A reinterpretation of mammalian sodium channel gating based on single channel recording. Nature **306**, 436–441.

Almers, W., and McCleskey, E. W. (1984): The nonselective conductance due to Ca channels in frog muscle: Ca-selectivity in a single file pore. J. Physiol. **353**, 585–608.

Almers, W., Fink, R., and Palade, P. T. (1981): Calcium depletion in frog muscle tubules: The decline of calcium current under maintained depolarization. J. Physiol. **312**, 177–207.

Almers, W., McCleskey, E. W., and Palade, P. T. (1984): A nonselective cation conductance in frog muscle membrane blocked by micromolar external Ca^{++}. J. Physiol. **353**, 565–583.

Armstrong, Clay M., (1981): Sodium channels and gating currents. Physiological Reviews. **61**, 644–682.

Armstrong, C. M., and Bezanilla, F. (1974): Charge movement associated with the opening and closing of the activation gates of the Na channels. J. Gen. Physiol. **63**, 533–552.

Armstrong, C. M., and Bezanilla, F. (1977): Inactivation of the sodium channel II. Gating current experiments. J. Gen. Physiol. **70**, 567–590.

Auld, V., Marshall, J., Goldin, A., Dowsett, A., Catterall, W., Davidson, N., and Dunn, R. (1985): Cloning and characterization of the gene for alpha subunit of the mammalian voltage-gated sodium channel. J. Gen. Physiol. **86**, 10a.

Barchi, R. L. (1983): Protein components of the purified sodium channel from rat skeletal sarcolemma. J. Neurochem. **40**, 1377–1385.

Barchi, R. L. and Murphy, L. E. (1981): Estimate of the molecular weight of the sarcolemma sodium channel using H_2O-D_2O centrifugation. J. Neurochem. **36**, 2097–3000.

Barchi, R. L., Cohen, S. A., and Murphy, L. E. (1980): Purification from rat sarcolemma of the saxitoxin-binding component of the excitable membrane sodium channel. Proc. Natl. Acad. Sci. USA 77, 1306–1310.

Barhanin, J., Giglio, J. R., Leopold, P., Schmid, A., Sampaio, S. V., and Lazdunski, M. (1982): *Tityus serrulatus* venom contains two classes of toxins. J. Biol. Chem. **257**, 12553–12558.

Barhanin, J., Schmid, A., Lombet, A., Wheeler, L. P., Lazdunski, M., and Ellory, J. C. (1983): Molecular size of different neurotoxin receptors on the voltage-sensitive Na^+ channel. J. Biol. Chem. **258**, 700–702.

Bean, B. P. (1984): Nitrendipine block of cardiac calcium channels: High-affinity binding to the inactivated state. Proc. Natl. Acad. Sci. USA **81**, 6388–6392.

Beneski, D. A., and Catterall, W. A. (1980): Covalent labeling of protein components of the sodium channel with a photoactivable derivative of scorpion toxin. Proc. Natl. Acad. Sci. USA 77, 639–643.

Benzer, T. I., and Raftery, M. A. (1973): Solubilization and partial characterization of the tetrodotoxin binding component from nerve axons. Biochem. Biophys. Res. Commun. **51**, 939–944.

Blaustein, M. P. (1975): Effects of potassium, veratridine and scorpion venom on calcium accumulation and transmitter release by nerve terminals *in vitro*. J. Physiol. *247*, 617–655.

Bolger, G. T., Gengo, P. J., Luchowki, E. M., Siegel, H., Triggle, D. J., and Janis, R. A. (1982): High affinity binding of a calcium channel antagonist to smooth and cardiac muscle. Biochem. Biophys. Res. Commun. **104**, 1604–1609.

Borsotto, M., Barhanin, J., Norman, R. I., and Lazdunski, M. (1984): Purification of the dihydropyridine receptor of the voltage-dependent Ca^{2+} channel from skeletal muscle transverse tubules using (+) [^{3}H] PN 200-110,. Biochem. Biophys. Res. Commun. **122**, 1357–1365.

Brum, G., Flockerzi, V., Hofmann, F., Osterrieder, W. and Trautwein, W. (1983): Injection of catalytic subunit of cAMP-dependent protein kinase into isolated cardiac myocytes. Pflügers Archiv. **398**, 147–154.

Cachelin, A. B., de Peyer, J. E., Kokubun, S., and Reuter, H. (1983): Ca^{2+} channel modulation by 8-bromocyclic AMP in cultured heart cells. Nature **304**, 462–464.

Cahalan, M. D. (1975): Modification of sodium gating in frog myelinated nerve fibres by *Centruroides sculpturatus* scorpion venom. J. Physiol. **244**, 511–534.

Campbell, K. P., Lipschutz, G. M., and Denney, G. H. (1984): Direct photoaffinity labeling of the high affinity nitrendipine-binding site in subcellular membrane fractions isolated from canine myocardium. J. Biol. Chem. **259**, 5384–5387.

Catterall, W. A. (1980): Neurotoxins that act on voltage-sensitive sodium channels in excitable membranes. Ann. Rev. Pharmacol. Toxicol., 15–43.

Catterall, W. A. (1986): Molecular properties of voltage-sensitive sodium channels. Ann. Rev. Biochem. **55**, 953–985.

Catterall, W. A., Morrow, C. S., and Hartshorne, R. P. (1979): Neurotoxin binding to receptor sites associated with voltage-sensitive sodium channels in intact, lysed, and detergent-solubilized brain membranes. J. Biol. Chem. **254**, 11379–11387.

Catterall, W. A., Morrow, C. S., Daly, J. W., and Brown, G. B. (1981): Binding of batrachotoxinin A 20-α-benzoate to a receptor site associated with sodium channels in synaptic nerve ending particles. J. Biol. Chem. **256**, 9822–9827.

Costa, M. R. C., and Catterall, W. A. (1984a): Cyclic AMP-dependent phosphorylation of the α subunit of the sodium channel in synaptic nerve ending particles. J. Biol. Chem. **259**, 8210–8218.

Costa, M. R. C., and Catterall, W. A. (1984b): Phosphorylation of the subunit of the sodium channel by protein kinase C. Cell. Mol. Neurobiol. **4**, 291–297.

Couraud, F., Jover, E., Dubois, J. M., and Rochat, H. (1982): Two types of scorpion toxin receptor sites, one related to the activation, the other to the inactivation of the action potential sodium channel. Toxicon **20**, 9–16.

Curtis, B. M., and Catterall, W. A. (1983): Solubilization of the calcium antagonist receptor from rat brain. J. Biol. Chem. **258**, 7280–7283.

Curtis, B. M. and Catterall, W. A. (1984): Purification of the calcium antagonist receptor of the voltage-sensitive calcium channel from skeletal muscle transverse tubules. Biochemistry **23**, 2113–2118.

Darbon, H., Jover, E., Couraud, F., and Rochat, H. (1983): Photoaffinity labeling of α- and β-scorpion toxin receptors associated with rat brain sodium channel. Biochem. Biophys. Res. Commun. **115**, 415–422.

Feller, D. J., Talvenheimo, J. A., and Catterall, W. A. (1985): The sodium channel from rat brain. Reconstitution of voltage-dependent scorpion toxin binding in vesicles of defined lipid composition. J. Biol. Chem. **260**, 11542–11547.

Ferry, D. R., Goll, A., and Glossman, H. (1983a): Putative calcium channel molecular weight determination by target size analysis. Naunyn-Schmedeberg's Arch. Pharmacol. **323**, 292–297.

Ferry, D. R., Goll, A., and Glossman, H. (1983b): Calcium channels: evidence for oligomeric nature by target size analysis. Embo. J. **2**, 1729–1732.

Ferry, D. R., Rombusch, M., Goll, A., and Glossmann, H. (1984): Photoaffinity labelling of Ca^{2+} channels with [^{3}H] azidopine. FEBS Lett. **169**, 112–167.

Flockerzi, U., Mewes, R., Ruth, P., and Hofmann, F. (1983): Phosphorylation of purified bovine cardiac sarcolemma and potassium-stimulated calcium uptake. Eur. J. Biochem. **135**, 132–142.

Fosset, M., Jaimovich, E., Delpont, E., and Lazdunski, M. (1983): [^{3}H] Nitrendipine receptors in skeletal muscle. J. Biol. Chem. **258**, 6086–6092.

Glossman, H., and Ferry, D. R. (1983a): Solubilization and partial purification of putative calcium channels labelled with [^{3}H]-nimodipine. Naunyn-Schmiedeberg's Arch. Pharmacol. **323**, 279–291.

Glossman, H., Ferry, D. R., and Boschek, C. B. (1983b): Purification of the putative calcium channel from skeletal muscle with the aid of [^{3}H]-nimodipine binding. Naunyn-Schmiedeberg's Arch. Pharmacol. **323**, 1–11.

Hagiwara, S., and Byerly, L. (1981): Calcium channel. Ann. Rev. Neurosci. **4**, 69–125.

Hartshorne, R. P., and Catterall, W. A. (1981): Purification of the saxitoxin receptor of the sodium channel from rat brain. Proc. Natl. Acad. Sci. USA **78**, 4620–4624.

Hartshorne, R. P., and Catterall, W. A. (1984): The sodium channel from rat brain. Purification and subunit composition. J. Biol. Chem. **259,** 1667–1675.

Hartshorne, R. P., Coppersmith, J., and Catterall, W. A. (1980): Size characteristics of the solubilized saxitoxin receptor of the voltage-sensitive sodium channel from rat brain. J. Biol. Chem. **255,** 10572–10575.

Hartshorne, R. P., Messner, D. J., Coppersmith, J. C., and Catterall, W. A. (1982): The saxitoxin receptor of the sodium channel from rat brain. Evidence for two nonidentical β subunits. J. Biol. Chem. **257,** 13888–13891.

Hartshorne, R. P., Keller, B. U., Talvenheimo, J. A., Catterall, W. A., and Montal, M. (1984): Functional reconstitution of the purified brain sodium channel in planar lipid bilayers. Proc. Natl. Acad. Sci. USA **82,** 240–244.

Henderson, R., and Wang, J. H. (1972): Solubilization of a specific tetrodotoxin-binding component from garfish olfactory nerve membrane. Biochemistry **11,** 4565–4569.

Hess, P., and Tsien, R. W. (1984): Mechanism of ion permeation through calcium channels. Nature **309,** 453–456.

Hille, B. (1971): The permeability of the sodium channel to organic cations in myelinated nerve. J. Gen. Physiol. **58,** 599–619.

Hille, B. (1972): The permeability of the sodium channel to metal cations in myelinated nerve. J. Gen. Physiol. **59,** 637–658.

Hodgkin, A. L., and Huxley, A. F. (1952): A quantitative description of membrane current and its application to conduction and excitation in nerve. J. Physiol. **117,** 500–544.

Huang, L. Y. M., Moran, N. and Ehrenstein (1984): Gating kinetics of batrachotoxin-modified sodium channels in neuroblastoma cells determined from single channel measurements. Biophys. J. **45,** 313–322.

Janis, R. A., and Scriabine, A. (1983): Sites of action of Ca^{2+} channel inhibitors. Biochem. Pharmacol. **32,** 3499–3507.

Jover, E., Couraud, F., and Rochat, H. (1980): Two types of scorpion neurotoxins characterized by their binding to two separate receptor sites on rat brain synaptosomes. Biochem. Biophys. Res. Commun. **95,** 1697–1614.

Katz, B., and Miledi, R. (1969): Tetrodotoxin-resistant electric activity in presynaptic terminals. J. Physiol. **203,** 459–487.

Kikkawa, U., Takai, Y., Minakuchi, R., Inohara, S., and Nishizuka, Y. (1982): Calcium activated, phospholipid-dependent protein kinase from rat brain. J. Biol. Chem. **257,** 13341–13348.

Kistler, J., Stroud, R. M., Klymkowsky, M. W., Lalancette, R. A., and Fairclough, R. H. (1982): Structure and function of an acetylcholine receptor. Biophys. J. **37,** 371–383.

Kraner, S. D., Tanaka, J. C., and Barchi, R. L. (1985): Purification and functional reconstitution of the voltage-sensitive sodium channel from rabbit T-tubular membranes. J. Biol. Chem. **260,** 6341–6347.

Krueger, B. K., Ratzlaff, R. W., Strichartz, G. R., and Blaustein, M. P. (1979): Saxitoxin binding to synaptosomes, membranes, and solubilized binding sites from rat brain. J. Membrane Biol. **50,** 287–310.

Krueger, B. K., Worley, J. F. III, and French, R. J. (1983): Single sodium channels from rat brain incorporated into planar bilayers. Nature **303,** 172–175.

Lee, K. S., and Tsien, R. W. (1983): Mechanism of calcium channel blockade by verapamil, D600, diltiazem and nitrendipine in single dialysed heart cells. Nature **302,** 790–794.

Levinson, S. R., and Ellory, J. C. (1973): Molecular size of the tetrodotoxin binding site estimated by irradiation inactivation. Nature New Biology **245,** 122–123.

Llinas, R., Yarom, Y., and Sugimori, M. (1981): Isolated mammalian brain in vitro: new technique for analysis of electrical activity of neuronal circuit function. Fed. Proc. **40,** 2240–2245.

Lombet, A., Norman, R. I., and Lazdunski, M. (1983): Affinity labeling of the tetrodotoxin-binding component of the Na^+ channel. Biochem. Biophys. Res. Commun. **114,** 126–130.

Messner, D. J., and Catterall, W. A. (1985): The sodium channel from rat brain: separation and characterization of subunits. J. Biol. Chem. **260,** 10597–10604.

Messner, D. J., and Catterall, W. A. (1986): The sodium channel from rat brain. Role of the $\beta 1$ and $\beta 2$ subunits in saxitoxin binding. J. Biol. Chem. **261,** 211–215.

Meves, H., Rubly, N., and Watt, D. D. (1982): Effect of toxins isolated from the venom of the scorpion *Centruroides sculpturatus* on the Na currents of the node of Ranvier. Pflügers Arch. Physiol. **393,** 56–62.
Miller, J. A., Agnew, W. S., and Levinson, S. R. (1983): Principal glycopeptide of the tetrodotoxin/saxitoxin binding protein from *Electrophorus electricus*: isolation and partial chemical and physical characterization. Biochemistry **22,** 462–470.
Montal, M. (1974): Formation of bimolecular membranes from lipid monolayers. Meth. Enzymol. **32,** 545–554.
Murphy, K. M. M., Gould, R. J., Largent, B. L., and Snyder, S. H. (1983): A unitary mechanism of calcium antagonist drug action. Proc. Natl. Acad. Sci. USA **80,** 860–864.
Nakayama, H., Withy, R. M., and Raftery, M. A. (1982): Use of a monoclonal antibody to purify the tetrodotoxin binding component from the electroplax of *Electrophorus electricus*. Proc. Natl. Acad. Sci. USA **79,** 7575–7579.
Narahashi, T. (1974): Chemicals as tools in the study of excitable membranes. Physiol. Rev. **54,** 813–889.
Noda et al., (1984): Primary structure of *Electrophorus electricus* sodium channel deduced from cDNA sequence. Nature **312,** 121–127.
Norman, R. I., Borsotto, M., Fosset, M., Lazdunski, M., and Ellory, J. C. (1983a): Determination of the molecular size of the mitrendipine-sensitive Ca^{2+} channel by radiation inactivation. Biochem. Biophys. Res. Commun. **111,** 878–883.
Norman, R. I., Borsotto, M., Fosset, M., Lazdunski, M., and Ellory, J. C. (1983a): Determination of the molecular size of the nitrendipine-sensitive Ca^{2+} channel by radiation inactivation. Biochem. Biophys. Res. Commun. **111,** 878–883.
Popot, J. and Changeux, J. (1984): Nicotinic receptor of acetylcholine: structure of an oligomeric integral membrane protein. Physiological Reviews **64,** 1162–1237.
Reuter, H. (1974): Localization of beta adrenergic receptors, and effects of noradrenaline and cyclic nucleotides on action potentials, ionic currents and tension in mammalian cardiac muscle. J. Physiol. **242,** 429–451.
Reuter, H. (1979): Properties of two inward membrane currents in the heart. Ann. Rev. Physiol. **41,** 413–424.
Reuter, H. (1983): Calcium channel modulation by neurotransmitters, enzymes and drugs. Nature **301,** 569–574.
Ribeiro, J. A., and Sebastiao, A. M. (1984): Enhancement of tetrodotoxin-induced axonal blockade by adenosine, adenosine analogues, dibutyryl cyclic AMP and methylxanthines in the frog sciatic nerve. Br. J. Pharmac. **85,** 309–313.
Ritchie, J. M., and Rogart, R. B. (1977): The binding of saxitoxin and tetrodotoxin to excitable tissue. Rev. Physiol. Biochem. Pharmacol. **79,** 1–49.
Rosemblat, M., Hidalgo, C., Vergara, C. and Ikemoto, N. (1981): Immunological and biochemical properties of transerse tubule membranes isolated from rabbit skeletal muscle. J. Biol. Chem. **256,** 8140–8148.
Rosenberg, R. L., Tomiko, S. A., and Agnew, W. S. (1984a): Single-channel properties of the reconstituted voltage-regulated Na channel isolated from the electroplax of *Electrophorus electricus*. Proc. Natl. Acad. Sci. USA **81,** 5594–5598.
Rosenberg, R. L., Tomiko, S. A., and Agnew, W. S. (1984b): Reconstitution of neurotoxin-modulated ion transport by the voltage-regulated sodium channel isolated from the electroplax of *Electrophorus electricus*. Proc. Natl. Acad. Sci. USA **81,** 1239–1243.
Sánchez, J. A., and Stefani, E. (1978): Inward calcium current in twitch muscle fibers of the frog. J. Physiol. **283,** 197–209.
Schwarzkroin, P. A., and Slawsky, M. (1977): Probable calcium spikes in hippocampal neurons. Brain Res. **135,** 157–161.
Talvenheimo, J. A., Tamkum, M. M., and Catterall, W. A. (1982): Reconstitution of neurotoxin-stimulated sodium transport by the voltage-sensitive sodium channel purified from rat brain. J. Biol. Chem. **257,** 11868–11871.
Tamkun, M. M., Talvenheimo, J. A., and Catterall, W. A. (1984): The sodium channel from rat brain. Reconstitution of neurotoxin-activated ion flux and scorpion toxin binding from purified components. J. Biol. Chem. **259,** 1676–1688.

Tanaka, J. C., Eccleston, J. F., and Barchi, R. L. (1983): Cation selectivity characteristics of the reconstituted voltage-dependent sodium channel purified from rat skeletal muscle sarcolemma. J. Biol. Chem. **258,** 7519–7526.

Triggle, D. J. (1982): Biochemical pharmacology of calcium blockers. In: Calcium Blockers: Mechanism of Actions and Clinical Applications (S. F. Flaim and R. Zelis, eds.), pp. 121–134. Urban and Schwarzenberg, Baltimore-Munich.

Tsien, R. W. (1983): Calcium channels in excitable cell membranes. Ann. Rev. Physiol. **45,** 341–358.

Tsien, R. W., Bean, B. P., Hess, P., and Nowycky, M. (1983): Calcium channels: mechanisms of β-adrenergic modulation and ion permeation. Cold Spring Harbor Symposia on Quantitative Biology. **XLVIII,** 201–212.

Unwin, P. N. T., and Zampighi, G. (1980): Structure of the junction between communicating cells. Nature **283,** 545–549.

Venter, J. C., Fraser, C. M., Schaber, J. S., Jung, C. Y., Bolger, G., and Triggle, D. J. (1983): Molecular properties of the slow inward calcium channel. J. Biol. Chem. **258,** 9344–9448.

Wang, G. K., and Strichartz, G. (1982): Simultaneous modifications of sodium channel gating by two scorpion toxins. Biophys. J. **40,** 175–179.

Weigele, J. B., and Barchi, R. L. (1982): Functional reconstitution of the purified sodium channel protein from rat sarcolemma. Proc. Natl. Acad. Sci. USA **79,** 3651–3655.

Windisch, H., and Tritthart, H. A. (1982): Isoproterenol, norepinephrine and phosphodiesterase inhibitors are blockers of the depressed fast Na^+-system in ventricular muscle fibers. J. Mol. Cell Cardiol. **14,** 431–434.

Fortschritte der Zoologie, Band 33 · Lüttgau (Hrsg.): Membrane Control
Gustav Fischer Verlag · Stuttgart · New York · 1986

Analysis of sodium channel function

Charles F. Stevens

Molecular Neurobiology, Yale Medical School, New Haven, Connecticut, USA

The elucidation of sodium channel structure/function relations requires a detailed knowledge of the conformational states available to the channel and the rates at which transitions between these states occur. Most studies of the sodium channel, however, have determined transition rates from a specific theory of sodium channel operation – the Hodgkin-Huxley equations, for example – so that the entire description must be correct in order to extract accurate values for any specific rate constants. We have been engaged in a program (Aldrich, Corey and Stevens, 1983; Aldrich and Stevens, 1983) whose goal is to decouple the determination of individual rate constants from the overall description of sodium channel behavior. Our objective has been to measure the rate constants, and their voltage dependence, for some conformational transitions in a way that does not depend on the details of other aspects of sodium channel operation.

We have studied the behavior of single sodium channels in cell attached patches on neuroblastoma cells (N1E115). The first latency of channel opening, the open time, the number of channel openings per depolarization epoch, and the number of channels in each patch are estimated. Large numbers of single channel records are averaged together to determine the probability of a channel being open (we call this function $p(t)$) and the macroscopic inactivation time constant τ_h (estimated by fitting an exponential to the declining phase of $p(t)$).

An equation for $p(t)$ has played a central role in our investigations:

$$p(t) = \int_0^t f(t-r)w(r)dr$$

In this equation, $p(t)$ is the probability of finding a channel open t ms after the onset of a depolarization, $f(t)$ is the probability that a channel first opens t ms after the start of the depolarization, and $w(t)$ is the probability that a channel will be open t ms after having opened for the first time. This equation enumerates the number of ways a channel can be open at time t.

The function $w(t)$ is composed of two parts:

$$w(t) = \exp(-t/D) + r(t)$$

where the exponential function specifies the probability that a channel will remain open t ms without closing, and the function $r(t)$ gives the probability that a channel will be open at t by having closed and then reopened.

We have shown that this equation for $p(t)$ is quite accurate in describing sodium channel behavior over a range of depolarizations when $r(t)$ is assumed to be zero. That is, we have claimed that sodium channels open only once over much of their voltage range.

Two other equations have been important for our analysis. They are

$$D = 1/(a+b)$$

and

$$F = a/(a+b).$$

Here *D* is the mean dwell time in the open state, *F* the probability that an open channel passes to the inactivated state when it makes a transition, *a* the transition rate from open to inactivated, and *b* the deactivation rate (open into closed but not inactivated).

These equations provide two relations for *a* and *b*; we have found ways of estimating both *D* and *F*, and thus for determining *a* and *b*. *F* has been estimated from the number of openings per depolarization epoch and from the equation

$$F = 1 - R/(1 - Q)$$

where *R* is the probability that an open channel will some time reopen and *Q* is the probability that a closed channel will pass into the inactivated state without ever opening. The quantity *R* in turn is given by

$$R = 1 - (1 - Q)D/I$$

where *I* is the integral of *p(t)* over a long depolarization and the other quantities have been defined in the preceding equations. This relation arises from a careful consideration of the convolution equation for *p(t)*.

We have applied these equations to estimate the transition rates *a* and *b*. Although not quite atheoretical, these estimates do not depend on the rest of the sodium channel behavior and so are, in that sense, model independent. We find that the deactivation rate *b* has a voltage dependence of about 3 elementary charges, and that inactivation is about an order of magnitude less voltage dependent (that is, about .3 charges passing through the applied membrane voltage will explain its voltage dependence). The rate at zero voltage is about 2 transitions/ms from the open to the inactivated state and about .0002 transitions/ms from open to closed. Thus inactivation is much faster than deactivation until the membrane potential approaches the resting level where deactivation, because of its rather large voltage dependence, starts to dominate.

These results imply that, over most of the voltage range, channels open only once and then inactivate. At the peak of the $\tau_h$curve channels reopen with a probability of around 1/4, and this reopening probability decreases to nearly zero for both hyper- and depolarizations. Because channels open only about one time for each depolarization, and because the inactivation rate of open channels is quite fast (around 2/ms), the process characterized by τ_h, ordinarily thought to represent inactivation, is in fact a slow step in channel opening rather than the time constant for open channels entering the inactivated state.

We conclude, then, that the closing transition involves the equivalent of about 3 elementary charges moving through the membrane electric field. According to the model of sodium channel gating proposed by Guy et al. (1986), only one or two charges would move for the conformational change of each domain. We suggest, therefore, that the movement of several domains is concerted in gating. As further functional studies are carried out so that the characteristics of sodium channel gating is better characterized, and as more detailed structural information becomes available, we anticipate that a view of the molecular mechanism of sodium channel gating will evolve.

References

Aldrich, R. W., Corey, D. P. and Stevens, C. F. A reinterpretation of mammalian sodium channel gating based on single channel recording. Nature **306:** 436–441, 1983.

Aldrich, R. W. and Stevens, C. F. Inactivation of open and closed sodium channels determined separately. Cold Spring Harbor Symposia on Quantitative Biology, Vol. **XLVIII,** pp. 147–153, 1983.

Guy, H. R., and Seetharamulu, P. Molecular Model of the Action Potential Sodium Channel. Proc. Natl. Acad. Sci. USA **83:** 508–512, 1986.

Fortschritte der Zoologie, Band 33 · Lüttgau (Hrsg.): Membrane Control
Gustav Fischer Verlag · Stuttgart · New York · 1986

Sodium current and gating current: Experiments on the node of Ranvier

HANS MEVES

I. Physiologisches Institut der Universität des Saarlandes, D-6650 Homburg/Saar, FRG

Since the development of the voltage clamp method for myelinated nerve fibres by DODGE and FRANKENHAEUSER (1958), macroscopic sodium currents of the node of Ranvier have been recorded by numerous scientists. Since NONNER, ROJAS and STÄMPFLI (1975) published the first records of gating currents from the frog node of Ranvier, considerable information about the intramembrane charge movement in the nodal membrane has been accumulated. Much of the earlier literature has been reviewed in articles by ALMERS (1978), NEUMCKE, NONNER and STÄMPFLI (1978) and ARMSTRONG (1981). The present article will concentrate on the experimental work published in the last five years. A main topic which has been dealt with during this period is the comparison of the time course of charge movement and sodium activation. Two other problems which have received interest are (a) the relation between charge immobilization and inactivation of the sodium permeability and (b) the dependence of inactivation rate on previous potential history.

Time course of gating current and time course of sodium activation

A convenient starting point for discussing this topic is Fig. 1 which is from the article by NEUMCKE et al. (1978). It shows the time course of the charge movement and the time course of the Na current, both normalized and plotted upwards, during a depolarization to −30 mV (A) or −6 mV (B). It is clear that the Na current rises with a considerable delay whereas the charge movement begins at t = 0; it is also clear that in A the Na current rises more slowly than the charge. Parameters which describe the kinetics quantitatively are given in the legend of Fig. 1. In A, the time constant of the charge movement is τ_{on} = 160μs; sodium activation m has a time constant τ_m = 231 μs and starts after a delay of 31 μs. In B, τ_m is smaller than τ_{on}. Similar results have been obtained by CHIU (1980) on rabbit nodes of Ranvier. Again, the time course of charge movement precedes the time course of the Na current. At E = −35 mV CHIU (1980) finds τ_{on} = 58 μs and τ_m = 180 μs and at E = −5 mV τ_{on} = 30 μs and τ_m = 43 μs (at a temperature of 24 °C).

Figs. 2 and 3 present a quantitative comparison between τ_m and τ_{on} for the squid giant axon and the frog node of Ranvier, respectively. In both preparations τ_m, the time constant of activation, reaches a maximum at −30 to −40 mV. At negative potentials τ_{on}, the time constant of the charge movement, is markedly smaller than τ_m whereas at positive potentials τ_{on} and τ_m coincide. Thus, the time course of sodium activation differs from the time

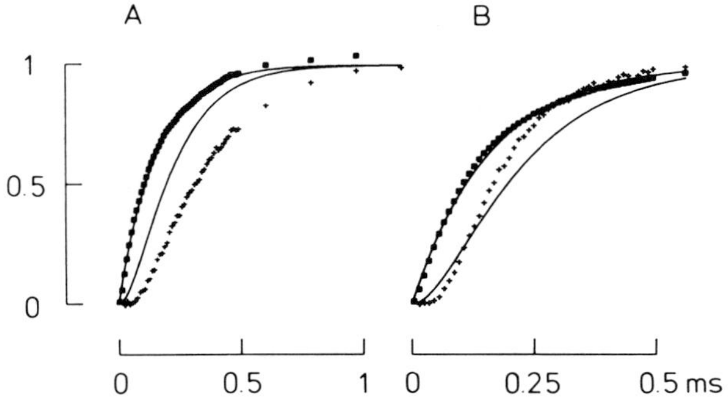

Fig. 1: Time course of charge movement and activation of sodium current in a node of Ranvier. A, depolarization from the holding potential (−98 mV) to E = −30 mV; B, depolarization to E = −6 mV. Gating current recorded in the presence of 300 nM tetrodotoxin (TTX) and numerically integrated; points ■ show the integrated on-response, normalized with respect to the charge value at the end of the record. Na current recorded in the presence of 6 nM TTX; gating current subtracted to obtain the pure Na current; points + show the pure Na current, divided by $\exp(-t/\tau_h)$, normalized and plotted upwards. Temperature 10 °C. The on-response has been fitted by a simple exponential function (τ_{on} = 160 μs in A, 158 μs in B), the second power of this function is also shown. The pure Na current $I_{Na}/\exp(-t/\tau_h)$ has been fitted by the expression

$$m^2 = [1-\exp(-(t-\delta t)/\tau_m]^2$$

with δt = 31 μs in A, 37 μs in B and τ_m = 231 μs in A, 105 μs in B (Neumcke, Nonner and Stämpfli, 1978; fit parameters from Table 1 of Neumcke, Nonner and Stämpfli, 1976).

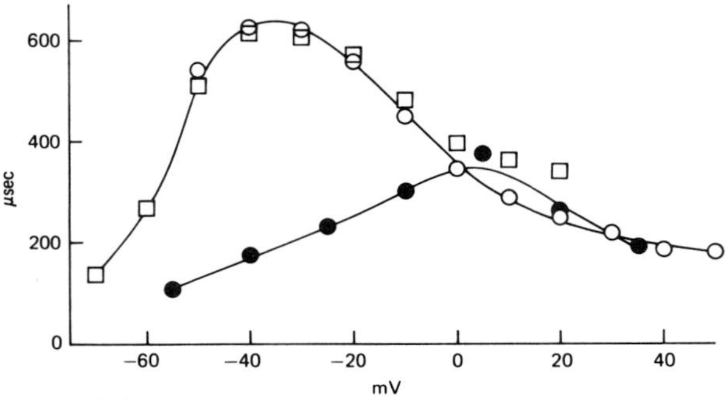

Fig. 2: Comparison of τ_m, time constant of activation of the sodium system, and τ_{on}, time constant of the on-response of the gating current, in a squid giant axon. τ_m for the turning-on and the turning-off of m is represented by o and □, respectively; τ_{on} is indicated by ●. All measurements on the same axon. Internal solution: 350 mM CsF + 400 mM sucrose. External solution for recording Na currents: artificial sea water with 4/5 of the Na replaced by Tris. External solution for recording gating currents: artificial sea water with all Na replaced by Tris and with 2 μM TTX. Temperature −0.1 °C (Keynes and Kimura, 1983).

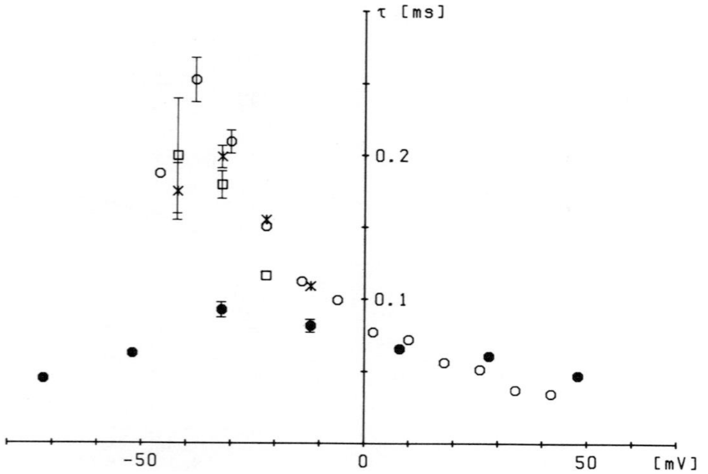

Fig. 3: Comparison of τ_m, time constant of activation of the sodium system, and τ_{on}, time constant of the on-response of the gating current, in the frog node of Ranvier. τ_m for the turning-on of m is represented by □, ○ and ∗; τ_{on} is indicated by ●. Points are average values (± standard error of the mean) from different nodes. Conditions for recording Na currents: Ringer + 6 nM TTX; ∗, average values from 6 nodes treated with 0.5 mM chloramine-T for 4–9 min; □, average values from 2 untreated nodes; ○, average values from Table 1 of NEUMCKE et al. (1976). Gating currents recorded in TMA-Ringer + 300 nM TTX (NaCl replaced by tetramethylammonium chloride (TMA)). Temperature 10 °C for ○ and 12 °C for all others (MEVES and RUBLY, 1986 and additional measurements).

course of charge movement in two respects: (a) it shows an initial delay which is not seen in the charge movement, (b) its time constant, at negative membrane potentials, is larger than the time constant of the charge movement.

As shown by symbols ∗ in Fig. 3, removal of inactivation by a brief treatment with chloramine-T (WANG, 1984) has no significant effect on τ_m, the time constant of activation. The time course of sodium activation is, however, profoundly altered by certain toxins. In nodes treated with batrachotoxin (BTX), the activation curve is shifted to more negative values of membrane potential so that Na inward currents can be elicited by test pulses to potentials as negative as −100 or −90 mV. These Na currents follow an exponential time course rather than the normal sigmoidal time course (KHODOROV, 1978; DUBOIS and SCHNEIDER, 1985). The same phenomenon (shift of activation curve, exponential time course) is observed in nodes treated with toxins III and IV from the scorpion *Centruroides sculpturatus* and subjected to a depolarizing conditioning pulse. Small test pulses elicit sodium currents which rise exponentially and start without a measurable delay (HU, MEVES, RUBLY and WATT, 1983). Fig. 4 shows the time course of the charge movement and the time course of the Na current in a node treated with 5 μg/ml *Centruroides sculpturatus* toxin IV. In A (without a depolarizing conditioning pulse), there is a pronounced delay between charge movement and rise of the Na current, similar to that in Fig. 1. In B (with a depolarizing conditioning pulse), both Na current and charge movement begin at t = 0 and both follow a simple exponential time course. A fundamental criterion that any gating current must satisfy is that it begins to flow at least by the time the channel opens (HILLE, 1976). In Fig. 4B, where both currents begin simultaneously at t =

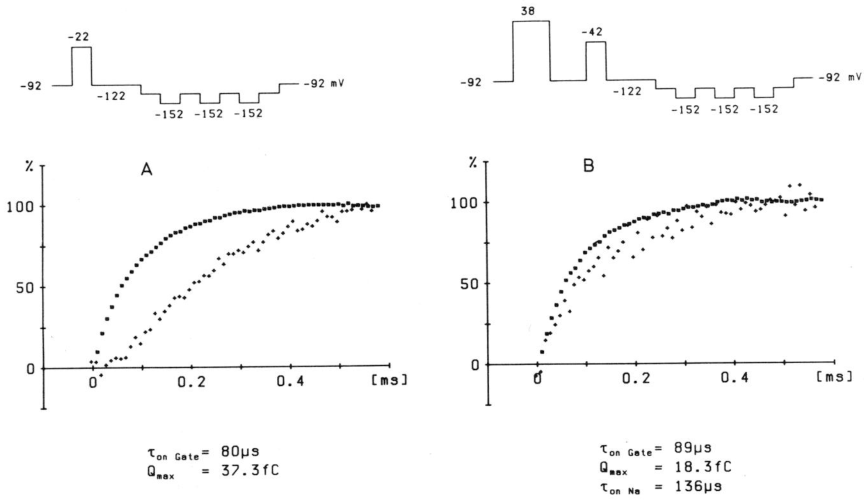

Fig. 4: Time course of charge movement and activation of sodium current in a node of Ranvier treated with 5 μg/ml toxin IV of *Centruroides sculpturatus*. Pulse program for measuring gating current or Na current shown on top. Test pulse to −22 mV (A) or to −42 mV (B). A, without conditioning pulse; B, with 15 ms conditioning pulse to 38 mV, followed by 40 ms pause. Gating current recorded in the presence of 300 nM TTX, integrated and normalized as in Fig. 1. Na current recorded in Na-poor Ringer (two thirds of Na replaced by Tris), divided by exp($-t/\tau_h$), normalized and plotted upwards. Temperature 12 °C (MEVES, RUBLY and WATT, 1986).

0, this criterion is still satisfied; also the rise of the Na current is still slower than the rise of the gating current ($\tau_{on\ Na} = 136\ \mu s$, $\tau_{on\ Gate} = 89\ \mu s$, $\tau_{on\ Na}/\tau_{on\ Gate} = 1.53$). A similar result is obtained with a test pulse to −62 mV ($\tau_{on\ Na} = 100\ \mu s$, $\tau_{on\ Gate} = 53\ \mu s$, $\tau_{on\ Na}/\tau_{on\ Gate} = 1.89$), whereas with a test pulse to −22 mV (which activates both modified and normal channels) the delay between charge movement and rise of Na current becomes more pronounced ($\tau_{on\ Na} = 238\ \mu s$, $\tau_{on\ Gate} = 88\ \mu s$, $\tau_{on\ Na}/\tau_{on\ Gate} = 2.70$). Observations similar to those on nodes treated with *C. sculpturatus* toxins have been reported for batrachotoxin-treated nodes by DUBOIS and SCHNEIDER (1985). In their case $\tau_{on\ Gate}$ is even slightly (1.15 times) larger than $\tau_{on\ Na}$.

In squid axons OXFORD (1981) observed an exponential rise of the Na current starting at t = 0 when the test pulse was preceded by another depolarizing pulse and the interval between the two pulses was short (e.g. 0.1 ms at 5 °C). The requirement for an exponentially rising Na current seems to be that the Na channels are still in a state close to the open state at the time when the test pulse is applied. This requirement seems to be fulfilled both in the experiment of Fig. 4B and in OXFORD's experiment.

Comparison between τ_{on} and τ_{off} for sodium activation and charge movement

As illustrated in Fig. 2, KEYNES and KIMURA (1983) found on squid axons that the time constant for the turning-on (○) and the time constant for the turning-off (□) of the Na activation variable m are not significantly different if both are measured at the same potential ($\tau_{m\ on} = \tau_{m\ off}$). A discrepancy between τ_{off} and τ_{on} was, however, reported by OXFORD (1981) who also studied Na currents and Na tail currents of the squid giant axon. As shown in his Fig. 4A, the tail current time constant continued to increase at more positive potentials whereas τ_m measured from I_{Na} turn-on decreased.

Our findings on the node of Ranvier (Fig. 5) support the conclusion of KEYNES and KIMURA (1983) that $\tau_{m\ on} = \tau_{m\ off}$. Fig. 5A shows a tail current record which was obtained by applying a brief strong depolarizing pulse (which served to activate the Na permeability) and repolarizing, at the peak of the Na inward current, to −22 mV. The tail current can be fitted by the sum of two exponentials (for numerical values of the time constants τ_1 and τ_2 see legend of Fig. 5) and a time-independent term. The time course of the tail current is not only determined by the change in the activation variable m but also by the change in the inactivation variable h. In particular, the initial fast phase of inactivation which occurs after a strong depolarizing prepulse (FRANKENHAEUSER, 1963; KOPPENHÖFER, 1967) may affect τ_1, the time constant of the first exponential. To inhibit inactivation we used chloramine-T, a substance which removes inactivation but has no significant effect on the time course of activation (WANG, 1984, see also Fig. 3). As illustrated by Fig. 5B, treatment with 0.5 mM chloramine-T for 5 min caused a reduction of the peak Na inward current to 77 % of the control value and had a marked effect on the time course of the tail current recorded at −22 mV. The tail current measured at 3 ms was twice as large as before. The division of the tail current into a fast initial and a slower second component became more evident and the time constant τ_1 became smaller (see legend of Fig. 5).

In Fig. 5C, average values of the first tail current time constant τ_1 from four chloramine-T-treated fibres are plotted against the postpulse potential (symbols o). The points reach a maximum at −32 mV and then decrease again. τ_1 equals $\tau_{m\ off}/2$ at large negative post-

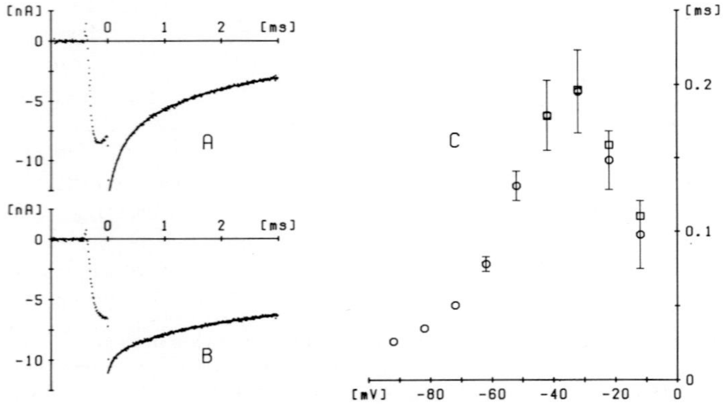

Fig. 5: A, Na current associated with a 0.4 ms pulse from holding potential (−92 mV) to 8 mV followed by repolarization to −22 mV. External solution contains 6 nM TTX to reduce series resistance artifact. K currents blocked by internal Cs (ends of fibre in 113 mM CsCl + 7 mM NaCl) and external TEA (12 mM). Three records averaged; TTX-insensitive current (measured with the same pulse sequence in the presence of 300 nM TTX) subtracted. B, same after treatment with 0.5 mM chloramine-T for 5 min. Tail currents fitted to two exponentials with $\tau_1 = 0.192$, $\tau_2 = 1.63$ ms in A, $\tau_1 = 0.113$, $\tau_2 = 1.86$ ms in B. C, fast tail current time constant (τ_1) plotted against postpulse potential (○) and time constant of the turning-on of Na activation ($\tau_{m\ on}$) at pulse potentials > −50 mV (□). Mean ± S. E. M. from four experiments. Temperature 12 °C (MEVES and RUBLY, 1985).

pulse potentials and $\tau_{m\ off}$ at small negative postpulse potentials. This is due to the fact that I_{Na} is proportional to

$$m^2 = [m_\infty - (m_\infty - m_o)\ \exp(-t/\tau_m)]^2.$$

For instance, with $m_o = 0.85$ (activating pulse to -12 mV) and $m_\infty = 0.6$ (postpulse potential -32 mV) the amplitude of the $\tau_{m\ off}/2$ component is only a fifth of the amplitude of the $\tau_{m\ off}$ component. In addition to the τ_1 values, Fig. 5C shows average values of $\tau_{m\ on}$ (symbols □), the time constant of the turning-on of the Na activation variable m. $\tau_{m\ on}$ was determined at four different potentials by fitting the equation

$$I_{Na} = I'_{Na}[1 - \exp(-(t - \delta t)/\tau_m)]^2\ [h_\infty - (h_\infty - 1)\exp(-(t - \delta t)/\tau_h)]$$

to the Na currents elicited by 5 ms depolarizing pulses. The $\tau_{m\ on}$ values are from the same four chloramine-T-treated fibres as the τ_1 values. The $\tau_{m\ on}$ values (symbols □) are not significantly different from the τ_1 values (symbols o) which in this potential range equal $\tau_{m\ off}$. It follows that $\tau_{m\ on} = \tau_{m\ off}$ at potentials between -12 and -42 mV.*

Without chloramine-T treatment, there was approximate agreement between τ_1 and $\tau_{m\ on}$ at -32 mV. This is illustrated by Fig. 6 which shows a tail current recorded at -32 mV (A) and the Na inward current elicited by a pulse to -32 mV (B). The quantitative analysis (see legend of Fig. 6) gave $\tau_1 = 0.171$ ms for the first phase of the tail current and $\tau_{m\ on} = 0.170$ ms for the turning-on of the activation variable m. However, at -22 mV τ_1 was much larger than $\tau_{m\ on}$. It seems that without chloramine-T treatment the τ_1 values measured at $E > -30$ mV are erroneously large due to contamination by the inactivation process.

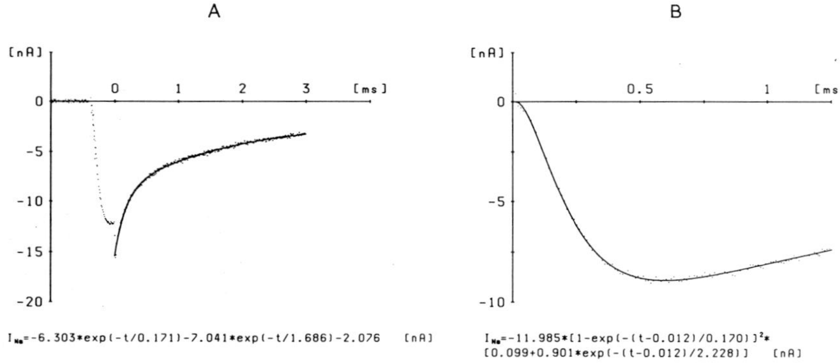

Fig. 6: Comparison of turning-off of m at -32 mV (A) and turning-on of m at -32 mV (B) in a fibre not treated with chloramine-T. A: Na current associated with a 0.4 ms pulse from holding potential (-92 mV) to -12 mV followed by repolarization to -32 mV. Tail current fitted to two exponentials with $\tau_1 = 0.171$, $\tau_2 = 1.686$ ms. B: Na current associated with a 5 ms pulse to -32 mV, only first 1.25 ms shown. Na current fitted with the equation

$$I_{Na} = -11.985\ [1\text{-}\exp(-(t-0.012)/0.170)]^2 \times [0.099+0.901 \times \exp(-(t-0.012)/2.228)][nA].$$

Solutions and temperature as in Fig. 5. Three records averaged; TTX-insensitive current subtracted (MEVES and RUBLY, unpublished).

* Fitting the tail currents with the same equation as used for the Na currents yields $\tau_{m\ on} = \tau_{m\ off}$ at -12 and -22 mV and $\tau_{m\ on} = \tau_{m\ off}/1.22$ at -32 mV (MEVES and RUBLY, 1986).

Likewise, in gating current experiments no significant difference between τ_{off} and τ_{on} (measured at the same potential) was found. Fig. 7A and B illustrate the method for determining the time constant of the turning-on (τ_{on}) and the turning-off (τ_{off}) of the gating current at the same potential. In A, a brief activating pulse (pulse potential 8 mV, pulse duration 0.2 ms) was followed by a 0.6 ms pulse to −32 mV. From the integrated gating current the time constant of the charge movement associated with the repolarization from 8 to −32 mV was determined as $\tau_{off} = 0.125$ ms. In B, the same 0.6 ms pulse to −32 mV without the preceding activating pulse was given. The time constant of the integrated charge movement associated with the depolarization to −32 mV was obtained as $\tau_{on} = 0.110$ ms, i. e. close to τ_{off}. Fig. 7C shows measurements of τ_{on} and τ_{off} on a single fibre over the voltage range −92 to 28 mV. The τ_{on} values (□) and the τ_{off} values (o) measured at the same potential are not significantly different. Close agreement between τ_{on} and τ_{off}, both measured at −32 mV, was observed in five fibres studied at 6–7.5 °C without treatment with chloramine-T and in four fibres investigated at 12 °C after treatment with chloramine-T.

Our finding $\tau_{off\ Gate} = \tau_{on\ Gate}$ is in conflict with the observations of DUBOIS and SCHNEIDER (1982) who found τ_{on} more than twice as large as τ_{off} at −30 mV (see Fig. 8 which is from DUBOIS and SCHNEIDER (1982) and shows $\tau_{on} = 0.24$ ms and $\tau_{off} = 0.10$ ms at −30 mV and 8°C). Comparison with Fig. 7C reveals that the discrepancy is mainly a

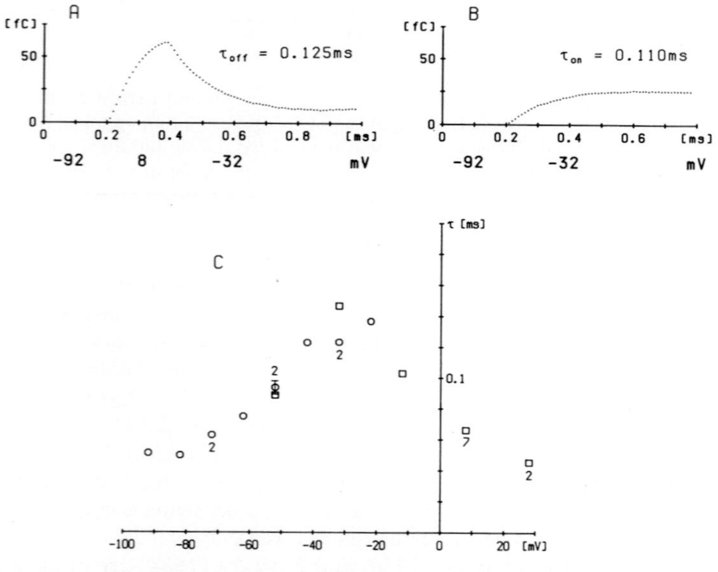

Fig. 7: Gating current experiment for determining the time constants of the turning-on (τ_{on}) and the turning-off (τ_{off}) of the charge movement at the same potential (−32 mV). A: integrated gating current obtained with two depolarizing pulses P1 and P2; P1 is a 0.2 ms pulse to 8 mV, P2 a 0.6 ms pulse to −32 mV. B: same as A, but without pulse P1. A and B: 64 records averaged, capacity and leakage current measured with hyperpolarizing pulses of amplitude −P1/2 and −P2/2 and subtracted. C: Time constants τ_{on} (□) and τ_{off} (O) measured with the method illustrated in A and B on an another fibre. Symbols represent individual measurements or averages from n measurements; in the latter case n, the number of measurements, is indicated. Except in one case, the SEM was within symbol size. Ringer + 12 mM TEA + 300 nM TTX. Temperature 7 °C (MEVES and RUBLY, 1986).

discrepancy of the τ_{on} values; our τ_{on} at −32 mV and 7 °C is 0.146 ms, i. e. only 61 % of the value given by DUBOIS and SCHNEIDER (1982), and τ_{off} at the same potential and temperature is 0.123 ms, i. e. close to the value given by DUBOIS and SCHNEIDER. It is not clear how the discrepancy of the τ_{on} values arises: pulse program, temperature, external solution, internal solution are the same or nearly the same in our experiments and in those of DUBOIS and SCHNEIDER. The only remaining possibility is that the discrepancy of the τ_{on} values arises from differences in the integration procedure. In this connexion, it is important to note that our essential result ($\tau_{on} = \tau_{off}$) is obtained regardless whether the integrated responses or the gating currents themselves are fitted.

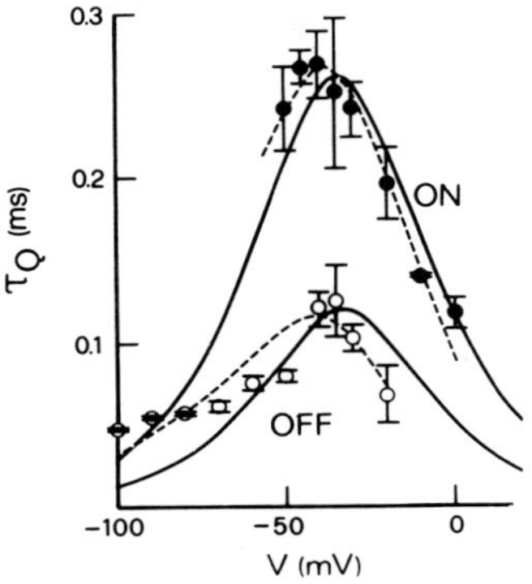

Fig. 8: Time constants τ_{on} (●) and τ_{off} (o) of the gating current plotted against membrane potential. The on charge movement was recorded during pulses of various amplitudes applied from the holding potential (−100 mV). The off charge movement was recorded during pulses of various amplitudes preceded by 0.2 ms depolarizations to 20 mV. Mean values and SEM of 2–9 determinations. Solid and dashed curves calculated from an energy barrier model. Temperature 8 °C (DUBOIS and SCHNEIDER, 1982).

If the τ_{on} values of DUBOIS and SCHNEIDER (1982) were right, the ratio τ_{on}/τ_m at −30 mV would be close to unity which would contradict the measurements of KEYNES and KIMURA (1983) on squid axons (Fig. 2), our measurements on frog nerve fibres (Fig. 3) and the measurements of CHIU (1980) on mammalian nerve fibres. DUBOIS and SCHNEIDER give $\tau_{on} = 0.24$ ms at −30 mV and 8 °C, corresponding (with a Q_{10} of 3) to $\tau_{on} = 0.192$ ms at 10 °C and $\tau_{on} = 0.156$ ms at 12 °C. Fig. 3 gives $\tau_m = 0.209$ ms at −30 mV and 10 °C (circles) and $\tau_m = 0.179$ at −32 mV and 12 °C (rectangles). Hence $\tau_{on}/\tau_m = 0.92$ and 0.87 at 10 and 12 °C, respectively. By contrast, $\tau_{on}/\tau_m = 0.32$ at −32 mV on squid axons (see Fig. 2), $\tau_{on}/\tau_m = 0.53$ at −32 mV in our measurements (see Fig. 3) and $\tau_{on}/\tau_m =$ 0.32 at −35 mV in CHIU's measurements (see his Table 3).

The τ_{on} values of NEUMCKE et al. (1976) and NONNER (1980) are in between our τ_{on} values and the τ_{on} values of DUBOIS and SCHNEIDER (1982). Table 1 of NEUMCKE et al. (1976) gives four τ_{on} values for −30 mV and 10 °C whose average is 0.153 ms, corresponding (with a Q_{10} of 3) to $\tau_{on} = 0.191$ ms at 8 °C. NONNER (1980) finds $\tau_{on} = 0.128$ ms at −32 mV and 13 °C (see Fig. 9B), corresponding (with a Q_{10} of 3) to $\tau_{on} = 0.222$ ms at 8 °C. Fig. 9B (which will be fully discussed in the following section) shows that a conditioning depolarization markedly diminishes τ_{on}, especially in the voltage range −40 to 0 mV; the strong dependence of τ_{on} on potential history could, at least partly, explain why different authors obtain different numerical values for τ_{on}.

Charge immobilization

As shown in Fig. 9, a depolarizing conditioning pulse of 2 ms duration has a marked effect on the charge movement. It reduces $Q_{on\ max}$, the maximum on-charge movement obtained with strong test pulses, to less than 50 % of its normal size but has no effect on Q_{on} measured with small test pulses. The slope of the Q_{on} (E) curve is considerably diminished. In addition, the time constant τ_{on} is reduced (see above). It appears that the depolarizing conditioning pulse has led to immobilization of those charges which are characterized by strongly voltage-dependent kinetics.

Treatment of the nerve fibre with a local anaesthetic has the same effect on the charge movement as a depolarizing conditioning pulse (GUSELNIKOVA et al. 1979; KHODOROV, 1981). Fig. 10A shows the $Q_{on}(V)$ curve measured under normal conditions (symbols o, curve 1), with a depolarizing conditioning pulse (symbols △) and after application of the local anaesthetic QX572 (symbols □). Points △ and □ are close together and are fitted with a

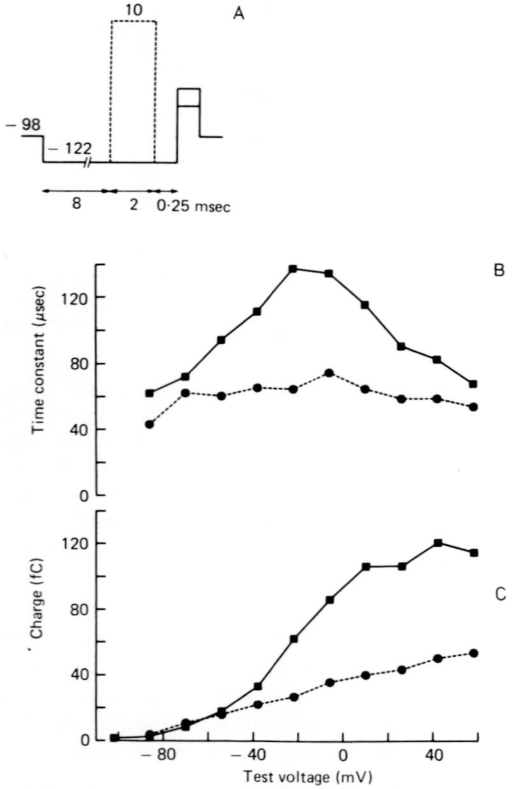

Fig. 9: Effect of a depolarizing conditioning pulse on the charge movement. A: pulse program including, or not, a conditioning pulse to 10 mV, followed by a 0.25 ms interval at −122 mV and a test pulse to various levels. B, time constant τ_{on} of the on-response plotted against test pulse voltage, without conditioning pulse (■) and with conditioning pulse (●). C, same for Q_{on}, the charge movement during the on-response. Temperature 13 °C (NONNER, 1980).

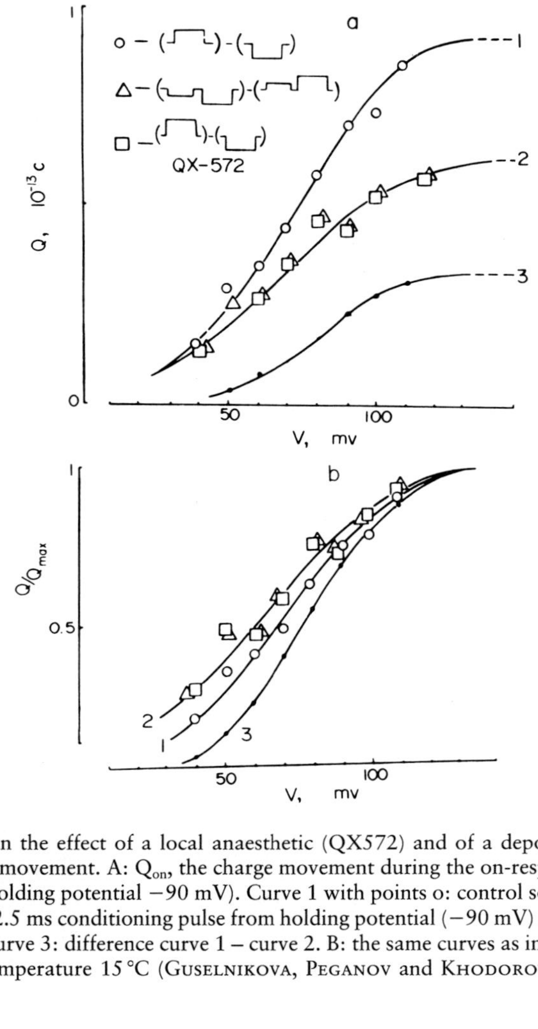

Fig. 10: Similarity in the effect of a local anaesthetic (QX572) and of a depolarizing conditioning pulse on the charge movement. A: Q_{on}, the charge movement during the on-response, plotted against test pulse voltage (holding potential −90 mV). Curve 1 with points o: control solution, no conditioning pulse. Curve 2: 2.5 ms conditioning pulse from holding potential (−90 mV) to −40 mV (△) or 0.2 mM QX572 (□). Curve 3: difference curve 1 – curve 2. B: the same curves as in A, but normalized to their maximum. Temperature 15 °C (GUSELNIKOVA, PEGANOV and KHODOROV, 1979; KHODOROV, 1981).

common curve (curve 2). This experiment suggests that there are two types of charges: charges which are sensitive to inactivation and local anaesthetics (curve 3 in Fig. 10A) and charges which are resistant to inactivation and local anaesthetics (curve 2 in Fig. 10A); the latter may be immobilized by slow inactivation. As shown by the normalized $Q_{on}(V)$ curves in Fig. 10B, the slope is largest for curve 3 and smallest for curve 2.

Similarly, the gating current of the squid giant axon can be divided into an inactivating and a non-inactivating component (for review see KEYNES, 1983). Only the inactivating component is affected by fast inactivation and local anaesthetics, but both components are reduced by slow inactivation. This has been shown by varying the holding potential for several minutes (BEKKERS, GREEFF, KEYNES and NEUMCKE, 1984). On the node of Ranvier, the effect of slow inactivation on the charge movement can be demonstrated by lengthening the interval between conditioning pulse and test pulse (which is only 0.25 ms in Fig. 9) to 20 ms (MEVES, RUBLY and WATT, 1986). On normal fibres the effect is small: A depolarizing conditioning pulse of 15 ms duration from the holding potential (−92 mV) to 38 mV reduces Q_{on} (measured after a 20 ms interval with a test pulse to 28 mV) only by the factor 0.949 ± 0.049 (mean ± SEM, n = 5). However, the effect becomes more pronounced on fibres treated with toxin III or IV (2.4–3.0 μg/ml) from the scorpion *Centruroides sculpturatus*: Here Q_{on} (measured with the same pulse program) is reduced by the factor 0.729 ± 0.060 (n = 5). It seems that the toxins make slow inactivation more pronounced.

Effect of previous history on the rate of inactivation

An effect of the previous potential history on the time course of inactivation has first been described by FRANKENHAEUSER (1963). As mentioned above, he found that after a short depolarizing prepulse the Na inward current inactivates in two phases, a fast initial phase and a slower second phase (see also KOPPENHÖFER, 1967). Two striking examples for the effect of previous history on the rate of inactivation are shown in Figs. 11 and 12. Fig. 11 repeats the «perturbation» experiment which SCHAUF and BAUMANN (1981) performed on *Myxicola* axons. The «perturbing» pulse is a 0.1 ms pulse to 58 or 108 mV superimposed on a depolarizing pulse to −32 mV. It causes a marked acceleration of the

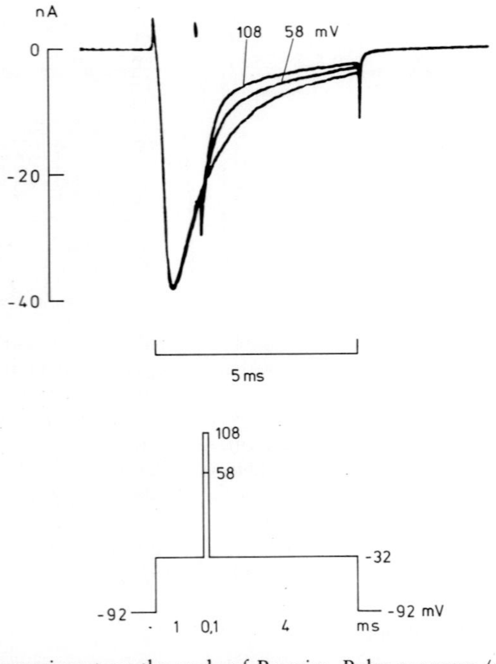

Fig. 11: Perturbation experiment on the node of Ranvier. Pulse program (see underneath records) consists of a 5.1 ms pulse from holding potential (−92 mV) to −32 mV with a 0.1 ms pulse to 58 or 108 mV superimposed. Ringer + 12 mM TEA. Cut ends of fibre in 113 mM CsCl + 7 mM NaCl. Temperature 12 °C (MEVES and RUBLY, unpublished).

rate of inactivation: the stronger the «perturbing» pulse, the more pronounced the acceleration. The acceleration is followed by a phase during which the decay of the Na current is slower than normal. Thus, the «perturbing» pulse has the same effect as the short depolarizing prepulse in the experiments of FRANKENHAEUSER (1963) and KOPPENHÖFER (1967). This is to be expected because omitting the initial 1 ms step to −32 mV in Fig. 11 leads to a pulse program like that used by FRANKENHAEUSER (1963) and KOPPENHÖFER (1967). The «perturbation» experiment was suggested to us by Dr. GILBERT BAUMANN from Duke University in Durham, North Carolina; its results are consistent with the aggregation model of BAUMANN (1981) which predicts that the «conductance kinetics depend on the perturbations that the gating system has experienced in its immediate past».

Fig. 12 shows a different type of experiment. The depolarizing conditioning pulse was much longer (500 ms duration) than the «perturbing» pulse (0.1 ms duration) in the experiment of Fig. 11. Between the conditioning pulse and the test pulse was a pause of 20 ms (Fig. 12A) or 100 ms (Fig. 12B). In spite of this long pause there was a clear effect of the conditioning pulse on the Na current elicited by the test pulse. The most conspicuous change was the reduction of the current remaining at the end of the 55 ms pulse, corresponding to a decrease of the time-independent term C. As can be seen from the fit parameters underneath the records, the conditioning pulse also reduced the size and time constant of the second exponential (parameters B and τ_2). A similar experiment on a fibre internally treated with KIO_3 in order to inhibit inactivation is shown in Fig. 9A of MEVES, RUBLY and WATT (1984). It appears that the inactivation process has s surprisingly long-lasting memory for the previous potential history.

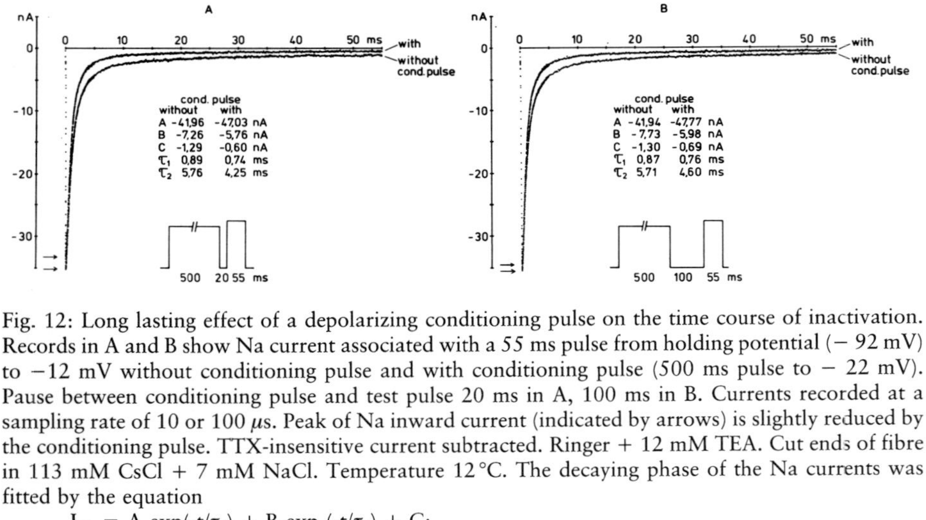

Fig. 12: Long lasting effect of a depolarizing conditioning pulse on the time course of inactivation. Records in A and B show Na current associated with a 55 ms pulse from holding potential (− 92 mV) to −12 mV without conditioning pulse and with conditioning pulse (500 ms pulse to − 22 mV). Pause between conditioning pulse and test pulse 20 ms in A, 100 ms in B. Currents recorded at a sampling rate of 10 or 100 μs. Peak of Na inward current (indicated by arrows) is slightly reduced by the conditioning pulse. TTX-insensitive current subtracted. Ringer + 12 mM TEA. Cut ends of fibre in 113 mM CsCl + 7 mM NaCl. Temperature 12 °C. The decaying phase of the Na currents was fitted by the equation

$$I_{Na} = A \exp(-t/\tau_1) + B \exp(-t/\tau_2) + C;$$

the fit parameters are given (MEVES and RUBLY, unpublished).

Suggestions for future experiments

Recently, two interesting findings on the node of Ranvier have been reported which clearly deserve more detailed investigation in future experiments. DUBOIS, SCHNEIDER and KHODOROV (1983) found that batrachotoxin causes an approximately threefold increase in steepness of the Q vs voltage relationship (an effect opposite to that of depolarizing conditioning pulses and local anaesthetics, see above) and a 50 mV negative shift of its midpoint. Batrachotoxin decreases the steepness factor k (defined as the number of mV required to change Q e-fold) from its normal value of 13.0 mV to 4.85 mV and shifts the potential at which $Q = Q_{max}/2$ from −32 mV (compare Figs. 9 and 10) to −83 mV. Whereas in untreated nodes the voltage dependence of Q is considerably less steep than the voltage dependence of the sodium conductance g_{Na} (NEUMCKE et al. 1976), the two curves coincide in batrachotoxin-treated fibres. DUBOIS et al. (1983) suggest «that batrachotoxin induces an aggregation of the charged gating particles associated with each channel and causes them to move as a unit having approximately three times the average valence of the individual particles». It will be interesting to see whether the observations on batrachotoxin-treated nodes are confirmed in other laboratories or with similarly acting chemical agents.

As described by NEUMCKE, SCHWARZ and STÄMPFLI (1985), sea anemone toxin ATX II (which inhibits inactivation of the sodium permeability) abolishes slow components of the on-response of the gating current. It is tempting to speculate that the slow ATX II-sensitive charge movement is in some way related to the process of inactivation. The question whether there is a component of gating current that is related to inactivation has repeatedly been discussed in the past, for instance by FRENCH and HORN (1983). If such a component could be definitely proved to exist, this would have important consequences for the modelling of the inactivation process. A detailed investigation of the slow components in the on-response of the gating current is therefore highly desirable.

References

Almers, W. (1978): Gating currents and charge movements in excitable membranes. Rev. Physiol. Biochem. Pharmacol. **82,** 96–190.

Armstrong, C. M. (1981): Sodium channels and gating currents. Physiol. Rev. **61,** 644–683.

Baumann, G. (1981): Novel kinetics in the sodium conductance system predicted by the aggregation model of channel gating. Biophys. J. **35,** 699–705.

Bekkers, J. M., Greeff, N. G., Keynes, R. D., Neumcke, B. (1984): The effect of local anaesthetics on the components of the asymmetry current in the squid giant axon. J. Physiol. **352,** 653–668.

Chiu, S. Y. (1980): Asymmetry currents in the mammalian myelinated nerve. J. Physiol. **309,** 499–519.

Dodge, F. A., Frankenhaeuser, B. (1958): Membrane currents in isolated frog nerve fibre under voltage clamp conditions. J. Physiol. **143,** 76–90.

Dubois, J. M., Schneider, M. F. (1982): Kinetics of intramembrane charge movement and sodium current in frog node of Ranvier. J. Gen. Physiol. **79,** 571–602.

Dubois, J. M., Schneider, M. F. (1985): Kinetics of intramembrane charge movement and conductance activation of batrachotoxin-modified sodium channels in frog node of Ranvier. J. Gen. Physiol. **86,** 381–394.

Dubois, J. M., Schneider, M. F., Khodorov, B. I. (1983): Voltage dependence of intramembrane charge movement and conductance activation of batrachotoxin-modified sodium channels in frog node of Ranvier. J. Gen. Physiol. **81,** 829–844.

Frankenhaeuser, B. (1963): Inactivation of the sodium-carrying mechanism in myelinated nerve fibres of *Xenopus laevis*. J. Physiol. **169,** 445–451.

French, R. J., Horn, R. (1983): Sodium channel gating: models, mimics, and modifiers. Ann. Rev. Biophys. Bioeng. **12,** 319–356.

Guselnikova, G., Peganov, E., Khodorov, B. (1979): Blockade of the gating currents in node of Ranvier under the action of the quaternary derivative of lidocaine (compound QX572). Dokl. Akad. Nauk. SSSR **244,** 1492–1494.

Hille, B. (1976): Gating in sodium channels of nerve. A. Rev. Physiol. **38,** 139–152.

Hu, S. L., Meves, H., Rubly, N., Watt, D. D. (1983): A quantitative study of the action of *Centruroides sculpturatus* toxins III and IV on the Na currents of the node of Ranvier. Pflügers Arch. **397,** 90–99.

Keynes, R. D. (1983): Voltage-gated ion channels in the nerve membrane. Proc. Roy. Soc. Lond. **B 220,** 1–30.

Keynes, R. D., Kimura, J. E. (1983): Kinetics of activation of the sodium conductance in the squid giant axon. J. Physiol. **336,** 621–634.

Khodorov, B. I. (1978): Chemicals as tools to study nerve fiber sodium channels; effects of batrachotoxin and some local anaesthetics. In: Membrane transport processes (D. C. Tosteson, Y. A. Ovchinnikov, R. Latorre, eds.), Vol. **1,** Raven Press, New York.

Khodorov, B. I. (1981): Sodium inactivation and drug-induced immobilization of the gating charge in nerve membrane. Prog. Biophys. molec. Biol. **37,** 49–89.

Koppenhöfer, E. (1967): Die Wirkung von Tetraäthylammoniumchlorid auf die Membranströme Ranvierscher Schnürringe von *Xenopus laevis*. Pflügers Arch. **293,** 34–55.

Meves, H., Rubly, N. (1985): Sodium tail currents at different post-pulse potentials in the voltage-clamped frog node of Ranvier. J. Physiol. **369,** 103 P.

Meves, H., Rubly, N. (1986): Kinetics of sodium current and gating current in the frog node of Ranvier. Pflügers Arch. **407,** 18–26.

Meves, H., Rubly, N., Watt, D. D. (1984): Voltage-dependent effect of a scorpion toxin on sodium current inactivation. Pflügers Arch. **402,** 24–33.

Meves, H., Rubly, N., Watt, D. D. (1986): Gating current experiments on frog nodes of Ranvier treated with *Centruroides sculpturatus* toxins or aconitine. Pflügers Arch. in preparation.

Neumcke, B., Nonner, W., Stämpfli, R. (1976): Asymmetrical displacement current and its relation with the activation of sodium current in the membrane of frog myelinated nerve. Pflügers Arch. **363,** 193–203.

Neumcke, B., Nonner, W., Stämpfli, R. (1978): Gating currents in excitable membranes. In: MTP International Review of Science, Biochemistry Series, Volume **2,** Series 2 (J. C. Metcalfe, ed.), pp. 129–155. University Park Press, Baltimore.

Neumcke, B., Schwarz, W., Stämpfli, R. (1985): Comparison of the effects of Anemonia toxin II on sodium and gating currents in frog myelinated nerve. Biochim. Biophys. Acta **814,** 111–119.

Nonner, W. (1980): Relations between the inactivation of sodium channels and the immobilization of gating charge in frog myelinated nerve. J. Physiol. **299,** 573–603.

Nonner, W., Rojas, E., Stämpfli, R. (1975): Displacement currents in the node of Ranvier. Voltage and time dependence. Pflügers Arch. **354,** 1–18.

Oxford, G. S. (1981): Some kinetic and steady-state properties of sodium channels after removal of inactivation. J. Gen. Physiol. **77,** 1–22.

Schauf, C. L., Baumann, G. (1981): Experimental evidence consistent with aggregation kinetics in the sodium current of *Myxicola* giant axons. Biophys. J. **35,** 707–714.

Wang, G. K. (1984): Irreversible modification of sodium channel inactivation in toad myelinated nerve fibres by the oxidant chloramine-T. J. Physiol. **346,** 127–141.

Fortschritte der Zoologie, Band 33 · Lüttgau (Hrsg.): Membrane Control
Gustav Fischer Verlag · Stuttgart · New York · 1986

The influence of SCN modified surface charges on nodal Na channels of frog nerve

B. Neumcke and R. Stämpfli

I. Physiologisches Institut der Universität des Saarlandes, D-6650 Homburg/Saar, FRG

Na channels in excitable membranes are gated by the electric field strength in the membrane phase. This electric field is not only determined by the voltage between the extra- and intracellular solutions but also by membrane surface potentials created by fixed negative charges on the outer and inner membrane surfaces. These surface potentials depend on the ionic composition of the solutions in contact with the membrane and thus can be altered by appropriate solution changes. As a result, the voltage dependence of the gating parameters is shifted along the voltage axis by an amount corresponding to a change of the surface potential at the «electrical field sensor» of the channel gate (for a review see Neumcke, 1981). A second effect of external membrane surface charges on Na channels is the modulation of the binding of the cationic Na channel blockers tetrodotoxin (TTX) and saxitoxin (STX) to receptors at the outer mouth of the channels (Ritchie and Rogart, 1977). Thirdly, surface charges may change the local concentration of permeant ions at the channel entrance and thus the channel conductance. Depending on the distance between surface charges and the components of the Na channel, the negative surface potential will affect various channel properties to a different degree. Thus, the mutual location of the field sensor of the channel gates, of the TTX, STX receptor and the channel entrance can be inferred from the strength of surface potential effects on voltage shifts of gating parameters, on TTX, STX binding and on Na channel conductance.

In myelinated nerve the density of external negative surface charges of the nodal membrane can be easily modulated by a change of the ionic composition of the extracellular solution. Addition of di- or trivalent cations neutralizes part of the negative charges, whereas replacement of Cl^- by NO_3^- or SCN^- anions produces a more negative surface potential. Hille et al. (1975) and Grissmer (1984a, b) have shown that such potential changes as sensed by the Na channel gates only partly affect the TTX, STX binding to Na channels, and they have estimated the fraction of the surface potential acting on the toxin receptor. In these experiments, macroscopic Na currents through all Na channels of a node of Ranvier were analysed from which a discrimination of surface potential effects on the number N of Na channels and the current i through a single channel was not possible. To overcome this difficulty we have recently performed measurements of non-stationary Na current fluctuations to study the effects of surface potential on individual Na channels (Neumcke and Stämpfli, 1984). The disadvantage of such a fluctuation analysis is that significant changes of N and i can be detected only for relatively large alterations of these channel parameters. This might have been the reason for our failure to detect surface potential effects on toxin binding in replacing Cl^- by NO_3^- and in the presence of the univalent TTX. Therefore, we have repeated similar fluctuation measurements under optimized experimental conditions (larger surface potential changes induced by replacement of Cl^- by SCN^- and by using the divalent STX instead of TTX). We now find a clear effect of surface potential on STX binding which, however, is smaller than derived previously from macroscopic Na currents. Hence, there must be a large separation between external surface charges and toxin receptor. Also, the entrance of the Na channel seems to be effectively shielded from these fixed membrane charges since we could not detect an effect of surface potential on channel conductance.

Methods

Single myelinated nerve fibres were dissected from the sciatic nerve of the frog *Rana esculenta* (STÄMPFLI and HILLE, 1976), and a node of Ranvier was voltage-clamped at 15 °C (NONNER, 1969). The internodal resistance needed for current calibration was determined from electrical measurements (SIGWORTH, 1980). Potentials are given as deviations, V, from the potential at which the steady-state Na inactivation h_∞ was approximately 0.7. To achieve an approximate compensation for changes of the external surface potential ψ_o in different extracellular solutions (see NEUMCKE and STÄMPFLI, 1984 and below), the holding potential V_H between test pulses was set to −28 mV in Ringer and to −44 mV in SCN-Ringer. K currents were blocked by tetraethylammonium chloride (TEA) in the extracellular and by CsCl in the intracellular solutions (see Solutions). Linear components of leakage and capacity currents were eliminated by an analogue circuit.

Solutions: Ringer's solution was composed of 110.5 mM NaCl, 2 mM $CaCl_2$ and 10 mM TEA. In SCN-Ringer NaCl was replaced by NaSCN. The ends of the nerve fibre were cut in a solution composed of 113 mM CsCl and 7 mM NaCl. Extra- and intracellular solutions were buffered with 4 mM morpholinopropanesulphonic acid and adjusted to pH 7.2 with NaOH. The junction potential of SCN-Ringer with respect to Ringer as measured with saturated KCl bridges was 1.2 mV (SCN-Ringer negative). Na^+ ion activities a_{Na} were 76.2 mM in Ringer and 70.7 mM in SCN-Ringer (measured with Orion Sodium Specific Electrode, Model 94-11). To study the effects of external surface potential on toxin binding to Na channels, the extracellular solutions contained 8 nM TTX or 4 nM STX. These toxins decreased the amplitude of Na currents and thereby minimized series-resistance artifacts and reduced interaction effects between neighbouring Na channels (NEUMCKE and STÄMPFLI, 1983).

Measurements and analysis: Peak Na currents I_{peak} at various depolarizations V were read off the oscilloscope for each solution. From the $I_{peak}(V)$ curves we determined i) Na reversal potentials V_{Na} as the intercepts with the voltage axis and ii) shifts ΔV between the descending parts of the curves in Ringer and SCN-Ringer.

The current i through a single open Na channel and the number N of Na channels per node were determined from non-stationary Na current fluctuations (SIGWORTH, 1980) as described by NEUMCKE and STÄMPFLI (1982). In these measurements a 45 ms prepulse to −32 mV was applied between the holding potential and the test pulse in Ringer and SCN-Ringer. The chord conductance $\gamma = i/(V-V_{Na})$ of a single channel was calculated from i, the potential V during the positive test pulse and the Na reversal potential V_{Na}. Channel numbers were corrected for the effects of the resistance R_s in series with the nodal membrane from equation (8) of NEUMCKE and STÄMPFLI (1982) with R_s = 220 kΩ for frog nodes (DROUIN and NEUMCKE, 1974).

Results

Figure 1 shows typical peak Na current voltage curves in Ringer and SCN-Ringer plus 8 nM TTX (part A) or 4 nM STX (part B). The figures illustrate negative shifts ΔV of approximately 20 mV between the descending parts of the $I_{peak}(V)$ curves in Ringer and SCN-Ringer whereas the Na reversal potentials V_{Na} are much less affected by the solution exchange. Mean ± SEM values of ΔV from 17 fibres are: $\Delta V = -19.0 \pm 0.3$ mV. Since only 1.2 mV of this shift is due to the liquid junction potential between Ringer and SCN-Ringer (see Solutions), we attribute the difference $\Delta \Psi_o = \Delta V + 1.2$ mV $= -17.8$ mV to a change of the external surface potential Ψ_o. On the other hand, the small negative shift of the Na reversal potential between both solutions ($\Delta V_{Na} = -2.1 \pm 1.0$ mV) can be attributed entirely to the liquid junction potential.

The maximum peak Na current in Ringer is reached near V = 60 mV, in SCN-Ringer near 40 mV. In the presence of TTX these maximum currents are larger in SCN-Ringer compared with Ringer (Fig. 1A), but in the presence of STX they are smaller (Fig. 1B). Similar ratios between maximum peak Na currents were found in all other experiments. The reason for the lower Na currents in STX is the stronger reduction of the number of unblocked Na channels by this divalent toxin (see below).

Examples of measurements of ensemble values of Na currents, I, and variances, var, of nonstationary Na current fluctuations are depicted in Fig. 2. The upper parts (A, C) of this figure show the kinetics of I in Ringer and SCN-Ringer and the lower parts (B, D) the corresponding values of var(I) obtained from measurements of var and I in the same time range. The fit of these var(I) values by a parabola (continuous curves) yields the single channel current i, the channel conductance γ and the number N of Na channels per node in both solutions (compare legend to Fig. 2). In the example shown in Fig. 2, the replacement of Ringer + 4 nM STX by SCN-Ringer + 4 nM STX yields a decrease of the channel conductance γ from 11.4 to 10.7 pS and a decline of the number of Na channels, N, not blocked by 4 nM STX from $17.3 \cdot 10^3$ to $14.0 \cdot 10^3$. The ratios of γ and N in SCN-Ringer with respect to Ringer from this and from more fibres are (mean values ± SEM, number of measurements in parenthesis): ratio $\gamma = 0.96 \pm 0.04$ (11), ratio N $= 0.96 \pm 0.07$ (11) in the presence of 8 nM TTX and ratio $\gamma = 0.93 \pm 0.05$ (10), ratio N $= 0.81 \pm 0.04$ (11) for 4 nM STX.

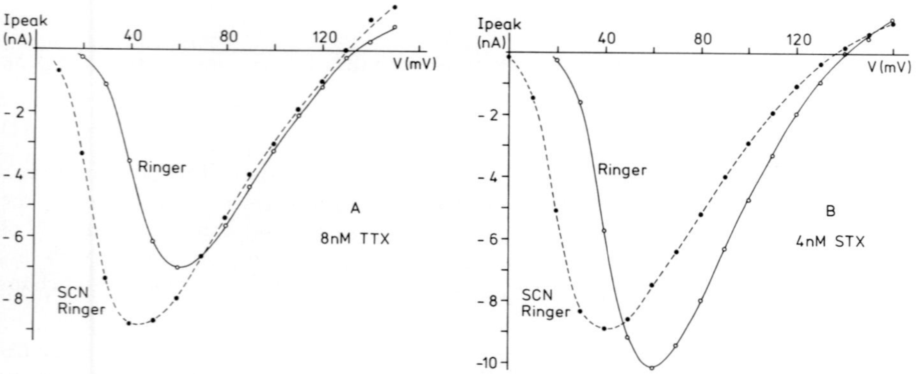

Fig. 1: Peak Na currents I_{peak} as function of depolarization V in Ringer and SCN-Ringer in the presence of 8 nM TTX (A) or 4 nM STX (B). Motor fibres 10/84 (A) and 26/84 (B).

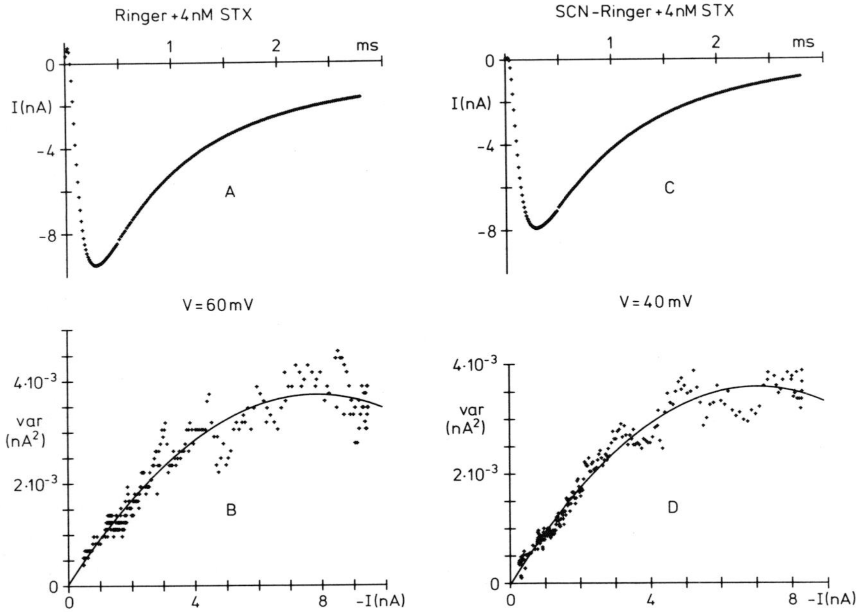

Fig. 2: Na currents I (A, C) and variances var (B, D) of Na current fluctuations in Ringer + 4 nM STX at V = 60 mV (A, B) and in SCN-Ringer + 4 nM STX at V = 40 mV (C, D). The curves in B, D represent fits by the relation var = $iI - I^2/N + c$, the fitted parameters are: $i = -0.944$ pA, $N = 16.6 \cdot 10^3$, $c = 3.68 \cdot 10^{-5}$ nA^2 (B) and $i = -1.033$ pA, $N = 13.6 \cdot 10^3$, $c = -2.56 \cdot 10^{-5}$ nA^2 (D). Channel conductances $\gamma = 11.4$ pS (B), 10.7 pS (D). Channel numbers N corrected for R_s effects: $17.3 \cdot 10^3$ (B), $14.0 \cdot 10^3$ (D). From same fibre as Fig. 1B.

Discussion

For N identical, non-interacting Na channels with only one conducting state the peak Na current can be written as:

$$I_{peak} = N \cdot i \cdot p_{max} \tag{1}$$

where p_{max} is the maximum probability of the open channel state. This probability is a function of the electric field strength at the Na channel gates which is determined by the test potential V and the external surface potential Ψ_o. On the other hand, the number N of Na channels not blocked by cationic extracellular toxins depends only on Ψ_o with less unblocked channels at more negative Ψ_o values. Hence, the fraction of unblocked channels is given by

$$N/N_{tot} = \frac{K}{K + c \exp(-\alpha z F \Psi_o/RT)} \tag{2}$$

where K is the intrinsic equilibrium dissociation constant, c the bulk concentration and z the valency of the toxin. The parameter α ($0 < \alpha < 1$) denotes the fraction of the surface potential Ψ_o acting on the toxin receptor, and F, R, T have their usual meaning (RT/F =

24.8 mV at 15 °C). From equation (2) one obtains the ratio of channel numbers induced by a change $\Delta\Psi_o$ of Ψ_o:

$$\text{ratio N} = \frac{K + c \exp(-\alpha z F \Psi_o/RT)}{K + c \exp[-\alpha z F(\Psi_o + \Delta\Psi_o)/RT]} \quad (3)$$

By introducing the apparent equilibrium dissociation constant

$$K^* = K \exp(\alpha z F \Psi_o/RT) \quad (4)$$

this ratio can be written as

$$\text{ratio N} = \frac{K^* + c}{K^* + c \exp(-\alpha z F \Delta\Psi_o/RT)} \quad (5)$$

Likewise, the current i through an open Na channel varies with the local concentration of Na^+ ions at the channel entrance and increases at more negative Ψ_o according to the BOLTZMANN relation

$$\text{ratio i} = \exp(-\beta F \Delta\Psi_o/RT) \quad (6)$$

In general, the coefficient β ($O < \beta < 1$) depends also on the location of the energy barriers within the channel (NEUMCKE, 1976). In Na channels, however, the highest barrier is located near the external membrane surface (HILLE, 1975). Under this condition β is independent of the channel structure and equal to the fraction of the surface potential Ψ_o sensed in the outer channel entrance.

In previous studies of HILLE et al. (1975) and GRISSMER (1984a, b), ratios of peak Na currents I_{peak} measured at strong depolarizations (which are equal to ratios of the Na conductance or Na permeability if there is no change in Na reversal potentials) were used to determine the fraction α of the external surface potential acting on the toxin receptor. In these evaluations it was assumed that surface potential changes do not affect the single channel current i ($\beta = 0$) and the maximum probability of the open channel state (ratio $p_{max} = 1$). As pointed out in the introduction, these assumptions are not necessary in our analysis since from nonstationary current fluctuations one can obtain the parameters N and i directly and separately.

In the presence of the univalent TTX the channel number N and the conductance γ were approximately equal in Ringer and SCN-Ringer (ratios N and γ not significantly different from unity) in accordance with our previous TTX experiments in Ringer and NO_3^- Ringer (NEUMCKE and STÄMPFLI, 1984). However, with the divalent STX the number N of unblocked Na channels was clearly lower in SCN-Ringer (ratio N = 0.81 ± 0.04). Inserting this value, z = 2 (thus ignoring the effects of the finite size of STX on z as described by CARNIE and MCLAUGHLIN, 1983), $K^* = 1.4$ nM (WAGNER and ULBRICHT, 1975), c = 4 nM and $\Delta\Psi_o = -17.8$ mV into Equ (5) yields $\alpha = 0.19$. Thus, only 19 % of the surface potential change is sensed by the toxin receptor. An even smaller $\Delta\Psi_o$ fraction seems to affect the channel conductance γ (ratio $\gamma = 0.93 \pm 0.05$). Since this γ ratio can already be accounted for by the reduced Na^+ ion activity a_{Na} in SCN-Ringer (ratio a_{Na} = 70.7 mM/76.2 mM = 0.93, see Methods), there is no detectable effect of external surface potential on the ion flux through open Na channels.

Our results are in qualitative, but not in quantitative agreement with previous determinations of surface potential fractions acting on Na channels (α between 0.3 and 0.5 estimated by HILLE et al., 1975, $\alpha = 0.46$ reported by GRISSMER, 1984a, b). The reason for the higher α values compared with our results ($\alpha = 0.19$) is not clear. The deviation cannot be explained by other experimental procedures or different Na currents, because our peak Na currents in Ringer and SCN-Ringer, as shown in Fig. 1A and B, are in agreement with those of GRISSMER (1984b) measured under almost identical conditions.

Instead, the higher α values derived from peak Na currents could be due to the above mentioned assumptions used in the analysis of macroscopic Na currents. Our low α value implies a relatively large separation of approximately 2 nm between external surface charges and the TTX, STX receptor. Moreover, the outer mouth of the Na channel seems to be effectively shielded from these negative surface charges since changes of the external surface potential have no detectable influence on the channel conductance. Our results are also of relevance to the current discussion on the location of the TTX, STX receptor. Since surface potential changes affect toxin binding and channel conductance to a different degree, it seems unlikely that the toxin receptor is located in the entrance of the Na channel. Instead, the toxin binding seems to occur at a site on the outer membrane surface near the channel as suggested by Kao and Walker (1982).

References

Carnie, S., McLaughlin, S. (1983): Large divalent cations and electrostatic potentials adjacent to membranes. A theoretical calculation. Biophys. J. **44**, 325–332.

Drouin, H., Neumcke, B. (1974): Specific and unspecific charges at the sodium channels of the nerve membrane. Pflügers Arch. **351**, 207–229.

Grissmer, S. (1984a): Effect of various cations and anions on the action of tetrodotoxin and saxitoxin on frog myelinated nerve fibres. Pflügers Arch. **402**, 353–359.

Grissmer, S. (1984b): Die Blockierung des Natriumstromes der markhaltigen Nervenfaser des Frosches *Rana esculenta* durch Tetrodotoxin und Saxitoxin und ihre Beeinflussung durch Kationen und Anionen. Doctoral dissertation. Universität des Saarlandes, Saarbrücken.

Hille, B. (1975): Ionic selectivity, saturation, and block in sodium channels. A four-barrier model. J. Gen. Physiol. **66**, 535–560.

Hille, B., Ritchie, J. M., Strichartz, G. R. (1975): The effect of surface charge on the nerve membrane on the action of tetrodotoxin and saxitoxin in frog myelinated nerve. J. Physiol. **250**, 34–35P.

Kao, C. Y., Walker, S. E. (1982): Active groups of saxitoxin and tetrodotoxin as deduced from actions of saxitoxin analogues on frog muscle and squid axon. J. Physiol. **323**, 619–637.

Neumcke, B. (1976): Surface charges on nerve membranes and artificial lipid bilayers. J. Electrochem. Soc. **123**, 1331–1334.

Neumcke, B. (1981): Surface charges on biological membranes. In: Membranes and intercellular communication (R. Balian, M. Chabre, P. F. Devaux, eds.), pp. 471–483. North-Holland, Amsterdam.

Neumcke, B., Stämpfli, R. (1982): Sodium currents and sodium-current fluctuations in rat myelinated nerve fibres. J. Physiol. **329**, 163–184.

Neumcke, B., Stämpfli, R. (1983): Alteration of the conductance of Na^+ channels in the nodal membrane of frog nerve by holding potential and tetrodotoxin. Biochim. Biophys. Acta **727**, 177–184.

Neumcke, B., Stämpfli, R. (1984): Heterogeneity of external surface charges near sodium channels in the nodal membrane of frog nerve. Pflügers Arch. **401**, 125–131.

Nonner, W. (1969): A new voltage clamp method for Ranvier nodes. Pflügers Arch. **309**, 176–192.

Ritchie, J. M., Rogart, R. B. (1977): The binding of saxitoxin and tetrodotoxin to excitable tissue. Rev. Physiol. Biochem. Pharmacol. **79**, 1–50.

Sigworth, F. J. (1980): The variance of sodium current fluctuations at the node of Ranvier. J. Physiol. **307**, 97–129.

Stämpfli, R., Hille, B. (1976): Electrophysiology of the peripheral myelinated nerve. In: Frog Neurobiology (R. Llinás, W. Precht, eds.), pp. 3–32. Springer Verlag, New York.

Wagner, H.-H., Ulbricht, W. (1975): The rates of saxitoxin action and of saxitoxin-tetrodotoxin interaction at the node of Ranvier. Pflügers Arch. **359**, 297–315.

Fortschritte der Zoologie, Band 33 · Lüttgau (Hrsg.): Membrane Control
Gustav Fischer Verlag · Stuttgart · New York · 1986

The sodium current in human skeletal muscle measured with the loose-patch clamp technique

F. Zite-Ferenczy, K. Matthias, S. R. Taylor* and R. Rüdel

Abteilung für Allgemeine Physiologie, Universität Ulm, Oberer Eselsberg, D-7900 Ulm, FRG

In several hereditary muscle diseases, such as myotonias (Rüdel and Lehmann-Horn, 1985) and periodic paralyses (Rüdel and Ricker, 1985), the fast sodium current of the muscle fiber membrane seems to be altered. To decide whether the number and availability of the sodium channels are abnormal in these diseases, knowledge of the physiological control values is necessary. Two studies of the sodium current in human muscle (DeCoursey, Bryant and Lipicky, 1982; Almers, Roberts and Ruff, 1984) have come to our knowledge, but neither of them was carried out with fibers having high resting potentials and at body temperature. Applying the loose-patch clamp technique (Almers, Stanfield and Stühmer, 1983a; Stühmer, Roberts and Almers, 1983) to biopsied human external intercostal muscle we have investigated the sodium current at 36 °C in fibers having a mean resting potential negative to −80 mV. The study was part of a program approved by the ethic commission of the Technical University of Munich and was carried out in abiding by the Helsinki convention.

Methods

During thoracotomy on 9 patients of either sex and with no known neuromuscular disease, muscle specimes containing intact fibers were removed and dissected as reported earlier (Kwieciński, Lehmann-Horn and Rüdel, 1984). Bundles of about 200 fibers were mounted in an experimental chamber filled with oxygenated (5 % CO_2) Bretag's (1969) interstitial solution from which the sugars were omitted for easier patching. The preparations were not enzymatically cleaned.

The original loose-patch clamp technique employing a single pipette (Almers et al., 1983a) was used for recording active membrane currents. The patch pipette having 6–20 μm tip diameter was mounted on the head stage of an amplifier whose output was connected to a circuit which subtracted capacitative currents and the current through the leak between membrane and pipette from the signal. The resulting active current transients were fed through a low-pass filter of 20 kHz corner frequency to a PDP 11/23 computer for data digitalization and storage. Data were collected with and without the current-

---

* On leave of absence from the Department of Pharmacology, Mayo Medical School, Rochester, Minnesota

correcting p/4 method (ALMERS et al., 1983a). Data reduction and evaluation were performed off-line. Only when the seal factor (sum of pipette and seal resistance divided by seal resistance) was < 1.8 a patch was used for current recording. Usually, the results of 5 consecutive identical tests were averaged. The resting potential, E_R, was measured with the conventional microelectrode technique after a patch clamp run was completed. Only results from fibers with a resting potential negative to -75 mV were included in this report. The data in Table 1 are the mean values $\pm$ S. E. from 43 fibers.

Results

Up to 4 hours after the biopsy it was difficult to find membrane patches from which large currents could be recorded, probably because the connective tissue prevented a close enough approach of the pipette to the membrane. Seven to fifteen hours after the biopsy, stable seals were obtained and the currents were reproducible. The transient inward currents flowing during 1.8 ms test pulses could be completely and reversibly blocked by TTX which indicates that they were carried by sodium. The amplitude of the sodium current measured at different patches of the same fiber and with the same pipette was very variable (Fig. 1). A similar variability was reported for frog muscle fibers (ALMERS et al., 1983a).

Fig. 2 illustrates the dependence of the current transients on the membrane potential E_m attained during the test pulse. With increasing test pulse amplitude, the time to peak current decreased, as generally observed in such experiments. The amplitude of the inward current increased, became maximal and then decreased as E_m approached E_{Na}, the sodium

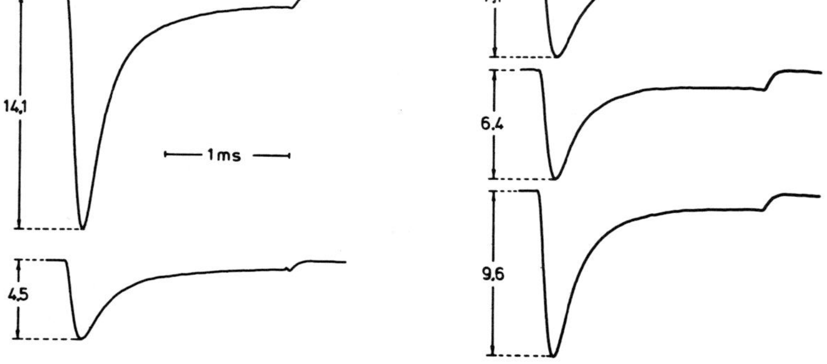

Fig. 1: Sodium current (I_{Na}) transients recorded from 8 approximately equidistant (~ 200 μm) patches along a fiber with resting potential $E_R = -82$ mV. Test depolarizations were square pulses of 80 mV amplitude and 1.8 ms duration. Each trace is the average of 5 consecutive tests.

equilibrium potential. E_{Na} could only be determined in 14 out of 43 fibers (Table 1). In the remaining cases the current transients flowing during test pulses to $E_m > 0$ mV were affected with artefacts which might have been caused by a non-linear increase of the leak current («rim currents», as discussed by ALMERS et al., 1984). Plots of the peak values of the sodium current, $I_{Na\ max}$, and the sodium conductance, g_{Na}, derived from the current transients of the left-hand panel, are shown in the right-hand panel of Fig. 2. A consistent finding with all fibers of this study was that the potentials for threshold and peak current were less negative than measured by ALMERS et al. (1984) with the improved loose-patch clamp. This might be explained by our stringent criterion of a good resting potential which made the use of hyperpolarizing holding potentials unnecessary. With the three-microelectrode voltage clamp, the threshold potential in human intercostal muscle was between −65 and −60 mV (LEHMANN-HORN et al., 1983). However, with this technique the potential at the current injection site is considerably less negative than the control potential, and since it is likely that the clamp does not fully suppress sodium currents elicited there, one would expect the threshold to be lower with this technique than with recording from a very small patch. We trust that the abscissa in Fig. 2 (and in 13 further experiments in which the reversal potential was determined) cannot be much off reality, because the mean current reversal potential of +60 mV agrees well with an E_{Na} = +60 mV calculated for an intracellular sodium concentration $\gamma_i^{-1} \cdot aNa_i = 0.59^{-1} \cdot 8$ mmol/l = 13.5 mmol/l measured in these fibers with Na-sensitive microelectrodes (LEHMANN-HORN et al., 1986).

To characterize the fast inactivation of the sodium channels, we determined the parameters h_∞ and τ_h in the usual way (details in legend to Fig. 3). In comparison with previous

Table 1: Comparison of present results with previous work on human skeletal muscle (mean ± S.E.).

	Present		Almers et al. (1984)	DeCoursey et al. (1982)
Method	Loose-Patch Voltage Clamp Single Pipette		Improved Loose-Patch Clamp Concentric Pipette	Vaseline Gap
Temperature (°C)	36		23	12
Resting potential (mV)	−80.9 ± 1.9	(n = 43)	−63 ± 3.6 (n = 6)	cut fibers
Sodium current parameters:				
Threshold potential (mV)	−42.9 ± 2.3	(n = 43)	−60	below −70
Peak amplitude (mA/cm²)	−8.2 ± 2.5	(n = 43)	−10.0 ± 2.8 (n = 6)	−2.4 ± 0.7 (n = 12)
Peak potential (mV)	−1.3 ± 5.1	(n = 43)	−30	~20
Time to peak (ms)	0.198 ± 0.05	(n = 9)	0.25	1
Reversal potential (mV)	+59.8 ± 4.2	(n = 14)	+40 ± 2.3 (n = 6)	+65 ± 6 (n = 8)
Inactivation parameters:				
Potential E_h at which $h_\infty = 1/2$ (mV)	−66.8 ± 2.9	(n = 33)	−86 ± 5.8 (n = 6)	−101 ± 4 (n = 14)
Slope k_h of h_∞-curve at E_h (mV)	7.3 ± 0.9	(n = 33)	5.9 ± 0.2 (n = 6)	10.1 ± 0.9 (n = 14)
Availability of Channels at E_m = −80 mV*	87%		27%	11%

* determined from E_h and k_h using $h_\infty = [1 + \exp \frac{(-80 - E_h)}{k_h}]^{-1}$

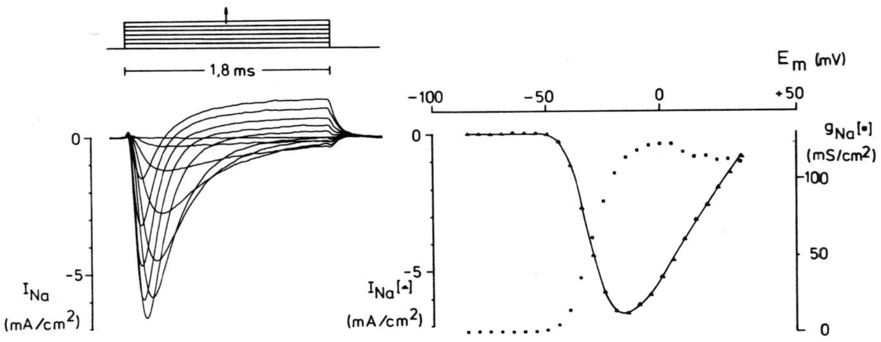

Fig. 2: Typical family of current transients from a fiber with $E_R = -85$ mV, obtained by test pulses to $E_m = -55, -45, -40, -35, -30, -25, -15, -5, +5, +15$ and $+30$ mV (left panel), and plots of $I_{Na\ max}$ (triangles) and sodium conductance $g_{Na} = I_{Na\ max}/(E_m - E_{Na})$ (squares) obtained from these transients vs. E_m (right panel).

measurements on human muscle, the steady-state inactivation curve was shifted towards less negative potentials (see Table 1). This result was to be expected, because the earlier investigators had attributed their relatively large steady-state inactivation at the physiological resting potential to experimental shortcomings now overcome. In 33 fibers we determined the potential E_h where h_∞ is 1/2 to −66.8 mV which is close to the E_h values found in rat muscles (ADRIAN and MARSCHALL, 1977: −70 mV; DUVAL and LÉOTY, 1980: −67 mV).

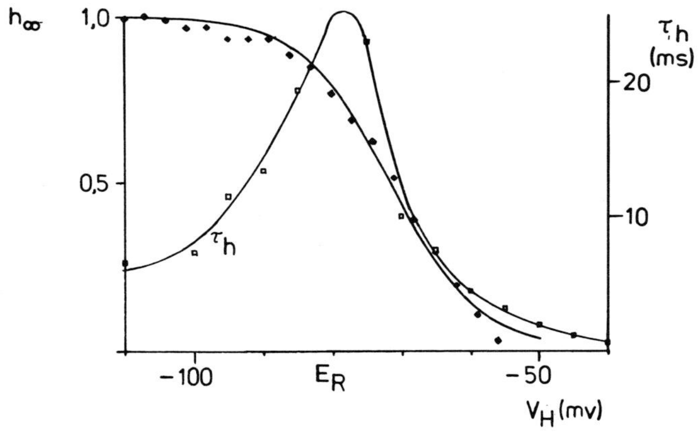

Fig. 3: The potential dependence of the inactivation parameters h_∞ and τ_h of a fiber with $E_R = -80$ mV. $I_{Na\ max}$ was determined during test pulses of 80 mV amplitude and 1.8 ms duration, preceded by prepulses of variable amplitude and duration. For the determination of h_∞, the prepulse duration was kept constant at 30 ms and for each prepulse potential the normalized $I_{Na\ max}$ (diamonds) was plotted against the membrane potential. For the determination of τ_h, the prepulse duration t was varied between 0.2 and 102 ms and for each prepulse potential, τ_h (squares) was calculated from $I_{Na\ max} = 1 - \exp -(t/\tau_h)$.

In 3 fibers we also investigated the temperature dependence of amplitude and time course of the sodium current. On cooling, $I_{Na\ max}$ decreased with a Q_{10} of 2.75, on rewarming it recovered only slowly. The measurements of the amplitude were difficult to perform, because the pipette resistance changed with temperature. Measurements of the time course were easier and showed that the time to peak sodium current increased with falling temperature. An Arrhenius plot of this parameter is shown in Fig. 4. In comparison to the time to peak measured by ALMERS et al. (1984) at 23 °C, our values are somewhat larger.

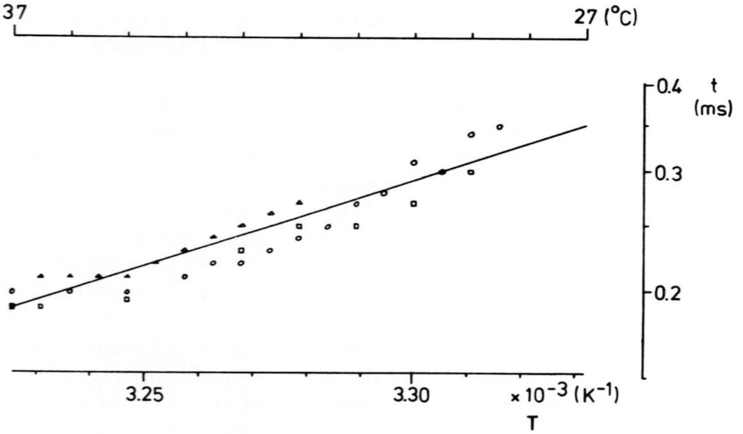

Fig. 4: Temperature dependence of the time to peak of I_{Na} during clamp steps of 80 mV amplitude. Different symbols represent 3 different fibers.

Discussion

The loose-patch clamp technique used by us differs from the sucrose gap method in that measurements of membrane parameters can be made with intact fibers and under physiological conditions. The advantage over the intracellular, two- or three-microelectrode clamp methods is that the time resolution is much better and that no twitches are provoked due to the small membrane area depolarized. Movement artefacts and fiber damage are thus avoided. The spacial homogeneity of the potential over the clamped area (containing several hundred sodium channels) has not been investigated as far as we know. It probably depends on the quality of the seal. In this respect, the improved method with two concentric pipettes (ALMERS et al., 1984) has unquestionable advantage over the single pipette method, especially for the case of large clamp steps up to the reversal potential for the sodium current. However, often enough we were able to record sodium outward currents using the single electrode clamp, and even when this was not possible, we could extrapolate the reversal potential reasonably well.

A serious shortcoming of the loose-patch clamp is that owing to the small area clamped, peculiar local phenomena are often encountered which are hard to explain. Thus, one is forced to selecting «good looking» results from a large number of measurements. We feel therefore obliged to discuss also the results we omitted from this report. A matter of major concern is the leak current which, in comparison to other methods, is extraordinarily large. For example, in our experiments the seal factor was about 1.5. With a mean pipette resistance of 270 kΩ, this corresponds to a seal resistance of about 540 kΩ. Attempts at an improved seal by pushing the pipette further against the preparation or by applying negative pressure to the back of the pipette resulted in reduction and instability of the sodium current. With this seal factor, 120 mV must be applied to the pipette to attain an 80 mV depolarization. The leak current is then about 148 nA. Assuming a patch area of the size of the mouth of the pipette (diameter ~ 8 μm), and a mean peak sodium current density of 8.2 mA/cm^2, it turns out that the leak current is 35 times larger than the peak sodium current of 4.1 nA. The question of how well the leak current is compensated thus becomes a decisive one.

With brief (< 1 ms) and small (< 2–5 mV) pulses, the leak current is appropriately compensated by the circuit. With longer and stronger pulses, the compensation is correct only when the leak current is constant in time and proportional to the applied voltage, i. e., when it has an ohmic characteristic. This means that the pipette and seal resistances should be independent of the total current density. In our experience this is not always so, perhaps because the resistance characteristic depends on the nature and thickness of the material lying between the pipette rim and the membrane proper. As a consequence, false «slow inward currents» may appear, as in the end of some of the traces of Fig. 1. These slow inward currents could not be consistently blocked by any of the known methods for identification of their ionic basis, and their current-voltage relationships could often not be explained by the laws of physics under the assumption that they are real membrane currents. Fortunately, such artefacts were small in the first 1–2 ms so that the simple compensation method seemed adequate for the measurement of the sodium current. But nearly always they affected the «delayed outward currents» flowing during test pulses lasting > 2 ms. For this reason we have strong reservations against «slow» or «delayed» currents recorded with the loose-patch clamp technique. Artefactual currents appeared already at low-amplitude hyperpolarizing pulses. This limited the application of the p/4 method to small test pulses. Apparently, not only the properties of the material within the seal, but also the net electric field strength within the membrane play a role.

An issue of particular interest with respect to the future investigation of the sodium channel in fibers from patients suffering from abnormal membrane depolarizations is concerned with the question whether channels in the state of ultra-slow inactivation (Almers, Stanfield and Stühmer, 1983b) may be reactivated with the help of the loose-patch clamp. Many of our fibers from normal individuals had a reduced resting potential, perhaps due to insufficient oxygenation or microinjury during dissection. When the resting potential was not lower than −60 mV, sodium currents could be recorded but the average maximum current density was markedly lower than in fibers with a high resting potential. As a rule, it was possible to determine the h_∞ curve which then reached a plateau only at a potential exceeding −100 mV. Hyperpolarizing prepulses lasting several minutes were ineffective when a brief (60 ms) pause was interposed between prepulse and test pulse. Sodium currents were practically absent in fibers having resting potentials lower than −60 mV, and it was not possible to re-establish the availability of sodium currents by hyperpolarizing the membrane by up to 80 mV for several minutes. Currents estimated by us to be artefacts were frequently encountered in such fibers.

Since with the loose-patch clamp the absolute amplitudes of the inward and outward currents are generally variable and since the reactivation of the sodium channels in depolarized membranes from non-diseased muscle does not lead to normal inactivation curves, this technique seems limited for the determination of abnormalities in diseased muscle.

Acknowledgments

We appreciate the help by Dr. W. STÜHMER in setting up the loose-patch clamp. The study was supported by the Deutsche Gesellschaft Bekämpfung der Muskelkrankheiten and by Schwerpunkt 25 («Muskelforschung») des Landes Baden-Württemberg.

References

Adrian, R. H., Marshall, M. W. (1977): Sodium currents in mammalian muscle. J. Physiol. **268**, 223–250.

Almers, W., Roberts, W. M., Ruff, R. L. (1984): Voltage clamp of rat and human skeletal muscle: measurements with an improved loose-patch technique. J. Physiol. **347**, 751–768.

Almers, W., Stanfield, P. R., Stühmer, W. (1983a): Lateral distribution of sodium and potassium channels in frog skeletal muscle: measurements with a patch-clamp technique. J. Physiol. **336**, 261–284.

Almers, W., Stanfield, P. R., Stühmer, W. (1983b): Slow changes in current through sodium channels in frog muscle membrane. J. Physiol. **339**, 253–271.

Bretag, A. G. (1969): Synthetic interstitial fluid for isolated mammalian tissue. Life Sci. **8**, 319–329.

DeCoursey, T. E., Bryant, S. H., Lipicky, R. J. (1982): Sodium currents in human skeletal muscle fibers. Muscle Nerve **5**, 614–618.

Duval, A., Léoty, C. (1980): Ionic currents in slow twitch skeletal muscle in the rat. J. Physiol. **307**, 23–41.

Kwieciński, H., Lehmann-Horn, F., Rüdel, R. (1984): The resting membrane parameters of human intercostal muscle at low, normal, and high extracellular potassium. Muscle Nerve **7**, 60–65.

Lehmann-Horn, F., Küther, G., Ricker, K., Grafe, P., Ballanyi, K., Rüdel, R. (1986): Adynamia episodica hereditaria with myotonia: a persistent sodium current and the effect of extracellular pH. Muscle Nerve, in press.

Lehmann-Horn, F., Rüdel, R., Ricker, K., Lorković, H., Dengler, R., Hopf, H. Ch. (1983): Two cases of adynamia episodica hereditaria: in vitro investigation of muscle cell membrane and contraction parameters. Muscle Nerve **6**, 113–121.

Rüdel, R., Lehmann-Horn, F. (1985): Membrane changes in cells from myotonia patients. Physiol. Rev. **65**, 310–356.

Rüdel, R., Ricker, K. (1985): The primary periodic paralyses. TINS **8**, 467–470.

Stühmer, W., Roberts, W. M., Almers, W. (1983): The loose patch clamp. In: Single Channel Recording (B. Sackmann, E. Neher, eds.) Plenum Press, New York.

Fortschritte der Zoologie, Band 33 · Lüttgau (Hrsg.): Membrane Control
Gustav Fischer Verlag · Stuttgart · New York · 1986

The mechanism of ion selectivity in calcium channels of skeletal muscle membrane

W. Almers, E. W. McCleskey and P. T. Palade

Dept. of Physiology and Biophysics, SJ-40; University of Washington, Seattle, WA 98195, USA

Voltage-dependent Ca channels are found in the cell membranes of all excitable cells. In response to cell membrane depolarization, they open to allow the influx of Ca, and thereby help to produce the increase in intracellular [Ca^{++}] that initiates a wide variety of physiologic responses. The contraction of skeletal muscle is one such response, but the Ca that triggers it originates entirely from the sarcoplasmic reticulum, an intracellular system of vesicles that releases Ca in response to cell membrane depolarization. Nevertheless, the muscle twitch is accompanied by Ca influx across the cell membrane, and this influx, however small (Curtis, 1966) and inessential for an individual twitch (Armstrong et al., 1972), probably occurs through voltage-dependent Ca channels.

Ca channels in skeletal muscle (Stanfield, 1977; Sanchez and Stefani, 1978; Almers and Palade, 1981) are located predominantly or exclusively in the membrane of the transverse tubules (Nicola-Siri et al., 1980; Almers et al., 1981) that pervade a skeletal muscle fibre like a network of inside-out nerve fibres and conduct the electric impulse from the sarcolemma into the fibre interior. Rather than directly providing Ca to the contractile proteins, they are probably involved in regulating the Ca content of a muscle cell in the long term. Specifically, they might provide a pathway for Ca influx to balance the extra Ca efflux from the cell that necessarily occurs when myoplasmic [Ca^{++}] rises during muscle activation. Ca channels in skeletal muscle are similar to those in other tissues, both in their selectivity among divalent cations (Almers and Palade, 1981) and in their pharmacologic properties (Palade and Almers, 1985). Their only unique feature is that they open in response to membrane depolarization about 10 to 100 times more slowly than Ca channels do in other tissues. Skeletal muscle is of special interest in the study of the Ca channel, because it promises to become for this channel what the electric organ of *Torpedo* has become for acetylcholine receptors: the most convenient tissue for extraction and purification (Catterall et al., this volume).

Functionally, Ca channels face an especially difficult task, namely to selectively transport a minority ion. In order to produce Ca^{++} influx without dissipating the important K and Na gradients across the cell membrane, Ca^{++} channels must, when open, selectively transport Ca^{++} and reject other small cations, such as Na^+ and K^+, even though these two ions are physiologically present at nearly one hundred times higher concentrations. Indeed, Ca channels under physiologic conditions are extremely efficient at excluding Na^+ and K^+. How is the high selectivity of Ca channels achieved? This paper will review recent work on skeletal muscle (Almers, McCleskey and Palade, 1984; Almers and McCleskey, 1984; McCleskey and Almers, 1985), leading to the conclusion that in Ca channels, the selectivity of ion transport results from the selective binding of Ca^{++}.

Methods

Membrane currents were recorded from small sections of isolated single frog muscle fibers with a whole-cell voltage clamp technique termed the Vaseline gap (HILLE and CAMPBELL, 1976). Throughout, muscle fibers were bathed in solutions that eliminated currents across the cell membrane through all ion channels except the Ca channel. The intracellular solutions contained high (> 40 mM) concentrations of the Ca-chelator EGTA, and the intracellular K^+ was replaced by mixtures of Na or Cs and the large organic cations tetraethyl- (TEA) or tetramethylammonium (TMA). TEA and Cs were included to block voltage-dependent K channels. Intracellular solutions reached the myoplasm by diffusion through the cut fibre ends. To prevent anion currents, extracellular solutions were Cl^--free and contained the impermeant anions methanesulfonate or EGTA as the main anions. 1 uM external tetrodotoxin was present throughout to block sodium channels. Throughout, membrane currents were corrected for leakage and capacitive currents, using a combination of analog and digital techniques. Details of experimental methods and composition of solutions are given elsewhere (ALMERS et al., 1984).

Results
General remarks on the selectivity of ion channels

How do Ca channels exclude monovalent cations? The question as to how ion channels discriminate among small inorganic cations has occupied physiologists for some time. In highly selective channels, such as Ca channels, ion size is clearly not the only, and probably not even the most important criterion (see, e.g., HILLE, 1975a, b), as one may appreciate by recalling that Na^+ and Ca^{++} have nearly identical crystal radii. Instead, ion channels must decide to pass or to reject an ion on the basis of the sum of electrostatic interactions between water, the permeating ion and the walls of the aqueous pore of the ion channel. Unfortunately, it is difficult to account for these interactions in any explicit way, so that even today, the molecular basis for ion selectivity is not completely understood. On a qualitative level, however, one may distinguish two mechanisms for ion selectivity that may operate singly or in combination (Fig. 1).

Early theories, such as EISENMANN'S (1962) theory of ion-sensitive glass electrodes, have attributed ion selectivity to the specific binding of a particular ion. Applied to transport through channels, one may suppose that the aqueous pore of the channel molecule (Fig. 1a) contains sites that bind the selected ion (circle) more tightly than they bind all others. Such pores will selectively extract this ion from mixed electrolytes and, under the appropriate conditions, transport it preferentially. This mechanism may be called *selectivity by affinity*. Selective binding of ligands by proteins, though not always understood, is a familiar theme in biochemistry, and there are many examples of proteins that bind Ca^{++} selectively and with high affinity.

To illustrate the concept in more detail, the drawing of Fig. 1a is translated into an «energy diagram» of the kind often used to calculate transport through ion channels (e. g. BEZANILLA and ARMSTRONG, 1972). Fig. 1b plots the potential energies of the two ions against distance along the pore when there is no membrane potential. The binding site is represented by an «energy well» (middle) and the barriers on either side represent factors such as the activation energy for partial dehydration that may be required before the ion may bind to the site, or the limitations on the rate at which ions may negotiate the narrow opening of the pore, or other factors. When selectivity occurs by affinity, then it is due to the deepest energy well being deeper for the selected ion than for all others.

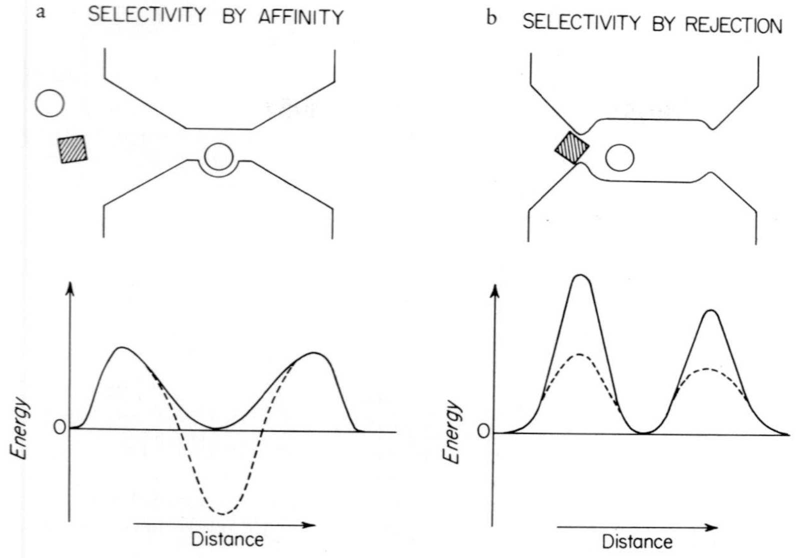

Fig. 1: Schematic drawing illustrating two mechanisms for selectivity of ion transport. Circle and square represent two different ions, which are both small enough to fit through the pore. The circle is meant to represent the ion that is transported preferentially. The dashed lines apply to the circle, the solid lines to the square.

Selectivity by affinity is perceived to have a fundamental problem: whatever force may selectively attract an ion into the aqueous pore of an ion channel will also tend to keep it there, thereby preventing rapid transport. This problem was stated succinctly in an appendix to an article by BEZANILLA and ARMSTRONG (1972), who showed that selectivity by affinity will not work in a pore containing a single binding site. Consequently, most workers imagine that ion channels achieve selectivity not by affinity, but instead by denying access to all but the selected ion (Fig. 1b). *Selectivity by rejection* is thought to occur at narrow places in the aqueous pore, which form «energy barriers» that are lower for the selected ion than for all others. Exclusion of ions by virtue of their large size would be the simplest example for this class of mechanisms.

Are Ca channels permeable to Na^+?

Fig. 2a, b shows membrane currents in solutions containing, besides an impermeant anion and varying amounts of Ca, only the large and nearly impermeant organic cation tetramethylammonium (TMA). In Fig. 2a, an inward current is seen to increase and decline; it was carried by Ca because it was strongly diminished when external $[Ca^{++}]$ was reduced (Fig. 2b). If Na^+ were significantly permeant, it should contribute to inward current. However, replacing the virtually impermeant TMA with Na caused no increase in inward current (compare Fig. 2a and c). Essentially all of the current in Fig. 2c must have been carried by Ca, since diminishing external $[Ca^{++}]$ (Fig. 2d) decreased inward current no less than was observed in the absence of Na^+. We consider that Fig. 2 confirms a

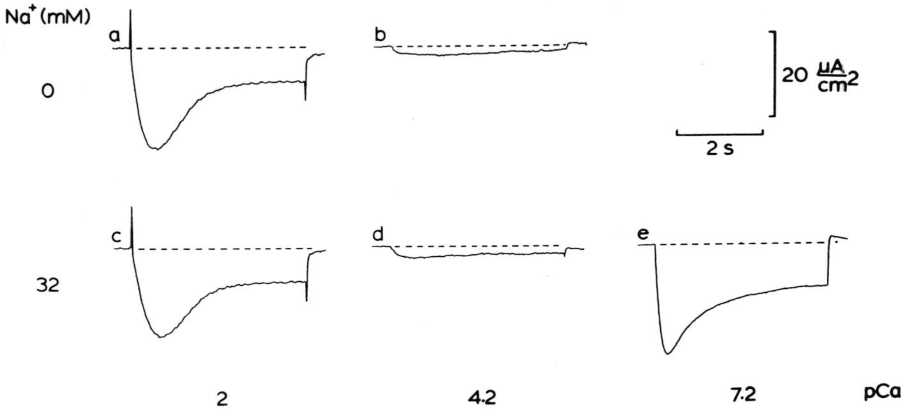

Fig. 2: Membrane currents with (*c–e*) and without Na^+ (*a* and *b*) as indicated. For each condition the potential during the depolarizing step (0 mV in *a* and *c* and −30 mV in *b, d* and *e*) was chosen to produce roughly maximal inward currents. Currents were recorded at external $[Ca^+]$ of 10 mM (*a* and *c*), approximately 60 uM (*b* and *d*) and approximately 60 nM (*e*). From ALMERS, MCCLESKEY and PALADE, 1984).

previous conclusion (REUTER and SCHOLZ, 1977), namely that, with external Ca^{++} concentration down to a few tens of micromolar, Ca channels are not measurably permeable to Na^+ and K^+.

Ca channels become permeable to many cations when external Ca is withdrawn

When we sought to eliminate also the small residual inward current in Fig. 2b, d by lowering external Ca^{++} into the submicromolar range with chelators, a large inward current unexpectedly returned (Fig. 2e). This current is carried by Na, since it is not seen when the large and impermeant tetraethylammonium (TEA^+) is the only external cation (not shown). Fig. 2 suggests that, nearly Na-impermeable at physiological $[Ca^{++}]$, Ca channels become freely Na permeable when external Ca^{++} is withdrawn. This conclusion has been reached also from work on snail neurons (KOSTYUK et al., 1983).

Fig. 3 shows currents carried through Ca channels not only by Na^+ (row a), but also by K^+ (row b), and Mg^{++} (row c). K^+ is known to be virtually impermeant at physiological external $[Ca^{++}]$ (LEE and TSIEN, 1982). Evidently all physiologically present metal cations can carry current through Ca channels when Ca is absent. In addition to Na and K, Li, Rb and Cs also are freely permeable under that condition (ALMERS et al., 1984). One piece of evidence that the currents in Fig. 2e and in Fig. 3 really do flow through Ca channels is their block by the specific Ca channel blocker nitrendipine, a well-known 1,4-dihydropyridine «Ca-antagonist» (Fig. 3 a4, b4, c4). Indeed, block of Ca-currents and Na-currents by nifedipine, a similar Ca-antagonist, follows identical dose-response curves. This and other evidence that currents such as in Fig. 3 flow through Ca channels has been reported and reviewed elsewhere (ALMERS and MCCLESKEY, 1984). Fig. 3 confirms that Na^+ and

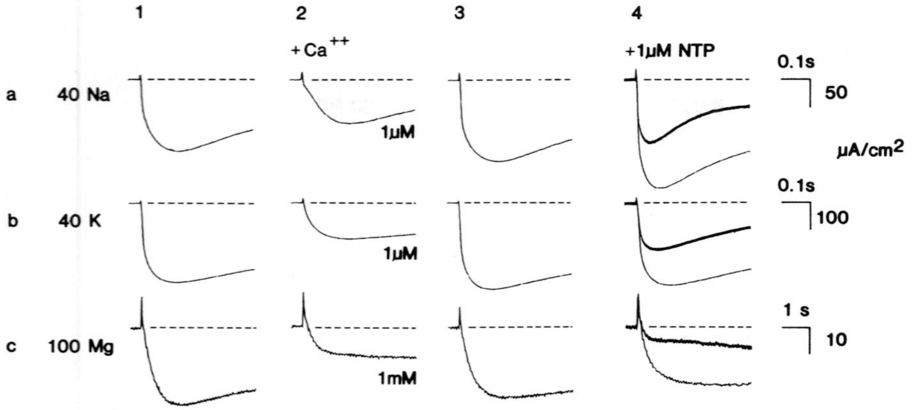

Fig. 3: Currents carried through the Ca channel by Na^+, K^+ or Mg^{++}. External [Ca^{++}] was about 63 nM (rows a, b) or less (c) except where indicated otherwise. Traces in rows a(1–3), b(1–3) and c(1–3) were recorded in the sequence shown, each from a different fiber; in a2, b2, external [Ca^{++}] was increased to 1 uM by adding 14.7 mM $Ca(CH_3SO_3)_2$; in c2, [Ca^{++}] was increased to 1 mM as specified below. Column 4: Na, K and Mg currents recorded just before (light) and 30–60 s after application of 1 uM nitrendipine (NTP; heavy traces); each panel of traces from a different fiber. The Na and K currents in rows a,b were recorded during voltage steps from −100 to −40 mV and with 40 mM external Na^+ or K^+, as indicated; fiber ends were cut in a solution containing, in mM, 40 Na-CH_3SO_3, 20 $(TEA)_2$EGTA, 50 arginine aspartate and 10 TEA-MOPS (pH = 7.0). Mg currents were recorded during steps from −80 mV to 0 (c1–3) or to 15 mV (c4); the external solution contained, in mM, 100 Mg-$(CH_3SO_3)_2$, 10 TEA-MOPS (pH = 7.0) plus either 1 $(TMA)_2$EGTA or, in c2, 1 Ca-$(CH_3SO_3)_2$; fiber ends were cut in 80 $(TEA)_2$-EGTA plus 10 TEA-MOPS buffer (pH = 7.0). In row c, the ordinate calibration applies to panels 1–3 only; for c4, the calibration bar represents 4 uA/cm^2. From McCleskey and Almers, 1985.

K^+ currents are strongly and reversibly reduced by 1 uM external Ca (Fig. 3 a2, b2); apparently the ability of Ca channels to reject monovalent cations is restored by adding trace amounts of external Ca^{++}.

Fig. 4 investigates this effect in more detail. Peak inward current at a fixed potential was measured with 32 mM external Na, as external [Ca^{++}] was varied over a 10^8 fold range. When [Ca^{++}] exceeds 30 uM, Ca^{++} is the main current carrier; indeed at pCa = 2, current is carried entirely by Ca^{++} (Fig. 2). At pCa > 5, however, we believe current to be carried by Na^+, since it is strongly reduced or abolished when Na is replaced by TMA or TEA. Na current diminishes when external [Ca^{++}] is increased. The block of Na current through Ca channels can be described as being due to one Ca^{++} binding to one channel with a dissociation constant of 0.7 uM (Almers et al., 1982, 1984). Similar dissociation constants have been inferred from measurements in snail neurons (0.3 uM, Kostyuk et al., 1983), in cardiac muscle (Hess and Tsien, 1984) and in neoplastic B-lymphocytes (2.0 uM, Fukushima and Hagiwara, 1985). Evidently, Ca blocks the passage of monovalent cations through Ca channels by binding to a high-affinity site.

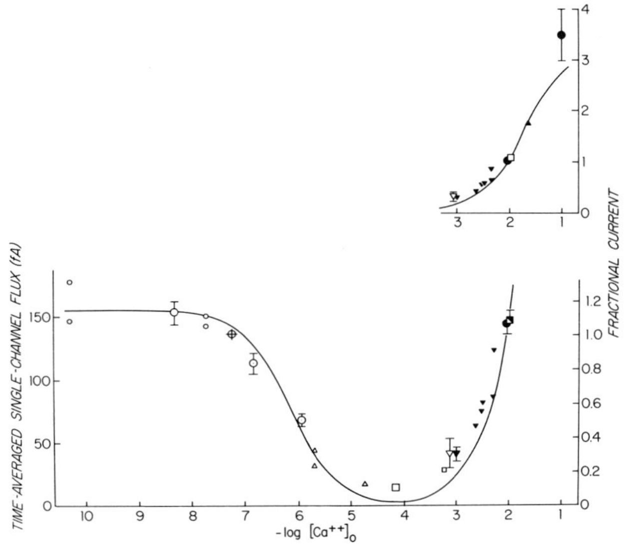

Fig. 4: Inward currents as a function of external [Ca^{++}]. The right hand ordinate gives current as a fraction of that measured at -log [Ca^{++}]$_o$ = 7.2. Open symbols in the presence, and filled symbols in the absence, of external Na$^+$. Large symbols are means of several measurements, small symbols are single measurements. Data are from Almers et al. (1984, their Fig. 9 and text) where details are given. Curves were calculated by the model illustrated in Fig. 7, using the procedures and parameters given in Almers and McCleskey (1984). The time-averaged single-channel fluxes predicted by the calculations are represented on the left-hand ordinate, with 136 fA/channel representing a fractional current of 1.0.

The ion selectivity of Ca channels is due to the selective binding of Ca

It is well known that many divalent cations can carry current through Ca channels when they completely replace external Ca^{++} (e. g., Hagiwara and Byerly, 1981). In skeletal muscle, Ba, Sr, Ca, Mn and even Mg are readily shown to be permeant, while Co and Ni are impermeant (Almers and Palade, 1981). When current is carried by a foreign divalent cation such as Mg^{++} (100 mM in Fig. 3, row c), it may be reversibly diminished by adding small amounts of Ca^{++} (Fig. c2). Similar results were obtained also when Sr^{++} (Veerecke and Carmeliet, 1971) and Ba^{++} carry current through Ca channels (Almers and McCleskey, 1984; Hess and Tsien, 1984). Evidently Ca blocks the passage of divalent as well as monovalent cations.

The findings discussed so far may be summarized. (1) In Ca channels, the well-known high permeability to Ba^{++}, and also that to Mg^{++}, is observed only in the absence of external Ca^{++}. (2) The well-known ability of Ca channels to exclude monovalent cations is seen only in the presence of external Ca^{++}. (3) Evidently, Ca^{++} blocks the passage of foreign cations through Ca channels. Without Ca^{++}, Ca channels are remarkably nonselective; all physiologically present inorganic cations are measurably permeant. (4) Ca channels carry high-affinity Ca binding sites, as judged by the block of Na currents through Ca channels by micromolar external Ca^{++}. These binding sites are specific, in that none of a number of other ions tested (Sr^{++}, Ba^{++}, Mg^{++}; KOSTYUK et al., 1983; Co^{++}, Cd^{++}, Mn^{++}, Sr^{++}, Mg^{++}, Ni^{++}; ALMERS et al., 1984) equals Ca^{++} in its potency in blocking Na current through Ca channels.

All these findings point to one conclusion: Ca channels are selective by binding Ca^{++} at a specific, high-affinity site. There is evidence suggesting that this is true not only in striated muscle and neurons, but also in other tissues, both in chordates and other phylae.

Ca channels are large pores

Evidently, the aqueous pore of Ca channels is innately unselective, and aquires its remarkable ability to reject foreign cations only when Ca is bound to a high-affinity site. Indeed, even the large organic cation TMA is measurably permeant when external Ca is absent. Fig. 5 shows membrane currents during steps to the indicated potentials, first in a solution with TEA as the only cation, then after substituting 80 mM TMA for TEA, and once again in pure TEA solution. With TMA, inward currents are clearly larger than with TEA. At potentials where currents in TEA are absent (−40 mV) or outward (− 30 mV), currents in TMA remain inward. Clearly, TMA is more permeant than TEA. The inward currents with TEA as the only external cation might suggest that even this ion is permeant. However, more experiments are needed to exclude that these extremely small inward currents are an erroneous result of a leak subtraction.

Fig. 5B plots peak current against potential; the values plotted are averages from two runs each in TEA, in TMA and in a TEA solution containing 5 mM Na^+ (traces not shown). The currents and reversal potentials observed in the 80 mM TMA and the 5 mM Na^+ solutions were about the same, hence TMA is 5/80 = 0.06 times as permeant as Na^+ in this experiment.

In the absence of external Ca, the Ca channel is permeable to many other monovalent organic cations, and even to the large divalent cation diaminobutane (MCCLESKEY and ALMERS, 1985). Particularly interesting are the four methylated amines (NH_4, CH_3NH_3, $(CH_3)_2NH_2$, $(CH_3)_3NH$, $(CH_3)_4N$), because these molecules are chemically similar, compact and of a fairly well-defined shape. In Fig. 6a the permeability of these compounds relative to that of Na was obtained from measurements of the reversal potential, and plotted against ion size. To determine ion size, we constructed Corey-Pauly-Koltum models of each ion, determined the volume of the smallest rectangular box that would accomodate it, and calculated the ion size as the length of a cube with that volume. Permeability to methylated ammonium derivatives is seen to diminish in a graded manner as ion size increases. TMA, the largest cation found to be clearly permeant, has a diameter of about 6 Å, hence the aqueous pore of the Ca channel at its narrowest point can be no smaller. Evidently the Ca channel is a large pore, much larger than is thought to be the case for K and Na channels on a similar experimental basis (HILLE, 1975b). Fig. 6b shows scale drawings of a 6 A diameter circle next to a Ca ion with an attached water molecule. Clearly the complex would fit through a pore that is large enough to pass TMA. The large pore size of the Ca channel fits with our view that this channel selects among inorganic cations mostly by binding rather than by rejection.

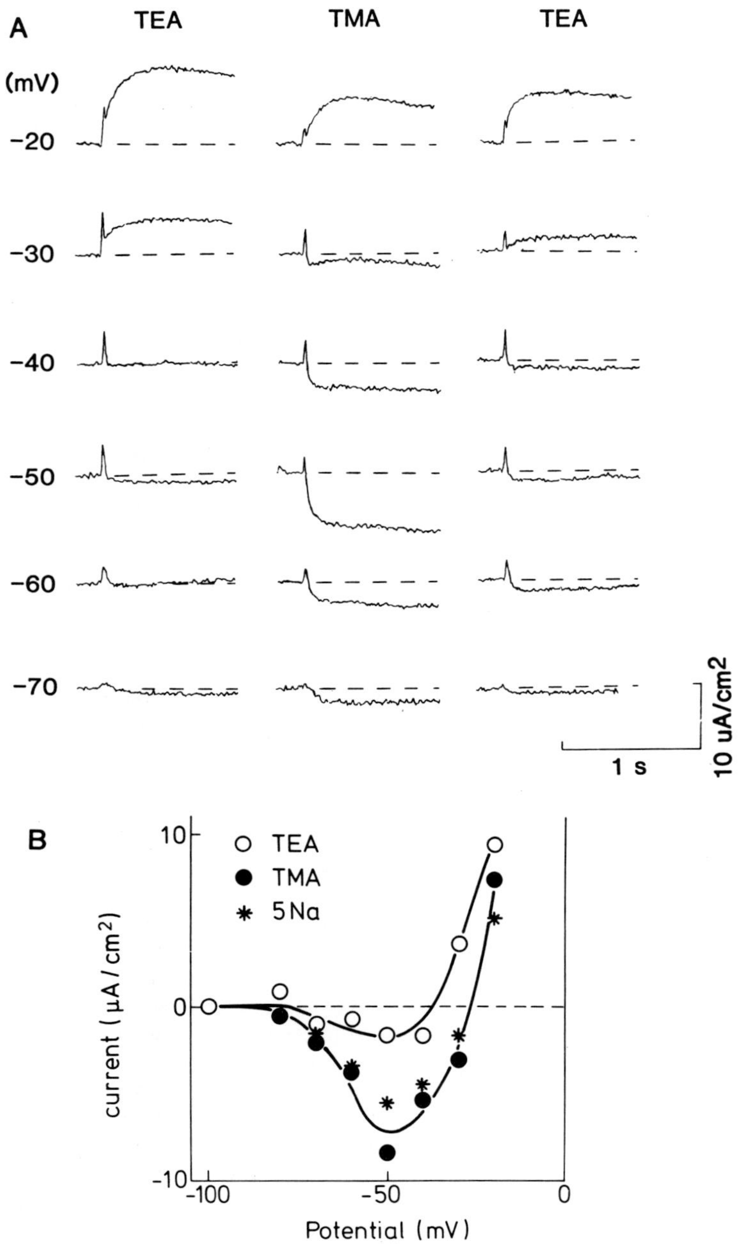

Fig. 5: (*A*) Membrane currents during jumps to the potentials given, with 80 mM TMA replacing external TEA, where indicated. (*B*) Peak current against voltage, with 80 mM TMA and 5 mM Na^+ replacing isosmolar amounts of TEA, as indicated. Solutions were applied in the sequence TEA, 80 mM TMA, 5 mM Na^+, TEA, 80 mM TMA, 5 mM Na^+; the values plotted are the average from the two runs in each solution. From MCCLESKEY and ALMERS, 1985.

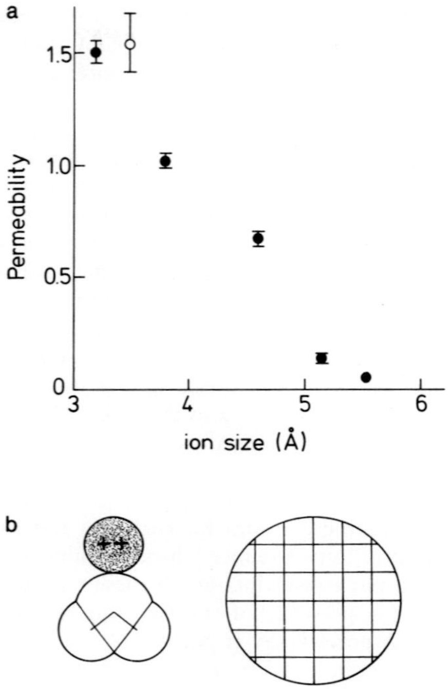

Fig. 6: Permeability ratios P_x/P_{Na} of hydrazinium (*circle*) and of ammonium and its four methylated derivatives (*dots*) were calculated from reversal potentials and are plotted as a function of ion size. Scale drawing of Ca^{++} and H_2O (*left*) and a 6 A pore (*right*). From McCleskey and Almers, 1985.

Discussion

How does Ca^{++} confer selectivity of ion transport on Ca channels? One possibility (Kostyuk et al., 1983) is that the Ca-specific site is an allosteric control site, that, on complexation with Ca^{++}, produces a structural change in the channel molecule or in a portion thereof. This structural change then transforms a nonselective into a selective channel. The hypothesis is difficult to exclude, and certainly explains that Ca channels appear highly selective under some conditions, and unselective under others. However, it makes no statements about the mechanism of selectivity.

Hess and Tsien (1984) and ourselves (Almers and McCleskey, 1984) explored instead an alternative view. Could it not be that the high-affinity binding site is a normal way-station for all ions during passage through the channel? And could it be that the selective binding of Ca^{++} at this site is, in fact, the essential feature that makes Ca channels selective? Indeed, the binding of Ca^{++} almost certainly occurs within the channel, since the block of monovalent cation permeability by Ca^{++} shows the characteristic voltage dependence expected when a permeant ion blocks by temporarily binding within the aqueous pore (Fukushima and Hagiwara, 1985; Nilius et al., 1986).

The problem that needs to be solved is the one posed by Armstrong et al., (1972): How can a channel preferentially transport the ion that it binds the tightest? The solution could be found in the literature on ion transport through «single-file» or «multi-ion pores» (Hille and Schwarz, 1978), such as the aqueous pores formed in lipid bilayers by the antibiotic, gramicidin-A. When gramicidin-A pores are exposed to only a single type of cation, they are freely permeable to all alkali metal ion, as well as to Tl^+. In ion mixtures, however, such pores act as though they were selectively permeable to Tl^+. Evidently, Tl^+ blocks the passage of ions other than Tl^+ through gramicidin-A channels (Neher, 1975; Eisenmann et al., 1978; Urban et al., 1980), just as Ca^{++} has now been found to block the passage of foreign cations through Ca channels. This and other findings on gramicidin-A channels were explained by assuming that the aqueous pore bears two ion binding sites, one at each end, to which permeating ions must bind in succession during passage (Urban et al., 1980; Urry et al., 1980). These ion binding sites are assumed to have a high affinity for Tl^+ and various lower affinities for the other permeant ions. Though both sites may be occupied simultaneously, ions may not pass each other inside the pore. High ion flux rates result because in a doubly-occupied pore, ions are expected to repel each other electrostatically so that their apparent affinity to the sites is reduced. Electrostatic repulsion helps ions dissociating from their sites, and hence enhances flux.

The mathematical statement of this physical picture is a model characterized by many rate constants, by one ion binding constant for each site and each ion, and by a factor telling how much the binding affinity is reduced during double occupancy. For gramicidin-A, there are enough data to put constraints on all these parameters. There is also direct experimental evidence for the presence of the two ion binding sites, as well as their positions in the gramicidin-A pore (Urry et al., 1982).

Similar concepts may be applied to Ca channels. If one accepts that the Ca site for blocking Na permeability lies within the aqueous pore and participates in ion transport, it is clear that there must be at least one more site. Firstly, a single site with 0.7 uM dissociation constant could not allow Ca ions to depart with the speed required to explain the observed high flux rates through single channels (Almers and McCleskey, 1984). Secondly, the relationship between current through Ca channels and the Ca concentration shows two affinities: one characterizing the block of Na current by Ca^{++}, and another describing the increase in Ca current seen when external $[Ca^{++}]$ is increased beyond 1 mM (Fig. 4).

Using the computer program of Begenisich and Cahalan (1980) and a pore with two sites, we were able to account quantitatively for the Ba/Ca and Na/Ca interaction in Ca channels observed experimentally (Almers and McCleskey, 1984). Our model is represented in Fig. 7, and shows our view of the Ca channel (Fig. 7a) along with energy diagrams for Na (dashed) and Ca^{++} (continuous), both drawn for a condition where the pore is empty and where there is no membrane potential. In our calculations, we assumed the distance between the two sites to be 10.5 Å, nearly the same as in a troponin-C molecule (Herzberg and James, 1985); the dielectric constant in the channel was taken as 20, one-quarter that in water. The affinity of at least one of the sites for Ca^{++} was experimentally determined ($K_D = 0.7\ \mu M$); the same value was assumed for the second site. With these constraints, one needs to assume a nearly diffusion-limited access of Ca^{++} from bulk fluid (entry rate constant $2 * 10^8/(M\ s)$ in our model) in order to obtain single-channel Ca fluxes of the magnitude observed experimentally (Fenwick et al., 1982). Nilius et al. (1986) have recently obtained a similar entry rate constant by direct measurement in cardiac Ca channels. Accordingly, the entry barriers in Fig. 7 represent mostly the diffusional limitation on access to the pore, and not primarily any physical or physicochemical obstacle.

Fig. 8 is a pictorial representation of this two-site model. For simplicity, assume that

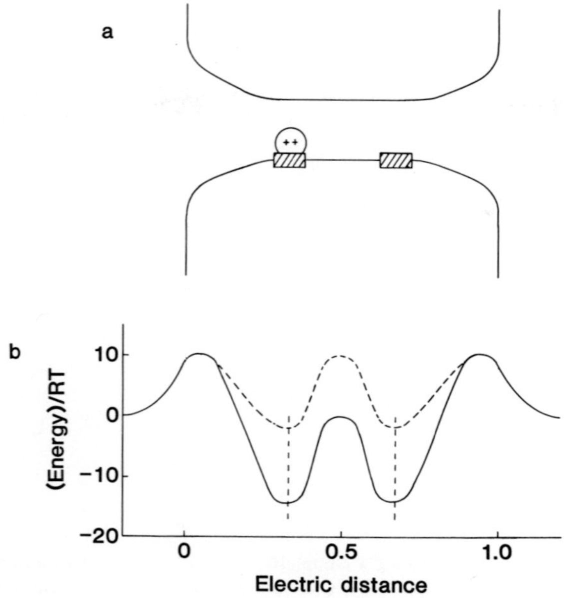

Fig. 7: *A*, schematic drawing of Ca channel with two binding sites (hatched), one of them complexed with a divalent cation. b, energy profile corresponding to a. The ordinate plots energy (in J/mole) divided by RT for an empty pore at zero membrane potential. The abscissa gives the fraction of the transmembrane potential experienced at any given point. From ALMERS and MCCLESKEY, 1984.

there is no membrane potential, and that net ion flux occurs because permeant ions are present on the left (outer) side of the pore only. The uppermost panel represents the pore when only a low-affinity ion is present, such as Na^+. Hopping from site to site, Na^+ is freely permeable. In the middle panels, a high-affinity ion (Ca^{++}) is also present; when it enters the pore, flux of Na^+ is blocked, since ions may not pass each other inside the pore. Neither is there much Ca-flux, since Ca^{++} is so tightly bound that it does not readily escape into the bulk fluid (though we assume that within the pore, Ca^{++} may move back and forth between vacant sites relatively easily). In this state, the pore passes only very small currents. In the lowermost panels, Ca^{++} is present at sufficient concentration to cause frequent double occupancy. Due to electrostatic repulsion, double occupancy is a relatively unstable state, where sooner or later one of the ions dissociates away. If the two Ca^{++} are bound with equal affinity, (as we assumed for simplicity), then the outer ion will leave in half of the cases; nothing is gained, and nothing is lost. In the other half of the cases, the inner ion will escape into the cytoplasm, generating Ca flux. Due to electrostatic repulsion, Ca^{++} finds it much easier (20 000 times easier in our model) to leave a doubly rather than a singly occupied pore, hence flux from singly-occupied pores is negligible by comparison, and flux should be nearly proportional to the number of pores doubly occupied by high-affinity ions. Note that co-occupation of the channel by Ca^{++} and Na^+ (or, under physiological conditions, also K^+) will still occur occasionally. However, neither Na^+ nor K^+ are bound tightly enough to stay sufficiently long to dislodge the resident Ca^{++}. Only another high-affinity ion has a significant chance of dislodging a resident high-affinity ion. Hence such a pore will, in ion mixtures, selectively transport the ion that is bound the tightest.

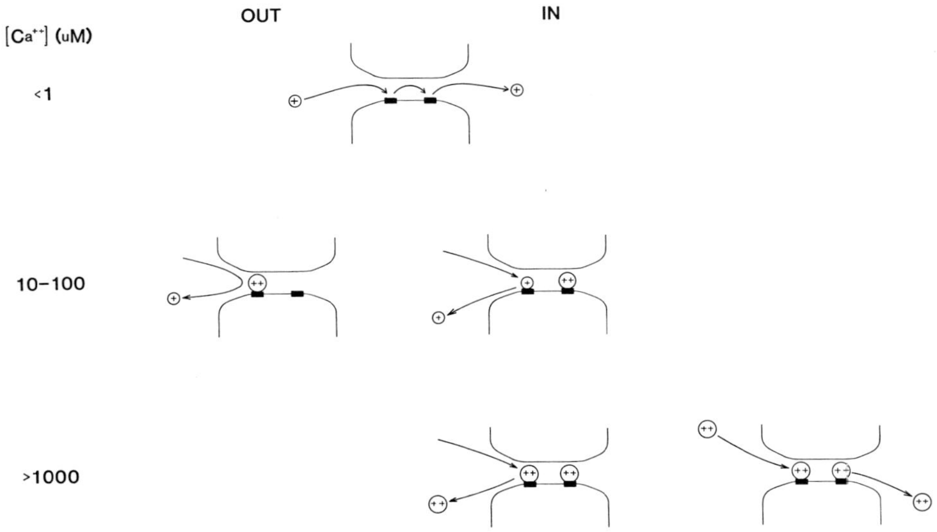

Fig. 8: Pictorial representation of how Ca channels pass Na^+ and other monovalent cations in the absence of Ca^{++}, but reject these ions when Ca^{++} is present. For explanation, see text.

To summarize, we believe that the ion selectivity of Ca channels is based on the selective binding of Ca^{++} to sites within an otherwise unselective pore. Though in animal cell membranes, the Ca channel is so far the only one for which such a mechanism has been recognized to apply, it seems possible that the highly selective K channels achieve their selectivity in a similar way. K channels are well known to be single-file pores (for review, see Hille and Schwarz, 1978).

For Ca channels, the problem of ion selectivity is now reduced to questions like: What is the structure of the Ca-selective sites? What special features make them prefer Ca^{++} over all other physiologic cations? And finally, how are the binding sites integrated into the aqueous pore? These questions will not be solved by electrophysiology alone, and require in addition the approaches of molecular biology.

Supported by grant # AMl7803 from the National Institutes of Health.

References

Almers, W., Fink, R., Palade, P. T. (1981): Calcium depletion in frog muscle tubules: The decline of calcium current under maintained depolarization. J. Physiol. (Lond.) **312**, 177–207.

Almers, W., McCleskey, E. W., Palade, P. T. (1982): Frog muscle membrane: a cation-permeable channel blocked by micromolar external Ca^{++}. J. Physiol. (Lond.) **332**, 52–53P.

Almers, W., McCleskey, E. W. (1984): Nonselective conductance in calcium channels of frog muscle: Calcium selectivity in a single-file pore. J. Physiol. (Lond.) **353**, 585–608.

Almers, W., McCleskey, E. W., Palade, P. T. (1984): A nonselective cation conductance in frog muscle membrane blocked by micromolar external calcium ions. J. Physiol. **353**, 565–583.

Almers, W., Palade, P. T. (1981): Slow calcium and potassium currents across frog muscle membrane: Measurements with a vaseline gap technique. J. Physiol. (Lond.) **312**, 159–176.

Armstrong, C. M., Bezanilla, F. M., Horowicz, P. (1972): Twitches in the presence of ethylene glycol bis(-aminoethyl ether)-N,N'-tetraacetic acid. Biochim. Biophys. Acta **267**, 605–608.

Begenisich, T. B., Cahalan, M. D. (1980): Sodium channel permeation in squid axons. I. Reversal potential experiments. J. Physiol. (Lond.) **307,** 217–242.

Bezanilla, F., Armstrong, C. M. (1972): Negative conductance caused by entry of sodium and cesium ions into the potassium channels of squid giant axons. J. Gen. Physiol. **60,** 588–608.

Catterall, W. A. (1986): Structure of voltage-sensitive sodium and Calcium channels. This volume.

Curtis, B. A. (1966): Ca fluxes in single twitch muscle fibers. J. Gen. Physiol. **50,** 255–267.

Eisenmann, G. (1962): Cation selective glass electrodes and their mode of operation. Biophys. J. **2,** 259–323.

Eisenmann, G., Sandblom, J., Neher, E. (1978): Interactions in cation permeation through the gramicidin channel. Biophys. J. **22,** 307–340.

Fenwick, E. M., Marty, A., Neher, E. (1982): Sodium and calcium channels in bovine chromaffin cells. J. Physiol. (Lond.) **331,** 599–635.

Fukushima, Y., Hagiwara, S. (1985): Currents carried by monovalent cations through calcium channels in mouse neoplastic B lymphocytes. J. Physiol. (Lond.) **358,** 255–284.

Hagiwara, S., Byerly, L. (1981): Calcium channel. Ann. Rev. Neurosci. **4,** 69–125.

Herzberg, O., James, M. N. G. (1985): Structure of the calcium regulatory muscle protein troponic-C at 2.8 A resolution. Nature **313,** 653–659.

Hess, P., Tsien, R. W. (1984): Mechanism of ion permeation through calcium channels. Nature **309,** 453–456.

Hille, B. (1975a): Ionic selectivity, saturation, and block in sodium channels. A four-barrier model. J. Gen. Physiol. **66,** 535–560.

Hille, B. (1975b): Ionic selectivity of Na and K channels of nerve membranes. In: Membranes: A series of advances. Vol. 3, G. Eisenmann, ed. Marcel Dekker, New York.

Hille, B., Campbell, D. T. (1976): An improved vaseline gap voltage clamp for skeletal muscle fibers. J. Gen. Physiol. **67,** 265–293.

Hille, B., Schwarz, W. (1978): Potassium channels as multi-ion, single-file pores. J. Gen. Physiol. **72,** 409–442.

Kostyuk, P. G., Mironov, S. L., Shuba, Ya. M. (1983): Two ion-selecting filters in the calcium channel of the somatic membrane of mollusc neurons. J. Membrane Biol. **76,** 83–93.

Lee, K. S., Tsien, R. W. (1982): Reversal of current through calcium channels in dialysed single heart cells. Nature **297,** 498–501.

McCleskey, E. W., Almers, W. (1985): The calcium channel in skeletal muscle is a large pore. Proc. Natl. Acad. Sci. USA **82,** 7149–7153.

Neher, E. (1975): Ionic specificity of the gramicidin channel and the thallous ion. Biochim. Biophys. Acta **401,** 540–544.

Nicola-Siri, L., Sanchez, J. A., Stefani, E. (1980): Effect of glycerol treatment on the calcium current of frog skeletal muscle. J. Physiol. (Lond.) **305,** 87–96.

Nilius, B., Hess, P., Lansman, J. B., Tsien, R. W. (1986): Two kinds of Ca channels in isolated ventricular cells from guinea pig heart. Progr. Zool. **33,** 75–82.

Palade, P. T., Almers, W. (1985): Slow calcium and potassium currents in frog skeletal muscle: their relationship and pharmacologic properties. Pflügers Arch. **405,** 91–101.

Reuter, H., Scholz, H. (1977): A study of the ion selectivity and the kinetic properties of the calcium dependent slow inward current in mammalian cardiac muscle. J. Physiol. (Lond.) **264,** 17–47.

Sanchez, J. A., Stefani, E. (1978): Inward calcium current in twitch muscle fibres of the frog. J. Physiol. (Lond.) **283,** 197–209.

Stanfield, P. R. (1977): A calcium-dependent inward current in frog skeletal muscle fibres. Pflügers Arch. **368,** 267–270.

Urban, B. W., Hladky, S. B., Haydon, D. A. (1980): Ion movements in gramicidin pores, an example of single-file transport. Biochim. Biophys. Acta **602,** 331–354.

Urry, D. W., Prasak, K. U., Tapane, T. L. (1982): Location of monovalent cation binding sites in the gramicidin channel. Proc. Natl. Acad. Sci. USA **79,** 390–394.

Urry, D. W., Venkatachalam, C. M., Spisni, A., Läuger, P., Khaled, A. (1980): Rate theory calculations of gramicidin single-channel currents using NMR-derived rate constant. Proc. Natl. Acad. Sci. USA **77,** 2028–2032.

Veerecke, J., Carmeliet, E. (1971): Sr action potentials in cardiac Purkinje fibres. II. Dependence of the Sr conductance on the external Sr concentration and Sr-Ca antagonism. Pflügers Arch. **322,** 73–82.

Fortschritte der Zoologie, Band 33 · Lüttgau (Hrsg.): Membrane Control
Gustav Fischer Verlag · Stuttgart · New York · 1986

Two kinds of Ca channels in isolated ventricular cells from guinea pig heart

B. Nilius, P. Hess*, J. B. Lansman* and R. W. Tsien*

Julius Bernstein Institute of Physiology, Martin Luther University Halle-Wittenberg, GDR-4020 Halle (Saale)
Department of Physiology, Yale University, School of Medicine, New Haven, CT, 06910, USA

In heart muscle, Ca-selective channels in the surface membrane are important for the control of many different cellular functions. Therefore, it is of interest to ask if heart cells possess a single or multiple types of Ca channel. Different types of Ca channels have already been described in noncardiac cells. Evidence has been given for the existence of two kinds of Ca channels coexisting in starfish eggs (Hagiwara et al., 1975), polychaete eggs (Fox and Krasne, 1984), cultured pituitary cells (Matteson and Armstrong, 1984, Cohen and McCarthy, 1985, Armstrong and Matteson, 1985), the ciliate Stylonychia (Deitmer, 1984), neuroblastoma cells (Tsunoo et al., 1984, 1985, Yoshii et al., 1985), vertebrate sensory neurones (Carbone and Lux 1984a, b, Nowycky et al., 1984a, b, Bossu et al., 1985, Fedulova et al., 1985) and skeletal muscle (Gota and Stefani, 1985).

In whole cell recordings from heart muscle cells, there is well-established evidence for the existence of a small and fast inactivating Ca-current coexisting in the same cell with the «conventional» large and slowly inactivating Ca current (Bean, 1985a, b). We could recently prove that also at the single channel level, two different types of Ca channels exist in heart muscle (Nilius et al., 1985). Here we describe some properties of a novel type of cardiac Ca channel.

Methods

Elementary Ca channel currents were recorded from cell-attached patches by the method of Hamill et al., 1981. The patch pipettes were filled with 110 $BaCl_2$ or 110 mM $CaCl_2$ (one patch with 50 mM $CaCl_2$) and 10 mM Hepes (pH 7.5 with TEA-OH). The resting potential of the isolated cells (ventricular cells from guinea pig, method of isolation described by Kao et al., 1980) was zeroed by exposing the cells to isotonic K-aspartat bathing solution.

Methods for filtering, storing, and analysing single channel recordings are described elsewhere (Hess et al., 1984).

Results

Figure 1 shows strikingly different channel activity recorded from the same patch if the holding potential was changed. At steps from a holding potential of −70 mV to a test potential of −20 mV (too negative to activitate the conventional Ca channel), openings appear as currents of about 0.5 pA amplitude (Fig. 1a). With 110 mM $BaCl_2$ in the patch pipette, the hitherto described conventional Ca channel is characterized by unitary currents of about 1.2 pA amplitude, showing brief openings in clusters throughout the depolarizing pulse from −50 to +10 mV (Fig. 1c). The driving force for Ba entry in the protocol shown in Figure 1a is higher than in Figure 1c, but the amplitude of the elemen-

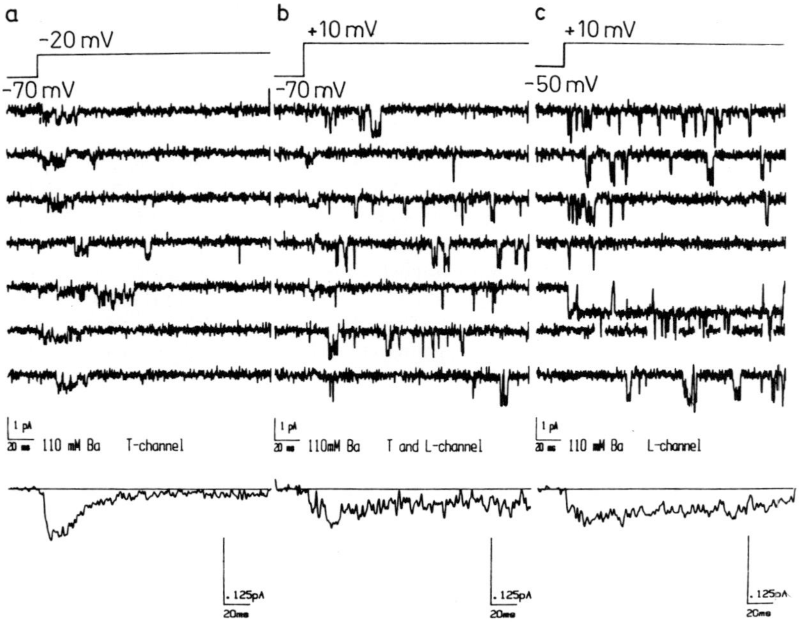

Fig. 1: Two different types of Ca channel in guinea pig ventricular cells in the same patch.
a) The novel type of Ca channel can be activated from holding potentials negative to −50 mV (holding potential −70 mV, step to −20 mV). The size of unitary currents is about 0.5 pA. Openings cluster at the beginning of the pulse. Note the smaller unitary currents in 1a than in 1c, in spite of the larger driving force and the different pattern of openings in comparison to the conventional Ca channel shown in 1c. The averaged current was obtained from 270 sweeps and shows a striking inactivation.
b) Two types of openings can be detected at steps from the same holding to more positive test potentials than in 1a (holding −70 mV, step to +10 mV). The averaged current (125 sweeps) is a mixture of a fast and a slowly inactivating current.
c) At a holding potential of −50 mV, only a large unitary current can be activated (holding −50 mV, test step to +10 mV). The conventional «L» type current is well maintained (averaged current from 294 sweeps). Cell-attached patch clamp recordings were obtained at 21 °C, 110 mM $BaCl_2$, 10 mM Hepes (pH 7.5 with TEA-OH) in the pipette, 140 mM K-aspartate, 10 mM EGTA, 10 mM Hepes (pH 7.5 with KOH) in the bath. Sampling rate 5 kHz, filtering 1 kHz, capacity and leakage currents were subtracted. Cell B 2 E.

tary currents is reduced. Therefore, there can be no doubt of the existence of two different Ba conducting channels in the same patch. In Figure 1b single channel activity of both types of Ca channels can be seen (step from −70 to +10 mV). The averaged current obtained from openings at negative membrane potentials decays rapidly (Fig. 1a). By contrast, the averaged current obtained from more positive test potentials is fairly well maintained. Because the current activated at negative potential is «tiny» and «transient», we call it «T-current» (T-channel). The hitherto-described type of cardiac Ca channel will be referred to as «L» channel (see NILIUS et al., 1985).

Figure 2 shows elementary current-voltage relationships for the L- and the T-channel. The «L» i-V relationship was recorded from 3 patches (13 points, 110 mM $BaCl_2$ in the pipette). A large slope conductance has been measured (20.6 pS). The reversal potential was estimated near +72 mV. The «T» i-V relationship was measured from 7 patches (26 points), but with 110 Ba or Ca in the pipette. A slope conductance of 7.5 pS was calculated; (reversal near 65 mV). The single channel conductance of the T-channel is considerably smaller than in the L-channel. Surprisingly, the T-channel conducts similar currents with either Ba or Ca (see also NILIUS et al., 1985).

In contrast to the conventional L-Ca channel, single channel currents through the T-channel can easily be recorded even in 50 mM Ca. Figure 3 shows an example for a one T-

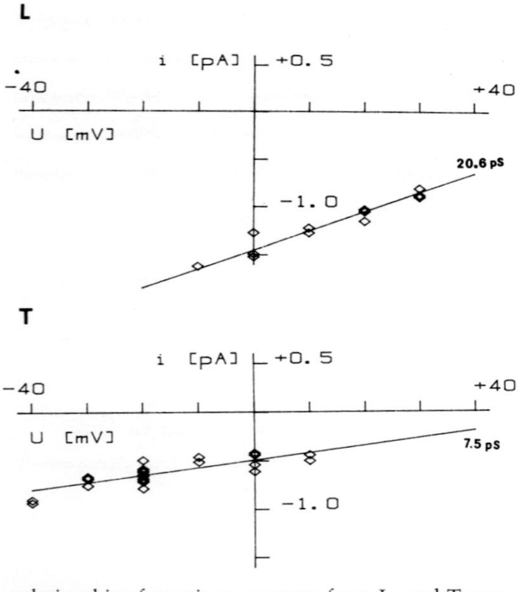

Fig. 2: Current-voltage relationships for unitary currents from L- and T-type.
top: L current-voltage relationship; 13 points (individual measurements of unitary L currents obtained from 3 patches). The holding potential in all records was between −60 and −40 mV. U is the test potential in mV. The slope of the regression line corresponds to a single L-channel conductance of 20.6 pS. The intercept with the abscisse (reversal potential) was calculated at 72.5 mV (110 mM Ba in the pipette; coefficient of regression 0.966).
bottom: T current-voltage relationship, 26 points, 7 patches. The holding potential was between −100 and −90 mV. U is again the test potential. From linear regression, a slope conductance of the T channel of 7.5 pS was calculated. The reversal potential was obtained at 65.3 mV (110 mM Ba or 110 mM Ca in the pipette, coefficient of regression 0.939).

channel patch. Typically, there is one burst per sweep. The openings cluster at the very beginning of the pulse. Sometimes we observed extremely long lasting waiting times to the first opening. The averaged current can be nicely fitted with a conventional m^2h-model. The maximum probability of the channel to open has been calculated from

$$P_{max} = \frac{I_{max}}{i \cdot N} \qquad (1)$$

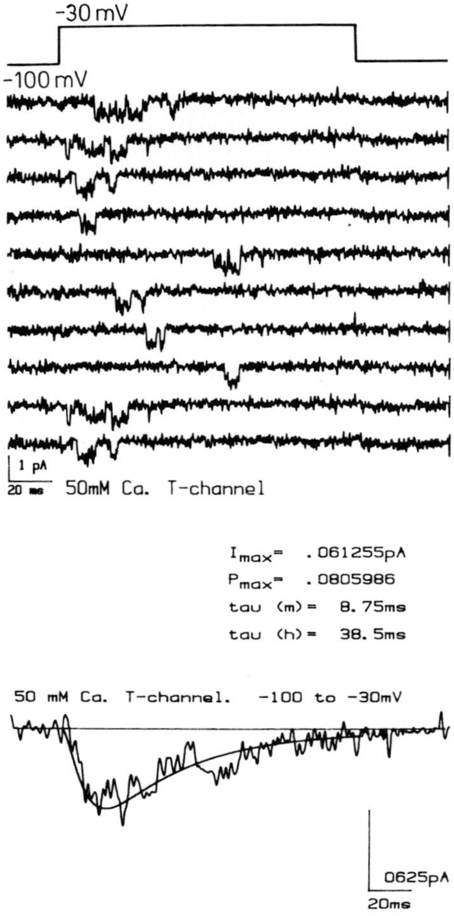

Fig. 3: T-channel activity recorded in 50 mM Ca.
top: Traces obtained from one channel patch. Note the clustering at the beginning of the depolarizing step from −100 mV to −30 mV. Sometimes long lasting first latencies can be recorded.
bottom: averaged current obtained from 215 sweeps. The current was fitted by use of an m^2h-model. I_{max} is the peak of the fitted current, tau(m) and (tau)h refer to the time constant of activation and inactivation, respectively. The maximum probability of the channel to open was calculated from P_{max}/ i(i = 0.76 pA). (same experimental conditions as in Figure 1, cell G 40 E.)

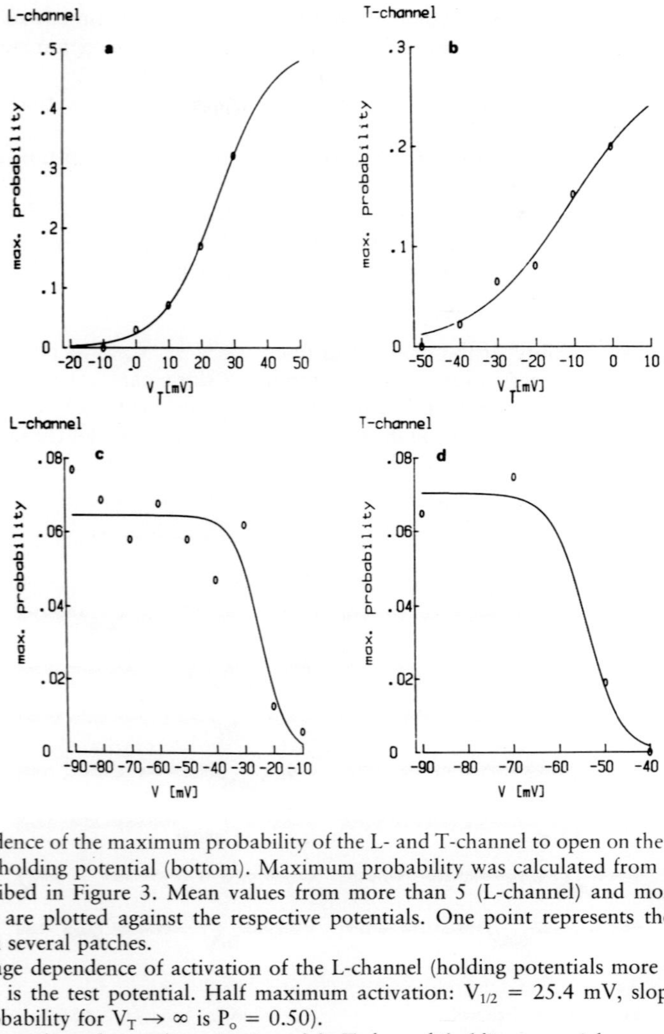

Fig. 4: Dependence of the maximum probability of the L- and T-channel to open on the test potential (top) and the holding potential (bottom). Maximum probability was calculated from averaged currents as described in Figure 3. Mean values from more than 5 (L-channel) and more than 8 (T-channel) cells are plotted against the respective potentials. One point represents the mean value obtained from several patches.
top, left: voltage dependence of activation of the L-channel (holding potentials more negative than -40 mV). V_T is the test potential. Half maximum activation: $V_{1/2} = 25.4$ mV, slope: -8.4 mV, maximum probability for $V_T \rightarrow \infty$ is $P_o = 0.50$).
top, right: voltage dependence of inactivation of the T-channel (holding potentials more negative than -80 mV), $V_{1/2} = -54.3$ mV, slope: $s = -12.5$ mV, $P_o = 0.29$).
bottom, left: voltage dependence of inactivation of the L-channel. V is the holding potential, 200 ms pulses were applied with a rate of 0.5 Hz (test potentials more positive than $+20$ mV). Half maximum steady state inactivation $V_{1/2} = -24.6$ mV, slope $= 4.6$ mV, $P_o = 0.07$.
bottom, right: steady state inactivation of the T-channel (test potentials more positive than -30 mV). $V_{1/2} = -54.3$ mV, $s = 3.8$ mV, $P_o = 0.07$.
The smooth lines are best fitted by use of equation (3) (Levenberg and Marquard algorithm, Brown and Dennis 1972).

I_{max} was obtained from the peak value of the fitted current, i was directly measured, N is the estimation of the number of channels in the patch. The macroscopic kinetic data were obtained from the best fits by use of equation (2)

$$I = a \cdot (1-\exp(-t/b))^2 \exp(-t/c) \tag{2}$$

(a, b, c are the parameters of the fit, b corresponds to the time constant of activation tau(m), c to inactivation tau(h)).

We found major differences in the voltage dependence of the two channel types as demonstrated in Figure 4. The voltage dependence of steady state activation and inactivation was analysed from the averaged currents and described by

$$P_{max} = P_o/(1 + \exp(V-V_{1/2})/s) \tag{3}$$

(P_o: maximum probability of the channel to open for $V \to \infty$, $V_{1/2}$: potential for half-maximum activation, inactivation, V: test potential, s: slope parameter in [mV]).

We calculated a half-maximum activation of the L-channel near +25 mV (110 mM Ba), but for the T-channel at −11 mV. Half-maximum inactivation of the L-channel could be

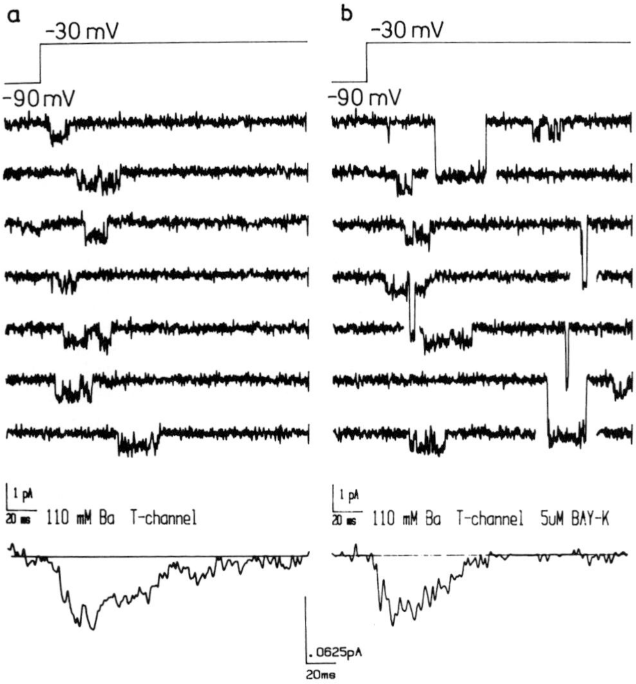

Fig. 5: Different effect of BAY-K 8644 on the two Ca channels.
a) Current traces with 110 mM Ba and 33 μM TTX in the pipette; averaged current from 234 sweeps. At −30 mV there are no detectable openings of the L-channel being present in the analysed patch.
b) Application of 5 μM BAY-K 8644 in the bath; same patch as left. Note the additional large amplitude (long-lasting) openings, indicating the additional activity of L-channels. The mean current was obtained from 134 sweeps with no detectable L-type activity. Note the lack of BAY-K 8644 effect on the T-channel, in constrast to the well known striking response of the L-channel to the Ca agonist. The experimental conditions are the same as in Figure 1. Cell B 3 D.

observed near −25 mV, for the T-channel near −54 mV. The T-channel steady state voltage relationships for activation and inactivation are shifted about 30 mV towards negative potentials.

One striking difference between T-type and L-type Ca channels concerns their sensitivity to dihydropyridines. It is well documented that the Ca agonist BAY-K 8644 promotes long lasting openings of the L-type Ca channel (Hess et al., 1984, Tsien et al., 1985).

Figure 5 shows unitary currents recorded from a patch with coexisting L- and T-type channels. At a test potential of −30 mV (holding potential −90 mV) in the absence of BAY-K 8644 (left), the recorded activity is typical for T-type channel openings as expected from the differing voltage ranges of activation (see also Fig. 4). After addition of 5 μM BAY-K 8644, depolarization to −30 mV evokes the same type of T activity, but with additional openings of the large conductance channel (right). Huge unitary currents (> 2 pA at −30 mV) are occasionally activated due to the drug-promoted leftward shift of the activation-voltage relationship for the L-channel. In the same sweeps the two types of Ca channels can easily be detected. The pattern of T openings is not changed by BAY-K 8644. The mean current constructed by averaging only those sweeps without L activity nicely matches the mean current before application of BAY-K 8644. The T-channel is insensitive to BAY-K 8644. We found the same lack of sensitivity of the T-channel to the Ca antagonist nimodipine. Also, a quite different pattern of sensitivity of both channels to other well-known Ca-modulating substances could be observed (Co, Cd, isoproterenol, forskolin, caffeine).

Conclusions

Ventricular cells possess at least two different types of Ca channels. The novel type of Ca channel (T-channel) conducts a tiny and fast decaying Ca or Ba current. It can survive in excised patches (Nilius et al., 1985) and, therefore, does not need the intact metabolical background of the whole cell, in contrast to the L-channel. It contributes only little to the Ca influx during the action potentials but could have some importance for pacemaking. However, the functional significance of the new channel is still obscure. The finding of multiple types of Ca channels can help to solve some long-standing puzzles why Ca channel modulating compounds have quite different effects in different tissues. The description of a different distribution of e. g. dihydropyridine sensitive (L) or insensitive (T) channels may help to explain different effects and to develop compounds with a greater tissue specificity.

Acknowledgements

We thank our colleagues M. C. Nowycky and A. P. Fox for helpful discussions and the USPHS and Miles Pharmaceuticals for support. The work was done at Yale, while B. Nilius was supported by a Fellowship from the International Research and Exchanges Board.

References

Armstrong, C. M., Matteson, D. R. (1985): Two distinct populations of calcium channels in a clonal line of pituitary cells. Science **227**, 65–66.

Bean, B. P. (1985a): Two kinds of calcium channels in atrial cells from dog and frog hearts. Biophys. J. **47**, 497a (Abstr.)

Bean, B. P. (1985b): Two kinds of calcium channels in canine atrial cells. J. Gen. Physiol. **86**, 1–30.
Bossu, J. L., Feltz, A., Thomann, J. M. (1985): Depolarization elicits two distinct calcium currents in vertebrate sensory neurons. Pflügers Arch. **403**, 360–368.
Brown, K. M., Dennis, J. E. Jr. (1972): Derivative free analogues of the Levenberg-Marquard and Gauss algorithms for nonlinear least squares approximation. Numer. Math. **18**, 289–297.
Carbone, E., Lux, H. D. (1984a): A low voltage-activated calcium conductance in embryonic chick sensory neurons. Biophys. J. **46**, 413–418.
Carbone, E., Lux, H. D. (1984b): A low voltage-activated, fully inactivating Ca channel in vertebrate sensory neurons. Nature **310**, 501–502.
Cohen, C. J., McCarthy, R. T. (1985): Differential effects of dihydropyridines on two populations of Ca channels in anterior pituitary cells. Biophys. J. **47**, 513a (Abstr.)
Cota, G., Stefani, E. (1985): Fast and slow Ca channels in twitch muscle fibres of the frog. Biophys. J. **47**, 65a (Abstr.).
Deitmer, J. W. (1984): Evidence for two voltage-dependent calcium currents in the membrane of the ciliate *Stylonychia*. J. Physiol. (Lond.) **355**, 137–159.
Fedulova, S. A., Kostyuk, P. G., Veselovsky, N. S. (1985): Two types of calcium channels in the somatic membrane of newborn rat dorsal root ganglion neurones. J. Physiol. (Lond.) **359**, 431–446.
Fox, A. P., Krasne, S. (1984): Two calcium currents in *Neanthes arenaceodentatus* egg cell membrane. J. Physiol. (Lond.) **356**, 491–505.
Hagiwara, S., Ozawa, S., Sand, S. (1975): Voltage clamp analysis of two inward current mechanisms in the egg cell membrane of a starfish. J. Gen. Physiol. **65**, 617–644.
Hamill, O. P., Marty, A., Neher, E., Sakmann, B., Sigworth, F. J. (1981): Improved patch clamp technique for high-resolution current recording from cells and cell-free membrane patches. Pflügers Arch. **391**, 85–100.
Hess, P., Lansman, J. B., Tsien, R. W. (1984): Different modes of Ca channel gating behaviour favored by dihydropyridine Ca agonist and antagonist. Nature **311**, 538–544.
Kao, R. L., Christman, E. W., Luh, S. L., Krauhs, J. M., Tyero, G. F. O., Williams, E. H. (1980): The effects of insulin and anoxia on the metabolism of isolated, mature rat cardiac myocytes. Arch. Biochem. Biophys. **203**, 587–599.
Matteson, D. R., Armstrong, C. M. (1984): Evidence for two types of Ca channels in GH 3 cells. Biophys. J. **45**, 36a (Abstr.)
Nilius, B., Hess, P., Lansman, J. B., Tsien, R. W. (1985): A novel type of calcium channel in ventricular heart cells. Nature **316**, 443–446.
Nowycky, M. C., Fox, A. P., Tsien, R. W. (1984a): Two components of calcium channel current in chick dorsal root ganglion cells. Biophys. J. **45**, 36a (Abstr.)
Nowycky, M. C., Fox, A. P., Tsien, R. W. (1984b): Multiple types of calcium channels in dorsal root ganglion cells distinguished by sensitivity to cadmium and single channel properties. Soc. Neurosci. **10**, 526 (Abstr.).
Nowycky, M. C., Fox, A. P., Tsien, R. W. (1985a): Three types of calcium channels in chick dorsal root ganglion cells. Biophys. J. **47**, 67a (Abstr.).
Nowycky, M. C., Fox, A. P., Tsien, R. W. (1985b): Three types of neuronal calcium channels with different calcium agonist sensitivity. Nature **316**, 440–443.
Tsien, R. W., Hess, P., Lansman, J. B., Lee, K. S. (1985): Current views of cardiac calcium channels and their response to calcium antagonists and agonists. In: Cardiac Electrophysiology and Arrhythmias, ed. O. P. Zipes, J. Jalife, pp. 119–129, Grune & Stratton, Orlando.
Tsunoo, A., Yoshii, M., Narahashi, T. (1984): Two types of calcium channels in neuroblastoma cells and their sensitivities to cAMP. Soc. Neurosci. **10**, 527 (Abstr.).
Tsunoo, A., Yoshii, M., Narahashi, T. (1985): Differential block of two types of calcium channels in neuroblastoma cells. Biophys. J. **47**, 433 (Abstr.).
Yoshii, M., Tsunoo, A., Narahashi, T. (1985): Different properties of two types of calcium channels in neuroblastoma cells. Biophys. J. **47**, 433a (Abstr.)

Fortschritte der Zoologie, Band 33 · Lüttgau (Hrsg.): Membrane Control
Gustav Fischer Verlag · Stuttgart · New York · 1986

Macroscopic and elementary currents through cardiac calcium channels*

DIETER PELZER[1], ADOLFO CAVALIÉ[1], TERENCE F. McDONALD[2] and WOLFGANG TRAUTWEIN[1]

[1] II. Physiologisches Institut, Universität des Saarlandes, 6650 Homburg/Saar, FRG
[2] Department of Physiology and Biophysics, Dalhousie University, Halifax, Nova Scotia, Canada B3H 4H7

When Ca channels in cardiac membranes open in response to membrane depolarization, they allow Ca entry and, thus, contribute to impulse conduction, rhythmic activity and refractoriness (see ZIPES et al., 1980; ZIPES and JALIFE, 1985 for review articles). Since, however, the Ca ion is considered as a nearly universal messenger in living cells (RASMUSSEN and BARRETT, 1984), the entry of Ca through highly selective Ca channels (LEE and TSIEN, 1984) means more than just the transfer of depolarizing positive charge; Ca also serves as a chemical message (TSIEN et al., 1983). By controlling Ca entry in a steeply voltage-dependent manner (see McDONALD, 1982; REUTER, 1983, 1984; TSIEN, 1983; TRAUTWEIN and PELZER, 1985a, b for reviews), Ca channels act as transducers to convert electrical information to a chemical signal which, after being decoded by Ca-binding proteins inside the cell (CHEUNG, 1982; COHEN, 1982), results in processes such as excitation-contraction coupling (FABIATO, 1983). Moreover, these channels take an essential part in the control of numerous cellular Ca-dependent enzyme reactions, especially those involving phosphorylation (COHEN, 1982). Thus, in contrast to other ionic channels, Ca channels directly link membrane potential changes to variations in levels of a messenger substance (TSIEN et al., 1983), a role which seems to be unique.

Currents flowing through single Ca channels have been recorded from membrane patches of ventricular cells isolated from neonatal rat (REUTER et al., 1982; TSIEN et al., 1983) and adult guinea pig (CAVALIÉ et al., 1983, 1986; TSIEN et al., 1983; HESS et al., 1984; PELZER et al., 1985a, b; TRAUTWEIN and PELZER, 1985a, b; TSIEN et al., 1985b). The pipette solutions bathing the membrane patches contained 20-110 mM Ba because large driving forces are required for the generation of single Ca channel currents of resolvable amplitude, and the Ba ions completely block K channel activity (SAKMANN and TRUBE, 1984). High-Ca solutions create problems because the inclusion of Ba to block K channels may also partially block Ca flux due to an anomalous mole fraction effect on the Ca channel (HESS and TSIEN, 1984).

There are several reasons why one cannot simply take single Ca channel data from patches bathed in high-Ba solutions, scale them as appropriate, and draw conclusions

* Supported by the Deutsche Forschungsgemeinschaft (DFG), SFB 38 (Membranforschung), project Gl, and the Medical Research Council (Canada)

about whole-cell I_{Ca} under physiological conditions. First, high divalent ion concentrations are known to shift channel voltage dependencies to the right (FRANKENHAEUSER and HODGKIN, 1957; HILLE, 1968; OHMORI and YOSHII, 1977). Secondly, channel kinetics may be affected by ionic concentration, independent of voltage shifts. Thirdly, whole-cell currents through Ca channels may saturate to a varying degree at high external concentrations of divalent cations (WILSON et al., 1983). Finally, channel voltage dependencies in Ba may be far to the left of those in equimolar physiological concentrations of Ca (WILSON et al., 1983; BYERLY et al., 1985).

In this study, whole-cell Ca channel currents were measured from adult guinea pig ventricular myocytes bathed in 3.6 mM Ca, 3.6 mM Ba, and 90 mM Ba. We have estimated the shifts in voltage dependencies, as well as whole-cell current densities and relative ionic permeabilities. In cell-attached patch-clamp experiments, single Ca channel currents were recorded with 90 mM Ba in the patch pipettes. These results have been related to the whole-cell data, and allow inferences about the activation of whole-cell I_{Ba}, the reversal potential of the single-channel current, and the density of Ca channels in the myocyte membrane.

Methods

Preparation, experimental procedures and solutions, and data analysis

Ventricular myocytes were enzymatically dissociated from adult guinea pig hearts (cf. CAVALIÉ et al., 1983, 1986 for details of the method) and superfused with modified Tyrode's containing (in mM) NaCl 140, KCl 10.8, $CaCl_2$ 3.6, $MgCl_2$ 1, glucose 10, HEPES 5 (pH 7.4, temperature 34 °C). Single-channel currents were recorded by means of the patch-clamp technique from membrane patches in the cell-attached configuration (HAMILL et al., 1981). The pipette-filling solution (external membrane patch solution) contained (in mM) $BaCl_2$ 90, NaCl 2, KCl 10.8, TTX 0.02 and HEPES 5 (pH 7.4). Whole-cell currents were recorded after establishment of the seal and subsequent rupture of the membrane patch with short pulses of suction (HAMILL et al., 1981; SAKMANN and NEHER, 1983). The pipette-filling solution perfusing the cell interior contained (in mM) CsCl 112, $MgCl_2$ 8, Na_2ATP 5, Cs_2EGTA 10 and HEPES 10 (pH 7.2). Three external solutions were used (pH 7.4, temperature 34 °C): 3.6 mM Ca (modified Tyrode's as above); 3.6 mM Ba (modified Tyrode's with 3.6 mM Ba replacing 3.6 mM Ca); 90 mM Ba (same as pipette-filling solution for single-channel recordings). All three solutions contained 20 μM TTX to block Na channel currents.

Elementary and whole-cell currents were recorded on FM tape at speeds of 7.5 or 15 ips. The data were subsequently filtered with a 4-pole Bessel filter and digitized with a 12-bit A/D converter for off-line computer analysis. The cut-off frequency (−3 dB) of the filter was usually adjusted to 1/2 of the sampling frequency. The analysis of single-channel current records obtained during step depolarization of the membrane patch was performed after digital subtraction of capacitive and leakage currents by averaging records without channel openings and subtracting the average from each record in the series. The ensemble mean current was compiled by averaging all subtracted single-channel current records (90–210) of the series. The sampling frequency was 2.5 or 5 kHz (filter 1.25 or 2.5 kHz, −3 dB) for the computation of mean currents. Whole-cell data were sampled at 3–4 kHz (filter 1 kHz, −3 dB) except when otherwise indicated.

Interference from other currents

The experiments were performed on smaller-sized myocytes (C_m = 40–130 pF) to facilitate voltage control and internal perfusion. The pipette solution exchanging with the intracellular fluid contained 10 mM EGTA to keep intracellular divalent cation concentrations at a low level as well as 132 mM Cs to minimize outward currents. Na currents were suppressed with 20 μM tetrodotoxin and an inactivating holding potential (−50 mV).

A second type of Ca channel has recently been described in atrial (Bean, 1985) and ventricular (Nilius et al., 1985) cardiac cells. This channel activates and completely inactivates at potentials far negative to those regulating the classical Ca channel and would therefore contribute negligible current during depolarization from a holding potential of −50 mV (also see Lee et al., 1985). This reasoning does not just apply to currents from myocytes in low-Ca or Ba solutions. In 110 mM Ba, steady-state inactivation is 90% complete near −50 mV and the normal probability of the channel opening is < 0.2 at the voltage (−10 mV) eliciting maximal current (Bean, 1985).

Results

Whole-cell Ca channel currents in solutions containing 3.6 mM Ca, 3.6 mM Ba, or 90 mM Ba

Step depolarizations elicited Ca channel currents whose amplitudes and time courses were dependent on voltage and on the divalent cation species and concentration. Since current amplitude was also a function of cell size, we have decided to present suitably scaled records in many of the figures. Information on absolute values of current amplitudes and densities will be given in the next section of the results. In common with others who found that inactivation of Ca channel currents was not always appropriately described by one or two exponentials (Bean, 1985; Bechem and Pott, 1985; Lee et al., 1985), we have also quantified the rate of current decay in terms of half-time ($T_{1/2}$) to complete inactivation.

Figure 1 shows current signals taken during a series of depolarizing pulses from a holding potential of − 50 mV to increasingly more positive membrane potentials in the presence of 3.6 mM external Ca (A) and 3.6 mM external Ba (B). At low divalent cation concentrations, activation of inward Ca and Ba current became significant beyond −40 mV. The inward Ca current was maximal near +5 mV, whereas the potential of maximal inward Ba current (V_{peak}) was close to 0 mV. With clamp pulses beyond +10 mV, both inward Ca and Ba current progressively diminished. The time courses of activation and inactivation of both inward Ca and Ba current were progressively accelerated by increasing depolarization. In 90 mM Ba solution (Fig. 2), the voltage-dependent properties of inward Ba current were qualitatively the same. However, threshold was around −10 mV and V_{peak} was near +25 mV. Beyond +80 mV, the current signal changed gradually from a decaying inward current to a decaying outward current; at the potentials around the reversal potential (E_{rev}), a rapid activation of current was followed by fast inactivation, whether the current was inward- or outward-directed. At E_{rev} itself, inward current carried by Ba must be offset by outward current carried by Cs or Na (contributions from other external cations and internal Ba would be negligible). On the assumption that the difference between internal and external surface potentials (see Meves and Vogel, 1973) in heart cells is small (Lee and Tsien, 1984), a modification of the latter authors' constant field expression for E_{rev} is

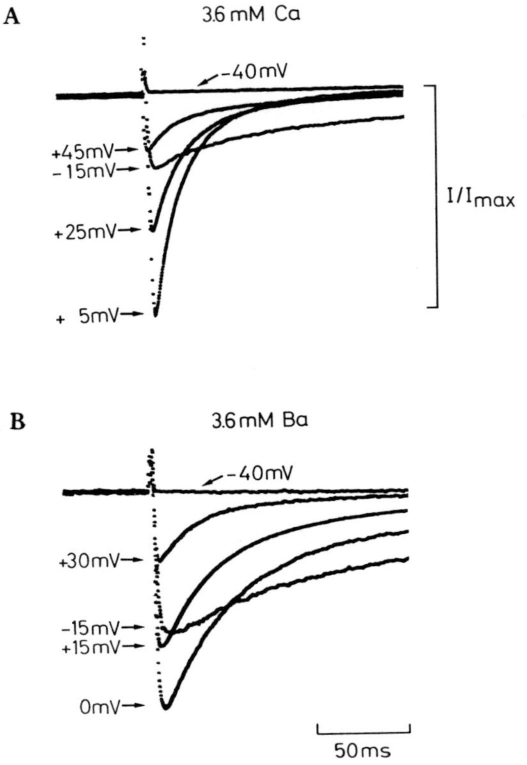

Fig. 1: Whole-cell calcium channel currents from guinea pig ventricular cells bathed in 3.6 mM Ca (A) and 3.6 mM Ba (B) solution. The currents were recorded during 300 ms depolarizations (at 0.2–0.5 Hz) to the denoted voltages from a holding potential of −50 mV. Note that I_{Ca} inactivates faster than I_{Ba}. Maximal peak currents were between 1 and 2 nA in these myocytes; the current families have been scaled for comparative reasons.

$$E_{rev} = \frac{RT}{2F} \ln \frac{4\, P_{Ba}\, a^{o}_{Ba}}{P_{Cs}\, a^{i}_{Cs} + P_{Na}\, a^{i}_{Na}} \,, \qquad (1)$$

where ion activities (a) can be estimated from concentrations by taking activity coefficients (γ) as $\gamma_{90Ba} = 0.26$, and $\gamma_{Cs} = \gamma_{Na} = 0.75$. With $E_{rev} = +94$ mV (Fig. 3B), and assuming $P_{Na} \sim 3\, P_{Cs}$ (FUKUSHIMA and HAGIWARA, 1985), the calculated P_{Ba}/P_{Cs} is 1,430. E_{rev} in 3.6 mM Ba solution can be calculated with this P_{Ba}/P_{Cs} and a higher activity coefficient (0.36). The result, +55 mV, forms a satisfactory extrapolation of the I–V curve in figure 3B.

The rate of inactivation was also a function of voltage whether cells were bathed in Ca or Ba solutions. At low divalent cation concentrations, the $T_{1/2}$ inactivation was 5–6 times faster at +10 mV than at −15 mV (Fig. 3A). In 90 mM Ba solution, there was no current at −15 mV and the current at +10 mV inactivated about twice as slowly as the current at −15 mV in 3.6 mM Ba (Fig. 3A). Currents in 90 mM Ba inactivated more quickly at potentials above +10 mV, the asymptotic $T_{1/2}$ being around 15–20 ms at high positive potentials (Fig. 2). This asymptotic $T_{1/2}$ inactivation in 90 mM Ba was 15–30 times shorter

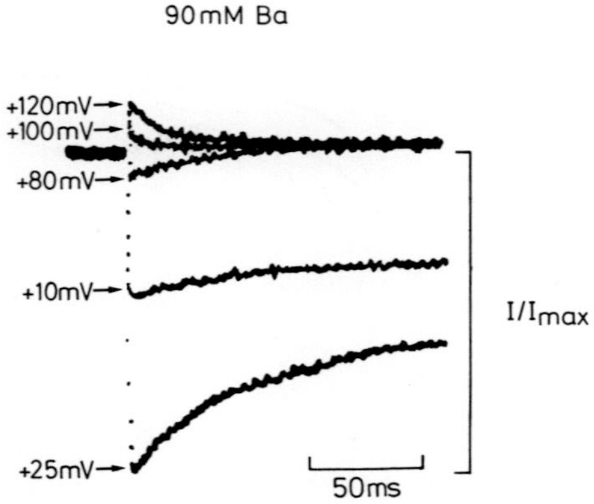

Fig. 2: Whole-cell calcium channel currents from a guinea pig ventricular cell bathed in 90 mM Ba solution. The currents were recorded during 300 ms depolarizations (at 0.2 Hz) to the denoted voltages from a holding potential of −50 mV. The peak inward current at +25 mV was roughly 10 nA.

than the $T_{1/2}$ at +10 to +15 mV. For comparison, our asymptotic $T_{1/2}$ at high positive potentials in 3.6 mM Ba solution was 14–18 times shorter than the $T_{1/2}$ at −20 mV whereas the asymptotic τ's of KASS and SANGUINETTI (1984) in Purkinje fibres (5.4 mM Ba) were about 20 times shorter than at −20 mV. In summary, the foregoing suggests that the high Ba concentration shifts the voltage dependence of the inactivation rate by 30–35 mV in the positive direction.

Whole-cell I–V relations were constructed after measuring the peak currents accompanying 300 ms depolarizations and normalizing them with reference to the largest peak current in that solution (I/I_{max}). Example relations from myocytes superfused with 3.6 mM Ca (solid curve), 3.6 mM Ba (dashed curve) or 90 mM Ba (dotted curve) are shown in figure 3B. The threshold potential near −40 mV, the potential at one-half I_{max} ($V_{1/2}$; −19 mV), and the potential at I_{max} (V_{peak}; −2 mV) in 3.6 mM Ba were 5–10 mV negative to the values in 3.6 mM Ca. The 3.6 mM Ba parameters were shifted to the right by approximately 30 mV in 90 mM Ba solution. Six additional I–V determinations were similar to those in figure 3B. In summary, whether one chooses V_{peak} or $V_{1/2}$ (GILBERT, 1971; OHMORI and YOSHII, 1977) as the indicator of relative screening action on membrane surface charges, the conclusion is that Ca is more effective than Ba, and that a 25-fold increase in Ba concentration depresses the surface potential by about 30 mV.

The symbols in figure 3B represent normalized values from non-perfused ventricular cells isolated from hearts of adult guinea pigs (open upright triangles, 3.6 mM Ca, unpublished observation) and rats (open rhombs, 2.5 mM Ca, from MITCHELL et al., 1983), guinea pig ventricular tissue (open reversed triangles, 1.8 mM Ca, from HINO and OCHI, 1980; open circles, 2.5 mM Ca, unpublished observation), and calf cardiac Purkinje fibres bathed in 5.4 mM Ca (open squares) and 5.4 mM Ba solution (filled squares, from KASS and SANGUINETTI, 1984). Apparently, the intracellular dialysis with the artificial solution used (see Methods section for composition) does not significantly affect the shape of the whole-cell I–V relation, the location of the inward current maximum (V_{peak}), or the extrapolated reversal potential (E_{rev}).

The likely reason for the large positive shift in V_{peak} with high Ba is a shift in the voltage dependence of Ca channel kinetics, specifically of the activation, since the relatively slow

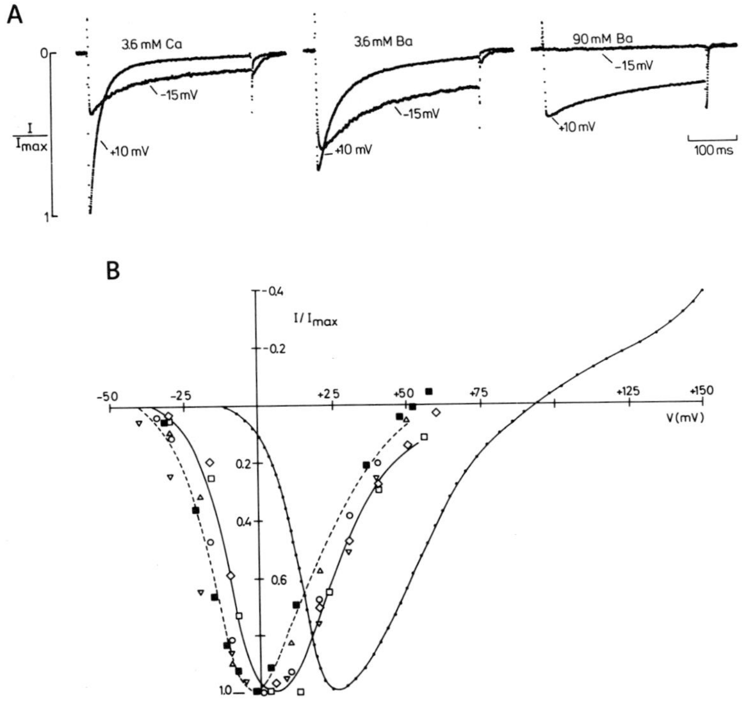

Fig. 3: The voltage dependence of whole-cell Ca channel currents. (A) Currents recorded during 300 ms pulses from −50 mV to −15 and +10 mV in myocytes bathed in solutions containing (left to right) 3.6 mM Ca, 3.6 mM Ba, and 90 mM Ba. The records have been scaled by reference to the maximum currents measured in the respective I–V determinations. These occurred at +6 mV (3.6 mM Ca), −2 mV (3.6 mM Ba), and +26 mV (90 mM Ba). (B) I–V relations of whole-cell Ca channel current from three different cells bathed in solutions containing 3.6 mM Ca (solid line), 3.6 mM Ba (dashed line), and 90 mM Ba (dotted line). Voltage pulses were applied from −50 mV to potentials V for 300 ms at 0.2 Hz. I was measured with respect to zero current and then normalized (I/I_{max}). The symbols represent values from other myocytes and tissues (see text for detailed explanation).

inactivation of I_{Ba} limits its influence on current amplitude. The records in figures 1 to 3 indicate that activation, as judged by the time to peak, speeds up with positive potential in all three test solutions. In addition, the records in figures 3 and 4Aa illustrate that the time to peak at +10 mV is much slower in 90 mM Ba than in 3.6 mM Ba. This is borne out by the plot of time to peak versus voltage from measurements on six myocytes (Fig. 4A, b). There was little difference between the values determined in 3.6 mM Ca (not shown) and 3.6 mM Ba (filled circles), but the curve fitted by eye to the 90 mM Ba data (filled triangles) required a negative shift of 30 mV in order to superimpose the 3.6 mM Ba data. When sampled at a high rate (Fig. 4B), the inward current records in the presence of 90 mM external Ba showed a clear delay in the activation of whole-cell Ca channel current. This result is contrary to earlier studies in multicellular cardiac tissue (cf. REUTER and SCHOLZ, 1977; MCDONALD, 1982) and single ventricular cells (cf. ISENBERG and KLÖCKNER, 1980), where activation of cardiac Ca channels was described as a simple first-order process. However, it is consistent with a recent report from guinea pig ventricular cells

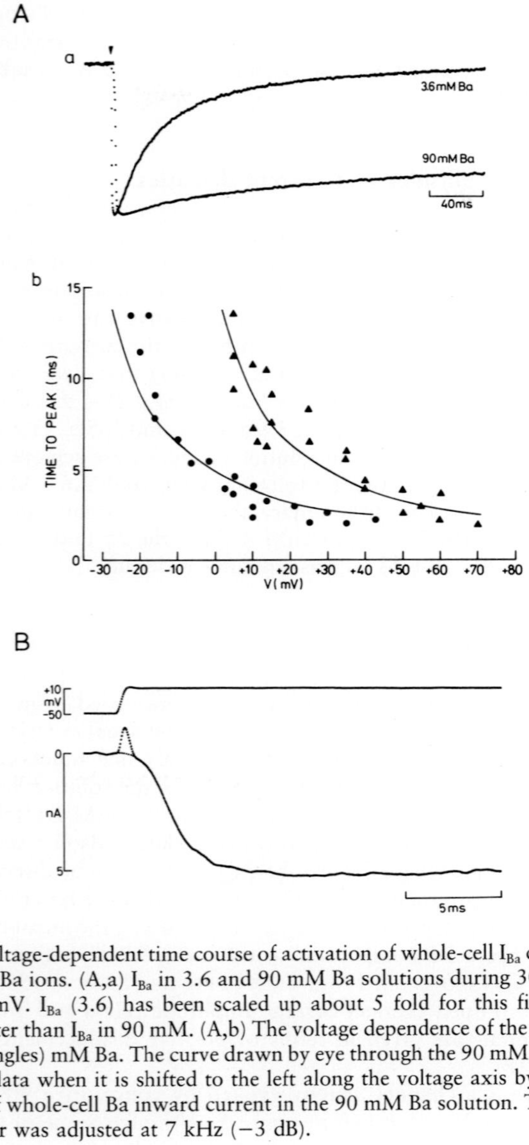

Fig. 4: Shift in the voltage-dependent time course of activation of whole-cell I_{Ba} due to a neutralization of surface charge by Ba ions. (A,a) I_{Ba} in 3.6 and 90 mM Ba solutions during 300 ms depolarizations from −50 to +10 mV. I_{Ba} (3.6) has been scaled up about 5 fold for this figure; it activates and inactivates much faster than I_{Ba} in 90 mM. (A,b) The voltage dependence of the time to peak I_{Ba} in 3.6 (circles) and 90 (triangles) mM Ba. The curve drawn by eye through the 90 mM Ba data superimposes on the 3.6 mM Ba data when it is shifted to the left along the voltage axis by 30 mV. (B) Sigmoid activation kinetics of whole-cell Ba inward current in the 90 mM Ba solution. The sampling rate was 25 kHz and the filter was adjusted at 7 kHz (−3 dB).

bathed in 2–5 mM Ca and Ba solutions (Lee and Tsien, 1984) and most of the reports from neuronal preparations (see Kostyuk, 1981 and Hagiwara and Byerly, 1981 for reviews), where a multi-step process was indicated by the sigmoid onset of Ca channel current following voltage steps. In addition, the observed delay is consistent with recent observations that openings of cardiac Ca channels occur in bursts (Reuter et al., 1982; Cavalié et al., 1983, 1986; Tsien et al., 1983; Pelzer et al., 1985a, b; Trautwein and Pelzer, 1985a, b; Tsien et al., 1985b). Sigmoid activation kinetics and bursts of single-channel activity can both be explained by a model of the channel's opening pathway in which two short-lived closed states precede the open state. The transition rate constants between these states are voltage-dependent and the whole process takes place on a milliseconds time scale.

Relative current amplitudes and current densities

After consideration of Ca channel current rundown (see LEE and TSIEN, 1984; CAVALIÉ et al., 1985 for references, time course and magnitude) and anomalous mole fraction effects (HESS and TSIEN, 1984) during an exchange of bath solutions (see MCDONALD et al., 1986 for details), a useful way of describing relative current amplitudes is to take account of the surface charge alterations by comparing the currents at V_{peak} rather than at an arbitrary voltage. With this approach, and assuming that 1 μF indicates 1 cm^2 membrane surface area, the current densities were (mean ± SE): 29.4 ± 2.6 $\mu A/cm^2$ (n = 13) for 3.6 mM Ca, 28.6 ± 3.0 $\mu A/cm^2$ (n = 12) for 3.6 mM Ba, and 288 ± 33 $\mu A/cm^2$ (n = 7) for 90 mM Ba. In three myocytes, in which all solution changes were achieved consecutively, the mean current densities at V_{peak} in the test solutions were 30.0 (3.6 mM Ca), 33.6 (3.6 mM Ba) and 311 (90 mM Ba) $\mu A/cm^2$. In summary, there was no significant difference between current densities in 3.6 mM Ca and 3.6 mM Ba, and the 25-fold increase in external Ba concentration produced a 10-fold increase in current density.

Single-channel currents

Ca channel currents in guinea pig myocytes were recorded from cell-attached membrane patches. Only the results from patches that by the usual criteria (cf. CAVALIÉ et al., 1983; TRAUTWEIN and PELZER, 1985b) contained only one functional channel are reported here. The solution inside the patch pipette, i. e., the solution bathing the external surface of the patch membrane, was identical to the 90 mM Ba solution used as the superfusate in some of the whole-cell experiments. It should also be noted that in contrast to the whole-cell technique where the membrane potential can be directly ascertained, the potential of the patch membrane cannot. One assumes that the latter has the same resting potential (RP) as the cell independent of the solution bathing the membrane patch and that the cell in question has a RP comparable to the mean RP of similar cells impaled with microelectrodes (cf. CAVALIÉ et al., 1983; TRAUTWEIN and PELZER, 1985a, b), or a RP that can be estimated from open channel current amplitude (HESS and TSIEN, 1984). In this section, patch potentials are given in terms of positive displacements (depolarizations) from pipette zero (RP).

Examples of single Ca channel activity evoked by consecutive 900 ms voltage steps (arrows) to RP + ΔV mV are shown in figure 5. Although some of the current sweeps contained no channel openings (blank traces), the remainder had openings which, at patch membrane potentials around RP+75 mV (Fig. 5B, a), usually occurred within the first 10 ms, were grouped into bursts and clusters of bursts, and were less likely to be observed during the second half of a pulse (CAVALIÉ et al., 1986; PELZER et al., 1985a; TRAUTWEIN and PELZER, 1985a, b). Independent of the time or duration of an opening, the amplitudes of the unitary current events clustered around a mean unit amplitude. The blank sweeps reflect conditions where the Ca channel is unavailable for opening; one corresponding to steady-state voltage inactivation and the other to dephosphorylation (CAVALIÉ et al., 1986; PELZER et al., 1985a). When reasonable numbers of both types of response were

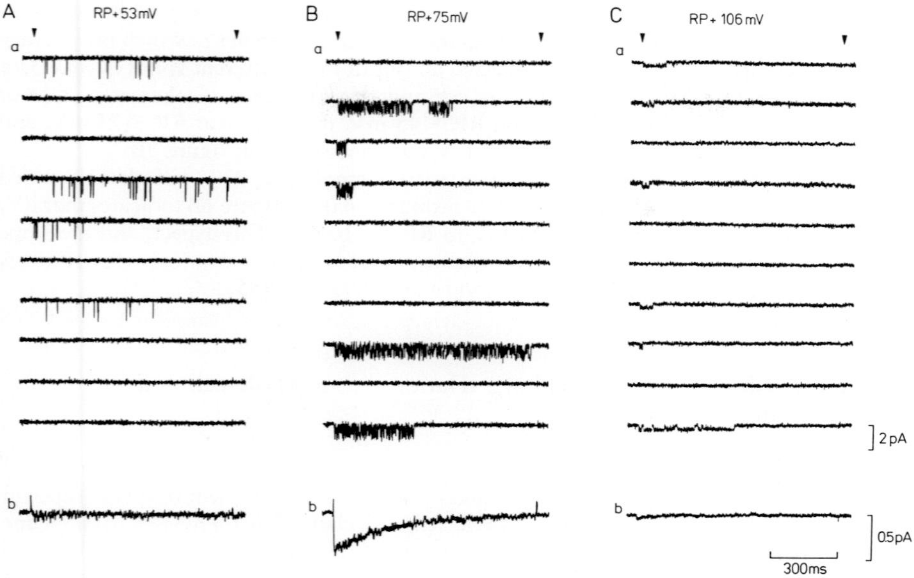

Fig. 5: Elementary (parts a) and ensemble average (parts b) calcium channel currents from a guinea pig ventricular cell. The cell-attached recording pipette contained 90 mM Ba. The currents were recorded during 900 ms depolarizations (marked by arrows on top of each panel) at 0.2 Hz to the denoted voltages (RP +53 mV in A; RP +75 mV in B; RP +106 mV inC) from the pipette zero potential.

present in an ensemble, blank records and traces with openings tended to group into sequences of consecutive single Ca channel current sweeps as a function of the conditioning holding membrane potential and phosphorylation (Cavalié et al., 1986; Pelzer et al., 1985a).

Figure 5 furthermore illustrates that the elementary Ca channel current amplitude (i) was dependent on the pipette voltage, declining by about 75 % between RP+53 mV (A, a) and RP+106 mV (C, a). In addition, there was a voltage-dependent change in the pattern of the openings during the pulse. The latency to first opening, as well as the time during which openings could be observed (i. e., cluster lifetime), was shortest at the higher potentials.

Large numbers of consecutive records (n = 90–210) were grouped into ensembles and averaged to obtain single-channel average currents (I*). The average currents at voltages between RP + 53 mV and RP + 106 mV from the example patch are shown in parts b of figure 5. The salient features of this assembly are that 1) the amplitude of the average current was small at RP + 53 mV, peaked at RP + 75 mV, and declined again at more positive potentials, 2) the time to peak declined with potential being 17.5 ms at RP + 53 mV, 7.3 ms at RP + 75 mV, 3.9 ms at RP + 91 mV (not shown), and 2.4 ms at RP + 106 mV, 3) the average current inactivated completely at the more positive voltages, and 4) the $T_{1/2}$ inactivation declined sharply with voltage from about 550 ms at RP + 62 mV (not shown) to 205 ms at RP + 75 mV, 85 ms at RP + 91 mV (not shown) and about 35 ms at RP + 106 mV. Therefore, in regard to the four features above, the average currents in this patch closely resembled the behaviour of the whole-cell currents in 90 mM Ba solution.

The symbols in figure 6A represent data gathered from six patches in which the average current was computed for ensembles collected at four or more different voltages. The data points are connected by curves drawn by eye and these produce a coherent picture of I*(V): the threshold potential lies around RP + 45 mV, the V_{peak} near RP + 75 mV, and the overall shape resembles the whole-cell I–V relations shown in figure 3B.

The voltage dependence of the elementary current amplitude, i(V), was also evaluated from these six experiments. The straight line fitting the data in figure 6B indicates that i(V) is fairly linear over the range RP + 15 mV to RP + 110 mV. This aspect, and the slope conductance of 21 pS, are in good agreement with earlier reports on heart cells (REUTER et al., 1982; CAVALIÉ et al., 1983; TRAUTWEIN and PELZER, 1985a).

Superimposition of current-voltage relations from whole-cell and single-channel experiments

A useful way of comparing the various current-voltage relations is to superimpose them with reference to their V_{peak} values. Figure 6C shows that this alignment results in superimposition of the descending limbs of the whole-cell I–V relations in 3.6 mM Ba (dashed line) and 90 mM Ba (dotted line) solutions. The courses of the ascending limbs agree less well, presumably because the shift in V_{peak} (~ 30 mV) produced by increasing the Ba concentration to 90 mM is less than the shift in E_{rev} (~ 40 mV). The 3.6 mM Ca I–V relation (solid line) superimposes the other descending limbs, and then tracks slightly to the right of the 3.6 mM Ba ascending limb.

The current-voltage relations of the average single-channel currents in figure 6A were normalized with reference to the amplitude at RP + 75 mV and sampled at regular voltage intervals. The sampled values (mean ± SE, n = 6) are indicated by the filled circles in figure 6C. At voltages negative to V_{peak}, I*(V) strongly resembles the whole-cell relations. At more positive voltages, I*(V) corresponds more closely with the 3.6 mM Ba relation than with the 90 mM one. The explanation may again involve the driving force. In the patch-clamp experiments, the major intracellular cation is K, not Cs as in the whole-cell experiments, and Ca channel permeability to the outward movement of K is thought to be several times larger than to Cs (LEE and TSIEN, 1982, 1984; FUKUSHIMA and HAGIWARA, 1985).

The close match-up of the single-channel and whole-cell current data suggests that V_{peak} of the I*–V relation may be similar to V_{peak} of the I–V relation in 90 mM Ba, i. e., RP + 75mV intra-pipette potential ≃ + 25 mV absolute membrane potential. This implies that the cells examined in the patch-clamp experiments had an average RP of approximately −50 mV, a value that is significantly lower than that expected for cardiac myocytes bathed in 10.8 mM K medium (BUSTAMENTE et al., 1981; PELZER et al., 1984). However, the myocytes used in the patch-clamp experiments were not stimulated, and ISENBERG and KLÖCKNER (1982) have reported that similarly prepared cells require regular stimulation for repolarization to an E_K-like RP.

Although the current through open single channels is larger near RP than at V_{peak} (Figs. 5 and 6B), the average current near RP is obviously much smaller (Figs. 5 and 6A). The reason is that the probability (P) of a channel opening near RP is very small, and this factor is an important determinant of the average current amplitude. The relation between these parameters can be expressed as

$$I^*(V) = P(V) \cdot N \cdot i(V), \qquad (2)$$

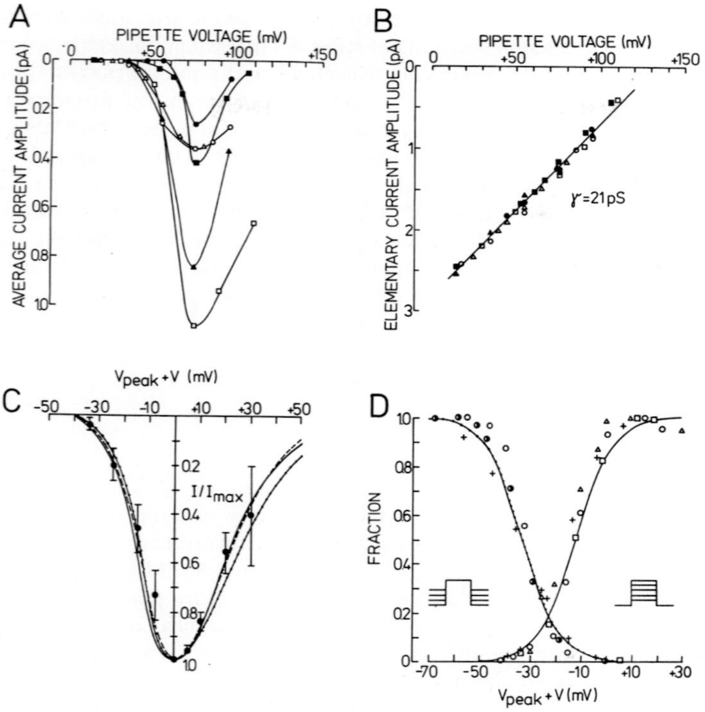

Fig. 6: Voltage dependencies of the average current (I*) and the elementary current amplitude (i). (A) Average currents from different membrane patches (n = 6). Curves between the symbols were drawn by eye. (B) Elementary current amplitudes from patches in (A). Each data point represents the mean of more than 50 single-channel current amplitude measurements at the respective voltage. The slope of the line indicates a single-channel conductance of 21 pS (90 mM Ba). Comparison of whole-cell and single-channel data after conversion of experimental voltages (absolute; RP-related) to V_{peak} + V. (C) Superimposition of I–V curves by alignment of the V_{peak} values. Whole-cell I–V relations in 3.6 mM Ca (dotted line), 3.6 mM Ba (dashed line) and 90 mM Ba (solid line); average single-channel currents (circles; mean ± SE from sampling of the curves in Fig. 6 A). (D) Relative probability (P) of opening of single Ca channels. The holding potential was kept constant at pipette zero (RP) and pulses were applied to different test potentials (right inset). P(V) (solid line) was determined as the number of depolarizations eliciting a channel opening in an ensemble of single-channel current records; this count was then normalized to the maximum. The influence of the holding potential on single-channel P is illustrated by the dotted curve. The test potential was kept constant at RP +85 mV and pulses were applied from different holding pipette potentials (left inset). P(V) was again determined as the number of depolarizations eliciting a channel opening in the ensemble of single-channel current records and normalized relative to the maximum. Fractional maximum P's in these patches were 0.94 (solid curve) and 0.93 (dotted curve). The symbols represent steady-state activation and inactivation determinations on cardiac myocytes and tissues bathed in physiological Ca solutions (see text for further explanation).

an assumption being that channels operate independently of each other. If N = 1, P(V) can be obtained by analyzing ensembles of single-channel current records and calculating the fraction of depolarizations that elicited a channel opening at each voltage. The solid curve in figure 6D represents the normalized P(V) relation obtained from trains of depolarizing voltage-clamp steps to increasingly more positive membrane potentials (right inset). There is a high probability of channel opening at RP + 85 mV when pulses are applied from the usual holding potential of RP ± 0 mV. However, when the holding potential was moved to more positive potentials (left inset), there was a reduction in the proportion of records having openings at RP + 85 mV. This influence of holding potential on the probability of opening is indicated by the dotted curve in figure 6D. The normalized voltage scale facilitates a direct comparison with the steady-state activation variables (d_∞) and the steady-state inactivation relations (f_∞) of I_{Ca} from internally-perfused (half-filled circles) and non-perfused (open triangles) guinea pig ventricular cells, guinea pig (open circles) and cat (crosses) ventricular tissue (unpublished observations), and calf cardiac Purkinje fibres (open squares, from Kass and Sanguinetti, 1984). All cells and tissues have been bathed in 2.5–5.4 mM Ca solutions. As with the I–V and I*–V relations (see Figs. 3 and 6C), the position of the symbols indicates the good accord with the voltage-dependent kinetic parameters of single channels, single cells and intact tissue.

Conclusions

1. Although the shape of the whole-cell I–V relation was independent of the bathing solution, this was not the case with the location of the inward current maximum (V_{peak}). In comparison to the V_{peak} values in 3.6 mM Ba, those in 3.6 mM Ca were 5–10 mV more positive, and those in 90 mM Ba were about 30 mV more positive. The shift in V_{peak} produced by high Ba was mirrored in magnitude by the shifts of the voltage-dependent activation and inactivation parameters of whole-cell currents. Thus, Ca channel kinetics in cardiac ventricular myocytes bathed in Ba solutions do not seem to be affected by a large increase in external Ba concentration. The shifts are solely explicable by a neutralization of surface charge by the divalent cations (9–14.3 Å between charges, also see Ohmori and Yoshii, 1977; Hagiwara and Ohmori, 1982; Wilson et al., 1983; Byerly et al., 1985).

2. Recent studies on the reversal potential of Ca channel currents (Lee and Tsien, 1982, 1984) and on ion permeation (Hess and Tsien, 1984) led the latter authors to conclude that cardiac Ca channels are multi-ion single-file pores. The selectivity of the channel for divalent cations comes from the strong binding of divalent cations to Ca channels which usually excludes monovalent cations from the channel, whereas current flow ensues from repulsion between ions in doubly occupied channels. Observations compatible with the ion permeation model proposed by Hess and Tsien (1984) included (a) a depression of current during Ca/Ba solution exchange reflecting a mutual block by one ion species of the flux of the other, (b) a high divalent to monovalent ion permeability, and (c) rectification of the outward limb of the I–V relation due to a voltage-dependent extrusion of divalent cations from the Ca channel, making the channel more permeable to monovalent ions.

3. Estimated current densities at V_{peak} were similar for myocytes in 3.6 mM Ca and 3.6 mM Ba, indicating similar current-carrying abilities of Ca and Ba for cardiac channels, and about 10 times larger in 90 mM Ba. When related to the difference in Ba activity between the two Ba solutions, roughly 18-fold, there was obviously a strong dependence of peak I_{Ba} on external Ba over this range. A comparable result has been reported by Hagiwara and Ohmori (1982) for rat pituitary cells (9-fold increase in I_{Ba} for 5–100 mM Ba), and Byerly et al. (1985) concluded that I_{Ba} in snail neurones is almost linearly related to Ba concentration between 1 mM and 30 mM. The latter conclusion was applicable whether or not one assumed that the mouth of the Ca channel sees the same shift in surface potential as the gating mechanism (also see Ohmori and Yoshii, 1977). The strong concentration dependence is also reflected by single Ca channel current amplitudes in

heart cells; in patch-clamp experiments there was a 4.6-fold increase in i for Ba concentrations between 20 mM and 90 mM (PELZER et al., 1985 b). This range can be extended by comparing i from ensemble noise analysis of whole cells (HESS and TSIEN, 1984) with i from single-channel patches (HESS et al., 1984), the result being a 9.8-fold difference between 10 mM (noise analysis) and 110 mM external Ba (patch).

4. Average currents (I*) calculated from ensembles of records of single Ca channel current had voltage-dependent time courses resembling those of whole-cell I_{Ba}. Single-channel I*–V relations were superimposable on whole-cell I–V curves suggesting that voltage-dependent single-channel parameters (probability of opening, elementary current amplitude) can be related to the voltage-dependent macroscopic current parameters (activation, instantaneous I–V relation) when scaled by channel number.

5. The close tracking of I*(V) with the whole-cell I–V relations suggests that E_{rev} for I* lies 55–70 mV positive to V_{peak}, i. e., between +80 and +95 mV absolute membrane potential. If we take the expression for E_{rev} (eq. 1 with P_{Ba}/P_{Cs} = 1,430), insert $P_K a^i_K$ for $P_{Cs} a^i_{Cs}$, and set a^i_K and a^i_{Na} respectively at 105 and 6 mM (BAUMGARTEN et al., 1981; SHEU and FOZZARD, 1982), the upper E_{rev} estimate of +95 mV (absolute potential) is obtained with $P_K = P_{Na} = P_{Cs}$, and the lower one of +80 mV (absolute potential) with $P_K = P_{Na} = 3\ P_{Cs}$. FUKUSHIMA and HAGIWARA (1985) have estimated that the permeability ratios for the Ca channel in mouse lymphocytes are P_K/P_{Cs} = 2.3 and P_{Na}/P_{Cs} = 2.9. The use of these permeabilities leads to an E_{rev} of +84 mV (absolute potential). The shape of the whole-cell I–V curve in 90 mM Ba suggests that the underlying i–V relation veers to the right in its final approach to E_{rev}. However, this may be a consequence of internal Cs, and the more permeable internal K in the single-channel experiments might prevent this drift (see Fig. 6 in FUKUSHIMA and HAGIWARA, 1985). In fact, a linear extrapolation of the i–V relation to zero current intersects the voltage axis at +82 mV (absolute potential); this agrees with the E_{rev} of +84 mV calculated above. In guinea pig myocytes treated with BAY K 8644, TSIEN et al. (1985a) found E_{rev} ~ +65 mV for open single channels with 20 mM Ba in the patch pipette. The same laboratory reported E_{rev} ~ +73 mV for whole-cell Ca channel currents in 20 mM Ba during internal perfusion with Cs (LEE and TSIEN, 1984). These values are completely in line with our estimates above and indicate that the reversal potentials of single Ca channel currents are as expected from whole-cell Ca channel currents, at least over the range 20–90 mM external Ba.

6. The density of Ca channels in myocytes was calculated from whole-cell I_{Ba} (90 mM) and average current through single channels. The mean $I^*(V_{peak})$ was 0.55 pA and the mean $I_{Ba}(V_{peak})$ was 288 $\mu A/cm^2$. The outcome, 3–5 channels/μm^2, agrees with two other recent estimates in neonatal rat ventricular cells (TSIEN et al., 1983) and snail neurones (LUX and BROWN, 1984) and results in a distance of 0.45–0.58 μm between Ca channels. This raises the question of why patches with membrane areas of ~ 3 μm^2 demonstrate activity from more than one channel in only 1.54 % (11 patches with 2–5 Ca channels) of all trials (total of 715 membrane patches with pipette-membrane seal resistances >10 GΩ, PELZER et al., 1985c). In the case of heart cells, Ca channel density might be very much higher in the T-tubular membrane than in the rest of the surface membrane. However, we cannot exclude the possibility that the mechanical deformation of the membrane aspirated into the patch pipette (cf. SAKMANN and NEHER, 1983) might have silenced nearly all the channels contained in the patch. Both alternatives would explain another disturbing statistics: 88.53 % (633) of the 715 membrane patches with high-resistance seals achieved in our laboratory over the past two years did not exhibit any single Ca channel activity whatever (PELZER et al., 1985c).

References

Baumgarten, C. M., Cohen, C. J., McDonald, T. F. (1981): Heterogeneity of intracellular potassium activity and membrane potential in hypoxic guinea pig ventricle. Circ. Res. **49,** 1181–1189.

Bean, B. P. (1985): Two kinds of calcium channels in canine atrial cells. Differences in kinetics, selectivity, and pharmacology. J. Gen. Physiol. **86,** 1–30.

Bechem, M., Pott, L. (1985): Removal of calcium current inactivation in dialysed guinea-pig atrial cardioballs by Ca chelators. Pflügers Arch. **404,** 10–20.

Bustamente, J. O., Watanabe, T., McDonald, T. F. (1981): Single cells from adult mammalian heart: Isolation procedure and preliminary electrophysiological studies. Can. J. Physiol. Pharmacol. **59,** 907–910.

Byerly, L., Chase, P. B., Stimers, J. R. (1985): Permeation and interaction of divalent cations in calcium channels of snail neurons. J. Gen. Physiol. **85,** 491–518.

Cavalié, A., Ochi, R., Pelzer, D., Trautwein, W. (1983): Elementary currents through Ca^{2+} channels in guinea pig myocytes. Pflügers Arch. **398,** 284–297.

Cavalié, A., McDonald, T. F., Pelzer, D., Trautwein, W. (1985): Temperature-induced transitory and steady-state changes in the calcium current of guinea pig ventricular myocytes. Pflügers Arch. **405,** 294–296.

Cavalié, A., Pelzer, D., Trautwein, W. (1986): Fast and slow gating behaviour of single calcium channels in cardiac cells: Relation to activation and inactivation of calcium-channel current. Pflügers Arch. **406,** 241–258.

Cheung, W. Y. (1982): Calmodulin. Sci. Am. **246,** 48–56.

Cohen, P. (1982): The role of protein phosphorylation in neural and hormonal control of cellular activity. Nature (Lond.) **296,** 613–620.

Fabiato, A. (1983): Calcium-induced release of calcium from the cardiac sarcoplasmic reticulum. Am. J. Physiol. **245,** C1–C14.

Frankenhaeuser, B., Hodgkin, A. L. (1957): The action of calcium on the electrical properties of squid axons. J. Physiol. (Lond.) **137,** 218–244.

Fukushima, Y., Hagiwara, S. (1985): Currents carried by monovalent cations through calcium channels in mouse neoplastic B lymphocytes. J. Physiol. (Lond.) **358,** 255–284.

Gilbert, D. L. (1971): Fixed surface charges. In: Biophysics and physiology of excitable membranes (W. J. Adelman Jr., ed.), pp. 359–378. Van Nostrand Reinhold, New York.

Hagiwara, S., Byerly, L. (1981): Calcium channel. Ann. Rev. Neurosci. **4,** 69–125.

Hagiwara, S., Ohmori, H. (1982): Studies of calcium channels in rat clonal pituitary cells with patch electrode voltage clamp. J. Physiol. (Lond.) **331,** 231–252.

Hamill, O. P., Marty, A., Neher, E., Sakmann, B., Sigworth, F. J. (1981): Improved patch-clamp techniques for high-resolution current recording from cells and cell-free membrane patches. Pflügers Arch. **391,** 85–100.

Hess, P., Lansman, J. B., Tsien, R. W. (1984): Different modes of Ca channel gating behaviour favoured by dihydropyridine Ca agonists and antagonists. Nature (Lond.) **311,** 538–544.

Hess, P., Tsien, R. W. (1984): Mechanism of ion permeation through calcium channels. Nature (Lond.) **309,** 453–456.

Hille, B. (1968): Charges and potentials at the nerve surface. Divalent ions and pH. J. Gen. Physiol. **51,** 221–236.

Hino, N., Ochi, R. (1980): Effect of acetylcholine on membrane currents in guinea-pig papillary muscle. J. Physiol. (Lond.) **307,** 183–197.

Isenberg, G., Klöckner, U. (1980): Glycocalyx is not required for slow inward calcium current in isolated rat heart myocytes. Nature (Lond.) **284,** 358–360.

Isenberg, G., Klöckner, U. (1982): Calcium tolerant ventricular myocytes prepared by preincubation in a «KB medium«. Pflügers Arch. **395,** 6–18.

Kass, R. S., Sanguinetti, M. C. (1984): Inactivation of calcium channel current in the calf cardiac Purkinje fiber. Evidence for voltage- and calcium-mediated mechanisms. J. Gen. Physiol. **84,** 705–726.

Kostyuk, P. G. (1981): Calcium channels in the neuronal membrane. Biochimica et biophysica acta **650,** 128–150.

Lee, K. S., Tsien, R. W. (1982): Reversal of current through calcium channels in dialysed single heart cells. Nature (Lond.) **297,** 498–501.

Lee, K. S., Tsien, R. W. (1984): High selectivity of calcium channels in single dialysed heart cells of the guinea-pig. J. Physiol. (Lond.) **354,** 253–272.

Lee, K. S., Marban, E., Tsien, R. W. (1985): Inactivation of calcium channels in mammalian heart cells: Joint dependence on membrane potential and intracellular calcium. J. Physiol. (Lond.) **364,** 395–411.

Lux, H. D., Brown, A. M. (1984): Patch and whole cell calcium currents recorded simultaneously in snail neurons. J. Gen. Physiol. **83,** 727–750.

McDonald, T. F. (1982): The slow inward calcium current in the heart. Ann. Rev. Physiol. **44,** 425–433.

McDonald, T. F., Cavalié, A., Trautwein, W., Pelzer, D. (1986): Voltage-dependent properties of macroscopic and elementary calcium channel currents in guinea pig ventricular myocytes. Pflügers Arch. **406,** 437–448.

Meves, H., Vogel, W. (1973): Calcium inward currents in internally perfused giant axons. J. Physiol. (Lond.) **235,** 225–265.

Mitchell, M. R., Powell, T., Terrar, D. A., Twist, V. W. (1983): Characteristics of the second inward current in cells isolated from rat ventricular muscle. Proc. R. Soc. Lond. B. **219,** 447–469.

Nilius, B., Hess, P., Lansman, J. B., Tsien, R. W. (1985): A novel type of cardiac calcium channel in ventricular cells. Nature (Lond.) **316,** 443–446.

Ohmori, H., Yoshii, M. (1977): Surface potential reflected in both gating and permeation mechanisms of sodium and calcium channels of the tunicate egg cell membrane. J. Physiol. (Lond.) **267,** 429–463.

Pelzer, D., Trube, G., Piper, H. M. (1984): Low resting potentials in single isolated heart cells due to membrane damage by the recording microelectrode. Pflügers Arch. **400,** 197–199.

Pelzer, D., Cavalié, A., Trautwein, W. (1985a): Activation and inactivation of single calcium channels in cardiac cells. Exp. Brain Res., in press.

Pelzer, D., Cavalié, A., Trautwein, W. (1985b): Cardiac Ca channel currents at the level of single cells and single channels. Basic Res. Cardiol. **80** (Suppl. 2), 65–70.

Pelzer, D., Hescheler, J., Cavalié, A., Trautwein, W. (1985c): Electrical estimate of calcium channel density in single ventricular cells from hearts of adult guinea pigs. Pflügers Arch. **403,** R48.

Rasmussen, H., Barrett, P. Q. (1984): Calcium messenger system: An integrated view. Physiological Reviews **64,** 938–984.

Reuter, H. (1983): Calcium channel modulation by neurotransmitters, enzymes and drugs. Nature (Lond.) **301,** 569–574.

Reuter, H. (1984): Ion channels in cardiac cell membranes. Ann. Rev. Physiol. **46,** 473–484.

Reuter, H., Scholz, H. (1977): A study of the ion selectivity and the kinetic properties of the calcium-dependent slow inward current in mammalian cardiac muscle. J. Physiol. (Lond.) **264,** 17–47.

Reuter, H., Stevens, C. F., Tsien, R. W., Yellen, G. (1982): Properties of single calcium channels in cardiac cell culture. Nature (Lond.) **297,** 501–504.

Sakmann, B., Neher, E. (1983): Single-channel recording. Plenum, New York.

Sakmann, B., Trube, G. (1984): Voltage-dependent inactivation of inward-rectifying single-channel currents in the guinea-pig heart cell membrane. J. Physiol. (Lond.) **347,** 659–683.

Sheu, S. S., Fozzard, H. A. (1982): Transmembrane Na^+ and Ca^{2+} electrochemical gradients in cardiac muscle and their relationship to force development. J. Gen. Physiol. **80,** 325–351.

Trautwein, W., Pelzer, D. (1985a): Voltage-dependent gating of single calcium channels in the cardiac cell membrane and its modulation by drugs. In: Calcium and cell physiology (D. Marmé, ed.), pp. 53–93. Springer Verlag, Berlin, Heidelberg, New York, Tokyo.

Trautwein, W., Pelzer, D. (1985b): Gating of single calcium channels in the membrane of enzymatically isolated ventricular myocytes from adult mammalian hearts. In: Cardiac electrophysiology and arrhythmias (D. P. Zipes, J. Jalife, eds.), pp. 31–42. Grune & Stratton, Orlando, London.

Tsien, R. W. (1983): Calcium channels in excitable cell membranes. Ann. Rev. Physiol. **45,** 341–358.

Tsien, R. W., Bean, B. P., Hess, P., Nowycky, M. C. (1983): Calcium channels: Mechanisms of β-adrenergic modulation and ion permeation. Cold Spring Harbor Symposia on Quantitative Biology **XLVII,** 201–212.

Tsien, R. W., Hess, P., Lansman, J. B. (1985a): Ventricular calcium current at the level of single cells and single channels: Reversal of single-channel current. In: The electrophysiology of single cardiac cells (D. Noble, T. Powell, eds.), in press. Academic Press, London, New York.
Tsien, R. W., Hess, P., Lansman, J. B., Lee, K. S. (1985b): Current views of cardiac calcium channels and their response to calcium antagonists and agonists. In: Cardiac electrophysiology and arrhythmias (D. P. Zipes, J. Jalife, eds.), pp. 19–29. Grune & Stratton, Orlando, London.
Wilson, D. L., Morimoto, K., Tsuda, Y., Brown, A. M. (1983): Interaction between calcium ions and surface charge as it relates to calcium currents. J. Membr. Biol. 72, 117–130.
Zipes, D. P., Bailey, J. C., Elharrar, V. (1980): The slow inward current and cardiac arrhythmias. Martinus Nijhoff Publishers, The Hague.
Zipes, D. P., Jalife, J. (1985): Cardiac electrophysiology and arrhythmias. Grune & Stratton, Orlando, London.

Fortschritte der Zoologie, Band 33 · Lüttgau (Hrsg.): Membrane Control
Gustav Fischer Verlag · Stuttgart · New York · 1986

Interaction of Ca-release and transmembrane Ca current in guinea pig atrial cardioballs

LUTZ POTT and SIEGFRIED MECHMANN

Department of Cell Physiology, Ruhr-University Bochum, 4630 Bochum, FRG

One of the central problems in cardiac cellular physiology is the regulation of the free intracellular Ca concentration (Ca_i) not only in terms of a diastolic homeostasis but also with regard to a graded systolic increase, which controls the contractile force of the heart and might be involved in determining the cardiac action potential (for reviews see NOBLE, 1984; DIFRANCESCO and NOBLE, 1985). There are several mechanisms contributing to this Ca_i-regulation in a cardiac cell. In the surface membrane there are at least three different Ca-transporting mechanisms: the voltage-dependent Ca-channel, which allows the passive movement of Ca-ions along their electrochemical gradient into the cell (for reviews see MCDONALD, 1982; TSIEN, 1983; REUTER, 1984); an active Ca-pump, which, by ATP-utilization, transports Ca-ions uphill out of the cell (CARONI and CARAFOLI, 1980), and a Na^+/Ca^{++} countertransport, which is supposed to transport Ca ions out of the cell using the Na-gradient as energy source, but which might also transport Ca-ions into the cell, depending on the driving forces of both ions involved and the stoichiometry of the carrier (reviewed by MULLINS, 1979; REUTER, 1982; EISNER and LEDERER, 1985). Inside the cell, apart from buffering by Ca-binding molecules, Ca-ions can be actively sequestered by the sarcoplasmic reticulum (SR) and – upon an appropriate signal – can be released from this intracellular storage system (e. g. CHAPMAN, 1983; FABIATO, 1983). There is strong evidence that Ca-ions have also a regulatory function with regard to some of these Ca_i controlling mechanisms: Increase in Ca_i can cause inactivation of Ca-channels in a variety of excitable preparations (for review see ECKERT and CHAD, 1984) including cardiac cells (NILIUS and HENČEK, 1983; KASS and SANGUINETTI, 1984; MENTRARD et al., 1984; BECHEM and POTT, 1985; LEE et al., 1985). The physiological signal causing Ca-release from the SR is very likely to be an increase in myoplasmic free Ca-concentration via transmembrane Ca-current (FABIATO, 1983, 1985). The experiments described in this article were performed in order to study interactions between transmembrane I_{Ca} and Ca-release from SR.

Methods

Tight-seal voltage clamp experiments were performed on single atrial myocytes from hearts of adult guinea pigs by means of patch clamp pipettes (HAMILL et al., 1981; MARTY and NEHER, 1983). The cells were isolated by an enzyme perfusion technique now common in many laboratories (e. g. POWELL and TWIST, 1976; BECHEM et al., 1983). Before being used experimentally the isolated myocytes were kept in cell culture for 3–14 days. Under this condition spherical cells with a diameter between 15 and 25 μm (‹cardioballs›) are obtained which, due to their size and geometry, are highly suited for voltage clamp and internal dialysis. The details of the isolation and culture conditions have been described previously (BECHEM et al., 1983).

One hour before the experiment the culture medium was replaced by a solution of the following composition (mM): NaCl 140, CsCl 2.0; $MgCl_2$ 1.0; $CaCl_2$ 2.0; Hepes/NaOH 10, pH7.4. The patch clamp pipettes were filled with a solution containing: Cs Citrate 65; CsCl 20; Na_2ATP 1.0; c-AMP 0.1 $MgCl_2$ 1.0; EGTA 1.0. The pH was adjusted to 7.2 with CsOH. All experiments were performed at room temperature (21–23 °C). Voltage clamp measurements were performed by means of a patch clamp amplifier (List LM/EPC 7). Voltage and current signals were stored on analog tape (Racal 4DS) at 7.5 or 15 ips and later analysed using an IBM PC at appropriate sampling rates (1–10 kHz).

Results

Immediately after destroying the membrane under the tip of the recording pipette by a suction pulse to get electrical and diffusional access to the inside of a cell, Ca currents evoked by step changes of the membrane potential from −50 mV into the range of I_{Ca}-activation (e.g. 0 to + 10 mV) are small or barely detectable (BECHEM and POTT, 1985). For this reason the dialysing fluid was supplemented with cAMP (0.1 mM). Upon dialysis with cAMP/ATP-containing solution within 1 to 5 minutes a gradual increase in I_{Ca}-amplitude for a given depolarization is observed. Thus, Ca current investigated in the present study almost completely represents its cAMP-modulated ‹state›. Because of Ca-channel rundown, a phenomenon which has been described in various excitable cells dialysed or perfused with artificial solutions (e.g. FENWICK et al., 1982), I_{Ca}-amplitude reaches a plateau of ca. 5–10 minutes in duration and then gradually decays. The measurements to be described were performed before a rundown of the Ca current by more than about 30 % had occurred.

The typical characteristics of Ca current recorded from a cell dialysed with the solution listed above is shown in Fig. 1A. The dependence of peak inward current on membrane potential is similar to previous studies on single myocytes investigated with conventional microelectrodes (e.g. ISENBERG and KLÖCKNER, 1982; MITCHELL et al., 1983; JOSEPHSON et al., 1984) or suction pipettes containing only EGTA as Ca-chelating agent (e.g. MATSUDA and NOMA, 1984). Inactivation of I_{Ca}, however, is very much slower under the present experimental conditions than hitherto described for cardiac I_{Ca}. For small to moderate depolarizatons inactivation is negligible or virtually absent, whereas in the voltage range of maximum I_{Ca}-flow (0 to +10 mV) a slow monophasic decay of the current is observed whose halftime ranges from about 100 ms to several seconds, depending on the current density of the individual cell (in the experiment shown $t_{1/2}$ at +5 mV is 340 ms).

This unusual inactivation behaviour of I_{Ca}, which closely resembles that described previously when Ba^{++} or Na^{+} are used as charge-carrying ions through Ca-channels (LEE and TSIEN, 1984; HESS and TSIEN, 1984), does not represent a particular property of the cultured cells used in the present study, but is due to loading of the cells with citrate, a low-affinity but fast Ca-buffering ligand. If EGTA or related compounds such as nitrilotriacatic acid are used in concentrations up to 20 mM as the only intracellular Ca-chelating compounds, Ca currents at membrane potentials between 0 and +10 mV always display a rapid initial component of inactivation ($t_{1/2} < 10$ ms). Qualitatively, the contribution of this fast component to the time-course of inactivation is reduced with increasing

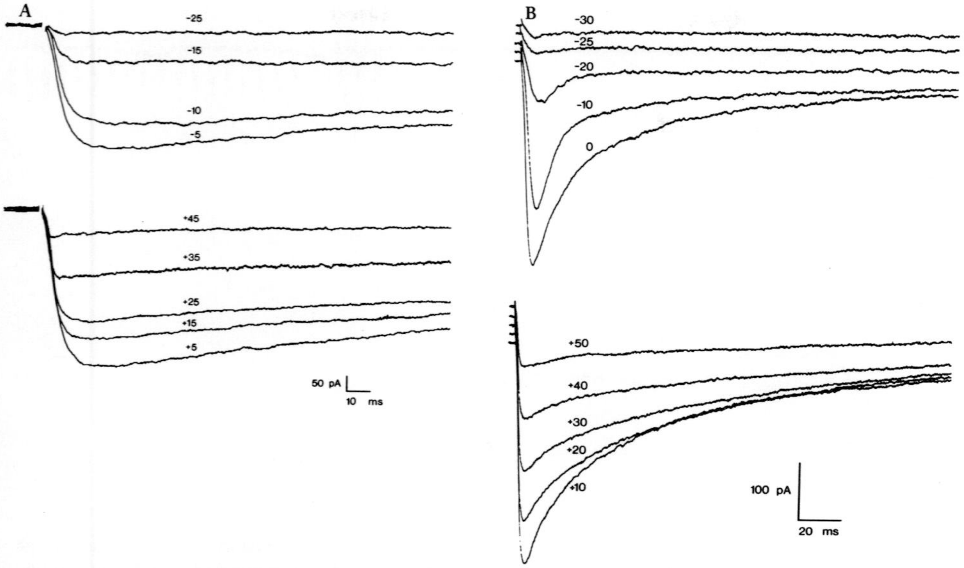

Fig. 1: Typical Ca currents recorded from a myocyte dialysed with either Citrate solution (A; cf. Methods) or a solution containing EGTA (20 mM) as only Ca-chelating ligand (B; the complete composition of this solution was (mM): CsCl 120, EGTA 20, $MgCl_2$ 5, Na_2ATP 1, c-AMP 0.1; Hepes/CsOH 10 pH 7.2). The holding membrane potential ws −45 mV in A and −50 mV in B. Both current-voltage relations were determined during maximum enhancement of I_{Ca} by c-AMP before significant rundown was detected. Linear leakage currents were subtracted by addition of a scaled current response upon a hyperpolarizing voltage step of 20 mV.

depolarization. Sample recordings of Ca-currents obtained under such condition (20 mM $EGTA_i$) are shown in Fig. 1B. On the other hand, dialysis with dipicolinate (DPA), an anion with similar Ca-binding properties as citrate but a very different molecular structure, results in slowly inactivating Ca currents indistinguishable from those measured in citrate-loaded cells.

This residual inactivation can further be slowed or completely abolished by conditions which, for a given depolarization, reduce the amplitude of I_{Ca}, such as partial inhibition by blocking ions (Co^{++}, Cd^{++}), spontaneous rundown, i.e. prolonged cell dialysis or a conditioning depolarization (BECHEM and POTT, 1985). Under neither of the conditions described above did I_{Ca} inactivation show any symptom of being dependent on membrane potential. The experimental results obtained from cells dialysed with citrate, however, clearly support the concept of Ca_i-dependent inactivation of I_{Ca}, which has first been suggested for Ca current in Paramecium (BREHM and ECKERT, 1978) and snail neurons (TILLOTSON, 1979) and has later been extended to various excitable cells (for review see ECKERT and CHAD, 1984).

The properties of I_{Ca}-inactivation in citrate-dialysed cells are reproducibly found if depolarizing voltage steps of 100–200 ms duration are applied at a frequency of 0.1 s^{-1} or less. If longer lasting depolarizations into the voltage range of maximum I_{Ca}-flow or higher frequencies are used, a second fast component of inactivation can be found. Two examples of this «sudden inactivation» are illustrated in Fig. 2. In A the cell was depolarized from

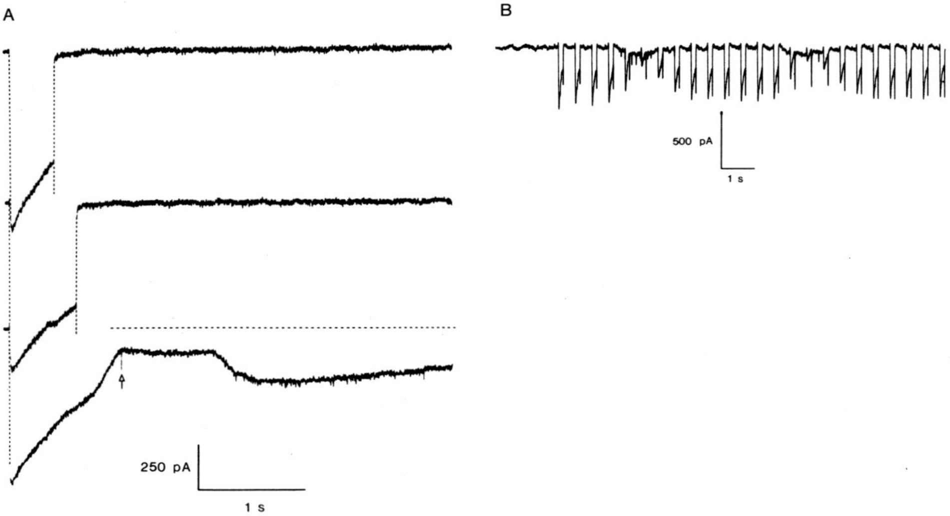

Fig. 2: Sudden inactivation of Ca current by prolongation of the duration of the depolarizing voltage step. A. The membrane potential was stepped to 0 mV from a holding potential of −50 V for 400 ms, 600 ms and 1 s (from top to bottom). The arrow at the lower trace marks the end of the (1 s) depolarization. (The fast upstrokes have been retouched). B. Cyclic inactivation of I_{Ca} during repetitive depolarization. Membrane potential was stepped (3 s^{-1}; duration: 150 ms) from −50 to 0 mV. The rapid current change at the end of Ca-inward currents consisting of the capacitive current and Ca-tail current is not adequately resolved at this time resolution.

the holding potential (−50 mV) to +5 mV at 0.1 s^{-1}. Clamp steps of 400 and 600 ms in duration elicit Ca currents with slow monophasic inactivation as described above. Upon an increase of the duration of the depolarizing pulse to 1 s, however, a sudden reduction of I_{Ca} occurs about 700 ms after the beginning of the step. After repolarization the holding current (at −50 mV) is shifted in the inward direction by about 200 pA. In this particular experiment a further phasic shift of the inward current occurred after another 2 s. A different experimental protocol, which consistently manifests this type of inactivation, namely repetitive depolarization, was used in the experiment depicted in 2 B. This cell was depolarized to 0 mV at 2 s^{-1} with pulses of 150 ms in duration. The first 4 Ca currents elicited by this train are more or less identical. The 5th inward current is much smaller in amplitude and inactivates much faster than the preceeding ones. The Ca current upon the 6th depolarization is almost completely inactivated. Thereafter the current amplitude recovers within 5 depolarizations almost to its initial value. After another 5 depolarizations the same sequence is observed. Like the sudden inactivation shown in 2 A, this cyclic reduction of I_{Ca}-amplitude is paralleled by transient inward shifts of the holding current. Observation of the cell through the microscope during such measurements reveals a vigorous contraction whenever these current changes occur, which is never observed upon activation of a ‹normal› Ca current, suggesting the primary event to be a sudden rise in Ca_i.

At certain combinations of rate and frequency of depolarization a given change in membrane potential may elicit a ‹normal›, i. e. monophasically inactivating Ca current, or currents displaying sudden inactivation at various times after the beginning of the voltage step. In the experiment illustrated in Fig. 3 the cell was depolarized once every 6 seconds to

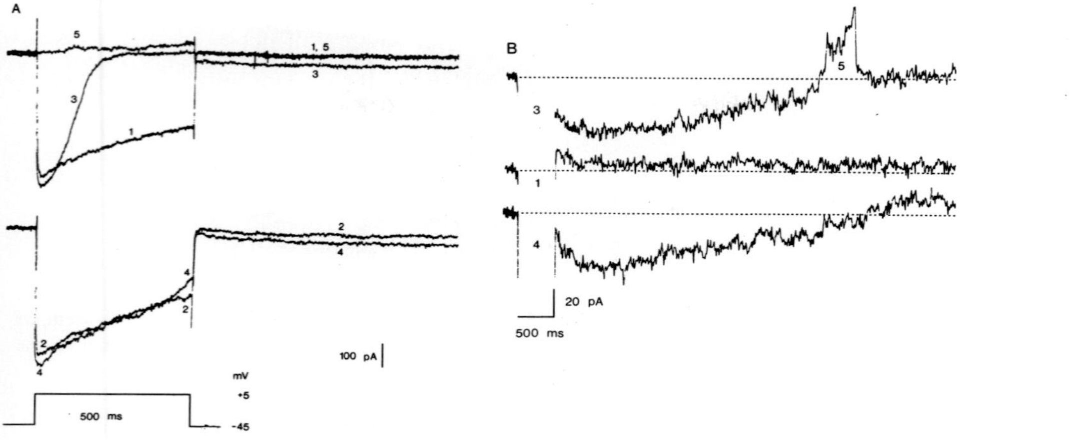

Fig. 3: Identical depolarization can evoke Ca-currents with different patterns of inactivation. A. Ca-inward currents elicited by voltage clamp depolarizations (1 every 6 seconds; duration 500 ms) from −45 mV to + 5 mV. B. Membrane current after repolarization at higher gain and slower time scale. The numbers correspond to A.

+5 mV (duration 500 ms). This results either in normal Ca currents (A 1,2) or currents with sudden inactivation which may be detected some tens of ms after the beginning of the pulse (3) or after up to ca. 400 ms later (5). As described in 2A, after termination of the clamp pulse the holding current at −50 mV is shifted in the inward direction if sudden inactivation is detected but not after a ‹normal› Ca current. The time course of this transient inward current is shown in Fig. 3B on a higher gain and slower time scale. If the depolarizing step is applied before complete decay of this current (4 in 3 A and B) no Ca current can be elicited in this cell.

The finding that «sudden inactivation» is favoured by long-lasting or repetitive Ca-current activation suggests that it reflects a Ca-dependent process which, however, is not directly caused by Ca-entry but by Ca-release from intracellular stores via a mechanism which has been studied extensively in skinned cardiac cells (e. g. Fabiato, 1985). A possible contribution of Ca-induced Ca-release from sarcoplasmic reticulum to the phenomena described in Figs. 2 and 3 was studied by means of caffeine, a substance which has been shown to release Ca ions from the SR and to prevent their re-accumulation in the SR of cardiac and skeletal muscle (Weber and Herz, 1968; Jundt et al., 1975). To ensure a rapid onset of action of this substance, it was applied from an extracellular capillary (tip diameter ca 5 μm) which contained the drug (10 mM dissolved in normal extracellular solution) by pressure ejection close (< 20 μm) to the surface of the cell. The effect of rapid superfusion of a cell with caffeine-containing solution is shown in Fig. 4. In accordance with previous studies on aggregates of neonatal cardiac myocytes (Clusin, 1984), caffeine causes a single transient shift of the holding current (at −50 mV) in the inward direction. In addition to this inward current, in all 12 experiments of this type rapid current fluctuations are detected which, on a faster time scale, turn out to reflect the opening and closing of an ionic channel with large unitary conductance (220–270 pS). Since the maximum number of simultaneous openings found in all experiments was 4, it seems rather likely that each cell possesses only a few of this novel type of channel. This – and the large

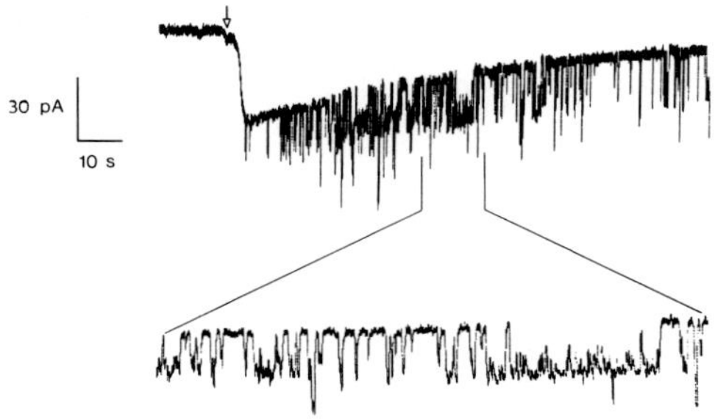

Fig. 4: Effect of caffeine on membrane holding current. Caffeine (10 mM)-containing extracellular solution was applied to the surface of the cell as described in the text at the time indicated by the arrow. Membrane potential was held at −50 mV.

conductance – might also serve as an explanation for the unique observation that single channel current events can be resolved in a whole-cell voltage clamp experiment. The properties of this ionic channel will be described in detail elsewhere. From Fig. 4 it is clear, however, that it does not represent the unitary current event underlying the transient inward current evoked by caffeine, since the first openings can be detected only after the early rising phase of this current.

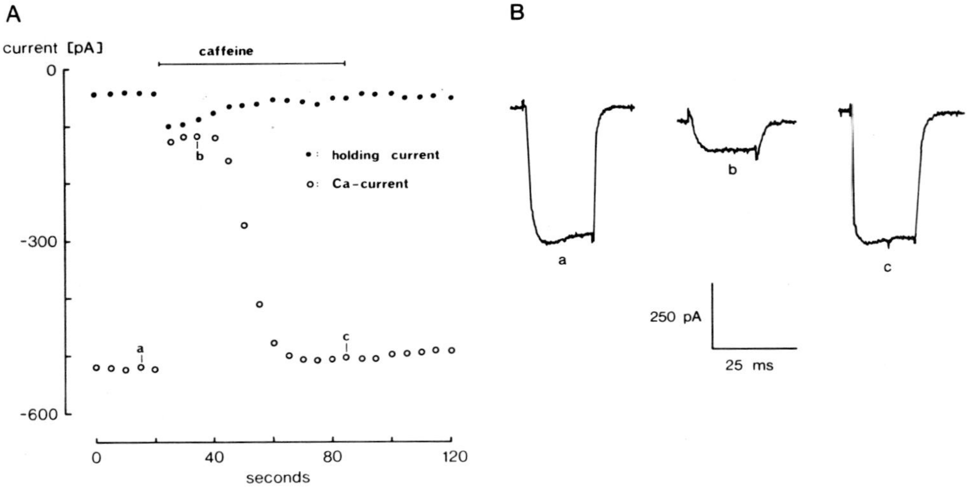

Fig. 5: Effect of caffeine on I_{Ca}-amplitude. Ca current was elicited by step changes to 0 mV from a holding potential of −50 mV (frequency: 0.25 s^{-1}; pulse duration 25 ms). With these pulse parameters neither sudden inactivation nor transient inward current was evoked in this cell. A. Plot of holding current and Ca current against time of the experiment (t=0 corresponds to the time when the c-AMP dependent enhancement of I_{Ca} had reached its maximum, which was about 6 minutes after starting dialysis of the cell. Caffeine was applied as described in the text during the period of time indicated. B. Ca currents recorded at the times marked a–c in A.

The caffeine-evoked transient inward current is paralleled by a reduction in I_{Ca}-amplitude at a given membrane depolarization. In Fig. 5 from a different cell, peak I_{Ca} evoked by short (25 ms; frequency 0.2 s^{-1}) depolarizing pulses to 0 mV and holding current have been plotted against time. (The pulse protocol used did not cause «sudden inactivation» or transient inward currents in the cell studied.) At t=10 s the cell was superfused with caffeine-containing solution as described above. This causes a reduction of I_{Ca}-amplitude in this cell by about 77 %. In 5 different experiments of this kind, reduction of I_{Ca}-amplitude (at 0 or +5 mV) ranged from 64 % to 100 %. In the presence of caffeine, I_{Ca} recovers in parallel to the decline of the transient inward current. This clearly suggests that Ca-release from SR may cause inactivation of Ca channel current.

The effect of Ca-release on I_{Ca} becomes particularly evident if Ca currents before caffeine application are compared with currents measured in presence of caffeine after both, the holding current and I_{Ca}-amplitude, have recovered to their control level, i. e. when no release should take place. In the experiment illustrated in Fig. 6 a frequency of depolarizing voltage clamp steps (from −50 to 0 mV; duration 200 ms) was chosen (0.2 s^{-1}) which resulted in Ca currents consistently followed by a transient inward current after repolarization. Although a distinct transition from «normal» to «sudden inactivation» was not prominent in this particular cell, the occurrence of transient inward current was taken as a sign of Ca-release (cf. Figs. 2 and 3). Superfusion of the cell with caffeine-containing solution first causes an inward shift of the holding current by ca. 60 pA which is paralleled by an almost complete inactivation of I_{Ca} (not shown). Both current changes recover within about 60 seconds in the presence of caffeine. Ca inward current evoked by an identical depolarization now inactivates more slowly, after repolarization there is scarcely any transient inward current detectable. (Note, however, the openings of the large ionic channel under this condition.) Although the difference between Ca currents observed in

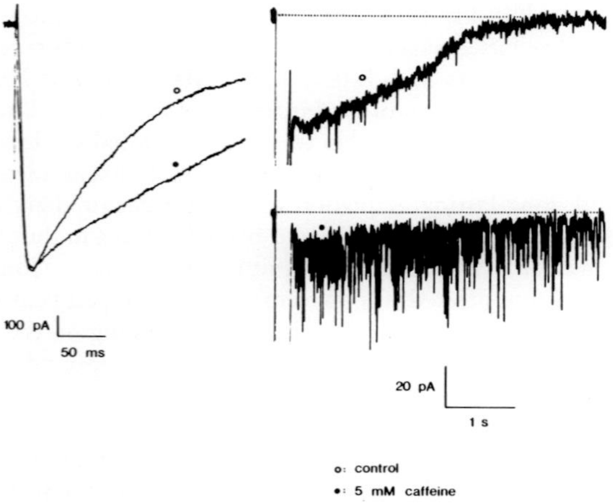

Fig. 6: Effect of caffeine on inactivation of I_{Ca}. From the holding potential (−50 mV) the cell was depolarized to 0 mV at a rate of 0.2 s^{-1} (duration 250 ms). The resulting Ca currents (O) were consistently followed by a transient inward current after repolarization. Extracellular application of caffeine (5 mM) first caused a shift of the holding current by ca. 60 pA, paralleled by a complete suppression of I_{Ca} (not shown; cf. Fig. 5). The traces marked by the closed circles were recorded 70 seconds after starting superfusion of the cell with caffeine-containing solution, when both, the holding current and I_{Ca}-amplitude, had recovered to their control levels.

normal extracellular solution and in the presence of caffeine was not consistently as pronounced as in this particular experiment, a qualitatively similar effect was observed in 8 experiments of this type, provided depolarization parameters were chosen which caused Ca-currents followed by a transient inward current indicating Ca-release from SR.

These results clearly demonstrate that interactions between transmembrane Ca current and sarcoplasmic Ca release can be detected in voltage-clamped single cardiac cells. Prolonged or repetitive activation of Ca-current can cause Ca release from SR, which in turn causes Ca-dependent inactivation of I_{Ca}. In addition, a membrane current is activated which is supposed to reflect Ca-extrusion from the cell via Na^+/Ca^{++}-exchange (MECHMANN and POTT, 1986).

Discussion

In the present study inactivation of classical Ca-current was investigated in single atrial myocytes from hearts of adult guinea-pigs. The spherical cells were dialysed with a solution containing a high concentration (65 mM) of citrate. Under this condition I_{Ca}-inactivation has been shown to be considerably slowed or virtually absent, depending on the amplitude of I_{Ca} at a given membrane potential (BECHEM and POTT, 1985). Whereas in previous investigations inactivation of cardiac I_{Ca} has been described as purely voltage dependent in terms of a Hodgkin-Huxley formalism (for review see: TRAUTWEIN, 1973; REUTER, 1979; MCDONALD, 1982), more recent studies suggest the co-existence of both, voltage and Ca-entry-dependent inactivation (KASS and SANGUINETTI, 1984; LEE et al., 1985). In citrate-loaded myocytes, however, no effect of the depolarization as such on relaxation of I_{Ca} was detected. Inactivation in the voltage range of maximum I_{Ca}-flow is slow or virtually absent, but displays a fast component if EGTA (20 mM) is used as Ca-chelating compound. The latter observation is in line with several recent studies on dialysed single myocytes (e. g. HESS and TSIEN, 1984; MATSUDA and NOMA, 1984) and is supposed to reflect the slow kinetics of Ca-buffering by EGTA (cf. THOMAS, 1982). Thus in an EGTA buffered cell it is not possible to impose a global Ca-load by a long-lasting depolarization, because I_{Ca} is partly switched off due to a subsarcolemmal rise in Ca^{++}.

On the other hand, long-lasting activation of I_{Ca} in a citrate-dialysed cell results in a global rise in total Ca. For a depolarization to 0 mV of 500 ms in duration (cf. Fig. 2), the time integral of I_{Ca} may be in the order of magnitude of 2×10^{-10} Coulomb, corresponding to a rise of the total (unbuffered) Ca concentration in a typical cardioball of 20 μm in diameter in the order of 3×10^{-4} M or even higher, depending on the accessible volume. With 65 mM citrate and 1 mM EGTA as only Ca-binding compounds, this would cause a free Ca-concentration of 3.1×10^{-7} M.

However, since apart from citrate and 1 mM EGTA the cell also contains natural Ca-binding molecules in unknown concentrations, and, in addition, there is slow equilibration of the intracellular solution with that in the recording pipette, the true free Ca_i cannot be predicted. The threshold for Ca-induced Ca-release from cardiac SR was determined as less than 5×10^{-7} M in skinned canine Purkinje cells (FABIATO, 1985). The conditions for Ca-release, however, depend on several factors. The amount of Ca^{++} released in skinned cells was found to be not only dependent on the amplitude of the triggering Ca^{++}-increase but also on the rate of this change and the previous Ca-load of the SR and other factors such as free Mg^{++} or the presence of calmodulin. Because none of these parameters was controlled in the present study, nor was a signal measured which could be calibrated in terms of free Ca^{++}-changes, a direct comparison between the conditions causing Ca-release in dialysed cells and skinned cell fragments with a highly defined environment seems to be inadequate at present. Nevertheless, the observation that maintained or repetitive activation of I_{Ca} can cause Ca-release from the SR is in line with the concept of Ca-induced Ca-release. The changes in membrane current due to Ca-release were accompanied by a strong contraction of the cell, indicating a rise in free Ca^{++} to at least 10^{-6} M (see above). This sudden rise in Ca_i causes partial or complete inactivation of Ca current. This is in line with previous attempts for estimating the Ca-affinity of the hypothetical binding site involved in Ca-dependent inactivation. For Helix neurons, PLANT et al., (1983) suggested a dissociation constant in the order of 7×10^{-7} M for this site, which they assumed to cause a closing of a Ca-channel if occupied by a Ca ion. More recent reports suggest a more complex mechanism of Ca-current inactivation (e.g. CHAD and ECKERT, 1985).

In the present study Ca-release from SR has been found to exert a massive effect on Ca current. To what extent cardiac I_{Ca} is affected by Ca-release also under more physiological conditions, i.e. in cells with a normal composition of the cytoplasm, is unknown. In a recent publication on rate dependent changes of I_{Ca} in isolated intact (i.e. non-dialysed) myocytes, the possibility of such interactions between Ca-current and Ca-release is indicated (MITCHELL et al., 1985). In analogy to the present results an increase in the frequency of depolarizations can cause a reduction in I_{Ca}-amplitude which seems to be related to Ca-release, and which is accompanied by an inward shift of the holding current. A transient inhibitory effect of caffeine on I_{Ca} has also been detected in voltage clamped Purkinje fibers (HESS and WIER, 1984).

The ionic nature of the transient inward current following Ca-release, which in a similar way can be evoked in aggregates of cultured neonatal myocytes (CLUSIN, 1983) and which shows some properties in common with oscillatory currents of cardiac steroids (e.g. KASS et al., 1978; KARAGUEUZIAN and KATZUNG, 1982), has not been further analysed in the context of the present investigation. For these currents two underlying ionic mechanisms are being discussed: a Ca-activated unspecific cation channel (cf. COLQUHOUN et al., 1981) or Na^{+}/Ca^{++}-exchange, which is supposed to be electrogenic i.e. to carry charges across the membrane due to its stoichiometry of $\geq 3\ Na^{+}/1\ Ca^{++}$ (for review see MULLINS, 1979; REUTER, 1982; EISNER and LEDERER, 1985). From measurements of the transient inward current under somewhat different conditions strong evidence has been presented recently that it is carried by Na^{+}/Ca^{++}-exchange rather than a gated ionic channel (MECHMANN and POTT, 1986).

Acknowledgements

We thank Mrs. U. MÜLLER for technical assistance. This work was supported by the Deutsche Forschungsgemeinschaft (SFB 114, TP A8). The development of the cell culture technique was rendered possible by a grant to L. P. from the Ministerium für Wissenschaft und Forschung Nordrhein-Westfalen.

References

Bechem, M., Pott, L. (1985): Removal of Ca current inactivation in dialysed guinea-pig atrial cardioballs by Ca chelators. Pflügers Arch. **404,** 10–20.
Bechem, M., Pott, L., Rennebaum, H. (1983): Atrial muscle cells from hearts of adult guinea-pigs: a new preparation for cardiac cellular electrophysiology. Europ. J. Cell. Biol. **31,** 366–369.
Brehm, P., Eckert, R. (1978): Calcium entry leads to inactivation of calcium channel in *Paramecium*. Science **202,** 1203–1206.
Caroni, P., Carafoli, E. (1980): An ATP-dependent Ca^{2-} pumping system in dog heart sarcolemma. Nature (Lond.) **283,** 765–767.
Chad, J., Eckert, R. (1985): Calcineurin, a calcium-dependent phosphatase, enhances Ca-mediated inactivation of Ca current in perfused snail neurons. Biophys. J. **47,** 266a.
Chapman, R. A. (1983): Control of cardiac contractility at the cellular level. Am. J. Physiol. **245,** H535–H552.
Clusin, T. C. (1983): Caffeine induces a transient inward current in cultured cardiac cells. Nature (Lond.) **301,** 248–250.
Colquhoun, D., Neher, E., Reuter, H ., Stevens, C. F. (1981): Inward current channels activated by intracellular Ca in cultured cardiac cells. Nature (Lond.) **294,** 752–754.
DiFrancesco, D., Noble, D. (1985): A model of cardiac electrical activity incorporating ionic pumps and concentration changes. Phil. Trans. R. Soc. (Lond.) **307,** 353–398.
Eckert, R., Chad, J. E. (1984): Inactivation of Ca channels. Progr. Biophys. Molec. Biol. **44,** 215–267.
Eisner, D. A., Lederer, W. J. (1985): Na-Ca exchange: stoichiometry and electrogenicity. Am. J. Physiol. **248,** C189–C202.
Fabiato, A. (1983): Calcium-induced release of calcium from the cardiac sarcoplasmic reticulum. Am. J. Physiol. **245,** H1–H14.
Fabiato, A. (1985): Time and calcium-dependence of activation of calcium release from the sarcoplasmic reticulum of a skinned cardiac Purkinje cell. J. Gen. Physiol. **85,** 247–289.
Fenwick, E. M., Marty, A., Neher, E. (1982): Sodium and calcium channels in bovine chromaffin cells. J. Physiol. (Lond.) **331,** 599–635.
Hamill, O. P., Marty, A., Neher, E., Sakmann, B., Sigworth, F. J. (1981): Improved patch clamp technique for high-resolution current recording from cells and cell-free membrane patches. Pflügers Arch. **391,** 85–100.
Hess, P., Tsien, R. W. (1984): Mechanism of ion permeation through calcium channels. Nature (Lond.) **309,** 453–456.
Hess, P., Wier, W. G. (1984): Excitation-contraction coupling in cardiac Purkinje fibers. Effects of caffeine on the intracellular Ca^{++} transient membrane currents and contraction. J. Gen. Physiol. **83,** 417–433.
Isenberg, G., Klöckner, U. (1982): Calcium currents of isolated bovine ventricular myocytes are fast and of large amplitude. Pflügers Arch. **395,** 30–41.
Josephson, I. R., Sanchez-Chapula, J., Brown A. M. (1984): A comparison of calcium currents in rat and guinea-pig single ventricular cells. Circ. Res. **54,** 144–156.
Jundt, H., Porzig, R., Reuter, H., Stucki, J. W. (1975): The effect of substances releasing calcium ions on sodium-dependent calcium efflux from guinea-pig auricles. J. Physiol. **246,** 229–253.
Karagueuzian, H. S., Katzung, B. G. (1982): Voltage-clamp studies of transient inward current and mechanical oscillations induced by ouabain in ferret papillary muscle. J. Physiol. (Lond.) **327,** 255–271.
Kass, R. S., Sanguinetti, M. C. (1984): Inactivation of calcium channel current in the calf cardiac Purkinje fiber. Evidence for voltage and calcium-mediated mechanism. J. Gen. Physiol. **84,** 705–726.
Kass, R. S., Tsien, R. W., Weingart, R. (1978): Ionic basis of transient inward current induced by strophantidin in cardiac Purkinje fibers. J. Physiol. (Lond.) **281,** 209–226.
Lee, K. S., Tsien, R. W. (1984): High selectivity of calcium channels in single dialysed heart cells of the guinea-pig. J. Physiol. (Lond.) **354,** 253–272.
Lee, K. S., Marban, E., Tsien, R. W. (1985): Inactivation of calcium channels in mammalian heart

cells: joint dependence of membrane potential and intracellular calcium. J. Physiol. (Lond.) **364,** 398–411.
Marty, A., Neher, E. (1983): Tight-seal whole-cell recording. In: B. Sakman, E. Neher (eds.) Single channel recording. Plenum, New York § London. pp. 107–122.
Matsuda, A., Noma, A. (1984): Isolation of calcium current and its sensitivity to monovalent cations in dialysed ventricular cells of the guinea-pig. J. Physiol. (Lond.) **357,** 553–573.
McDonald, T. F. (1982): The slow inward calcium current in the heart. Ann. Rev. Physiol. **46,** 425–434.
Mechmann, S., Pott, L. (1986): Identification of Na-Ca exchange current in single cardiac myocytes. Nature (Lond.) **319,** 597–599.
Mentrard, D., Vassort, G., Fischmeister, R. (1984): Calcium-mediated inactivation of the calcium conductance in cesium-loaded frog heart cells. J. Gen. Physiol. **83,** 105–131.
Mitchell, M. R., Powell, T., Terrar, D. A., Twist, V. W. (1983): Characteristics of the second inward current in cells isolated from rat ventricular muscle. Proc. Roy. Soc. Lond. B **219,** 447–469.
Mitchell, M. R., Powell, T., Terrar, D. A., Twist, V. W. (1985): Influence of a change in stimulation rate on action potentials in rat ventricular cells. J. Physiol. (Lond.) **364,** 113–130.
Mullins, L. J. (1979): The generation of electric current in cardiac fibers by Na-Ca exchange. Am. J. Physiol. **236,** 103–110.
Nilius, B., Henček, M. (1983): Current-dependent slow channel inactivation in heart muscle. Gen. Physiol. Biophys. **2,** 217–224.
Noble, D. (1984): The surprising heart: A review of recent progress in cardiac electrophysiology. J. Physiol. (Lond.) **353,** 1–50.
Plant, T. D., Standen, N. B., Ward, T. A. (1983): The effects of injection of calcium ions and calcium chelators on calcium channel inactivation in *Helix* neurons. J. Physiol. (Lond.) **224,** 189–212.
Powell, T., Twist, V. W. (1976): A rapid technique for the isolation and purification of adult cardiac muscle cells having respiratory control and a tolerance to calcium. Biochem. Biophys. Res. Commun. **72,** 7733–7739.
Reuter, H. (1979): Properties of two inward membrane currents in the heart. Ann. Rev. Physiol. **41,** 413–424.
Reuter, H. (1982): Na-Ca counter-transport in cardiac muscle. In: A. N. Martonosi (ed.) Membranes and transport. Plenum, New York. pp. 623–631.
Reuter, H. (1984): Ionic channels in cardiac cell membranes. Ann. Rev. Physiol. **46,** 473–484.
Thomas, M. V. (1982): Techniques in calcium research. Academic press, New York.
Tillotson, D. (1979): Inactivation of Ca conductance dependent on entry of Ca ions in molluscan neurons. Proc. Natl. Acad. Sci. **76,** 1497–1500.
Trautwein, W. (1973): Membrane currents in cardiac muscle. Physiol. Rev. **53,** 793–835.
Tsien, R. W. (1983): Calcium channels in excitable membranes. Ann. Rev. Physiol. **46,** 341–358.
Weber, A., Herz, R. (1968): The relationship between caffeine contracture of intact muscle and the effect of caffeine on reticulum. J. Gen. Physiol. **52,** 750–759.

Fortschritte der Zoologie, Band 33 · Lüttgau (Hrsg.): Membrane Control
Gustav Fischer Verlag · Stuttgart · New York · 1986

Properties of two voltage-dependent calcium channels in a ciliate

JOACHIM W. DEITMER

Institut für Zoologie I, Universität Düsseldorf, D-4000 Düsseldorf, FRG

Introduction

Calcium-dependent electrogenesis is the most variable and wide-spread form of electrical excitation. Calcium channels are ubiquitous, from unicellular organisms to mammals, and both ontogenetically and phylogenetically they often precede sodium channels. There is good evidence now to believe that they are the «original» mode of cellular excitation, and that sodium channels are a specialization in electrically excitable tissues to achieve a very fast impulse propagation.

Since the first reports of Ca-dependent excitability in crustacean muscle (FATT and KATZ, 1953; FATT and GINSBORG, 1958) there have been numerous studies on Ca action potentials and Ca currents in a great variety of species. The course of research on Ca-dependent excitability has been nicely described in a recent book by HAGIWARA (1983). In the last few years several reviews on the structural entity in the cell membrane related to this form of excitation, the voltage-dependent Ca channel, have been published (KOSTYUK, 1980; HAGIWARA and BYERLY, 1981; REUTER, 1983; TSIEN, 1983).

The diversity of properties displayed by Ca-dependent electrogenesis has long lead to speculations whether one or more types of Ca channels exist. The first indication of two types of Ca-dependent inward currents came from a voltage-clamp study on starfish eggs (HAGIWARA et al., 1975). In rat brain synaptosomes a fast and a slow entry of divalent cations was observed, suggesting the presence of two Ca pathways across the presynaptic membrane (NACHSHEN and BLAUSTEIN, 1982). It was only quite recently, however, that the identification of two different Ca currents – and thus presumably two Ca channels – was studied in more detail (DEITMER, 1983; 1984; CARBONE and LUX, 1984a, b; FOX and KRASNE, 1984; ARMSTRONG and MATTESON, 1985; BEAN, 1985; BOSSU et al., 1985; FEDULOVA et al., 1985; NILIUS et al., 1985). Even three types of Ca channels have been postulated in vertebrate sensory neurones (NOWYCKY et al., 1985). The large number of publications on the presence of several types of voltage-dependent Ca channels in one cell signals the wide interest in this phenomenon. Indeed, various Ca currents in different parts of the membrane appear to play a major role in determining the firing pattern of electrically excitable cells (LLINAS and YAROM, 1981; JAHNSEN and LLINAS, 1984; GRAUBARD and ROSS, 1985). In addition, other Ca-dependent membrane currents, such as e.g. the Ca-induced K currents (MEECH, 1978), exert a direct influence on the cell's electrical behaviour.

Thus, Ca ions, which play a major role in the transduction of cellular signals, such as contraction, secretion and ciliary motility, appear to enter the cells through membrane channels, which vary in properties and in their distribution in the membrane. Ca influx could be gated and controlled by various types of Ca channels. With the elucidation of more detailed channel properties, in particular by single channel analysis (see e. g. LUX and NAGY, 1981; FENWICK et al., 1982; CAVALIÉ et al., 1983; NELSON et al., 1984; WORLEY et al. 1986), the classification of Ca channels may soon go beyond the description of two or three types. While the Na-dependent excitation is still thought to be based on one type of Na channel described by HODGKIN and HUXLEY, (1952), Ca channels exhibit a diversity which is more like that of K channels. The latter occur in virtually all living cells in multiple forms, and by now at least four different types have been well characterized (HILLE, 1984).

In the present account the main properties of two voltage-dependent Ca channels in the ciliate *Stylonychia* are summarized. Hypotrichous ciliates are regarded as belonging to the most highly advanced unicellular organisms: They have a more differentiated morphology, and the ciliary system is more elaborate than in other ciliates. Cilia of hypotrichous ciliates are usually grouped into clusters of 5 to 80, forming rod-like cirri and velum-shaped membranelles. This differentiation, and the specific location of membranelles and cirri, provides a highly developed locomotor system. Sensory reception and electrical excitation of the cell membrane lead to the activation of ciliary organelles and thereby determine cellular behaviour (MACHEMER and DEITMER, 1986). The presence of two types of voltage-dependent Ca channels may be directly related to different behavioural patterns on a cellular level, which makes this simple, but rather sophisticated organism a unique model to study functional characteristics of Ca channels.

Methods

The experiments were performed on the ciliate *Stylonychia mytilus* syngen I (Hypotricha), which was cloned and cultured in Pringsheim solution at 18 °C. The cells were fed with the phytomonad alga *Chlorogonium elongatum* every three days. For experimentation, cells were washed and equilibrated in the normal experimental solution containing 1 mM $CaCl_2$ or 1 mM $BaCl_2$, 1 mM KCl, and 1 mM TRIS-HCl or 1 mM HEPES (N-2-hydroxyethyl piperazine-N'-ethanesulphonic acid) to give a pH of 7.4 ($\pm$ 0.1). The plant lectin concanavalin A (Sigma, grade IV) was prepared as stock solution of either 100 μg/ml or 400 μg/ml. To these stock solutions concanavalin A was added to the experimental solution just before use to give a concentration of 0.5 μg/ml, which corresponds to 5 × 10exp-9 M of the tetrameric form of concanavalin A. The experiments were carried out with the experimental chamber (volume less than 1 ml) held at a temperature of 17 to 18 °C by means of a constant perfusion of a microscope cooling table.

Electrical recording

The cells were penetrated by two microelectrodes (borosilicate capillaries with filament, outer diameter 1 mm), one electrode being filled with 1 M KCl for membrane potential recording, the other one filled with 2 M K-citrate for current injection. A third microelectrode, filled with 1 M KCl, was placed outside the cell for differential measuring of the membrane potential. The resistance of the electrodes was 10–60 MOhms in normal experimental solution. The voltage clamp was performed by means of a feed-back system using a high-gain differential amplifier (AD 171 K). The membrane currents were monitored by a current-voltage converter connected to the bath via a 1 M KCl-agar bridge and displayed on an oscilloscope. De- and hyperpolarizing square wave voltage steps were applied; the voltage was usually clamped to a stable steady-state within 100–300 μs during a 10 mV step. The time-to-peak of the early inward currents was 1.5–4.5 ms or more. Thus, the clamp was sufficiently fast to record the peak inward current free of capacitative transients.

In control experiments, K outward currents were reduced or inhibited with blocking agents, such as tetraethylammonium, 4-aminopyridine or internal Cs (brought into the cell via the intracellular current injecting microelectrode).

Results and discussion

The cellular structure and location of ciliary organelles of *Stylonychia* are shown in Fig. 1A, B. The cell is approximately 250 μm in length (up to 350 μm in some strains), 40–50 μm in width, and 15–20 μm in its dorso-ventral extension. The organization of the membranellar band, which surrounds the anterior pole of the cell and which extends to the oral groove, suggests that its main function might be to provide a feeding water current (MACHEMER, 1966). Ventral and marginal cirri serve cellular locomotion. Recent high-speed cinematography of cirri and membranelles of *Stylonychia* under membrane voltage clamp revealed that these two types of organelles display different motor responses to the same voltage stimuli (DEITMER, MACHEMER and MARTINAC, 1983; 1984). Membranelles

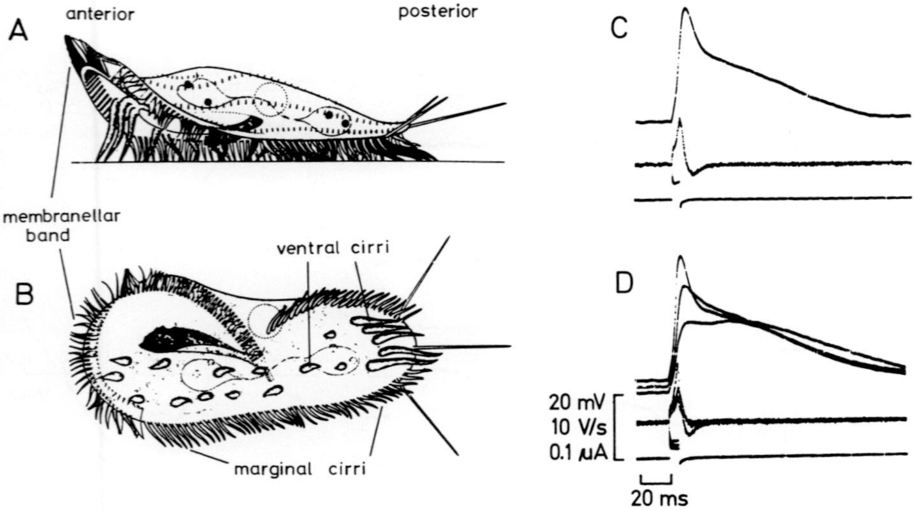

Fig. 1: Drawing of the hypotrich ciliate *Stylonychia* as viewed from the lateral (A) and ventral (B) side, after MACHEMER in GRELL (1973). The different ciliary organelles, membranelles and cirri, are indicated. Single (C) and superimposed (D) action potentials (upper traces), their first derivatives (dV/dt, middle traces), and the intracellularly injected current pulses (lower traces) are shown. In (D) pulses of three different amplitudes were injected for triggering the composite action potential to demonstrate the graded character of the first peak and the apparent all-or-none character of the second peak. From DEITMER, 1983.

continuously beat at a frequency of around 40 Hz irrespective of the voltage stimulus applied, while ventral and marginal cirri respond to membrane polarization with a change in direction and frequency of their power stroke. In contrast to membranelles, cirri are inactive at a membrane potential value near the cell's resting potential, which is around −50 mV.

Depolarization of the membrane by brief outward current pulses evokes an action potential that characteristically contains two components, a large, graded peak and a second smaller, all-or-none peak or shoulder (Fig. 1C, D). A very similar compound action potential can be elicited by mechanically stimulating the anterior part of the cell. In the latter case a depolarizing mechanoreceptor potential gives rise to the action potential (Peyer and Machemer, 1978; Peyer and Deitmer, 1980).

Both components of the action potential are dependent upon extracellular Ca (Peyer and Machemer, 1977). The amplitudes of the first and the second peak vary with the extracellular Ca concentration. If extracellular Ca is replaced by Mg, Co or Mn, no action potential can be elicited. If, however, Sr or Ba replaces Ca, action potentials of increased amplitude and duration are generated. The action potential remains unaffected by changes in the extracellular Na and Cl concentration. All these properties of membrane excitability meet the criteria of Ca spikes (Hagiwara, 1975). Voltage clamp experiments on the ionic selectivity of the early inward current have confirmed the conclusion that the inward currents are carried by Ca, Sr and Ba, but not by Mg, Mr or Co (Peyer and Deitmer, 1980; Deitmer, 1983, 1984; Ballanyi and Deitmer, 1984).

In voltage clamp experiments, the cell membrane was held at its resting potential of −50 mV and depolarized in steps of various amplitudes and of 50 ms in duration (Fig. 2A). Depolarizations of only 2–3 mV were sufficient to elicit a small transient inward

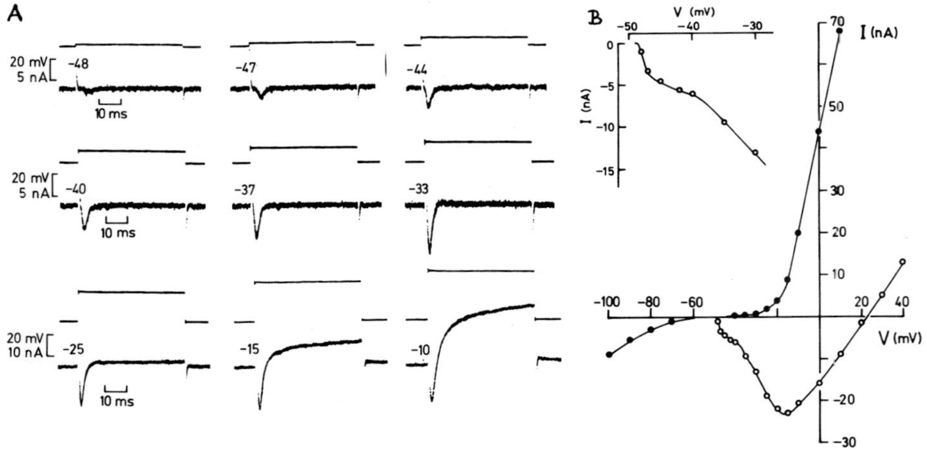

Fig. 2: (A) Membrane currents (lower traces) recorded following 50 ms depolarizing voltage-clamp pulses (upper traces) to potentials indicated by the figures between the traces (holding potential: −50 mV). Inward currents are recorded even with small depolarizations, while a net outward current appears only at a membrane potential of −25 mV and above. (B) Current-voltage relationship of the cell membrane: The early, fast, transient current (open circles), the current at the end of 50 ms long de- and hyperpolarizing pulses (filled circles). Note the two maxima in the inward current-voltage relationship. From Deitmer, 1984.

current (up tp 3 nA), which increased with further depolarization. Fig. 2B shows typical current-voltage relationships. There is a first maximum of the inward current at a membrane potential near −45 mV and another maximum near −17 mV. The inset of Fig. 2B shows part of the inward current-voltage relationship, i. e. up to −30 mV, on an enlarged scale to show the low-threshold current more clearly. The two maxima of the inward current-voltage relationship will be referred to as inward current I and inward current II, or, more briefly, current I and current II, respectively.

The ‹steady-state› current-voltage relationship revealed a strong outward-going rectification upon depolarization beyond −20 mV and a moderate inward-going rectification upon hyperpolarization of the membrane (Fig. 2B). Both types of rectification decreased considerably when Ca was replaced by Mg (Peyer and Deitmer, 1980). A fast outward current was sometimes evident at a membrane potential of between −35and −20 mV.

In an attempt to isolate the Ca component of the inward current, drugs known to block K channels, such as Cs, tetraethylammonium and 4-aminopyridine were used in some experiments (see Deitmer, 1984). The outward currents were considerably reduced, but not completely inhibited, by these substances. A fast, transient outward current apparent in some cells could be abolished. The inward currents, however, remained virtually unaltered except for a somewhat slower decay due to the reduction of outward current. The inward current-voltage relationship was not changed and still showed two distinct maxima.

Effects of anorganic Ca antagonists

When Ca was partially replaced by Co or Mn in the external solution, the inward current was substantially reduced. The outward current was activated with a slower time course in the presence of Co or Mn, levelling into a steady-state of smaller amplitude. This may indicate the influence of Ca inward currents on the K outward current suggested for this cell (Peyer and Deitmer, 1980). The voltage dependence of the inward currents remained essentially unchanged by Co (or Mn). The reduction by Co of the second maximum of the inward current-voltage curve was, however, relatively larger than that of the first maximum. With 0.5 and 1.0 mM Co, the peak inward current I was reduced to 62 % and 29 %, while the peak current II was reduced to 32 % and 6 %, respectively (Deitmer, 1984). The reduction of the external Ca concentration to 0.5 and 0.1 mM, to keep the divalent cation concentration constant in these experiments, reduced the peak of both inward currents to 90 % and 65 %, respectively, in control experiments (without Co). This suggests that inward current I is less sensitive to Co than inward current II.

In a series of experiments, $CdCl_2$ at concentrations between 10exp-6 M and 10exp-4 M was added to the normal solution. Cd also reduced both types of inward currents, but again with different efficacy. Inward current I was less sensitive to Cd and was reduced to 50 % by approximately 10exp-4 M Cd, while inward current II was already reduced to 50 % by 10exp-5 M Cd. When Ca was completely replaced by Co or Mn (nominally Ca-free), no inward currents could be elicited by membrane depolarizations. Increasing the external Ca concentration, on the contrary, produced larger inward currents.

Inactivation of the two types of inward currents

Inward current I decayed with a similar time course when either Ca, Sr or Ba acted as charge carrier. This is in sharp contrast to inward current II, which decayed rapidly in Ca-

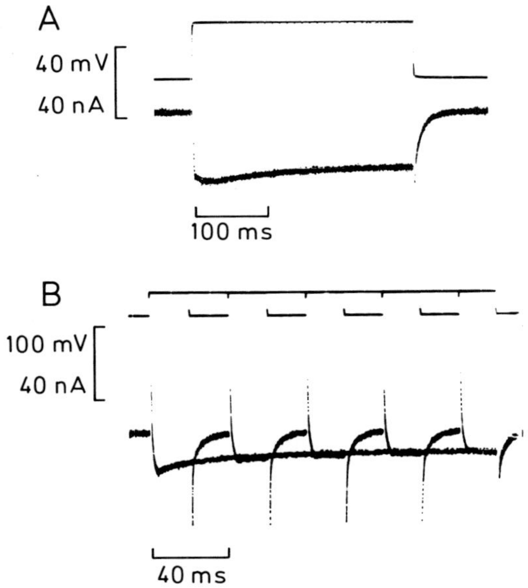

Fig. 3: Voltage-clamp steps from −50 mV to −20 mV in Ca-free Ba solution. There is little inactivation of the Ba inward current during a 300 ms long pulse (A), and equally little inactivation during five 20 ms pulses, or one 180 ms long pulse (B, traces superimposed).

and Sr-solution, even in the presence of K channel blockers, but relatively slowly and incompletely in Ba-solution (Fig. 3A). In Ca-free Ba-solution a large inward current II was maintained over hundreds of milliseconds or even seconds. The amplitude of inward current II when carried by Ba ions was the same if one long, 180 ms, or multiple short, 20 ms, voltage steps depolarized the membrane (Fig. 3B). This seems to rule out inactivation of the inward current, also when carried by Ca, due to extracellular depletion of the charge-carrying ion, as was found for the Ca current in the T-tubules of frog skeletal muscle (ALMERS et al., 1981). The inactivation of inward current II in Ca-solution depended in a U-shaped manner upon the voltage of the conditioning prepulse (DEITMER, 1984), as was also shown in *Paramecium* (BREHM and ECKERT, 1978), and in many other preparations (for ref. see ECKERT and CHAD, 1984), where inactivation of the Ca inward current was directly related to the influx of Ca into the cell and/or to accumulation of Ca at the inner membrane side. A characteristic of Ca-dependent inactivation is that in Ba-solution these inward currents showed much less or no inactivation at all.

The inactivation found for inward current I appears to be voltage-dependent, thus inactivation was the same with Ca or Ba as charge carrier (DEITMER, 1986). A similar voltage-dependent inactivation of Ca and Ba currents has been described in other preparations, e. g. in the egg cell of the marine polychaete *Neanthes* (FOX, 1981), and in cultured mouse myeloma cells (FUKUSHIMA and HAGIWARA, 1983). Hence, Ca channels with different inactivation mechanisms have been found in different species, in *Stylonychia* these occur in the same cell.

Effect of varying the holding potential

Another distinct feature of inward current I is its dependence on the holding potential (DEITMER, 1986). When the holding potential was varied from −50 mV to values between −40 mV and −70 mV, the activation of current I was shifted parallel to the holding potential along the voltage axis, the shift being 8 mV/10 mV change in holding potential. Inward current II remained unaffected in its voltage course by varying the holding potential.

The voltage shift of current I with different holding potentials could not only be explained with the removal of voltage-dependent inactivation. Amplitude and rate of rise were maximal with a holding potential of −55 mV and similar or even smaller for more negative holding potentials. The availability of a fast outward current with more negative holding potentials might have contributed to an apparent voltage shift of the inward current. This can be excluded, however, since a fast outward current is activated only at potentials more positive to −35 mV, while current I is fully activated at potentials negative to −35 mV. In addition, a shift of outward currents with varying holding potentials was never observed.

Both inward currents *did* shift along the voltage axis when the divalent cation concentration was altered in the external solution. This would be expected, particularly in these low ionic fesh-water substitute solutions, from the surface potential hypothesis (MCLAUGHLIN et al., 1971). An effect of the holding potential on the voltage course of current I could be explained if membrane potential changes could alter the surface charges at the membrane (MCLAUGHLIN and HARARY, 1974). There is as yet no direct evidence, however, which supports this mechanism for the observed potential-dependent shift of current I in *Stylonychia*.

Inhibition of current I by concanavalin A

Incubation of *Stylonychia* in fluorescin-labeled concanavalin A (Con A, 0.5 μg/ml) produced a strong fluorescence of the membranelles but comparatively weak fluorescence of the other compound cilia and of the somatic membrane (IVENS and DEITMER, 1986). Compared to untreated cells, the frequency of spontaneous back-and-forth movements, indicative for the generation of spontaneous action potentials, was reduced in the presence of 0.5 μg/ml Con A. The two-peak action potential lost its second component in the presence of Con A. In voltage-clamp experiments Con A inhibited inward current I, but not current II. The recordings in Fig. 4 show membrane currents in Ba-solution before and after the addition of Con A. Due to the different kinetics of the two currents in Ba-solution, the selective inhibition of only current I can be clearly demonstrated.

The inhibitory effect of Con A on current I was prevented by 10–30 mM α-methyl D-mannoside, indicating that the Con A effect was mediated by binding to specific sugar residues on the excitable membrane. The lectin wheat germ agglutinin (20 μg/ml) was ineffective. The succinylated dimeric derivative of Con A, which fails to produce capping in lymphocytes and fibroblasts (see NICOLSON, 1974), did not inhibit Ca current I. Thus, the two inward currents can now be chemically separated by their different sensitivity to concanavalin A (IVENS and DEITMER, 1986). The selective inhibition of only inward current I indicates that this Ca channel itself or its immediate membrane environment is different from Ca channel II in terms of Con A-specific carbohydrate residues.

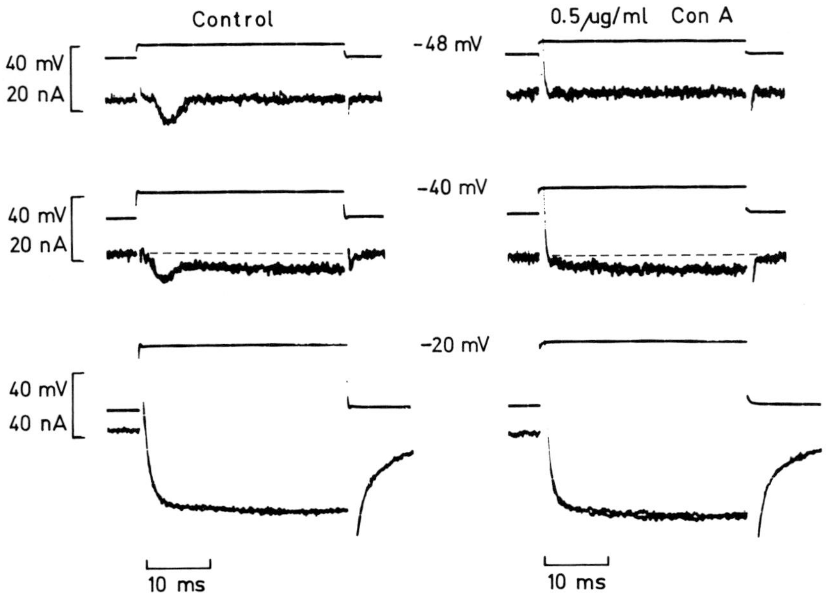

Fig. 4: Membrane inward currents in Ba solution during voltage clamp pulses from −55 mV to −48 mV, −40 mV and −20 mV in the absence (control, left) and in the presence of 0.5 µg/ml concanavalin A (right). All traces are two superimposed recordings. From Ivens and Deitmer, 1986.

Localization of the two channels

It has been known since the work of Jennings and Jamieson (1902) that hypotrichous ciliates can survive the release of their membranellar band, which often occurs under stress. The action potential recorded from a cell devoid of its membranellar band has lost its second component (Fig. 5A). The first, graded, peak of the action potential appears unaffected, thus leading to a shortening of the total action potential duration. When recording membrane currents from a cell without a membranellar band, no inward currents were elicited upon small depolarizations: Inward current I was absent (Fig. 5B). The inward current-voltage relationship revealed a single peak at −18 mV, typical for current II, but no inward current I (Fig. 5C).

From the different types of compound cilia forming functionally different motor organelles in this ciliate, the possibility of an inhomogeneous distribution of Ca channels in the membrane was further tested. For this, cells were cut transversely, or parts of the cells were removed to obtain cell fragments (Deitmer, 1984). The remaining anterior or posterior cell parts were used for intracellular recording. When the anterior third or half of a cell was removed and recorded from the intact posterior part, the first, graded, peak of the action potential remained virtually unaffected, while the second, all-or-none, peak disappeared. If, however, the posterior third or half of a cell was removed to record from an intact anterior part with its functional membranellar band, the action potential had still two peaks. In voltage clamp experiments inward current I was always absent in cells

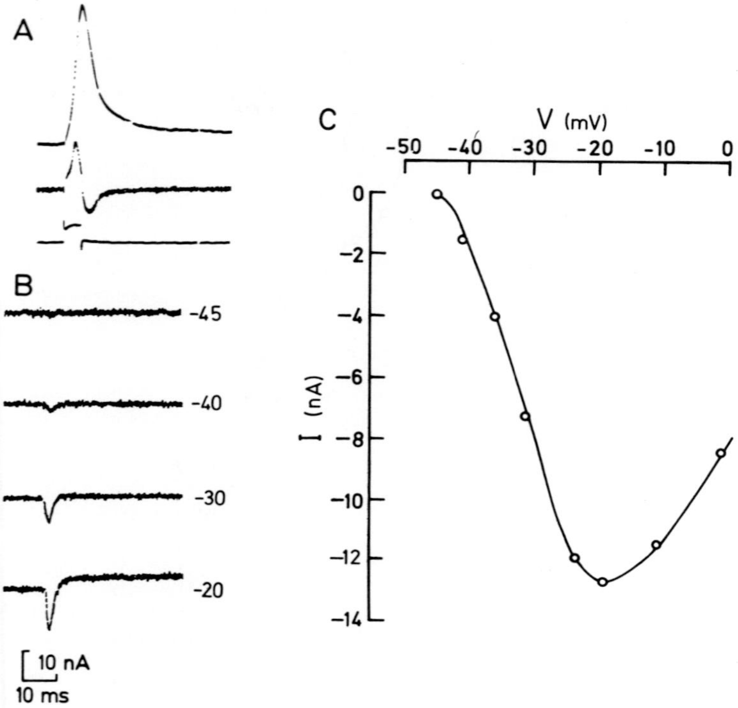

Fig. 5: Records in the standard Ca solution from a cell which had released its membranellar band. (A) Action potential (upper trace) and its first derivative (dV/dt, middle trace), elicited by a 10 ms long intracellular current pulse (lower trace). (B) Membrane inward currents of the same cell obtained during voltage-clamp steps to various potentials (indicated by figures on the right) from a holding potential of −50 mV. No inward current I could be recorded, as indicated by the absence of inward current at −45 mV. (C) The inward current-voltage relationship of this cell had only a single maximum at −18 mV, typical for current II. From Deitmer, 1984.

without the anterior part, i. e. without their membranellar band. In the inward current-voltage relationship two peaks only occurred in cells with their anterior part intact, but only the peak of current II was present in cell fragments devoid of the membranellar band (Fig. 6).

This strongly suggests that the two Ca channels reside in different parts of the cell membrane, one in the membrane of the membranelles, and the other presumably in the membrane of the cirri. This is confirmed by recording from cells prior to encystment which had resorbed all their ciliary organelles except a few cirri and single cilia. In these rounded, almost ‹deciliated› cells, a small component of Ca current II remained (< 10 %), while current I was completely absent (Deitmer, unpublished). In addition, very young cells, i. e. up to 30 min after cell division, have a relatively larger amount of current I than current II, suggesting that the membrane inward currents are coupled to the morphogenetic development of different ciliary organelles (Deitmer et al., 1985).

The presence of two types of voltage-dependent Ca channels in the membrane of *Stylonychia* is likely to be functionally significant. The low threshold and steep activation

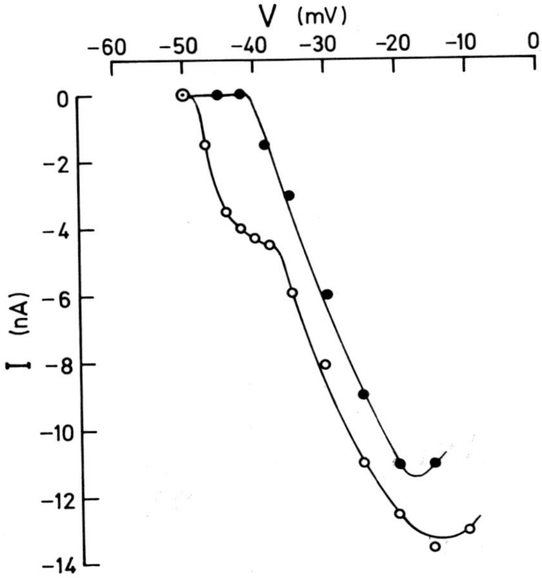

Fig. 6: The inward current-voltage relationship of an anterior cell fragment (open circles) showing the maxima of both current I and current II, and of a posterior cell fragment (filled circles) showing only the maximum of current II. From Deitmer, 1984.

of inward current I may be involved in the generation of spontaneous action potentials. Each action potential triggers a back-and-forth movement in these cells due to Ca influx into the cilia (Eckert, 1972), and is thus tightly coupled to cellular behaviour. These spontaneous movements of the cells may optimize food collection by means of a more efficient biotope screening.

This would, however, not explain the need for a localization of the two types of voltage-dependent inward currents. The distribution of the Ca channels in different parts of the membrane might also be related to the control of ciliary activity in the two types of motor organelles (Deitmer et al., 1984). It is therefore tempting to speculate that inward current I, restricted to the membranelles, is involved in controlling membranellar activity, while inward current II is related to controlling the beating activity of ventral and marginal cirri.

Conclusion

The membrane of the ciliate *Stylonychia* contains two different types of voltage-dependent calcium channels, which can be distinguished by a variety of properties (Table 1). The different localization of the two inward currents indicates that they are related to controlling different motor organelles. Hence, the existence of two voltage-dependent Ca currents may provide separate gears for independent motor control of membranelles and cirri, respectively. The two Ca channels in this unicellular organism would thus directly be related to cellular behaviour.

Table 1: Properties of the two Ca channels

	selective for	inhibited by	$V_{0.5}$ of activation	mode of inactivation	localization	% of total inward current
Channel I	Ca, Sr, Ba	Co, Mn $Cd(K_{0.5} \sim 10^{-4}M)$ Concanavalin A (0.5 μm/ml)	−47 mV (at $V_h = -50$ mV; variable with V_h)	voltage-dependent	memebranelles	20%
Channel II	Ca, Sr, Ba	Co, Mn $Cd(K_{0.5} \sim 10^{-5}M)$	−33 mV	Ca-dependent	cirri (?)	80%

Acknowledgements

The experimental work was carried out at the Ruhr-Universität Bochum and was supported by the Deutsche Forschungsgemeinschaft, SFB 114, TP A5. The receipt of a Heisenberg-Fellowship from the DFG is gratefully acknowledged.

References

Almers, W., Fink, R. and Palade, P. (1981): Calcium depletion in frog muscle tubules: the decline of calcium current under maintained depolarization. J. Physiol. **312**, 177–207.

Armstrong, C. M. and Matteson, D. R. (1985): Two distinct populations of calcium channels in a clonal line of pituitary cells. Science **227**, 65–67.

Ballanyi, K. and Deitmer, J. W. (1984): Concentration-dependent effects of Ba on action potential and membrane currents in the ciliate *Stylonychia*. Comp. Biochem. Physiol. **78A**, 575–581.

Bean, B. P. (1985): Two kinds of calcium channels in canine atrial cell. J. gen. Physiol. **86**, 1–30.

Bossu, J. L., Feltz, A. and Thomann, J. M. (1985): Depolarization elicits two distinct calcium currents in vertebrate sensory neurones. Pflügers Arch. **403**, 360–368.

Brehm, P. and Eckert, R. (1978): Calcium entry leads to inactivation of calcium channel in *Paramecium*. Science **202**, 1203–1206.

Carbone, E. and Lux, H. D. (1984a): A low voltage-activated fully inactivating Ca channel in vertebrate sensory neurones. Nature **310**, 501–502.

Carbone, E., Lux, H. D. (1984b): A low voltage-activated calcium conductance in embryonic chick sensory neurons. Biophys. J. **46**, 413–418.

Cavalié, A., Ochi, R., Pelzer, D. and Trautwein, W. (1983): Elementary currents through Ca channels in guinea pig myocytes. Pflügers Arch. **398**, 284–297.

Deitmer, J. W. (1983): Ca channels in the membrane of the hypotrich ciliate *Stylonychia*. In: The Physiology of Excitable Cells (A. D. Grinell, W. J. Moody, eds.), pp. 51–63. A. R. Liss Inc., New York.

Deitmer, J. W. (1984): Evidence for two voltage-dependent calcium currents in the membrane of the ciliate *Stylonychia*. J. Physiol. **355**, 137–159.

Deitmer, J. W. (1986): Voltage dependence of two inward currents carried by calcium and barium in the ciliate *Stylomychia mytilus*. J. Physiol. **380** (in press).

Deitmer, J. W., Ivens, I. and Pernberg, J. (1986): Changes in voltage-dependent calcium currents during the cell cycle of the ciliate *Stylonychia*. Expt. Cell Res. **162**, 549–554.

Deitmer, J. W., Machemer, H. and Martinac, B. (1983): Simultaneous recording of responses of membranelles and cirri in *Stylonychia* under membrane voltage clamp. J. Submicr. Cytol. **15**, 285–288.

Deitmer, J. W., Machemer, H. and Martinac, B. (1984): Motor control in three types of ciliary organelles in the ciliate *Stylonychia*. J. comp. Physiol. **154**, 113–120.

Eckert, R. (1972): Bioelectric control of ciliary activity. Science **176**, 473–481.

Eckert, R. and Chad, J. E. (1984): Inactivation of Ca channels. Progr. Biophys. molec. Biol. **44**, 215–267.

Fatt, P. and Ginsborg, B. L. (1958): The ionic requirements for the production of action potentials in crustacean muscle fibres. J. Physiol. **142**, 516–543.

Fatt, P. and Katz, B. (1953): The electrical properties of crustacean muscle fibres. J. Physiol. **120**, 171–204.

Fedulova, S. A., Kostyuk, P. G. and Veselovsky, N. S. (1985): Two types of calcium channels in the somatic membrane of newborn rat dorsal root ganglion neurones. J. Physiol. **359**, 431–446.

Fenwick, E. M., Marty, A. and Neher, E. (1982): Sodium and calcium channels in bovine chromaffine cells. J. Physiol. **331**, 597–635.

Fox, A. P. (1981): Voltage-dependent inactivation of a calcium channel. Proc. Natl. Acad. Sci. USA **78**, 953–956.

Fox, A. P. and Krasne, S. (1984): Two calcium currents in *Neanthes arenaceodendatus* egg cell membranes. J. Physiol. **356**, 491–505.

Fukushima, Y. and Hagiwara, S. (1983): Voltage-gated Ca channel in mouse myeloma cells. Proc. Natl. Acad. Sci. USA **80**, 2240–2242.

Grell, K. G. (1973): Protozoology, Springer Verlag, Heidelberg. pp. 1–554.

Graubard, K. and Ross, W. N. (1985): Regional distribution of calcium influx into bursting neurons detected with arsenazo III. Proc. Natl. Acad. Sci. USA **82**, 5565–5569.

Hagiwara, S. (1975): Ca-dependent action potential. In: Membranes, Vol 3 (G. Eisenman, ed.), pp. 359–381. Marcel Dekker, New York.

Hagiwara, S. (1983): Membrane Potential-Dependent Ion Channels in Cell Membrane, Raven Press, New York.

Hagiwara, S. and Byerly, L. (1981): Ca channel. Annu. Rev. Neurosci. **4**, 69–125.

Hagiwara, S., Ozawa, S. and Sand, O. (1975): Voltage clamp analysis of two inward current mechanisms in the egg cell membrane of a starfish. J. gen. Physiol. **65**, 617–644.

Hille, B. (1984): Ionic Channels of Excitable Membranes, Sinauer Assoc. Inc., Sunderland, Mass.

Hodgkin, A. L. and Huxley, A. F. (1952): Currents carried by sodium and potassium ions through the membrane of the giant axon of *Loligo*. J. Physiol. **116**, 449–472.

Ivens, I. and Deitmer, J. W. (1986): Inhibition of a voltage-dependent Ca current by concanavalin A. Pflügers Arch. **406**, 212–217.

Jahnsen, H. and Llinas, R. (1984): Ionic basis for the electroresponsiveness and oscillatory properties of guinea-pig thalamic neurones. J. Physiol. **349**, 227–247.

Jennings, H. S. and Jamieson, C. (1902): Studies on reactions to stimuli in unicellular organisms. X. The movements and actions of pieces of ciliate infusoria. Biol. Bull. **3**, 225–234.

Kostyuk, P. G. (1980): Calcium ionic channels in electrically excitable membrane. Neurosci. **5**, 945–959.

Llinas, R. and Yarom, Y. (1981): Electrophysiology of mammalian inferior olivary neurones *in vitro*. Different types of voltage-dependent ionic conductances. J. Physiol. **315**, 549–567.

Lux, H. D. and Nagy, K. (1981): Single channel Ca currents in *Helix pomatia* neurones. Pflügers Arch. **391**, 252–254.

Machemer, H. (1966): Zur Koordination und Wirkungsweise der Membranellen von *Stylonychia mytilus*. Arch. Protistenk. **109**, 257–277.

Machemer, H. and Deitmer, J. W. (1986): From structure to behaviour: *Stylonychia* as a model system for cellular physiology. Progr. Protistol. **2** (in press).

McLaughlin, S. and Harary, H. (1974): Phospholipid flip-flop and the distribution of surface charges in excitable membranes. Biophys. J. **14**, 200–208.

McLaughlin, S. G. A., Szabo, G. and Eisenman, G. (1971): Divalent ions and surface potential of charged phospholipid membranes. J. gen. Physiol. **58**, 667–687.

Meech, R. W. (1978): Calcium-dependent potassium activation in nervous tissues. Annu. Rev. Biophys. Bioeng. **7**, 1–18.

Nachshen, D. A. and Blaustein, M. P. (1982): Influx of calcium, strontium, and barium in presynaptic nerve endings. J. gen. Physiol. **79**, 1065–1087.

Nelson, M. T., French, R. J. and Krueger, B. K. (1984): Voltage-dependent calcium channels from brain incorporated into planar lipid bilayers. Nature **308**, 77–80.

Nicolson, G. L. (1974): The interactions of lectins with animal cell surfaces. Int. Rev. Cytol. **39**, 89–190.

Nilius, B., Hess, P., Lansman, J. B. and Tsien, R. W. (1985): A novel type of cardiac calcium channel in ventricular cells. Nature **316**, 443–446.

Nowycky, M. C., Fox, A. P. and Tsien, R. W. (1985): Three types of neuronal calcium channel with different calcium agonist sensitivity. Nature **316**, 440–443.

Peyer, J. E. de and Deitmer, J. W. (1980): Divalent cations as charge carriers during two functionally different membrane currents in the ciliate *Stylonychia*. J. exp. Biol. **88**, 73–89.

Peyer, J. E. de and Machemer, H. (1977): Membrane excitability in *Stylonychia*: properties of the two-peak regenerative Ca-response. J. comp. Physiol. **121**, 15–32.

Peyer, J. E. de and Machemer, H. (1978): Hyperpolarizing and depolarizing mechanoreceptor potentials in *Stylonychia*. J. comp. Physiol. **127**, 255–266.

Reuter, H. (1983): Calcium channel modulation by neurotransmitters, enzymes, and drugs. Nature **301,** 569–574.
Tsien, R. W. (1983): Calcium channels in excitable cell membranes. Annu. Rev. Physiol. **45,** 341–358.
Worley, J. F., Deitmer, J. W. and Nelson, M. T. (1986): Single nisoldipine-sensitive calcium channels from smooth muscle cells isolated from rabbit mesenteric artery. Proc. Natl. Acad. Sci. USA **83,** 5746–5750.

II. Session
Cellular control of channel incorporation and activation

Fortschritte der Zoologie, Band 33 · Lüttgau (Hrsg.): Membrane Control
Gustav Fischer Verlag · Stuttgart · New York · 1986

Xenopus oocytes as a tool for molecular cloning of the genes coding for neurotransmitter receptors and voltage-operated channels

K. Sumikawa, I. Parker and R. Miledi

Laboratory of Cellular and Molecular Neurobiology, Department of Psychobiology, University of California Irvine, Irvine, California 92717, USA

Application of the methods of molecular genetics to the nicotinic acetylcholine receptor (AChR) has given a deep insight into the structure of this multi-subunit receptor (Noda et al., 1982, 1983a, b; Devillers-Thiery et al., 1983; Claudio et al., 1982; Sumikawa et al. 1982, 1983; Mishina et al., 1984, 1985; White et al., 1985). There is every reason to suppose that these techniques will prove equally as powerful for study of the many different neurotransmitter receptors in the brain, providing that it is first possible to isolate the genes coding for the receptors.

Well established methods are available for the construction of clone libraries containing cDNA copies of mRNA (Maniatis et al., 1982). Thus, in principle, any gene coding for the neurotransmitter receptors or channels can be isolated from such a library, if a method for screening is available. Conventional techniques for cloning involve first the purification of the desired protein, and partial determination of its amino acid sequence. This is then used to prepare probes, such as antibodies or oligonucleotides, which are used to screen the libraries for their receptor or channel genes.

However, the low abundance of many neurotransmitter receptors and ion channels in the brain makes difficult the preparation of suitable probes. Instead, we are using a novel approach to screen a cDNA library for the presence of receptor or channel genes. This involves the translation of mRNA in *Xenoopus* oocytes followed by electrophysiological recording from the oocytes. *Xenopus* oocytes have been shown to be a highly efficient translation system of microinjected heterologous mRNA, and are able to faithfully execute posttranslational processes such as glycosylation, sequestration and secretion of appropriate products (Gurdon et al., 1971; Lane, 1983). Moreover, we have used this system to translate mRNAs coding for neurotransmitter receptors. For example, oocytes injected with poly$(A)^+$ mRNA extracted from *Torpedo* electric organ (the richest known source of the nicotinic AChR) efficiently assembled multi-subunit AChR which showed properties characteristic of the native AChR (Sumikawa et al., 1981). Furthermore, experiments using electrophysiological techniques revealed that the foreign receptor subunits are inserted into the oocyte's surface membrane where they form functional receptors (Barnard et al., 1982). We have also shown that the oocyte system could be used to monitor the purification of mRNA which was subsequently used to clone the gene coding for the α subunit of the AChR (Sumikawa et al. 1982; Sumikawa et al., 1983).

To see if the oocyte membrane was also able to acquire *de novo* some of the tansmitter

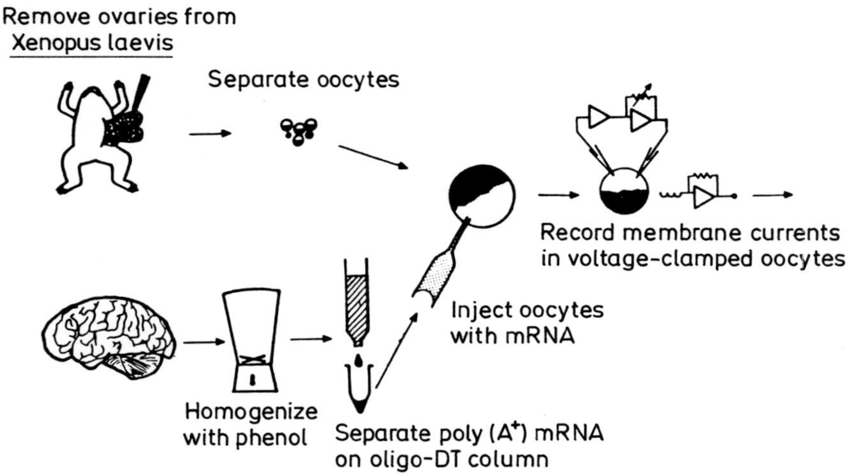

Fig. 1: Stages in the ‹transplantation› of neurotransmitter receptors into oocytes by the isolation and injection of mRNA from brain.

receptors which operate in the brain, we injected the oocytes with brain mRNA. The method used is shown diagramatically in Fig. 1. Essentially, poly $(A)^+$mRNA was extracted from the brain and injected into *Xenopus* oocytes. We, and subsequently others, found that the foreign mRNA was translated by the oocytes own protein synthesizing machinery, and that the products were correctly processed and incorporated into the oocyte membrane where they formed receptor-channel complexes that functioned like those in the cells from which the mRNA was extracted. Using this method oocytes have been induced to acquire most of the known receptors to transmitters, as well as the voltage operated channels (MILEDI et al., 1982, 1983; GUNDERSEN et al., 1983a, b, 1984a–c; SUMIKAWA et al., 1984a, b; HOUAMED et al., 1984). Thus, *Xenopus* oocytes provide us with a very sensitive and specific detector of mRNAs coding for neurotransmitter receptors and voltage operated channels and can, therefore, help us to purify these mRNAs. These can then be used for the construction of cDNA libraries as well as for screening for the genes coding for these proteins. We described here the initial step in our cloning strategy for neurotransmitter receptors and voltage operated-channels, that is the purification of mRNAs coding for these proteins.

Partial purification of mRNA coding for voltage-operated sodium and potassium channels

Xenopus oocytes that have been injected with whole poly$(A)^+$mRNA extracted from chick, rat or human brain acquire large numbers of Na^+ and K^+ channels, which are activated when the oocyte membrane is depolarized (GUNDERSEN et al., 1983b, 1984c). The content of specific mRNAs encoding voltage-operated channels can be assayed by measuring the maximal current elicited when the membrane of the poly$(A)^+$mRNA injected oocytes is depolarized. As Fig. 2 shows, the amplitude of the membrane current induced by membrane depolarization varies with the amount of mRNA injected and is

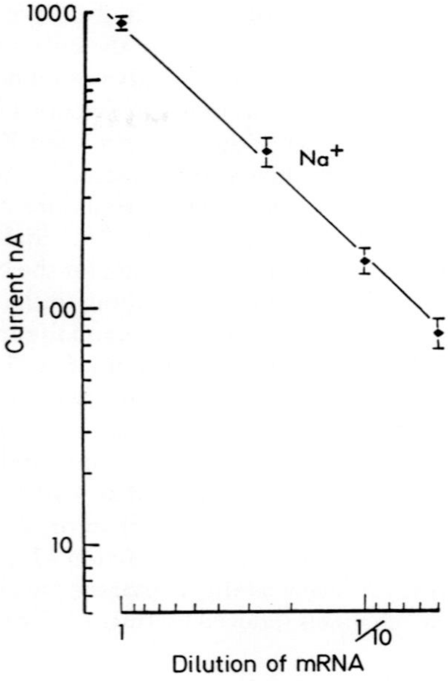

Fig. 2: Relation between amount of mRNA injected and mean size of voltage-operated sodium current, in oocytes injected with chick brain mRNA. Sizes of sodium currents were measured with depolarization to −10 mV.

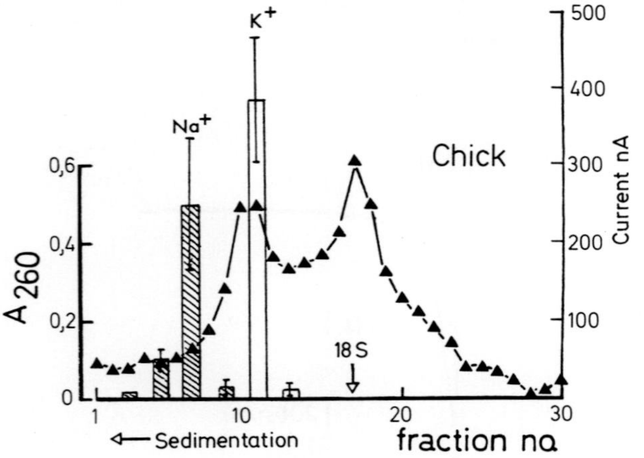

Fig. 3: Sedimentation profile of poly(A)$^+$ mRNA and profiles of voltage-activated responses induced by mRNA fractions derived from chick brain. Open columns represent the size of potassium currents induced by the corresponding fractions, shaded columns the size of sodium currents, and triangles the optical density of the messenger fractions at 260 nm.

directly proportional to the amount of mRNA injected over a large range. Thus, by translating the mRNA in the oocytes, and measuring the current elicited by membrane depolarization we can obtain a measure of the relative amount of a voltage-operated channel mRNA contained in different preparations, or fractions of mRNA.

In order to partially purify the mRNA coding for Na^+ and K^+ channels, total poly-(A)$^+$mRNA derived from chick or rat brain was fractionated by sucrose gradient centrifugation and the fractions were assayed for their ability to induce Na^+ and K^+ channels in the oocytes (Sumikawa et al., 1984a). As Fig. 3 shows, Na^+ and K^+ channels were synthesized by different mRNA fractions. The mRNA coding for the Na^+ channel sedimented much faster than that coding for the K^+ channel, resulting in the complete separation of the two mRNA species. That is, fraction 7 induced maximal numbers of Na^+ channels, while the mRNA expressing K^+ channels peaked at fraction 11. Sample currents are illustrated in Fig. 4, which shows membrane currents from two oocytes injected with either fraction 7 or fraction 11. Fraction 7 induced the appearance of the inward Na^+ current alone, which increased in size with depolarization to 0 mV and then declined at more positive potentials, being almost completely suppressed at +40 mV. Even at this potential there was no fast potassium current, indicating that fraction 7 contained no detectable amount of K^+ channel mRNA. In complete contrast, fraction 11 induced only the outward K^+ current, which increased progressively as the membrane was depolarized. At about 0 mV, at which potential the Na^+ channels induced by fraction 7 were maximally activated,

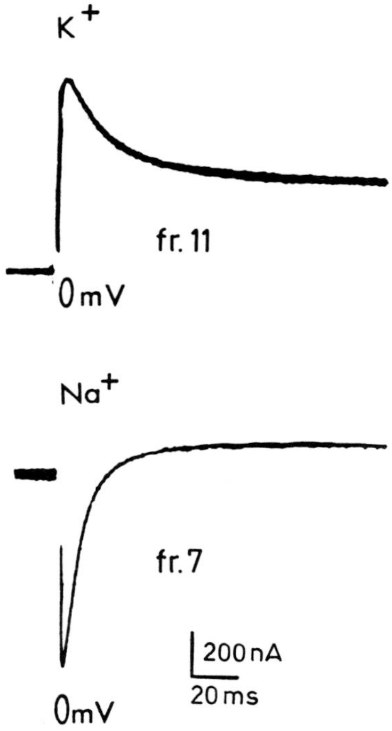

Fig. 4: Voltage-operated sodium and potassium currents recorded from two oocytes injected with fraction 11 (top) and fraction 7 (bottom) mRNA from chick brain. In this, and all other figures, downward deflexions correspond to inward membrane currents.

the oocytes injected with fraction 11 showed no inward current, suggesting that there was no detectable amount of Na^+ channel mRNA in this fraction. Different to this, oocytes injected with whole mRNA showed both the inward Na^+ and outward K^+ currents.

Partial purification of mRNA coding for the neurotransmitter receptors that are directly coupled to channels

In addition to the voltage operated channels, brain mRNA induces the oocyte membrane to acquire also functional neurotransmitter receptors. Of the several animal species tested so far, rat brain has yielded the mRNA most efficient in expressing receptors to neurotransmitters and related substances. Binding of these substances with the receptors induced by the mRNA causes membrane channels to open, and the consequent ionic current gives a measure of the number of channels opened. Furthermore, the amplitude of the current is directly proportional to the amount of mRNA injected, as illustrated for the receptor to kainate in Fig. 5.

We fractionated the rat brain mRNA by sedimentation in a sucrose gradient (Fig. 6). In order to assay the gradient fractions for the presence of neurotransmitter receptor mRNAs, these fractions were translated in the oocytes and the oocytes were examined electrophysiologically to determine the amount of functional receptors expressed. As shown in Fig. 7 and 10, the fractionated mRNAs were more potent than whole mRNA in expressing the receptors. Figures 7 and 8 show that the mRNA species coding for kainate,

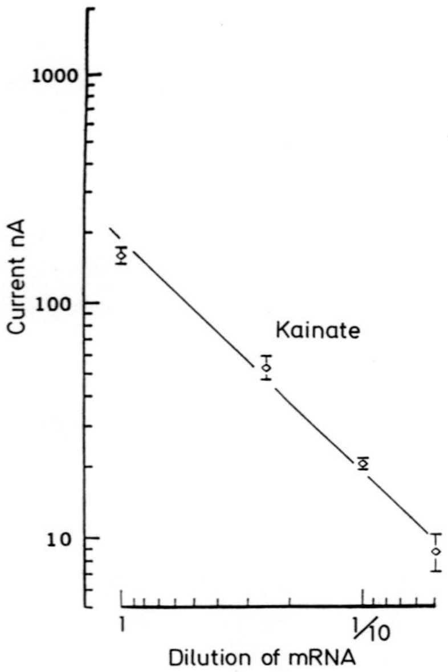

Fig. 5: Relation between amount of mRNA injected and mean size of kainate-activated currents in oocytes injected with rat brain mRNA. Responses were recorded to bath application of 10^{-4} M kainate, at a membrane potential of -60 mV.

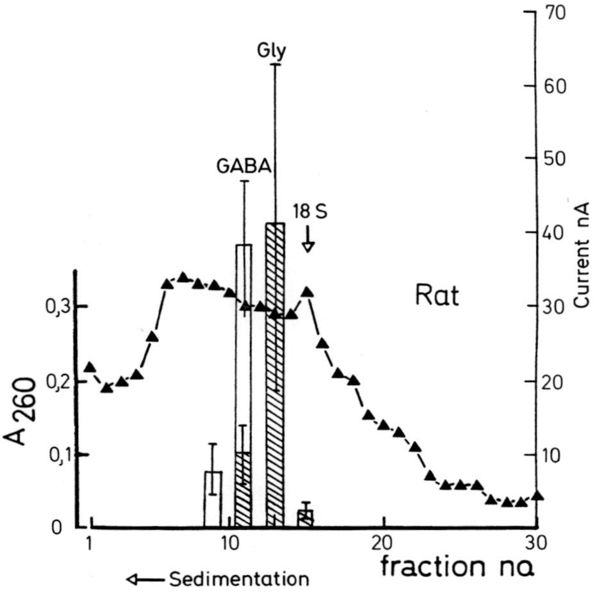

Fig. 6: Sedimentation profile at poly(A)$^+$mRNA and profiles of drug-activated responses induced by mRNA fractions derived from rat brain. Open columns represent size of GABA responses (1 mM) and shaded columns glycine responses.

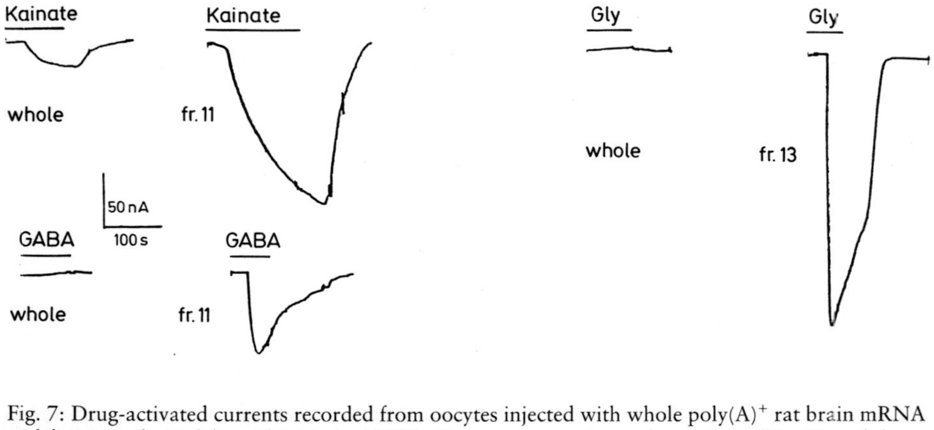

Fig. 7: Drug-activated currents recorded from oocytes injected with whole poly(A)$^+$ rat brain mRNA and fractions derived from the whole mRNA. Oocytes were voltage clamped at –60 mV, and drugs were bath applied at a concentration of 10^{-4} M kainate, and 1 mM GABA and glycine.

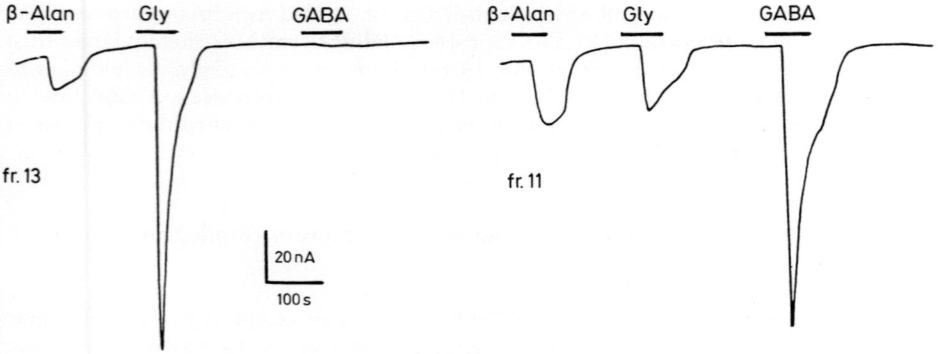

Fig. 8: Smooth chloride currents elicited by ‹inhibitory› amino acids in oocytes injected with rat brain mRNA fractions. Clamp potential was −60 mV. All drugs applied at a concentration of 1 mM.

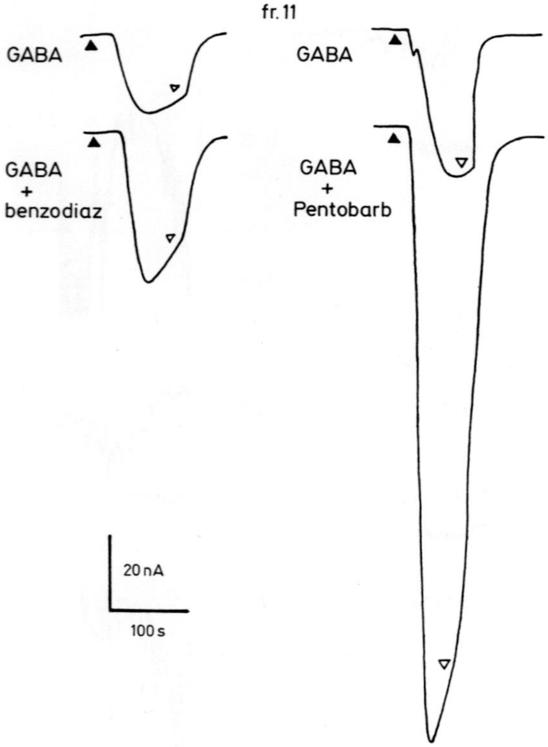

Fig. 9: Potentiation of responses to GABA by pentobarbital and flunitrazepam in an oocyte injected with rat brain mRNA fraction 11. Clamp potential was −60 mV. Drug concentrations were 10^{-5} M GABA, 10^{-4} M pentobarbital and 10^{-5} M flunitrazepam.

glycine, β-alanine or GABA, all of which elicit smooth inward membrane currents, were sedimented mainly in fractions 11 and 13, corresponding to mRNAs slightly larger than 18S rRNA. Oocytes injected with fraction 13 gave large responses to glycine and none to GABA, while oocytes injected with fraction 11 induced larger response to GABA than to glycine. The barbiturate pentobarbital and benzodiazepines potentiated the responses to GABA (Fig. 9), but not those to glycine.

Partial purification of mRNA coding for the receptors coupled to second messenger systems

The oocytes injected with total poly(A)$^+$mRNA expressed receptors to serotonin, muscarinic ACh and glutamate, all of which appear to be coupled to a second messenger system. The currents induced by these transmitters usually started after a long delay, showed oscillations and were carried largely by chloride ions. Screening of the different fractions for mRNA coding for these receptors indicated that the mRNAs coding for them are larger than 18S rRNA and here again the fractionated mRNA induced more receptors for these transmitters than the whole mRNA (Fig. 10).

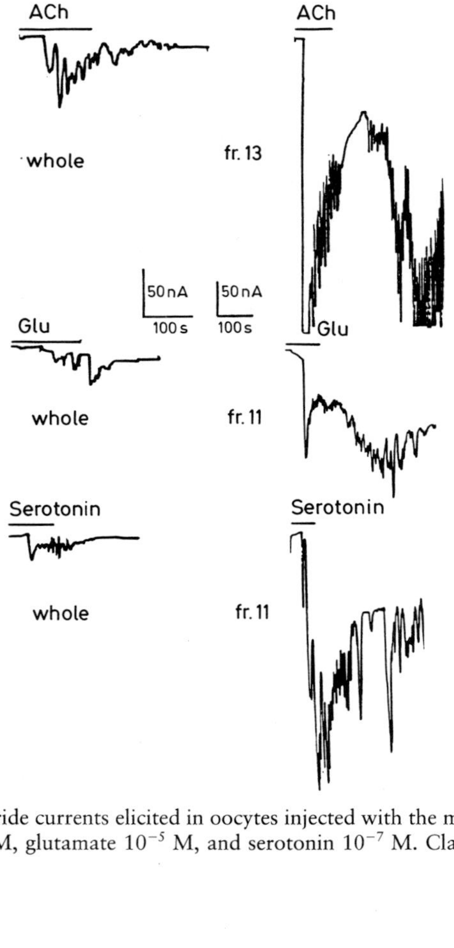

Fig. 10: Oscillatory chloride currents elicited in oocytes injected with the mRNA fractions indicated. ACh concentration 10^{-4}M, glutamate 10^{-5} M, and serotonin 10^{-7} M. Clamp potential −60 mV.

The mRNA fractions which gave maximum responses to glutamate, serotonin or ACh (muscarinic) peaked in fractions 11, 9 or 13, respectively. The mRNA coding for the glutamate receptor was sharply sedimented, while the mRNAs coding for the other receptors were widely spread among different fractions (SUMIKAWA et al., 1984a). Subsequently, we found that dopamine and norepinephrine also elicited oscillatory Cl^- currents in oocytes injected with fractions 10 or 11 (Fig. 11). Thus, the mRNA species sedimenting in fractions 9 to 13 encode receptors that function by activating a system that generates oscillatory chloride currents.

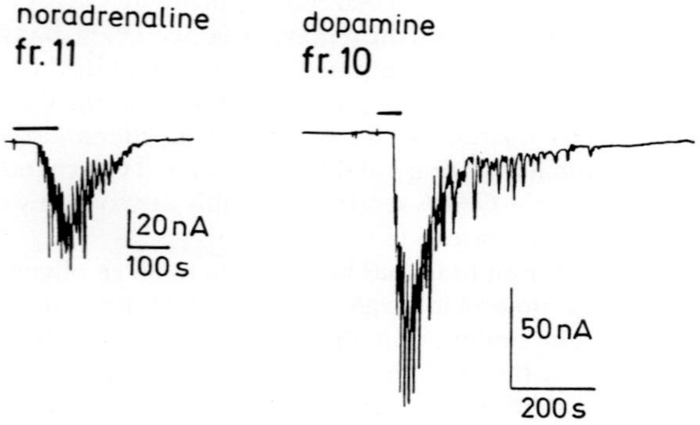

Fig. 11: Oscillatory chloride currents elicited by dopamine and noradrenaline in oocytes injected with the rat brain mRNA fractions indicated. Both agonists were bath applied at a concentration of 10^{-3} M. Clamp potential −60 mV.

Discussion

An important first step in receptor gene cloning is the partial purification of the mRNA coding for a receptor. This requires a sensitive and specific method to identify a particular mRNA fraction carrying the required mRNA. Our assay system, which involves the translation of mRNA in *Xenopus* oocytes followed by electrophysiological recording from the oocytes, requires the expression of functional receptors and channels, and this could pose considerable problems. For instance, a functional receptor could demand the expression of various protein subunits, or of a protein necessary to assemble the subunits into a functional receptor-channel complex. If these proteins were coded by messengers of very different length, then size fractionation of the mRNA could yield fractions incapable of expressing functional receptors. This was not the case, and the results obtained clearly demonstrate that fractionated mRNA is still effective in expressing many functional receptors and channels. In fact, we found that the fractionated mRNA was even more potent than total mRNA in expressing functional receptors and channels. For example, fractions 10 and 11 were capable of expressing norepinephrine and dopamine receptors, while whole mRNA hardly expressed these receptors (SUMIKAWA et al. 1984b). Moreover, expression of particular receptors or channels tended to be restricted to fractions containing messengers larger than 18S. Thus, our results suggest that the functional receptors or channels expressed are coded by a single mRNA species, or by several mRNAs of similar size.

It is interesting to note that the mRNAs coding for GABA, glycine and β-alanine receptors, all of which mediate synaptic transmission by opening Cl^- channels, sedimented in separate fractions. Fraction 13 gave responses to glycine and β-alanine but not GABA, while fraction 11 gave larger responses to GABA than to glycine, and a similar response to β-alanine. Thus, it seems very likely that GABA, β-alanine and glycine binding sites are on different proteins coded by separate mRNAs, but we still do not know whether their associated Cl^- channels are formed by the same proteins that carry the receptor sites, or by proteins coded by a separate mRNA.

It is known that barbiturates and benzodiazepines potentiate GABA mediated synaptic transmission in the central nervous system (Haefely et al., 1979; Barker et al., 1978). Since the responses to GABA in oocytes injected with rat brain mRNA fraction 11 were potentiated by barbiturates and benzodiazepines, it follows that the GABA receptor complex induced by this mRNA fraction must consist of a functional assembly, containing binding sites for GABA, modulating drugs and their associated Cl^- channels. This suggests that the proteins constituting the GABA receptor assembly are coded by one mRNA or by separate mRNAs of very similar sizes.

The Na^+ channel purified from brain has been shown to be an oligomeric protein with the largest subunit having a molecular weight of 260,000 (Hartshorne and Catterall, 1984). This agrees with our finding that the mRNA coding for Na^+ channel, which migrated near the bottom of the gradient, is the largest among the mRNAs coding for receptors and channels. In addition to the 260,000 subunit, the Na^+ channel contains two other subunits with molecular weights of 39,000 and 37,000 (Hartshorne and Catterall, 1984). It is thought that these subunits are coded by smaller mRNAs than that coding for the 260,000 subunit. Thus, it is likely the chick brain mRNA fraction 7 and rat brain mRNA fraction 5, both of which express functional Na^+ channels (Sumikawa et al. 1984), contain only large mRNAs, including that coding for the 260,000 subunit, but not mRNAs for the smaller subunits. This would suggest that only the largest subunit is required to form a functional Na^+ channel, or if one or both of the two small subunits are required, then the mRNAs coding for these subunits are usually large relative to the sizes of these proteins and are very similar in size to that for the heavy subunit.

It is interesting that most transmitters used here, except for kainate, open Cl^- channels. For instance, Cl^- channels are involved in the smooth responses to GABA, glycine and β-alanine, as well as in the slow oscillatory responses produced by ACh, serotonin, glutamate, dopamine and norepinephrine. The characteristics of the oscillatory membrane currents elicited by these different transmitters appear to be indistinguishable. However, the receptor molecules are entirely distinct, as shown by their very different pharmacological properties (Gundersen et al., 1984a), and because it was possible to partly separate the mRNAs coding for different receptors by size-sedimentation (Sumikawa et al., 1984a). Several characteristics of the oscillatory responses suggest that they are mediated by intracellular second messengers, which link receptor activation to channel opening. Furthermore, all these oscillatory responses are abolished when oocytes are injected intracellularly with the calcium chelating agent EGTA (Parker et al., 1985), suggesting that calcium may act as an intracellular second messenger in these receptor systems.

It is known that the native oocytes (not injected with mRNA) already contain a system that elicits oscillatory Cl^- currents, either spontaneously or during exposure to ACh (Kusano et al., 1982). Therefore, it could be that the mRNA injected into the oocytes merely causes the synthesis of transmitter binding proteins that link in to an already existing cascade that consists of an internal messenger system and Cl^- channels. Alternatively, it may be that the mRNAs coding for proteins that constitute the second messenger system and the Cl^- channels exist in different sizes and are sedimented in many fractions, including fractions 9 to 13, which are the ones that led to expression of receptors which trigger oscillatory Cl^- currents.

There are several ways in which one can go forward towards the cloning of receptors and channels without their prior purification. For instance, the sucrose gradient fraction that best expresses a particular receptor or channel in the oocytes will be subjected to a second fractionation procedure, and the most purified mRNA fraction will be used to construct a cDNA library. The cDNA clones can then be screened by a hybridization-selected translation method (PARNES et al., 1981), except that the mRNA hybridized to cDNA clones will be released, and then assayed by translation in the oocytes and subsequent electrophysiological recording from the oocytes. The receptor or channel cDNA clones will be identified because the mRNA released from them should induce the appearance of receptors or channels in the oocytes. If a functional receptor or channel consists of a single subunit or several identical subunits, screening should be relatively straightforward. On the other hand if the functional receptor is made by different subunits coded by mRNAs of very different sizes the screening will be more difficult, but not impossible. If oscillatory responses arise through a separate transmitter binding protein, a Cl^- channel and a second messenger system, then the oocytes may be a very good system for the study of the corresponding receptors, because the native (non-injected) oocytes already contain the Cl^- channel and the second messenger system to which the transmitter binding protein could link up, resulting in expression of functional responses to glutamate, ACh, serotonin, dopamine or norepinephrine.

References

Barnard, E. A., Miledi, R. and Sumikawa, K. (1982): Translation of exogenous messenger RNA coding for nicotinic acetylcholine receptors produces functional receptors in *Xenopus* oocytes. Proc. R. Soc. Lond. **B 215**, 241–246.

Barker, J. L. and Ransom, B. R. (1978b): Pentobarbitone pharmacology of mammalian central neurones grown in tissue culture. J. Physiol. **280**, 355–372.

Claudio, T., Ballivet, M., Patrick, J. and Heinemann, S. (1983): Nucleotide and deduced amino acid sequences of *Torpedo californica* acetylcholine receptor γ subunit. Proc. Natl. Acad. Sci. **80**, 1111–1115.

Devillers-Thiery, A., Giraudat, J., Bentaboulet, M. and Changeux, J. P. (1983): Complete mRNA coding sequence of the acetylcholine binding α subunit of *Torpedo marmorata* acetylcholine receptor: A model for the transmembrane organization of the polypeptide chain. Proc. Natl. Acad. Sci. **80**, 2067–2071.

Gundersen, C. B., Miledi, R. and Parker, I. (1983a): Serotonin receptors induced by exogenous messenger RNA in *Xenopus* oocytes. Proc. R. Soc. Lond. **B 219**, 103–109.

Gundersen, C. B., Miledi, R. and Parker, I. (1983b): Voltage-operated channels induced by foreign messenger RNA in *Xenopus* oocytes. Proc. R. Soc. Lond. **B 220**, 131–140.

Gundersen, C. B., Miledi, R. and Parker, I. (1984a): Glutamate and kainate receptors induced by rat brain messenger RNA in *Xenopus* oocytes. Proc. R. Soc. Lond. **B 221**, 127–143.

Gundersen, C. B., Miledi, R. and Parker, I. (1984b): Properties of human brain glycine receptors expressed in *Xenopus* oocytes. Proc. R. Soc. Lond. **B 221**, 235–244.

Gundersen, C. B., Miledi, R. and Parker, I. (1984c): Messenger RNA from human brain induces drug- and voltage-activated channels in *Xenopus* oocytes. Nature **308**, 421–424.

Gurdon, J. B., Lane, C. D., Woodland, H. R. and Marbaix, G. (1971): Use of frog eggs and oocytes for the study of messenger RNA and its translation in living cells. Nature 233, 177–182.

Haefely, W., Polc, P., Schaffner, R., Keller, H. H., Pieri, L. and Moehler, H. (1979): Facilitation of GABAergic transmission by drugs. In: GABA-Neurotransmitters. eds., Krogsgaard-Larsen, P., Schell-Krueger, J. and Kofod, H. New York: Academic Press. pp. 357–375.

Hartshorne, R. P. and Catterall, W. A. (1984): The sodium channel from rat brain. J. Biol. Chem. **259**, 1667–1675.

Houamed, K. M., Bilbe, G., Smart, T. G., Constanti, A., Brown, D. A., Barnard, E. A. and Richards, B. M. (1984): Functional expression of GABA, glycine and glutamate receptors in *Xenopus* oocytes by injection of rat brain mRNA. Nature **310**, 318–321.

Kusano, K., Miledi, R. and Stinnakre, J. (1982): Cholinergic and catecholaminergic receptors in the *Xenopus* oocyte membrane. J. Physiol. **328**, 143–170.

Lane, C. D. (1983): The fate of genes, messengers and proteins introduced into *Xenopus* oocyte. Curr. Top. in Devel. Biol. **18**, 89–116.

Maniatis, T., Fritsch, E. F. and Sambrook, J. (1982): Molecular cloning: A laboratory manual. Cold Spring Harbor Laboratory.

Miledi, R., Parker, I. and Sumikawa, K. (1982): Synthesis of chick brain GABA receptors by frog oocytes. Proc. R. Soc. Lond. **B 216**, 509–515.

Miledi, R., Parker, I. and Sumikawa, K. (1983): Recording of single γ-amino butyric acid and acetylcholine-activated receptor channels translated by exogenous messenger RNA in *Xenopus* oocytes. Proc. R. Soc. Lond. **B 218**, 481–484.

Mishina, M., Tobimatsu, T., Imoto, K., Tanaka, K., Fujita, Y., Fukuda, K., Kurasaki, M., Takahashi, H., Morimoto, Y., Hirose, T., Inayama, S., Takahashi, T., Kuno, M. and Numa, S. (1985): Location of functional regions of acetylcholine receptor α-subunit by site-directed mutagenesis. Nature **313**, 364–369.

Mishina, M., Kurosaki, T., Tobimatsu, T., Morimoto, Y., Noda, M., Yamamoto, T., Terao, M., Lindstrom, J., Takahashi, T., Kuno, M. and Numa, S. (1984): Expression of functional acetylcholine receptor from cloned cDNAs. Nature **307**, 604–608.

Noda, M., Takahashi, H., Tanabe, T., Toyosato, M., Furutani, Y., Hirose, T., Asai, M., Inayama, S., Miyata, T. and Numa, S. (1982): Primary structure of α-subunit precursor of *Torpedo californica* acetylcholine receptor deduced from cDNA sequence. Nature **299**, 793–797.

Noda, M., Takahashi, H., Tanabe, T., Toyosato, M., Kikyotani, S., Hirose, T., Asai, M., Takashima, H., Inayama, S., Miyata, T. and Numa, S. (1983a): Primary structures of β- and δ-subunit precursors of *Torpedo californica* acetylcholine receptor deduced from cDNA sequences. Nature **301**, 251.

Noda, M., Takahashi, H., Tanabe, T., Toyosato, M., Kikyotani, S., Furutani, Y., Hirose, T., Takashima, H., Inayama, S., Miyata, T. and Numa, S. (1983b): Structural homology of *Torpedo californica* acetylcholine receptor subunits. Nature **302**, 528–532.

Parker, I., Gundersen, C. B. and Miledi, R. (1985): Intracellular Ca^{2+}-dependent and Ca^{2+}-independent responses of rat brain serotonin receptors transplanted to *Xenopus* oocytes. Neurosci. Res. **2**, 491–496.

Parnes, J. R., Velan, B., Felsenfeld, A., Ramanathan, L., Ferrini, U., Appella, E. and Seidman, J. G. (1981): Mouse β_2-microglobulin cDNA clones: A screening procedure for cDNA clones corresponding to rare mRNAs. Proc. Natl. Acad. Sci. USA **78**, 2253–2257.

Sumikawa, K., Houghton, M., Emtage, J. S., Richards, B. M. and Barnard, E. A. (1981): Active multi-subunit ACh receptor assembled by translation of heterologous mRNA in *Xenopus* oocytes. Nature **92**, 862–864.

Sumikawa, K., Houghton, M., Smith, J. D., Bell, L., Richards, B. M. and Barnard, E. A. (1982): The molecular cloning and characterization of cDNA coding for the α subunit of the acetylcholine receptor. Nucleic Acids Res. **10**, 5809–5822.

Sumikawa, K., Miledi, R., Houghton, M. and Barnard, E. A. (1983): A study of the mRNA and genes coding for the nicotinic acetylcholine receptor. In: Cell Surface Receptors. Ed. Strange, P. G. Ellis Horwood:Chichester, England pp. 249–269.

Sumikawa, K., Parker, I. and Miledi, R. (1984a): Partial purification and functional expression of brain mRNAs coding for neurotransmitter receptors and voltage-operated channels. Proc. Natl. Acad. Sci. **81**, 7994–7998.

Sumikawa, K., Parker, I. and Miledi, R. (1984b): Messenger RNA from rat brain induces noradrenaline and dopamine receptors in *Xenopus* oocytes. Proc. Roy. Soc. **B 223**, 235–260.

Sumikawa, K., Parker, I. and Miledi, R. (1984c): Separate fractions of mRNA from *Torpedo* electric organ induce chloride channels and acetylcholine receptors in *Xenopus* oocytes. EMBO Journal **3**, 2291–2294.

White, M. M., Mayne, K. M., Lester, H. A. and Davidson, N. (1985): Mouse-*Torpedo* hybrid acetylcholine receptors: Functional homology does not equal sequence homology. Proc. Natl. Acad. Sci. USA **82**, 4852–4856.

Fortschritte der Zoologie, Band 33 · Lüttgau (Hrsg.): Membrane Control
Gustav Fischer Verlag · Stuttgart · New York · 1986

Ion channels and signal transmission

C. METHFESSEL and B. SAKMANN

Max-Planck-Institut für biophysikalische Chemie, Göttingen, FRG

An important function of biological membranes is to divide the organism into numerous individual cells. Cell membranes allow the differentiation of cells with various functions and thus the organisation of structures. On the other hand, membranes are a barrier to the continuous exchange of signals between different cells that is essential for the coordinated activity of the organism. This problem is solved by transport proteins, which are embedded in biological membranes. When turned on by a specific signal, these specialized proteins make the membrane permeable for ions and so mediate the flow of information across the cell membrane. The signal actually transversing the membrane can either be the flow of ions itself or the change of the electrical membrane potential that is caused by it. A change of membrane potential that is effected by an ion flow is also a basic mechanism for the distribution of signals within a cell, for example along a nerve axon or a muscle fibre.

Two mechanisms are conceivable for the transport of ions across a cell membrane. In a «carrier» scheme, a mobile hydrophobic protein within the membrane binds individual ions and shuttles them across the membrane. In a «channel» scheme, on the other hand, a larger protein molecule that is fixed in the membrane forms a small pore that passes through the membrane and has a hydrophilic lining. This channel then allows ions to diffuse across the membrane according to its selectivity and the electrochemical gradient for the various ion species. Over the last two decades it has become clear that, at least for rapid signaling such as in nervous systems, ion channels are the predominant mechanism.

Ion channels are not restricted to excitable cells like nerve and muscle cells however. They occur in the plasma membranes of virtually all kinds of cells investigated to date. Ion channels were found in the membranes of exo- and endocrine secretory cells, macrophages, lymphocytes, or the cells of parenchymal organs, and it is to be expected that there they also have signalling functions.

Voltage- and transmitter-gated channels

The most familiar ion channels are the electrically gated sodium and potassium selective channels of nerve fibres, first described by HODGKIN and HUXLEY (1952). These channels are responsible for the transmission of action potentials along the nerve fibre and insure that nerve fibres can transmit information quickly and reliably over distances that can exceed 1 m. At the nerve endings, specialized contacts, called synapses, mediate the transfer of signals between two or more cells. The elements of a synapse are the presynaptic membrane of the transmitting cell and the postsynaptic membrane of the receiving cell. At the presynaptic membrane of the transmitting cell, voltage-dependent calcium-selective channels induce the release of a chemical transmitter substance that diffuses to the membrane of the receiving cell. There, the transmitter can lead to a number of effects depending both on the nature of the transmitter substance and on the type of synapse. In every case, however, the transmitter is first bound by extracellular receptors in the postsynaptic membrane. These receptors then control the transport of ions through the postsynaptic membrane by turning ion channels, called «receptor channels», on or off. Depending on the specific kinds of ions involved this can excite or inhibit the receiving cell.

It should be pointed out that the distinction between voltage- and transmitter-gated channels is by no means rigorous. Voltage gated channels are frequently found to be modulated by transmitters, and the gating of most receptor channels is affected by the membrane potential. Different kinds of ion channels are selective for particular ions, such as calcium, potassium, sodium or chloride. Each kind of neuron has a specific set of membrane ion channels that are activated by changes in the electrical membrane potential or by chemical transmitters. Thus, the excitation of a neuron depends sensitively on the interaction of numerous different kinds of ion channels (ECCLES, 1957).

The endplate current

The best-studied example of transmitter-mediated signal transmission between cells is the synapse of the neuromuscular endplate, which is the switching point between a motor neuron and the muscle it innervates (fig. 1a). The mechanism of release of the transmitter substance acetylcholine has largely been clarified through the work of KATZ and MILEDI (KATZ, 1969). From the innervating motor neuron, acetylcholine is released in quantum packets of rather uniform size (fig. 1b). Secretion of one such packet, which contains between 2000 and 5000 molecules of acetylcholine, induces a current flow of 2–4 nA on the postsynaptic side. This miniature endplate current (fig. 1c) is the elementary unit of synaptic transmission. The excitatory endplate signal results from the superposition of 200 to 300 of such quanta. The endplate current has been studied intensively, and many of the properties of membrane ion channels were first discovered with it.

As late as 1970 it was unclear whether ion transport in biological membranes is by a carrier or channel mechanism. Then, by introducing the method of noise analysis of membrane current fluctuations, KATZ and MILEDI (1972) were able to show that the endplate current arises from the superposition of many elementary current pulses of a few milliseconds duration. The size of the elementary current pulses could be estimated and was found to be in the range of 2 pA. Thus, at least a thousand elementary current pulses must be superimposed to obtain a miniature endplate current (fig. 1c). The elementary ion current corresponds to a transport rate of about 10^7 monovalent ions per second. From studies on artificial membranes it was known, however, that carriers cannot transport more than about 10^5 ions per second. Therefore, only a channel mechanism was consistent with the experimental results.

The elementary current

The direct measurement of the elementary current passing through a single ion channel was made possible by the patch clamp technique (NEHER and SAKMANN, 1976; HAMILL et

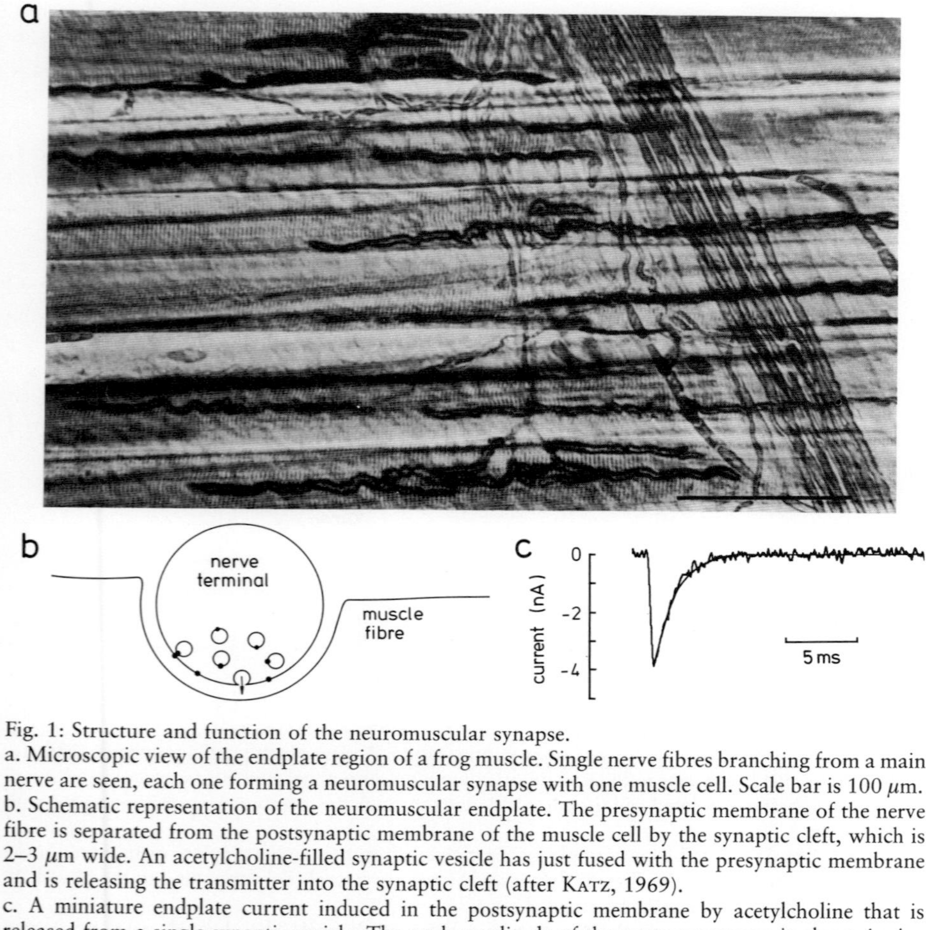

Fig. 1: Structure and function of the neuromuscular synapse.
a. Microscopic view of the endplate region of a frog muscle. Single nerve fibres branching from a main nerve are seen, each one forming a neuromuscular synapse with one muscle cell. Scale bar is 100 μm.
b. Schematic representation of the neuromuscular endplate. The presynaptic membrane of the nerve fibre is separated from the postsynaptic membrane of the muscle cell by the synaptic cleft, which is 2–3 μm wide. An acetylcholine-filled synaptic vesicle has just fused with the presynaptic membrane and is releasing the transmitter into the synaptic cleft (after KATZ, 1969).
c. A miniature endplate current induced in the postsynaptic membrane by acetylcholine that is released from a single synaptic vesicle. The peak amplitude of the current response is about 4 nA.

al., 1981). The measurement of current is limited to a minute «patch» of membrane, with an area of only about 10 μm^2. This is accomplished by pressing a glass pipette with a smooth rim against the membrane (fig. 2a). The pipette opening has a diameter of 1–2 μm. The pipette is filled with extracellular solution and contains in addition a small amount of acetylcholine. This measuring configuration allows the resolution of membrane currents that are smaller than one picoampere. Fig. 2b shows a current record from such a patch clamp experiment on the endplate region of a skeletal muscle fibre. In the presence of acetylcholine, the current switches at random from a low resting value to a well-defined higher level. When the current is at its resting or zero value, all ion channels within the membrane area under investigation are closed. Each downward current step represents the turn-on, and each upward current step the turn-off, of a single ion channel current. Since it is an inward current, the turn-on is shown downwards. The actual transition between the two states is very rapid and takes less than 10 μs. The amplitude of successive current steps

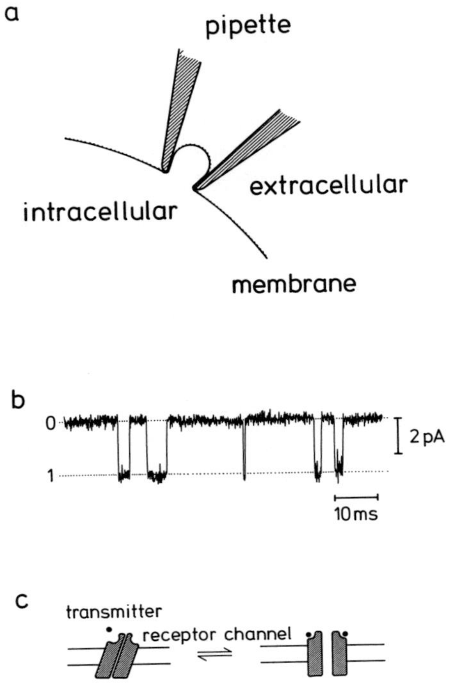

Fig. 2: Recording of single channel currents from the neuromuscular endplate.
a. Schematic representation of the recording configuration. A glass pipette with an opening diameter of 1–2 μm is filled with extracellular solution containing a small amount of acetylcholine. A small patch of membrane is isolated and the current flowing through the membrane patch is measured with an amplifier.
b. Current signal recorded from a single receptor channel in the muscle endplate membrane. In the presence of acetylcholine, the current fluctuates between two levels corresponding to the closed (0) and open (1) states of the receptor channel.
c. Schematic representation of the function of a receptor channel. The channel opens when two transmitter molecules are bound to the receptor but remains closed otherwise.

is constant, which shows that the channel has only two conductance states, open and closed. The duration of the individual openings, however, varies around a mean value of a few milliseconds. This is most simply interpreted if the channel has one or more binding sites for acetylcholine. When the binding sites are not occupied, the channel is closed. However, if acetylcholine occupies the binding sites, the channel opens (fig. 2c). The random opening of the channel therefore reflects the statistics of binding of acetylcholine to its receptor and the subsequent channel-opening reaction. As long as the channel is open, ions can pass through it driven by their electrochemical gradient across the membrane, and the size of the current indicates the average number of ions passing through in a given time interval.

Quite similar step-wise current events are seen in the membranes of other cells whenever the ion channels present are activated according to their specific mechanisms. Fig. 3 shows three examples. In fig. 3a, single channel currents through sodium and potassium selective channels in a pituitary cell are seen. Fig. 3b shows currents through a chloride selective channel that is activated in spinal neurones by GABA, a transmitter of inhibitory synapses in the central nervous system. This channel is gated in a very similar way as the acetylcholine channel from the endplate. It is closed in the absence of GABA and switches randomly between the open and closed states if GABA is present. Finally, fig. 3c shows the current through a potassium selective channel in a pituitary cell. On the cytoplasmic side of the membrane this channel has a binding site for calcium, and its switching pattern is regulated by the cytoplasmic calcium concentration as well as the membrane potential.

In summary, it has become clear that most of the currents that flow through biological membranes arise from the superposition of many elementary current pulses that can be measured in picoamperes. The durations of such elementary currents range from less than one millisecond to hundreds of milliseconds. The current through a single channel is characterized by a well defined amplitude and by the statistial distribution of current pulse durations. Therefore, the mechanism of ion transport through such channels can be studied by measuring the single channel current amplitude under various conditions of membrane potential and with different species and concentrations of transported ions. On the other hand, the mean duration of the current pulses, and the mean interval between

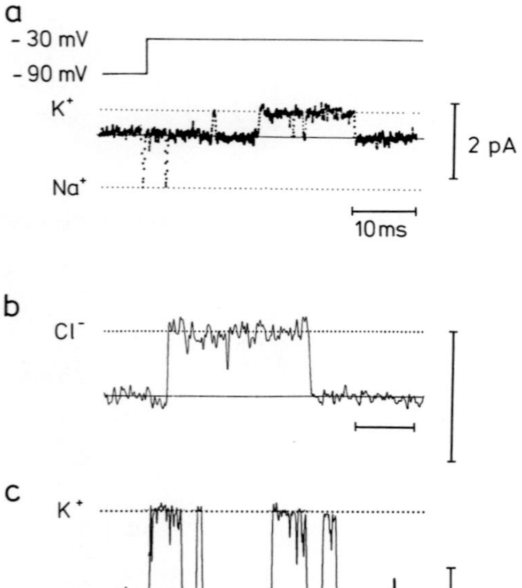

Fig. 3: Examples of single channel currents from various cell types.
a. Voltage-activated channels in a membrane patch from a rat pituitary cell. Following a depolarizing voltage step from −90 mV to −30 mV, inward sodium currents are activated first (downward deflections), followed by the delayed activation of outward potassium currents (upward deflections).
b. Single channel current record from a mouse spinal neuron. The outward (upward) current step is due to the turning-on of a chloride selective ion channel activated by the transmitter GABA.
c. Patch current record from a rat hippocampal neuron showing outward currents flowing through a calcium dependent potassium channel whose activity is controlled by the intracellular level of free calcium. The scale bars in each case represent 2 pA and 10 ms.

them, can give clues about the kinetics of the reactions controlling the switching of the channel. A statistical analysis of open and closed time intervals can reveal the kinetics of a single macromolecule.

Gating of ion channels

The succession of single channel openings and closings over a longer period of time can be analyzed with statistical methods. This allows detailed conclusions to be drawn about the reaction mechanism that controls the opening and closing of the channel (COLQUHOUN and HAWKES, 1977). It can be determined how many different open and closed configurations the channel can enter, what the average probability of occurrence is for these states, and what the rates of transitions between the states are. The simplest example, of course, is a channel that has only two states, of which one is closed and one is open. As the channel fluctuates between the two states, a sequence of current pulses («open») of variable duration and separated by irregular intervals («closed») will result. A short piece of such a fluctuation is shown in fig. 4a. From the measured distributions of open and closed interval durations, the probabilities of the open and closed states can be determined

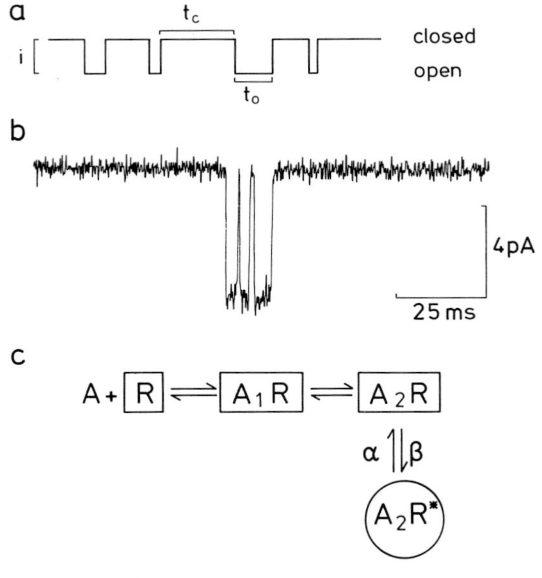

Fig. 4: Kinetic analysis of single channel current records.
a. The current flowing through a simple two-state channel switches randomly between two values that correspond to the open and closed channel states. The dwell times in the open state (t_o) and in the closed state (t_c) can be measured and a statistical analysis performed on them.
b. At high time resolution, the current flowing through a single endplate channel is seen to consist of a burst of several brief current pulses.
c. Reaction scheme describing the gating of single endplate channels. Closed states are shown by rectangles, the open state is shown by a circle. R = receptor, A = agonist. The channel can open after binding two acetylcholine molecules.

as well as the rates of the opening and closing reactions. However, the behavior of most biological ion channels is more complex, as they can enter a number of different open and closed states. This can be concluded from the distributions of open and closed durations that can only be fitted with two or more exponential functions. Again, the endplate channel can be used as an example (fig. 4b). At high time resolution, the single channel current is seen to be interrupted repeatedly for just a few hundreds of microseconds. These brief gaps can be attributed to statistical fluctuations from the open channel state A_2R^* into the short-lived closed state A_2R that occur within one episode of agonist binding to the channel (Fig. 4c). The much longer closed intervals, of many milliseconds, separating individual current pulses correspond to states of the channel molecule where only one acetylcholine molecule, or none at all, is bound (the states A_1R and R in the scheme of fig. 4c). Only a few simple assumptions are necessary to estimate the reaction rates, a and b, as well as the dissociation rate of acetylcholine from the channel from the duration and frequency of the short gaps (Colquhoun and Sakmann, 1985). Such calculations indicate that the endplate channel is turned on very rapidly, within a few microseconds, following the binding of two acetylcholine molecules. The opening rate is thus far greater than the closing rate. The probability of finding the channel in its open state is very high, about 95 %, whenever both acetylcholine binding sites are occupied. This is the case in normal neuromuscular transmission where the transient concentration of acetylcholine in the synaptic cleft can reach 1–3 μM, or ten times the binding constant of acetylcholine to the receptor. Thus, acetylcholine and its receptor channel together represent a highly effective switch.

Additional information can be obtained from a more detailed examination that reveals additional fine structure of the single-channel current pulses. When single channel ion currents are measured at high time resolution, the time course of the elementary current pulses is sometimes found to deviate from the ideal square-pulse shape. For example, endplate channels occasionally exhibit brief interruptions of the channel current that do not correspond to a complete closing of the channel. Instead, the current takes on a low intermediate value. Such «sublevels» suggest that one channel may have several different open, conducting states, some of which correspond to partial openings (Hamill and Sakmann, 1981). A different observation is that the current noise, or the fluctuation of the membrane current around its mean value, is greater when the channel is open than before the opening event. The additional current fluctuations have a characteristic time of the order of a few hundred microseconds and may indicate that the open channel does not have a completely rigid structure (Sigworth, 1985). Recently, detailed studies at high time resolution have revealed additional features about the gating of acetylcholine receptor channels (Colquhoun and Sakmann, 1985).

Structure of ion channels

It is now clear that specialized transport proteins embedded in the cell membrane are responsible for receptor functions and ion transport. The biochemical and biophysical structure and behavior of some of the proteins that constitute ion channels have been studied very extensively for many years. Ion channel proteins, like other membrane proteins, are amphiphilic so that they can be stably incorporated into the lipid bilayer of the cell membrane. They can be extracted from their native membrane by treatment with suitable detergents and separated from other proteins by their specific properties (Changeux, 1981). For example, acetylcholine receptor channels are separated by binding to α-bungarotoxin, and sodium channels can be purified by affinity chromatography using tetrodotoxin or saxitoxin. In general, such studies are difficult because ion channels make up only a very small proportion of the total protein content of a tissue and because the complex, amphiphilic channel proteins are delicate and require special, careful handling.

The best studied ion channel is the acetylcholine receptor channel (AChR) from the electric organ of certain species of fish, such as *Electrophorus* or *Torpedo* (CHANGEUX, 1981). In these organs, the AChR channel occurs at a very high concentration so that enough material for biochemical and biophysical studies can be obtained more easily than from other tissues, such as nerve or muscle tissues, where the ion channels make up only a very small fraction of the total protein content. The rather complicated supramolecular structure of the acetylcholine receptor has been clarified mostly by biochemical and electron microscopic techniques. The receptor-channel complex consists of five protein subunits of comparable molecular weight (between 40 and 60 kD), all of which pass through the membrane (KARLIN et al., 1983). There are four different types of subunit called the alpha, beta, gamma, and delta subunit, respectively. In the pentameric receptor-channel complex, each subunit occurs only once except for the alpha subunit which occurs twice and is assumed to carry the acetylcholine binding site (ZINGSHEIM et al., 1982). The primary structure of the protein subunits has been elucidated with the techniques of molecular biology by the cloning and sequencing of complementary DNA. Each subunit consists of about 500 amino acid residues. The sequences of the subunits show a high degree of homology, and each subunit contains 4–5 α-helical segments that are just long enough to span the membrane (NODA et al., 1983). It can be assumed that each subunit contributes one α-helix to form the lining of the ion channel, in a manner similar to the staves of a barrel. This would be consistent with electron microscopic results that suggest a receptor channel-complex as shown in fig. 5, with a hole passing through the center of a rosette (KISTLER et al., 1982).

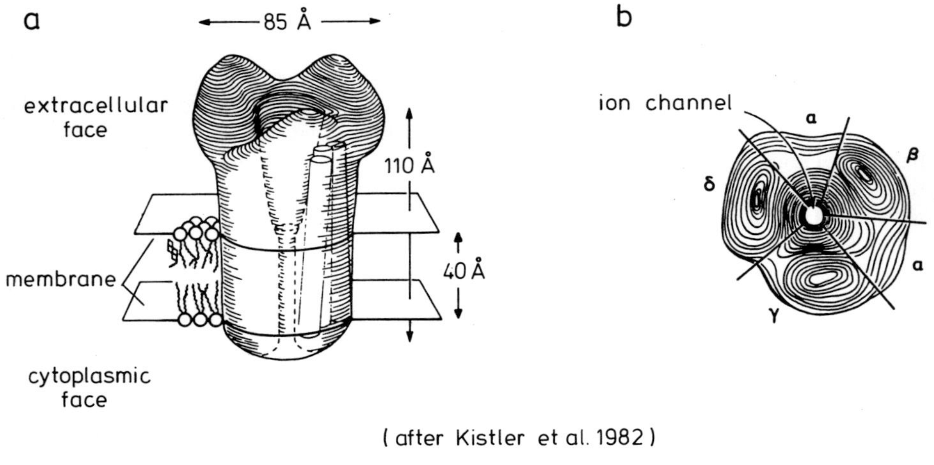

Fig. 5: Schematic representation of the acetylcholine receptor channel according to KISTLER et al. (1982).
a. Side view of the receptor-channel complex embedded in the membrane.
b. View from the extracellular side of the membrane.

Relation between structure and function of ion channels

For many years, an important goal in the study of ion channels has been to understand how the structure of ion channels determines their function. One approach has been to biochemically purify and characterize ion channels and then to reconstitute them into artificial lipid bilayer systems. For several ion channels, it has been shown that the purified protein, when reconstituted into lipid vesicles, will again control the flow of ions in the specific way (CHANGEUX, 1981), and techniques have been developed for single-channel current recording from receptors that have been reconstituted into planar lipid bilayers (MONTAL et al., 1981, BOHEIM et al., 1981).

A different approach to the study of structure and function of ion channels was opened by the use of *Xenopus* oocytes as host cells for the implantation of ion channels from other tissues by the injection of messenger RNA that codes for ion channels. Heterologous messenger RNA is translated into proteins with high efficiency when it is microinjected into immature oocytes of the clawed toad *Xenopus laevis* (GURDON et al., 1971). Moreover, the resulting protein products in general are found to be correctly processed by the oocyte including glycosylation, assembly of subunits and, in the case of membrane proteins, insertion into the cell membrane. As proteins, ion channels are synthesized by the translation of messenger RNA that codes for their specific amino-acid sequence. Therefore, it should be possible to implant ion channels into the oocyte membrane by supplying the oocyte with appropriate messenger RNA. SUMIKAWA, BARNARD, MILEDI and their coworkers have first demonstrated that this approach, which is illustrated in fig. 6, is

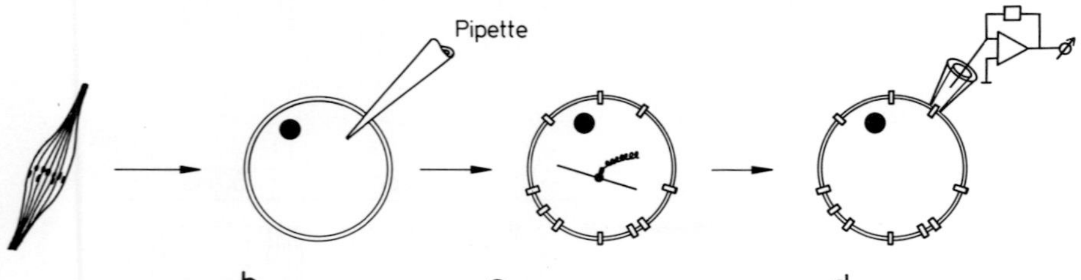

Fig. 6: The implantation of ion channels into frog oocytes for electrophysiological studies.

feasible (SUMIKAWA et al., 1981, BARNARD et al., 1982). Messenger RNA is extracted from cells that are actively synthesizing ion channels, such as growing nerve or muscle cells. The polyadenylated messenger RNA is separated by chromatography on an oligo-d(T) column and injected into *Xenopus* oocytes with a micropipette. A few days later, the cells are assayed for the presence of ion channels. In many cases, the oocytes exhibit a high activity of ion channels of the kinds normally found in the tissue from which the mRNA was taken. A wide variety of different ion channels was found to be implanted successfully into oocytes by this method (GUNDERSEN et al., 1984).

The efficiency of ion channel synthesis is increased by the use of channel-specific mRNA. Using cloned cDNA templates in conjunction with the SP6 promoter and bacteriophage SP6 RNA-polymerase as an *in vitro* translation system, large amounts of specific messenger RNA coding for only one precisely defined protein can be obtained. This has been achieved for the acetylcholine receptor channels from both *Torpedo californica* electric organ and calf muscle (MISHINA et al., 1985). When such specific mRNA is injected into oocytes, the corresponding protein is synthesized at a high rate. For ion channels, such as the acetylcholine receptor, this leads to a very high density of receptor channels in the oocyte membrane. Such oocytes are extremely sensitive to cholinergic agonists, and it is easy to study the transport and gating behavior of the channels in detail with high resolution patch clamp recordings. Fig. 7 shows patch clamp current recordings

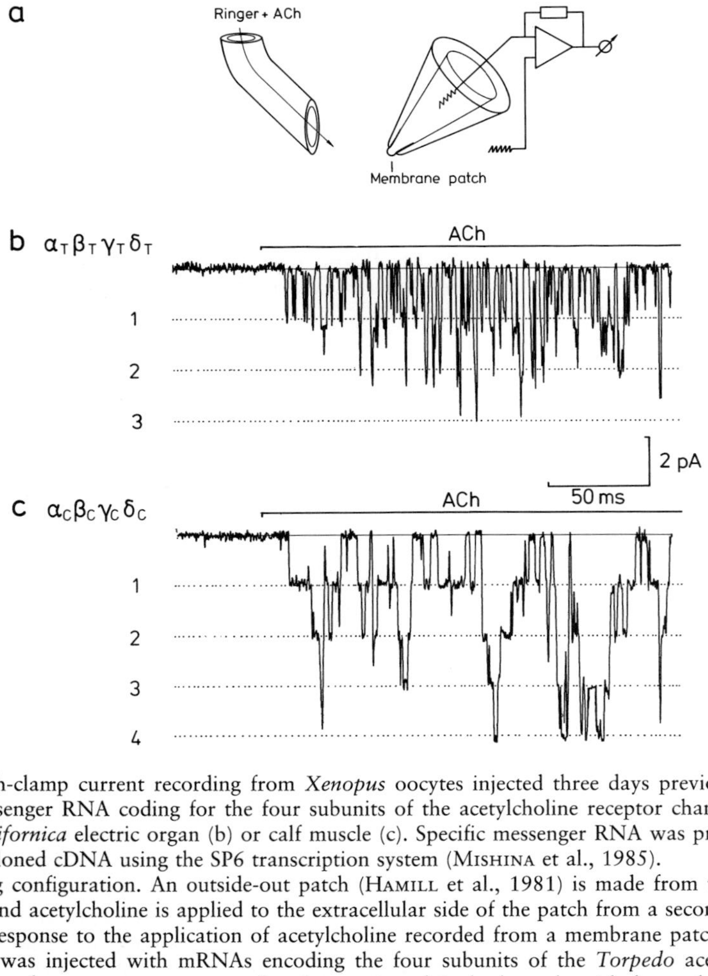

Fig. 7: Patch-clamp current recording from *Xenopus* oocytes injected three days previously with specific messenger RNA coding for the four subunits of the acetylcholine receptor channels from *Torpedo californica* electric organ (b) or calf muscle (c). Specific messenger RNA was produced *in vitro* from cloned cDNA using the SP6 transcription system (MISHINA et al., 1985).
a. Recording configuration. An outside-out patch (HAMILL et al., 1981) is made from the oocyte membrane and acetylcholine is applied to the extracellular side of the patch from a second pipette.
b. Current response to the application of acetylcholine recorded from a membrane patch from an oocyte that was injected with mRNAs encoding the four subunits of the *Torpedo* acetylcholine receptor. Inward current steps correspond to the opening of single channels, with the total number of open channels as indicated on the left.
c. Response to ACh of a patch from an oocyte injected with the mRNAs encoding the calf acetylcholine receptor, recorded under similar conditions as (b).

from oocytes injected with *Torpedo* and calf AChR messages. Outside-out patches were made from oocytes injected three days previously with a mixture of the specific mRNAs coding for all four subunits of either the calf or the *Torpedo* AChR. When acetylcholine is applied to the outside-out patch from a second pipette, characteristic stepwise current pulses are seen in both cases, with a single channel conductance of 40 pS in frog Ringer's solution at 20 °C. Interestingly, the *Torpedo* AChR channel, while resembling the more familiar mammalian channels in many ways, also exhibits some differences. For example, the mean open duration of *Torpedo* AChR currents is clearly much shorter than for the mammalian AChR. Also, for the calf muscle AChR the opening duration depends on the membrane potential, leading to inward rectification in the whole-cell current-voltage relationship. By contrast, the duration of *Torpedo* AChR current pulses is virtually independent of the potential, and accordingly no rectification is seen (SAKMANN et al., 1985).

Modification of ion channels

Once the complementary DNA encoding an ion channel is available and its nucleotide sequence is determined, it becomes possible to modify the protein by introducing specific mutations into the cDNA clones. By suitable methods of site-directed mutagenesis or «genetic engineering», virtually any desired change in the cDNA can be made that will lead to a corresponding change in the mRNA derived from it. If such mutated mRNA is injected into oocytes and expressed, channel proteins with a defined modification of their primary structure will be produced. Recently, this approach was used successfully to map regions of the α-subunit of the *Torpedo* AChR channel that are essential to the function of the receptor (MISHINA et al., 1985). By deleting short pieces at various locations on the cDNA, it could be shown that the putative transmembrane segments are required for channel operation but not for toxin binding. Also, the importance of possible disulfide bridges was assayed by the replacement of various cysteine residues by other amino acids.

A variation of this approach was used to assign certain aspects of channel function to one of the AChR subunits (SAKMANN et al., 1985). Instead of specific mutations of a single peptide chain, the four subunits of the AChR from two species, calf and *Torpedo*, were recombined in new ways to produce «hybrid» AChR channel complexes. As described above, the AChR from *Torpedo* electric organ and calf muscle differ in their gating behavior, and the question was whether these differences could be ascribed to a particular channel subunit. Messenger RNAs for hybrid channels were produced by mixing together only three of the *Torpedo* AChR subunit mRNAs and adding the fourth homologous calf mRNA. For example, «α-hybrid» mRNA was prepared by mixing the RNA encoding the calf α-subunit with the *Torpedo* β-, γ-, and δ-RNAs, the «δ-hybrid» RNA contained the *Torpedo* α-, β- and γ-RNA together with calf δ-message, and so forth. These mixtures were injected into oocytes and the resulting channels studied electrophysiologically. Although all four mixtures led to the expression of active AChR channels, only the α- and δ-hybrids showed a level of activity that was comparable with that of the parental receptors. Of these, the α-hybrid channels behaved rather like the *Torpedo* channel, with brief openings whose duration was not voltage-dependent. The δ-hybrid channels, on the other hand, closely resembled the calf receptor in showing a long, voltage-dependent open duration (fig. 8). From this, it was concluded that the δ-subunit must carry the structural features responsible for certain steps of channel gating that determine the average duration of the elementary current.

Clearly, the combination of molecular biology with the high resolution of the patch clamp technique is a powerful approach to the study of the relation between the structure and function of ion channels.

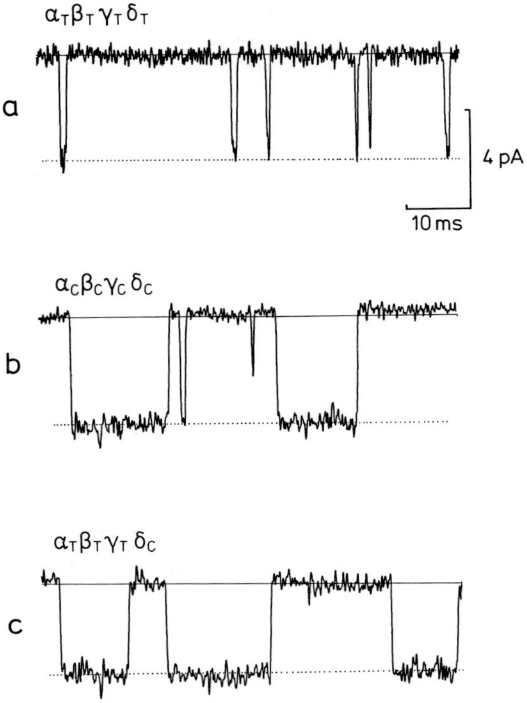

Fig. 8: Sample records of single channel currents from outside-out patches of oocytes injected previously with different combinations of specific mRNAs coding for calf or *Torpedo* AChR receptor subunits. The mRNA combination used is indicated above each trace.
a. *Torpedo* AChR channel, showing brief openings with a mean duration of 0.6 ms at −100 mV membrane potential.
b. Longer openings of the calf AChR channel. The mean duration at −100 mV is 8.6 ms.
c. The «delta-hybrid» channel, consisting of calf δ-subunit together with the *Torpedo* α, β- and γ-subunits. Although only one subunit is of bovine origin, the channel gating behaviour is similar to that of the calf channel.

References

Barnard, E. A., Miledi, R., Sumikawa, K. (1982): Translation of exogenous messenger RNA coding for nicotinic acetylcholine receptors produces functional receptors in *Xenopus* oocytes. Proc. Roy. Soc. Lond. **B 215**, 241–246.

Boheim, G., Hanke, W., Barrantes, F. J., Eibl, H., Sakmann, B., Fels, G., Maelicke, A. (1981): Agonist-activated ionic channels in acetylcholine receptor reconstituted into planar lipid bilayers. Proc. Nat. Acad. Sci. USA **78**, 3586–3590.

Changeux, J. P. (1981): The acetylcholine receptor: an «allosteric» membrane protein. Harvey Lect. **75**, 85–254.

Colquhoun, D., Hawkes, A. G. (1977): Relaxation and fluctuations of membrane currents that flow through drug-operated channels. Proc. Roy. Soc. Lond. **B199**, 231–262.

Colquhoun, D., Sakmann, B. (1985): Fast events in single-channel currents activated by acetylcholine and its analogues at the frog muscle end-plate. J. Physiol. **369**, 501–557.

Eccles, J. C. (1957): The physiology of nerve cells. John Hopkins, Baltimore.
Gunderson, C. B., Miledi, R., Parker, I. (1984): Messenger RNA from human brain induces drug- and voltage-operated channels in *Xenopus* oocytes. Nature **308,** 421–424.
Gurdon, J. B., Lane, C. D., Woodland, H. R., Marbaix, G. (1971): Use of frog eggs and oocytes for the study of messenger RNA and its translation in living cells. Nature **233,** 177–182.
Hamill, O. P., Marty, A., Neher, E., Sakmann, B., Sigworth, F. J. (1981): Improved patch-clamp techniques for high-resolution current recording from cells and cell-free membrane patches. Pflügers Arch. **391,** 85–100.
Hamill, O. P., Sakmann, B. (1981): Multiple conductance states of single acetylcholine receptor channels in embryonic muscle cells. Nature **294,** 462–464.
Hodgkin, A. L., Huxley, A. F. (1952): Currents carried by sodium and potassium ions through the membrane of the giant axon of *Loligo*. J. Physiol. **116,** 449–472.
Karlin, A., Holtzman, E., Yodh, N., Lobel, P., Wall, J., Hainfeld, J. (1983): The arrangement of the subunits of the acetylcholine receptor of *Torpedo californica*. J. Biol. Chem. **258,** 6678–6681.
Katz, B. (1969): The release of neural transmitter substances. University Press, Liverpool.
Katz, B., Miledi, R. (1972): The statistical nature of the acetylcholine potential and its molecular components. J. Physiol. **224,** 665–699.
Kistler, J., Stroud, R. M., Klymkowsky, W., Lalancette, R. A., Fairclough, R. H. (1982): Structure and function of an acetylcholine receptor. Biophys. J. **37,** 371–383.
Mishina, M., Kurosaki, T., Tobimatsu, T., Morimoto, Y., Noda, M., Yamamoto, T., Terao, M., Lindstrom, J., Takahashi, T., Kuno, M., Numa, S. (1984): Expression of functional acetylcholine receptor from cloned cDNAs. Nature **307,** 604–608.
Mishina, M., Tobimatsu, T., Imoto, K., Tanaka, K., Fujita, Y., Fukuda, K., Kurasaki, M., Takahashi, H., Morimoto, Y., Hirose, T., Inayama, S., Takahashi, T., Kuno, M., Numa, S. (1985): Location of functional regions of acetylcholine receptor α-subunit by site-directed mutagenesis. Nature **313,** 364–369.
Montal, M., Darszon, A., Schindler, H. (1981): Functional reassembly of membrane proteins in planar lipid bilayers. Quart. Rev. Biophys. **14,** 1–79.
Neher, E., Sakmann, B. (1976): Single-channel currents recorded from membrane of denervated frog muscle fibres. Nature **260,** 799–802.
Noda, M., Takahashi, H., Tanabe, T., Toyosato, M., Kikyotani, S., Furutani, Y., Hirose, T., Takashima, H., Inayama, S., Miyata, T., Numa, S. (1983): Structural homology of *Torpedo californica* acetylcholine receptor subunits. Nature **302,** 528–532.
Sakmann, B., Methfessel, C., Mishina, M., Takahashi, T., Takai, T., Kurasaki, M., Fukuda, K., Numa, S. (1985): Role of acetylcholine receptor subunits in gating of the channel. Nature **318,** 538–543.
Sigworth, F. (1985): Open channel noise I. Noise in acetylcholine receptor currents suggests conformational fluctuations. Biophys. J. **47,** 709–720.
Sumikawa, K., Houghton, M., Emtage, J. S., Richards, B. M., Barnard, E. A. (1981): Active multisubunit ACh receptor assembled by translation of heterologous mRNA in *Xenopus* oocytes. Nature **292,** 862–864.
Zingsheim, H. P., Barrantes, F. J., Frank, J., Hänicke, W., Neugebauer, D. Ch. (1982): Direct structural localization of two toxin-recognition sites on an ACh receptor protein. Nature **299,** 81–84.

Fortschritte der Zoologie, Band 33 · Lüttgau (Hrsg.): Membrane Control
Gustav Fischer Verlag · Stuttgart · New York · 1986

Rat brain sodium channels recorded from *Xenopus* oocytes

W. Stühmer, C. Methfessel, V. Witzemann and B. Sakmann

Max-Planck-Institut für biophysikalische Chemie, Göttingen, FRG

Oocytes from *Xenopus laevis* provide an efficient expression system for membrane channels from brain (Gundersen et al., 1984). This system was used to characterize the conductance and gating properties of rat brain Na channels. Poly $(A)^+$ RNA extracted from rat brain was microinjected into *Xenopus laevis* oocytes. After an incubation period of four to six days, the oocytes were voltage clamped with a standard two electrode clamp. Most of the oocytes had expressed sodium and potassium channels by that time. The oocytes with large sodium current densities were patch-clamped (Hamill et al., 1981, Sigworth and Neher, 1980) for recording of single Na-channel currents.

Isolation and injection of mRNA

Total RNA from whole rat brain was isolated using the guanidinium isothiocyanate method (Glisin et al., 1974). After proteinase K treatment and phenol extraction poly $(A)^+$ rich RNA was obtained upon chromatography on oligo (dT)-cellulose from Collaborative Research Inc. (USA) (Aviv and Leder, 1972). The activity of the isolated mRNA was tested by an in vitro translation assay using the reticulocyte lysate system (Pelham and Jackson, 1976) purchased from NEN (Dreieich, FRG) followed by analyzing the newly synthesized proteins on polyacrylamide gels. 50 nl of poly $(A)^+$ RNA at 0.5 $\mu g/\mu l$ were microinjected into each oocyte and after a period of four to six days oocytes were tested for channel expression (Gundersen et al., 1984).

Sodium channel expression in the oocyte membrane

a) Whole cell currents

Fig. 1 shows currents elicited by step depolarizations from a holding potential of -100 mV. The depolarizing pulses clamped the oocytes to potentials ranging from -60 mV to $+50$ mV in steps of 10 mV. Currents flowing after application of 100 nM tetrodotoxin (TTX) were subtracted.

Recordings similar to the ones obtained from voltage gated sodium channels in other membranes can be seen. Peak inward currents flowed at a test pulse potential around zero millivolts and the activation was half complete at -22 mV. The reversal potential for sodium started off at potentials as positive as 160 mV and decreased down to 55 mV

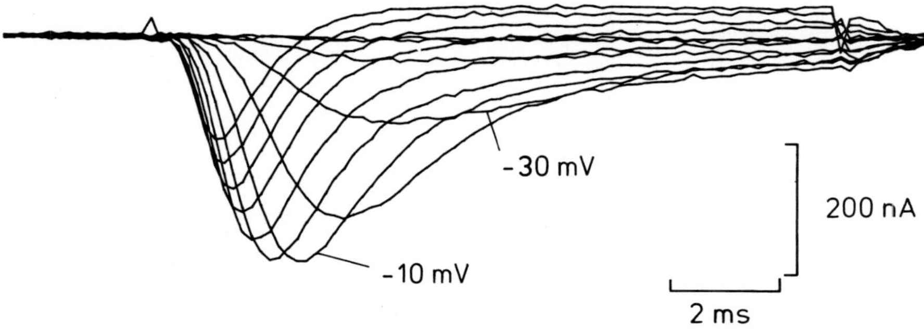

Fig. 1: Currents flowing in response to depolarizing potential steps from −60 to 50 mV in steps of 10 mV. The holding potential was −100 mV. Temperature 20 °C. TTX insensitive currents were subtracted. Normal frog Ringer's solution in the bath.

during the course of long experiments (10–20 min). We attribute this to sodium accumulation and leakage into the oocytes.

The potential dependent inactivation of sodium currents is shown in Fig. 2. The normalized peak sodium currents are plotted as a function of prepulse potentials lasting 20 ms. The data points are fitted with the function:

Eq. 1. $$\frac{I_{Na}}{I_{Na}^{MAX}} = \frac{1}{1 + e^{(V_{1/2} - V_{PP})/a}}$$

giving a potential of −48 mV at which half of the channels are inactivated.

We also tested the sensitivity of the transient inward current to TTX. The data was well fitted by assuming a single binding site for TTX with a dissociation constant of 8 nM.

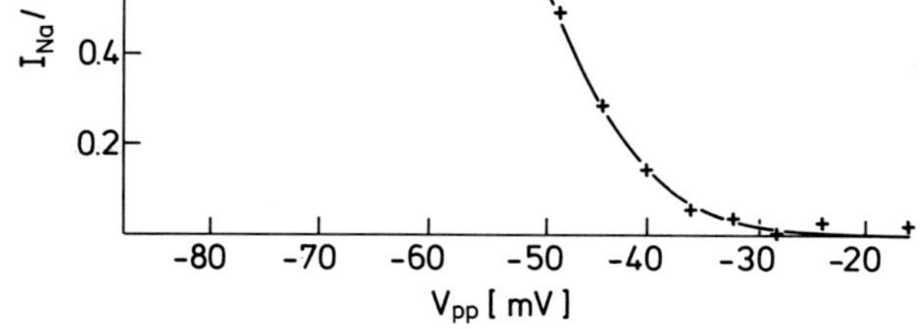

Fig. 2: Potential dependence of the steady state inactivation. After a 20 ms prepulse of variable amplitude (abscissa), a test pulse to 0 mV was applied. The peak sodium current flowing during this test pulse was normalized and plotted as the ordinate. The data points are fitted by a function according to Eq. 1 giving a = 4.73 and $V_{1/2}$ = −48 mV, the potential at which half of the channels are inactivated.

b) Single channel currents

Oocytes with high sodium current densities were selected for single channel recording. For this purpose the vitelline envelope was removed after shrinking the oocyte in a hypertonic solution. This procedure exposes the membrane proper, a requirement to obtain good seals between the patch pipette and the oocyte plasma membrane. Fig. 3a shows current responses of a membrane patch to consecutive depolarizing voltage steps of 20 ms duration as indicated by the arrows. In most records one or several brief inward current pulses are observed following the onset of the voltage step. These inward current pulses show the hallmarks of elementary Na-channel currents as they are observed in other electrically excitable membranes:

1. The sum of 180 responses shows an initial fast increase followed by a much slower decay (Fig. 3b).
2. The distribution of current step amplitudes at a given test potential is characterized by a single peak (Fig. 3c).
3. The current voltage relation is linear over a 30 mV range of membrane potential indicating a single channel conductance of 22 pS (Fig. 3d). and
4. The durations of elementary Na-channel currents are exponentially distributed with a mean duration of 0.4 ms (Fig. 3e).

Thus both the conductance and gating properties of the Na-channels implanted into the oocyte membrane following rat-brain poly $(A)^+$ RNA microinjection agree, to a first approximation, with the observations on Na-channels in membranes from peripheral cells such as rat muscle cells (SIGWORTH and NEHER, 1980).

Conclusions

The expression of Na-channels in Xenopus oocytes following microinjection of poly $(A)^+$ RNA provides a novel way to characterize Na-channels from brain by pharmacological and biophysical methods which cannot be applied to mature brain cells (GUNDERSEN et al., 1984). With the methods described here it is possible to compare quantitatively the properties of Na-channels originating from a variety of primary tissues under identical conditions. We did this with mRNA obtained from rat skeletal muscle and rat brain and have provided an initial description of whole cell sodium currents from rat brain. This has shown that the macroscopic behaviour of these currents is comparable to that of peripheral tissues such as rat skeletal muscle. No indication of a TTX resistant transient current component was obtained. Also, the behaviour of single channel currents corresponded to that of muscle Na-channels suggesting that possibly brain and muscle Na-channels are similar molecular entities.

The Na-channel currents described here were recorded following expression of Na-channels after injection of total poly $(A)^+$ RNA. So far it is not known whether functional brain Na-channels are composed of several subunits (HARTSHORNE and CATTERALL, 1984) or if it is a single polypeptide as suggested for heart and *Electrophorus* electric organ Na-channels (ROSENBERG et al., 1984). The use of mRNA fractionated according to size (SUMIKAWA et al., 1984) or of specific mRNA made from cDNA templates (NODA et al., 1984) will help to decide this question.

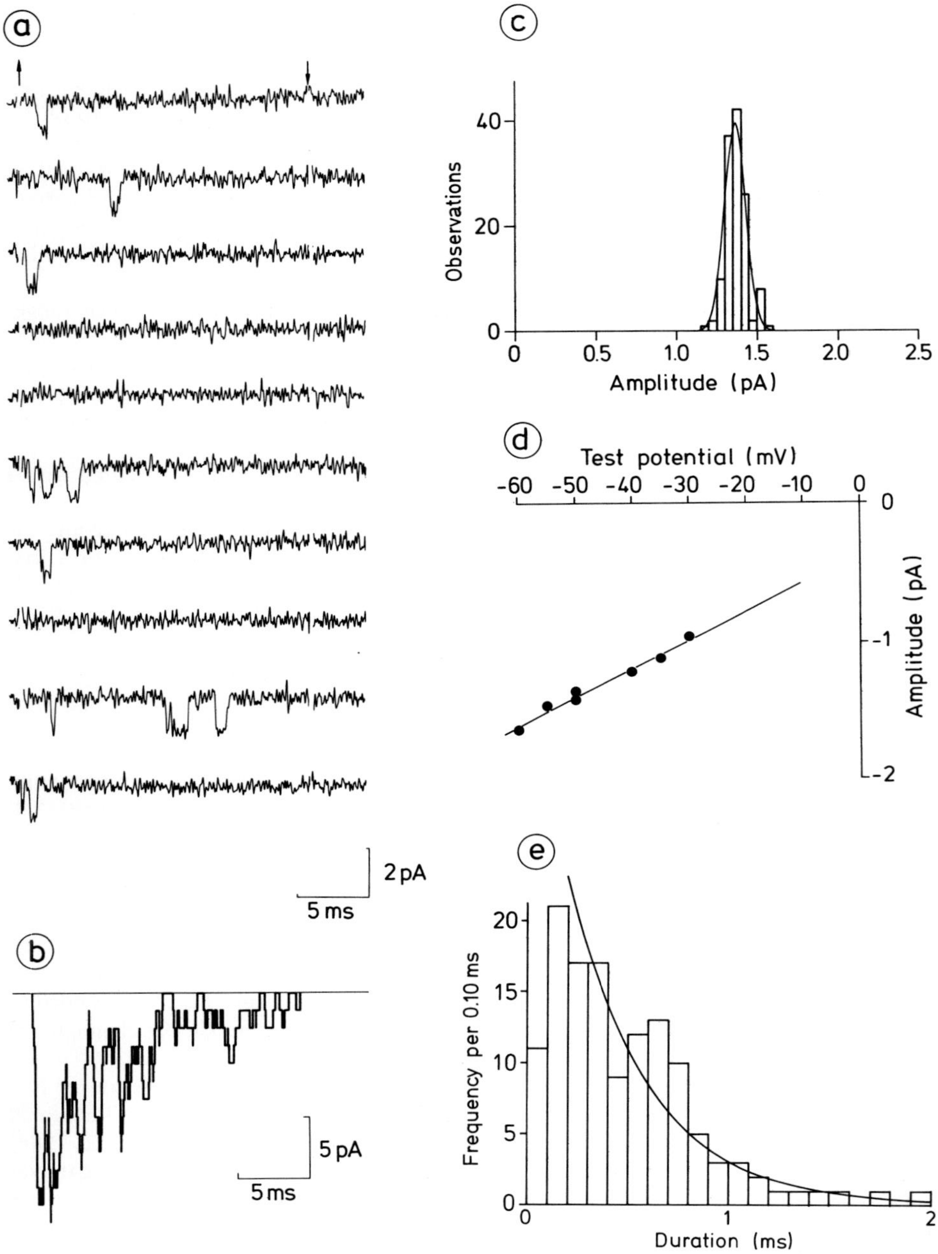
a
2 pA
5 ms
b
5 pA
5 ms
c
Observations
40
20
0
0 0.5 1.0 1.5 2.0 2.5
Amplitude (pA)
d
Test potential (mV)
-60 -50 -40 -30 -20 -10 0
0
-1
-2
Amplitude (pA)
e
Frequency per 0.10 ms
20
15
10
5
0
0 1 2
Duration (ms)

References

Aviv, H., Leder, P. (1972): Purification of biologically active globin messenger RNA by chromatography on oligothymidylic acid-cellulose. Proc. Natl. Acad. Sci. USA **69**, 1408–1412.

Glisin, V., Crkvenjakov, R., Byus, C. (1974): Ribonucleic acid isolated by cesium chloride centrifugation. Biochemistry **13**, 2633–2637.

Gundersen, C. B., Miledi, R., Parker, I. (1984): Messenger RNA from human brain induces drug- and voltage-operated channels in *Xenopus* oocytes. Nature **308**, 421–424.

Hamill, O. P., Marty, A., Neher, E., Sakmann, B., Sigworth, F. J. (1981): Improved patch-clamp techniques for high resolution current recording from cells and cell-free membrane patches. Pflügers Arch. **391**, 85–100.

Hartshorne, R. P., Catterall, W. A. (1984): The sodium channel from rat brain – purification and subunit composition. J. Biol. Chem., **259**, 1667–1675.

Noda, M., Shimizu, S., Tanabe, T., Takai, T., Kayano, T., Ikeda, T., Takahashi, H., Nakayama, H., Kanaoka, Y., Minamino, N., Kangawa, K., Matsuo, H., Raftery, M. A., Hirose, T., Imayama, S., Hayashida, H., Miyata, T., Numa, S. (1984): Primary structure of *Electrophorus electricus* sodium channel deduced from cDNA sequence. Nature **312**, 121–127.

Pelham, H. R. B., Jackson, R. J. (1976): An efficient mRNA dependent translation system for reticulocyte lysates. Eur. J. Biochem. **67**, 247–256.

Rosenberg, R. L., Tomiko, S. A., Agnew, W. S. (1984): Single-channel properties of the reconstituted voltage-regulated Na channel isolated from the electroplax of *Electrophorus electricus*. Proc. Natl. Acad. Sci. USA **81**, 5594–5598.

Sigworth, F. J., Neher, E. (1980): Single Na^+ channel currents observed in cultured rat muscle cells. Nature **287**, 447–449.

Sumikawa, K., Parker, I., Miledi, R. (1984): Partial purification and functional expression of brain mRNAs coding for neurotransmitter receptors and voltage-operated channels. Proc. Natl. Acad. Sci. USA **81**, 7994–7998.

Fig. 3: Conductance and gating properties of single Na channel currents in oocytes following injection of rat brain poly $(A)^+$ RNA. Temperature 20 °C, cell attached recordings. Pipette solution is normal frog Ringer's solution.

a. Current responses in one patch following 55 mV depolarizing steps from an estimated holding potential of –100 mV. The turning on and off of the potential step is indicated by arrows. Low pass filtering at 2 kHz(–3dB).

b. Summed current response to 180 consecutive potential steps. Same experiment as in a.

c. Distribution of elementary current amplitudes fitted by a Gaussian fit giving a mean of 1.34 ± 0.07 pA. Estimated test potential was –45 mV, as in a.

d. Current-voltage relation of single Na channels. Mean amplitudes of elementary currents are plotted as function of test potential. Oocyte resting membrance potential, measured by intracellular microelectrode, was added to pipette potentials to obtain test potentials on abscissa. Different experiment as in a.

e. Distribution of elementary current durations. The fit by a single exponential yields an apparent mean duration of 0.4 ms. Same experiment as in a.

Fortschritte der Zoologie, Band 33 · Lüttgau (Hrsg.): Membrane Control
Gustav Fischer Verlag · Stuttgart · New York · 1986

Expression of functional mouse band 3 protein in oocytes of *Xenopus laevis*

P. Hanke, M. Morgan, R. Grygorczyk, A. Tintschl, H. Fasold, H. Passow

Max-Planck-Institut für Biophysik, 6000 Frankfurt am Main, FRG

The oocytes of *Xenopus laevis* mature in the follicles of the ovaries until they reach the prophase of the first meiotic division. Further development is then arrested until a hormonal signal induces the maturation process to go to completion. In the prophase-arrested state little translation of the oocyte's endogenous mRNA takes place. However, foreign mRNA injected into the oocytes successfully competes with the endogenous mRNA, and translation products will be formed. Since the oocytes contain the necessary machinery for post-translational processing and intracellular transport, the transport proteins synthesized from injected mRNA will be moved to the plasma membrane where their functional state can be studied.

The expression of many channel-forming proteins from a large variety of different sources in oocytes of *Xenopus laevis* has been reported in the literature. Their insertion into the oocyte's membrane has been demonstrated by means of sensitive electrophysiological measurements. We have demonstrated the insertion of the so-called band 3 protein, synthesized by means of injected mRNA from anemic mouse spleen. Two fractions of the oligo-(dT)-purified and density gradient centrifugation-fractionated mRNA led to the expression of mouse band 3 as demonstrated by immunoprecipitation with polyclonal antibodies against mouse band 3. In contrast to channel forming proteins, the band 3 protein mediates anion exchange without giving rise to a membrane conductance. Hence, we were compelled to measure anion fluxes by means of radioactively labeled isotopes. We found that $^{36}Cl^-$ influx into the injected oocytes was increased 2–4 fold, and that the increment could be abolished by stilbene disulfonates, specific inhibitors of anion transport in red blood cells. To document our findings, Fig. 1 shows an autoradiogram of SDS-PAGE of immunoprecipitates of extracts of oocytes injected with mouse spleen mRNA, using anti-band 3 antibodies. Fig. 2 demonstrates the increase of anion uptake in the mRNA-injected oocytes and the abolishment of the increment by the anion transport inhibitor 4,4'-dinitro stilbene-2,2'-disulfonate.

The results presented in this abstract have been published in extenso elsewhere (Morgan, M., Hanke, P., Grygorczyk, R., Tintschl, A., Pasold, H., Passow, H. (1985): EMBO J. 4, 1927–1931).

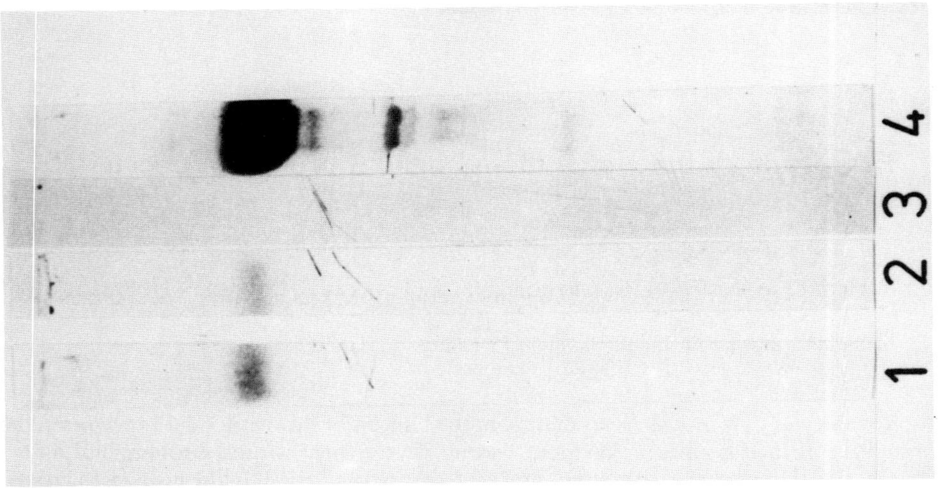

Fig. 1: Autoradiogramm of SDS-Page of immunoprecipitates of extracts of oocytes microinjected with mouse spleen mRNA using anti-band 3 antibodies (lanes 1 and 2). Lane 3 shows the control with preimmune serum, and lane 4 shows $^3H_2DIDS$ labelled mouse erythrocyte ghosts.

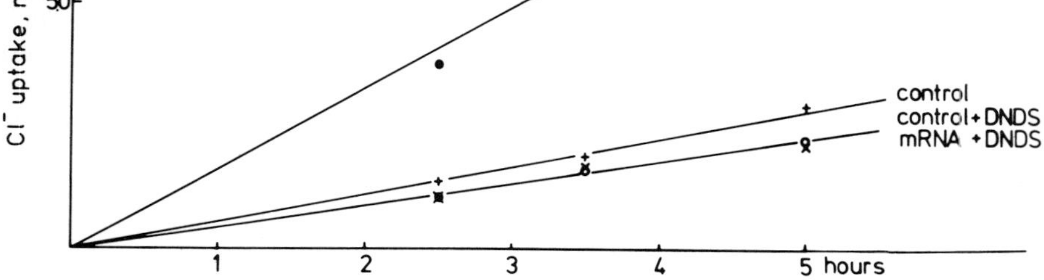

Fig. 2: Effect of microinjected mRNA from mouse spleen on Cl^- uptake by prophase-arrested fully grown oocytes from Xenopus laevis. C and C + DNDS: controls in Barth's medium without and with 0.4 mM DNDS, respectively. mRNA and mRNA + DNDS: oocytes containing mRNA in Barth's medium without and with 0.4 mM DNDS, respectively. 20 °C (according to MORGAN et al., 1985).

Fortschritte der Zoologie, Band 33 · Lüttgau (Hrsg.): Membrane Control
Gustav Fischer Verlag · Stuttgart · New York · 1986

Cardiac calcium channels and their transmitter modulation

W. Trautwein*, M. Kameyama*, J. Hescheler* and F. Hofmann**

* II. Institute of Physiology, ** Institute of Biochemistry, University of the Saarland, 6650 Homburg, Saar, FRG

Calcium ions play a key role in the transmission of signals across the plasma membrane and within the cell (2nd messenger). They control both, synthesis and secretion of transmitters and hormones (Katz, 1969), the activity of many enzymes (Cohen, 1982) and the contraction of the muscle (Fabiato and Fabiato, 1979). Chemical or electrical stimulus can increase the intracellular Ca concentration from the resting value (ca. 10^{-7}M) by a factor of about 100. The increase occurs primarily by a Ca current (I_{Ca}) through Ca selective channels in the sarcolemma and secondarily by Ca release from the SR (Fabiato, 1983). In addition, part of the depolarizing current for the spontaneous impulse generation in the SA node is carried by Ca ions. Thus I_{Ca} controls the two most important parameters of cardiac performance, the rate and the contractile force.

Rate and force are modulated by the sympathetic and cholinergic innervation or their transmitters epinephrine, norepinephrine and acetylcholine, respectively. Changes in the amplitude of the Ca current play an important role in this modulation. The underlying mechanisms of the regulation of the amplitude of I_{Ca} are the topic of this lecture. We report effects of intracellular dialysis of cAMP, ATP-analogues and several enzymes. Emphasis will be given to the phosphorylation hypothesis which explains the increase in I_{Ca} by phosphorylation of a Ca channel protein. In this context we will focus our attention not only on the increase of I_{Ca} by β-adrenergic stimulation but also on the question whether under control conditions phosphorylation is a requirement for the Ca channel to pass ions on depolarization. The last part deals with the mechanism of the muscarinic inhibition of the Ca current. It will be shown that inhibition is due to activation of the inhibitory transducer protein N_i of the adenylate cyclase and consequently by a decrease in intracellular cAMP.

Methods

A. Preparation and solutions

Ventricular myocytes were prepared from hearts of adult guinea pigs by collagenase treatment as described elsewhere (Kameyama et al., 1985). The Tyrode solution contained (in mM): NaCl 112, $NaHCO_3$ 24, KCl 5.4, $CaCl_2$ 1.8, $MgCl_2$ 1.0, glucose 10 and HEPES 5. The solution was equilibrated with 95 % O_2 and 5 % CO_2, the pH was 7.4. For whole cell current recording and cell dialysis with cAMP, ATP-derivatives and enzymes, the internal solution in the pipette contained (in mM): K-aspartate 80, KCl 50, KH_2PO_4 10, $MgSO_4$ 1, HEPES 5, Na_2ATP 3, EGTA 0.02; pH was adjusted to 7.3–7.4 by KOH. For recording single Ca channel activity the pipette in the cell-attached configuration contained (in mM) $BaCl_2$ 90, NaCl 2, KCl 4, HEPES 5, TTX 0.02, pH adjusted to 7.4. The pipette resistances were between 5 and 10 Mohm.

B. Drugs and enzymes

L(-)-Isoprenaline (ISP, 1 mM, Sigma, St. Louis, MO, USA) was dissolved in distilled water containing 1 mM ascorbic acid. Adenosine-3',5'-cyclic monophosphate (cAMP; Serva, Heidelberg, FRG) and 3-isobutyl-l-methylxantine (IBMX, Sigma) were also dissolved in distilled water as 1 mM stock solutions and were stored below −18 °C. 5'-Adenylyl-imidodiphosphate (AMP-PNP; lithium salt, Böhringer, Mannheim, FRG) and adenosine-5'-(-thio)-triphosphate (ATPγS; lithium salt, Serva, Heidelberg, FRG) were substituted for ATP in the pipette solution. 2.4-Dinitrophenol (DNP, Sigma) was directly dissolved in the internal solution. Pertussis toxin (islet-activating protein, PT) was kindly supplied to us by Dr. K. JAKOBS, Heidelberg, and Dr. G. SCHULTZ, Berlin).

The catalytic subunit of cAMP-dependent protein kinase II (C subunit) was obtained from bovine heart as previously described (BEAVO et al., 1974a; HOFMANN, 1980). The heat-stable inhibitor protein of cAMP-dependent protein kinase (PKI) was prepared from bovine cardiac muscle according to the method of ASHBY and WALSH (1972).

The catalytic subunits of PPase-l and −2A were supplied to us by Dr. G. MIESKES, Göttingen. They were purified from rabbit skeletal muscle as previously described (TUNG et al., 1984). The protein contents of PPase-l and −2A were 1.6 and 1.5 mg/ml, respectively. The activity of the PPases was measured in an assay with phosphorylase A as substrate (TUNG et al., 1984; INGEBRITSEN et al., 1983). One unit of the PPase released 1 nmole phosphatate per min from phosphorylase A. The activities were 32,000 U/ml for PPase-l and 24,000 U/ml for PPase-2A. The inhibitor 2 of PPase-1 (PI-2) was prepared from rabbit skeletal muscle and the activity (usually 5,000 U/ml) was measured as the ability to inhibit the activity of PPase-1 (GRUPPOSO et al., 1985). The enzymes were stored at –18 °C in a solution containing 50% glycerol, 25 mM Tris-HCl, 0.5 mM dithioerythriol (DTE) and several protease inhibitors at pH 7.0 include framed sentence. Before the experiment, the phosphatases and PI2 were dialysed against the pipette solution without ATP, creatine phosphate (CP) and creatine phosphokinase (CPK). After dialysis the activity of enzyme was reduced to 21±3% (n = 5). The enzyme solution was supplemented with ATP, CP and CPK immediately before the experiment. Considering possible protease activity or oxidation, 1 mM phenylmethylsulphonyl-fluoride (PMSF), 0.25 mM benzamidine, 2μg/ml leupeptin and 0.5 mM dithioerythritol (DTE) were added to the enzyme-containing pipette solution.

C. Current recording

Heat-polished patch electrodes were prepared from Pyrex glass capillaries according to HAMILL et al. (1981). The electrodes had an inside tip diameter of 2–4 μm and a resistance of 2–5 MOhm when filled with the internal solution. After establishing a 10–40 GOhm seal by suction, the membrane patch was either preserved for single channel recording or disrupted by further suction of −30 to −60 cm H_2O for whole-cell current recording. The same electrode was used both for the measurement of membrane current (single electrode voltage clamp) and the cell dialysis. Cells were held at their resting potential of −80 to −84 mV. Membrane currents were elicited by test pulses (duration 200–300 ms), preceded by a conditioning pulse to −40 mV (duration 100–200 ms) to inactivate fast sodium current. The amplitude of I_{Ca} was measured as peak inward current with reference to zero potential. The membrane capacity of each cell was measured and a specific membrane capacity of 1 $\mu F/cm^2$ was assumed in order to estimate the area of the surface membrane and to calculate the current density. Action potentials and membrane currents (single channel and whole cell current) were displayed on a storage oscilloscope (Tektronix 5113) and were stored on magnetic tape (Hewlett Packard 3964) for later computer analysis (Nicolet MED-80)

D. Internal dialysis of cells

For the intracellular perfusion of the cells the electrode tip was perfused via a thin heat-pulled polyethylene tube (tip diameter 10–40 μm) connected with a stainless steel tube which was inserted into the glass pipette (Soejima and Noma, 1984, Trautwein and Kameyama, 1986). The tip of the plastic tube was as close to the pipette tip as 80–200 μm. The solution in the pipette tip was changed by applying negative pressure (−20 to −50 cm H_2O) to the back end of the pipette and, simultaneously, positive pressure (90–100 kPa) to the inner polyethylene tube. During this procedure a slight swelling of the cell was often observed on the TV monitor, without any sign of a change in the GOhm seal.

E. Efficacy of cell dialysis

The diffusion of molecules from the pipette into the cell was simulated in a simplified compartment model (Kameyama et al., 1985). The calculated intracellular concentrations for C-subunit (M_r 40.000) were 50 % and 90 % of the pipette concentration 4.2 and 13 min after the start of cell dialysis. Similar concentrations are expected for PPase-1 (M_r 33.000) or PPase-2 (M_r 31.000). For cAMP the intracellular concentration after 3 min dialysis was calculated to 90% of the pipette concentration.

Results

The rationale of the experiments described here follows from the scheme in Fig. 1 which indicates that in analogy to the β-adrenergic relation of the glycogen metabolism, the increase in I_{Ca} is thought to be mediated by a cascade reaction (for reviews see Tsien, 1977, 1983; Drummond and Severson, 1979; Reuter, 1983; Levitan, 1985): a β-adrenergic agonist activates adenylate cyclase to produce cAMP which in turn dissociates the inactive holoenzymes of cAMP-dependent protein kinase (cAMP-PK) to yield active catalytic subunit (C subunit). Finally, C subunit catalyses the phosphorylation of a protein within, or close to, the Ca channel. This hypothesis is supported by the observation that application of membrane-permeable cAMP analogues or direct intracellular application of cAMP elevates the plateau of the action potential which has been shown to be due to an increased I_{Ca} (reviewed by Tsien, 1983; Trautwein et al., 1982; Reuter, 1983, Nargeot et al.,

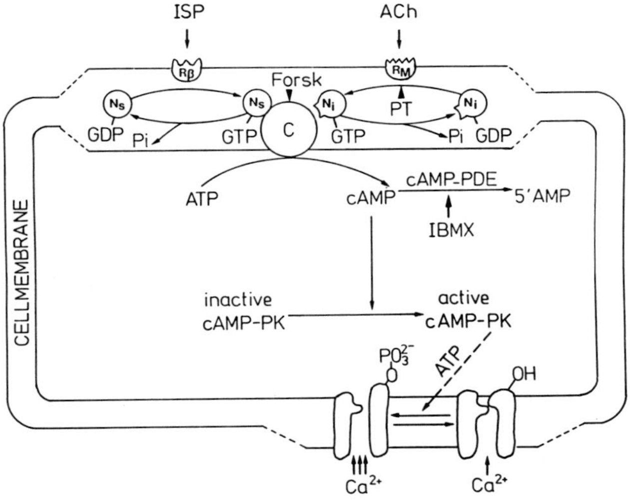

Fig. 1: Simplified scheme of the β-adrenergic and muscarinic action on the Ca channel. R_β,β-adrenergic receptor; R_M, muscarinic receptor; N_s and N_i, stimulatory and inhibitory transducer protein; C, catalytic subunit of adenylate cyclase; cAMP-phosphodiesterase, cAMP-PK, cAMP-dependent protein kinase. For explanation, see text. From HESCHELER et al., 1986.

1983). Another piece of evidence is the observation of an increase in I_{Ca} by injection of C subunit (OSTERRIEDER et al., 1982; BRUM et al., 1983). As the final step of the cascade, phosphorylation of a Ca channel-related protein should result in a larger amplitude of I_{Ca}. The nature of the protein and its relation to the Ca channel is controversial (RINALDI et al., 1981; FLOCKERZI et al., 1983; HORNE et al., 1984).

Whole cell and single channel activity on β-adrenergic stimulation

Epinephrine or isoprenaline (ISP) increases the amplitude of the whole-cell I_{Ca} in a concentration-dependent manner, the threshold concentration being 2×10^{-9}M, and maximum increase occurs with 10^{-6}M in the bath solution (Fig. 2A, C and 4A). The threshold potential, the potential at which the current is maximum (around 0 mV), the apparent reversal potential and the time course of inactivation are only negligibly affected.

The amplitude of a current (I), for example the whole cell current in Fig. 2A, is given by the product $I = N \cdot i \cdot p(t)$, where N is the number of the channels, i the amplitude of the single channel current and p(t) the probability that the channel is open at time t. Increase in I_{Ca} could result from a larger N, i or p(t), or any combination of them. The patch-clamp technique allows to measure these three parameters directly before and during β-stimulation. The current traces in response to step depolarization in Fig. 2Ba show burst-like activity of channel openings having an i of 1.1 pA. However, 4 out of 8 pulses failed to elicit channel activity resulting in empty traces or blanks. Bath application of 1μM adrenaline did not alter i but reduced the number of blanks (Fig. 2 Da) and increased the open state probability p(t) during activity, resulting in a 3-fold increase in the ensemble

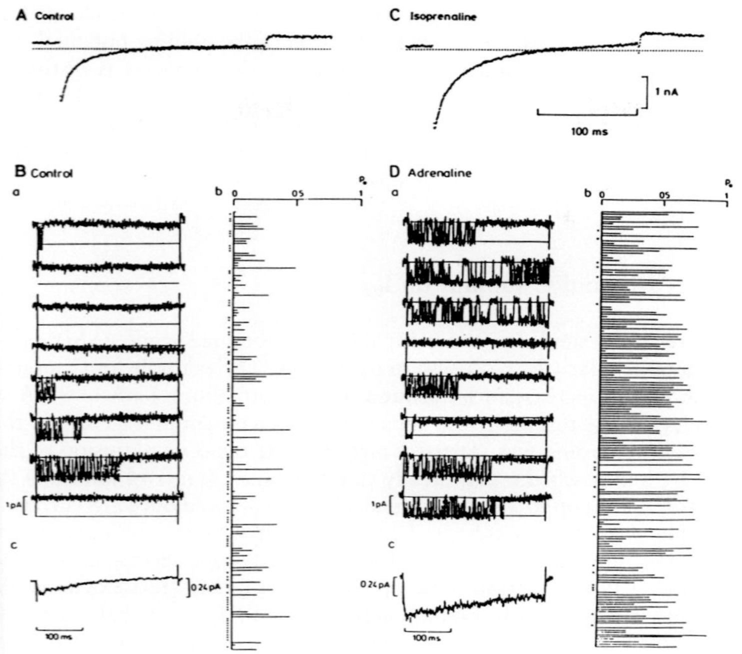

Fig. 2: A and C, whole-cell Ca current before and after application of 5×10^{-8}M ISP, respectively. B and D, single Ca channel activity in response to step depolarizations before (Ba) and in presence of 1 μM adrenaline (Da). Horizontal lines indicate the amplitude of the single channel current determined by amplitude histograms. Bb and Db, opening probability (integrated activity of each trace) on successive depolarizations. Dots mark blanks. Bc and Dc, average currents of 180 traces.

average current (Fig. 2Bc, Dc). In this experiment, where one channel was active in the patch (N = 1), adrenaline failed to increase N over 180 depolarizing pulses (no superpositions of channel openings). In other experiments β-stimulation never produced activity when under control conditions no channel activity was detectable (BRUM et al., 1984; see also CACHELIN et al., 1983). It is unlikely, therefore, that an increase in the total number of channels contributes to the increase in the whole-cell Ca current caused by β-adrenergic stimulation.

The increase in p(t), i.e. the fraction of time the channel is open during a depolarizing pulse, is shown for 180 consecutive traces (2 s interval) as vertical bars for the control run (Fig. 2Bb) and during β-stimulation (Fig. 2Db). The adrenaline-induced increase in open state probability in traces with activity is due to prolongation of the open time from about 1 ms to 2 ms, shortening of the closed time between bursts to about one half and a prolongation of the cluster duration (BRUM et al., 1984; CACHELIN et al., 1983). Dots beneath the base lines in Fig. 2Bb and Db represent a failure of channel activity (blanks). In the control, blanks tended to occur in clusters, suggesting that the transition between «available» and «non-available» states of the channel is a slow process (order of seconds). Obviously, adrenaline increased the number of traces having a higher value of p_o and reduced the number of blanks. The underlying mechanism might be a slow transition process between the «available» and the «non-available» state of the channel. Although the occurrence of blanks is also modified by the level of the holding potential (CAVALIÉ et al., 1983; 1986; TRAUTWEIN and PELZER, 1985), the slow process is distinct from the voltage-dependent inactivation process since the latter is not significantly affected by β-adrenergic stimulation (REUTER, 1974). If the adrenaline-induced decrease of the number of blanks is mediated by phosphorylation of a membrane protein, the effect might be denoted as removal of «chemical inactivation».

Effects of cAMP and C subunit on I_{Ca}

I_{Ca}-voltage relations similar to those for ISP were obtained when cAMP or C subunit were applied intracellularly by perfusion of the pipette. The example for C subunit (3 μM) in Fig. 3Ab shows an increase in I_{Ca} around 0 mV from about 1 nA to 3 nA without a significant change of the threshold and apparent reversal potential (Fig. 3B). In this experiment, the current recording was started 5 min after the onset of perfusion of the suction pipette when I_{Ca} had reached a new steady state (between 5 and 14 min, n = 24) which was attained for 10 min up to 2 h in different cells. The delayed outward current (I_K), seen at -42 mV (Fig. 3A), is also enhanced by C subunit whereas the outward current at negative potentials (inward rectifier, -98 mV in Fig. 3A) is unaffected. Very similar results were obtained with ISP and intracellular application of cAMP (KAMEYAMA et al., 1985).
The dose-related increase of I_{Ca} on bath application of ISP or cell dialysis with cAMP or C subunit is shown in Fig. 4A. In the 3 dose-effect curves the control value of I_{Ca} was

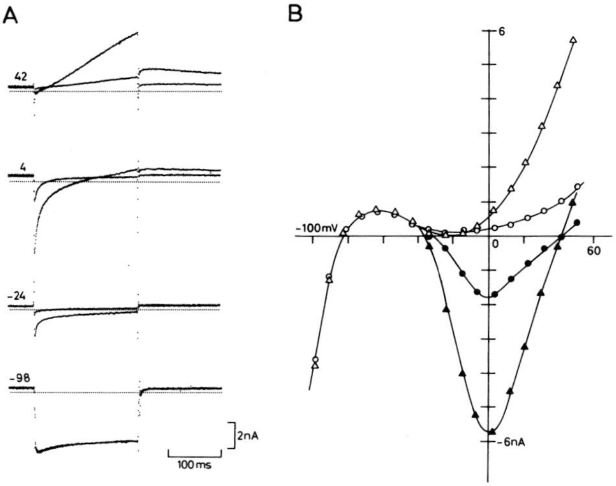

Fig. 3: Effects of internally applied C subunit on the membrane current. A. Current traces in response to 200 ms steps from V_H of -39 mV to potentials indicated on each trace before (smaller currents) and about 5 min after perfusion with 3.3 μM C subunit (larger currents). B. I–V relations for the same cell as in A. Circles are control and triangles are after C subunit dialysis. Filled and opened symbols represent peak inward current and the current level at the end of the test pulse, respectively. From KAMEYAMA et al., 1985.

around 9 $\mu A/cm^2$, and the maximum concentration of either of these agents increased I_{Ca} close to 35 $\mu A/cm^2$. The dose-response relation for ISP in Fig. 4A indicates a threshold at about 10^{-9}M and saturation at 10^{-6}M. Such high doses of ISP were not applied repeatedly to the same cell, since repeated or prolonged exposure to high concentrations resulted in a smaller response of I_{Ca} (tachyphylaxis or desensitization, cf. STILES and LEFKOWITZ, 1984). When cAMP was applied intracellularly by perfusion of the pipette tip, the threshold concentration was about 1 μM. The effects of low concentrations of cAMP (1–3 μM) on I_{Ca}, however, were variable and the increased amplitude of I_{Ca} often tended to decrease again during continuous dialysis of the cells, presumably because of the activity of phosphodiesterase. Therefore, 10 μM 3-isobutyl-l-methylxanthine (IBMX), a phosphodiesterase inhibitor, was added to the pipette solution. IBMX alone increased I_{Ca} by 40 %, presumably by accumulation of endogenous cAMP. With IBMX in the pipette, concentrations of cAMP higher than 3 μM produced regularly a significant increase in I_{Ca}. The broken curve (in Fig. 4B) gives the estimated relation between low cAMP concentrations in the pipette and I_{Ca} amplitude in the absence of IBMX. The curve indicates a threshold concentration around 1 μM cAMP. The half-maximal effect was obtained with 5 μM cAMP and the maximal effect occurred at 15–30 μM cAMP with or without IBMX in the pipette. The maximum level was not further increased by additional superfusion with 10^{-6} M ISP. The cAMP concentrations in the pipette which regulate the amplitude of I_{Ca} may be compared with biochemical measurements. The basal level of cAMP in the myocyte is reported to be around 1 μM (WATANABE and BESCH, 1975; DOBSON et al., 1976; TSIEN and WEINGART, 1976; TERASAKI and BROOKER, 1977), and about half the amount of cAMP is present in free form (TERASAKI and BROOKER, 1977). Therefore, an ideal dialysis of the cell with cAMP of more than 0.5–1 μM would produce an increase in I_{Ca}. In the absence of IBMX the threshold concentration of cAMP in the pipette was estimated from the broken line in Fig. 4Ab to be around 1 μM, and hence the free cAMP concentration inside the cell during dialysis might have been close to the pipette concentration. The estimated range of the intracellular cAMP concentration of 0.5–5 μM, in which I_{Ca} has been enhanced, is close to those measured in vitro during β-adrenergic stimulation of cardiac cells (approximately 0.5–2 μM, DOBSON et al., 1976; TERASAKI and BROOKER, 1977).

The dose-response curve for C subunit in Fig. 4C was constructed from results obtained from 24 cells in which 0.5–100 μM C subunit were internally applied. The threshold concentration of the enzyme was less than 0.5 μM and the half-maximal and maximal effects were obtained with 0.95 and 3–4 μM in the pipette, respectively. From biochemical measurements (HOFMANN et al., 1977; CORBIN et al., 1977) the intracellular concentration of C subunit was estimated to 0.6–1.3 μM. Therefore, about 1 μM C subunit seems to be enough to increase I_{Ca} to the maximum level in response to ISP or cAMP. This value is similar to that for the intracellular concentration of C subunit which, due to the slow diffusion of C subunit, was estimated to be half of that in the pipette (1.5–2 μM) (cf. KAMEYAMA et al., 1985). The small discrepancy between the biochemical and the present data might arise from binding of the protein kinase II, a predominant isozyme in the guinea pig heart (CORBIN and KEELY, 1977), to particulate materials (presumably sarcolemma) of the cell (CORBIN and KEELY, 1977; CORBIN et al., 1977; TERASAKI and BROOKER, 1977). If such a compartmentalization exists, the actual concentration of active C subunit of the endogenous enzyme would be higher in the vicinity of the sarcolemma than that measured in homogenized preparations.

There is no ready explanation for the steepness of the dose-response relation between C subunit and I_{Ca}. Possible reasons might be: 1. Existence of a protein-kinase inhibitor which abolishes the effect of low concentration of C subunit (cf. KREBS and BEAVO, 1979); 2. The

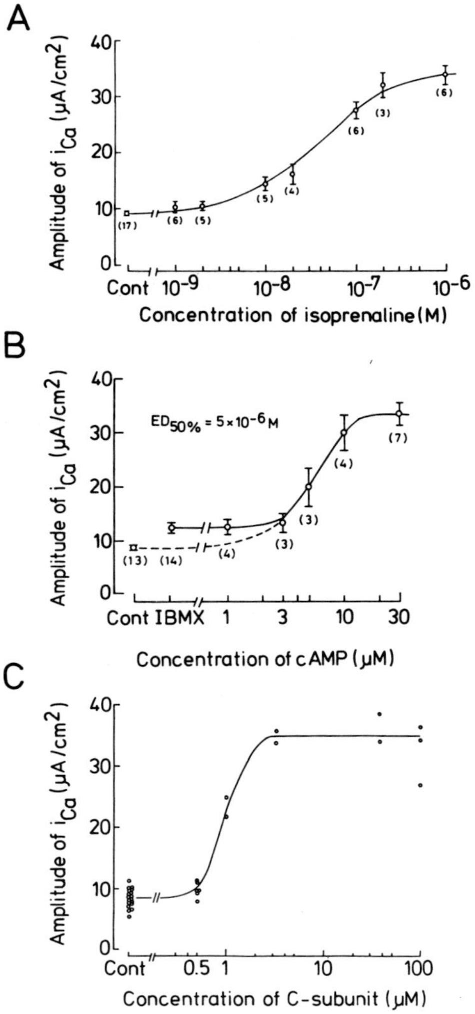

Fig. 4: Dose-response curves for ISP, cAMP and C subunit vs. I_{Ca}. A–C, abscissa: concentrations in log scale of ISP, cAMP and C (pipette concentrations); ordinate: amplitude of I_{Ca} in terms of current density (mean±SEM, number of experiments). The continuous curve in A was drawn according to a half-maximal concentration of 3.8×10^{-8}M and a slope factor of 1. B. Dialysis of cAMP was carried out together with 10 µM IBMX in the pipette. In controls, I_{Ca} was measured without cAMP in the absence (Cont) and presence (IBMX) of 10 µM IBMX. The continuous curve was drawn by eye. Broken line represents an estimated relation between cAMP and I_{Ca} in the absence of IBMX and the estimated curve had a slope factor of 2.2. C. The continuous curve was drawn by eye. The slope factor was about 3. The intracellular concentration of diffused C subunit was estimated as 50 % of that in the pipette (see Methods). From KAMEYAMA et al., 1985.

substrate protein which modulates the Ca channel activity might have multiple phosphorylation sites; 3. Activity of protein phosphatase which counteracts the effect of C subunit may be reduced by the subunit (cf. COHEN, 1982). These possibilities are not mutually exclusive, so that more than one mechanism might underlie the steepness of the dose-response relation between C subunit and I_{Ca}.

From the data of Fig. 4 the relation between bath concentration of ISP and intracellular cAMP concentration can be inferred by plotting concentrations of each of the compounds equally effective to increase I_{Ca}. The relationship shown in Fig. 5A can be fitted to a curve having a half-maximal concentration of 7.1×10^{-8} M ISP and a slope factor of 0.85. The fit is based on the assumption that the level of free intracellular cAMP in the absence of β-stimulation and on maximum β-stimulation amounts to 0.7 μM and 7.5 μM, respectively. The ISP-cAMP relation is similar to the ISP-I_{Ca} relation curve, suggesting that the increase in I_{Ca} by ISP is directly related to the increase in cAMP. In support of this idea, IBMX did strongly enhance the effect of ISP on I_{Ca}, i. e. in the presence of IBMX a suprathreshold concentration of ISP produced a nearly maximal increase in I_{Ca}. The ISP-cAMP relation agrees well with biochemical measurements where in guinea pig ventricular cells ISP increased the cAMP level with a half-maximum concentration of 10^{-8} to 10^{-7}M.

The relationship between cAMP concentration and the protein kinase activity, derived from Fig. 4B and C, shows the enzyme to be half-maximally activated by 5 μM cAMP in the cell (Fig. 5B). This value is higher than that reported for *in vitro* studies (WALSH et al.,

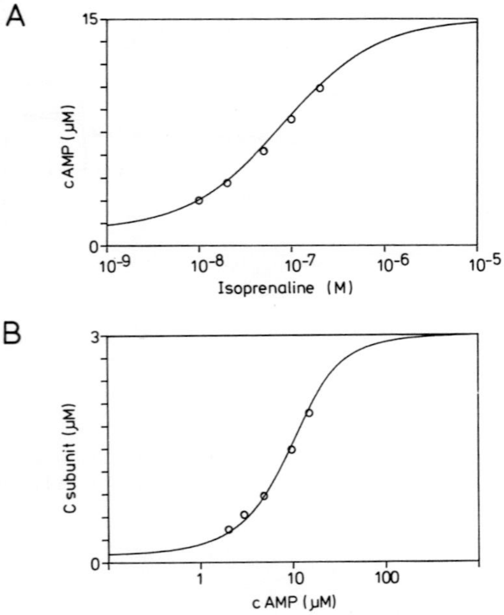

Fig. 5: Estimated relations between ISP vs. cAMP (A) and cAMP vs. free C subunit (B). Circles were obtained from Fig. 4A and B and Fig. 4B and C by finding concentrations of two agents which produced identical increase in I_{Ca}. Concentrations of cAMP and C subunit were halved to represent intracellular concentration. The continuous curves drawn with the parameters given in the text. From KAMEYAMA et al., 1985.

1968; Beavo et al., 1974b; Keely et al., 1975; Hofmann et al., 1975), presumably due to the presence of inhibitory nucleotides, such as AMP and GDP, which affect the binding of cAMP to R (regulatory) subunit of the enzyme (Kuo and Greengard, 1969), and/or a higher concentration of the enzyme in the cell than that studied in vitro (Beavo et al., 1974b; Hofmann et al., 1975). The continuous curve in Fig. 5B was computed according to the reaction scheme (Corbin et al., 1978) for the dissociation of the holoenzyme cAMP-PK into the R and C subunits:

$$R_2C_2 + 4\ cAMP \longrightarrow R_2\ cAMP_4 + 2C$$

assuming a total concentration of cAMP-PK of 2 μM and a dissociation constant for cAMP binding of 8 μM. The experiments with C subunit suggest that this enzyme phosphorylates a Ca channel-related protein, but it does not give information whether other kinases can also exert this effect. This problem can be approached by dialysing cells with PKI, a specific inhibitor of C subunit during β-stimulation (Kameyama et al., 1986a). As shown in Fig. 6, 1 μM PKI completely supresses the enhancement of I_{Ca} by 5×10^{-8} M ISP, suggesting that other kinases can hardly play a significant role in the enhancement of I_{Ca} by ISP. Similar but less pronounced effects were obtained by dialysing β-stimulated myocytes with the regulatory subunit of cAMP-dependent protein kinase which is known to bind the active catalytic subunit.

The results described in this section suggest that β-adrenergic stimulation enhances I_{Ca} via the cascade agonist receptor binding, activation of adenylate cyclase and increase in cAMP level. This increase leads to a higher activity of C subunit of cAMP-PK. The final step in this chain of events, the phosphorylation of a channel-related protein, is the topic of the following section.

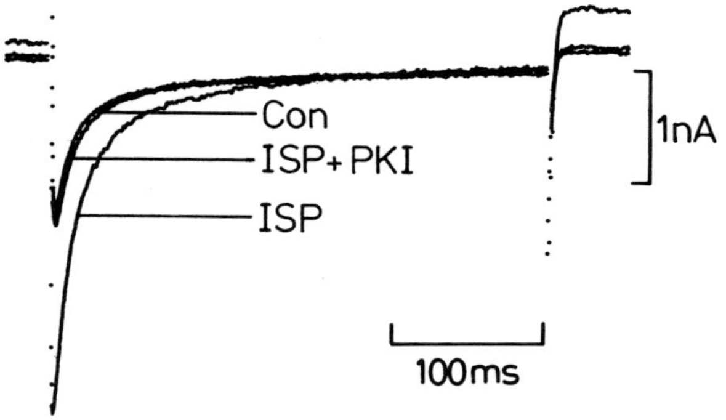

Fig. 6: Effect of PKI on ISP enhanced I_{Ca}. Superimposed current traces in response to test pulses (duration 300 ms) from −40 mV to 0 mV; control, 5×10^{-8}M ISP and in presence of ISP dialysis of the cell with 1 μM PKI.

The phosphorylation hypothesis

The problem of Ca channel phosphorylation as the final step in the enhancement of I_{Ca} by β-stimulation was studied by dialysing cells with ATP analogues (Kameyama et al., 1985), phosphatases or phosphatase inhibitor (Kameyama et al., 1986a, b). Cells were dialysed with a non-hydrolysable ATP analogue, AMP-PNP (adenylylimidodiphosphate) or with ATPγS (adenosine-γ(thio)-triphosphate) which is a substrate of the protein kinase but produces thiophosphorylated protein which is less subject to dephosphorylation (cf. Yount, 1975). In the case of AMP-PNP, absence or depression of the ISP response and in the case of ATPγS, facilitation of the ISP effect on I_{Ca} were expected. The result of an experiment with AMP-PNP is shown in Fig. 7A. In this cell I_{Ca} was increased 3-fold by 10^{-7}M ISP when the normal pipette solution contained 3 mM ATP. After the cell had been dialysed with 5 mM AMP-PNP-containing pipette solution free of ATP for 4 min, the stimulatory effect of the same concentration of ISP on I_{Ca} was markedly depressed. Since AMP-PNP has been reported to be catalyzed by adenylate cyclase to form cAMP and imidodiphosphate (cf. Yount, 1975), this result is consistent with the idea that the hydrolysis of γ-phosphate of ATP is involved in the action of ISP on I_{Ca}. The residual response of I_{Ca} to ISP in the presence of AMP-PNP suggested that in this condition ATP was still reproduced and utilized in the cell. Even more pronounced effects of AMP-PNP on β-stimulated I_{Ca} were observed when cells were dialysed with both AMP-PNP and 50 μM dinitrophenol (DNP) which blocks endogenous ATP production (see Fig. 7B). In this condition, dialysis of 3 μM C-subunit which produces a large increase in Ca current in the control (cf. fig. 3) produces only a small and slow increase in the amplitude of I_{Ca}.

Fig. 10A shows the effect of dialysing the cell with ATPγS on I_{Ca}. In the absence of β-stimulation the amplitude rises slowly during dialysis of 5 mM ATPγS, presumably because of a shift of the dynamic equilibrium between phosphorylation and dephosphorylation towards the former state. Twelve min after the beginning of the experiment a relatively low concentration of ISP (10^{-8}M) produced a maximum enhancement of I_{Ca}; thus the presence of ATPγS greatly facilitates the effect of ISP on I_{Ca}. Also, when ISP was washed out, the return of I_{Ca} to the control level was greatly delayed (more than 10 min in the ATPγS dialysed cells vs. 3 min in the control cells).

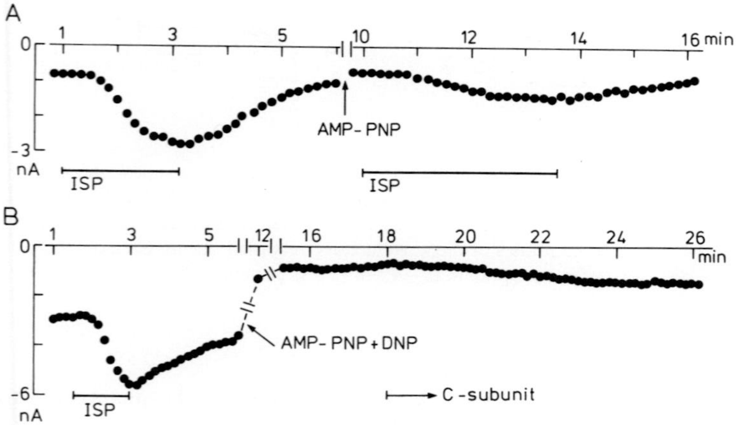

Fig. 7: Effects of non-hydrolysable ATP on ISP- or C-subunit induced I_{Ca} increase. A. Time course of the amplitude of I_{Ca} in response to ISP before and after internal dialysis of 5 mM AMP-PNP. ISP (10^{-7}M) was superfused during the period indicated by bars on the graph. Holding potential (V_H) = −40 and test potential (V_T) = −1 mV. B. Experiment similar to A, but 3 μM C subunit was applied after the dialysis of 5 mM AMP-PNP and 50 μM DNP. V_H = −39 and V_T = 0 mV. Abscissa represents the time after the start of intracellular recording for A and B. From Kameyama et al., 1985.

These results strongly suggest that protein-phosphorylation is involved in the β-adrenergic enhancement of I_{Ca}. Another approach is to dialyse the cell with the phosphatase which dephosphorylates the channel-related protein and thereby depresses the ISP-induced increase in I_{Ca}. We have indeed observed that the catalytic subunits of phosphatase-1 and -2A (PPase-1 and -2A, cf. COHEN, 1982; INGEBRITSEN et al., 1983b), which are intrinsic protein phosphatases in cardiac muscle, do reverse the ISP-induced enhancement of I_{Ca}. In the experiment shown in Fig. 8, 5×10^{-8}M ISP increased I_{Ca} nearly 3-fold. When, in the presence of ISP, the cell was dialysed with catalytic subunit of PPase-1 (about 2.0 μM), the amplitude of I_{Ca} returned nearly to the control level within 7–10 min. The effect seems to be dose dependent since a lower concentration of PPase (about 0.22 μM) had a smaller depressing effect on I_{Ca}. Samples of PPase-1 and -2A which had no activity in the assay (see Methods) were ineffective in reducing the amplitude of ISP-enhanced I_{Ca}. Similarly, alkaline-phosphatase and acid-phosphatase were without effect.

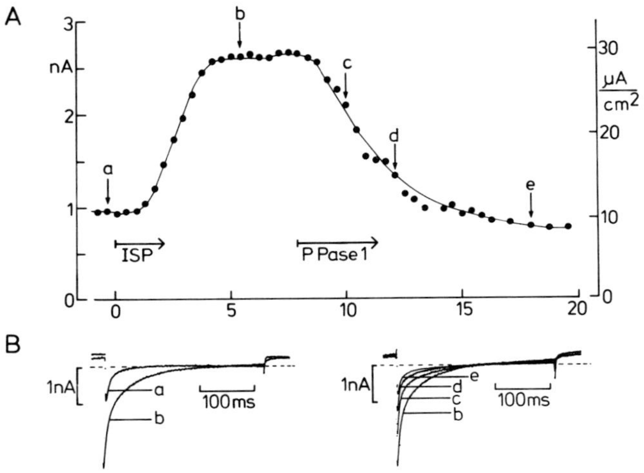

Fig. 8: Effects of PPase-1 on isoprenaline-enhanced I_{Ca} in the guinea pig ventricular single myocyte. A. Time course of the amplitude of I_{Ca} on external application of 5×10^{-8}M ISP (Sigma, St. Louis USA), and internal dialysis with 6,400 U/ml (2.0 μM) PPase-1. ISP and PPase-1 were applied at the time indicated in the figure. B. Examples of the current trace recorded during the experiment at the times indicated in A (a–e). Conditional potential, –40 mV; test potential, 0 mV. From KAMEYAMA et al., 1986b.

Although PPase-1, besides PPase -2A, is the predominant phosphatase in cardiac muscle, the effect of the enzyme on intracellular application does not prove that PPase-1 dephosphorylates Ca channel protein under physiological conditions. This question can be answered by dialysing the myocyte with a specific inhibitor of PPase-1, PPase-inhibitor-2 (PI-2; cf. COHEN, 1982; INGEBRITSEN and COHEN, 1983a, b; HUANG and GLINSMANN, 1976). The experiment in Fig. 9 shows under control conditions during dialysis of the inhibitor a slight but steady increase of I_{Ca} and on application of a relatively small concentration of ISP (10^{-8}M) an increase of I_{Ca} which is much larger than in the absence of PI-2 (cf. Fig.3). This observation suggests that endogenous PPase-1 is inhibited by PI-2 result-

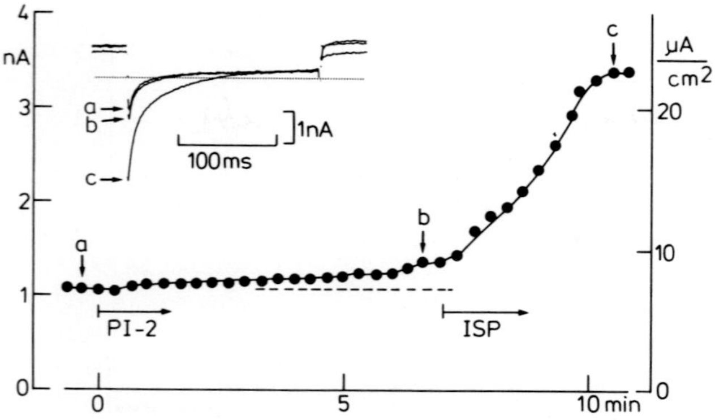

Fig. 9: Effects of PI-2 on the amplitude of I_{Ca} and the response of I_{Ca} to ISP. The time course of the amplitude of I_{Ca} during dialysis with PI-2 (1,000 U/ml) and external application of 10^{-8}M ISP are shown. Inset shows current traces recorded at the times indicated in the figure (a–c). Conditioning potential, −39 mV; test potential, 1 mV. From Kameyama et al., 1986b.

ing in an increased phosporylated state of Ca channel protein. In our experiment, PPase-2A had similar effects as PPase-1. However, it remains to be settled whether PPase-2A dephosphorylates the Ca-channel regulating protein under physiological conditions. This could be tested by cell dialysis with an antibody against PPase-2A.

These results show that there is a dynamic equilibrium between Ca-channel protein phosphorylation and dephosphorylation which can be shifted in either direction, i. e. towards the more phosphorylated state by cAMP-dependent protein kinase and PI-2 or towards the dephosphorylated state by PPase-1 and -2A.

Phosphorylation and basal amplitude of the I_{Ca}

All the measures which suppress the enhancement of I_{Ca} by ISP, like cell dialysis with AMP-PNP, proteinkinase inhibitor, regulatory subunit of cAMP-PK (Kameyama et al., 1986a), PPase-1 or -2A, have a relatively small depressing effect on the amplitude of control I_{Ca}, i. e. in the absence of β-stimulation (see Figs. 6, 7, 8). The amplitude of the control I_{Ca} was never reduced by more than 30 %. These observations suggested that either channel phosphorylation is not a prerequisite for channel opening or another kinase is involved in the maintainance of the phosphorylated state of the Ca-channel. An experiment to decide between these alternatives is shown in Fig. 10. The control part (A) has already been described: ATPγS increased the amplitude of control I_{Ca} and facilitated the ISP response. When, however, prior to the dialysis of ATPγS, the cell was dialysed with PKI (1 μM), ATPγS increased only little, if at all, the amplitude of I_{Ca} (6 % in 8–9 min). The ISP response (5×10^{-8}M) was much less in B compared with the control in A, indicating that cAMP-PK was inhibited. Since we have shown in Fig. 6 that PKI completely suppresses the ISP response and thereby the cAMP-PK, it is unlikely that other kinases are appreciably involved in channel protein phosphorylation. Hence the experiment in Fig. 10B indicates that phosphorylation is not a prerequisite for channel opening.

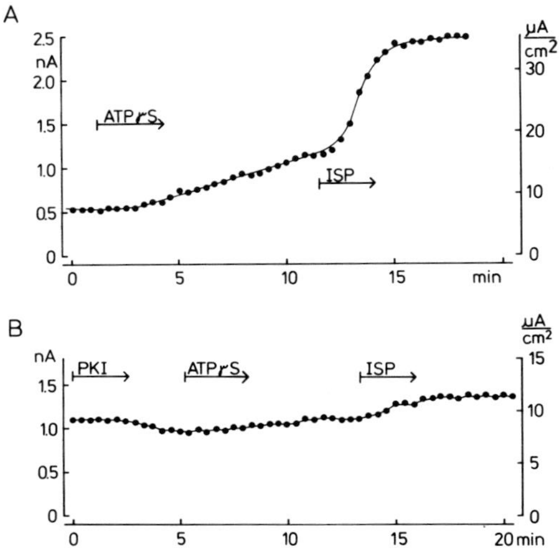

Fig. 10: Effects of ATPγS on I_{Ca} in the presence or absence of PKI. Time course of I_{Ca} is illustrated. A. The cell was dialysed with 5 mM ATPγS at the time 1.2 min. After 11.5 min, 5×10^{-8}M ISP was applied to the bath. B. The cell was dialysed with 1 μM PKI beginning at time zero. After 5 min, the dialysate was changed to PKI+ 5 mM ATPγS-containing solution. Finally at time 13.3 min, 5×10^{-8}M ISP was applied. V_H and V_T were −40 and 0 mV, respectively, for A and B. From KAMEYAMA et al., 1986a.

Muscarinic inhibition of I_{Ca}

It is well known that ACh has little if any effect on the ventricular action potential (HOFFMAN and SUCKLING, 1953; SCHMIDT, 1958) but lowers its plateau level in the β-stimulated cell (BAILEY et al., 1979; BIEGON and PAPPANO, 1980; JOSEPHSON and SPERELAKIS, 1982). This observation could mean that ACh depresses the Ca current in the β-stimulated cell but not under control conditions. The hypothesis is tested by the dose-response relation in absence and presence of 2 different concentrations of ACh (Fig. 11). When ISP is virtually absent or at maximum ISP concentrations, ACh does not, or only a little, reduce I_{Ca} but at intermediate ISP concentrations, especially the half maximum concentration, ACh clearly reduces the amplitude of I_{Ca}. This result, together with the biochemical observation of a decrease in intracellular cAMP content by ACh (BIEGON and PAPPANO, 1980), led us to search for the mechanism of the muscarinic inhibition along the cascade outlined in Fig. 1. In a first series of experiments, myocytes were dialysed with 5×10^{-6}M cAMP or 10^{-6}M C subunit of the cAMP-dependent protein kinase, both resulting in a 2 to 2.5-fold increase of I_{Ca} corresponding to the effect of 5×10^{-8}M ISP which was markedly suppressed by ACh (see Fig. 11). In contrast to the ISP-stimulated cell, no significant effect of 10^{-5}M ACh was observed on the cAMP or C subunit-dialysed cell. The results suggested that ACh has neither an effect on protein kinase nor a direct inhibitory action on the Ca channel (for a detailed description of these experiments see HESCHELER et al., 1986).

A different result was, however, obtained when the intracellular cAMP concentration was increased either by the phosphodiesterase blocker IBMX or by bath application of

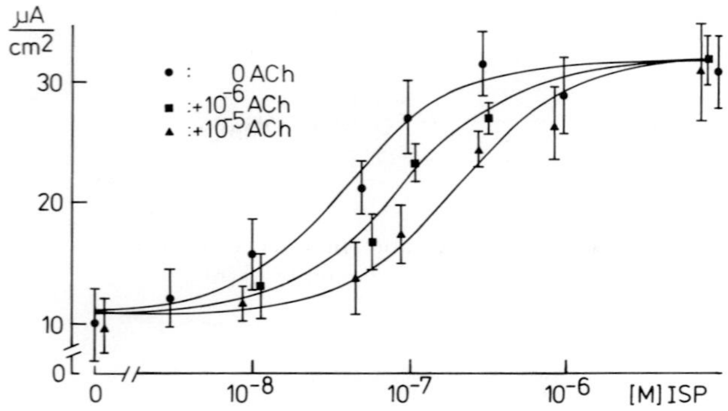

Fig. 11: Relationship between ISP concentration (abscissa) and I_{Ca} density (ordinate) at different ACh concentrations. Filled circles: control: (no ACh); squares with 10^{-6}M ACh; triangles; with 10^{-5}M ACh. The smooth curves were calculated from the equation: $I_{Ca} = (I^*-I_0) \times ISP^n/(ED_{50\%}{}^n + ISP^n) + I_0$, where I^* and I_0 were the maximally-enhanced and the basal I_{Ca} density, respectively. The $ED_{50\%}$ for ISP was 4×10^{-8}M in the control, 9×10^{-8}M in presence of 10^{-6}M and 2×10^{-7}M in presence of 10^{-5} ACh. Apparent Hill coefficients (n) varied between 1.1 and 1.2. From HESCHELER et al., 1986.

forskolin which activates directly the catalytic subunit of the adenylate cyclase (SEAMON and DALY, 1983; SEAMON and WETZEL, 1984; RODGER and SHAHID, 1984). Under both experimental conditions which increase the amplitude of I_{Ca}, ACh exerts an inhibitory effect i.e. it reduces the amplitude of I_{Ca}. This is shown in the experiment of Fig. 12A where forskolin increased I_{Ca} from 1.3 to 3.5 nA and additional application of 10^{-5}M ACh inhibited 54 % of the increase of I_{Ca} by forskolin. The results with IBMX and forskolin suggest that ACh inhibits the cAMP production i.e. acts somewhere between the muscarinic receptor and the catalytic subunit of the adenylate cyclase. Therefore, we studied the role of the transducer proteins N_i and N_s which mediate the signal from the β-receptor (stimulating, N_s) and muscarinic receptor (inhibitory, N_i) to the catalytic subunit of the adenylate cyclase. Both transducer proteins which have GTPase activity bind and hydrolyse GTP during their turnover between the activated and inactivated states (for review see RODBELL, 1980; GILMAN, 1984). These steps can be affected by dialysing cells with a non-hydrolysable GTP derivative. GMP-PNP (5'-guanylyl-imido-diphosphate) competes with GTP for the binding sites of both N_s and N_i and thereby produces persistent activation of these proteins (JAKOBS et al., 1979; SELINGER and CASSEL, 1981) which results in uncoupling the external signals from the adenylate cyclase activity. We have indeed observed that in cells dialysed with GMP-PNP the ISP response on I_{Ca} was blocked and ACh was ineffective to decrease I_{Ca}. When, however, forskolin (10^{-6}M) was applied to the GMP-PNP-dialysed cell, the amplitude of I_{Ca} rose from 2.1 to 3.2 nA and further addition of ACh did not reduce I_{Ca} (Fig. 12B) as it did in the absence of GMP-PNP (Fig. 11A). It should be noted that dialysis of GMP-PNP increased I_{Ca} (compare controls in Fig. 11A and B) presumably because of a larger effect of the stimulated N_s protein than the stimulated N_i protein on the catalytic subunit of the adenylate cyclase.

GMP-PNP activates both stimulatory and inhibitory transducer proteins of the adenylate cyclase. More specifically, the polypeptide pertussis toxin (PT) is thought to block only the inhibitory transducer protein by ADP ribosylation (UI, 1984; WOLFF et al., 1984). Block of the ACh effect on I_{Ca} was observed by incubating the cells with 5×10^{-7}g/ml

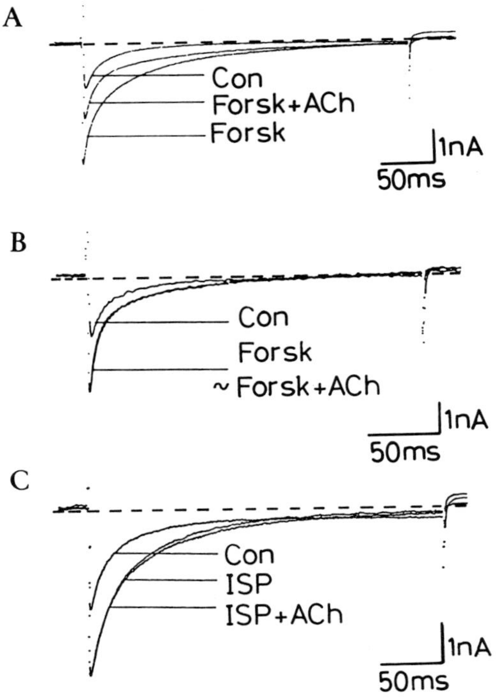

Fig. 12: Muscarinic effects on the forskolin-stimulated I_{Ca} and effects of dialysis with the non-hydrolysable GTP-derivative GMP-PNP and of incubation of the cell in pertussis toxin-containing solution. A. Non-dialysed cell: Forsk (10^{-6}M) enhanced I_{Ca} and additional ACh (10^{-5}M) reduced the amplitude. B. GMP-PNP (10^{-3}M) dialysed cell: the basal I_{Ca} was augmented to 2.3 nA and Forsk (10^{-6}M) increased the current amplitude as in A. In contrast to A 10^{-5}M ACh did not reduce I_{Ca}. C. Current traces in a cell incubated with 5×10^{-7} g/ml PT for 5 h at 23 °C. 5×10^{-8}M ISP increased I_{Ca} 1.7-fold. ACh (10^{-6}M) was ineffective to depress the enhanced current. From Hescheler et al., 1986.

PT for 5 h at 22 °C or 1.5 h at 36 °C. In Fig. 12C, obtained from a cell incubated in PT, the control current, the current after bath application of 5×10^{-8}M ISP and the current after application of 5×10^{-8}M ISP + 10^{-5}M ACh are superimposed. ISP enhanced I_{Ca} from 1.9 to 3.3 nA suggesting intact stimulatory transducer proteins. There was, however, no significant effect of ACh on the β-stimulated I_{Ca} in the cell preincubated in PT-containing solution. These results are in line with biochemical studies of the muscarinic stimulation of the N_i protein (Jakobs et al., 1979) and with measurements of a decrease in intracellular cAMP concentration on muscarinic inhibition (Linden et al., 1985). Even in non β-stimulated cells a decrease of intracellular cAMP by acetylcholine was observed (Linden et al., 1985). As mentioned above, we did not find a decrease in the amplitude of I_{Ca} by acetylcholine in control cells. The discrepancy might be explained by the very small I_{Ca} response to low doses of intracellular cAMP (Fig. 4Ab).

The results described in this section strongly suggest that the inhibition of I_{Ca} by ACh is due to a decrease of intracellular cAMP concentration via the activation of the transducer protein N_i which inhibits the catalytic subunit of the adenylate cyclase.

Conclusions

1. β-adrenergic agonists, as isoprenaline (ISP), increase the slow inward Ca current. On the single channel level, the enhancement of I_{Ca} was due to an increase of the open probability p_o (decrease of the number of blanks), both the total number of channels and the single channel amplitude remaining the same.

2. I_{Ca} was also enhanced when cAMP or C-subunit of cAMP-dependent protein kinase (cAMP-PK) was internally applied, and the effects of all three of these compounds were not additive, suggesting that β-adrenergic agonists influence the Ca-channel via a cascade mechanism with a phosphorylation of a Ca channel-regulating protein as a final step. Plots of concentrations vs. I_{Ca} amplitude were established and compared with biochemical data.

3. The phosphorylation hypothesis was tested by cell dialysis with different ATP-analogues, the regulatory subunit (R) and the inhibitor (PKI) of cAMP-PK and protein phosphatases 1 and 2A. Measures which suppress phosphorylation (the non-hydrolysable ATP-analogue AMP-PNP, PKI, R-subunit and phosphatases) suppress the ISP enhancement of I_{Ca}, and those which enhance phosphorylation (the dephosphorylation resistant ATP-analogue ATPγS, C-subunit and inhibitor of phosphatase 1) augment the ISP response.

4. When AMP-PNP, R-subunit, PKI or phosphatases are applied to non-β-stimulated cells, I_{Ca} was not completely reversed, suggesting that the Ca channel has a ‹basal› activity in the dephosphorylated state. This corresponds with the observation that single Ca channels with a low p_o are more affected by β-adrenergic stimulation than those with high p_o under control conditions. Low p_o values might correspond to the dephosphorylated state, high p_o values to the phosphorylated state.

5. Muscarinic agonists, as acetylcholine (ACh), inhibit I_{Ca}, enhanced by submaximal ISP-concentrations (no effect on control I_{Ca} and maximally stimulated I_{Ca}). It is plausible that the muscarinic action occurs at the level of the inhibitory transducer protein N_i, since a) ACh was ineffective when I_{Ca} was increased by cAMP or C-subunit and b) since the ACh-inhibition of the adenylate cyclase was blocked by dialysing the cell with non-hydrolysable GTP or incubation in pertussis toxin.

References

Ashby, C. D., Walsh, D. A. (1972): Characterization of the interaction of a protein inhibitor with adenosine 3',5'monophosphate-dependent protein kinase. J. Biol. Chem. **247:** 6637–6642.

Bailey, J., Watanabe, A., Besch, H., Lythrop, D. (1979): Acetylcholine antagonism of the electrophysiological effects of isoproterenol on canine cardiac purkinje fibers. Circ. Res. **44:** 378–382.

Beavo, J. A., Bechtel, P. J., Krebs, E. G. (1974a): Preparation of homogeneous cyclic AMP-dependent protein kinase and its subunits from rabbit skeletal muscle. Methods Enzymol **38:** 299–308.

Beavo, J. A., Bechtel, P. J., Krebs, E. G. (1974b): Activation of protein kinase by physiological concentration of cyclic AMP. Proc. Natl. Acad. Sci. USA **71:** 3580–3583.

Biegon, R., Pappano, A. (1980): Dual mechanism for inhibition of calcium-dependent action potentials in avian ventricular muscle. Circ. Res. **46:** 353–362.

Brum, G., Flockerzi, V., Hofmann, F., Osterrieder, W., Trautwein, W. (1983): Injection of catalytic subunit of cAMP-dependent protein kinase into isolated cardiac myocytes. Pflügers Arch. Eur. J. Physiol. **398:** 147–154.

Brum, G., Osterrieder, W., Trautwein, W. (1984): β-adrenergic increase in the calcium conductance of cardiac myocytes studied with the patch clamp. Pflügers Arch. Eur. J. Physiol. **401:** 111–118.

Cachelin, A. B., De Peyer, J. E., Kokubun, S., Reuter, H. (1983): Calcium channel modulation by 8-bromo-cyclic AMP in cultured heart cells. Nature **304:** 462–464.

Cavalié, A., Ochi, R., Pelzer, D., Trautwein, W. (1983): Elementary currents through Ca channels in guinea pig myocytes. Pflügers Arch. Eur. J. Physiol. **398:** 284–297.

Cavalié, A., Pelzer, D., Trautwein, W. (1986): Fast and slow gating behaviour of single calcium channels in cardiac cells: Relation to whole-cell calcium channel current. Pflügers Arch. Eur. J. Physiol. **406:** 241–258.

Cohen, P. (1982): The role of protein phosphorylation in neural and hormonal control of cellular activity. Nature **296:** 613–620.

Corbin, J. D., Keely, S. L. (1977): Characterization and regulation of heart adenosine 3':5'-monophosphate-dependent protein kinase isozymes. J. Biol. Chem. **252:** 910–918.

Corbin, J. D., Sugden, P. H., Lincoln, T. M., Keely, S. L. (1977): Compartmentalization of adenosine 3':5'-monophosphate and adenosine 3':5'-monophosphate-dependent protein kinase in heart tissue. J. Biol. Chem. **252:** 3854–3861.

Corbin, J. D., Sugden, P. H., West, L., Flockhart, D. A., Lincoln, T. M. (1978): Studies on the properties and mode of action of the purified regulatory subunit of bovine heart adenosine 3':5'-monophosphate-dependent protein kinase. J. Biol. Chem. **253:** 3997–4003.

Dobson, J. G., Ross, J., Mayer, S. E. (1976): The role of cyclic adenosine 3':5'-monophosphate and calcium in the regulation of contractility and glycogen phosphorylase activity in guinea pig papillary muscle. Circ. Res. **39:** 388–395.

Drummond, G. I., Severson, D. L. (1979): Cyclic nucleotides and cardiac function. Circ. Res. **44:** 145–153.

Fabiato, A., Fabiato,F. (1979): Calcium and cardiac excitation-contraction coupling. Ann. Rev. Physiol. **41:** 473.

Fabiato, A. (1983): Calcium-induced release of calcium from the cardiac sarcoplasmic reticulum. Am. J. Physiol. **245** (Cell. Physiol. **4**) C1–C14.

Flockerzi, V., Mewes, R., Ruth, P., Hofmann, F. (1983): Phosphorylation of purified bovine cardiac sarcolemma and potassium-stimulated calcium uptake. Eur. J. Biochem. **135:** 131–142.

Gilman, A. (1984): G proteins and dual control of adenylate cyclase Cell **36:** 577–579.

Grupposo, P., Johnson, G., Constantinides, M., Brautigan, D. (1985): Phosphorylase phosphatase regulatory subunit. Western blotting with immunoglobulins against inhibitor-2 reveals a protein of M_r = 60.000. J. Biol. Chem. **260:** 4288–4294.

Hamill, O. P., Marty, A., Neher, E., Sakmann, B., Sigworth, F. J. (1981): Improved patch-clamp techniques for high resolution current recording from cells and cell-free membrane patches. Pflügers Arch. Eur. J. Physiol. **391:** 85–100.

Hescheler, J., Kameyama, M., Trautwein, W. (1986): On the mechanism of mucarinic inhibition of the cardiac Ca current. Pflügers Arch. Eur. J. Physiol. **407:** 182–189.

Hoffman, B., Suckling, E. (1953): Cardiac cellular potentials: effect of vagal stimulation and acetylcholine Am. J. Physiol. **173:** 312–320.

Hofmann, F. (1980): Apparent constants for the interaction of regulatory and catalytic subunit of cAMP-dependent protein kinase I and II. J. Biol. Chem. **255:** 1559–1564.

Hofmann, F., Beavo, J. A., Bechtel, P. J., Krebs, E. G. (1975): Comparison of adenosine 3':5'-monophosphate-dependent protein kinase from rabbit skeletal muscle and bovine heart muscle. J. Biol. Chem. **250:** 7795–7780.

Hofmann, F., Bechtel, P. J., Krebs, E. G. (1977): Concentrations of cyclic AMP-dependent protein kinase subunits in various tissues. J. Biol. Chem. **252:** 1441–1447.

Horne, P., Triggle, D. J., Venter, J. C. (1984): Nitrendipine and isoproterenol induce phosphorylation of a 42,000 dalton protein that co-migrates with the affinity labelled calcium channel regulatory subunit. Biochem. Biophys. Res. Comm. **121:** 890–898.

Huang, F. L., Glinsmann, W. H. (1976): Separation and characterization of two phosphorylase phosphatase inhibitors from rabbit skeletal muscle. Eur. J. Biochem. **70:** 419–426.

Ingebritsen, T. S., Stewart, A. A., Cohen, P. (1983): The protein phosphatases involved in cellular regulation: Measurement of type-1 and type-2 protein phosphatases in extracts of mammalian tissues; an assessment of their physiological roles. Eur. J. Biochem. **132:** 297.

Ingebritsen, T. S., Cohen, P. (1983a): The protein phosphatases involved in cellular regulation. Eur. J. Biochem. **132:** 255–261.

Ingebritsen, T. S., Cohen, P. (1983b): Protein phosphatases: Properties and role in cellular regulation. Science **221:** 331–338.

Jakobs, A., Aktories, K., Schulz, G. (1979): GTP-dependent inhibition of cardiac adenylate cyclase by muscarinic cholinergic agonists. Naunyn Schmiedebergs Arch. Pharmacol. **310:** 113–119.

Josephson, I., Sperelakis, N. (1982): On the ionic mechanism underlying adrenergic, cholinergic antagonism in ventricular muscle. J. gen. Physiol. **79:** 69–86.

Kameyama, M., Hofmann, F., Trautwein, W. (1985): On the mechanism of β-adrenergic regulation of the Ca channel in guinea-pig heart. Pflügers Arch. Eur. J. Physiol. **405:** 285–293.

Kameyama, M., Hescheler, J., Hofmann, F., Trautwein, W. (1986a): Modulation of Ca current during the phosphorylation cycle in the guinea pig heart. Pflügers Arch. **407:** 123–128.

Kameyama, M., Hescheler, J., Mieskes, G., Trautwein, W. (1986b): Protein phosphatases regulate the Ca channel in guinea pig heart. Pflügers Arch. Eur. J. Physiol. **407:** 461–463.

Katz, P. (1969): The release of neurotransmitter substances. Liverpool University Press, Liverpool, UK.

Keely, S. L., Corbin, J. D., Park, C. R. (1975): On the question of translocation of heart cAMP-dependent protein kinase. Proc. Natl. Acad. Sci. USA **72:** 1501–1504.

Krebs, E. G., Beavo, J. A. (1979): Phosphorylation-dephosphorylation of enzymes. Ann. Rev. Biochem. **48:** 923–959.

Kuo, J. F., Greengard, P. (1969): Cyclic nucleotide-dependent protein kinases, IV. Widespread occurrence of adenosine 3′:5′-monophosphate-dependent protein kinase in various tissues and phyla of the animal kingdom. Proc. Natl. Acad. Sci. USA **64:** 1349–1355.

Levitan, I. (1985): Phosphorylation of ion channels. J. Membrane Biol. **87:** 177–190.

Linden, J., Hollen, C., Patel, A. (1985): The mechanism by which adenosine and cholinergic agents reduce contractility in rat myocardium. Correlation with cyclic AMP and receptor densities. Circ. Res. **56:** 728–735.

Nargeot, J., Nerbonne, J., Engels, J., Lester, H. (1983): Time course of the increase in myocardial slow inward current after a photochemically generated concentration jump of intracellular cAMP. Proc. Natl. Acad. Sci. **88:** 2395–2399.

Osterrieder, W., Brum, G., Hescheler, J., Trautwein, W., Hofmann, F., Flockerzi, V. (1982): Injection of subunits of cyclic AMP-dependent protein kinase into cardiac myocytes modulates Ca^{2+} current. Nature **298:** 576–578.

Reuter, H. (1974): Localization of β-adrenergic receptors, and effects of noradrenaline and cyclic nucleotides on action potentials, ionic currents and tension in mammalian cardiac muscle. J. Physiol. **242:** 429–451.

Reuter, H. (1983): Calcium channel modulation by neurotransmitters, enzymes and drugs. Nature **301:** 569–574.

Rinaldi, M. L., Le Peuch, C. J., Demaille, J. G. (1981): The epinephrine-induced activation of the cardiac slow Ca^{2+} channel is mediated by the cAMP-dependent phosphorylation of calciductin, a 23000 M_r sarcolemma protein. FEBS Lett **129:** 277–281.

Rodbell, M. (1980): The role of hormone receptors and GTP-regulatory proteins in membrane transduction. Nature **284:** 17–22.

Rodger, I. W., Shahid, M. (1984): Forskolin, cyclic nucleotides and positive inotropism in isolated papillary muscles of the rabbit. Br. J. Pharmac. **81:** 151–159.

Schmidt, R. F. (1958): Über die Acetylcholin-Empfindlichkeit verschiedener Herzabschnitte. Naunyn Schmiedebergs Arch. Exp. Path. Pharmacol. **233:** 531–540.

Seamon, K., Daly, J. (1983): Forskolin, cyclic AMP and cellular physiology. (TIPS-March 1983).

Seamon, K., Wetzel, B. (1984): Interaction of forskolin with dually regulated adenylate cyclase. Adv. Cyclic Nucleotide Res. **17:** 91–99.

Selinger, Z., Cassel, D. (1981): Role of guanine nucleotides in hormonal activation of adenylate cyclase. Adv. Cyclic Nucleotide Res. **14:** 15–22.

Soejima, M., Noma, A. (1984): Mode of regulation of the ACh-sensitive K-channel by muscarinic receptor in rabbit atrial cells. Pflügers Arch. Eur. J. Physiol. **400:** 424–431.

Stiles, G. L., Lefkowitz, R. J. (1984): β-adrenergic receptors: Biochemical mechanisms of physiological regulation. Physiol. Rev.**64:** 661–743.

Terasaki, W. L., Brooker, G. (1977): Cardiac adenosine 3':5'-monophosphate. J. Biol. Chem. **252:** 1041–1050.

Trautwein, W., Pelzer, D. (1985): Voltage-dependent gating of single calcium channels in the cardiac cell membrane and its modulation by drug. In: Marmé D. (ed.). Calcium and cell physiology. Springer, Berlin, Heidelberg, New York, Tokyo, pp. 53–93.

Trautwein, W., Kameyama, M. (1986): The mechanism of β-adrenergic regulation of Ca channels: Intracellular injection and patch-clamp studies. In *Electrophysiology of single cardiac cells*, Ed. Noble, D. and Powell, T., Academic Press, London.

Trautwein, W., Taniguchi, J., Noma, A. (1982): The effect of intracellular cyclic nucleotides and calcium on the action potential and acetylcholine response of isolated cardiac cells. Pflügers Arch. Eur. J. Physiol. **392:** 307–314.

Tsien, R. W. (1977): Cyclic AMP and contractile activity in heart. Adv. Cyclic Nucleotide Res. **8:** 363–420.

Tsien, R. W. (1983): Calcium channels in excitable cell membranes. Ann. Rev. Physiol. **45:** 341–358.

Tsien, R. W., Weingart, R. (1976): Inotropic effect of cyclic AMP in calf ventricular muscle studied by a cut end method. J. Physiol. **260:** 117–141.

Tung, L., Resink, T., Hemmings, B., Shenolikar, S., Cohen, P. (1984): The catalytic subunits of protein phosphatase-1 and phosphatase-2A are distinct gene products. Eur. J. Biochem. **138:** 635–641.

Ui, M. (1984): Islet-activating protein, pertussis toxin: a probe for functions of the inhibitory guanin nucleotide regulatory component of adenylate cyclase. TIPS 5: 277.

Walsh, D. A., Perkins, J. P., Krebs, E. G. (1968): An adenosine 3′-5′-monophosphate-dependent protein kinase from rabbit skeletal muscle. J. Biol. Chem. **243:** 3763–3774.

Watanabe, A. M., Besch, H. R. Jr. (1975): Interaction between cyclic adenosine monophosphate and cyclic guanosine monophosphate in guinea pig ventricular myocardium. Circ. Res. **37:** 309–317.

Wolff, J., Hope-Cook, G., Goldhammer, A., Londos, C., Hewlett, E. (1984): Bordetella pertussis: multiple attacks on host cell cyclic AMP regulation. Adv. Cyclic Nucleotide Res. **17:** 161–172.

Yount, R. G. (1975): ATP analogs. Adv. Enzymol. **34:** 1–56.

III. Session
Electro-effector coupling

Fortschritte der Zoologie, Band 33 · Lüttgau (Hrsg.): Membrane Control
Gustav Fischer Verlag · Stuttgart · New York · 1986

Membrane charge movement and excitation contraction coupling in skeletal muscle

M. F. Schneider, B. J. Simon,, G. Szücs and W. Melzer

Department of Physiology, University of Rochester, School of Medicine and Dentistry, Rochester, N. Y. 14642, USA and
Cardiovascular Section, Gerontology Research Center, 4940 Eastern Avenue, Baltimore, MD 21224, USA

Introduction and background

Electrical depolarization of a skeletal muscle fibre initiates a chain of events that results in a transformation of the fibre from a state of rest to a state of mechanical activity (see Lüttgau and Stephenson, 1986 for overall review). Later events in the depolarization contraction coupling process include release of calcium ions from the sarcoplasmic reticulum (SR), the intracellular calcium sequestering organelle in muscle, and an elevation of the cytosolic free calcium concentration $[Ca^{2+}]$. This promotes binding of calcium ions to regulatory sites on thin filament troponin molecules, thereby removing an inhibition of mechanochemical interaction between the thick and thin contractile filaments and allowing shortening and force generation. Relaxation is produced by the cessation of SR calcium release, a lowering of $[Ca^{2+}]$ and dissociation of calcium from troponin. Skeletal muscle is thus specialized for relatively large and rapid movements of calcium from SR to myoplasm. These intracellular releases of internally stored calcium ions in skeletal muscle are strictly controlled by membrane voltage and appear to be independent of movement of any ions, including calcium, into the cell from the external bathing solution (Lüttgau and Spiecker, 1979; Miledi, Parker and Zhu, 1984; Curtis and Eisenberg, 1985).

Under physiological conditions the depolarization that initiates calcium release is produced by an action potential that propagates along the fibre and into the transverse tubules (TT) a system of tubular invaginations of the fibre surface membrane. Under experimental conditions any sufficient depolarization of the transverse tubules can initiate calcium release from the SR in the absence of an action potential. The TT membrane is closely apposed to the terminal cisternae of the sarcoplasmic reticulum but is apparently structurally and electrically distinct from the SR membrane. The mechanism underlying the control of SR calcium release by the voltage across the TT membrane appears to involve at least three components: (1) voltage sensors in the TT membrane that can detect and respond to changes in TT membrane potential, (2) calcium channels in the SR membrane that can be opened to allow calcium ions to move out passively from SR to myoplasm down a large electrochemical gradient and (3) a system for coupling the TT voltage sensor to the SR calcium channel.

A general mechanism for sensing and responding to changes in membrane potential was suggested by Hodgkin and Huxley (1952) who hypothesized the existence of charged or dipolar molecules within the membrane. Changes in the voltage across the membrane would cause such intramembrane charges to redistribute within the membrane, producing some change in functional properties of the system controlled by the intramembrane molecules and giving rise to a small transmembrane charge movement current (I_Q). The basic properties of intramembrane charge movements and the resulting currents have been reviewed elsewhere (cf. Almers, 1978; Adrian, 1978; Schneider, 1981). Since I_Q is small compared to other membrane ionic and capacitative currents, a variety of precautions and procedures have to be employed to block membrane ionic currents and to substract both any remaining ionic current and the charging current for the membrane's linear capacitance in order to extract I_Q currents (cf. Horowicz and Schneider, 1981a). The fast charge movement current detected in squid axons (Armstrong and Bezanilla, 1973) serves as the gating current for sodium channels (Armstrong, 1981). The results reviewed here indicate that the slower I_Q detected in frog skeletal muscle (Schneider and Chandler, 1973) is involved in control of SR calcium release.

The intramembrane charge movement in skeletal muscle was initially thought to be involved with depolarization-contraction coupling because its kinetics and voltage dependence seemed to be roughly appropriate and because it was too slow to gate sodium channels (Schneider and Chandler, 1973). It was subsequently observed that charge movement disappears during depolarizations lasting tens of seconds and reappears only after seconds or tens of seconds of repolarization (Chandler, Rakowski and Schneider, 1976). The fact that the time courses of disappearance and reappearance of charge movement during prolonged depolarization and repolarization (Chandler et al., 1976) were similar to the time courses of development of the mechanically refractory state during prolonged depolarization and of recovery from mechanical refractoriness on repolarization (Hodgkin and Horowicz, 1960; Caputo, 1972 a and b) was an early indication that muscle charge movement is involved in the control of calcium release. Additional early support for the hypothesis that charge movement serves as a voltage sensor for calcium release was provided by the observation that when a fibre was repolarized after a period of prolonged depolarization, the voltage and time dependence of restoration of microscopically just detectable contraction was consistent with the voltage dependence of charge movement (Adrian, Chandler and Rakowski, 1976). Finally, microscopically just detectable contraction of fully polarized fibres was produced when a set «threshold» amount of charge had been moved by a pulse depolarization of the fibre. The threshold amount of charge movement for producing detectable contraction was constant for pulses of different amplitudes and for pulses to a given voltage immediately preceded by various prepulses (Horowicz and Schneider, 1981b). These results are all consistent with charge movement being the voltage sensor for SR calcium release. However, the mechanical response is several steps removed from calcium release so that a more direct comparison of charge movement and calcium release was needed.

Methods

Transient changes in cytosolic free calcium concentration in response to fibre depolarization have been monitored in muscle by introducing either calcium dependent photoproteins or metallochromic calcium indicators into individual muscle fibres (cf. Blinks, Wier, Hess and Prendergast, 1982). In our laboratory we have used the metallochromic indicator antipyrylazo III (Scarpa, Brinley and Dubyak, 1978) to monitor myoplasmic calcium transients produced by voltage clamp depolarization (Kovács, Rios and

SCHNEIDER, 1979, 1983). The experiments were carried out on single frog muscle fibres that were cut at both ends, mounted across two vaseline gaps to isolate both cut ends from the intact middle section and stretched so as to remove essentially all regions of overlap of the thick and thin contractile filaments. This large amount of stretch was essential for the elimination of mechanical movements which would otherwise have introduced large artifacts in the optically recorded calcium transient.

The free calcium concentration monitored by a calcium indicator comprises only a small fraction of the calcium actually released from the SR, a much larger fraction being bound to various myoplasmic constituents. Two general procedures have been used to calculate SR calcium release from measured free calcium transients. BAYLOR, CHANDLER and MARSHALL (1983) used literature values for concentrations and rate constants of the principal known muscle calcium binding proteins to calculate total calcium release from measured myoplasmic calcium transients. In our laboratory we have developed a complementary procedure (MELZER, RIOS and SCHNEIDER, 1984; SCHNEIDER, RIOS and MELZER, 1985). We analyze the calcium movements in muscle using three major components (Fig. 1): calcium release from the SR, the cytosolic pool of «fast calcium» and the

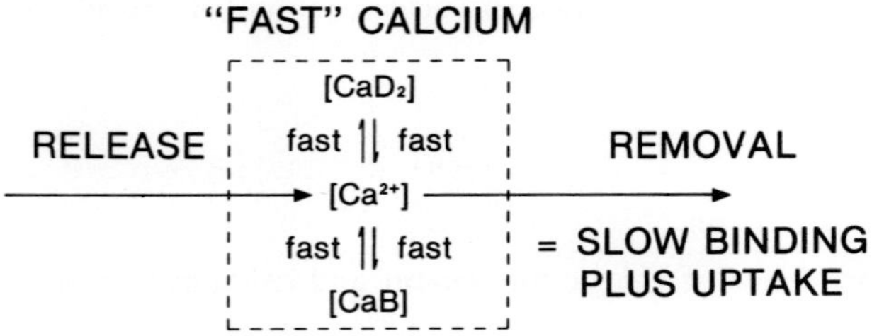

Fig. 1: Scheme for analyzing intracellular calcium movements in muscle fibres. CaD_2 and CaB represent calcium complexes with dye and with rapidly equilibrating intrinsic binding sites (SCHNEIDER et al., 1985).

overall system for removing calcium from the fast calcium pool. Fast calcium refers to the sum of the free calcium plus the calcium bound to all rapidly equilibrating binding sites in the fibre and removal refers to both slow binding and transport out of the myoplasm. Assuming calcium release to be turned off shortly after fibre repolarization, we use the time course of decay of free calcium following pulses of various durations and amplitudes to characterize the overall calcium removal capability of the fibre under investigation (MELZER, RIOS and SCHNEIDER, 1984, 1986a). Once the calcium removal system has been characterized, the rate of calcium release can be calculated as the sum of the rate of change of fast calcium plus the rate of removal of calcium from the fast calcium pool (MELZER et al., 1984; SCHNEIDER et al., 1985).

Fig. 2 shows the calcium transient produced by a 200 ms duration depolarizing pulse to −20 mV and the rate of calcium release calculated previously by MELZER et al. (1984) from the calcium transient. One immediate conclusion from this analysis was that calcium release from the SR reaches a maximum rate relatively early after the start of a depolarizing pulse and then declines appreciably during the pulse. This decline of release during a pulse was observed independent of whether the free calcium declined or increased during the pulse (MELZER et al., 1984) and appears to be due to a partial inactivation of the SR calcium channels responsible for calcium release (MELZER et al., 1984; SIMON, SCHNEIDER and SZÜCS, 1985).

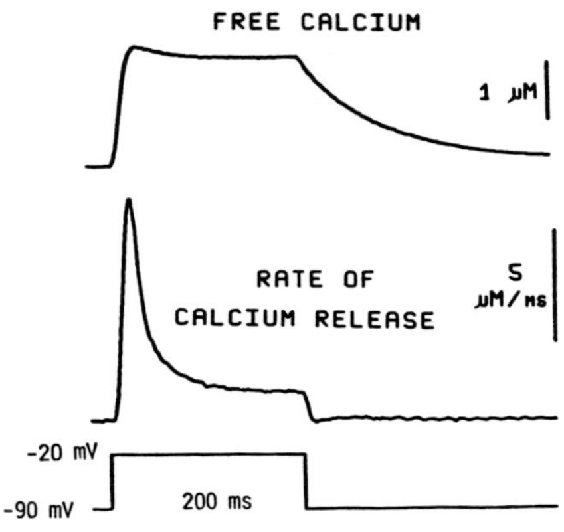

Fig. 2: Calcium transient recorded from a muscle fibre and the calculated underlying time course of calcium release from the sarcoplasmic reticulum. The calcium release was produced by a 200 ms voltage clamp depolarization to −20 mV from a holding potential of −90 mV. Data obtained from Melzer et al., 1984, fibre B140.

Results and discussion

Voltage dependence of charge movement and calcium release

Fig. 3 presents the steady state voltage dependence of charge movement and the voltage dependence of the peak rate of calcium release. It has been noted previously that the time course of decline of the rate of calcium release during a pulse and the ratio of peak to final level of rate of release during a pulse are both independent of pulse voltage over much of the voltage range (Melzer et al., 1984). In that case the voltage dependence of peak rate of release should provide a fairly accurate measure of the steady state voltage dependence of activation of SR calcium channels without having to make corrections for channel inactivation. This justifies the direct comparison of the voltage dependence of peak rate of release with that of charge movement in studies of steady state characteristics.

Fig. 3 shows that charge movement becomes significant at more negative voltages than calcium release and also has a less steep voltage dependence than release (Melzer, Schneider, Simon and Szücs, 1986b). However, both release and charge movement appear to saturate at roughly similar positive membrane potentials. These results are consistent with a gating system for calcium release having more than one step that produces charge movement but in which only the final step actually controls the opening of the SR calcium channel (Melzer et al., 1986b; Armstrong, 1981, reviews an analogous interpretation of gating of sodium channels in axon membranes). The theoretical curves fit to the data in Fig. 3 correspond to the three state two transition model shown in the figure, in which only the second transition influences directly the opening of SR calcium channels but in which both transitions involve charge movements. Fits of the three state model to data such as that in Fig. 3 from several different fibres were all quite good and indicated that the same amount of charge movement was produced by each of the two transitions but that the midpoint voltage for the first transition was 30 to 50 mV more negative than the midpoint voltage for the second transition (Melzer et al., 1986b).

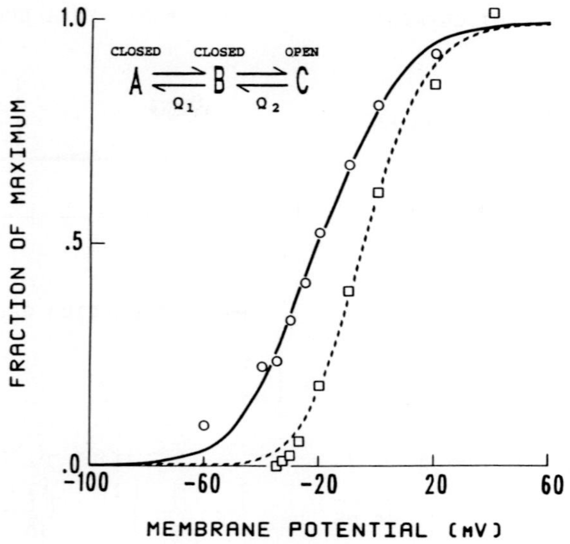

Fig. 3: Voltage dependence of intramembrane charge movement (circles) and peak rate of calcium release (squares). The theoretical curves give the best fit to the data of the three state model shown in the inset. The best fit values of the midpoint voltages for the first and second transitions were −33 and −5 mV and the charge moved in each of the two transitions was approximately equal. From MELZER et al., 1986b.

In principle, the presence of charge movement for pulses to voltages at which calcium release is negligible (Fig. 3) could be due to charge movement unrelated to calcium release or could indicate the existence of charge movements that are part of the voltage sensing mechanism for calcium release but are preliminary to the final step that actually controls the opening of the channel (above). The latter interpretation is supported by two observations concerning the effects of subthreshold prepulses. If a given test pulse was immediately preceded by a subthreshold prepulse (1), the test pulse duration required to produce detectable contraction was decreased (HOROWICZ and SCHNEIDER, 1981b) and (2) the latency before the start of the test pulse calcium transient was decreased without other changes, providing the test pulse was relatively long (SCHNEIDER, RIOS and KOVÁCS, 1981). The decrease in the test pulse duration for contraction or in the latency of the test pulse calcium transient were both quantitatively consistent with the time required to move the prepulse charge at the test pulse voltage (HOROWICZ and SCHNEIDER, 1981b; SCHNEIDER et al., 1981), indicating that prepulse charge is likely to be involved as a preliminary step in the mechanism controlling SR calcium release.

The charge movement that directly controls calcium release

We have recently devised an experimental protocol to isolate the component of charge movement arising from the final transition that directly controls the SR calcium channel (MELZER et al., 1986b). We employ a prepulse to a voltage very close to the voltage at which calcium release begins to be detectable and follow the prepulse immediately by

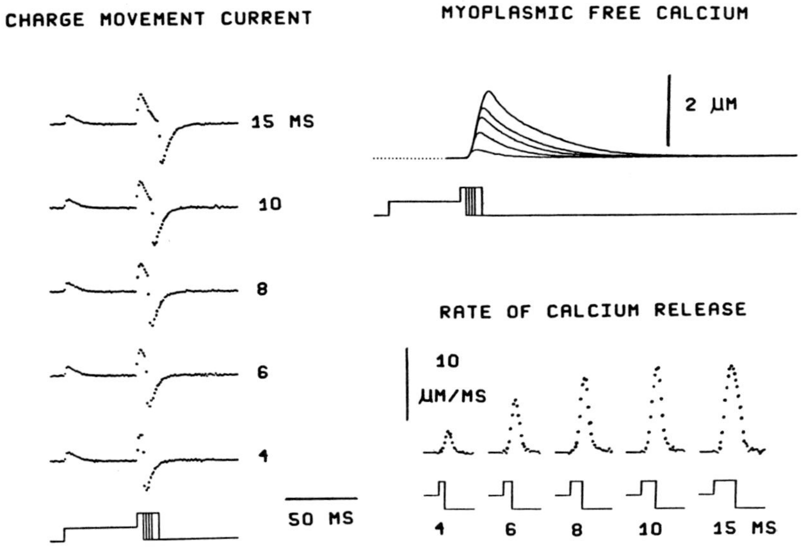

Fig. 4: Charge movement current, calcium transients and rates of SR calcium release from an experiment designed to study the role of suprathreshold charge movement in the control of SR calcium channels. The prepulse moves most of the subthreshold charge and does not activate calcium release. Charge moved during the immediately following test pulse should be predominately that component of charge movement which is directly involved in controlling the opening of SR calcium channels. See text and Melzer et al., 1986b for details.

various larger test pulses. Fig. 4 (top right) illustrates calcium transients obtained with this protocol using test pulses to the same voltage but having different durations. The records of rate of calcium release calculated for each calcium transient are shown at the bottom right and the charge movement current records for the same pulses are at the left. In addition to data such as that in Fig. 4, similar data were obtained in the same fibre for the same prepulse but different test pulse amplitudes. When all results from this fibre were combined (Fig. 5) we obtained a strikingly linear relationship between peak rate of calcium release and test pulse charge movement (Melzer et al., 1986b). Thus, once the charge of the preliminary transitions has been moved by the prepulse, a given amount of additional charge moved by the test pulse activates calcium release to the same extent, independent of test pulse amplitude or duration. This is as expected if the test pulse charge movement arises predominantly from the transition that directly controls calcium release.

Conclusions and questions

We believe that the present results provide strong evidence that activation of SR calcium release in skeletal muscle is closely regulated by intramembrane charge movement. A major remaining question concerns the nature of the system for coupling T tubule charge movement to the SR calcium channel. A direct macromolecular mechanical link as suggested by Chandler et al. (1976) would be consistent with currently available data on charge movement and calcium release if the link were displaced only by the last charge moving transition. Alternatively, a diffusable messenger might serve to transmit the signal

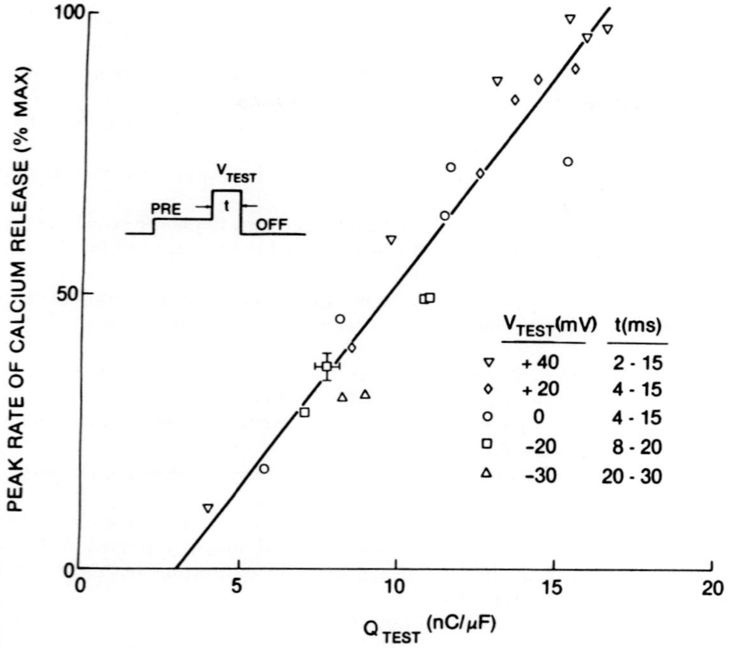

Fig. 5: Peak rate of calcium release as a function of the charge moved by the test pulse. Data obtained using the stepped ON pulse protocol in the upper inset. Each symbol represents a different test pulse voltage, with the voltages and durations as given in the lower inset. All prepulses were to −50 mV for 50 ms. From MELZER et al., 1986b.

from TT to SR, with liberation of the messenger being tightly controlled by the last charge transition. The messenger molecule would also have to be rapidly removed in order to account for the rapid turn off of release (RIOS, 1984) when a fibre is repolarized and charge is returned to its resting position in the TT membrane. It has recently been demonstrated that inositol 1,4,5-trisphosphate is capable of activating calcium release in skinned skeletal muscle fibres (VERGARA, TSIEN and DELAY, 1985) and in isolated SR vesicles (VOLPE, SALVIATI, DI VIRGILIO and POZZAN, 1985). Whether the liberation and breakdown of inosoitol 1,4,5-trisphosphate and the resynthesis of its precursor are sufficiently rapid to account for the kinetics of activation of muscle calcium release remains to be determined. In any case, if inositol 1,4,5-trisphosphate or any other diffusable messenger is involved, it seems that its liberation must be controlled by some molecular rearrangement associated with voltage dependent intramembrane charge movement.

Acknowledgements

We thank Drs. E. G. LAKATTA and R. C. GREULICH of the Gerontology Research Center for providing space, support services and a stimulating environment for carrying out part of this project. This work was supported by research grants from the Muscular Dystrophy Association and the U.S. Public Health Service (R01-NS13842). Dr. SIMON was the recipient of a fellowship from the Muscular Dystrophy Association.

References

Adrian, R. H., Chandler, W. K. and Rakowski, R. F. (1976): Charge movement and mechanical repriming in striated muscle. J. Physiol. **254:** 361–388.

Adrian, R. H. (1978): Charge movement in the membrane of striated muscle. Ann. Rev. Biophys. Bioeng. 7: 85–112.

Almers, W. (1978): Gating currents and charge movements in excitable membranes. Rev. Physiol. Biochem. Pharmacol. **82:** 96–190.

Armstrong, C. M. (1981): Sodium channels and gating currents. Physiol. Rev. **61:** 644–683.

Armstrong, C. M. and Bezanilla, F. (1973): Currents related to movement of the gating particles of the sodium channels. Nature, **242:** 459–461.

Baylor, S. M., Chandler, W. K. and Marshall, M. W. (1983): Sarcoplasmic reticulum calcium release in frog skeletal muscle fibres estimated from arsenazo III calcium transients. J. Physiol. **344:** 625–666.

Blinks, J. R., Weir, W. G., Hess, P. and Prendergast, F. G. (1982): Measurement of Ca^{2+} concentration in living cells. Prog. Biophys. Molec. Biol. **40:** 1–114.

Caputo, C. (1972a): The effect of low temperature on the excitation-contraction phenomena of frog single muscle fibres. J. Physiol. **223:** 461–482.

Caputo, C. (1972b): The time course of potassium contractures of single muscle fibres. J. Physiol. **223:** 483–505.

Chandler, W. K., Rakowski, R. F. and Schneider, M. F. (1976): Effects of glycerol treatment and maintained depolarization on charge movement in skeletal muscle. J. Physiol. **254:** 285–316.

Curtis, B. A. and Eisenberg, R. S. (1985): Calcium influx in contracting and paralyzed frog twitch muscle fibers. J. Gen. Physiol. **85:** 383–408.

Hodgkin, A. L. and Horowicz, P. (1960): Potassium contractures in single muscle fibres. J. Physiol. **153:** 386–403.

Hodgkin, A. L. and Huxley, A. F. (1952): A quantitative description of membrane current and its application to conduction and excitation in nerve. J. Physiol. **117:** 500–544.

Horowicz, P. and Schneider, M. F. (1981a): Membrane charge movement in contracting and non-contracting skeletal muscle fibres. J. Physiol. **314:** 565–593.

Horowicz, P. and Schneider, M. F. (1981b): Membrane charge moved at contraction thresholds in skeletal muscle fibres. J. Physiol. **314:** 595–633.

Kovács, L., Rios, E. and Schneider, M. F. (1979): Calcium transients and intramembrane charge movement in skeletal muscle fibres. Nature (Lond.) **279:** 391–396.

Kovács, L., Rios, E. and Schneider, M. F. (1983): Measurement and modification of free calcium transients in frog skeletal muscle fibres by a metallochromic indicator dye. J. Physiol. **343:** 161–196.

Lüttgau, H. Ch. and Stephenson, G. D. (1986): Ion movements in skeletal muscle in relation to the activation of contraction. In: Physiology of Membrane Disorders 2^n ed., T. E. .Andreoli, J. F. Hofmann, D. D. Fanestil and S. G. Schultz, eds. Plenum Publishing Corporation, 449–468.

Lüttgau, H. Ch. and Spiecker, W. (1979): The effects of calcium deprivation upon mechanical and electrophysiological parameters in skeletal muscle fibres of the frog. J. Physiol. **296:** 411–429.

Melzer, W., Rios, E. and Schneider, M. F. (1984): Time course of calcium release and removal in skeletal muscle fibres. Biophys. J. **45:** 637–641.

Melzer, W., Rios, E. and Schneider, M. F. (1986a): The removal of myoplasmic free calcium following calcium release in frog skeletal muscle. J. Physiol. **372:** 261–292.

Melzer, W., Schneider, M. F., Simon, B. J. and Szücs, G. (1986b): Intramembrane charge movement and calcium release in frog skeletal muscle. J. Physiol. **373:** 481–511.

Miledi, R., Parker, I. and Zhu, P. H. (1984): Extracellular ions and excitation-contraction coupling in frog twitch muscle fibres. J. Physiol. **351:** 687–710.

Rios, E. (1984): Off gating of calcium release in skeletal muscle. J. Gen. Physiol. **84:** 40a.

Scarpa, A., Brinley, F. J. and Dubyak, G. (1978): Antipyrylazo III, a «middle range» Ca^2 metallochromic iondicator. Biochemistry **17:** 1378–1386.

Schneider, M. F. (1981): Membrane charge movement and depolarization-contraction coupling. Ann. Rev. Physiol. **43:** 507–517.

Schneider, M. F. and Chandler, W. K. (1973): Voltage dependent charge movement in skeletal muscle: a possible step in excitation-contraction coupling. Nature, Lond. **242:** 244–246.

Schneider, M. F., Rios, E. and Kovács, L. (1981): Calcium transients and intramembrane charge movement in skeletal muscle. In: The Regulation of Muscle Contraction: Excitation-Contraction Coupling. A. D. Grinnell and M. A. B. Brazier, eds. Academic Press, Inc., New York, 131–142.

Schneider, M. F., Rios, E. and Melzer, W. (1985): Use of a metallochromic indicator to study intracellular calcium movements in skeletal muscle. Cell Calcium **6:** 109–118.

Simon, B. J., Schneider, M. F. and Szücs, G. (1985): Inactivation of SR calcium release in frog skeletal muscle is mediated by calcium. J. of Gen. Physiol. **86:** 36a.

Vergara, J., Tsien, R. Y. and Delay, M. (1985): Inositol 1,4,5-trisphosphate: A possible chemical link in excitation-contraction coupling in muscle. Proc. Natl. Acad. Sci. USA. **82:** 6352–6356.

Volpe, P., Salviati, G., Di Virgilio, F. and Pozzan, T. (1985): Inositol 1,4,5-trisphosphate induces calcium release from sarcoplasmic reticulum of skeletal muscle. Nature **316:** 347–349.

Fortschritte der Zoologie, Band 33 · Lüttgau (Hrsg.): Membrane Control
Gustav Fischer Verlag · Stuttgart · New York · 1986

The role of Ca^{2+} in inactivation and paralysis of excitation-contraction coupling in skeletal muscle

H. Ch. Lüttgau, G. Gottschalk and Dorothea Berwe

Department of Cell Physiology, Ruhr-University, D-4630 Bochum 1, FRG

During an action potential an inward flow of Ca^{2+} ions takes place through the T-tubular membrane of skeletal muscle fibres (e. g. Stefani and Chiarandini, 1982). This Ca^{2+} influx is too small to activate the contractile system directly. However, it might trigger the release of Ca^{2+} from the sarcoplasmatic reticulum (s. r.). Several lines of evidence exist which show that an increase in myoplasmic Ca^{2+} promotes the release of Ca^{2+} from the sarcoplasmic reticulum (for review see Lüttgau and Stephenson, 1986). Direct tests about the role of external Ca^{2+} in force activation, however, led to apparently controversial observations.

Several authors (Armstrong, Bezanilla and Horowicz, 1972; Lüttgau and Spiekker, 1979) showed that twitches and contractures could still be obtained when the extracellular Ca^{2+} concentration was reduced to extremely low values by applying the Ca^{2+} chelator EGTA. Under these conditions the electro-chemical gradient for Ca^{2+} was no longer inwardly directed so that an efflux rather than an influx of Ca^{2+} should occur upon depolarization. In addition Gonzalez-Serratos, Valle-Aguilera, Lanthrop and Del Carmen Garcia (1982) blocked the tubular Ca^{2+} channels with the organic Ca^{2+} antagonist diltiazem and were still able to produce normal potassium contractures.

These results show that the normal force activating process can take place in the absence of a Ca^{2+} influx. However, it is known that removal of external Ca^{2+} has distinct effects on force kinetics. It shortens the plateau of potassium contractures, accelerates force inactivation, impedes restoration, and shifts the steady state potential dependence of force inactivation to more negative potentials (Lüttgau and Spiecker, 1979; Cota and Stefani, 1981; Graf and Schatzmann, 1984). After long-lasting depolarization periods in «Ca^{2+}-free» solutions restoration may fail completely (for review see Frank, 1982), in particular when external Ca^{2+} is not replaced by an equivalent amount of Mg^{2+} to prevent an increase in external surface charge density (Barrett and Barrett, 1978). In the following we will describe these additional effects of Ca^{2+} removal in more detail. We hope that our results and their interpretation may help to settle continued controversy about the role of external Ca^{2+} in force activation.

Preliminary accounts of some of the experiments described here were presented at a meeting of the Physiological Society (Gottschalk and Lüttgau, 1985).

Methods

The experiments were done with single fibres from the *M. lumbricalis digiti IV* of the frog as described in detail elsewhere (CAPUTO and FERNANDEZ DE BOLAÑOS, 1979; GOMOLLA, GOTTSCHALK and LÜTTGAU, 1983). Isometric force was measured under voltage-clamp control with the help of two flexible internal microelectrodes. The external solution contained TEA sulphate which ensured a uniform potential along the whole fibre during point depolarizations (BERWE and FELDMEYER, 1984). Normal solution (in mM): K_2SO_4 1.25; TEA sulphate 40; $CaSO_4$ 8 ($Ca^{2+} \sim 4$ mM); MOPS 5; sucrose 113 and TTX 1×10^{-7} g/ml). In the «Ca^{2+}-free» solution Ca^{2+} was replaced by an «equivalent» amount of Mg^{2+} to prevent an alteration in external surface charge density (DÖRRSCHEIDT-KÄFER, 1976). This solution contained (in mM): K_2SO_4 1.25; TEA sulphate 40; $MgSO_4$ 17.4 (free $Mg^{2+} \sim 7$); EGTA 1; MOPS 5; Saccharose 101, and TTX 1×10^{-7} g/ml.

Results

The paralysed state

Depolarization induces a phasic contracture in skeletal muscle fibres. A few seconds of maximum force are followed by a spontaneous relaxation. The force controlling system is then in a refractory state, i. e. the release of Ca^{2+} from the reticulum is blocked or «inactivated». After a *short* depolarization period the ability to develop force can be restored within seconds by repolarizing the fibre. Restoration is delayed after a *longer-lasting* depolarization (HODGKIN and HOROWICZ, 1960). Removal of external Ca^{2+} appears to be an additional factor which impedes restoration. In the following, experiments will be described which suggest that during a depolarization the force controlling system turns from the active into the inactive state and if the depolarization continues into a secondary inactivate state. The latter state resembles the so-called paralysed state observed in fibres poisoned with the Ca^{2+} antagonist D600 (EISENBERG, MCCARTHY and MILTON, 1983).

In Fig. 1 the development of paralysis is shown. The fibre was clamped for 5 min at −90 mV. Subsequently we applied a pulse program consisting of cycles in which a long-lasting depolarization alternated with a shorter repolarization period at −90 mV. The first depolarization (Fig. 1, upper row) induced a roughly normal contracture showing the characteristic plateau. The second contracture was slightly smaller and almost without a plateau and during the third depolarization a force response was hardly detectable. In normal external solutions maximum force can be restored within about 20 s if the depolarization has lasted for 30 s or less. The combined treatment of the fibre with the «Ca^{2+}-free» solution and repetitive long-lasting depolarizations turned the system into a secondary refractory state from which it did not recover during a restoration period of 1.5 min at −90 mV. However, hyperpolarizing the membrane to −150 mV for only one min brought about a nearly complete restoration of force as shown by the subsequent depolarization (Fig. 1, upper row). Using the same or only slightly different depolarization-repolarization cycles as in Fig. 1 we observed great variations in the speed at which fibres were paralysed. Generally, 2–3 cycles were sufficient. However, often more cycles were needed, and occasionally we were unable to reach a complete paralysis. In the lower row of Fig. 1 the fibre had reached an incomplete paralysed state, and repolarization periods of 5 and 1.5 min at −90 induced no restoration. However, a restoration time of 1 min at −150 mV generated a partial recovery. A subsequent restoration phase of 2 min which immediately followed the short test depolarization removed paralysis nearly completely as revealed by the final depolarization.

In a few experiments we observed no restoration even after restoration times of up to 30 min at −150 or −120 mV. This could mean that restoration is no longer possible once an advanced stage of paralysis is reached or that under some conditions even longer restoration times are needed. However, it is also possible that these fibres were damaged.

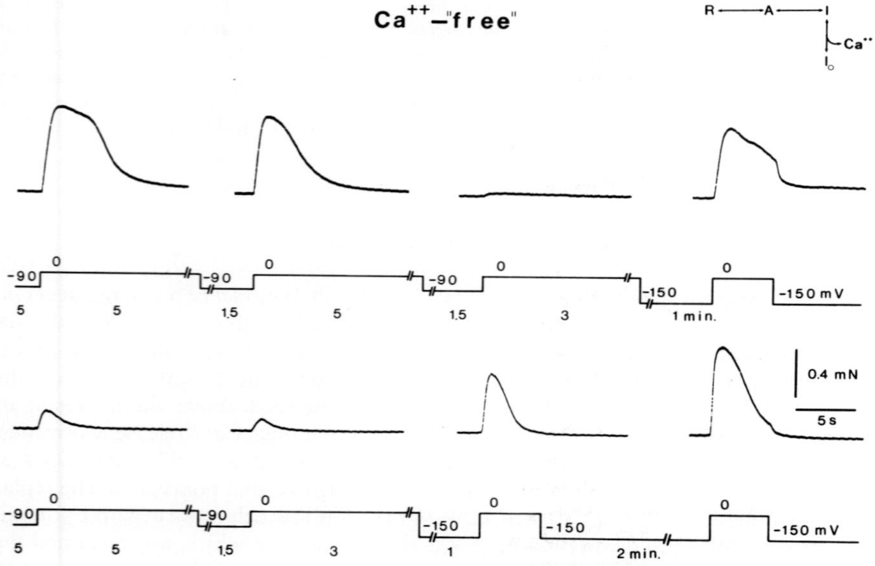

Fig. 1: Paralysis and restoration from paralysis in a solution with Ca^{2+} replaced by an equivalent amount of Mg^{2+} («Ca^{2+}-free»-solution, see Methods). The time scale of the pulse program (in min) differs from that of the contractures (time scale on the right). The lower row shows another fibre which had been turned into a partially paralysed state by a preceding depolarization. (T = 7 °C)

State diagram

As a working hypothesis for the design of further experiments we used the four state model shown in the inset of Fig. 1. Following Schneider and Chandler (1973) we assume that a voltage sensitive system (including mobile charged groups) is located in the T-tubular membrane which in some way controls the release of Ca^{2+} from the s. r. It can exist in three states (Hodgkin and Horowicz, 1960): Resting, active and inactive. Probably the inactive state corresponds to immobilized charges (see Rakowski, 1981). At negative membrane potentials the system exists in the resting state. Upon depolarization it turns first into the active state, which allows the release of Ca^{2+} from the s. r., and then into the inactive state, in which this release becomes blocked (Fig. 1, inset). New in this concept is our additional proposal that the coupling system in the T-tubular membrane possesses a potential dependent binding site for Ca^{2+}. We assume that the affinity for Ca^{2+}

is high at negative membrane potentials and becomes low in the depolarized state so that Ca^{2+} can dissociate. This dissociation turns the system into a secondary inactive state which is called the paralysed state (see Eisenberg et al., 1983). The dissociation can slowly be reversed after repolarizing the membrane. Since a removal of external Ca^{2+} is accompanied by a decrease in internal free Ca^{2+} (López, Alamo, Caputo, DiPolo and Vergara, 1983) the shift into the paralysed state should occur faster in «Ca^{2+}-free» solutions.

Slow inactivation of conductance has been observed in different ionic channels. The force controlling system described here resembles in this respect the sodium channel in excitable membranes. In the sodium channel fast inactivation could be impaired by the internal application of pronase while slow inactivation still took place. These results and further findings suggest that fast and slow inactivation are processes which occur in parallel and independently of each other rather than in a sequential manner (Rudy, 1978; Bezanilla, Taylor and Fernandez, 1982). In our state diagram we propose a sequential process but we can not exclude a parallel development of I and I_o ($A \longleftrightarrow I \longleftrightarrow I_o$; $A \longleftrightarrow I_o$).

The potential dependence of force inactivation

The state diagram shown above was derived from Hille's model of a voltage-dependent block of Na^{+} channels by local anesthetics (Hille, 1977; Bean, Cohen and Tsien, 1983). The same concept has recently also been applied to explain the action of Ca^{2+} antagonists upon Ca^{2+} channels (Bean, 1984). Following the theoretical approach of these authors a voltage-dependence of Ca^{2+} binding as described above should result in a hyperpolarizing shift of the availability of the system to induce Ca^{2+} release. Corresponding experiments had been performed by Lüttgau and Spiecker (1979) and Cota and Stefani (1981) with contractures induced by increasing external potassium. The replacement of external Ca^{2+} by Mg^{2+} caused a 20–30 mV shift towards more negative potentials of the ‹steady state› inactivation curve. Fig. 2 shows results in which we confirmed these experiments under voltage-clamp conditions. In a first series a conditioning pulse of 60 s was applied to establish a new distribution between resting and inactive sites. Subsequently the remaining availability of resting sites was checked by a full depolarization. In the presence of Ca^{2+} inactivation becomes detectable beyond -50 mV and reaches completion near -30 mV with a midpoint potential around -40 mV. Replacement of Ca^{2+} by Mg^{2+} shifted the inactivation curve by about 20 mV to more negative potentials.

When the conditioning pulse was prolonged from 60 to 240 s we measured a midpoint voltage in the Ca^{2+}-containing solution of -50 mV and a corresponding shift of the curve by 20 mV to more negative potentials when Ca^{2+} was replaced by Mg^{2+}. The results show that after a conditioning pulse of 60 s the system is not yet in a steady state, since a prolongation shifted the curve further towards more negative potentials. Therefore we assume that during the first 60 seconds mainly inactivation takes place and that during a prolonged conditioning pulse inactivated sites shift into the paralysed state, even when Ca^{2+} is present in the external solution. Altogether the experiments confirmed the earlier findings that removal of external Ca^{2+} causes an acceleration of the inactivation process indicated by the shift of the inactivation curve towards more negative potentials.

The large shift of the force availability curve during conditioning pulses of only one minute, observed in a «Ca^{2+}-free» solution, appears to be in contradiction with the relative slow development of the fully paralysed state (Fig. 1). The following experiment (Fig. 3) shows that this shift takes place because at a holding potential of -90 mV the system exists already in a partially paralysed state even though maximum force can still be

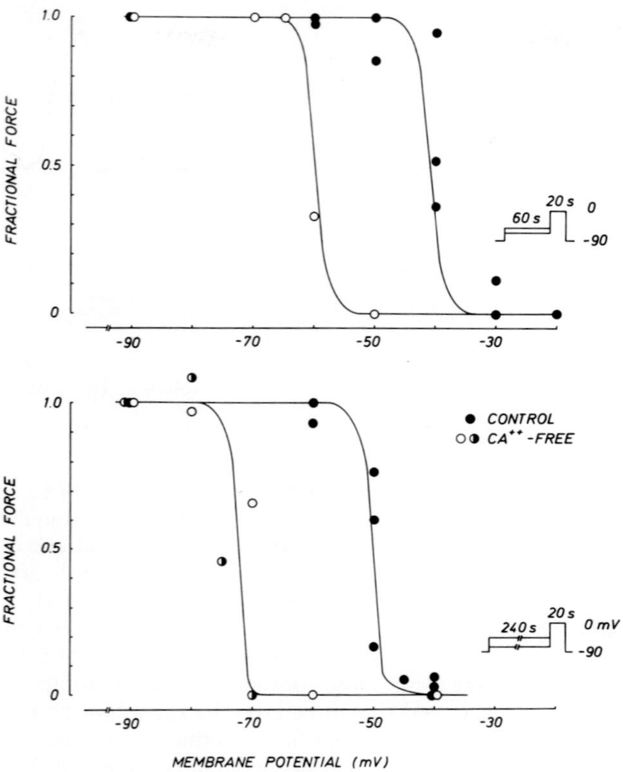

Fig. 2: The potential dependence of force inactivation. Isometric force, related to maximum force of the corresponding fibre, is plotted on the ordinate against the membrane potential during the conditioning pulse on the abscissa. The conditioning pulses lasted for 60 s (above) or 240 s (below), respectively. ● Solution with normal Ca^{2+}, ○ ◑ solutions in which Ca^{2+} was replaced by an «equivalent» amount of Mg^{2+}. ◑ These data (see BERWE, 1985) were obtained in the «Ca^{2+}-free» solution from fibres which had been left for 60 min in a «Ca^{2+}-free» solution which contained in addition 62 μM Quin-2. (T = 6.3–7 °C)

reached upon depolarizing the fibre from −90 to zero. Applying a holding potential of −120 mV instead of −90 mV we obtained nearly maximum force after a 60-second conditioning pulse at −50 mV and about 30 % at −40 mV (Fig. 3). Thus, hyperpolarizing the fibre from −90 to −120 mV restored further coupling sites and the availability curve approached that in the solution with normal Ca^{2+}. Force generation is a saturable indicator of the availability of functional coupling sites, which explains that additional repriming by hyperpolarization mainly prolongs the plateau phase of the contractures without further increasing maximum force. In agreement with this interpretation a shortening of the plateau was always observed when Ca^{2+} was replaced by Mg^{2+} in the external solution (LÜTTGAU and SPIECKER, 1979). Following the state diagram shown in Fig. 1, we regard the shift of the availability curve as a consequence of the transition of inactive sites to the paralysed state. This disturbs the potential-dependent equilibrium between resting and active/inactive sites so that more resting sites become activated and subsequently inacti-

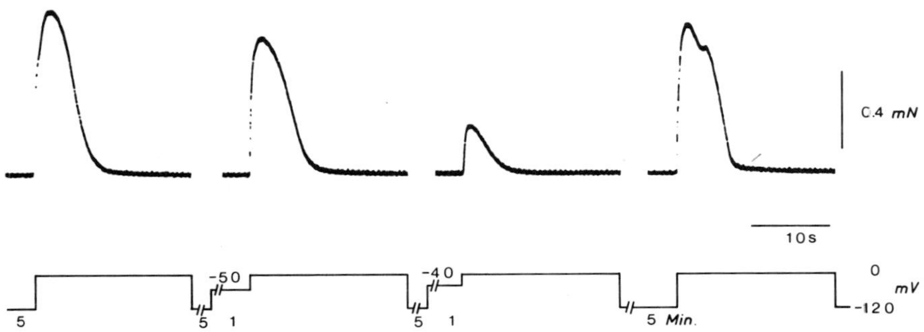

Fig. 3: The effect of a restoration period of 5 min at a more negative potential (−120 mV) on the potential dependence of force inactivation in a «Ca^{2+}-free» solution. The conditioning pulses (−50 and −40 mV) lasted for 1 min. (T = 7 °C)

vated. If we accept the concept of a potential-dependent binding of Ca^{2+}, the shift of the availability curve by roughly 50 mV following the change of sites from the inactivated into the paralysed state should provide some information about the differences in the dissociation constants between the high affinity state at negative potentials and the low affinity state at more positive potentials (compare HILLE, 1977; BEAN et al., 1983, and BEAN, 1984, concerning the potential-dependent binding of local anesthetics and Ca^{2+} antagonists to Na^{+}- and Ca^{2+}-channels). According to BEAN (1984) the shift Δ V should depend on the difference between the dissociation constant in the high affinity state (D_H) and that in the low affinity state (D_L) and should be given by the following equation: $\Delta V = k \ln (D_H/D_L)$, in which k represents the slope factor of the curves. Taking a value for k of 5 mV the equation leads to a difference in dissociation constants by 2–3 orders of magnitude. In order to explain the large effect of Ca^{2+} removal on this system, it appears reasonable to assume that the dissociation constant of the low affinity state corresponds to the internal free Ca^{2+} concentration in the resting state. This value is in the order of 10^{-7} to 10^{-6} Molar so that in the high affinity state a dissociation constant in the nmolar range should be attained. These data sound reasonable. However, it has to be kept in mind that force is only an indirect measure of Ca^{2+} release. In particular, force soon reaches a saturation value. The foregoing calculations should therefore only be regarded as an illustration of our concept.

In an earlier publication LÜTTGAU and SPIECKER (1979) tried to interpret shifts in the potential dependence of force inactivation with an alteration in surface charge density at the inner side of the membrane, the latter being controlled by a Ca^{2+} activated phosphorylation process. This concept includes an interesting regenerative element. However, it is incapable of explaining recovery from paralysis by hyperpolarization and the effects of the Ca^{2+} antagonist D600 (see GOTTSCHALK and LÜTTGAU, 1985).

Discussion

The model presented in the results provides a plausible explanation of the controversial effects of Ca^{2+} removal upon force activation. When fibres are stimulated by action potentials or short depolarization steps from a relatively negative holding potential, force can be produced for long periods of time, even in the presence of extremely high concentrations of EGTA (LÜTTGAU and SPIECKER, 1979). The shift into the paralysed state is prevented or at least delayed when the potential is mainly kept at negative values. During longer lasting depolarizations, however, in particular if they are repeated and follow insufficient restoration intervals, the fibres turn into the paralysed state. In the early stage of paralysis restoration is possible if the fibre is hyperpolarized for some time.

Models of excitation-contraction coupling in which Ca^{2+} dissociates from some site in the tubular membrane have been proposed before. In an extension of the well-known charge movement concept (CHANDLER, RAKOWSKI and SCHNEIDER, 1976) GRAF and SCHATZMANN (1984) suggested that Ca^{2+} imparts positive charge to the postulated gating molecule in the T-tubular membrane. If the fibre is depolarized, these charges move into the outside position thus activating in some way the release of Ca^{2+} from the sarcoplasmic reticulum. In this position Ca^{2+} is believed to dissociate from the coupling molecule into the «Ca^{2+}-free» tubular space. This decrease in charge accelerates the subsequent shift into the refractory position at the inner side of the membrane. The authors propose that, after Ca^{2+} has dissociated, the molecule remains blocked in this position in which it is not accessible to external *or* internal Ca^{2+}. The system remains in the refractory state even when the membrane is repolarized and external Ca^{2+} is readmitted. The model explains paralysis as well as the acceleration of force inactivation in «Ca^{2+}-free» solutions. In its present form, however, it does not provide an explanation for the observed slow shift into the paralysed state even in the presence of external Ca^{2+} and the relief from paralysis by hyperpolarizing the fibre.

The two models described so far deal with the control of Ca^{2+} release by a system located in the T-tubular membrane. They provide no answer concerning the transfer of the signal to the Ca^{2+} channels in the sarcoplasmic reticulum. In this way they differ from a third model in which a depolarization induced dissociation of Ca^{2+} from the T-tubular membrane is also assumed to take place. This model, which can be traced back to ideas proposed by HEILBRUNN and WIERCINSKI (1947), has been further advanced in a series of recent publications mainly by FRANK (e. g. FRANK, 1982). The author suggests that Ca^{2+} released from the T-tubular wall bridges the gap between the T-system and the sarcoplasmic reticulum by «triggering» the release of Ca^{2+} from the terminal cisternae. This idea is attractive since it is known that an increase in myoplasmic Ca^{2+} promotes the release of Ca^{2+} from the sarcoplasmic reticulum. The major shortcoming of this model is that it does not explain how force remains strictly under the control of the membrane potential of the tubular wall once force begins to develop by a Ca^{2+}-induced Ca^{2+} release. This has clearly been apprehended by FABIATO. In his recent reviews (e. g. FABIATO and BAUMGARTEN, 1984) he proposed several concepts about the way in which all-or-none responses could be avoided.

An alternative model about the way in which the gap between T-system and sarcoplasmic reticulum is bridged has recently been presented by VERGARA, TSIEN and DELAY (1985) who proposed that $InsP_3$ operates as a second messenger to activate Ca^{2+} release from the sarcoplasmic reticulum. In this context it would be of interest to learn how much Ca^{2+} might influence steps in the phosphatidyl-inositol cycle.

References

Armstrong, C. M., Bezanilla, F. M. and Horowicz, P. (1972): Twitches in the presence of ethylene glycol bis (β-aminoethyl ether)-N,N258-tetraacetic acid. Biochim. Biophys. Acta **267**, 605–608.

Barrett, J. N. and Barrett, E. F. (1978): Excitation-contraction coupling in skeletal muscle: Blockade by high extracellular concentrations of calcium buffers. Science **200**, 1270–1272.

Bean, B. P., Cohen, C. J. and Tsien, R. W. (1983): Lidocaine block of cardiac sodium channels. J. Gen. Physiol. **81**, 613–642.

Bean, B. P. (1984): Nitrendipine block of cardiac calcium channels: High-affinity binding to the inactivated state. Proc. Natl. Acad. Sci. USA **81**, 6388–6392.

Berwe, D. (1985): Thesis, Faculty of Biology Ruhr-University Bochum.

Berwe, D. and Feldmeyer, D. (1984): Investigation of force restoration in short toe muscle fibres under voltage-clamp control. Pflügers Arch. **402**, R46.

Bezanilla, F., Taylor, R. E. and Fernandez, J. M. (1982): Distribution and kinetics of membrane dielectric polarization. 1. Long-term inactivation of gating currents. J. Gen. Physiol. **79**, 21–40.

Caputo, C. and Fernandez de Bolaños, P. (1979): Membrane potential, contractile activation and relaxation rates in voltage clamped short muscle fibres of the frog. J. Physiol. **289**, 175–189.

Chandler, W. K., Rakowski, R. F. and Schneider, M. F. (1976): Effects of glycerol treatment and maintained depolarization on charge movement in skeletal muscle. J. Physiol. **254**, 285–316.

Cota, G. and Stefani, E. (1981): Effects of external calcium reduction on the kinetics of potassium contractures in frog twitch muscle fibres. J. Physiol. **317**, 303–316.

Dörrscheidt-Käfer, M. (1976): The action of Ca^{2+}, Mg^{2+} and H^{+} on the contraction threshold of frog skeletal muscle. Pflügers Arch. **362**, 33–41.

Eisenberg, R. S., McCarthy, R. T. and Milton, R. L. (1983): Paralysis of frog skeletal muscle fibres by the calcium antagonist D-600. J. Physiol. **341**, 495–505.

Fabiato, A. and Baumgarten, C. M. (1984): Methods for detecting calcium release from the sarcoplasmic reticulum of skinned cardiac cells and the relationships between calculated transsarcolemmal calcium movements and calcium release. In: Physiology and Pathophysiology of the Heart (N. Sperelakis ed.), pp. 215–254. Martinus Nijhoff Publishing, Boston.

Frank, G. B. (1982): Roles of extracellular and «trigger» calcium ions in excitation-contraction coupling in skeletal muscle. Can. J. Physiol. Pharmacol. **60**, 427–439.

Gomolla, M., Gottschalk, G. and Lüttgau, H. Ch. (1983): Perchlorate-induced alterations in electrical and mechanical parameters of frog skeletal muscle fibres. J. Physiol. **343**, 197–214.

Gonzalez-Serratos, H., Valle-Aguilera, R., Lathrop, D. A. and Del Carmen Garcia, Maria (1982): Slow inward calcium currents have no obvious role in muscle excitation-contraction coupling. Nature **298**, 292–294.

Gottschalk, G. and Lüttgau, H. Ch. (1985): The effect of D600 and Ca^{2+} deprivation on force kinetics in short toe muscle fibres of the frog. J. Physiol. **371**, 170 p.

Graf, F. and Schatzmann, H. J. (1984): Some effects of removal of external calcium on pig striated muscle. J. Physiol. **349**, 1–13.

Heilbrunn, L. V. and Wiercinski, F. J. (1947): The action of various cations on muscle protoplasm. J. cell. Physiol. **29**, 15–32.

Hille, B. (1977): Local anesthetics: Hydrophilic and hydrophobic pathways for the drug-receptor reaction. J. Gen. Physiol. **69**, 497–515.

Hodgkin, A. L. and Horowicz, P. (1960): Potassium contractures in single muscle fibres. J. Physiol. **153**, 386–403.

López, J. R., Alamo, L., Caputo, C., DiPolo, R. and Vergara, J. (1983): Determination of ionic calcium in frog skeletal muscle fibers. Biophys. J. **43**, 1–4.

Lüttgau, H. Ch. and Spiecker, Wiltrud (1979): The effects of calcium deprivation upon mechanical and electrophysiological parameters in skeletal muscle fibres of the frog. J. Physiol. **296**, 411–429.

Lüttgau, H. Ch. and Stephenson, D. G. (1986): Ion Movements in Skeletal Muscle in Relation to the Activation of Contraction. In: Physiology of Membrane Disorders (T. E. Andreoli, J. F. Hoffman, D. D. Fanestil, eds.), pp. 449–468.

Rakowski, R. F. (1981): Immobilization of membrane charge in frog skeletal muscle by prolonged depolarization. J. Physiol. **317**, 129–148.

Rudy, B. (1978): Slow inactivation of the sodium conductance in squid giant axons. Pronase resistance. J. Physiol. **283,** 1–21.
Schneider, M. F. and Chandler, W. K. (1973): Voltage dependent charge movement in skeletal muscle: A possible step in excitation-contraction coupling. Nature **242,** 244–246.
Stefani, E. and Chiarandini, D. J. (1982): Ionic channels in skeletal muscle. Annu. Rev. Physiol. **44,** 357–372.
Vergara, J., Tsien, R. Y. and Delay, M. (1985): Inositol 1,4,5-trisphosphate: A possible chemical link in excitation-contraction coupling in muscle. Proc. Natl. Acad. Sci. USA **82,** 6352–6356.

Fortschritte der Zoologie, Band 33 · Lüttgau (Hrsg.): Membrane Control
Gustav Fischer Verlag · Stuttgart · New York · 1986

Electromotor coupling in cilia

Hans Machemer

Arbeitsgruppe Rezeptoren, Fakultät für Biologie, Ruhr-Universität, D-4630 Bochum 1, FRG

1. Introduction

The cilium of eukaryotic cells is the most advanced motile organelle among non-muscular machines. Nine doublets of microtubules are arranged parallel to each other to form a cylinder, which encloses two microtubules within a central sheath. The 9+2 structure, or ciliary axoneme, is ubiquitous in the animal and plant kingdoms and may have evolved together with microtubule-regulated processes such as mitosis and meiosis (Margulis, 1981; Sleigh, 1985).

Ciliary movement bears interesting similarities to muscular function: mechanical forces are generated by an intracellular sliding-filament mechanism which works in a unidirectional manner (Afzelius, 1959; Satir, 1968; Sleigh, 1971; Sale and Satir, 1977). The ciliary membrane includes voltage-sensitive Ca channels, and ionic Ca is an intracellular messenger of the electromotor coupling process. In the unicellular eukaryotes, the exploitation of electric membrane signals for the generation of rapid motor responses is very evident in ciliary structures, but may also occur in systems involving acto-myosin such as cytoplasmic streaming (see Sleigh, 1984).

The present paper focuses on basic mechanisms in electromotor coupling of cilia. Accounts of the structure and function of protozoan and metazoan cilia have been given in previous reviews (Doughty and Dryl, 1981; Gibbons, 1981; Hausmann, 1983; Machemer, 1974a, 1977; Naitoh, 1982; Naitoh and Sugino, 1984; Sanderson, 1984; Satir, 1984; Sleigh, 1974a, b, Sleigh and Barlow, 1982; Takahashi et al., 1982). Therefore, only some principles of the ciliary machine will be recalled here. Emphasis is given to topics of controversy and to so far unanswered questions.

2. Principles of the ciliary machine

2.1. Elementary building blocks

Axonemal microtubules are hollow cylinders of 25 nm diameter composed of polymerized dimers of α- and β-tubulin. The microtubular doublet consists of one complete microtubule (13 tubulin protofilaments; A-tubule) and one incomplete microtubule (10 protofilaments; B-tubule) which shares a wall with the complete microtubule. Nine doublets arise from the ciliary basal body (kinetosome) which provides a firm anchorage for the peripheral axonemal structures. Pairs of transverse dynein arms originate from each A-tubule and extend towards the neighbouring B-tubule with a periodicity of 24 nm. The inner and outer dynein arms have a hook-like appearance in fixed preparations; the outer arms may be composed of three subunits, two of which are Mg-ATPases. Outer and inner dynein arms can generate active sliding between the doublets they are bridging (GIBBONS and GIBBONS, 1973), but they show different ATPase competence (HUANG et al., 1979). Neighbouring doublets are interconnected by highly elastic nexin links, with a longitudinal periodicity of 86 nm, at the inner side of the axonemal cylinder (WARNER, 1976).

2.2. Dynein cycle

The dynein arm cycle, as inferred from a variety of biochemical and ultrastructural studies, is illustrated in Fig. 1. An arm extends perpendicularly from doublet N binding to doublet N+1 in the absence of ATP (rigor state). Upon access of ATP the bridge is opened on doublet N+1 (standard configuration). With the hydrolysis of ATP the arm reextends and tilts towards the ciliary base (extended form). The arm binds to the new site, and ADP is released. Binding leads to conformational contraction of the arm molecule, so that doublet N+1 slides towards the ciliary tip relative to doublet N (SALE and SATIR, 1977; SALE and GIBBONS, 1979; SATIR et al., 1981).

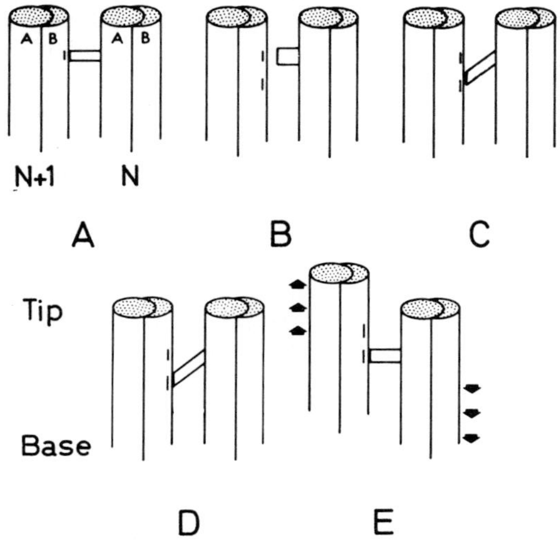

Fig. 1: Morphological correlates of the dynein cycle. A. Absence of ATP leaves the dynein arm of doublet N bound to doublet N+1 (rigor state). B. Opening of bridge and shortening of the dynein arm upon access of ATP (standard configuration). C. Hydrolysis of ATP leads to a re-extension and tilting of the dynein arm towards the ciliary base. D. Reattachment of the extended arm; release of ADP + P_i. E. Shortening and tipward swing of the dynein arm to a rigor-state position leads to a 16 nm relative sliding of doublets. After SATIR et al., 1981.

2.3. Sliding and bending

The unidirectional active sliding between one pair of doublets gives rise to bending of the cilium, because the proximally fixed microtubules retain a constant length and spatial arrangement (Fig. 2). Unipolarity of active swings of the dynein arms together with the geometry of the axoneme imply that quasi-antipodes of active doublets are passive back-sliders. Thus, agonist and antagonist mechanisms (for active sliding and for backsliding) coincide in the axonemal structure.

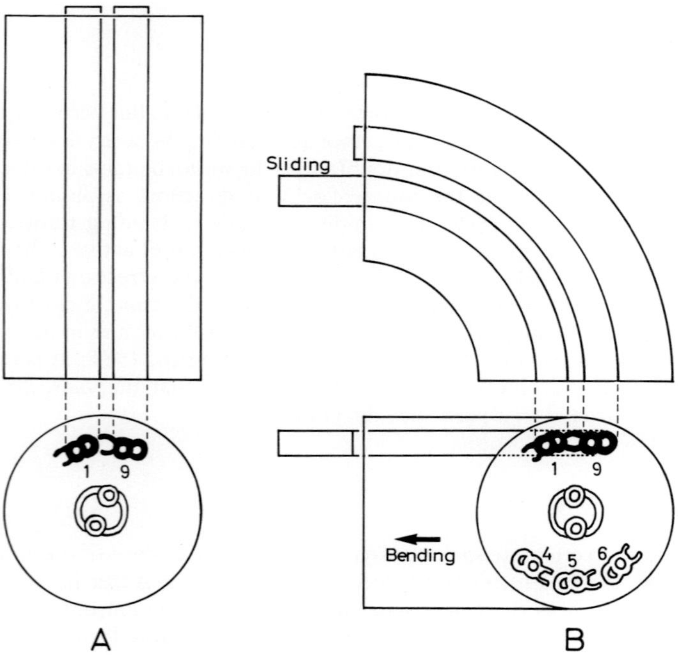

Fig. 2: Sliding and bending. Section of the ciliary shaft seen in side view (top) and from tip to base in cross-section (bottom) prior to (A) and following active sliding between one pair of microtubular doublets (B). Doublet 1 slides in the direction of the ciliary tip. With bases of 9 and 1 fixed the sliding between the pair of doublets translates into bending of the axoneme (arrow). It is presumed that the planes of sliding and of bending are parallel to each other. Due to bending the central pair reorients so that the common plane of the central tubules is perpendicular to the plane of bending. The quasi-antipodes of doublet-pair 9/1 (= 4, 5, 6) are passive sliders during this direction of bending, because the active sliding process is unipolar (Fig. 1). The scheme ignores overlapping in space of sliding at any instant of time (doublets 7/8, 8/9, 1/2 and 2/3 being active sliders together with 9/1, and doublets 3/4 and 6/7 being passive sliders together with 4/5 and 5/6.

2.4. Axonemal twisting

Sliding displacement between adjacent doublets is limited to 40 nm in a beating cilium (Warner, 1976). Translation of microtubular sliding into ciliary bending requires that the axoneme is not subject to major twisting. Electronmicroscopic studies have indicated the occurrence of twists in various axonemes; however, interpretations of the twist configuration is difficult due to the possible intervention of deformations during the experimental treatment. Previous quantitative analysis of quiescent planar S-shaped spermatozoa indicates that local twists play a minor role, if any, in ciliary function (OMOTO and BROKAW, 1983). Calculations of the contribution of dynein activity to twist within the axoneme have shown that the cumulative twist should not exceed a few degrees (HINES and BLUM, 1985). Thus, the structural framework of the axoneme, including nexin links and radial spokes, appears to be well suited for effective sliding-to-bending translation.

2.5. Sliding transfer and gyration

Ciliary bending is commonly not restricted to a single plane, but occurs in three dimensions. This type of movement is possible, since active sliding between one pair of doublets is transferred to neighbouring pairs of doublets. In the protozoa (also in echinoderms and tunicates) the cilium gyrates in the counterclockwise direction, as observed from tip to base, while it performs the cycle. The unidirectionality of bending transfer during the ciliary cycle suggests a unipolar time-staggered translocation of active sliding circling the axoneme (1/2 → 2/3 → 3/4 → ... 9/1). The counterclockwise direction of ciliary gyration appears to be invariable for one type of cell. The reverse direction, a clockwise gyration, has been observed in some phyla: in the lamellibranch molluscs and in mammal tracheal epithelia (AIELLO and SLEIGH, 1972; SANDERSON and SLEIGH, 1981). It is interesting, in view of the enantiomorphic structure of the axoneme, that unipolar, circular sliding transfer is not restricted to a particular direction.

2.6. Planar beating

Invertebrate and vertebrate spermatozoa may exhibit excursions of the axoneme in one plane (BROKAW, 1974; ISHIJIMA and MOHRI, 1985). The same is true for some compound ciliary structures such as the comb plates in ctenophores, the abfrontal cirri in lamellibranch gills and the cirri in the sedentarian polychaete *Sabellaria*. Planar bending patterns of spermatozoan axonemes include minor helical components (HIRAMOTO and BABA, 1978; WOOLLEY, 1979). Spermatozoa may be experimentally induced to generate helical bending (BROKAW, 1966). Planar or quasi-planar bending of the axoneme can arise from mechanical restraints to, and/or alteration in the program of, local sliding amplitude and rate of transfer of active sliding to new doublets. It is thought to result from functional adaptation of the basically three-dimensional rotary sliding machine.

2.7. Core of axoneme

The two central microtubules do not extend into the basal body. One microtubule arises from the basal granule (axosome), the other is distinctly detached from the granule (DUTE and KUNG, 1978). Curved projections from the central tubules give rise to an apparent helical structure (central sheath) to which the radial spokes extend from the A-tubule of the peripheral doublets. The periodicity of the spokes varies between 20 and 64 nm and appears to be related to the periodicity of the central sheath (WARNER, 1970, 1974).

Structural analysis of spoke configuration between A-tubules and sheath has shown that the spoke heads undergo an attachment-detachment cycle in bent regions of the axoneme and are detached distal to a bend, while sliding proceeds (WARNER and SATIR, 1974). The tentative localization of a ciliary dynein fraction at the spoke heads (DOUGHTY, 1979) awaits substantiation.

2.8. Rotation of the central complex

Structural analysis has shown that the central microtubules bend side-by-side, i. e. with the common plane of the tubules being normal (90°) to the axonemal bending plane (TAMM and HORRIDGE, 1970). In *Paramecium* the common plane of the central tubules rotates with the bending reorientations during the ciliary cycle (Fig. 3A); it also follows the helical deformation of the axoneme (OMOTO and KUNG, 1980). Central-tubule rotation has been directly demonstrated in the marine alga *Micromonas* (OMOTO and WITMAN, 1981). The existence of rotation of the central apparatus is indirect evidence, from mechanical considerations, that a major sliding capacity between the central tubules does not exist. Core rotation potentially includes rotation of the axosome in the manner of a socket, or an axial rotation of the inserted microtubule about the fixed axosome. Rotational movement may be limited to bidirectional swinging in those axonemes which exhibit a pronounced steady inclination during activity, such as the cirri in *Stylonychia* (Fig. 3C).

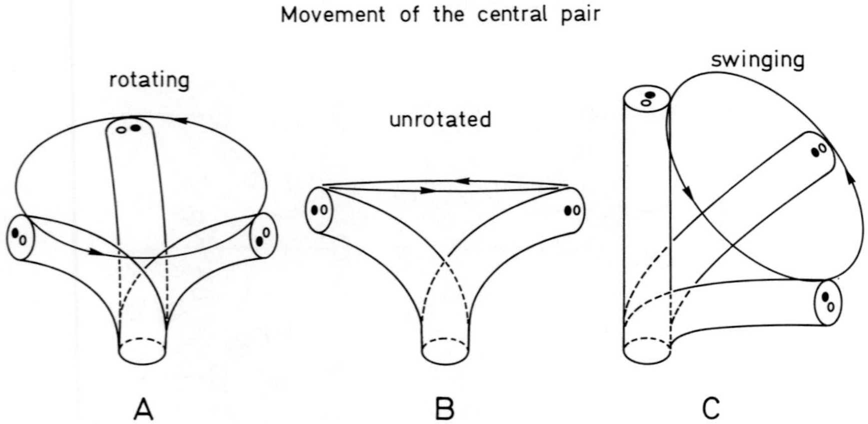

Fig. 3: Movement of the central pair of microtubules during ciliary gyration. A. The central complex rotates during the cycle of a cilium or flagellum, when bending of the axoneme is omnidirectional; this rotation is presumed to be a passive response to mechanical strain upon the central pair of microtubules; strain is minimal when the common plane of the microtubules is perpendicular to the bending plane. B. No rotation of the central complex occurs upon quasi-planar performance of the cycle as seen in ctenophores (Fig. 4) and many spermatozoa. C. Ciliary movement including pronounced inclination of the axoneme Fig. 14B, C) may impose mechanical restraints upon rotation of the central complex so that it swings bidirectionally, but does not rotate.

2.9. Role of the central complex

The system of radial spokes and tangential nexin links secures the integrity of the axoneme during local strain from sliding-to-bending transformation. Since the central complex can rotate, an active role of the complex in regulating the ciliary cycle has been suggested (OMOTO and KUNG, 1980). Geometric considerations imply that during rotation of the complex one central tubule is juxtaposed to the most active pair of doublets (i. e. with maximum sliding rate); the other central tubule is near the principle pair of backsliders (Fig. 2B).

The discovery of reduced axonemal structures in 3-dimensionally motile flagella of gregarine gametes (6+0, *Lecudina tuzetae*, SCHREVEL and BESSE, 1975; 3+0, *Diplauxis hatti*, PRENSIER et al., 1980) and eel spermatozoa (9+0, *Anguilla anguilla*, GIBBONS et al., 1983) has shown that the central complex is not essential for regular sliding transfer. Although mutants of *Chlamydomonas* with the central tubules and radial spokes missing were paralyzed (ADAMS et al., 1981), suppressor mutations restored motility in the absence of central structures (HUANG et al., 1982). An inhibitory function of the central complex was suggested by observations of reduced beating frequency in a *Chlamydomonas* mutant with missing spoke-heads (BROKAW et al., 1982). On the other hand, the highest beating frequency ever recorded in axonemal structures (95 Hz) is from a 9+0 eel flagellum (GIBBONS et al., 1983).

It is interesting to note that rotation of the central complex is unlikely to regulate temporal and spatial polarization of the ciliary cycle: (1) each of the central tubules meets the 9 doublets in sequence during the cycle (Figs. 2B, 3A); (2) the central tubules of comb-plate cilia in the ctenophore *Pleurobrachia* do not rotate during a 180° reversal in planar beat direction (TAMM and TAMM, 1981) (Figs. 3B, 4); (3) proximal inclination of active cirri in *Stylonychia* prohibits a full (360°) rotation of the central complex during the 3-dimensional cycle (MACHEMER and SUGINO, 1986) (Fig. 3C).

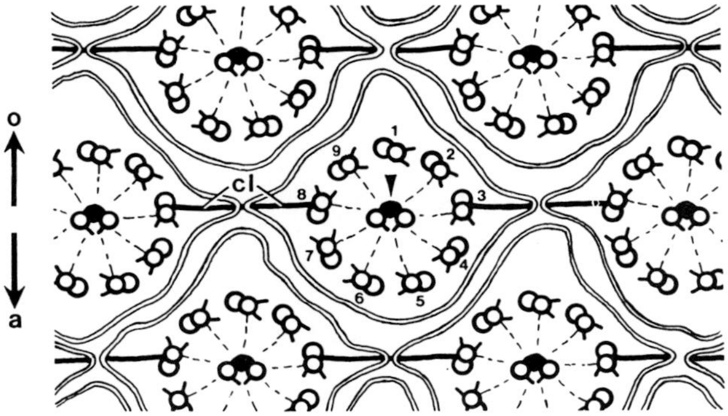

Fig. 4: Active or passive role of the central pair? Cross-sections of comb-plates of the ctenophore *Pleurobrachia* seen base-to-tip show compartmenting lamellae (cl), which interconnect the axonemes, running at right angle to the plane of bending. A dense midfilament at one side of the central pair (arrowhead) serves as marker for the orientation of the central complex (AFZELIUS, 1961). This orientation is the same during oral (o) or aboral (a) direction of the power stroke (arrows) indicating that the central pair does not regulate the ciliary cycle (TAMM and TAMM, 1981). In addition, mechanical considerations suggest that the compartmenting lamellae, which interconnect doublets (3 and 8) of neighbouring axonemes, determine the planar performance of beating of the comb-plate.

An overview of the properties of the ciliary machine identified so far suggests that the basically simple mechanical design incorporates some complex functions. Variations in ciliary responses further indicate the existence of sophisticated mechanisms controlling ciliary motion.

3. Ciliary responses in demembranated preparations

3.1. The two-machine hypothesis

The pioneering results of HOFFMANN-BERLING (1955) in reactivation of glycerinated axonemes with Mg-ATP have been confirmed in a variety of ciliated protozoan and

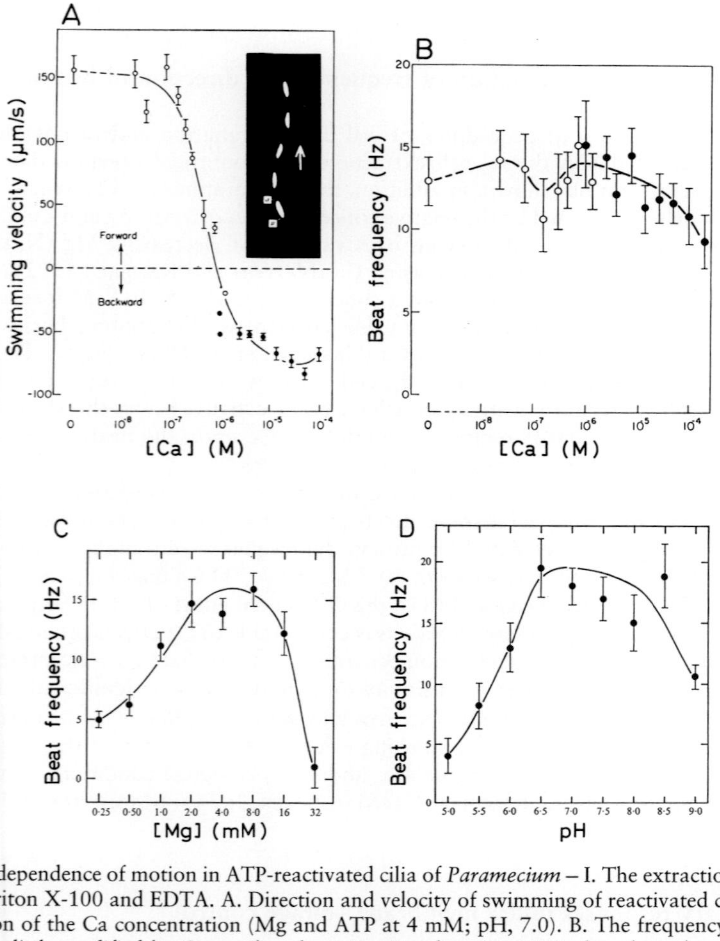

Fig. 5: Ion dependence of motion in ATP-reactivated cilia of *Paramecium* – I. The extraction medium included Triton X-100 and EDTA. A. Direction and velocity of swimming of reactivated cell models as a function of the Ca concentration (Mg and ATP at 4 mM; pH, 7.0). B. The frequency of ciliary beating was little modified by Ca, so that the swimming direction (A) is thought to be primarily a function of Ca-regulated beat orientation. C. Mg at concentrations between 2 mM and 8 mM was most effective in reactivating ciliary frequency. D. The frequency of reactivated cilia was maximal near pH values of 7 and 8, and steadily declined with rising acidity. A, B, NAITOH and SUGINO, 1984; C, D, NAITOH and KANEKO, 1973.

metazoan cells (see GOLDSTEIN, 1974). According to the earlier literature ionic magnesium plays a major role in regulating ciliary frequency. In glycerinated paramecia addition of Ca to Zn-ATP induced an anteriad reorientation (maximally 50°) of the nonbeating cilia; this led to the hypothesis that the cilium incorporates two ATP-energized mechanisms, one employing Mg, the other using Ca (NAITOH, 1969).

Separation of an orientational response from the frequency response was confirmed in *Paramecium* after demembranation by the detergent Triton-X (NAITOH and KANEKO, 1972) and in live cells using nickel-paralyzed cilia (NAITOH, 1966; ECKERT and NAITOH, 1970). According to the two-machine hypothesis, locomotion by means of cilia results from the combined action of intraciliary Mg and Ca in regulating two axonemal functions: the frequency (being Mg-dependent; «beating mechanism») and orientation of the ciliary power stroke (being Ca-dependent); «reversal mechanism»; NAITOH, 1982) (Fig. 5).

3.2. Ca-dependent regulation of frequency and direction of beating

Recent modification of procedures of cell demembranation and reactivation (use of EGTA instead of EDTA during cell extraction) has confirmed previous data based on EDTA-buffering, but has shown, in addition, that preparations of ATP-reactivated *Paramecium* models are affected by the relative concentrations of both Mg and Ca. Cell models of *Paramecium* were induced to swim backwards upon decreasing Mg (NAKAOKA and TOYOTAMA, 1979) as well as by increasing Ca (NAITOH and KANEKO, 1972) (Fig. 6).

Raising as well as lowering Ca from a concentration of 6×10^{-7} M increased ciliary frequency. Ca concentrations below that value led to forward swimming; backward swimming was observed above 6×10^{-7} M Ca (NAKAOKA et al., 1984) (Fig. 6). The results of various reactivation procedures may depend on preservation or degradation of those proteins which confer Ca-sensitivity on ciliary cyclic activity. It was shown, for example, that calmodulin antagonists removed the effect of Ca upon the beating frequency in a concentration-dependent manner (NAKAOKA et al., 1984).

Demembranation of *Chlamydomonas* using EGTA for Ca-buffering and subsequent Mg-ATP reactivation showed that Ca affects at least two parameters of the flagellum: the degree of beating asymmetry and frequency; the frequency of a highly asymmetric beat was near 50 Hz at Ca concentrations of 10^{-9} M; at 10^{-4} M Ca flagellar beat at 70 Hz was symmetric (OMOTO and BROKAW, 1985); the differential effect of Ca on flagellar frequency and beating pattern of *Chlamydomonas* is comparable to Ca effects observed in cilia of *Paramecium*, since flagellar inactivation occurred at intermediate Ca concentrations (10^{-5} M) (BESSEN et al., 1980). The Ca-sensitivity for inactivation was significantly different in the two flagella of *Chlamydomonas* (KAMIYA and WITMAN, 1984). The data using EGTA-buffering during extraction give supporting evidence to the view that the frequency and directional responses of the axoneme are, under physiological conditions, coupled by a common regulating agent, intraciliary Ca (MACHEMER, 1974b; MACHEMER and DE PEYER, 1982).

4. Ciliary responses under membrane voltage control

Ciliary activity is under control of the membrane potential according to extensive experimental work in protozoan and metazoan cells (see AIELLO, 1974; ECKERT, 1972; MACHEMER, 1977; MACHEMER and DE PEYER, 1977; MACKIE, 1970; NAITOH, 1982;

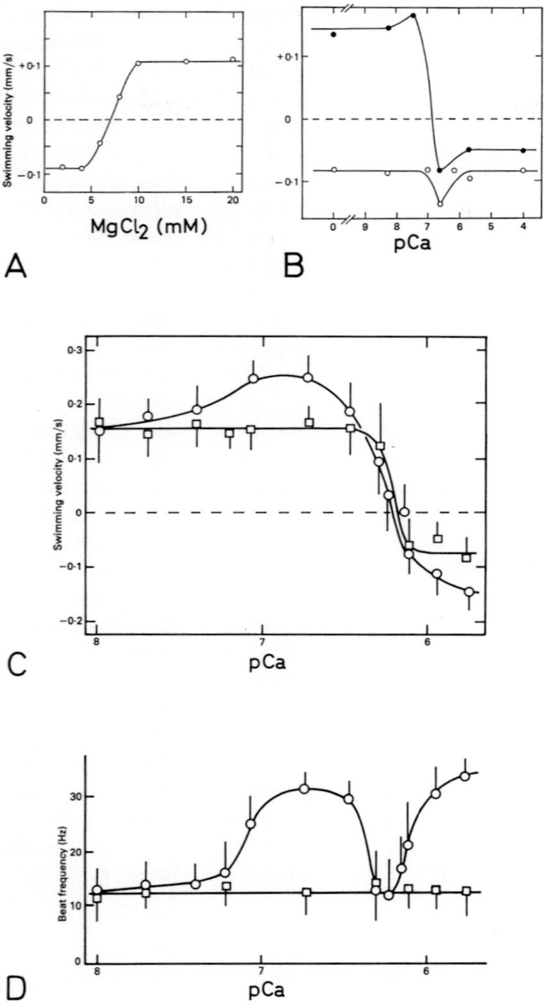

Fig. 6: Ion dependence of motion in ATP-reactivated cilia of *Paramecium* – II. Demembranation by Triton in the presence of EDTA or EGTA. A. A variation in Mg concentration with no Ca present affected the swimming direction and velocity inversely to Ca (see B; Fig. 5A). B. The effect of Ca upon the swimming direction and velocity was dependent upon the level of Mg (open circles, 4 mM, closed circles, 15 mM). C. Swimming of model cells as a function of Ca after extraction using EGTA (circles) and EDTA (squares); reactivation with 8 mM Mg and 4 mM ATP. Both methods confirm Ca-effects on the direction of beating. An effect on swimming velocity was shown using EGTA buffering. D. Ca-dependence of beat frequency. Meaning of symbols as in (C). It is seen that EGTA-buffering during demembranation preserves a Ca-sensitivity of cyclic beating, which is presumably lost upon extraction in the presence of EDTA. Between Ca concentrations of 10^{-7} M and 2×10^{-6} M the frequency profile resembles that following a positive-going voltage ramp (Fig. 7). The frequency minimum at 6×10^{-7} M coincides with the reversal in swimming direction (C, compare Fig. 7). A, B, Nakaoka and Toyotama, 1979; C, D, Nakaoka et al., 1984.

Naitoh and Sugino 1984; Saimi, 1977). Regulation of the cilia may also be mediated by the endocrine system (Sanderson and Sleigh, 1982), by modulators and neurotransmitters (Murakami, 1983), and cyclic AMP (Gaber and Kopf, 1980; Murakami, 1983). 5-Hydroxytryptamine is without effect in model cilia of *Mytilus* (Sanderson and Satir, 1982). In many of these cases, a separation of the signalling chain from the electric membrane response has not been critically demonstrated. In *Paramecium* injected cyclic AMP was ineffective in raising ciliary frequency, when the membrane potential was clamped at the resting potential, although the same substance raised the frequency and hyperpolarized the membrane of the unclamped cell (Hennessey et al., 1985).

A large body of electrophysiological data has been accumulated suggesting that depolarization of the membrane may activate ciliary Ca channels which allows Ca to accumulate in the intraciliary space, thereby mediating the motor response of the cilium. Ciliary responses following membrane hyperpolarization are distinctly different from those following depolarization. No excitable channels are activated (or deactivated) with hyperpolarization.

The current terminology of ciliary responses includes traditional expressions such as «normal beating», «ciliary reversal» and «augmentation». In addition, there exists a growing number of descriptive terms («quiescence», Aiello, 1960; Gibbons and Gibbons, 1980; Tamm and Moss, 1985; «inactivation», Machemer, 1974; «relaxation», Mackie et al., 1974; «stationary», Sleigh, 1974; «arrest» or «stoppage», Takahashi and Murakami, 1968; Mackie, 1970; Sleigh and Barlow, 1982; «intermediate beat cycle», «at rest», Sleigh and Barlow, 1982; «laydown», Tamm and Moss, 1985; «silent reorientation», De Peyer and Machemer, 1983; «inclination», Machemer and Sugino, 1986). Many of these responses are associated with changes in membrane polarization.

Two generalizing terms have been coined for the characterization of motor responses of previously resting cirri in *Stylonychia*: «depolarization-dependent ciliary activation» (DCA), and «hyperpolarization-dependent ciliary activation» (HCA) (Machemer and de Peyer, 1982). This nomenclature is useful for the detection of homologies among various motor responses. In the following, ciliary responses will be discussed including «DCA» and «HCA» as organizing principles. Experiments employing voltage-clamp techniques will be mainly referred to, because judging electromotor coupling in cilia is difficult, unless the membrane potential is under direct control (see also section 5).

4.1. Ciliary frequency profile

The frequency of beating may rise following depolarization and hyperpolarization. Fig. 7 gives overviews of ciliary motor responses to positive-going voltage ramps for two different ciliates and different types of ciliary organelles. In *Stylonychia* the frequency of the cirri, but not of the membranelles, rises with rising voltage stimuli (Fig. 7A). The cirri as well as the membranelles are compound structures formed from many independent and complete cilia. Different types of ciliary organelles of one cell may vary in sensitivity to the same voltage: the marginal cirri show smaller latencies and larger peak frequencies to hyperpolarization and depolarization than the frontal cirri which arise from the ventral surface of the cell.

Cilia of *Paramecium* have, in principle, similar frequency characteristics; however, normal activity at the resting membrane potential occurs along the «hyperpolarizing» slope of the frequency profile; ciliary inactivity occurs with small depolarizations (Fig. 7B).

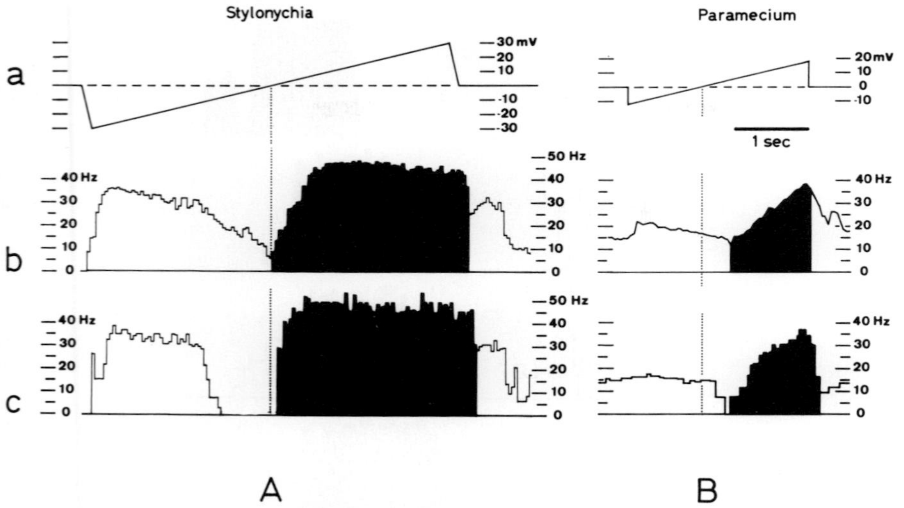

Fig. 7: Ciliary responses in *Stylonychia* (A) and *Paramecium* (B) to bipolar voltage ramp. a. Time course of the holding potential under voltage-clamp (continuous line) with reference to the membrane resting potential (dashed line). b. Frequency response of cilia averaged, c., of single cilium or cirrus. A. Cirral activity in *Stylonychia* is minimal, typically zero, at the membrane resting (= zero current) potential. The frequency rises with negative or positive deflections from the resting potential. The frequency-voltage relation following depolarization is particularly steep. The voltage range of inactivation varies in individual cirri (see Fig. 9). White histogram bars indicate posteriad, black bars anteriad direction of the power stroke observed in side view. B. A similar frequency profile of cilia in *Paramecium* is shifted along the voltage axis so that the ciliary frequency at membrane rest is between 10 and 20 Hz with the power stroke pointing posteriorly; ciliary inactivation occurs at small depolarizations. Similarities between the frequency histograms and the cell reactivation studies (Fig. 6C, D) suggest that the intraciliary Ca concentration is controlled by the membrane potential. MACHEMER and DE PEYER, 1982.

«Inactivity» of cilia in *Paramecium* and «rest» of the cirri in *Stylonychia* are presumably homologous motor phenomena.

Application of different rates of membrane polarization illustrates that a particular ciliary frequency couples to a particular membrane potential (Fig. 8). Cirri of *Stylonychia* are in an inactive state in a small range of voltage near the resting potential. Ciliary frequency during HCA relates less steeply with membrane polarization than frequency during DCA, and the frequency maximum of HCA remains clearly below the maximum of DCA (Figs. 7–9). Threshold for activation of the cyclic response are subject to positional influence within the same type of ciliary organelle: those cirri inserting more posteriorly along the cell axis showed the relatively largest threshold voltage (Fig. 9); this applies to DCA as well as to HCA.

Testing electromotor coupling in cilia by means of clamped voltage ramps is complicated due to time-dependent properties of the ciliary motor and of the membrane. First, the minimal time period of a momentary frequency response is around 20 ms (assuming the frequency to be at 50 Hz) and may rise to hundreds of milliseconds for low beating frequencies. High rates of potential changes tend to distort, or even suppress, the ade-

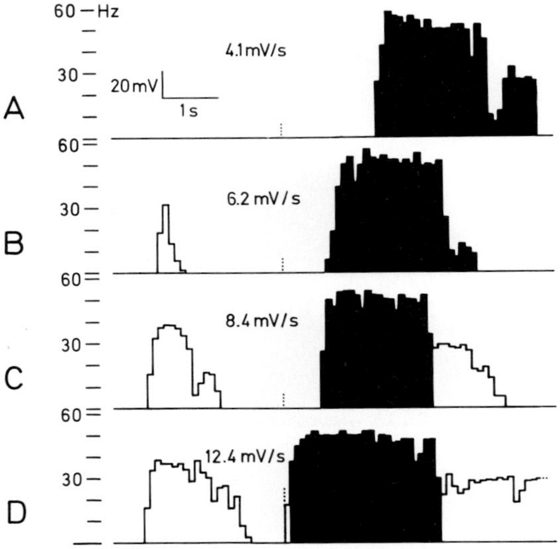

Fig. 8: A qualitative test of the voltage-dependence of ciliary frequency applying voltage ramps of appropriate rates of rise to *Stylonychia* (A–D). The graph illustrates that the responses are primarily voltage-, not time-dependent. Same symbols as in Fig. 7. DE PEYER and MACHEMER, 1983.

quate, i. e. voltage-coupled, ciliary motor response. Thus, a rapid 20 mV positive sawtooth ramp (160 mV/s) applied to the *Paramecium* membrane induced a direct transition from normal to high-rate reversed beating of the cilia comparable to events following an action potential (Fig. 10A). Only with slower ramps was the occurrence of voltage-dependent inactivity and the voltage-graded frequency response of the cilium revealed (Fig. 10B, C).

Second, ciliary motor responses to low rates of membrane polarization are subject to membrane accomodation and/or ion accumulation or depletion in the ciliary space. In

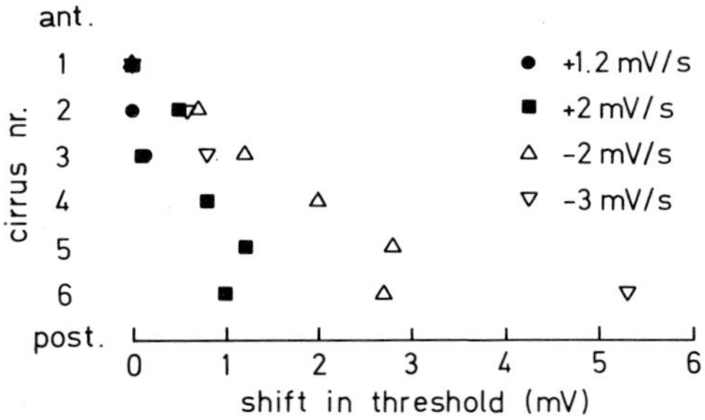

Fig. 9: An antero-posterior gradient in voltage-dependent cyclic activation. Six marginal cirri were selected within an 80 μm distance along the antero-posterior axis of *Stylonychia* (36 % of cell length), the distance between two evaluated cirri being 13 to 20 μm. The diagram shows that the threshold voltage grew in the posterior direction for depolarizing and hyperpolarizing stimulation; the shifts in threshold were larger for hyperpolarizing (open symbols) than for depolarizing stimulation (closed symbols). DE PEYER and MACHEMER, 1983).

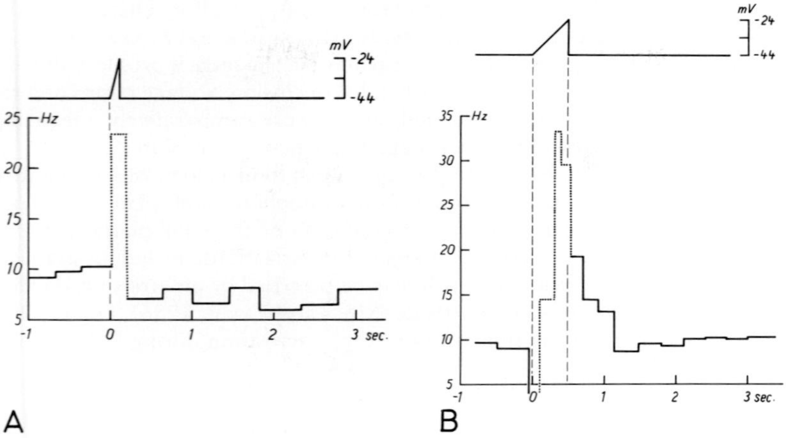

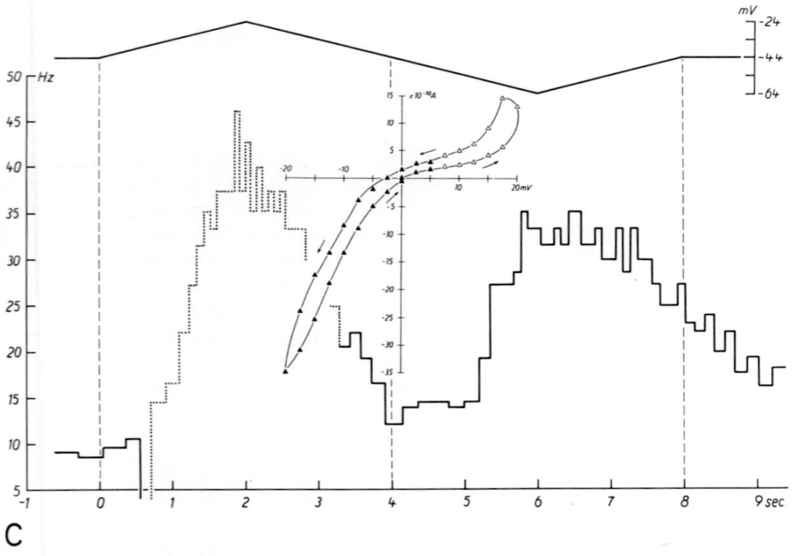

Fig. 10: Limits of electromotor coupling in cilia. A. A rapid sawtooth depolarization (160 mV/s) from the zero-current potential (−44 mV) under voltage-clamp induced the cilia in *Paramecium* to switch directly from normal beating near 10 Hz to reversed beating at 23 Hz (dotted histogram); this sequence resembles events following an action potential (Fig. 12). B. Depolarizations at reduced rate (40 mV/s; C, 10 mV/s) allowed the ciliary response to follow the time-course of the voltage, i. e. to insert inactivation prior to gradual activation of reversed beating. C. With increasingly low rates of membrane polarization the frequency response tended to lag behind the voltage signal; at the same time the I/V relation shifted along the voltage axis (inset). MACHEMER, 1975.

Paramecium voltage-dependent motor responses, DCA as well as HCA, relaxed during voltage steps sustained over one-minute periods (MACHEMER and ECKERT, 1975). Similar time-dependent effects are apparent in the asymmetric frequency profile following slow symmetric triangular voltage ramps (Fig. 10C). In conclusion, voltage ramps of intermediate velocities, ranging between 5 mV/s and 20 mV/s are comparatively adequate, albeit non-ideal, stimuli for representing the voltage-frequency relationship.

Voltage-clamp techniques have not yet been applied to metazoan cilia for electromotor correlations. Recent intracellular recordings from ctenophore comb-plate cells suggest that membrane depolarization can activate cyclic activity of the combplates in the normal (aboral) and reversed (oral) direction. Larger depolarizations, including graded action potentials, induce reversed beating, which may be preceded by an arrest or «laydown» in the direction of the «reversed» power stroke (Moss and TAMM, 1986) (Fig. 11). Reversed beating of the combplate bears similarities to cyclic activation during DCA in ciliates.

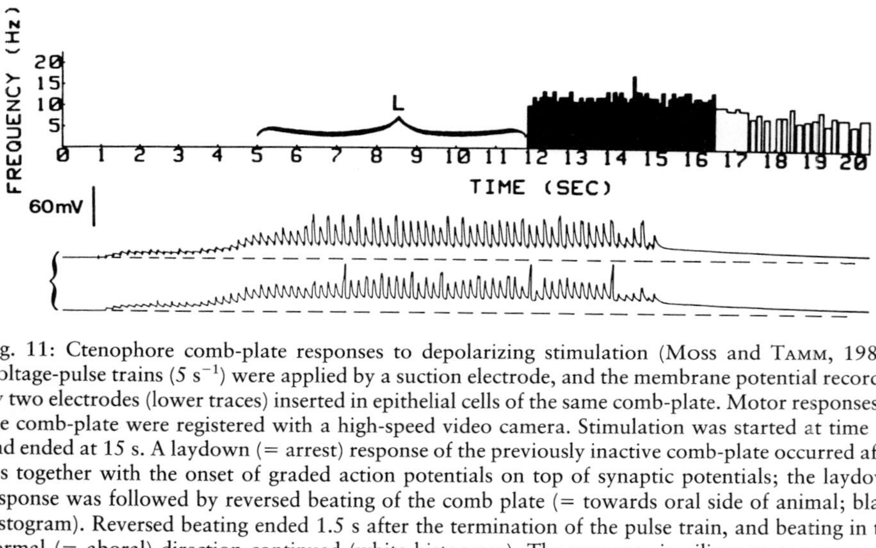

Fig. 11: Ctenophore comb-plate responses to depolarizing stimulation (Moss and TAMM, 1986). Voltage-pulse trains (5 s^{-1}) were applied by a suction electrode, and the membrane potential recorded by two electrodes (lower traces) inserted in epithelial cells of the same comb-plate. Motor responses of the comb-plate were registered with a high-speed video camera. Stimulation was started at time 1 s and ended at 15 s. A laydown (= arrest) response of the previously inactive comb-plate occurred after 4 s together with the onset of graded action potentials on top of synaptic potentials; the laydown response was followed by reversed beating of the comb plate (= towards oral side of animal; black histogram). Reversed beating ended 1.5 s after the termination of the pulse train, and beating in the normal (= aboral) direction continued (white histogram). The sequence in ciliary motor responses resembles that observed in ciliates following rising depolarization (Figs. 7, 8, 18B).

4.2. Inactivation

A transient loss of cyclic and orientational responses of the cilium was observed in *Paramecium* which had been induced by depolarizing stimulation to beat in reverse (MACHEMER and ECKERT, 1973). A frequency-time plot from high-speed cine records of non-clamped cells shows that following depolarization the frequency of reversed beating decreases exponentially, then cyclic activity breaks down to be resumed and increased to the prestimulus level with the power stroke reoriented in the normal direction (Fig. 12). Because the time course of ciliary activity after termination of depolarization is thought to be associated with a gradual decrease in transiently raised intraciliary Ca, it was hypothesized that ciliary inactivation is due to Ca concentrations slightly elevated above

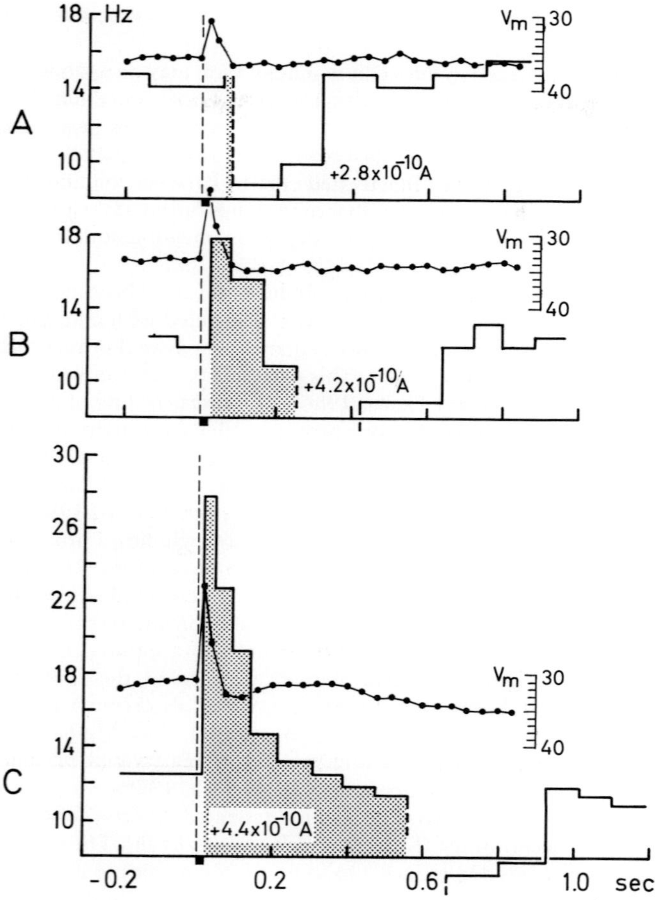

Fig. 12: Ciliary reversal and transient inactivation following depolarizing 20-ms constant current stimulation in *Paramecium*. Time course of the membrane potential (filled circles) and of the ciliary frequency (histogram) were registered. A. Response to weak depolarization. The cilia simultaneously reversed orientation (shaded area) without completing a cycle; cyclic activity in the normal direction was resumed at a low level. B, C. Rising depolarization increased the peak frequency and duration of reversed beating; the cyclic activity declined exponentially to be followed by inactivation (absence of cyclic activity) and resumption of normal beating starting at a low level (white histogram). This sequence of motor events: reduction in reversed beating → inactivation → rise in normal beating, is presumed to be regulated by the decrease in intraciliary Ca, which had been raised due to depolarization-induced Ca influx. MACHEMER, 1974b.

normal. Voltage-clamp experiments using depolarizing voltage steps of 1 mV to 3 mV in fact showed that the frequency of normal beating was reduced and eventually dropped to zero in the course of one second (MACHEMER and ECKERT, 1975). Depolarizing voltage ramps of sufficiently low rate of rise also induced the cilia to inactivate during weak depolarization (Figs. 7, 10). Mg-ATP reactivation experiments of demembranated paramecia have indicated that minimal locomotion and reversal in swimming direction occurs at Ca concentrations slightly raised to a value below 10^{-6} M (NAITOH and KANEKO, 1972; NAKAOKA et al., 1984).

According to the voltage-clamp data ciliary inactivation may be a labile motor response intervening between reversed and normal cyclic activity of the cilium. Inactivated cilia «lack all signs of polarized cyclic beating, ... extend more or less perpendicularly to the cell surface and perform irregular movements at low frequency and amplitude» (MACHEMER, 1974b). Properties of inactivated cilia in *Paramecium* and their occurrence between two active states have suggested that mutual inhibition of the processes of normal and reversed ciliary activation, and no energy-depletion phenomenon, interrupts the cyclic beating of the cilium (MACHEMER, 1977).

A re-normalizing changeover from stimulus-induced reversed beating to normal beating of comb-plates of the ctenophore *Pleurobrachia* is associated with a peculiar transition in beat form showing a «flagellar» pattern with equally propagated symmetrical bends during the cycle (SLEIGH and BARLOW, 1982). This pattern has been confirmed previously and termed «intermediate» (MOSS and TAMM, 1986). The transient loss of polarization of the ctenophore beat cycle is reminiscent of one aspect of ciliary inactivity in *Paramecium* and may indicate an equivalence of these patterns (SLEIGH and BARLOW, 1982).

A diagnosis somewhat similar to that of inactivation of cilia in *Paramecium* has been applied to «quiescence» in sea urchin sperm (GIBBONS and GIBBONS, 1980). Quiescence of demembranated and Mg-ATP reactivated sperm flagella including a pronounced principal bend was induced by adding 10^{-4} M Ca to the reactivation medium. Reactivated quiescent spermatozoa were mechanically fragile; disruption and microtubule sliding occurred spontaneously or upon gentle agitation indicating that the axoneme remained potentiated for active sliding. Reduction of Ca by EGTA-buffering or supraoptimal concentrations of Ca (such as 1 mM) removed the quiescent state from most of the sperm models which resumed active swimming. Spermatozoan quiescence was also removed by a reduction of Mg-ATP below 0.3 mM; this is an interesting observation, since Mg has been reported to affect the forward or backward swimming velocity of reactivated *Paramecium* models (zero velocity near 7 mM Mg; NAKAOKA and TOYOTAMA, 1979).

A quiescence in each of the two flagella in reactivated *Chlamydomonas* occurred at vastly different Ca concentrations (KAMIYA and WITMAN, 1984). The comparatively high concentrations of Ca required to induce quiescence in some types of flagella are suggestive of a possible relationship to ciliary arrest responses (SLEIGH and BARLOW, 1982; see following section). It is noteworthy that such generalization from model cilia remains speculative, since the ionic requirements of the reactivated axoneme may not fully correspond to the viable system.

Ciliary inactivation in some cells is easily identified, such as the resting posture of cirri in the hypotrich ciliates (Fig. 13); these cirri show a voltage-dependent frequency profile comparable to *Paramecium*, although slightly shifted along the voltage scale (Fig. 7). A high-frequency low-amplitude vibration of marginal cirri has been observed in *Stylonychia* termed «Restschwingung» (residual oscillation), which may precede or follow rapid high-amplitude activity of the cirri (MACHEMER, 1969b). A possible interpretation of residual oscillation is that some of the component cilia of the cirrus are in the inactive state so that they mechanically inhibit the active cilia.

In lamellibranch molluscs the lateral cilia of excised gill filaments are inactive («quiescent») inclining frontally at 60° (GRAY, 1924). The cilia of the isolated preparation resume beating after addition of serotonin (5-hydroxytryptamine) to the medium (AIELLO, 1960). A discrimination between ciliary inactivity and the arrest response in the lamellibranch gill is possible, since inactive cilia assume the more inclined arrest position following mechanical stimulation (MOTOKAWA and TAKAHASHI, 1974). Branchial cilia of the

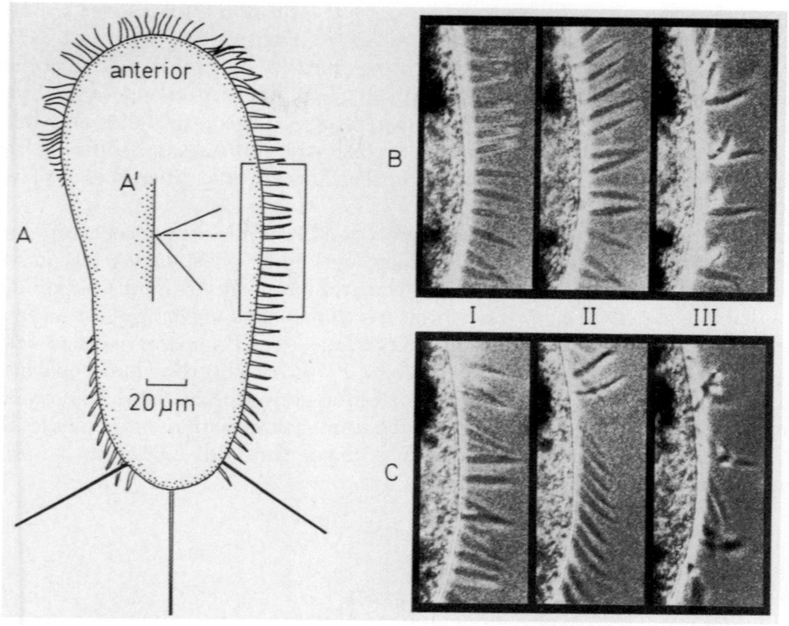

Fig. 13: Voltage-dependent inclination of nonbeating cilia. The marginal cirri of *Stylonychia* (A) were recorded on cine film (frame in A), while the cell was linearly depolarized or hyperpolarized at an extremely low rate under voltage-clamp. B. Inclination response during the depolarizing ramp. Starting from a neutral posture (I), the cirri gradually reoriented anteriorly (II); with rising depolarization they started rapid cyclic beating (III). Compare Fig. 18B. C. Inclination response during the hyperpolarizing ramp. I, neutral posture; II, end of the nonbeating inclination; III, cyclic activation. Compare Fig. 18A. Inset A': Range of observed inclination responses. Note that the inclination remains voltage-coupled unlike the cyclic ciliary movement which can occur in the absence of shifts in membrane potential. DE PEYER and MACHEMER, 1983.

ascidian *Corella* also exhibit three different states of activity: normal beating, arrest (with the cilia inclined opposite to the power stroke), and the «relaxed» state which consists of cilia straightened perpendicularly to the cell surface (MACKIE et al., 1974). A transient «rest» has also been reported from cilia of the lateral gill bars in the chordate *Branchiostoma* (BONE, 1958). Parts of the gill bars were found to be at rest or «feebly vibrating». Stimulation by suspended particles led to continued rest of the cilia. Anaesthetics such as benzamine hydrochloride, urethane or magnesium chloride induced a resumption of cyclic activity, including metachronal coordination, of the cilia. Comparison with the lamellibranch gill suggests that the anaesthetics used as well as serotonin have modulated membrane functions of the epithelial cell to remove ciliary inactivation. This regulation may involve Ca (TSUCHIYA, 1977) and/or cyclic AMP (MURAKAMI, 1983).

There are reports of experimental suppression of the amplitude of flagellar beating, where the functional relationship to inactivation is not clear. (1) A reduction of the bending amplitude of demembranated and reactivated sea urchin sperm flagella by CO_2 was not associated with a decrease in beating frequency (BROKAW, 1977). CO_2-inhibition was even more pronounced during digestion by trypsin of the reactivated axoneme presumably due to weakening of the flagellar structure (BROKAW and SIMONICK, 1977). The observations have been interpreted as indicating mutual sliding inhibition. (2) Echinoderm spermatozoa were rendered quiescent by applying low pH (MOHRI and YASUMASU, 1963). Live as well as Triton-extracted and reactivated sperm flagella straightened while inactivated at pH 5.3, and resumed beating after introduction of the same solution at pH 8.2; the principal bend and the reverse bend of the flagellum showed differences in pH-sensitivity (GOLDSTEIN, 1979).

An axoneme inactivates following depletion in ATP. While the concentration of ATP is assumed to be kept at or above the millimolar level under physiological circumstances, a rapid transfer of demembranated sea urchin sperm into a reactivation solution devoid of ATP has led to a variety of rigor wave forms which remained unchanged for several hours; upon addition of 10^{-6} M ATP the rigor waves relaxed, and the sperm flagella straightened over a period of 30 min (GIBBONS and GIBBONS, 1974). An electronmicroscopic inspection of rigor wave axonemes after appropriate fixation showed that the dynein crossbridges were maintained throughout the ring of doublets in analogy with rigor in muscle (compare Fig. 1). It appears that axonemal rigor induced by depletion of ATP is not a basis of the phenomena of inactivity described above.

4.3. Ciliary inclination

A noncyclic, voltage-coupled orientational response of the cilium has been recently isolated by applying voltage ramps of extremely low rate of rise (DE PEYER and MACHEMER, 1983). The marginal cirri of *Stylonychia* gradually shifted in the anterior direction with rising depolarization; the shift was posteriad with increasing hyperpolarization (Fig. 13). The slow reorientation of the cirri from the neutral posture at the membrane resting potential was called «silent», because of its noncyclic nature. These reorientations of the cirri occurred in a range of +25° and −50° at voltages near the membrane resting potential. Within this range the responses (ciliary bending restricted to the base of the shaft) resemble those of a sensitive analog voltmeter. In unclamped cells membrane potential fluctuations induce the marginal cirri to swing forwards and backwards at low amplitudes; these movements may represent voltage-coupled, noncyclic reorientations or «inclinations».

Previous high-speed cine recording of cirral movements at axial view has shown that voltage-coupled inclination occurs during cyclic ciliary activity as well; here, inclination does not coincide with the direction of the ciliary power stroke (MACHEMER and SUGINO, 1986) (Fig. 14). Ciliary inclination and the power stroke have a common property: being orientational responses with bending limited to the proximal shaft. Inclination differs from the power stroke in that it is a steady-state response coupled to the voltage stimulus, which tilts the beating cone (Fig. 14B, C) or the nonbeating cilium (Fig. 13).

Inclination is a property of the proximal shaft and characterized by (1) the angle of tilt (from the neutral posture i. e. normal to cell surface) and (2) its orientation (proceeding counterclockwise from posterior = 0°). Because ciliary responses have not been qantitatively registered in three dimensions, the angle and the orientation of inclination are difficult to identify. Side views of ciliary organelles, such as those represented in Fig. 13, give perspectives, but no accurate values of inclination. Restrictions in viewing the orientation of cilia, and the rapid ciliary responses to stimulation, are presumably the reasons, why ciliary inclination has commonly not been separated from cyclic polarization of the cilium.

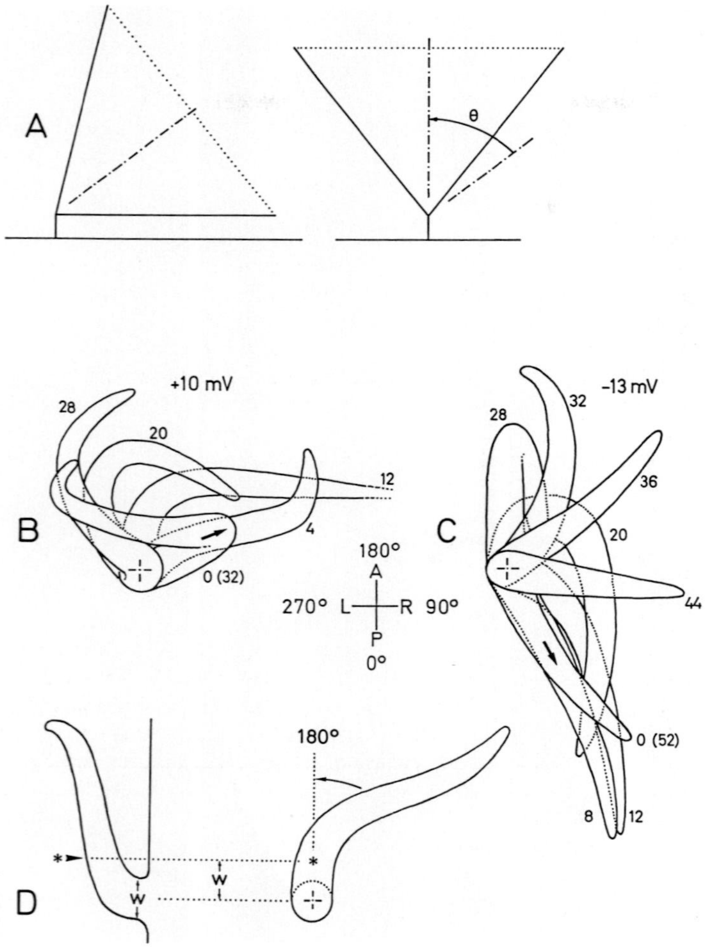

Fig. 14: Inclination and polarization as components of the ciliary cycle. A. Scheme of the beating cone of a cilium in side view, inclined (left) and corrected for the inclination angle θ (right). B. DCA of a frontal cirrus of *Stylonychia*, seen tip-to-base, during a +10 mV step; the cycle is inclined anteriorly (A) and polarized along the left-right axis (L–R). C, HCA during a −13 mV step; the inclination is towards the right, the polarization along the antero-posterior axis (A–P). Numbers near selected images of the cirrus give the time in milliseconds during the cycle; arrows indicate the apparent beat direction near the end of the power stroke (compare beat directions Fig. 22). D. Determination of the reference point for measurement of cirral orientation, expressed as an angle proceeding counterclockwise from posterior (= 0°). MACHEMER and SUGINO, 1986.

A rapid ciliary reorientation («arrest», «laydown») follows depolarizing stimulation of comb-plates of the ctenophore *Pleurobrachia* (MURAKAMI, 1972; SLEIGH and BARLOW, 1982; MOSS and TAMM, 1986). Two types of orientational ciliary responses to electric-field stimulation have also been described in different developmental stages of echinoderm larvae: following onset of the cathodic stimulus normal ciliary beating in the blastula or

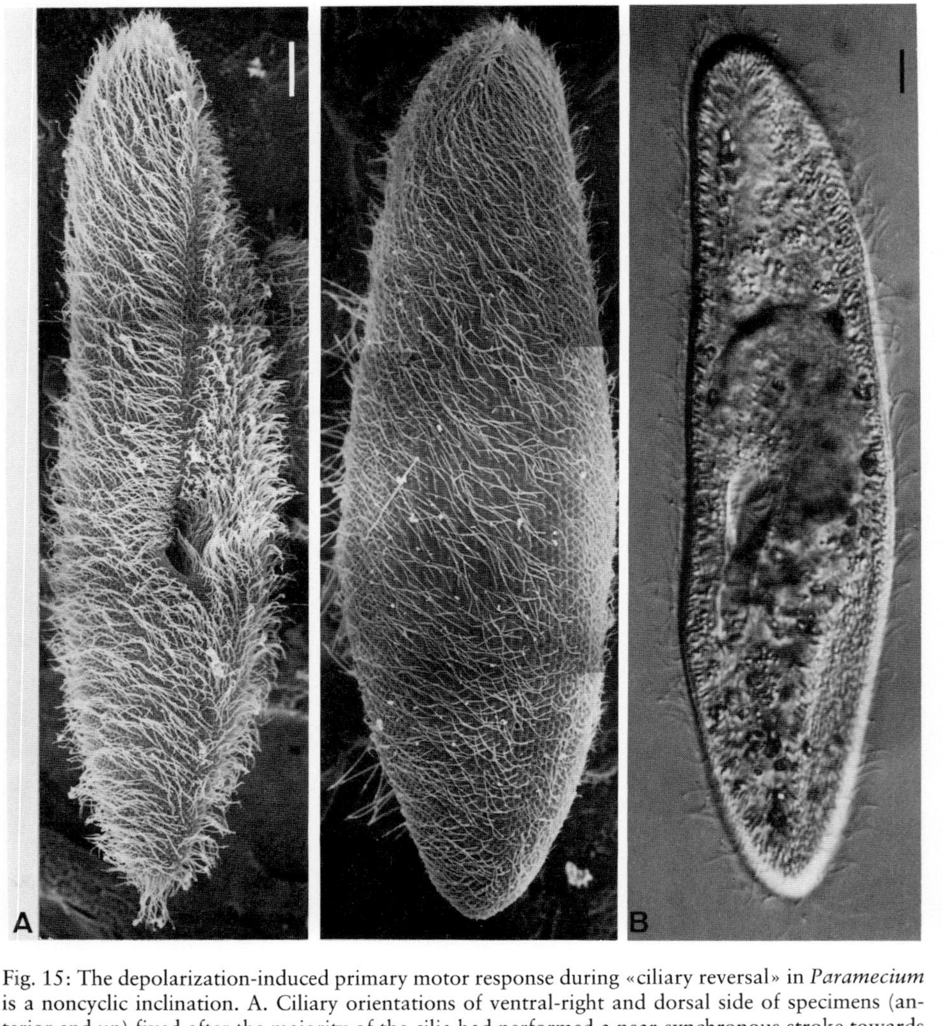

Fig. 15: The depolarization-induced primary motor response during «ciliary reversal» in *Paramecium* is a noncyclic inclination. A. Ciliary orientations of ventral-right and dorsal side of specimens (anterior end up) fixed after the majority of the cilia had performed a near-synchronous stroke towards the anterior and left side. Note that tail cilia did not reverse. OGURA, unpublished. B. Live cell with primary reversal response in profile view exposed by electronic flash; anterior end up. Note the simultaneous occurrence of the ciliary response, which throws the cell in the backward direction (passive divergence of inactive tail cilia). Bar, 10 μm. MACHEMER, 1970.

gastrula stage was halted in a straight and largely upright posture («primitive response»). In the more advanced pluteus the same type of stimulus induced reversed cyclic beating (BABA, 1975). Beating centered about the static orientational response of the previous larval stage. Depolarizing stimulation of the lamellibranch gill leads to an «arrest response» of the lateral cilia which is a rapid and synchronized reorientation opposite to the normal (abfrontal) beat direction (TAKAHASHI and MURAKAMI, 1968). A similar arrest response has been documented in the gastropod veliger larva *Mangelia* (MACKIE et al.,

1976) and the branchial cilia of the ascidians *Ciona* (TAKAHASHI et al., 1973) and *Corella* (MACKIE et al., 1974). Synchronization of the previously metachronally coordinated cilia in these tissues suggests a direct coupling of the response to the membrane potential. Mg-ATP reactivation of Triton-X extracted tissue of the mussel gill has shown that the arrest response of lateral cilia is elicited with Ca concentrations rising above 10^{-7} M (TSUCHIYA, 1977); induction of arrest in laterofrontal and frontal cilia required an at least 100-fold higher Ca concentration (WALTER and SATIR, 1978; SANDERSON and SATIR, 1982).

The separation of orientations of ciliary inclination and of the power stroke resolves some paradigms of motor events during DCA in *Paramecium*.

(1) Records of instantaneously fixed as well as live cells indicate that the primary orientational response of the cilia is towards the anterior and left side of the cell (Fig. 15), while the first cycle completed «in reverse» ends with a power stroke towards the anterior and right side (MACHEMER, 1974b). It was previously assumed that the first orientational response following depolarization is a synchronized power stroke, and that the orientation of the power stroke can change by a major angle within the course of one cycle (MACHEMER, 1974a). In accordance with a suggestion by SLEIGH and BARLOW (1982) the primary ciliary reorientation to rapid voltage shifts is re-interpreted as an inclination (Fig. 16) with cyclic activation (return stroke) starting after termination of this response.

(2) Weak depolarizing stimuli applied to the free or clamped ciliate membrane can

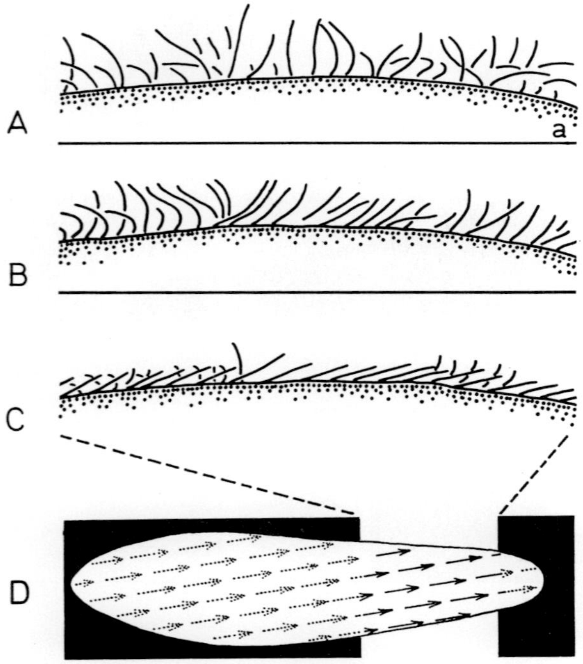

Fig. 16: Transition from a metachronous cyclic activity (A) to a synchronous «reversal» of cilia in *Paramecium* (B, C) following membrane depolarization; the anterior end (a) is towards the right. The three sequential frames from a high-speed cine record occurred at 4 ms intervals. D. Diagram illustrating the anterior left orientation of the cilia after performance of the inclination response; the light area corresponds to the section shown in the frames. After MACHEMER and ECKERT, 1977.

trigger what has been termed an «incomplete reversal response» (MACHEMER, 1974b): the cilia swing anteriorly, but fail to complete a cycle in reverse; instead, a cycle is performed at much reduced rate in the «normal» direction (Fig. 12A). A revised interpretation of this observation is that weak depolarization induced an anteriad inclination response, but was insufficient for cyclic activation of the cilia.

(3) Depolarization-induced activation of cirri in *Stylonychia* decays exponentially (DE PEYER and MACHEMER, 1982a). Re-orientation of the cirral cycle (seen in side view), which is gradually reset from anteriad to posteriad, may occur in the course of this decay (Fig. 17D). The apparent uncoupling of the frequency response from the directional response (compare Figs. 7 and 17D) applies to inclination of the cycle, not to the power stroke which was not determined in these experiments.

A separation of voltage thresholds for ciliary inclination and cyclic activation has been clearly demonstrated in the marginal cirri of *Stylonychia* by applying clamped low-rate voltage ramps of either polarity (DE PEYER and MACHEMER, 1983). With a few millivolts of polarization the cirri started to reorient in proportion to the rising voltage («silent

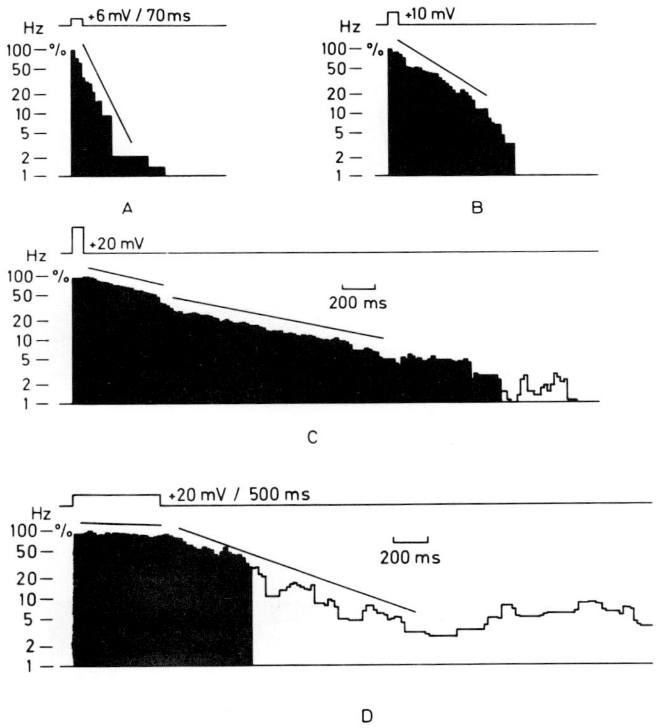

Fig. 17: Time course of DCA in *Stylonychia* following variations in amplitude and duration of voltage steps. The time of exponential decay of DCA (black histogram bars) was dependent upon the step amplitude (A–C), not upon the step duration (D). The decay was minimal during the depolarization. In (D) the anterior inclination of the cirrus, as seen in side view, was terminated while the frequency declined. An uncoupling between cyclic and inclination responses is also seen in Figs. 8D, 10B, C. DE PEYER and MACHEMER, 1982a.

reorientation»); rapid cyclic activation of the cirri began after the membrane polarization had been raised further (Fig. 18).

A consequence of discrimination between inclination and power stroke is that these responses operate in more limited ranges of angles than had been previously assumed for the power stroke in *Paramecium* (around 200°, MACHEMER, 1974b). Preliminary evaluations of data from cirri in *Stylonychia* suggest that this range may be 120° or less for both inclination and power stroke, the sector of inclination being shifted counterclockwise with respect to the sector of the power stroke (SUGINO and MACHEMER, 1986).

Previous experiments using nickel to eliminate cyclic beating of live cilia in *Paramecium* have been interpreted as demonstrating the separation of the power stroke from cyclic activity (NAITOH, 1966; ECKERT and NAITOH, 1970). Reorientations of nonbeating cilia

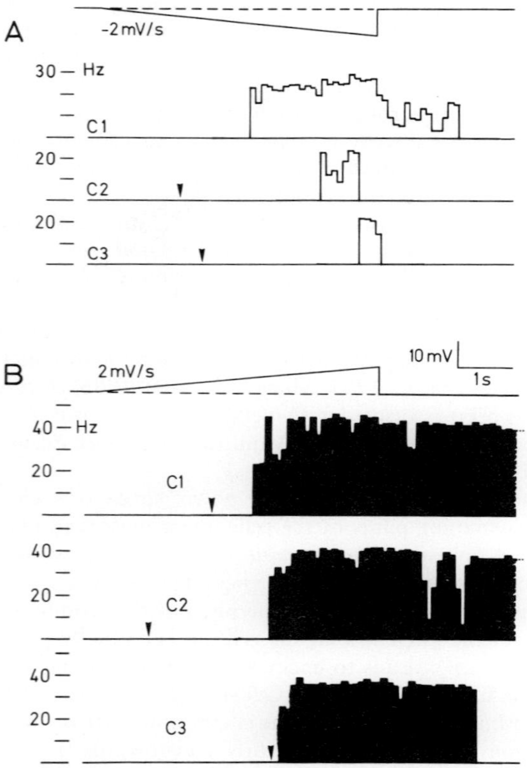

Fig. 18: Separation in thresholds for activation of the inclination response (arrowhead) and of cyclic activity following low-rate hyperpolarizing (A) and depolarizing (B) voltage ramps. The white histogram bars represent HCA (cyclic beating of the cirri towards the posterior cell end); black bars = DCA (beating towards the anterior cell end. Three marginal cirri (Fig. 13) were selected for evaluation and numerated according to their location in the antero-posterior direction (C1–C3). It is seen that the voltage for activation of the inclination response scattered, but was generally less than the threshold for the cyclic response (No inclination was separable from cyclic activation during hyperpolarization in the most anterior cirrus (C1)). In all cirri the cyclic activity started in a burst-type manner with frequencies near maximum. DE PEYER and MACHEMER, 1983.

in demembranated models of *Paramecium* immersed in Mg-free Ca-ATP solutions (NAITOH and KANEKO, 1972) have led to the conclusion that Ca regulates the orientation of the power stroke (see section 3.1). Published documents of nonbeating live or model cilia of *Paramecium* show limited ranges of ciliary reorientations, which in fact resemble those of inclination, but are less well comparable to cilia at the end of a power stroke. It may be speculated that ciliary inclination in ciliates, the primitive response of echinoderm larvae, and the arrest and laydown responses seen in several ciliated tissues are homologous voltage-coupled, Ca-dependent, noncyclic motor responses of the cilia.

4.4. Orientation of the power stroke

Performance of the ciliary cycle includes temporal and spatial polarization, which has been traditionally addressed by differentiating between a «power stroke» (or effective stroke) and a «return stroke» (or recovery stroke)[1]. The power stroke occurs with a basal bend, the straight ciliary shaft swinging at large amplitude and commonly at increased angular velocity; the return stroke occurs with the cilium bent over to one side and a pronounced bending wave travelling from base to tip. Membrane depolarization can induce a reorientation of the direction of the power stroke in ciliate protozoa and some metazoa which has led to the term «ciliary reversal».

Correlations between the ciliary beat orientation and the membrane potential were first established by KINOSITA (1954) in *Opalina*. A *Paramecium* reverses the direction of swimming upon depolarizing stimulation, such as immersion in solutions with high K concentration. The reversal in swimming occurs because the ciliary power stroke is reoriented from a posterior to an anterior direction. In ctenophores prey capture or a depolarizing current lead to a reversal of the power strokes of the comb-plate cilia from an aboral to an oral direction (TAMM and MOSS, 1985; MOSS and TAMM, 1986). A reversal in the direction of ciliary beating has been associated with membrane depolarization in echinoderm larvae (*Strongylocentrotus*, MACKIE et al., 1969) and tunicates (*Oikopleura*, *Diplosoma*, GALT and MACKIE, 1971).

Alterations in the orientation of the ciliary power stroke of various ciliates have been deduced from the swimming paths of the cells under dark-field illumination (PARDUCZ, 1959; DRYL, 1961). A non-stimulated *Paramecium caudatum* swims forward along a left-handed helix due to locomotive forces of cilia beating towards the posterior and right side. Minor depolarizing stimulation decreases the pitch of the swimming helix; rising hyperpolarization increases the pitch so that the cell may eventually proceed along a straight line. A major depolarization leads to backward swimming along a right-handed helix.

Osmium-tetroxide fixation techniques (GELEI, 1926; PARDUCZ, 1951) applied to backward swimming paramecia revealed that the ciliary power stroke was shifted in the counterclockwise direction now pointing anteriorly and towards the right (160°; PARDUCZ, 1959; MACHEMER, 1969a). Extreme premortal stimulation by the fixing agent even shifted coordinated beating towards the anterior and left direction (190°; PARDUCZ, 1956). Electronic-flash photographs of live cells under Nomarski illumination have confirmed the rapid-fixation data (MACHEMER, 1972a–c). It was shown that the orientation of the ciliary power stroke is deducible from profile views of the metachronal wave system lining the cell border (MACHEMER, 1974a).

---

1 Preference is given to the descriptive terms in accordance with RINGO (1967), who applied them to describe flagellar movements of *Chlamydomonas*.

According to high-speed cine recording experiments on *Paramecium* in which the membrane potential was displayed on the film, the power stroke shifts in the counterclockwise direction with positive-going membrane polarization, and shifts in the clockwise direction when the membrane potential is negative-going (MACHEMER, 1974b, MACHEMER and ECKERT, 1977). A common orientation during depolarization is near 160°, during hyperpolarization 0°. It was noted that ciliary beat orientation becomes uncoupled from the membrane potential after termination of brief voltage shifts (MACHEMER and ECKERT, 1973; MACHEMER, 1974b). Following an action potential and rapid counterclockwise reorientation of the power stroke, the beating direction gradually reorients in the clockwise direction after repolarization; the direction of beating may even transiently overshoot the resting orientation (MACHEMER and ECKERT, 1977). Similar conditions apply to hyperpolarizing stimulation: clockwise reorientation, followed by delayed counterclockwise renormalization. Orientational and frequency responses to hyperpolarization are distinctly slower than following depolarization; they involve a larger latency, rise more slowly to peak and often decay more gradually (MACHEMER, 1974b, DE PEYER and MACHEMER, 1982a, b).

4.5. Temporal polarization of the cycle

The ciliary cycle proceeds, in principle, along the surface of a «beating cone» with the vertex located on the ciliary origin. The angular velocity of the cilium varies during the cycle: often it is increased during the power stroke as compared to the return stroke.

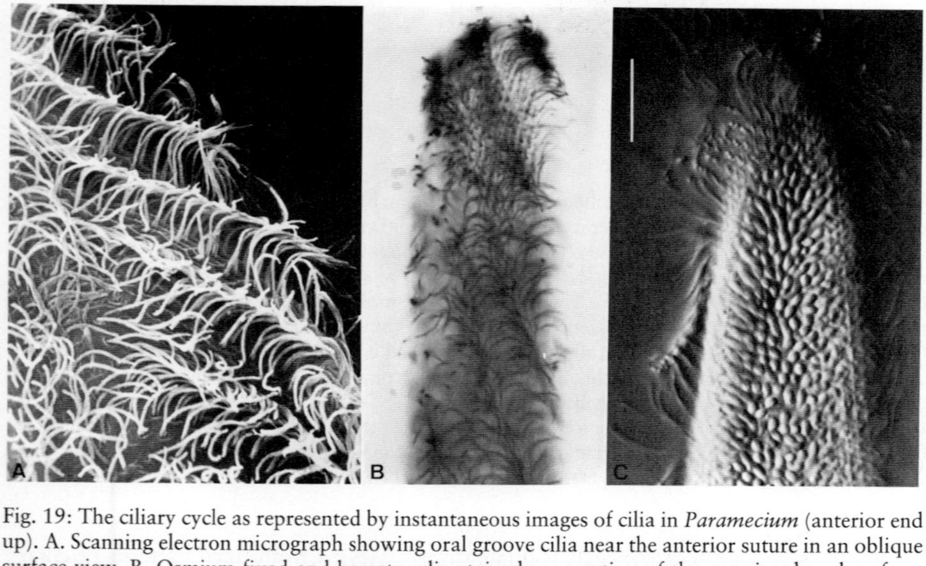

Fig. 19: The ciliary cycle as represented by instantaneous images of cilia in *Paramecium* (anterior end up). A. Scanning electron micrograph showing oral groove cilia near the anterior suture in an oblique surface view. B. Osmium-fixed and hematoxylin-stained preparation of the anterior-dorsal surface. The direction of the power stroke is towards the posterior and right (= parallel to the wave fronts; also in A). The return stroke is indicated by sickle-shaped cilia. C. Electronic-flash micrograph of a live cell; a profile of the cycle of pairs of cilia in the anterior oral groove (left) is seen from the left side; a modified wave system on opposite side of the cell indicates a different viewing angle. Bar, 10 μm. A. HAUSMANN, 1985; B, C, MACHEMER, 1970.

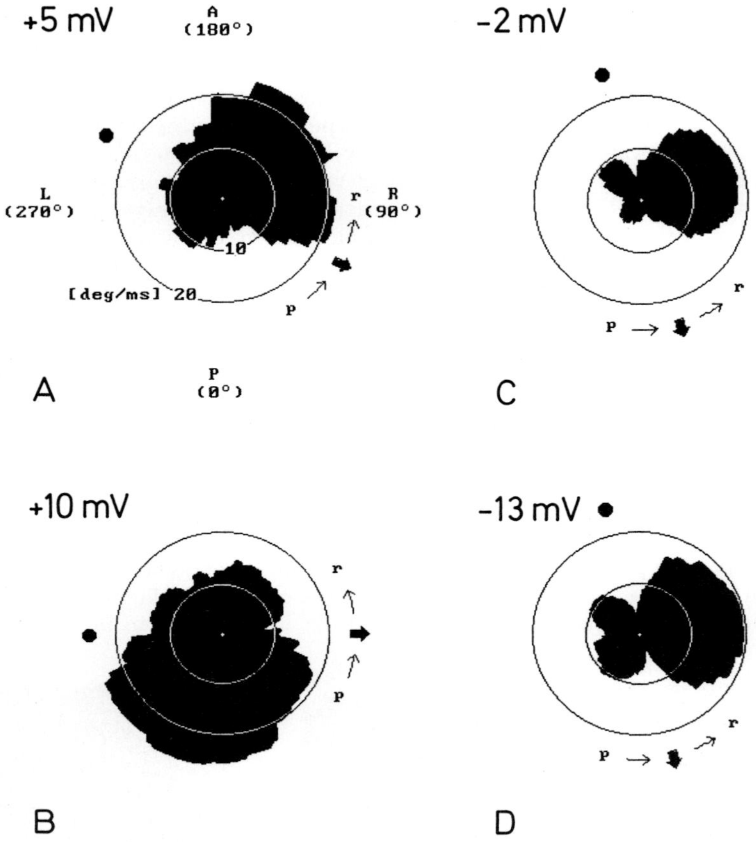

Fig. 20: Polarization in time of the ciliary cycle as a function of the membrane potential under voltage clamp. Polar plots show highly structured directional change rates of the basal shaft of a frontal cirrus in *Stylonychia*. Data from axial-view records of cirri on high-frequency cine film (250 frames/s). The reference point of bending orientation was determined at a distance from the cirral base center equalling the cirral width (Fig. 14D). The plots give projections of the angular velocity upon a plane parallel to the cell surface («normalized angular velocity») after correction for inclination of the cycle (Fig. 14A). Wide arrow, orientation of power stroke; filled circle, orientation of return stroke; light arrows indicate direction of the cycle during the return stroke (r) and the power stroke (p). Angle of cirral orientation refers to the topography of the cirrus (P, posterior; R, right; A, anterior; L, left). A, B. Responses to depolarizing voltage steps (+5 mV: 6 cycles averaged, 17 Hz; +10 mV: 13 cycles, 34 Hz). C, D. Responses to hyperpolarizing voltage steps (−2 mV: 11 cycles, 11 Hz; −13 mV: 12 cycles, 22 Hz). See text. A, C, Sugino and Machemer, unpublished. B, D, Machemer and Sugino, 1986.

Temporal polarization of the cycle is qualitatively assessed from fixed patterns of ciliary activity (Fig. 19). Viewing a ciliary population in profile, more cilia are commonly seen as being involved in the return stroke than in the power stroke; this indicates that the return stroke was slower than the power stroke (Fig. 19C). In general, temporal components of the cycle are difficult to separate from ciliary postures in space in fixed preparations of metachronally coordinated cilia.

Cyclic reorientations of the cilium are normalized (i. e., separated from variations in beating amplitude), after correction for inclination (Fig. 14), and upon projection of the ciliary cycle on a plane parallel to the cell surface. A normalized angular velocity of the basal shaft, the «directional change rate» is a direct measure of beat polarization in time (Machemer and Sugino, 1986).

Fig. 20 illustrates some directional change rates of a cirrus following variation of the step amplitude and polarity under voltage-clamp. The display shows that in fact the temporal course of the cycle is voltage-dependent; the power stroke rotated counterclockwise with rising depolarization (A, B); it showed essentially no shift following hyperpolarization (C, D). It should be noted that the orientation of the power stroke appears under different perspective, being changed following correction for inclination (compare Fig. 14). The present data suggest that directional change rates are much differentiated in the course of a cycle; patterns may have been dramatically rotated (Fig. 20A, B) or remain topographically stable, while modified in detail (C, D; note posterior left wing of display).

The directional response during the cycle is more complex than has been previously assumed; fast reorientations are not limited to the power stroke, nor do slow rates of reorientation occur exclusively during the return stroke. Upon hyperpolarization the directional change rate of the return stroke may even exceed that of the power stroke. Pronounced depressions in directional change were seen at the end of the power stroke following depolarization, and at the end of power and return strokes following hyperpolarization.

4.6. Spatial polarization of the cycle

An inspection of Fig. 19 confirms that the protozoan cilium performs a counterclockwise conical pathway. The gyration tends to be flattened during the power stroke (troughs of waves in A, lines of crowded cilia in B, diverging ciliary pattern in C), but bulges out during the return stroke (crests in A, curved ciliary shapes in B, converging pattern in C). Spatial polarization of the cilium was reconstructed using wire models of the ciliary cycle generalized from micrographs of cilia in *Paramecium* (Fig. 21). The diagrams suggest that the cilium follows a deformed ellipsoidal cycle; quantitative evaluation is difficult because the beating cone is inclined (towards the anterior and right; Fig. 21D).

Cinematographic recording of the ciliary cycle at axial view and correction for inclination (Fig. 14A) has led to more accurate approximations of spatial polarization, of the orientation of the power stroke, and to direct demonstrations of their voltage-dependence (Fig. 22). Polarization was defined as the ratio of major versus minor amplitude of the cycle (Machemer and Sugino, 1986). The orientation of the major amplitude determines the direction of the power stroke. Extremes in orientations in inclined cilia (see, e. g., dashed tangents to ellipse in Fig. 22B) are no reliable indicators of the power stroke orientation. The major amplitude and beat polarization increased with rising depolarization of the membrane (Fig. 22A, B); rising hyperpolarization very little modified the course of the ciliary cycle (Fig. 22C, D), but it raised the frequency (see section 4.1.).

Comparison of data relating to spatial and temporal polarization shows that, in general, the major amplitude corresponds to minimal directional change rate, and vice versa (Figs. 20, 22).

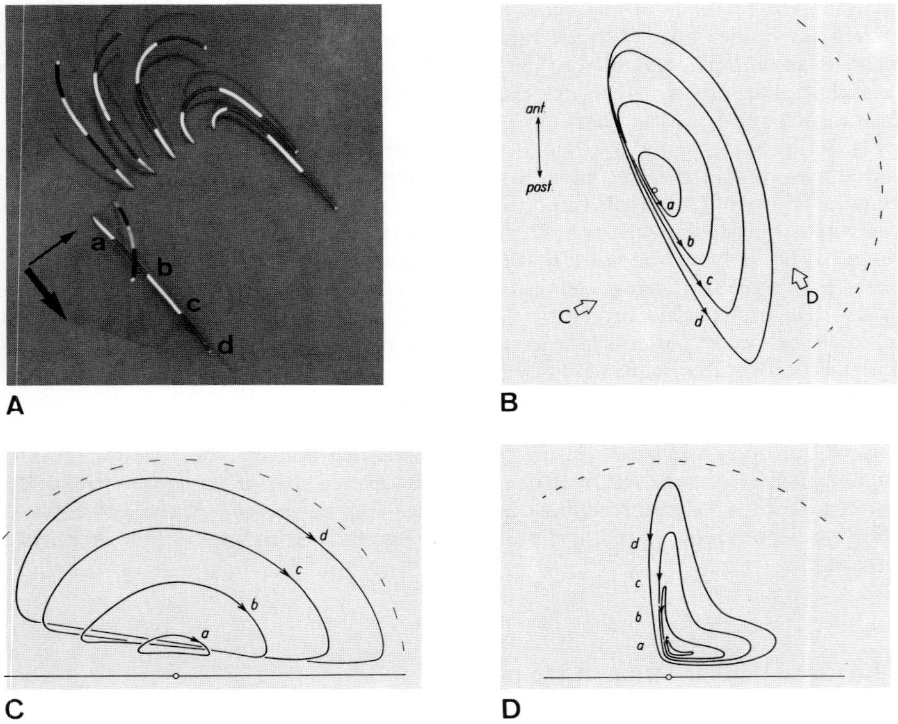

Fig. 21: Qualitative assessment of spatial polarization of the ciliary cycle. A. Stages of the ciliary cycle in non-stimulated *Paramecium* as represented by wire models. The model cilia were marked to identify cyclic tracks of four equally spaced points on the cilium (a–d). The heavy arrow indicates the direction of the power stroke; the light arrow gives the direction of the metachronal wave. B. Tracks as seen in surface view; ant., post., anterior and posterior directions. The radius of the interrupted arc equals the ciliary length. C. Side view of the cycle as marked by the light arrow C in (B). D. View in the direction of the return stroke as marked by arrow D in (B). Modified after Machemer, 1972c.

Fig. 22: Spatial polarization of the ciliary cycle following stimulation under voltage-clamp. Data corresponding to those shown in Fig. 20. Closed trajectory represents the nonplanar basis of the beating cone with the slant height of the cone equalling the length (L) of the cirrus. The shaded ellipse is a normal (90°) section through the beating cone at 1/3 of cirral length. The dashed line shows the major amplitude seen prior to correction for inclination. Major and minor diameters of the ellipse (A, B) give relative amplitudes (major amplitude, $\alpha = 2\tan^{-1}(3A/2L)$; minor amplitude, $\beta = 2\tan^{-1}(3B/2L)$). The ratio of major to minor amplitude represents the spatial polarization of the cycle. A, B. Responses to depolarizing voltage steps before, A', B', after correction for inclination. With rising depolarization the amplitude and polarization of beating increased, and the orientation of the power stroke was shifted counterclockwise. C, D. Responses to hyperpolarizing voltage steps before, C', D', after correction for inclination. Note the prominent amplitude and polarization of the beat, which remained largely unmodified by the stimulus amplitude. Sugino and Machemer, unpublished.

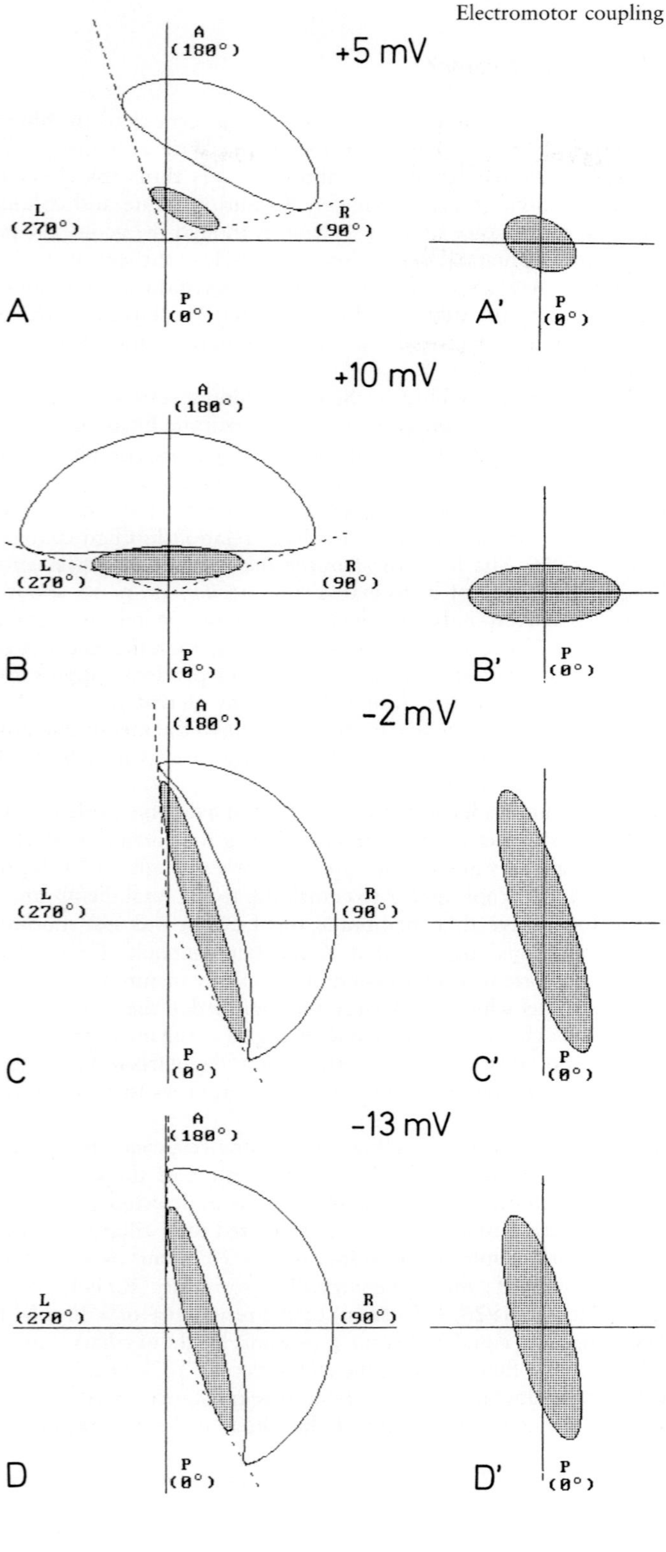
+5 mV
A
(180°)
L
(270°)
R
(90°)
P
(0°)
A
A'
P
(0°)
+10 mV
A
(180°)
L
(270°)
R
(90°)
P
(0°)
B
B'
P
(0°)
-2 mV
A
(180°)
L
(270°)
R
(90°)
P
(0°)
C
C'
P
(0°)
-13 mV
A
(180°)
L
(270°)
R
(90°)
P
(0°)
D
D'
P
(0°)

5. Is the cilium a good cable?

Coupling of the ciliary motor response to a stimulus-generated membrane signal requires appropriate conducting properties of the cilium. With a diameter of 250 nm and length ranging between 10 and 100 μm the cilium is a very thin cable. In analogy to cilia, T-tubules of striated muscle (typical diameter, 80 nm) generate and conduct an action potential radially over a distance of up to 50 μm. Although the geometric parameters of the T-tubule are extreme, potential decay along the tubule in the steady-state was approximated at 10% or less (ADRIAN et al., 1969), so that excitation-contraction coupling is presumably not limited by the tubular cable constants. There is good reason to assume that cables of comparable properties have evolved in nature, wherever this was a prerequisite for physiological function.

DUNLAP (1977) observed a doubling of the value of input resistance (from 40 MΩ to 80 MΩ) following deciliation of *Paramecium* by chloral hydrate. Introducing 5% ethanol for physiological deciliation, the deciliation of the cell was more complete (OGURA, 1977), and effects of the deciliating drug were separable from effects of deciliation upon the electric properties of the membrane. It was shown that neither the resting potential nor the resting input resistence nor the late current/voltage relationship had changed due to the removal of 5000 to 6000 cilia from the *Paramecium* surface (MACHEMER and OGURA, 1979). The input capacitance of a deciliated *Paramecium* drops to about 50% of the untreated cell, which corresponds to calculations of the geometric membrane surface contributed by the cilia. The results of ethanol deciliation upon the passive electric properties of the ciliate membrane have recently gained independent support from work in *Didinium*, a *Paramecium* predator. Although the cilia of *Didinium* are longer and restricted to two circular girdles, the deciliated cell retained the membrane potential, input resistance and late I/V relation, and the input capacitance was near 60% of the control cells (PAPÉ and MACHEMER, 1986).

The deciliation experiments have so far been the best available evidence suggesting that the ciliary membrane is unlike the membrane covering the somatic surface. The specific resistance of the resting ciliary membrane appears to be very high (so far, beyond quantitative assessment), since it did not appear to contribute to the total membrane resistance. It is also interesting to observe that membrane rectification was not modified following deciliation by ethanol. This suggests that K rectifier channels, for inward as well as outward K current, are rare or even missing in the ciliary membrane.

The sole type of channel which has been so far identified in the viable ciliary membrane is a voltage-sensitive Ca channel. This channel is closed at the membrane resting potential and following hyperpolarization; it activates upon depolarization of the membrane (NAITOH, 1979). Thus, the resting ciliary membrane appears to be essentially non-conducting for ions.

A conservative assumption of the ciliary membrane resistance is that it exceeds the somatic resistance by a factor of 20 (the shunting effect of the ciliary resistance, 5% reduction in total resistance, will presumably remain undetected). Thus, a conjectured total ciliary input resistance of 1 GΩ and the calculated total ciliary surface of 4×10^{-4} cm^2 give a specific ciliary membrane resistance of 4×10^5 Ωcm^2 or a resistance of $r_m = 5 \times 10^9$ Ωcm per unit length of cilium. The intraciliary resistivity (R_i) is approximated using measurements by GELFAN (1926) (150 Ωcm) or the resistsivity of a 30 mM KCl solution (250 Ωcm). Assuming R_i to equal 200 Ωcm, r_i (for unit lenght of ciliary compartment) is 5×10^{11} Ω/cm. Because the fluid space of the cilium is only 50% or less of the total space, this is an underestimate; doubling the calculated core resistance ($= 10^{12}$ Ω/cm) may give a more realistic value. Since the resistivity of the outer medium is negligible, the length constant for a cilium of «infinite» length, calculated according to $\lambda^2 = r_m/r_i+r_o$, approximates 0.7 to 1 mm.

Ciliary conductance increases, and the length constant drops during depolarization. Assuming that a depolarization by 30 mV to −5 mV (Ca driving force = 120 mV) induces a peak inward Ca current of 8 nA across the total ciliary surface (4×10^{-4} cm^2) of *Paramecium,* λ will be reduced to 87 μm which still supplies 89% of the signal amplitude at the tip of the cilium. A similar calculation of the cable properties of depolarized membranelles in *Stylonychia* leads to a λ of 170 μm and 82% in signal amplitude at the tip of a 35 μm membranelle (IVENS, 1986). With length constants varying in these ranges, cilia and flagella will transmit the membrane potential in the excited as well as non-excited state without major losses. It is interesting to note that giant cilia of ctenophore combplates which can reverse beating direction due to Ca influx (NAKAMURA and TAMM, 1985) are up to 1 mm long. Ultimately, the cable properties may be a limiting factor for ciliary length.

In spite of the inferred favourable conditions for electric coupling of the cilia to the cell soma, reservations regarding a possible insufficient space clamp control during voltage-clamp experiments have not been ruled out by direct evidence. A cilium, which is not fully under membrane potential control, may generate action potentials which eventually invade other ciliary membranes, so that the recorded membrane currents and observed ciliary motor responses are unrelated to the command stimulus.

Several arguments suggest that this possibility is less likely: (1) A free swimming cell colliding with a mechanical obstacle at the anterior end generates a receptor potential in the soma membrane which triggers an action potential in the ciliary membrane followed by a synchronized reversal response of the cilia. Insufficient passive invasion of the receptor potential into the cilium interferes with the generation of a stimulus-graded and pointed action potential as well as ciliary motor response. (2) Under voltage-clamp the early inward current rises with depolarization in a conventional manner. No voltage artifacts from invaded action potentials have been observed. Insufficient clamp of the ciliary space would not allow the establishment of I/V relationships unless the ciliary Ca channels are restricted to the ciliary base; however, properties of the ciliary machine (active sliding along the total axoneme) and the time course of membrane currents related to input capacitance in reciliating paramecia (MACHEMER and OGURA, 1979) are favouring an even distribution of ciliary Ca channels. (3) The quantified ciliary motor response (number of cycles activated = «ciliary work») is correlated with the amplitude of the voltage-clamp step (DE PEYER and MACHEMER, 1982a, b). In summary, until direct evidence becomes available, the data from deciliation experiments and general arguments suggest that the cilium can conduct a voltage signal without major losses in amplitude.

6. Compartmentation of ciliary and somatic spaces

Since a cilium encloses a minor volume largely claimed by the axoneme, the neighbouring somatic space hosts a large number of mitochondria, Golgi vesicles, ER and other components supporting the ciliary metabolism. It has been shown that diffusion of phosphorylated nucleotides between the ciliary base and tip can fulfill ATP requirements (NEVO and RIKMENSPOEL, 1970); charges can presumably leave the ciliary environment using the somatic space as an ion sink. Voltage-activated inward Ba current, for example, which passes across the ciliary channel, continues for a long time with no signs of major shift in equilibrium potential (BREHM and ECKERT, 1978; DE PEYER and DEITMER, 1980;

Pape and Machemer, 1986). It would seem, therefore, that the movement of molecules and ions between the ciliary and somatic spaces is not controlled.

This assumption is presumably not applicable to Ca. Ciliary and somatic functions, although supportive of each other, pose a mutual risk. Because the ciliary total space is covered by an enormous area of membrane, malfunction of this membrane such as extreme leakage of Ca and other ions may lead to rapid cell death. Consequently, many ciliates shed their cilia under extreme conditions using preexisting breaking lines at the ciliary base (Blum, 1971). The cilia are regrown within a few hours, after the environment has normalized (Ogura, 1981). Ionic disturbances near the inner face of the soma membrane (Tillotson and Gorman, 1980; Zucker and Stockbridge, 1983; Chad et al., 1984) are a potential source of disequilibration of ions and other molecules regulating the ciliary function. Little is known about the requirements of the ciliary enzyme system; however, isolated and purified ciliary membranes incorporated in artificial lipid membranes had electric properties unlike those of the living ciliary membrane (Boheim et al., 1982; Ehrlich et al., 1984).

Voltage-clamp experiments testing sensory-motor coupling in *Stylonychia* have shown that ionic calcium from somatic or ciliary sources does not interfere with processes in the neighbouring compartment. An anteriorly applied mechanical stimulus activates a Ca-conducting somatic channel generating a depolarizing receptor potential (De Peyer and Machemer, 1978a; Ogura and Machemer, 1980). When the stimulus was positioned near a marginal cirrus, while the cell was held at the level of the resting potential under voltage-clamp, the cirrus (including any other cirri) remained inactive, although a local Ca receptor current of at least 10 nA was recorded. The common ciliary activation occurred only with stimulation of the free membrane or displacements of the clamped voltage (De Peyer and Machemer, 1978b). The results are direct evidence of the failure of transiently raised somatic Ca to invade the highly Ca-sensitive cilium. Raised intraciliary Ca presumably does not affect the somatic Ca gradient, since ciliary Ca current from depolarizing step pulses did not depress a subsequent Ca receptor current (Deitmer, 1983). A possible interpretation of these data is, that a Ca pump monitoring ciliary Ca concentrations is located at the transition between the ciliary and the somatic membrane as suggested previously (Blum and Hines, 1983). Although Ca deposits have been identified in areas of ciliary membrane granules (Plattner, 1975; Tsuchiya and Takahashi, 1976), direct evidence of the existence and location of the ciliary Ca pump is still missing.

7. Pathways of electromotor coupling

Among ciliary responses to membrane polarization those following depolarization are common in the animal kingdom, and many of these responses have been related to Ca as mediator (Sleigh and Barlow, 1982). Motor responses to hyperpolarization have so far only been investigated in the ciliate protozoa, but some of the parameters of HCA may not be restricted to unicellular organisms. In the following sections four major components of the ciliary response: frequency, inactivation, inclination, and orientation of the power stroke, will be considered with respect to the ways in which they can be controlled by the voltage signal.

7.1. Depolarization controls Ca-mediated regulation of cyclic ciliary activity

Voltage-dependent Ca channels of the cilia in *Stylonychia* may activate upon depolarizations of 2 mV or more (De Peyer and Machemer, 1977; Deitmer 1984). In *Para-*

mecium a regenerative upstroke from electrotonic deflection of the membrane is detectable with depolarizations beyond 5 mV (MACHEMER and ECKERT, 1973). Two types of voltage-dependent Ca channels have been identified in ciliates: one (classical) channel which is characterized by a wide range of threshold, a graded membrane response and Ca-dependent inactivation (BREHM and ECKERT, 1978a); a different channel has a low threshold,

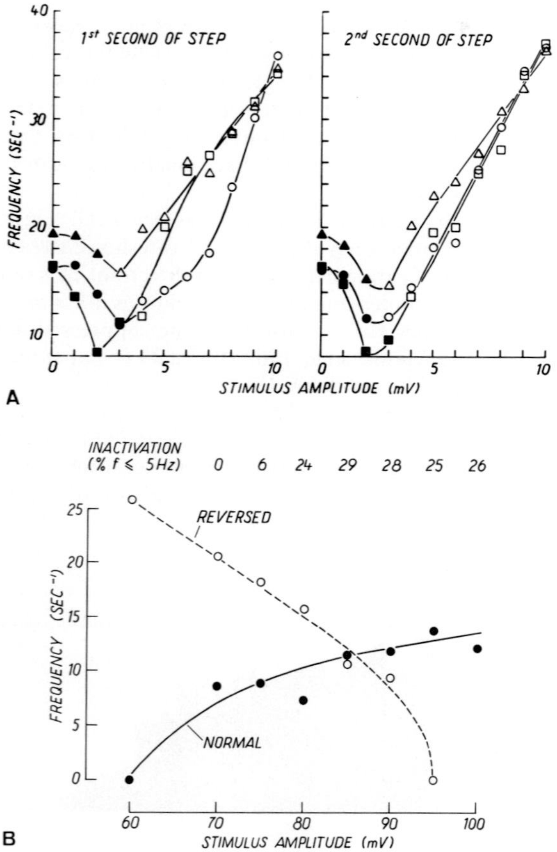

Fig. 23: Depolarization, inferred Ca influx and motor responses of cilia in *Paramecium*. A. Frequency responses of three identified cilia (different symbols) following small steps of 2-second duration from the holding (= resting) potential. The graph shows that rising depolarization decreased the frequency of normal beating (black symbols) and/or increased the frequency of reversed beating (open symbols; this sequence was voltage- and time-dependent (compare data points during first and second 1-s period of step). B. Large positive steps from the holding (= resting) potential generated two patterns of movement: some cilia showing reversed beating and other cilia showing normal beating. With steps rising towards the Ca equilibrium potential the reversed beating frequency decreased and/or normal beating increased. The percentage of inactivated cilia was maximal at step potentials of 80–90 mV. The time dependence of responses corresponded to that seen with small step amplitudes (data not shown). The results suggest that Ca slowly accumulates in the cilium during small and very large positive voltage steps thereby producing the sequence in motor responses «decrease in normal beating → inactivation → increase in reversed beating». MACHEMER and ECKERT, 1975.

all-or-none response properties and voltage-dependent inactivation; the latter channel occurs in *Stylonychia* and is presumably restricted to specialized ciliary organelles (Deitmer, 1984).

Inactivation of ciliary beating has been shown to occur with small and very large depolarizations. Ciliary frequency of *Paramecium* declined from the resting level near 20 Hz with depolarizing voltage steps between 1 mV and 3 mV (Fig. 23A). The decline developed with time and frequency eventually dropped to zero Hz; reversed beating often arose following inactivation over step periods of 2 seconds. A reverse sequence in motor events was seen with positive voltage steps rising towards the Ca equilibrium potential (Fig. 23B). It was concluded, therefore, that gradually rising intraciliary Ca regulates the drop in normal beating frequency, ciliary inactivation, and a rise in frequency of reversed beating (Machemer and Eckert, 1975). Conversely, it follows that a decrease in Ca concentration from the raised level regulating ciliary inactivation, can activate the frequency of normal beating in *Paramecium*.

Inactivity is a typical state of cirri in a resting *Stylonychia* cell (Figs. 7A, 13). When the membrane potential is depolarized beyond a critical threshold, the cirri begin to incline anteriorly, then activate cyclic beating in the anterior direction. This sequence in responses is homologous to depolarization-dependent ciliary responses in *Paramecium*; it is presumably due to a rise in intraciliary Ca, because it can be suppressed during large positive voltage steps (De Peyer and Machemer, 1982a) (Fig. 24) comparable to similar tests in *Paramecium* (Machemer and Eckert, 1973).

Comparisons with cell-reactivation studies in *Paramecium* (see Naitoh and Sugino, 1984; Nakaoka et al., 1984), in *Chlamydomonas* (Hyams and Borisy, 1978; Kamiya and Witman, 1984; Omoto and Brokaw, 1985) and in sea urchin sperm (Gibbons and Gibbons, 1980) suggest a general pattern of Ca-dependence of the axonemal response:

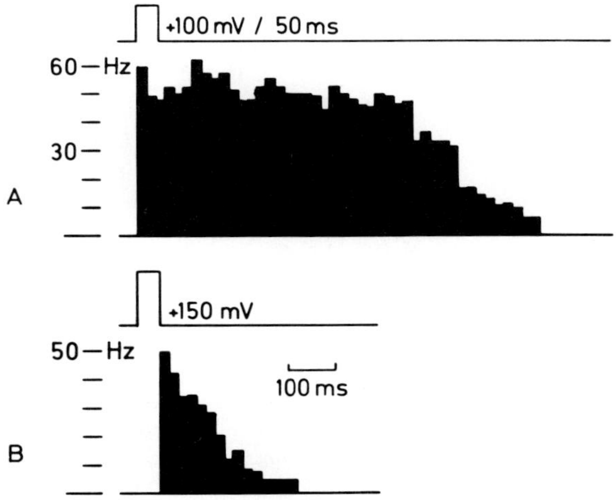

Fig. 24: Suppression and «off-response» of cyclic activation of cirri following very large positive voltage steps in *Stylonychia*. A. With +100 mV step DCA was activated conventionally and persisted for 830 ms. B. DCA was suppressed during a +150 mV step; brief activation of DCA was registered after step termination suggesting that the Ca driving force was insufficient during the step, but a residual Ca influx occurred after restoration of this force. De Peyer and Machemer, 1982a.

normal cyclic activity at a resting Ca concentration near 10^{-7} M, and a depolarization-induced «reversed» beating following raised Ca-concentrations up to 10^{-4} M; ciliary inactivation and quiescence occur at intermediate levels of intraciliary Ca. This model corresponds, in some respects, to stimulus-induced classes of ciliary beat patterns which have been previously suggested by SLEIGH and BARLOW (1982). A coupling of the family of cyclic responses (normal beating → inactivation → reversed beating) to rising membrane depolarization has so far been demonstrated only in *Paramecium* and *Stylonychia*; in the latter cell normal beating occurs only with hyperpolarization (Fig. 7). The sequence in renormalizing ciliary responses following depolarization in *Corella* (relaxed state → normal beating; MACKIE et al., 1974) compares to those in *Paramecium* (inactivation → normal beating) and suggests a similar coupling to Ca and thereby to depolarization.

The manner by which Ca can rise, decrease or eventually suppress the ciliary cyclic activity remains a matter of speculation. It has been proposed that Ca modulates axonemal function *via* the central complex (see SATIR, 1984), but direct evidence is missing (see also section 2.9). The properties of radial spokes which connect to the central complex in bent regions and are detached in straight regions (WARNER and SATIR, 1974) suggest a supporting mechanical function during the cycle (see, however, following section).

Sliding-activation of Triton-extracted, Mg-ATP reactivated and trypsin-incubated axonemes of *Paramecium* did not indicate that Ca can affect the rate of sliding between microtubular doublets (MOGAMI and TAKAHASHI, 1983). On the assumption that Ca is less likely to affect ciliary frequency by means of passive restraints or active modulation of the sliding rate, it may be hypothesized that the rate of sliding transfer between neighbouring pairs of doublets is regulated by Ca.

7.2. Depolarization controls Ca-mediated regulation of orientational ciliary responses

Overviews of the noncyclic inclination (or arrest) responses reported in the literature have shown that this type of ciliary motor activation is related to depolarization and/or rise in intraciliary Ca concentration (SLEIGH and BARLOW, 1982; see section 4.3). The orientation of inclination is graded with the size of the depolarization (Figs. 13, 22) and presumably with intraciliary Ca. The property of inclination, axonemal bending restricted to the proximal shaft, suggests that Ca can «set», distally to the bend, a certain amount of steady-state sliding displacement between particular doublets. Inclination is maintained during cyclic ciliary activation (Fig. 14), so that a steady active sliding displacement is also accounted for during cyclic sliding activation. Separation of the steady and the cyclic process in *Stylonychia* (Figs. 13, 18D), and in metazoan preparations showing depolarization-dependent arrest, suggests that Ca regulates these responses by means of two mechanisms. It is possible that Ca-controlled steady radial-spoke connections near the basal bend account for the maintenance of inclination during cyclic activity of the axoneme. In accordance with this speculation, trypsin-digested, reactivated sea urchin sperm produced Ca-independent symmetric bending waves (BROKAW and GIBBONS, 1974). The geometric and structural postulates of this hypothesis are testable.

The second orientational parameter of ciliary activity, the power stroke, including temporal and spatial polarization of the cycle, has been related to the intraciliary Ca concentration (see section 3). While supporting evidence from live and Mg-ATP reactivated cells is compelling, a rather complex implication of this hypothesis is that the total bending program of the ciliary cycle (not only the power stroke direction) is rotated in a graded relationship to depolarization and intraciliary Ca. Two principal ways of thinking have been applied to this view: either, a Ca-regulated orientational mechanism is superimposed upon a Mg-regulated cyclic beating mechanism; the structural correlate of such Ca-machine could be the central complex including the radial-spoke system (see NAITOH and SUGINO, 1984; SATIR, 1984). Alternatively, each of the 9 doublets, including the associated sets of dynein arms and radial spokes, is differently tuned to varying Ca concentrations, so that for a given Ca concentration the amount, and the rate of transfer, of active sliding (to the neighbouring pair of doublets) is re-assigned to particular doublets (MACHEMER, 1977).

A crucial testing point of these two working hypothesis may be whether or not the frequency response of the cilium can be experimentally uncoupled from cyclic polarization of the ciliary beat, so as to separate the presumed «orientation machine» from the presumed «frequency machine». Previous cell-reactivation experiments in *Paramecium* have shown that Mg as well as Ca can affect the swimming direction (NAKAOKA and TOYOTAMA, 1979) and Ca as well as Mg can modulate ciliary frequency (NAKAOKA et al., 1984); these data suggest that the cyclic ciliary responses may be coupled, because they are subject to the same regulating mechanism, Ca together with Mg. Mg is presumed to be kept at high ($\geq 10^{-4}$ M) concentrations in the cilium; therefore, raised Ca so far remains the sole candidate for regulation of the frequency and directional responses of the cilium controlled by depolarization of the membrane.

7.3. Is hyperpolarization-dependent ciliary activation mediated by calcium?

Ciliary responses induced by membrane hyperpolarization (HCA) are unrelated to Ca influx. Hyperpolarization increases the driving force for Ca by a few percent, but HCA is presumably not a function of raised intraciliary Ca as suggested previously (ECKERT, 1972). If this were the case, rising hyerpolarization of the membrane should produce a sequence of ciliary frequency responses comparable, in principle, to that following depolarization. Inspection of Fig. 7 shows that this is not the case in *Paramecium*, while it may occur in *Stylonychia*; however, the directional response following hyperpolarization shifts in the clockwise direction, while the shift is counterclockwise following depolarization (MACHEMER, 1974b).

HCA shares some properties with depolarization-induced ciliary activity (DCA) such as (1) a voltage-graded activation of ciliary frequency (Fig. 7); (2) decay of the frequency response being coupled to the size of the voltage stimulus (Fig. 25, compare with Fig. 17); (3) a common counterclockwise resetting of inclination and beat orientation with positive-going polarization of the membrane (MACHEMER, 1974b; Figs. 13, 22). It should be noted that the frequency-voltage relation near the resting potential of *Paramecium* is a continuous function of the membrane potential (Figs. 7B, 23A). An interesting difference between HCA and DCA is that cyclic activation of the cilium involves a larger latency, and the rise to peak activity occurs at a comparatively slower rate following hyperpolarization (MACHEMER, 1974b; DE PEYER and MACHEMER, 1982a, b) (Figs. 12, 17, 25).

Comparison of electric and ciliary motility data in ciliates has led to the hypothesis that Ca can regulate the ciliary motor responses throughout the physiological range of membrane potentials (MACHEMER, 1974b, 1977; MACHEMER and DE PEYER, 1982). The hypothesis assumes that depolarization increases intraciliary Ca due to activation of Ca channels, and that hyerpolarization leads to decreases in free Ca and/or Ca bound to the axoneme. The observed differences in motor activation kinetics of DCA and HCA agree with the fact that rapid Ca fluxes are possible along, but not against the inward electrochemical gradient of this cation.

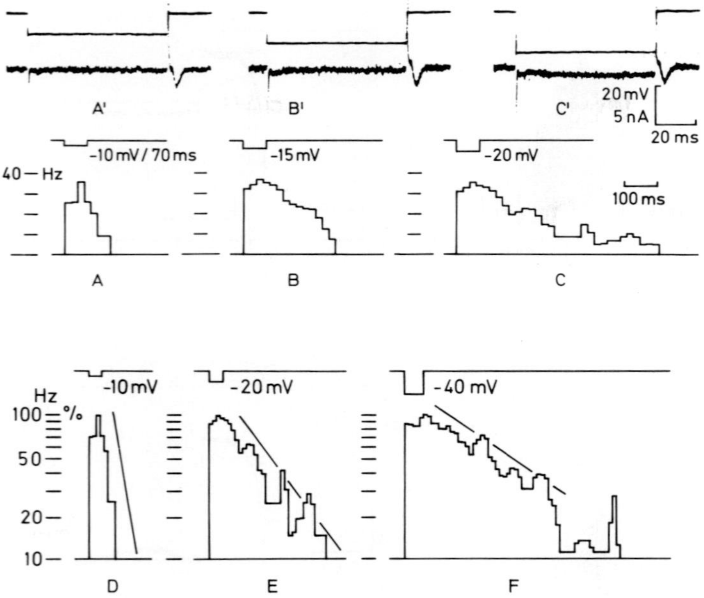

Fig. 25: Activation of ciliary activity following hyperpolarizing voltage steps in *Stylonychia*. Note (1) the passive nature of the membrane current (noisy traces) during the voltage step (A'–C'); (2) rising of the frequency response over 50-ms period (A–C); (3) a −10mV pulse was sufficient for maximal activation; (4) the rate of exponential decline of the cyclic response after pulse end was dependent upon the stimulus amplitude (D–F). De Peyer and Machemer, 1982b.

Hyperpolarization-dependent reduction in intraciliary Ca may occur following a drop in Ca conductance and/or Ca pumping (Eckert et al. 1976), but there is evidence that the resting g_{Ca} of the ciliary membrane is not reduced by hyperpolarization (Naitoh, 1979; personal communication). A reduction in Ca_i by hyperpolarization has been reported from squid axon (Baker, 1972). A reduction of small depolarizations or a substantial drop in the Ca driving force can raise normal ciliary beating in *Paramecium* (Fig. 23). Experiments exploring interactions of DCA and HCA under voltage-clamp have shown that a hyperpolarizing step directly following a depolarizing step reduced the duration of DCA, but failed to induce the regular HCA response (Machemer and de Peyer, 1982) (Fig. 26). This is supporting evidence of the «all-calcium hypothesis» of ciliary motor regulation. On the other hand, a «subtractive effect» of mechanisms regulating DCA and HCA does not necessarily imply Ca as the sole regulator.

Reactivation of detergent-permeabilized cell models has shown that a reduction as well as an increase in Ca can raise the ciliary frequency (see section 3). In particular, the frequency of Mg-ATP reactivated cilia increased, and the velocity of forward swimming *Paramecium* models rose with free Ca decreasing from 6×10^{-7} M to 2×10^{-7} M Ca (Nakaoka et al., 1984). These values correspond to a decrease in number of free Ca ions per cilium from 60 to 20 (ciliary length assumed to be 10 μm). Greater amounts of Ca bound to membrane-associated and axonemal proteins may equilibrate with free calcium, so that eventually Ca bound to the axoneme can regulate the motor response following hyperpolarization.

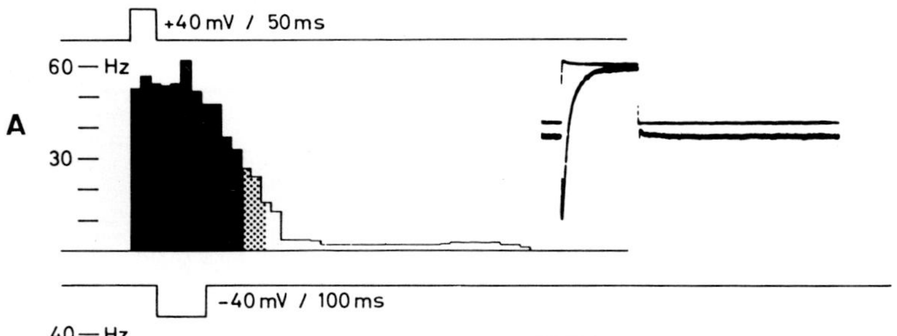

Fig. 26: «Subtractive effect» upon ciliary activation of coupled depolarizing and hyperpolarizing voltage steps in *Stylonychia*. A. A large depolarizing voltage step induced maximal early inward Ca current (inset) and vigorous cyclic beating towards the anterior end of the cell (DCA, black histogram bars; shaded area: DCA in part of the cirri). B. Motor response to a hyperpolarizing step was a typical cyclic activation with the power stroke directed posteriorly (HCA, white histogram bars). C. Subsequent combination of both steps served to reduce the duration of DCA, and to suppress HCA (inset depicts occurrence of large early current). D. A single hyperpolarization at the end of a stimulus series proved that suppression of HCA in (C) was due to the depolarizing prepulse. The simplest explanation of the subtractive effect is that hyperpolarization decreased the previously raised intraciliary Ca. MACHEMER and DE PEYER, unpublished.

An alternative hypothesis explaining HCA assumes that loops of current enter the cilium during membrane hyperpolarization and cause an electrophoretic redistribution of charged particles in the ciliary space (BREHM and ECKERT, 1978b). A crude approximation of passive current for a minimal motor response of a cilium suggests that this is an unlikely mechanism for regulating ciliary functions; assuming that 5 % of the charge of a minimal effective hyperpolarization[2] can enter the cilia (see section 5), the average charge per

2 The frontal cirrus in *Stylonychia* was activated by a 2 mV hyperpolarization after 40 ms (SUGINO and MACHEMER, unpublished) corresponding to a charge of 1.6×10^{-12}C. *Stylonychia* includes about 10.000 cilia averaging 20 μm in length.

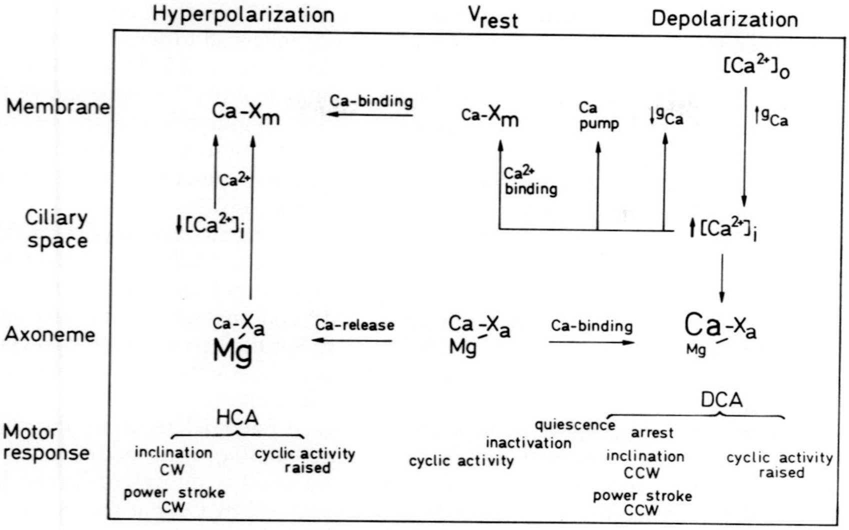

Fig. 27: Conjectured pathways of electromotor coupling in cilia suggesting that graded membrane signals can be translated, by means of ionic Ca, to graded alteration of Ca-Mg binding to a protein (X_a) near the axonemal sliding sites. The summarizing diagram shows the resting and two polarized states of the membrane. Signal processing occurs at three levels: the membrane, the ciliary space and the axoneme. The motor responses, HCA or DCA, include maximally two directional responses (inclination, direction of power stroke; CW, clockwise, CCW, counterclockwise shifts), one cyclic response, and inactivation (the absence of pronounced directional and cyclic activity). Other well documented ciliary responses are included. Depolarization activates voltage-sensitive ciliary Ca channels so that Ca_i can rise in a graded manner. Raised intraciliary Ca inactivates the Ca conductance, increases Ca pumping, and successfully competes with Mg_i for binding to an axonemal modulating protein (X_a). An increased ratio of Ca/Mg binding to X_a can specifically regulate active sliding and thereby signal the stimulus-specific motor response (DCA). Hyperpolarization may lead to increased binding of intraciliary free Ca such as to a voltage-sensitive, membrane-integrated protein (X_m), thereby affecting the equilibrium of free and bound axonemal Ca; some Ca is released from the axonemal protein and replaced by Mg. A decreased ratio of Ca/Mg bound to X_a signals the production of HCA.

cilium corresponds to 50 monovalent ions. With 10^7 cations being present in one cilium (the K_i concentration is near 40 mM; De Peyer and Machemer, 1978a) it is difficult to imagine how a minor displacement of charges along the cilium can affect axonemal function. Moreover, long cilia having a larger surface area than short cilia, should be more sensitive to membrane hyperpolarization. The reverse relationship was observed: activation of the marginal cirri of *Stylonychia* (25 μm) is associated with a shorter latency and higher frequency response than that of the longer frontal cirri (55 μm) (Deitmer et al., 1984).

A hypothetical selective entrance into the ciliary space of 50 H^+ ions would be equivalent to a change in intraciliary pH from 7.0 to 6.7 which may be a reasonable signal for inducing HCA. Modifications in pH are nevertheless unlikely candidates for regulating the ciliary motor, since reactivation experiments were performed at buffered neutral pH. Naitoh and Kaneko (1973) found that an increase in pH from 5.0 to 7.0 induced a graded rise in frequency of reactivated cilia; this observation does not correspond to the pH-hypothesis. It has been reported that reduction in pH of the medium between 9.6 and 5.6 and raising the pH between 4.7 and 5.6 can induce enhanced forward swimming of *Paramecium* (DRYL, 1961). Previous tests on live *Paramecium* of pH-effects ranging between 6.3 and 7.7 (including control mixes of two solutions of pH 7.0) have shown that forward swimming of *Paramecium* is augmented for up to 20 min following the mechanical disturbance, irrespective of a step-up or step-down in pH (MACHEMER-RÖHNISCH and MACHEMER, unpublished). Experiments recording ciliary activity under voltage-clamp and controlled intracellular pH may crucially test the pH-hypothesis.

Biochemical and behavioural studies of *Paramecium* showing an increase of cyclic AMP in parallel with stimulus-induced HCA have indicated that cyclic AMP may be an intracellular messenger of ciliary responses following membrane hyperpolarization (GUSTIN et al., 1983; SCHULTZ et al., 1984). Injections of cyclic AMP and analogs into the cell under voltage-clamp, showed an increase in outward current, but no increase in normal ciliary activity (HENNESSEY et al., 1985). It was concluded that cyclic AMP can hyperpolarize the membrane, but cannot bypass hyperpolarization to induce HCA.

Comparisons of current views of how the membrane potential regulates the ciliary motor show a general agreement that Ca is the major regulating agent for DCA, but the manner by which the various ciliary functions are coordinated is not well understood. So far the available evidence suggests that HCA is also regulated by Ca, but this matter still awaits a thorough explanation. On the basis of available data a scheme of the possible universal electromotor control of cilia by Ca is illustrated in Fig. 27: processing of two electrical signals (hyperpolarization, depolarization) occurs at three levels: the membrane, the ciliary space and the axoneme. Axonemally bound Ca is thought to be at the center of ciliary motor control. The motor response, HCA or DCA, can include two directional responses (inclination, direction of power stroke), one cyclic response, and inactivation. In essence, the diagram explains how graded membrane signals can be translated, by means of ionic Ca, into graded alterations of Ca-Mg binding to axonemal sliding sites. The manner by which Ca-Mg binding to nine different axonemal sliding sites can produce a specific motor response in three dimensions remains unknown at present.

8. Perspectives

The electrophysiological control of the ciliary response has been a challenge for multidisciplinary approaches, and ultimate solutions of current research questions may eventually result from common efforts. This paper deals with basic questions of structure, function and biophysics of the ciliary organelle employing the comparative approach. At the present time, an increasingly realistic view of how the cilium moves in space and time is emerging due to improving techniques of data recording and processing. It is expected that a detailed knowledge of the ciliary function under membrane potential and environmental control will provide crucial clues as to how the sliding machinery works. Another frontier, an integrated effort of biochemistry, genetics and ultrastructural analysis has been successfully probing into the molecular design of the cilium using increasingly *in vitro* assays. Because of its universal presence in early eukaryotic life, the little rotary sliding machine has assumed key roles in cellular interactions with the environment. Understanding the ciliary motor response will help to solve questions of far-reaching biological and medical relevance[3].

---

3 An illustration of this view is the recent finding that the kinocilium of the vertebrate ampullary hair cell can produce minor inclination responses to polarizing stimulation (THURM and RÜSCH, 1985).

Acknowledgments

This paper was supported by the Deutsche Forschungsgemeinschaft, SFB 114, TP A5. I thank Professor M. A. Sleigh for critically reading the manuscript.

References

Adams, G. M. W., Huang, B., Piperno, G., Luck, D. J. L. (1981): The central pair microtubular complex of *Chlamydomonas* flagella: polypeptide composition as revealed by analysis of mutants. J. Cell Biol. **91**, 69–76.

Adrian, R. H., Costantin, L. L., Peachey, L. D. (1969): Radial spread of contraction in frog muscle fibres. J. Physiol. **204**, 231–257.

Afzelius, B. A. (1961): The fine structure of the cilia from ctenophore swimming plates. J. Biophys. Biochem. Cytol. **9**, 383–394.

Aiello, E. (1960): Factors affecting ciliary activity on the gill of the mussel *Mytilus edulis*. Physiol. Zool. **33**, 120–135.

Aiello, E. (1974): Control of ciliary activity in Metazoa. In: Cilia and flagella (M. A. Sleigh, ed.), pp. 353–376, Academic Press, London, New York.

Aiello, E., Sleigh, M. A. (1972): The metachronal wave of lateral cilia of *Mytilus edulis*. J. Cell. Biol. **54**, 493–506.

Baba, S. A. (1975): Developmental changes in the patterns of ciliary response and the swimming behavior of some invertebrate larvae: In: Swimming and flying in nature (T. Y. T. Wu, C. J. Brokaw, C. Brennen, eds.), vol. I, pp. 317–323, Plenum, New York.

Bessen, M., Fay, R. B., Witman, G. B. (1980): Calcium control of waveform in isolated flagellar axonemes of *Chlamydomonas*. J. Cell Biol. **86**, 446–455.

Blum, J. J. (1971): Existence of a breaking point in cilia and flagella. J. Theor. Biol. **33**, 257–263.

Blum, J. J., Hines, M. H. (1983): Diffusion of Ca^{2+} and the quiescent response of sea urchin sperm flagella. J. Theor. Biol. **100**, 511–523.

Boheim, G., Hanke, W., Methfessel, C., Eibl, H., Kaupp, U. B., Maelicke, A., Schultz, J. E. (1982): Membrane reconstitution below lipid phase transition temperature. In: Transport in biomembranes: model systems and reconstitution (R. Antolini, ed.), pp. 87–97, Raven Press, New York.

Bone, Q. (1958): Nervous control of cilia in *Amphioxus*. Nature (Lond.) **181**, 193–194.

Brehm, P., Eckert, R. (1978a): Calcium leads to inactivation of calcium channel in *Paramecium*. Science, **202**, 1203–1206.

Brehm, P., Eckert, R. (1978b): An electrophysiological study of the regulation of beat frequency in *Paramecium*. J. Physiol. **283**, 557–568.

Brokaw, C. J. (1966): Effects of increased viscosity on the movements of some invertebrate spermatozoa. J. Exp. Biol. **45**, 113–139.

Brokaw, C. J. (1974): Movement of the flagellum of some marine invertebrate spermatozoa. In: Cilia and flagella (M. A. Sleigh, ed.), pp. 93–109, Academic Press, London, New York.

Brokaw, C. J. (1977): CO_2-inhibition of the amplitude of bending of Triton-demembranated sea urchin sperm flagella. J. Exp. Biol. **71**, 229–240.

Brokaw, C. J., Luck, D. J. L., Huang, B. (1982): Analysis of the movement of *Chlamydomonas* flagella: the function of the radial-spoke system is revealed by comparison of wild-type and mutant flagella. J. Cell. Biol. **92**, 722–732.

Brokaw, C. J., Simonick, T. F. (1977): Motility of Triton-demembranated sea urchin sperm flagella during digestion by trypsin. J. Cell Biol. **75**, 650–665.

Chad, J. E., Deitmer, J. W., Eckert, R. (1984): Spatio-temporal characteristics of Ca^{2+} dispersal following its injection into *Aplysia* neurons. Biophys. J. **45**, 181a.

Deitmer, J. W. (1983): Ca channels in the membrane of the hypotrich ciliate *Stylonychia*. In: The physiology of excitable cells (A. Grinnell, W. J. Moody, eds.), pp. 51–63, Liss, New York.

Deitmer, J. W., Machemer, H., Martinac, B. (1984): Motor control in three types of ciliary organelles in the ciliate *Stylonychia*. J. Comp. Physiol. A **154**, 113–120.

De Peyer, J. E., Deitmer, J. W. (1980): Divalent cations as charge carriers during two functionally different membrane currents in the ciliate *Stylonychia*. J. Exp. Biol. **88**, 73–89.

De Peyer, J. E., Machemer, H. (1978a): Hyperpolarizing and depolarizing mechanoreceptor potentials in *Stylonychia*. J. Comp. Physiol. **127**, 255–266.

De Peyer, J. E., Machemer, H. (1978b): Are receptor-activated ciliary motor responses mediated through voltage or current? Nature **276**, 285–287.

De Peyer, J. E., Machemer, H. (1982a): Electromechanical coupling in cilia I. Effects of depolarizing voltage steps. Cell Motility **2**, 483–496.

De Peyer, J. E., Machemer, H. (1982b): Electromechanical coupling in cilia II. Effects of hyperpolarizing voltage steps. Cell Motility **2**, 497–508.

De Peyer, J. E., Machemer, H. (1983): Threshold activation and dynamic response range of cilia following low rates of membrane polarization under voltage-clamp. J. Comp. Physiol. **150**, 223–232.

Doughty, M. J. (1979): Control of ciliary activity in *Paramecium* – IV. Ca^{2+} modification of Mg^{2+} dependent dynein ATPase activity. Comp. Biochem. Physiol. **64B**, 255–266.

Doughty, M. J., Dryl, S. (1981): Control of ciliary activity in *Paramecium*: an analysis of chemosensory transduction in a eukaryotic unicellular organism. Progr. Neurobiol. **16**, 1–115.

Dryl, S. (1961): The velocity of forward movement of *Paramecium caudatum* in relation to pH of medium. Bull. Acad. Pol. Sci. Cl. II, **9**, 71–74.

Dunlap, K. (1977): Localization of calcium channels in *Paramecium caudatum*. J. Physiol. **271**, 119–133.

Dute, R., Kung, C. (1978): Ultrastructure of the proximal region of somatic cilia in *Paramecium tetraurelia*. J. Cell Biol. **78**, 451–464.

Eckert, R. (1972): Bioelectric control of ciliary activity. Science, N. Y. **176**, 473–481.

Eckert, R., Naitoh, Y. (1970): Passive electrical properties of *Paramecium* and problems of ciliary coordination. J. Gen. Physiol. **55**, 467–483.

Ehrlich, B. A., Finkelstein, A., Forte, M., Kung, C. (1984): Voltage-dependent calcium channels from *Paramecium* cilia incorporated into planar lipid bilayers. Science **225**, 427–428.

Gaber, D. L., Kopf, G. S. (1980): The regulation of spermatozoa by calcium and cyclic nucleotides. Adv. Cyclic Nucleotide Res. **13**, 251–306.

Galt, C. P., Mackie, G. O. (1971): Electrical correlates of ciliary reversal in *Oikopleura*. J. Exp. Biol. **55**, 205–212.

Gelfan, S. (1926): The electrical conductivity of protoplasm and a new method of its determination. Univ. Calif. Publs. Zool. **29**, 453.

Gelei, J. von (1926): Eine neue Osmium-Toluidinmethode für Protistenforschung. Mikrokosmos **20**, 97–103.

Gibbons, B. H., Gibbons, I. R. (1973): The effect of partial extraction of dynein arms on the movement of reactivated sea urchin sperm. J. Cell Science **13**, 337–357.

Gibbons, B. H., Gibbons, I. R. (1974): Properties of flagellar «rigor waves» formed by abrupt removal of adenosine triphosphate from actively swimming sea urchin sperm. J. Cell Biol. **63**, 970–985.

Gibbons, B. H., Gibbons, I. R. (1980): Calcium-induced quiescence in reactivated sea urchin sperm. J. Cell Biol. **84**, 13–27.

Gibbons, B. H., Gibbons, I. R., Baccetti, B. (1983): Structure and motility of the 9+0 flagellum of eel spermatozoa. J. Submicrosc. Cytol. **15**, 15–20.

Gibbons, I. R. (1981): Cilia and flagella of eukaryotes. J. Cell Biol. (Suppl.) **91**, 107–124.

Gibbons, I. R., Gibbons, B. H. (1974): The fine structure of rigor wave axonemes from sea-urchin sperm flagella. J. Cell Biol. **63**, 110a.

Goldstein, S. F. (1974): Isolated, reactivated and laser-irradiated cilia and flagella. In: Cilia and flagella (M. A. Sleigh, ed.), pp. 111–130, Academic Press, London, New York.

Goldstein, S. F. (1979): Starting transients in sea urchin sperm flagella. J. Cell Biol. **80**, 61–68.

Gray, J. (1924): The mechanism of ciliary movement. IV. The relation of ciliary activity to oxygen consumption. Proc. R. Soc. Lond. (Biol.) **96**, 95–114.

Gustin, M. C., Bonini, M. N., Nelson, D. L. (1983): Membrane potential regulation of cAMP: Control mechanism for the swimming behaviour in *Paramecium*. Soc. Neurosci. Abstr. **9**, 167.

Hausmann, K. (1983): Flagellen- und Cilienbewegung: Kenntnisstand zum 9+2-Muster. BIUZ **13**, 161–169.

Hausmann, K. (1985): Protozoologie. pp. 1–351, Thieme, Stuttgart.
Hennessey, T., Machemer, H., Nelson, D. L. (1985): Injected cyclic AMP increases ciliary beat frequency in conjunction with membrane hyperpolarization. Eur. J. Cell Biol. **36**, 153–156.
Hines, M., Blum, J. J. (1985): On the contribution of dynein-like activity to twisting in a three-dimensional sliding filament model. Biophys. J. **47**, 705–708.
Hiramoto, Y., Baba, S. A. (1978): A quantitative analysis of flagellar movement in echinoderm spermatozoa. J. Exp. Biol. **76**, 85–104.
Hoffmann-Berling, H. (1955): Geißelmodelle und Adenosintriphosphat. Biochim. Biophysica Acta **16**, 146–154.
Huang, B., Piperno, G., Luck, D. J. L. (1979): Paralyzed flagella mutants of *Chlamydomonas reinhardtii* defective for axonemal doublet microtubule arms. J. Biol. Chem. **254**, 3091–3099.
Huang, B., Ramanis, Z., Luck, D. J. L. (1982): Suppressor mutations in *Chlamydomonas* reveal a regulatory mechanism for flagellar function. Cell **28**, 115–124.
Ishijima, S., Mohri, H. (1985): A quantitative description of flagellar movement in golden hamster spermatozoa. J. Exp. Biol. **114**, 463–475.
Ivens, I. (1986): Different properties of two voltage-dependent inward currents in the ciliate *Stylonychia mytilus*. J. Physiol. (in press).
Kamiya, R., Witman, G. B. (1984): Submicromolar levels of calcium control the balance of beating between the two flagella in demembranated models of *Chlamydomonas*. J. Cell Biol. **98**, 97–107.
Kinosita, H. (1954): Electric potentials and ciliary response in *Opalina*. J. Fac. Sci. Univ. Tokyo, Sect. IV, **7**, 1–14.
Machemer, H. (1969a): Regulation der Cilienmetachronie bei der Fluchtreaktion von *Paramecium*. J. Protozool. **16**, 764–771.
Machemer, H. (1969b): Filmbildanalysen 4 verschiedener Schlagmuster der Marginalcirren von *Stylonychia*. Z. Vergl. Physiol. **62**, 183–196.
Machemer, H. (1970): In-vivo studies on ciliary activity and metachrony in *Paramecium multimicronucleatum*. Habilitationsschrift, pp. 1–98, Fachbereich Biologie, Eberhard-Karls-Universität Tübingen.
Machemer, H. (1972a): Properties of polarized beat in *Paramecium*. Acta Protozool. **11**, 295–300.
Machemer, H. (1972b): Temperature influences on ciliary beat and metachronal coordination in *Paramecium*. J. Mechanochem. Cell. Motil. **1**, 57–66.
Machemer, H. (1972c): Ciliary activity and the origin of metachrony in *Paramecium*: Effects of increased viscosity. J. Exp. Biol. **57**, 239–259.
Machemer, H. (1974a): Ciliary activity and metachronism in Protozoa. In: Cilia and flagella (M. A. Sleigh, ed.), pp. 199–286, Academic Press, London, New York.
Machemer, H. (1974b): Frequency and directional responses of cilia to membrane potential changes in *Paramecium*. J. Comp. Physiol. **92**, 293–316.
Machemer, H. (1975): Modification of ciliary activity by the rate of membrane potential changes in *Paramecium*. J. Comp. Physiol. **101**, 343–356.
Machemer, H. (1977): Motor activity and bioelectric control of cilia. Fortschr. Zool. **24**, 195–210.
Machemer, H., de Peyer, J. E. (1982): Analysis of ciliary beating frequency under voltage-clamp control of the membrane. Cell Motility (Suppl.) **1**, 205–210.
Machemer, H., Eckert, R. (1973): Electrophysiological control of reversed ciliary beating in *Paramecium*. J. Gen. Physiol. **61**, 572–587.
Machemer, H., Eckert, R. (1975): Ciliary frequency and orientational responses to clamped voltage steps in *Paramecium*. J. Comp. Physiol. **104**, 247–260.
Machemer, H., Eckert, R. (1977): Electromechanical coupling of ciliary activity in *Paramecium*. Fortschr. Zool. **24**, 211–215.
Machemer, H., Ogura, A. (1979): Ionic conductances of membranes in ciliated and deciliated *Paramecium*. J. Physiol. **296**, 49–60.
Machemer, H., Sugino, K. (1986): Parameters of the ciliary cycle under membrane voltage control. Cell Motil. Cytoskel. **6**, 89–95.
Mackie, G. O. (1970): Neuroid conduction and the evolution of conducting tissues. Q. Rev. Biol. **45**, 319–322.

Mackie, G. O., Paul, D. H., Singla, C. M., Sleigh, M. A., Williams, D. E. (1974): Branchial innervation and ciliary control in the ascidian *Corella*. Proc. R. Soc., Ser. B, **187**, 1–35.
Mackie, G. O., Singla, C. L., Thiriot-Quievreux, C. (1976): Nervous control of ciliary activity in gastropod larvae. Biol. Bull. **151**, 182–199.
Mackie, G. O., Spencer, A. N., Strathmann, R. (1969): Electrical activity associated with ciliary reversal in an echinoderm larva. Nature (London) **223**, 1383–1385.
Margulis, L. (1981): Symbiosis in cell evolution. pp. 1–419, Freeman & Company, San Franscisco.
Mohri, H., Yasumasu, I. (1963): Studies on the respiration of sea-urchin spermatozoa. J. Exp. Biol. **40**, 573–586.
Moss, A. G., Tamm, S. L. (1986): Electrophysiological control of ciliary motor responses in the ctenophore *Pleurobrachia*. J. Comp. Physiol. A **158**, 311–330.
Motokawa, T., Takahashi, K. (1974): Response of nonbeating cilia of *Mytilus* to mechanical stimulation. J. Fac. Sci. Univ. Tokyo (Sect. 4) **13**, 233–242.
Murakami, A. (1972): Movement and control of cilia. (in Japanese) The Cell **4**, 17–24.
Murakami, A. (1983): Control of ciliary beat frequency in *Mytilus*. J. Submicrosc. Cytol. **15**, 313–316.
Murakami, A., Takahashi, K. (1975): Correlation of electrical and mechanical responses in nervous control of cilia. Nature (London) **257**, 48–49.
Naitoh, Y. (1966): Reversal response elicited in nonbeating cilia of *Paramecium* by membrane depolarization. Science N. Y. **154**, 660–662.
Naitoh, Y. (1969): Control of the orientation of cilia by adenosine-triphosphate, calcium and zinc in glycerol-extracted *Paramecium caudatum*. J. Gen. Physiol. **53**, 517–529.
Naitoh, Y. (1979): Membrane currents in voltage-clamped *Paramecium* and their relations to ciliary motion. Acta Protozool. **18**, 1–6.
Naitoh, Y. (1982): Protozoa. In: Electrical conduction and behaviour in ‹simple› invertebrates (G. A. B. Shelton, ed.), pp. 1–48, Clarendon Press, Oxford.
Naitoh, Y., Kaneko, H. (1972): Reactivated Triton-extracted models of *Paramecium*: modification of ciliary movement by calcium ions. Science N. Y. **176**, 523–524.
Naitoh, Y., Kaneko, H. (1973): Control of ciliary activities by adenosine triphosphate and divalent cations in Triton-extracted models of *Paramecium caudatum*. J. Exp. Biol. **58**, 657–676.
Naitoh, Y., Sugino, K. (1984): Ciliary movement and its control in *Paramecium*. J. Protozool. **31**, 31–40.
Nakamura, S., Tamm, S. L. (1985): Calcium control of ciliary reversal in ionophore-treated and ATP-reactivated comb plates of ctenophores. J. Cell. Biol. **100**, 1447–1454.
Nakaoka, Y., Toyotama, H. (1979): Directional change of ciliary beat effected with Mg^{2+} in *Paramecium*. J. Cell. Sci. **40**, 207–214.
Nakaoka, Y., Tanaka, H., Oosawa, F. (1984): Ca^{2+}-dependent regulation of beat frequency of cilia in *Paramecium*. J. Cell Sci. **65**, 223–231.
Nevo, A. C., Rikmenspoel, R. (1970): Diffusion of ATP in sperm flagella. J. Theor. Biol. **26**, 11–18.
Ogura, A. (1977): Non-lethal deciliation of *Paramecium* with ethanol. M. Sc. Thesis., pp. 1–10, Faculty of Science, University of Tokyo.
Ogura, A. (1981): Deciliation and reciliation in *Paramecium* after treatment with ethanol. Cell Structure and Function **6**, 43–50.
Ogura, A., Machemer, H. (1980): Distribution of mechanoreceptor channels in the *Paramecium* surface membrane. J. Comp. Physiol. **135**, 233–242.
Omoto, C. K., Brokaw, C. J. (1983): Quantitative analysis of axonemal bends and twists in the quiescent state of *Ciona* sperm flagella. Cell Motility **3**, 247–259.
Omoto, C. K., Brokaw, C. J. (1985): Bending patterns of *Chlamydomonas* flagella: II. Calcium effects on reactivated *Chlamydomonas* flagella: Cell Motility **5**, 53–60.
Omoto, C. K., Kung, C. (1980): Rotation and twist of the central-pair microtubules in the cilia of *Paramecium*. J. Cell Biol. **87**, 37–46.
Omoto, C. K., Witman, G. B. (1981): Functionally significant central-pair rotation in a primitive eukaryotic flagellum. Nature (London) **290**, 708–710.
Pape, H. C., Machemer, H. (1986): Electrical properties and membrane currents in the ciliate *Didinium*. J. Comp. Physiol. A **158**, 111–124.

Parducz, B. (1951): Die Fixation als Reizwirkung in der Tätigkeit der Zellorganellen. Acta Biol. Acad. Sci. Hung. **3,** 1–17.

Parducz, B. (1956): Reizphysiologische Untersuchungen an Ziliaten. V. Zum physiologischen Mechanismus der sog. Fluchtreaktion und der Raumorientierung. Acta Biol. Acad. Sci. Hung. **7,** 73–99.

Parducz, B. (1959): Reizphysiologische Untersuchungen an Ziliaten. VIII. Ablauf der Fluchtreaktion bei allseitiger und anhaltender Reizung. Ann. Hist. Nat. Mus. Natl. Hung. **51,** 227–246.

Plattner, H. (1975): Membrane-intercalated particle aggregates associated with Ca^{2+}-binding sites in *Paramecium*. J. Cell Sci. **18,** 257–269.

Prensier, G., Vivier, E., Goldstein, S., Schrevel, J. (1980): Motile flagellum with a ‹3+0› ultrastructure. Science N. Y. **207,** 1493–1494.

Ringo, D. I. (1967): Flagellar motion and fine structure of the flagellar apparatus in *Chlamydomonas*. J. Cell Biol. **33,** 543–571.

Saimi, Y. (1977): Electrophysiological studies on the control of the ciliary movement in *Mytilus edulis L.*. pp. 1–69, Doctoral Thesis, Faculty of Science, University of Tokyo.

Sale, W. S., Gibbons, I. R. (1979): Study of the mechanism of vanadate inhibition of the dynein cross-bridge cycle in sea urchin sperm flagella. J. Cell Biol. **82,** 291–298.

Sale, W. S., Satir, P. (1977): Direction of active sliding of microtubules in *Tetrahymena* cilia. Proc. Natl. Acad. Sci. USA **74,** 2045–2049.

Sanderson, M. J. (1984): Cilia. In: Biology of the integument, vol 1, Invertebrates (J. Bereiter-Hahn, A. G. Matoldsy, K. S. Richards, eds.), pp. 17–42, Springer-Verlag, Berlin, Heidelberg, New York, Tokyo.

Sanderson, M. J., Satir, P. (1982): Multiple effects of ethanol and 5-hydroxytryptamine on the gill cilia of *Mytilus edulis*. Cell Motility **2,** 215–224.

Sanderson, M. J., Sleigh, M. A. (1981): Ciliary activity of cultured rabbit tracheal epithelium; beat pattern and metachrony. J. Cell Sci. **47,** 331–347.

Sanderson, M. J., Sleigh, M. A. (1982): The function of respiratory tract cilia. In: The lung and its environment (G. Bonsignore, G. Cumming, eds.), pp. 81–120, Plenum Press, New York.

Satir, P. (1968): Studies on cilia – III. Further studies on the cilium tip and a «sliding filament» model of ciliary motility. J. Cell Biol. **39,** 77–94.

Satir, P. (1984): The generation of ciliary motion. J. Protozool. **31,** 8–12.

Satir, P., Wais-Steider, J., Lebduska, S., Nasr, A., Avolio, J. (1981): The mechanochemical cycle of the dynein arm. Cell Motility **1,** 303–327.

Schrevel, J., Besse, C. (1975): Un type flagellaire fonctionnel de base 6+0. J. Cell Biol. **66,** 492–507.

Schultz, J. E., Grünemund, R., von Hirschhausen, R., Schönefeld, U. (1984): Ionic regulation of cyclic AMP levels in *Paramecium tetraurelia*. FEBS Lett. **167,** 113–116.

Sleigh, M. A. (1971): Cilia. Endeavour **30,** 11–17.

Sleigh, M. A. (1974a): Patterns of movement of cilia and flagella. In: Cilia and flagella (M. A. Sleigh, ed.), pp. 79–92. Academic Press, London, New York.

Sleigh, M. A. (1974b): Metachronism of cilia in Metazoa. In: Cilia and flagella (M. A. Sleigh, ed.), pp. 287–304, Academic Press, London, New York.

Sleigh, M. A. (1984): Motile systems of ciliates. Protistologica **20,** 299–305.

Sleigh, M. A. (1985): Origin and evolution of flagellar movement. Cell Motility **5,** 137.

Sleigh, M. A., Barlow, D. I. (1982): How are different ciliary beat patterns produced? In: Procaryotic and eukaryotic flagella (W. B. Amos, J. G. Duckett, eds.), Symp. Soc. Exp. Biol. **35,** 139–157.

Takahashi, K., Baba, S. A., Murakami, A. (1973): The ‹excitable› cilia of the tunicate *Ciona intestinalis*. J. Fac. Sci. Univ. Tokyo (Sect. IV) **13,** 123–137.

Takahashi, K., Murakami, A. (1968): Nervous inhibition of ciliary motion in the gill of the mussel, *Mytilus edulis*. J. Fac. Sci. Univ. Tokyo (Sect. 4) **11,** 359–372.

Takahashi, K., Shingyoji, C., Kamimura, S. (1982): Microtubule sliding in reactivated flagella. In: Procaryotic and eucaryotic flagella (W. B. Amos, J. G. Duckett, eds.). Symp. Soc. Exp. Biol. **35,** 159–177.

Tamm, S. L., Horridge, G. A. (1970): The relation between the orientation of the central fibrils and the direction of beat in cilia of *Opalina*. Proc. R. Soc. Lond. Ser. B. Biol. Sci. **175,** 219–233.

Tamm, S. L., Moss, A. G. (1985): Unilateral ciliary reversal and motor responses during prey capture by the ctenophore *Pleurobrachia*. J. Exp. Biol. **114,** 443–461.
Tamm, S. L., Tamm, S. (1981): Ciliary reversal without rotation of axonemal structures in ctenophore comb plates. J. Cell Biol. **89,** 495–509.
Thurm, U., Rüsch, A. (1985): Motor activities of ampullary kinocilia. Pflügers Arch. **405** (Suppl. 2), R56, 204.
Tillotson, D., Gorman, A. L. F. (1980): Nonuniform Ca^{2+} buffer distribution in a nerve cell body. Nature (London) **286,** 816–817.
Tsuchiya, T. (1977): Effects of calcium ions on Triton-extracted lamellibranch gill cilia: ciliary arrest response in a model system. Comp. Biochem. Physiol. **56A,** 353–361.
Tsuchiya, T., Takahashi, K. (1976): Localization of possible calcium-binding sites in the cilia of *Paramecium caudatum*. J. Protozool. **23,** 523–526.
Walter, M. F., Satir, P. (1978): Calcium control of ciliary arrest in mussel gill cells. J. Cell Biol. **79,** 110–120.
Warner, F. D. (1970): New observations on flagellar fine structure. J. Cell Biol. **47,** 159–182.
Warner, F. D. (1974): The fine structure of the ciliary and flagellar axoneme. In: Cilia and flagella (M. A. Sleigh, ed.), pp. 11–37, Academic Press, London, New York.
Warner, F. D. (1976): Ciliary inter-microtubule bridges. J. Cell Sci. **20,** 101–114.
Warner, F. D., Satir, P. (1974): The structural basis of ciliary bend formation. Radial spoke positional changes accompanying microtubule sliding. J. Cell Biol. **63,** 35–63.
Woolley, D. M. (1979): Interpretations of the pattern of sperm tail movements. In: The spermatozoon (D. W. Fawcett, J. M. Bedford, eds.), pp. 69–79, Urban & Schwarzenberg, Baltimore, München.
Zucker, R. S., Stockbridge, N. (1983): Presynaptic calcium diffusion and the time course of transmitter release and synaptic facilitation at the squid giant synapse. J. Neurosci. **3,** 1263–1269.

Fortschritte der Zoologie, Band 33 · Lüttgau (Hrsg.): Membrane Control
Gustav Fischer Verlag · Stuttgart · New York · 1986

Control of quantal transmitter release from nerve terminals by depolarization

J. Dudel

Physiologisches Institut der Technischen Universität München, Biedersteiner Strasse 29, D-8000 München 40, FRG

As suggested originally by Katz and Miledi (1967), the release of synaptic transmitter quanta from nerve terminals is generally believed to be controlled by the intracellular Ca-concentration: depolarization of a terminal by an action potential causes a Ca-inflow, which raises the intracellular Ca-concentration, $[Ca]_i$, from the very low resting level and allows release. If a second stimulus follows, ‹residual Ca› from the previous one may add, and will cause facilitation of release from the second stimulus (Katz and Miledi, 1968). Already Katz and Miledi discussed quantitative difficulties with the theory of control of release by $[Ca]_i$ alone. The duration of phasic release of a few ms is very different from that of facilitation, which may last for seconds. Although release seems to depend in some range on $[Ca]_i^4$ (Dodge and Rahamimoff, 1967), it is difficult to see that both the time course of release and of facilitation are caused by a slowly declining $[Ca]_i$ (see also Datyner and Gage, 1980, Dudel et al., 1983). In addition, double pulse facilitation could maximally reach a factor $F = 2^4 = 16$, if release depends on $[Ca]_i^4$. However, ‹early facilitation› measured for short pulse intervals (or doubling pulse duration) reached values of $F = 54$ (Katz and Miledi, 1968) and > 100 in crayfish and frog (Dudel, 1983a, 1984a). Such high facilitations are not compatible with a control of release by $[Ca]_i^4$. For these and other reasons it has been proposed that release is not controlled by $[Ca]_i$ alone, but also by an additional potential dependent factor (Datyner and Gage, 1980, Llinás et al., 1981, Dudel et al., 1983, Dudel, 1984a, b, H. Parnas et al., 1986, I. Parnas et al., 1986). On the other hand, Zucker and Stockbridge (1983) and Stockbridge and Moore (1984) seem to be able to describe release and facilitation for the squid giant synapse and the frog's neuromuscular junction as controlled by $[Ca]_i$ alone, assuming that only a very small zone next to the membrane is involved. In the following, a number of lines of evidence will be discussed which support the idea of control by an additional non-$[Ca]_i$ potential dependent factor.

Methods

The preparations were the opener muscle of the first walking leg of crayfish *(Astacus leptodactylus, Astacus astacus)*, or the cutaneus pectoris muscle of small frogs *(Rana esculenta)*. The preparations were set up as described by Dudel (1983a, 1984a). They were superfused with normal bathing solution, to which $2 \cdot 10^{-7}$ M tetrodotoxin was added to prevent excitations. Recording was by means of a macro-patch-clamp electrode with about 50 μm inner tip diameter. Through the same electrode current pulses could be applied which shifted mainly the extracellular potential around the terminal. Terminals thus could be depolarized, eliciting release (Fig. 1), or also hyperpolarized.

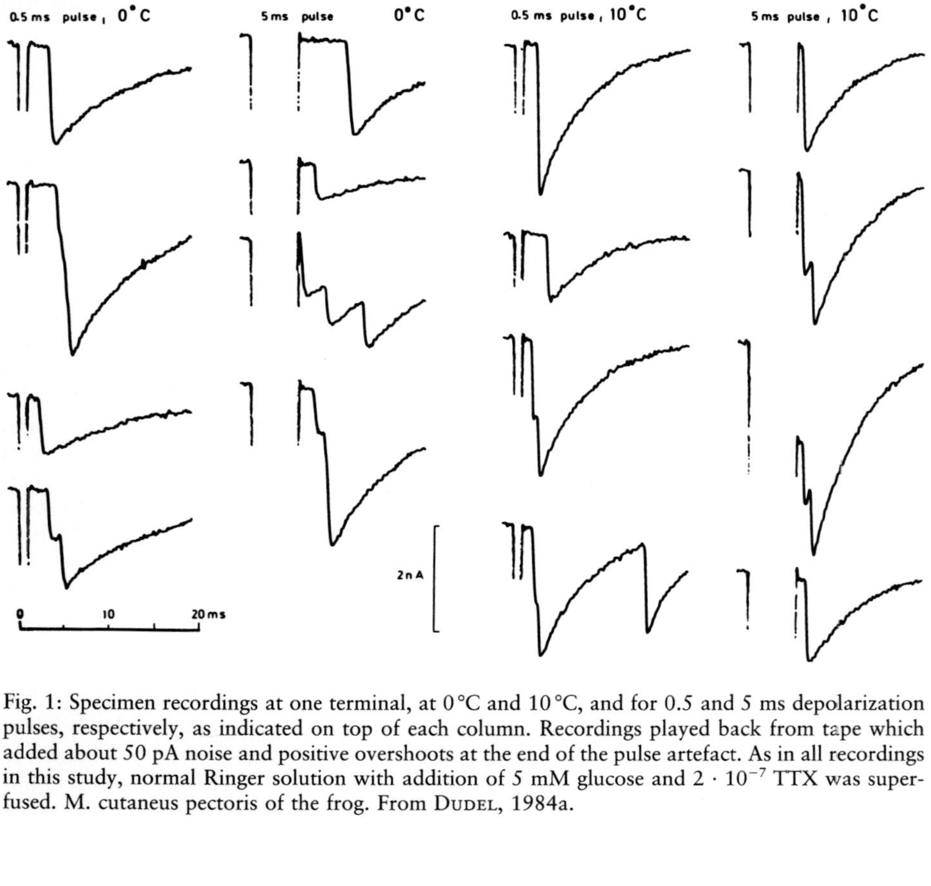

Fig. 1: Specimen recordings at one terminal, at 0 °C and 10 °C, and for 0.5 and 5 ms depolarization pulses, respectively, as indicated on top of each column. Recordings played back from tape which added about 50 pA noise and positive overshoots at the end of the pulse artefact. As in all recordings in this study, normal Ringer solution with addition of 5 mM glucose and $2 \cdot 10^{-7}$ TTX was superfused. M. cutaneus pectoris of the frog. From DUDEL, 1984a.

Double-pulse experiments

If one wants to study the dependence of release on intracellular Ca^{2+}-concentration, $[Ca]_i$, it is not possible to determine changes of $[Ca]_i$ directly in the very small terminals of neuromuscular junctions. Assuming that facilitation in double pulses is due to ‹residual Ca›, one can use the extent of facilitation as an indicator of changes in $[Ca]_i$. Release will depend on the change in $[Ca]_i$, which is expressed as $d[Ca]_{ir}$ in units of the resting $[Ca]_i$, $[Ca]_{ir}$, on a saturation related constant $K_L = k_L\,[Ca]_{ir}$, on the cooperativity ℓ of release with respect to $[Ca]_i$, and on the maximal possible release $\hat{L}_{Ca}$:

(1) $$L_{Ca} = \hat{L}_{Ca}\left(\frac{d+1}{k_L + d+1}\right)^{\ell}$$

(H. Parnas et al., 1982, I. Parnas et al., 1982b). The dependence of L_{Ca} on $d[Ca]_i$ is plotted in Fig. 2. If after a second identical depolarization $[Ca]_i$ will reach the value $2d[Ca]_{ir}$ (disregarding decay of $[Ca]_i$ for short intervals), the double pulse facilitation F_d will be given by the release L_{Ca} after the second pulse divided by the release after the first pulse:

2) $$F_d = \left(\frac{(2d+1)\,(k_L+d+1\,)}{(k_L + 2d+1)\,(d+1)}\right)^{\ell}$$

and this is also plotted in Fig. 2.

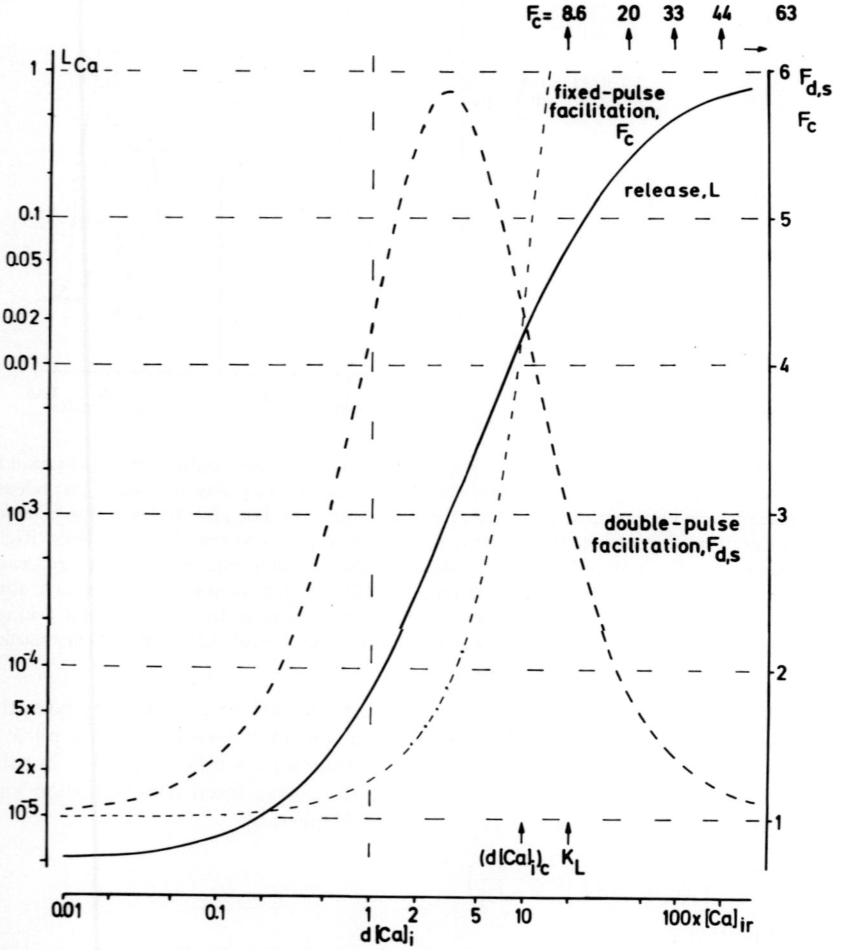

Fig. 2: Theoretical plots of release L_{Ca}, double pulse facilitation F_d and fixed-pulse facilitation F_c in dependence of the Ca-inflow during the first pulse, $d[C]a_i$, in units of resting $[Ca]_i$, $[Ca]_{ir}$. Curves according to eq. (1), (2) and (3), respectively, with $K_L = 20\ [Ca]_{ir}$. The F_c-curve runs out of scale and reaches the values indicated above, saturating at a facilitation of 63.

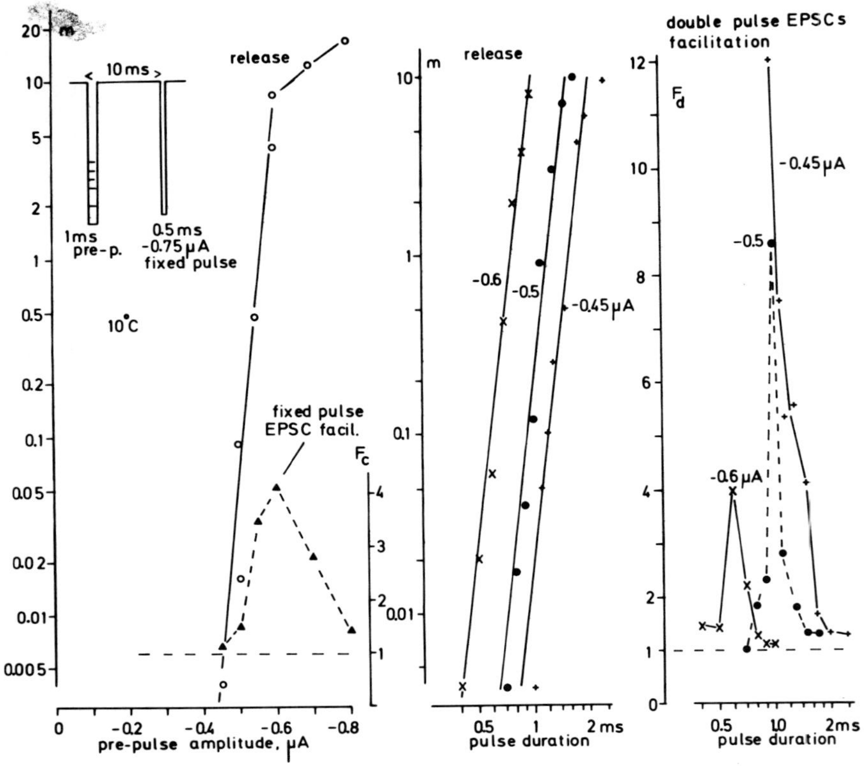

Fig. 3: Left hand: Release m (quanta/stimulus, logarithmic scale) and fixed pulse EPSC facilitation F_c in dependence on the amplitude of a 1 ms prepulse. Parameters of the pulses in inset. F_c = (release after fixed pulse preceded by prepulse): (release after fixed pulse). Middle plot: Release m in dependence on pulse duration, double-logarithmic plot. Amplitude of pulses at the respective lines. Right hand plot: double-pulse facilitation F_d in dependence on pulse duration (logarithmic scale), recorded together with release in the middle plot, same pulse amplitudes and symbols. F_d = (release after second pulse) : (release after first pulse). All recordings at same site, at 10 °C. Each point average from 128 to 2048 recordings. Excitation blocked by tetrodotoxin, as in all experiments. Frog muscle.

In the double-pulse facilitation experiments, both pulses are equal, i. e. they have the same amplitude and duration. In another type of facilitation experiment, a first pulse is varied in amplitude or duration, which will lead to different Ca-inflows $d[Ca]_{ir}$, but the second pulse is kept constant, causing an inflow $c[Ca]_{ir}$ by a fixed depolarization amplitude and duration. This fixed pulse facilitation F_c is given by:

$$3) \qquad F_c = \left(\frac{(c+d+1)\ (k_L+c+1)}{(k_L+c+d+1)\ (c+1)} \right)^{\ell}$$

which is also plotted in Fig. 2.

As seen in Fig. 2, these two types of facilitations have a fundamentally different dependence on $d[Ca]_i$: F_c rises as long as d[Ca]i rises in an S-shaped manner similar to L_{Ca}. F_d, on the other hand, rises to a maximum and falls again to 1 on increasing $d[C]a]_i$, and the shape of F_d is approximately proportional to the slope of L_{Ca} in dependence on $d[Ca]_i$.

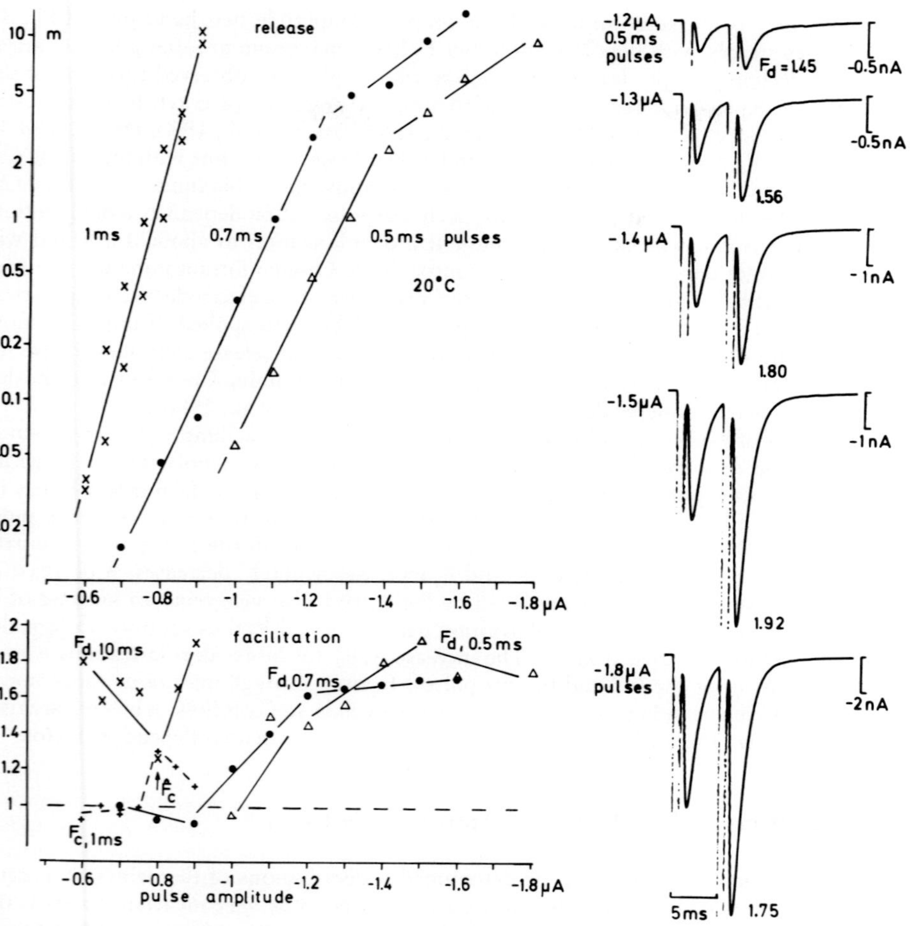

Fig. 4: Upper plot: Release m (logarithmic scale) in dependence on depolarization pulse amplitude, the pulse durations are marked at the curves. Lower plot: Double pulse facilitation F_d measured together with the releases above, same symbols. Fixed pulse facilitation F_c (x) was measured also with a 1 ms prepulse and a −0.55 μA, 2 ms fixed pulse. On the right hand specimen recordings of average releases by the 0.5 ms pulses with the amplitudes indicated left of each trace. After the second EPSC the value of facilitation F_d is given. Note the different amplitude calibrations! All recordings at 20 °C. Interval of double pulses 5 ms. Frog muscle.

In the experiment of Fig. 3, the two types of facilitation are compared. In the right hand part, pulse duration was varied which means that depolarization stayed constant and only Ca-inflow changed. Release increased very steeply with pulse duration, with a double logarithmic slope of about 8 (corresponding to an early facilitation > 200). Double-pulse facilitation F_d showed maxima at a specific pulse duration, depending on the level of depolarization. This agrees with the prediction for the $d[Ca]_i$ dependence of F_d inFig. 2. If F_c is determined in dependence on duration of the first pulse (fixed amplitude), it rises with pulse duration and reaches a saturation level (not illustrated), as also predicted in Fig. 2.

However, if F_c is measured in dependence on pulse amplitude (left hand plot of Fig. 3), release rises steeply with depolarization, but F_c has a maximum at $-0.6\ \mu A$ depolarization, and declines sharply for larger depolarizations. We have observed this type of depolarization dependence regularly in neuromuscular junctions of crayfish, rock lobster and frog (DUDEL et al., 1983, H. PARNAS et al., 1986, DUDEL et al., 1984, DUDEL, 1983b, 1984b). Since F_c, according to equation 3 and to Fig. 2 rises monotone with increasing Ca-inflow, it is concluded that at the peak of F_c Ca-inflow has a maximum, and that Ca-inflow declines for larger depolarizations. Such a depolarization dependence of Ca-inflow is to be expected: it will have a maximum at a depolarization to about 0 mV and will decline for larger depolarizations which approach the Ca-equilibrium potential (see e. g. Llinás et al., 1981). Taking account of the seal resistance of the electrode, such depolarizations are to be expected at the current amplitudes which were applied. If thus Ca-inflow has a maximum at the peak of F_c, it is very remarkable that release continues to rise for larger depolarizations. This increase in release in spite of declining Ca-inflow must be due to a non-Ca potential dependent control factor (H. PARNAS et al., 1986).

The effects of variations in depolarization on double pulse facilitation F_d are shown in Fig. 4. Release rises steeply with depolarization, the necessary depolarization range increasing for lower pulse duration. For the 1 ms pulse, fixed pulse facilitation F_c has its maximum at $-0.8\ \mu A$ depolarization (and the same would be found for other pulse durations, see DUDEL et al., 1983). Double pulse facilitation for the 1 ms pulse is a mirror image of F_c:F_d declines while F_c rises, and F_d increases while F_c decreases. A decrease of F_d with increasing Ca-inflow is predicted by Fig. 2, and also vice-versa an increase of F_d when Ca-inflow declines. The depolarization dependence of F_d thus supports the conclusions on Ca-inflow drawn from F_c. The increase in F_d for larger depolarizations is even more impressive for the 0.7 and 0.5 ms pulses: F_d rises throughout a large range above $-0.8\ \mu A$ (specimens in Fig. 4) and thus suggests a decline in Ca-inflow, while release rises throughout this range, which must be due to the non-Ca potential dependent factor.

Other effects of the release promoting non-Ca factor

The time course of release can be determined if distributions of the delays of quantal releases are measured (Fig. 5). This time course proves to be very invariant towards the level of depolarization and the amount of release, which vary by a factor of 200 in Fig. 5; the same result was obtained for crayfish (H. PARNAS et al., 1986). If release and its time course were determined by Ca-inflow alone, one would expect that larger Ca-inflow would lead to a prolongation of release, but this is not observed. Even if the level of $[Ca]_i$ is raised by a series of prepulses to result in a facilitation of 50, the time course of release is not affected (H. PARNAS et al., 1986). Also these results lead to the conclusion that the time course of release must be determined by the non-Ca release promoting, potential dependent factor – as shown by H. PARNAS et al., 1986 in an explicit model.

Another unexpected finding suggests a similar interpretation. If prepulses are placed before a fixed releasing pulse (insert in Fig. 6), hyperpolarizing such prepulses reduce release by the fixed depolarization, and depolarizing such prepulses, which are themselves sub-threshold for release, increase release (Fig. 6). The same is true for the respective post-pulses. The results of Fig. 6 could be due to electrotonic interaction: if, for instance, the hyperpolarizing prepulse would generate a slowly declining potential change, the pre-hyperpolarization would diminish the depolarization during the releasing pulse and a reduction of release should be expected. However, the extracellular depolarizations by our pulses should decline very rapidly (KATZ and MILEDI, 1967). An experimental control of such effects can be obtained by measuring the facilitation of a succeeding release elicited by a fixed pulse, which is found to be unaffected by the sub-threshold pre- and post-pulses. The same observations were also made in crayfish junctions (I. PARNAS et al., 1986, also Fig. 9). We have called the effect of the pre- or post-pulses ‹modulation›. If the prepulses are set with an interval before the releasing pulse, the extent of modulation declines with a

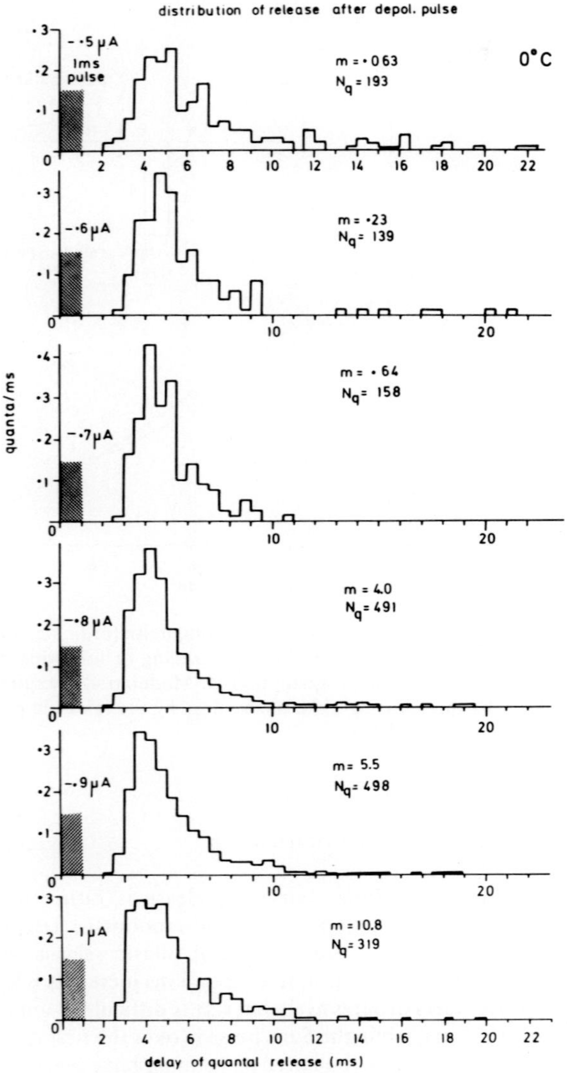

Fig. 5: Distributions of delays of release after the beginning of 1 ms depolarization pulse, the amplitude of the pulse is indicated in the single graphs. For each distribution, the average quantum content m of the EPSC and the number of quantal delays evaluated, N_q, are presented. The ordinates are normalized to quanta/ms, i. e., the number of delays observed in a certain time interval (bin width, here 0.5 ms) was divided by N_q · (bin width in ms). Frog muscle. From DUDEL, 1984a.

time course which is about the same as that of the decay of phasic release at the same temperature (Fig. 5) (DUDEL, 1984b, I. PARNAS et al., 1986). Modulation obviously cannot be due to changes of Ca-inflow. It can be explained by the build-up and dissipation of the same potential-dependent non-Ca factor mentioned above, which also has been shown in a quantitative model (I. PARNAS et al., 1986).

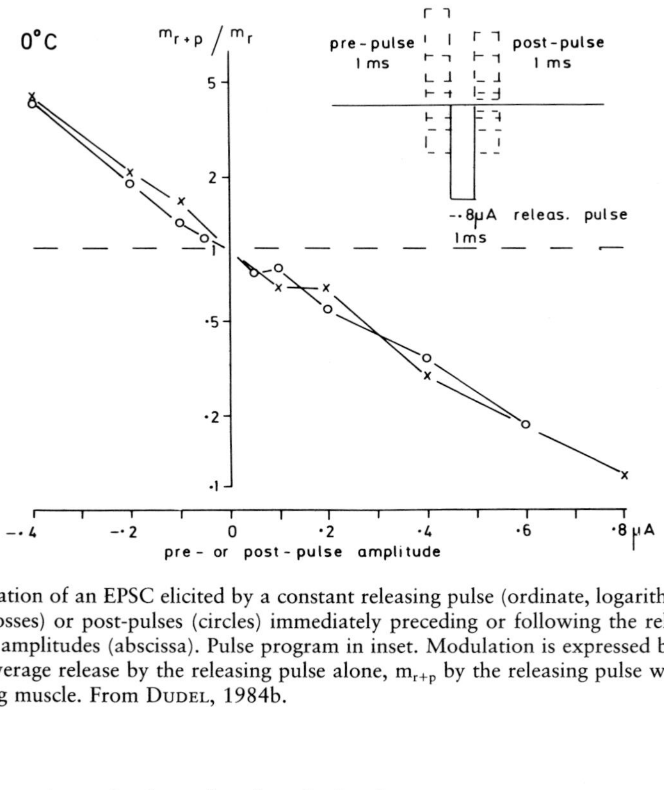

Fig. 6: Modulation of an EPSC elicited by a constant releasing pulse (ordinate, logarithmic scale) by pre-pulses (crosses) or post-pulses (circles) immediately preceding or following the releasing pulse, with different amplitudes (abscissa). Pulse program in inset. Modulation is expressed by m_{r+p}/m_r, in which m_r is average release by the releasing pulse alone, m_{r+p} by the releasing pulse with preceding pre-pulse. Frog muscle. From DUDEL, 1984b.

Short repression of release by depolarization

As demonstrated in Fig. 5, the time course of release is rather independent of the amplitude of the eliciting depolarization and of the amount of release. However, the duration of depolarization shifts the time course of phasic release. As seen in Fig. 7, prolongation of the releasing depolarization from 2 to 5 ms increases release by a factor of more than 100, but release starts progressively later. It is difficult to understand why the 2 ms pulse elicits release at 3.5 ms, while the 5 ms pulse evokes the first releases after 5.5 ms: releases triggered by the first 2 ms of the latter pulse must have been delayed by 2 ms or suppressed altogether by the continuing depolarization. This ‹latency shift› has been observed by all who have changed pulse duration and measured the time course of release (KATZ and MILEDI, 1967, DATYNER and GAGE, 1980, 1982, DUDEL, 1984a). The latency shift has been ascribed already by KATZ and MILEDI (1967) to tail Ca-currents: during large depolarizations Ca-inflow is suppressed and occurs mainly shortly after repolariza-

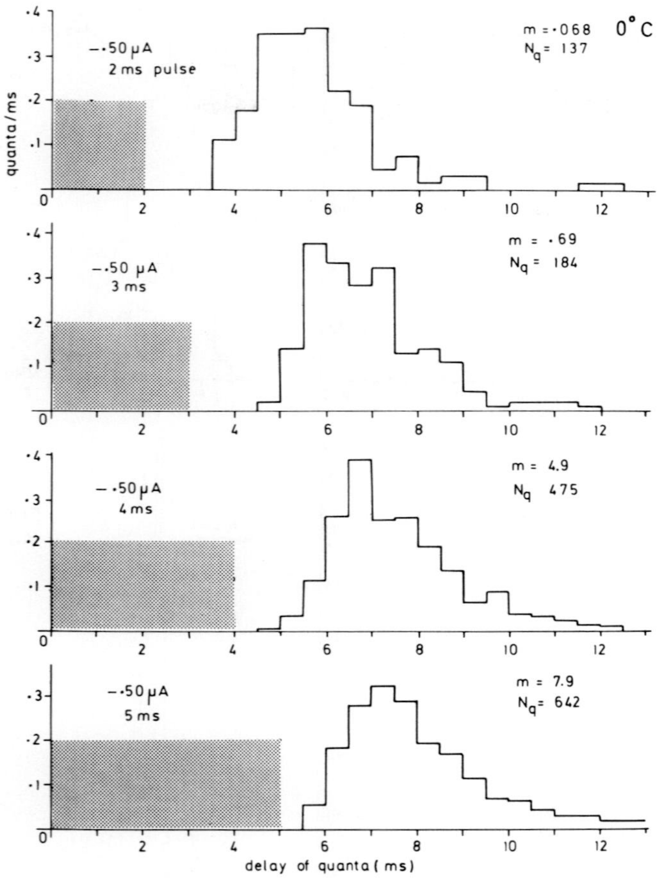

Fig. 7: Distributions of delays of quantal releases in one terminal after a pulse of −0.50 µA amplitude and 2 ms, 3 ms, 4 ms, 5 ms duration, as indicated in the single plots. Frog muscle. From DUDEL, 1984a.

tion. Only this tail current then would evoke release. However, the depolarizations in the experiment of Fig. 7 were very small, much below the level of peak facilitation F_c.

In order to exclude the possibility that latency shifts were due to tail currents, small post-pulses were used to produce the latency shifts. In the experiment of Fig. 8, a fixed test pulse of −0.6 µA and 1 ms was applied throughout, which generated the control distribution of release drawn in each of the plots. The average release by this pulse m_t = 0.15 quanta/stimulus was low, at about 1/100 of the saturation level. If post-pulses of −0.1 µA and 1 to 4 ms duration were added, they produced increasing delays of the first releases, and also shifts of the medians of the distributions. By themselves, −0.1 µA pulses in this terminal, which should depolarize by less than 10 mV, would not cause any release and probably not raise Ca inflow at all. The shifts in the delays of release generated by the post-pulses were highly significant (statistical analysis not illustrated). Obviously these small depolarizations were able to delay or to prevent release for several milliseconds.

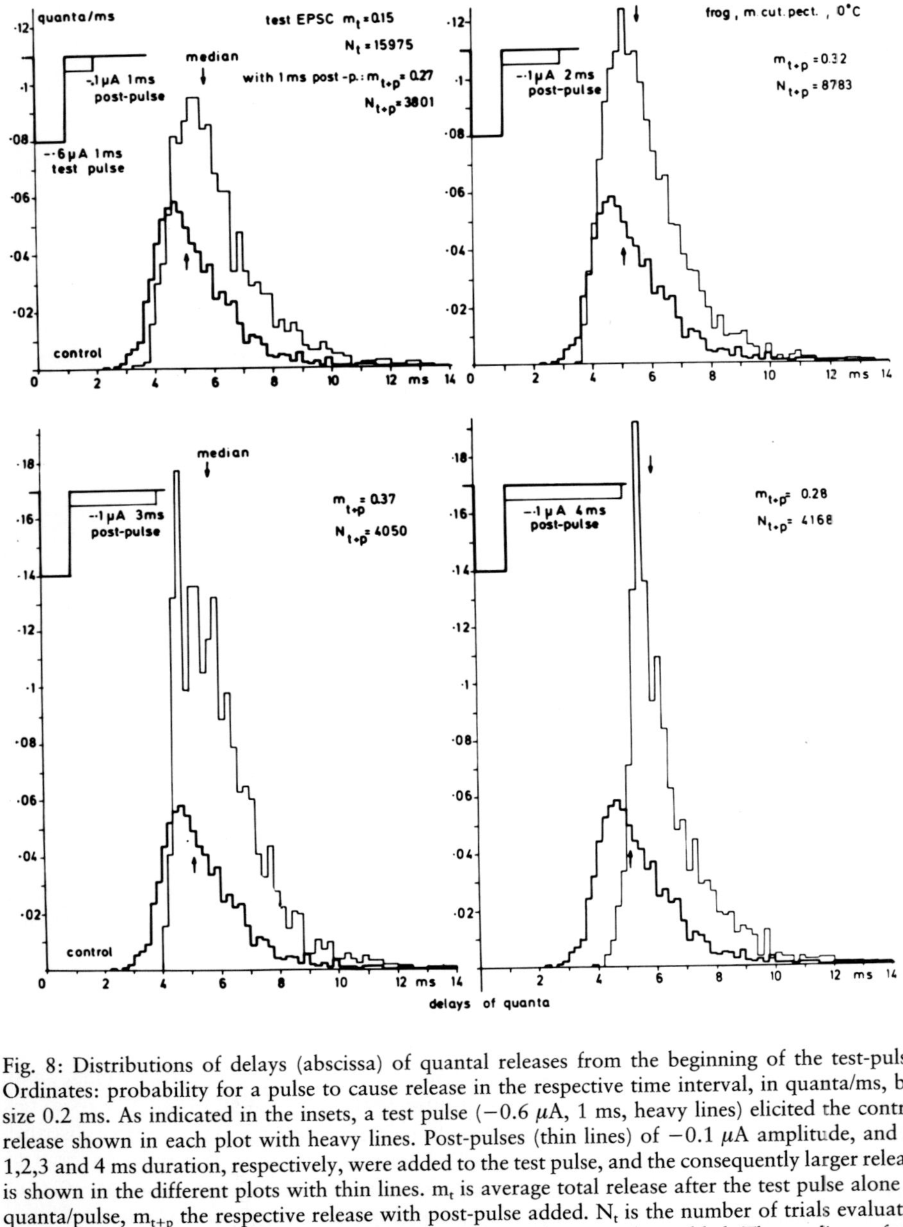

Fig. 8: Distributions of delays (abscissa) of quantal releases from the beginning of the test-pulse. Ordinates: probability for a pulse to cause release in the respective time interval, in quanta/ms, bin size 0.2 ms. As indicated in the insets, a test pulse (−0.6 µA, 1 ms, heavy lines) elicited the control release shown in each plot with heavy lines. Post-pulses (thin lines) of −0.1 µA amplitude, and of 1,2,3 and 4 ms duration, respectively, were added to the test pulse, and the consequently larger release is shown in the different plots with thin lines. m_t is average total release after the test pulse alone in quanta/pulse, m_{t+p} the respective release with post-pulse added. N_t is the number of trials evaluated with test pulse alone, and N_{t+p} the respective number with post-pulses added. The medians of the control distribution are indicated by an upward, of the distributions obtained with added post-pulses by a downward arrow. Terminal from m. cut. pectoris of the frog, 0 °C. Normal bathing solution with 2 × 10^{-7} M tetrodotoxin, like in all experiments.

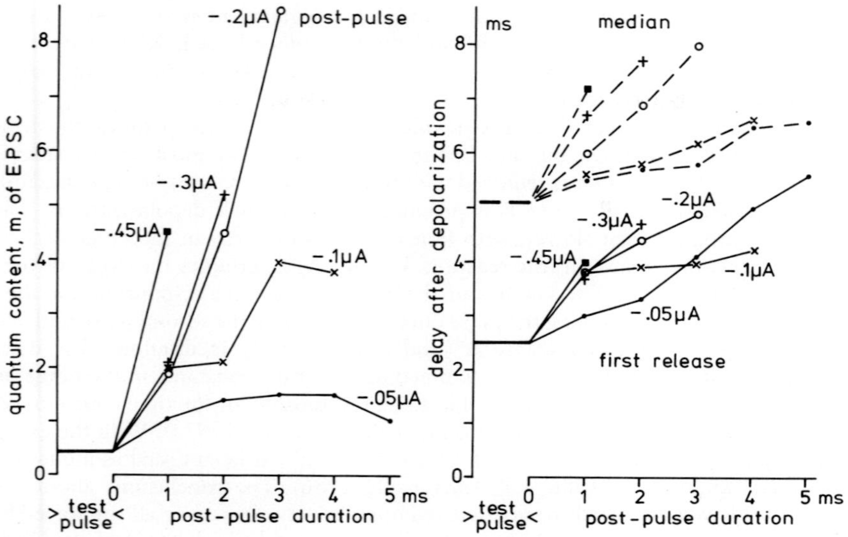

Fig. 9: Plots of dependence of average quantum content m, time of first quantal release and median delay in dependence on the duration of post-pulses. The amplitudes of the post-pulses are indicated at the respective curves. Test pulse $-45\ \mu A$, 1 ms. Crayfish motor nerve terminal, 0 °C.

Results of a similar, more extensive experiment of this type on crayfish muscle are shown in Fig. 9. The fixed test-pulse caused low release of $m = 0.04$ quanta/stimulus, the first releases appeared after 2.5 ms, and the median of the distribution of releases was 5.1 ms. Post-pulses with durations up to 5 ms and amplitudes of -0.05, -0.1, -0.2, -0.3 and $-0.45\ \mu A$, respectively, were added and increased release accordingly. The delay of first releases increased with pulse duration and amplitude, and the same occurred for the medians. With the very small depolarization (< 5 mV) produced by the $-0.05\ \mu A$ post-pulse, the first releases could be delayed to more than the median of the control distribution. It must be concluded that a very depolarization-sensitive mechanism in the membrane represses release for a short, but definite period.

Discussion

The results reported above, and others which could not be included, are best summarized by the scheme of the release process in Fig. 10. Depolarization causes the well known inflow of Ca, indicated by $Ca_o \xrightarrow{d} Ca_i$, and on re- or hyperpolarization Ca will reequilibrate, $Ca_i \xrightarrow{h} Ca_o$. The model thus includes the generally assumed mechanism of control of release by $[Ca]_o$, and the facilitations (but not ‹early facilitation›) are assumed to be due to residual $[Ca]_i$. The non-Ca depolarization dependent release promoting factor mentioned above is named activator A. It has (at least) two ineffective prestages A_1 and A_2, which are converted to the activator A^* by depolarization (d), and back towards A_1 by re- or hyperpolarization (h). The two prestages A_1 and A_2 are necessary to account for the modulation phenomenon: by the chain of prestages subthreshold prepulses can affect the level of A_2 even if given with some interval before the releasing pulse. A^* and Ca_i are assumed to combine to a complex (A^*Ca_i), and n (equivalent to ℓ in equ. 1–3) such complexes will react with a repressor R* and effect quantal release L. R* is generated from R by re- or hyperpolarization, $R \xrightarrow{h} R^*$, and R* is low or absent during depolarization, $R^* \xrightarrow{d} R$, preventing release.

The different systems play their specific role in the control of release due to the details of their potential dependencies, but also due to their kinetics. The most rapid system is the repression, at 0 °C repression is removed with time constants < 1 ms on repolarization. In addition, the repression $R^* \longrightarrow R$ is produced by very small depolarizations. The activator system reacts a bit slower, with time constants of decay in the range of 1 ms (at 0 °C). With this time constant, the reaction $A^* \longrightarrow A_2$ determines the decay of the time course of phasic release. The kinetics of the activator also are responsible for the time course of modulation. Doubling the pulse duration or adding the second pulse with a delay of up to 1 ms will greatly increase A* and generate ‹early facilitation›. The decay of increased $[Ca]_i$ after repolarization is assumed to have time constants in the range of 100 ms, and this slow decay of $[Ca]_i$ is thought to be responsible for the time course of double pulse facilitation which can last for seconds (I. PARNAS et al., 1982a). With the exception of repression, the scheme of control of release in Fig. 10 has been tested as a quantitative model (H. PARNAS et al., 1986, I. PARNAS et al., 1986). The conclusions about the behaviour of this system, which were discussed qualitatively above, are all supported by the quantitative model. As far as we know, it is the only model which can describe, with one set of parameters, the fixed time course of phasic release and large and long-lasting facilitations, the increase of release for large depolarizations for which Ca-inflow declines, early facilitation, as well as modulation of release by de- or hyperpolarizing pre- or post-pulses.

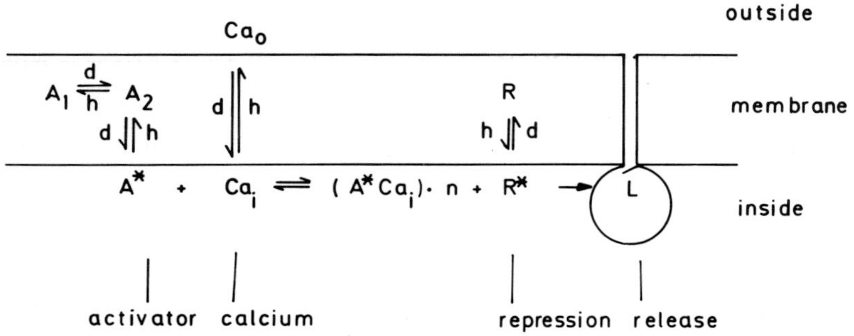

Fig. 10: Hypothetical reaction scheme for the control of release. The activator A* has two inactive prestages A_1 and A_2, which convert to A* on depolarization (d) and to A_1 on re- or hyperpolarization (h). Triggered by depolarization, Ca flow through the membrane from Ca_o to Ca_i. The repressor R becomes available for reaction (R*) by re- or hyperpolarization. The reaction of n · (A^* Ca_i) with R* triggers release L.

References

Datyner, N. B., Gage, P. W. (1980): Phasic secretion of acetylcholine at a mammalian neuromuscular junction. J. Physiol. (Lond.) **303**, 299–314.

Datyner, N. B., Gage, P. W. (1982): Secretion of acetylcholine in response to graded depolarization of motor nerve terminals. J. Physiol. (Paris) **78**, 412–432.

Dodge, F., Rahamimoff, R. (1967): Cooperative action of calcium ions in transmitter release at the neuromuscular junction. J. Physiol. (Lond.) **193**, 419–432.
Dudel, J. (1983a): Graded or all-or-nothing release of transmitter quanta by local depolarizations of nerve terminals on crayfish muscle? Pflügers Arch **398**, 155–164.
Dudel, J. (1983b): Transmitter release triggered by a local depolarization in motor nerve terminals of the frog: role of calcium entry and of depolarization. Neurosci. Lett. **41**, 133–138.
Dudel, J. (1984a): Control of quantal transmitter release at frog's motor nerve terminals. I. Dependence on amplitude and duration of depolarization. Pflügers Arch. **402**, 225–234.
Dudel, J. (1984b): Control of quantal transmitter release at frog's motor nerve terminals. II. Modulation by de- or hyperpolarizing pulses. Pflügers Arch. **402**, 235–243.
Dudel, J., Parnas, I., Parnas, H. (1983): Neurotransmitter release and its facilitation in crayfish muscle. VI. Release determined by both, intracellular calcium concentration and depolarization of the nerve terminal. Pflügers Arch. **399**, 1–10.
Dudel, J., Parnas, I., Cohen, I., Franke, Ch. (1984): Excitability and depolarization – release characteristics of excitatory nerve terminals in a tail muscle of spiny lobster. Pflügers Arch. **401**, 293–296.
Katz, B., Miledi, R. (1967): The release of acetylcholine from nerve endings by graded electric pulses. Proc. Roy. Soc. (Lond.) B **167**, 23–38.
Katz, B., Miledi, R. (1968): The role of calcium in neuromuscular facilitation. J. Physiol. (Lond.) **195**, 481–492.
Llinás, R., Steinberg, I., Walton, K. (1981): Relationship between presynaptic calcium current and postsynaptic potential in squid giant synapse. Biophys. J. **33**, 323–352.
Parnas, H., Dudel, J. Parnas, I. (1982): Neurotransmitter release and its facilitation in crayfish. I. Saturation kinetics of release, and of entry and removal of calcium. Pflügers Arch. **393**, 1–14.
Parnas, H., Dudel, J., Parnas, I. (1986): Neurotransmitter release and its facilitation in crayfish. VII. Another voltage dependent process beside Ca entry controls the time course of phasic release. Pflügers Arch. **406**, 121–130.
Parnas, I., Parnas, H., Dudel, J. (1982a): Neurotransmitter release and its facilitation in crayfish. II. Duration of facilitation and removal processes of calcium from the terminal. Pflügers Arch. **393**, 232–236.
Parnas, I., Parnas, H., Dudel, J. (1982b): Neurotransmitter release and its facilitation in crayfish. V. Basis for synapse differentiation of the fast and slow type in one axon. Pflügers Arch. **395**, 261–270.
Parnas, I., Parnas, H., Dudel, J. (1986): Neurotransmitter release and its facilitation in crayfish. VIII. Modulation of release by hyperpolarizing pulses. Pflügers Arch. **406**, 131–137.
Stockbridge, N., Moore, J. W. (1984): Dynamics of intracellular calcium and its possible relationship to phasic transmitter release and facilitation at the frog neuromuscular junction. J. Neurosci. **4**, 803–811.
Zucker, R. S., Stockbridge, N. (1983): Presynaptic calcium diffusion and the time courses of transmitter release and synaptic facilitation at the squid giant synapse. J. Neurosci. **3**, 1263–1269.

Fortschritte der Zoologie, Band 33 · Lüttgau (Hrsg.): Membrane Control
Gustav Fischer Verlag · Stuttgart · New York · 1986

Protein kinase C and exocytosis

P. F. BAKER

M. R. C. Secretory Mechanisms Group, Department of Physiology, King's College London, Strand, London WC2R 2LS., UK

The surface membranes of cells are in a state of flux: new membrane is constantly being added by exocytosis and old membrane retrieved by endocytosis. Exocytosis is the process by which intracellular vesicles fuse with the inner face of the plasma membrane. It serves two functions: to add new membrane to the cell surface and to release into the extracellular fluid substances previously stored within the vesicle. Many workers divide exocytosis into two types, continuous and triggered: the former provides for the steady turnover of membrane components and the latter for sudden changes either in membrane composition or in the release of biologically active molecules. This last aspect includes chemical transmission in the nervous system and the release of a wide variety of hormones and enzymes. This paper will be concerned entirely with triggered exocytosis as virtually nothing is known at the present time about the properties of continuous exocytosis.

The technique of fast freezing has provided some useful morphological insights into early events in exocytosis (CHANDLER and HEUSER, 1980; ORNBERG and REESE, 1981; SCHMIDT et al., 1983). It appears that membrane fusion occurs focally to generate a very narrow pore between the vesicle interior and the external solution. The diameter of this pore rapidly increases giving rise to an Ω profile of the kind seen in transmission electronmicrographs. In some cases the vesicle continues to flatten until it can only be distinguished from the rest of the plasma membrane by the use of markers specific for vesicle membrane components (LINGG et al., 1983).

Although in no instance do we yet know the mechanism of exocytosis, there is growing evidence that even within triggered exocytosis there must be a number of variations on the basic theme. This is particularly clear in those cells that contain more than one population of secretory vesicle, the contents of which can be released selectively. Thus platelets contain two separate populations of vesicles the contents of which can be released differentially in response of thrombin (KNIGHT, NIGGLI and SCRUTTON, 1984) and there is growing evidence for something similar in many nerves where the pattern of nerve impulses seems to determine which population of vesicles is recruited (see CUELLO, 1982; BARTFAI, 1985).

All triggered exocytosis must comprise three major steps (i) generation of the trigger; (ii) a receptor for detecting the trigger and (iii) a mechanism for coupling the receptor to the initiation of exocytosis. Traditionally, calcium has occupied an almost unique position as trigger for exocytosis; but recently conditions have been found in a variety of secretory cells where exocytosis can be initiated with little or no change in free Ca, opening up the possibility of multiple controls for exocytosis (see RINK and HALLAM, 1984). At the present time, the bulk of the data can be rationalized within a framework in which these multiple controls operate through a single enzyme, protein kinase C. In this paper I shall review this evidence and indicate how one enzyme can be used to generate all the observed variations in secretory control.

Exocytosis in permeable cells

One of the major problems in studying exocytosis is that it occurs at an intracellular site that is relatively inaccessible to experimental manipulation. The demonstration of exocytosis in permeable cell preparations (BAKER and KNIGHT, 1978; KNIGHT and BAKER, 1982) overcame many of these problems and has permitted a detailed analysis of a number of the intracellular factors that control exocytosis.

Permeabilization can be achieved in a number of ways. Populations of cells can be exposed to brief high-voltage pulses (BAKER and KNIGHT, 1978) or treated with a variety of chemicals including detergents (BROOKS and TREML, 1983; WILSON and KIRSCHNER, 1983; DUNN and HOLZ, 1983) complement (SCHWEITZER and BLAUSTEIN, 1980) and ATP (COCKCROFT and GOMPERTS, 1979) and in favourable situations secretion in single cells can be monitored either optically or electrically after attachment to a patch-clamp perfusion pipette (NEHER and MARTY, 1982). Each method has its strong and weak points. Detergents generate large holes, but also interfere with exocytosis (BAKER and KNIGHT, 1981) which seriously limits the usefulness of preparations prepared in this way. In contrast, the high-voltage technique generates cells that are stable and continue to respond for up to an hour but the holes are rather small. Most of the experimental data discussed below was obtained on cells rendered ‹leaky› by exposure to brief high-voltage pulses. These include four mammalian cell preparations: adrenal medullary cells, platelets, β- cells and exocrine pancreas.

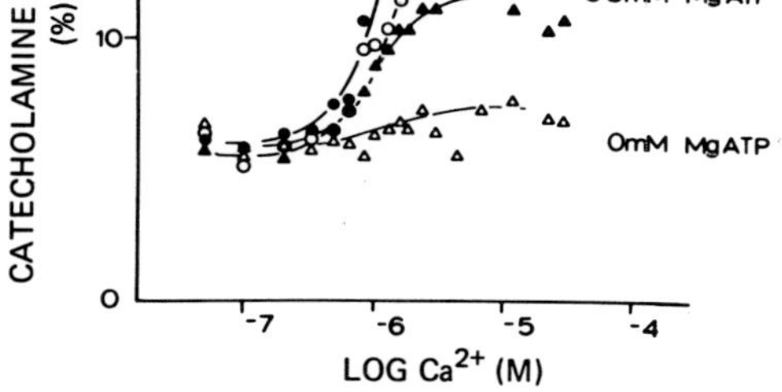

Fig. 1: Dependence on Mg-ATP of catecholamine release from permeable bovine adrenal medullary cells. Cells suspended in K glutamate medium and rendered permeable by exposure to 10 × 2KV pulses τ–200 μsec (see KNIGHT and BAKER, 1982). Note that lowering Mg-ATP reduces the extent of secretion but not its apparent affinity for Ca. From KNIGHT and BAKER, 1982.

In all cases, provided Mg-ATP is present, exocytosis is activated by Ca in the micromolar range of concentrations. The requirement for Mg-ATP is remarkably specific and half-maximal activation of exocytosis needs 100 μM to 1 mM of nucleotide. The shape of the nucleotide activation curve is consistent with a single nucleotide binding site. As each exocytotic event is the all-or-nothing release of the contents of a single secretory vesicle, this might imply that each exocytotic event requires one molecule of Mg-ATP. The Ca-activation curve is steeper and, in the adrenal medulla, consistent with a requirement for 2 Ca ions. Mg-ATP affects the extent of exocytosis, but not its apparent affinity for Ca (Fig. 1).

The sensitivity of exocytosis to a wide range of agents has been examined in detail in bovine adrenal medullary cells (see Table 1). Somewhat surprisingly, it is little affected by agents that alter the cytoskeleton. It is also unaffected by a variety of protease inhibitors and persists under conditions where the pH gradient and potential across the vesicle membrane have been collapsed (KNIGHT and BAKER, 1985 a). It can be inhibited by chaotropic anions, by raising free Mg, by -SH reagents such as N-ethylmaleimide and by a number of more specific inhibitors discussed below.

One of the most striking features of Ca-dependent exocytosis in ‹leaky› cells is its sensitivity to certain phorbol esters. The response to phorbol esters takes at least three different forms (see Fig. 2): (1) a small increase in apparent affinity for Ca with little

Table 1: Properties of Ca^{2+}-dependent catecholamine release from ‹leaky› bovine adrenal medullary cells

(1) Activation half maximal at Ca^{2+} concentration of 1 μM		
(2) Requirement for Mg^{2+}-ATP is very specific: half maximal activation requires 1 mM.		
(3) Unaffected by:	(a)	agonists and antagonists of ACh receptors
	(b)	Ca^{2+}-channel blocker D600 (100 μM)
	(c)	agents that bind to tubulin (colchicine, vinblastine 100 μM)
	(d)	cytochalasin B (1 mM)
	(e)	inhibitors of anion permeability (SITS, DIDS, 100 μM)
	(f)	protease inhibitors TLCK (1 mM); leupeptin (1 mM)
	(g)	cyclic nucleotides (cAMP, cGMP, 1 mM)
	(h)	S-adenosyl methionine (5 mM)
	(i)	phalloidin (1 mM)
	(j)	vanadate (10^{-4}M)
	(k)	leu- and Met enkephalins; substance P (100 μM)
	(l)	somatostatin (1 μM)
	(m)	NH_4Cl (30 mM)
(4) Inhibited by:	(a)	chaotropic anions : SCN > Br > Cl
	(b)	detergents (complete inhibition after 10 min incubation with 10 μg/ml of digitonin; Brij 58 or saponin)
	(c)	trifluoperazine (complete inhibition with 20 μg/ml)
	(d)	high Mg^{2+} : small increase in apparent K_m for Ca^{2+} accompanies large reduction in Vmax.
	(e)	high osmotic pressure : large reduction in Vmax but no significant changes in the affinity for Ca^{2+}
	(f)	carbonylcyanid P-trifluormethoxyphenylhydrazone (FCCP) (45% inhibition by 10 μM)
	(g)	N-ethyl maleimide (NEM) (100% inhibition at 10^{-4}M)
	(h)	GTP-γ-S (50% inhibition at 5 μM)
	(i)	Botulinum toxin type D

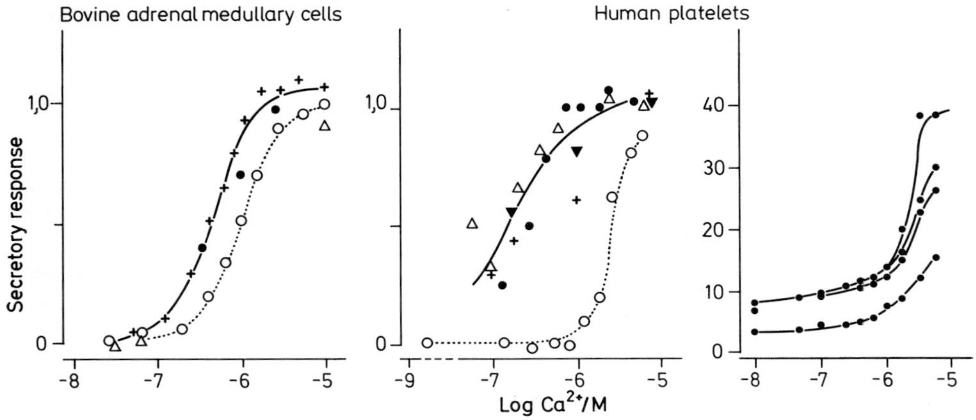

Fig. 2: Modification of Ca-dependent secretion in ‹leaky› cells by exposure to the phorbol ester TPA and other agents. Examples of the three classes of response that have been observed. A. the small leftward shift seen in catecholamine secretion from bovine adrenal medullary cells in presence of 3 nM TPA (◆), 100 μM dioctanoylglycerol (△) (from KNIGHT and BAKER, 1983). B. the marked leftward shift seen in 5-HT secretion from human platelets: 30 nM TPA (◆), 20 μM OAG (▲), 50 μM GTP-γ-S (◇) and C, the lack of any shift, only an increase in extent of exocytosis of N-acetylglucosaminidase also from platelets: 10 ng/ml TPA (○), 30 μg/ml DAG (▲), 0.5 u/ml, thrombin (◆). From KNIGHT et al., 1984.

change in the extent of secretion (2) a large increase in apparent affinity for Ca often associated with a small increase in the extent of secretion and (3) no change in the apparent affinity for Ca but a large increase in the extent of secretion. Catecholamine release from adrenal medullary cells provides a good example of the first type. 5HT secretion from platelets of the second and β-N-acetylglycosaminidase release also from platelets of the third.

It is these effects of phorbol esters which implicate protein kinase C in exocytosis because this enzyme is also activated by phorbol esters and there is an excellent correlation between those phorbol esters which activate C-kinase and those which alter the kinetics of exocytosis.

Protein kinase C: the enzyme

C-kinase was discovered by Nishizuka and his colleagues (TAKAI et al., 1979; KAIBUCHI, TAKAI and NISHIZUKA, 1981) who were the first to point out its very unusual requirements for activation: the presence simultaneously of calcium, diacylglycerol and a phospholipid. In the absence of diacylglycerol (DAG) the apparent affinity for Ca is very low; but increases dramatically on addition of DAG. Subsequently they showed that certain phorbol esters including 12-O-tetradecanoyl-phorbol-13-acetate (TPA or PMA) can substitute for DAG (CASTAGNA et al., 1982). Most phorbol esters are very lipid soluble; but working with the somewhat more hydrophilic molecule phorbol 12, 13 dibutyrate it has proved possible to isolate the phorbol receptor and this proves to be identical with protein kinase C (NIEDEL et al., 1983). Exposure of intact bovine adrenal medullary cells to [^{3}H] phorbol-12-13 dibutyrate reveals only 300 phorbol-binding sites per cell.

The close parallel between the properties of C-kinase and exocytosis suggests that the enzyme may be involved. This is strengthened further by two other findings: (1) like exocytosis, protein kinase C has a rather specific requirement for Mg-ATP, and (2) the effects of phorbol esters on exocytosis can be mimicked by analogues of DAG which also activate protein kinase C. A further feature of considerable interest to the present topic is that those phorbol esters that activate the enzyme also favour its transfer from the cytosol into membranes (KRAFT and ANDERSON, 1983).

Comparisons between the properties of protein kinase C determined in the test tube and exocytosis in ‹leaky› cells are fraught with problems. Two of the most important being lack of knowledge of the physiological substrates of the enzyme (it is conventionally assayed by phosphorylation of histone) and the very real possibility that its properties may change during isolation or when it no longer has membranes with which to associate. In addition, diacylglycerol is a generic term and it is possible that different forms of C-kinase prefer different members of the diacylglycerol family.

As the enzyme requires both Ca and DAG for activation, it is of interest to consider what would happen if the enzyme had a preferred order of binding of these two substrates. If we neglect the binding of phospholipid and Mg-ATP, there are three possibilities:

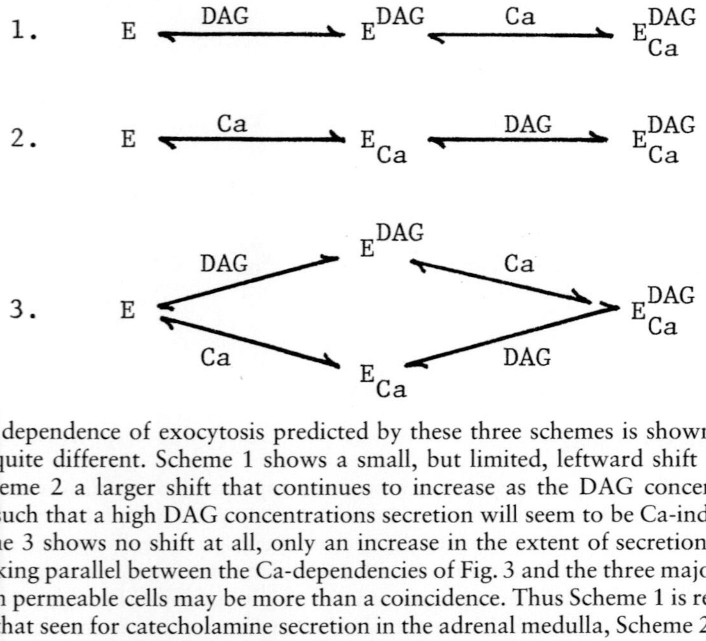

The Ca dependence of exocytosis predicted by these three schemes is shown in Fig. 3. They are quite different. Scheme 1 shows a small, but limited, leftward shift on adding DAG; Scheme 2 a larger shift that continues to increase as the DAG concentration is increased such that a high DAG concentrations secretion will seem to be Ca-independent; and Scheme 3 shows no shift at all, only an increase in the extent of secretion.

The striking parallel between the Ca-dependencies of Fig. 3 and the three major patterns observed in permeable cells may be more than a coincidence. Thus Scheme 1 is remarkably similar to that seen for catecholamine secretion in the adrenal medulla, Scheme 2 for 5-HT secretion in platelets and Scheme 3 for enzyme secretion in platelets. It is certainly a very interesting point that these apparently different kinetics can all be generated via the same enzyme simply by specifying different preferred orders of substrate binding. To take the platelet as a specific example, production of DAG will favour 5-HT secretion as DAG increases the sensitivity of this process for Ca; but not that for secretion of enzyme. Fig. 3. shows that this differential effect can be achieved simply by specifying Scheme 2 order of binding for 5-HT release and permitting random binding (Scheme 3) for enzyme secretion.

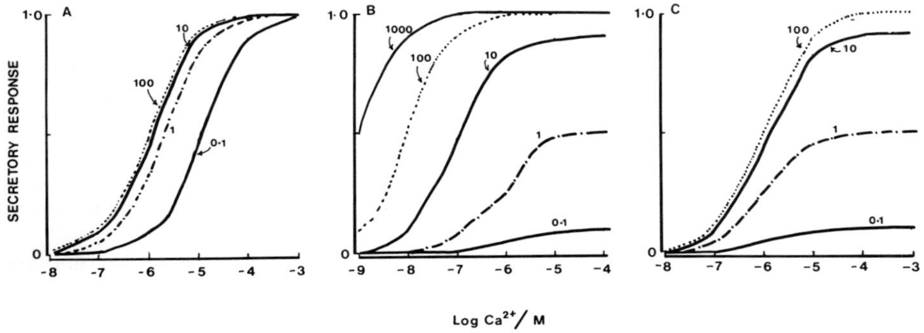

Fig. 3: Ca-dependence of secretion calculated on the assumption of ordered binding of DAG and Ca to protein kinase C. Numbers by the curves refer to DAG concentrations (μM).

For ease of calculating the curves, the affinity constants K_{Ca} and K_D for Ca and DAG respectively have been set at 1 μM.

A. $$E \underset{K_D}{\overset{DAG}{\rightleftharpoons}} E^{DAG} \underset{K_{Ca}}{\overset{Ca}{\rightleftharpoons}} E^{DAG}_{Ca} \qquad F_{E^{DAG}_{Ca}} = \frac{1}{1 + \frac{K_{Ca}}{Ca}\left(1 + \frac{K_D}{D}\right)}$$

B. $$E \underset{K_{Ca}}{\overset{Ca}{\rightleftharpoons}} E_{Ca} \underset{K_D}{\overset{DAG}{\rightleftharpoons}} E^{DAG}_{Ca} \qquad F_{E^{DAG}_{Ca}} = \frac{1}{1 + \frac{K_D}{D}\left(1 + \frac{K_{Ca}}{Ca}\right)}$$

C. $$E \overset{DAG}{\rightleftharpoons} E^{DAG} \overset{Ca}{\rightleftharpoons} E^{DAG}_{Ca}; \quad E \overset{Ca}{\rightleftharpoons} E_{Ca} \overset{DAG}{\rightleftharpoons} E^{DAG}_{Ca} \qquad F_{E^{DAG}_{Ca}} = \frac{1}{1 + \frac{K_D}{D} + \frac{K_{Ca}}{Ca}\left(1 + \frac{K_D}{D}\right)}$$

Is protein kinase C essential for exocytosis?

Inhibitors of C-kinase

In view of the data presented so far, it becomes important to establish whether protein kinase C is essential for exocytosis – or whether it merely plays a modulatory role. This is a difficult question to answer unequivocally because there are no really specific inhibitors of the kinase. The isolated kinase shares with calmodulin sensitivity to trifluperazine and other ‹so-called› calmodulin antagonists and can also be inhibited by high concentrations of amiloride and polymixin B. Exocytosis is also sensitive to these agents: but none of the inhibitors is specific enough to clinch the argument.

It is particularly striking that no inhibitor has been found that can remove the TPA-shift whilst leaving Ca-dependent exocytosis unaffected. Agents that inhibit exocytosis all leave a residual TPA-shift consistent with the view that the kinase is directly involved in exocytosis.

One preparation which does not conform to this pattern is the cortical reaction in the sea urchin egg. This is a Ca-dependent process (BAKER, KNIGHT and WHITAKER, 1980);

but it is neither strongly dependent on ATP nor affected by phorbol esters (unpublished data of P. F. BAKER). Whether this represents a quite different system or simply Scheme 1 working at saturating levels of DAG or something equivalent remains to be determined.

The source of DAG

If protein kinase C is essential for exocytosis, it is important to know from where it obtains the DAG essential for activation of the enzyme. Diacylglycerol can be produced in a variety of ways but the two sources that seem to predominate in most cells are phosphatidylinositol (PI) and phosphatidylcholine (PC). PI has received considerable attention recently because phospholipase C converts it into two biologically active products, the Ca-mobilising messenger IP_3 and DAG (BERRIDGE, 1984); but it should be stressed that PI is not the only source of DAG. As DAG is highly hydrophobic, it is likely to be almost entirely associated with membranes and breakdown of membrane phospholipid will serve to raise the local concentration of DAG. The lifetime of DAG in membranes will depend on the activities of other enzymes most notably diacylglycerol kinase which converts it to phosphatidic acid.

Rather little is known about the regulation of membrane levels of DAG. Recent interest in PI has begun to provide evidence that phospholipase C, like adenylate cyclase, may be subject to complex regulation which includes both extracellular signals such as hormones (see MICHELL, 1975) and intracellular messengers such as cyclic nucleotides (see KNIGHT and SCRUTTON, 1984) and there is growing evidence for involvement of GTP-binding proteins in linking hormone-binding to alterations in phospholipase C activity. Thus exposure of ‹leaky› cells to GTP-γ-S leads to breakdown of PI, with concomitant release of IP_3, and DAG and it is of considerable interest that exposure of Class 2 type secretory systems to GTP-γ-S mimics the actions of phorbol esters and DAG analogues in promoting exocytosis in an apparently Ca-independent fashion (see FERNANDEZ et al., 1984; HASLAM and DAVIDSON, 1984). It seems most likely that GTP-γ-S is promoting production of endogenous DAG in these cells.

How does protein kinase C facilitate exocytosis?

If protein kinase C is intimately involved with exocytosis, how does it act? The obvious possibility is that it phosphorylates a substrate which helps bring about membrane fusion; but although exocytosis requires Mg-ATP and many intracellular substrates are phosphorylated in a Ca-dependent fashion, a unique substrate whose phosphorylation closely parallels exocytosis in a number of different systems has yet to emerge. An alternative idea which merits close examination is that, in the presence of Mg-ATP, protein kinase C is, itself a fusigen. It partitions strongly into membranes in the presence of TPA (and probably DAG) and seems to associate with secretory vesicles in a Ca-dependent fashion (CREUTZ et al., 1983). It thus has the properties to act as a molecular bridge between secretory vesicle and plasma membrane and generation of such a bridge might be the first step towards the membrane fusion which underlies exocytosis. According to this scheme, phosphorylation may be concerned with membrane retrieval rather than exocytosis. The concept of protein kinase C as a membrane fusigen is highly speculative; but certainly worthy of experimental examination. The apparent requirement for 1 Mg-ATP could imply that one activated protein kinase C molecule effects exocytosis of one vesicle and the order of substrate binding to the enzyme might lead to apparently different patterns of exocytosis as discussed earlier.

The control of exocytosis

There seems overwhelming evidence that the classical control of exocytosis by Ca must now give rise to a more complex system in which at least two variables, Ca and DAG (and perhaps others), interact apparently through protein kinase C. Secretion in ‹leaky› cells can be divided into three classes on the basis of the effects of phorbol esters on the Ca-activation curve. There are:

Class 1 (equivalent to reaction Scheme 1). Characterized by rather little effect of phorbol esters, at most a small leftward shift in the Ca-activation curve. In these cells it seems likely that the major control of exocytosis may be exerted through Ca. Adrenal medullary cells provide a good example of this category and it will be of interest to discover whether other nerve cells behave similarly. In terms of the kinetic model, this may reflect a membrane-activated protein kinase C which only needs Ca for initiation of exocytosis. As such it would probably be a fast responding system. In order to achieve the observed sensitivity to Ca, the endogenous level of DAG would have to be maintained at a high level; but it is possible that some other more stable membrane component could satisfy this requirement in these cells. It is of interest that in the bovine adrenal medulla GTP-γ-S, which should raise endogenous levels of DAG, inhibits Ca-dependent exocytosis (KNIGHT and BAKER, 1985 b).

Class 2 (equivalent to reaction Scheme 2). Characterized by a large effect of TPA or DAG increasing the apparent affinity for Ca and bringing about a small increase in the extent of exocytosis. Control could be achieved either through large changes in Ca or DAG or, perhaps more likely, by a combination of smaller changes in the two. As DAG increases, the system will appear to become Ca-independent even though low concentrations of Ca are still required. This system may underlie secretion in platelets, neutrophils and mast cells where control of secretion can be exerted either via Ca at low levels of DAG or via DAG at low levels of Ca and where apparently Ca-independent secretion can be produced by GTP-γ-S.

Class 3 (equivalent to Scheme 3). Characterized by a lack of effect of phorbol esters and DAG on the sensitivity to Ca. These agents only affect the extent of secretion. The only example that has been studied in detail so far is enzyme secretion from the platelet (see KNIGHT, NIGGLI and SCRUTTON, 1984).

There seems no reason why vesicles representing these different classes might not co-exist in the same cell. Thus, in the human platelet it appears that Class 2 and Class 3 types of exocytosis co-exist and addition of DAG brings about secretion of the contents of the 5-HT-containing Class 2 vesicles with rather little effect on the enzyme-containing Class 3 vesicles which require a large rise in free Ca for activation. Behaviour of this type could underlie the differential release of stored materials which has been observed in a variety of cell types. For instance, in those nerves where low frequencies of stimulation preferentially release one transmitter and higher frequencies another, it is possible that low levels of Ca permit release of Class 1 or 2 type vesicles; but high levels of Ca are needed to release Class 3 type vesicles.

In conclusion, the evidence implicating protein kinase C in a number of exocytotic systems is so suggestive that it would seem to merit a major examination of the properties of the kinase in specific secretory systems. Is it, for instance, subject to modulation by other membrane proteins such as GTP-binding proteins (KNIGHT and BAKER, 1985 b)? In any such study it will be essential to use ‹leaky› cells or reconstituted systems because activation of protein kinase C in intact cells has a wide range of effects including alteration of Ca channels (see DE REIMER et al., 1985) which would tend to obscure actions on exocytosis itself. One tool which may provide helpful new information is botulinum toxin which blocks Ca-dependent exocytosis in cholinergic nerve terminals and cultured adrenal medullary cells apparently by acting downstream from the Ca transient and very close to the site of exocytosis. (Fig. 4, KNIGHT, TONGE and BAKER, 1985). It will be of interest to examine whether the toxin has any direct or indirect effects on protein kinase C activity in these systems.

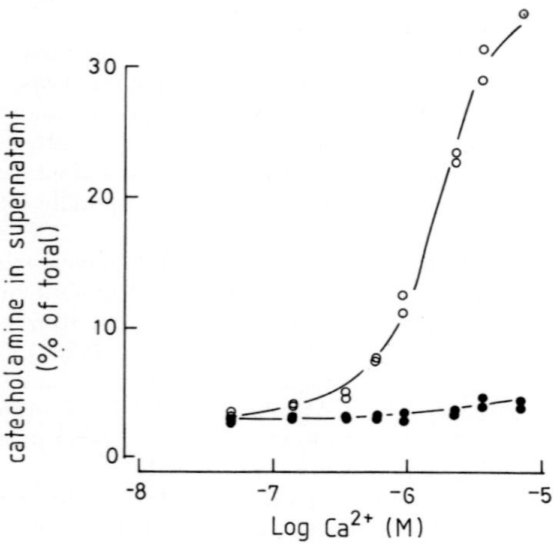

Fig. 4: Inhibition of Ca-dependent exocytosis by pretreatment of cultured bovine adrenal medullary cells with Botulinim toxin type D. Cells subsequently rendered permeable as described in the legend to Fig. 1. Control (○), toxin-treated (●). From KNIGHT, TONGE and BAKER, 1985.

References

Baker, P. F. and Knight, D. E.: Calcium-dependent exocytosis in bovine adrenal medullary cells with leaky plasma membranes. Nature Lond. **276**, 620–622. (1978)

Baker, P. F. and Knight, D. E.: Calcium control of exocytosis and endocytosis in bovine adrenal medullary cells. Phil. Trans. Roy. Soc. London B, **296**, 83–103. (1981)

Baker, P. F., Knight, D. E. and Whitaker, M.: The relation between ionized calcium and cortical granule exocytosis in eggs of the sea urchin *Echinus esculentus*. Proc. Roy, Soc. Lond. B. **207**, 149–161. (1980)

Bartfai, T.: Presynaptic aspects of the co-existence of classical neuro-transmitters and peptides. TIPS. August 1985, 331–334. (1985)

Berridge, M. J.: Inositol trisphosphate and diacyclycerol as second messengers. Biochem. J. **220**, 345–360. (1984)

Brooks, J. C. and Treml, S.: Catecholamine secretion by chemically-skinned cultured chromaffin cells. J. Neurochem. **40**, 468–473. (1983)

Castagna, M., Takai, Y., Kaibuchi, K., Sano, K., Kikkawa, U. and Nishizuka, Y.: Direct activation of calcium-activated phospholipid-dependent protein kinase by tumor-promoting phorbol esters. J. Biol. Chem. **257**, 7847–7871. (1982)

Chandler, D. E. and Heuser, J. E.: Arrest of membrane fusion events in mast cells by quick-freezing. J. Cell. Biol. **86**, 666–674. (1980)

Cockcroft, S. and Gomperts, B. D.: Activation and inhibition of calcium dependent histamine secretion by ATP ions applied to rat mast cells. J. Physiol. Lond. **296**, 229–243. (1979)

Creutz, C. E., Dowling, L. G., Sando, J. J., Villar-Palsi, C., Whipple, J. H. and Zeks, W. J.: Characterization of the chromobindins. Soluble proteins that bind to the chromaffin granule membrane in the presence of Ca^{2+}. J. Biol. Chem. **258,** 14 664–14 674. (1983)

Cuello, A. C.: *Co-transmission* Macmillan Press, London. (1982)

De Reimer, S. A., Strong, J. A., Albert, K. A., Greengard, P. and Kaczmarek, L. K.: Enhancement of calcium current in *Aplysia* neurones by phorbol ester and protein kinase C. Nature Lond. **313,** 313–316. (1985)

Dunn, L. A. and Holz, R. W.: Catecholamine secretion by digitonin-treated adrenal medullary chromaffin cells. J. Biol. Chem. **258,** 4989–4993. (1983)

Fernandez, J. M., Neher, E. and Gomperts, B. D.: Capacitance measurements reveal stepwise fusion events in degranulating mast cells. Nature Lond. **312,**453–455. (1984)

Haslam, R. J. and Davidson, M. M. L.: Guanine nucleotides decrease the free Ca^{2+} required for secretion of serotonin from permeabilized blood platelets. Febs. Lett. **174,** 90–95. (1984)

Kaibuchi, K., Takai, Y. and Nishizuka, Y.: Co-operative roles of various membrane phospholipids in the activation of calcium-activated, phospholipid-dependent protein kinase. J. Biol. Chem. **256,** 7146–7149. (1981)

Knight, D. E. and Baker, P. F.: Calcium-dependence of catecholamine release from bovine adrenal medullary cells after exposure to intense electric fields. J. Membrane Biol. **68,** 107–140. (1982)

Knight, D. E. and Baker, P. F.: The phorbol ester TPA increases the affinity of exocytosis for calcium in ‹leaky› adrenal medullary cells. Febs. Lett. **160,** 98–100. (1983)

Knight, D. E. and Baker, P. F.: The chromaffin granule protein pump and calcium-dependent exocytosis in bovine adrenal medullary cells. J. Membrane Biol. **83,** 147–156. (1985 a)

Knight, D. E. and Baker, P. F.: Guanine nucleotides and Ca-dependent exocytosis: studies in two adrenal cell populations. Febs. Lett. **189,**345–349. (1985 b)

Knight, D. E., Niggli, V. and Scrutton, M. C.: Thrombin and activators of protein kinase C modulate secretory responses of permeabilized human platelets induced by Ca^{2+}. Eur. J. Biochem. **143,** 437–446. (1984)

Knight, D. E. and Scrutton, M. C.: Cyclic nucleotides control a system which regulates Ca^{2+}-sensitivity of platelet secretion. Nature Lond. **309,** 66–68. (1984)

Knight, D. E., Tonge, D. A. and Baker, P. F.: Inhibition of exocytosis in bovine adrenal medullary cells by Botulinum toxin type D. Nature Lond. **317,** 719–721. (1985)

Kraft, A. S. and Anderson, W. B.: Phorbol esters increase the amount of Ca^{2+}, phospholipid-dependent protein kinase associated with plasma membrane. Nature London, **301,** 621–623. (1983)

Lingg, C., Fischer-Colbrie, R., Schmidt, W. and Winkler, H.: Exposure of an antigen of chromaffin granules on cell surface during exocytosis. Nature Lond. **301,** 610–611. (1983)

Michell, R. H.: Inositol phospholipids and cell surface receptor function. Biochem. biophys. Acta **415,** 81–147. (1975)

Neher, E. and Marty A. : Discrete changes of cell membrane capacitance observed under conditions of enhanced secretion in bovine adrenal chromaffin cells. Proc. Natl. Acad. Sci. USA **79,**6712–6716. (1982)

Niedel, J. E., Kuhn, L. J. and Vandenbark, G. R.: Phorbol diester receptor co-purifies with protein kinase C. Proc. Nat. Acad. Sci. USA **80,**36–40. (1983)

Ornberg, R. L. and Reese, T. S.: Beginning of exocytosis captured by rapid freezing of *Limulus* amebocytes. J. Cell. Biol. **90,** 40–54. (1981)

Rink, T. J. and Hallam, T.: What turns platelets on? TIBS, **12,**215–219. (1984)

Schmidt, W., Patzak, A., Lingg, G., Winkler, H. and Plattner, H.: Membrane events in adrenal chromaffin cells during exocytosis: a freeze-etching analysis after rapid cryofixation. Eur. J. Cell Biol. **32,** 31–37. (1983)

Schweitzer, E. S. and Blaustein, M. P.: The use of antibody and complement to gain access to the interior of presynaptic nerve terminals. Exp. Brain Res. **38,** 443–453. (1980)

Takai, Y., Kishimoto, A., Kikkawa, U., Mori, T. and Nishizuka, Y.: Unsaturated diacylglycerol as a possible messenger for the activation of calcium-activated, phospholipid-dependent protein kinase system. Biochem. Biophys. Res. Commun. **91,** 1218–1224. (1979)

Wilson, S. P. and Kirschner, N.: Calcium-evoked secretion from digitonin permeabilized adrenal medullary chromaffin cells. J. Biol. Chem. **258,** 4994–5000. (1983)

Fortschritte der Zoologie, Band 33 · Lüttgau (Hrsg.): Membrane Control
Gustav Fischer Verlag · Stuttgart · New York · 1986

Patch clamp studies on the role of calcium in secretion*

Erwin Neher

Max-Planck-Institut für biophysikalische Chemie, Abt. Membranbiophysik, Am Faßberg, D-3400 Göttingen, FRG

The classical concept of secretion assigns a predominant role to the calcium ion. Locke (1894) already found nearly one hundred years ago that signal transmission in a nerve-muscle preparation depends on the presence of calcium in the bath, and Cushing (1901) was able to identify the nerve endings as the sites of action. Our present view was primed by a series of outstanding papers by Katz and Miledi (see review by Katz, 1969). According to this concept, depolarisation of the nerve ending leads to an inflow of calcium through voltage-dependent channels, with a resulting increase in the concentration of intracellular calcium. The increased calcium level induces fusion of secretory vesicles with the plasma membrane. This concept was extended by Douglas (1969) and postulated to be the basic mechanism of stimulus-secretion coupling in a variety of cellular systems, both neuronal and non-neuronal. Mongar and Schild (1958) had already shown that histamine secretion in mast cells depends on the availability of calcium.

More recently, however, the central role of calcium has been questioned. It is now possible to monitor the intracellular concentration of free calcium $[Ca]_i$ in very small secretory cells by means of new fluorescence indicator dyes (Tsien, Pozzan and Rink, 1984). Measurements of this kind revealed cell types in which secretion can take place without any increase in $[Ca]_i$ (Rink, Sanchez and Hallam, 1983). In fact, an inverse relationship between $[Ca]_i$ and secretion was found in cells of the parathyroid (Shoback et al., 1984). Thus, new interest has been aroused regarding the relation between calcium, calcium-specific channels and the secretory process.

The patch clamp technique (Hamill et al., 1981) allows the study of ionic currents in small cells. Since most of the secretory cells of interest are small (5–10 μm diameter) this technique very often provides the only means of characterizing the changes in membrane permeability that precede secretion. Recently, a variant of this technique employing membrane capacitance measurement was described (Neher and Marty, 1982) which provides an electrical signal related to exocytosis. Thus, it is possible to study simultaneously on a single cell secretion and the ionic channels that control secretion. In the following, the patch-clamp technique, in particular capacitance measurements, will be briefly described. The question of calcium dependency will be discussed by comparing measurements made on two very different cell types.

---

* This is a translation of an article which appeared in German in Volume 2 of «Hauptvorträge der Tagungen der Deutsche Physiologischen Gesellschaft», Fischer Verlag.

The patch-clamp technique for electrophysiological measurements on small cells

The currents flowing through individual ion channels can only be resolved when the electrical measurement is confined to a very small membrane area. For this reason NEHER and SAKMANN (1976) measured currents flowing through fine glass pipettes placed onto the surface of muscle cells (see fig. 1, upper part). The mechanical contact between the pipette rim and the cell isolates the small patch of membrane covered by the pipette for the purpose of the electrical measurement. In this way ionic currents flowing through individual acetylcholine-activated channels were resolved. However, the seal obtained this way was usually not perfect, resulting in a shunt due to a thin film of electrolyte remaining between glass and membrane. This shunt compromised the fidelity of the signal and caused high background noise in the measurement. In order to make the method applicable to a variety of channels and preparations, the problem of the membrane-glass seal had to be solved. It was found that slight suction applied to the pipette often leads to a sudden and spontaneous improvement in seal resistance by factors of 100 to 1000, providing clean surfaces are used. Seal resistances in the range $10^9\ \Omega$ or gigaohm (gigaseal) became quite common, which greatly improved the measurements. As a result, elementary currents of many different types of ion channels have since been recorded at high resolution (see AUERBACH and SACHS, 1984, for review). Fig. 2 shows a representative example of a single channel recording from acetylcholine-activated channels in myoballs.

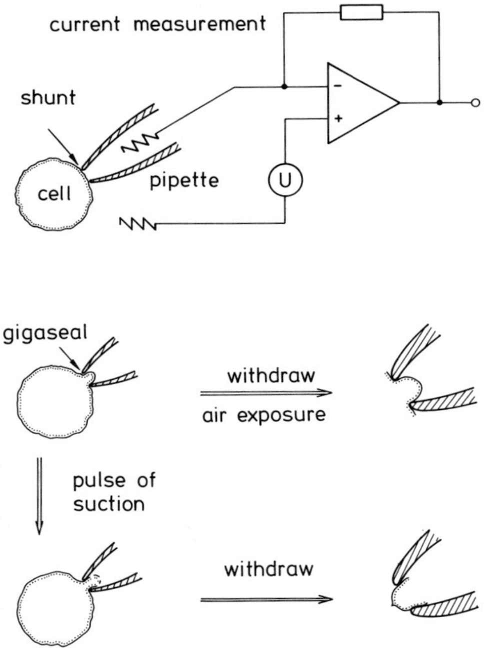

Fig. 1: Schematic diagram of different patch clamp configurations (see text). Reproduced from NEHER and STÜHMER, 1985.

The solution to the seal problem led to new ways of measuring membrane currents, which proved to be at least as important as single channel recording. This is illustrated in the lower part of fig. 1. The key to these different configurations was the finding that the gigaseal contact is not only electrically tight, but also mechanically very stable. The membrane patch enclosed in the pipette tip can be isolated from the cell by simple withdrawal of the pipette. Alternatively, a short pulse of suction or voltage applied to the pipette very often perforates the patch without rupture of the tight connection between pipette and cell membrane. A conducting pathway is thereby established between the pipette and the cell interior in a configuration which is very similar to conventional microelectrode recording. However, this kind of ‹microelectrode penetration› has proven to be much more gentle, and to provide more stable recordings than conventional penetrations – even on cells as small as erythrocytes (HAMILL, 1983). It has proven ideally suited for voltage- and current-clamp measurements on almost all cell culture preparations. The specific electrical parameters of this configuration allow voltage clamp conditions to be reached without the use of a second micropipette or a feedback amplifier, providing the cell is sufficiently small. Some numerical values may illuminate this: Membrane resistance of small cells, 10 to 20 μm in diameter is typically in the range 10–100 GΩ. This may drop during excitation to values between 100 MΩ and 1 GΩ. The access resistance of the cell (resistance between pipette and cell) can readily be made to be as small as 2–5 MΩ (MARTY and NEHER, 1983); it is thus always smaller than that of the membrane. Voltage signals applied to the

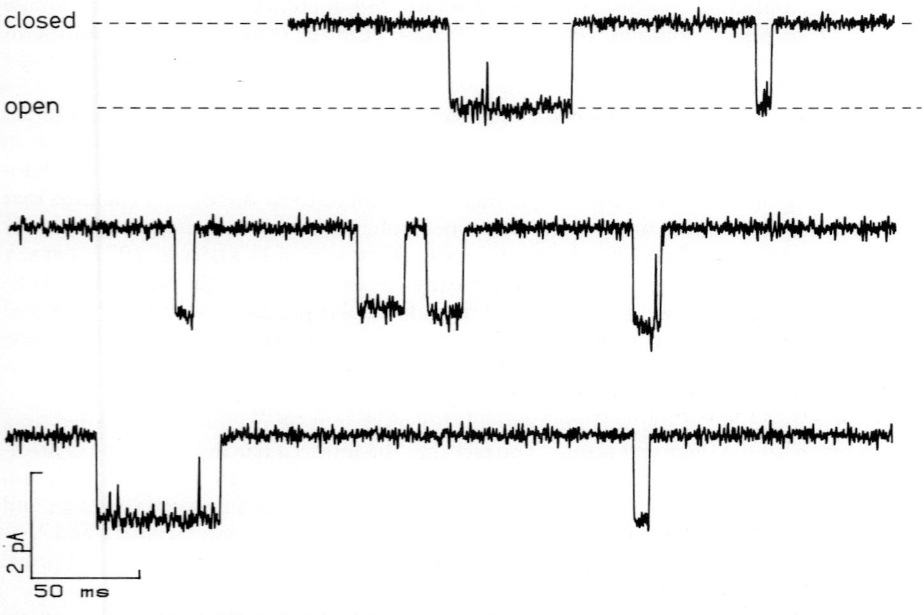

Fig. 2: Currents flowing through individual acetylcholine-activated ion channels in embryonic muscle membrane. Leading and trailing edges of downwardly directed current pulses mark the opening and closing of channels, respectively. The membrane patch under study most likely contained more than one channel. However, concentration of acetylcholin in the pipette (0.5 μM) was chosen low enough such that probability of simultaneous opening of several channels was low. Membrane voltage was –70 mV: temperature 12 °C. The recording was kindly supplied by Mr. S. HEINEMANN.

pipette are therefore impressed onto the cell membrane without appreciable voltage decrement, and the resulting currents can be considered voltage clamp currents. This type of voltage clamp is commonly referred to as ‹whole cell patch clamp recording›. Unfortunately this term is long and misleading – it refers to a patch that is no longer present. The technique is instead based on the tight seal which is established during patch formation. It will therefore be called ‹tight seal clamp› in the following.

There are several fundamental differences between conventional microelectrode recording and the tight seal clamp besides the ease with which voltage clamp conditions can be reached. These differences can emerge as advantages or as severe disadvantages, depending on the purpose of the measurement. They are pinpointed in the diagram of fig. 3 and elaborated upon in the following.

The main difference concerns the size relations between cell diameter and the pipette opening. Conventional microelectrodes have inside diameters in the range 0.1 μm or smaller, particularly if pipettes of high resistance (100 MΩ) are used, which is required when recording from small cells. They usually have a very small tapering angle. Both features are apt to reduce diffusional fluxes between pipette and cell. Patch pipettes, on the other hand, often have inside diameters in the range 1 μm and large tapering angles for low access resistance. This then also allows fast diffusional exchange between pipette and cell. Marty and Neher (1983) showed that intracellular potassium is replaced by sodium within seconds if pipettes are filled with solutions rich in sodium. For this reason, patch pipettes should be filled with solutions resembling the intracellular milieu. Filling with 3 M KCl, as is standard for microelectrodes, is not practical. Furthermore, most probably all diffusible cytoplasmic constituents will ‹wash out› and dilute into the practically infinite volume of the pipette solution. Neher and Almers (1986 b) showed that the fluorescent indicator dye fura-2 (Grynkiewicz et al., 1985) with molecular weight 831 exchanges within 20–60 seconds.

The question must be asked whether cellular functions can be maintained intact under such conditions. It is probably a lucky coincidence that the traditional signal mediators in electrophysiological measurements (Na-channels, K-channels, transmitter-activated channels) are integral membrane proteins and therefore immune to ‹washout›. Ca-channels that are subject to a somewhat more complicated metabolic regulation were found to be slowly ‹washed out› in internally perfused giant neurones (Kostyuk and Krishtal, 1977; Byerly and Hagiwara, 1982), an effect which is greatly enhanced in the tight-seal clamp (Fenwick et al., 1982 b). It should be expected that all cellular processes regulated by second messengers or cofactors such as cyclic AMP, inositol-trisphosphate, calcium and guanine nucleotides should be greatly impaired by washout. The interruption of the stimulus-secretion pathway in mast cells discussed below serves as an example.

The phenomenon of the washout should, however, not be exclusively regarded as a disadvantage of the tight seal clamp. The fact that the intracellular milieu can be controlled and supplemented by appropriate compositions or additions to the pipette solution opens up possibilities for reconstitution of labile regulatory mechanisms (Kameyama and Trautwein, 1985). Technical advances such as intrapipette perfusion (Soejima and Noma, 1984) or selective perforation of patches (Lindau and Fernandez, 1986) will prove very valuable in this context.

Another difference between microelectrode measurements and the tight-seal clamp relates to the tight seal itself. Cell penetration with microelectrodes inevitably leads to some membrane damage and leak. Even under very favourable circumstances this leak will probably range between 100 MΩ and 1 GΩ. For instance, microelectrode recordings from single chromaffin cells (Brandt et al., 1976) resulted in values for input resistance (parallel combination of membrane resistance and leak) in the range 300 MΩ to 500 MΩ. The

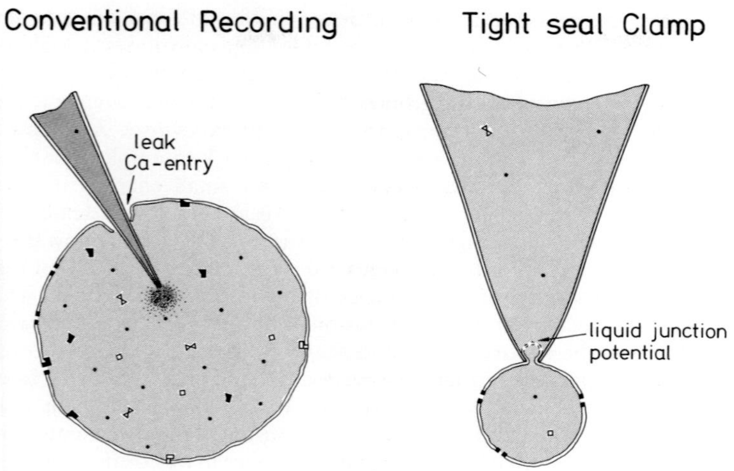

Fig. 3: Schematic pinpointing differences between conventional microelectrode recording and tight seal clamp. The drawing is supposed to: 1) emphasize differences in relative sizes; 2) illustrate that there are many regulatory components (second messengers; soluble regulatory proteins; guanine nucleotides; calcium) inside the cell which are being diluted in the tight seal clamp; 3) show differences in the ionic strengths of filling solutions.

tight seal clamp allowed values as high as 10 to 50 GΩ. (Fenwick et al., 1982 a). This implies that in the former measurements the input resistance was greatly influenced by leak. The leak also provides a pathway for the inflow of calcium into the cell. Elevated $[Ca]_i$ can then activate calcium-dependent potassium channels such that an adequate resting potential appears in spite of the presence of large leakage currents.

A final difference between patch pipettes and conventional microelectrodes results from the relatively low ionic strength of standard pipette filling solutions. The strong electrolyte (particularly concentrated KCl) shunts liquid junction potentials at the pipette tip. With patch pipettes offset potentials up to approximately 15 mV have to be allowed for (Marty and Neher, 1983).

Capacitance measurements for studying secretory processes

The commonly accepted mechanism of exocytosis – fusion of secretory granules with the plasma membrane – implies an increase in surface area as the membrane of the vesicle is incorporated into the outer membrane. This increase can be monitored by measuring membrane capacitance. According to the basic laws of electricity, the capacitance of a condenser is proportional to its area. The cell membrane can be approximated quite well by such a condenser with the bimolecular lipid leaflet as the dielectric. Values for specific membrane capacitance in a variety of biological membranes are all close to 1 $\mu F/cm^2$ (Almers, 1978), a quantity which relates the measured capacity change to a change in surface area. Jaffe et al. (1978) and Gillespie (1979) have demonstrated some time ago that secretory processes can be monitored this way.

Any current measurement can be used for determination of capacitance by employing standard techniques of circuit analysis. The patch clamp constitutes a high resolution current measurement which can thus be easily converted into a high resolution capacitance measurement. By optimizing the background noise of such a measurement, Neher and Marty (1982) tried to resolve the elementary process of exocytosis. A patch-clamp apparatus was combined with a phase-sensitive detector (lock-in amplifier). This method provided highest resolution, but was accurate only for small changes in capacitance. Thereby a resolution in the range 1–5 fF (1 fF = 10^{-15} Farad) was achieved, varying according to the measurement configuration. Fig. 4 shows schematically how this quantity relates to the signals expected for two different cell types. Chromaffin cells of the adrenal medulla contain catecholamine-storing vesicles of up to 0.4 μm diameter. This would result in a capacitance increment per vesicle fusion of up to 5 fF. This value is close to the limit of resolution specified above. Neher and Marty (1982) succeeded in recording such individual events in cell-attached patches, where background noise is lowest. However, the frequency of occurrence of events was very low. In the whole-cell (tight seal clamp) recording, however, the summated response of many fusion events after stimulation could be readily detected. However, background noise was higher in this configuration such that the elementary process could not be characterized.

This situation suggested the use of a preparation with larger storage granules, such as the mast cell. The histamine-containing mast cell granules have an average diameter of 0.7 μm (HELANDER and BLOOM, 1974), which is about twice the size of the chromaffin granules. Thus, a four-fold signal is expected in the measurement of surface area, which can well be resolved. Fig. 5 shows the initial phase of a mast cell degranulation (see below) where each step-like change in capacitance reflects the fusion of a single vesicle with the plasma membrane. The individual steps are not all of the same size. The distribution of step sizes could be accurately predicted from the morphometrically determined distribution of vesicle diameters (FERNANDEZ, NEHER and GOMPERTS, 1984).

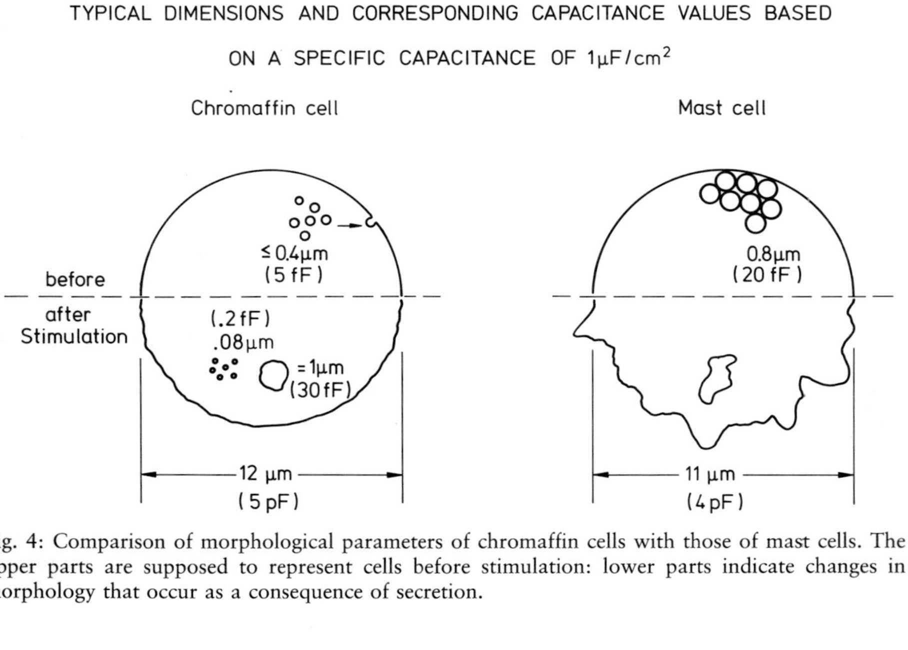

Fig. 4: Comparison of morphological parameters of chromaffin cells with those of mast cells. The upper parts are supposed to represent cells before stimulation: lower parts indicate changes in morphology that occur as a consequence of secretion.

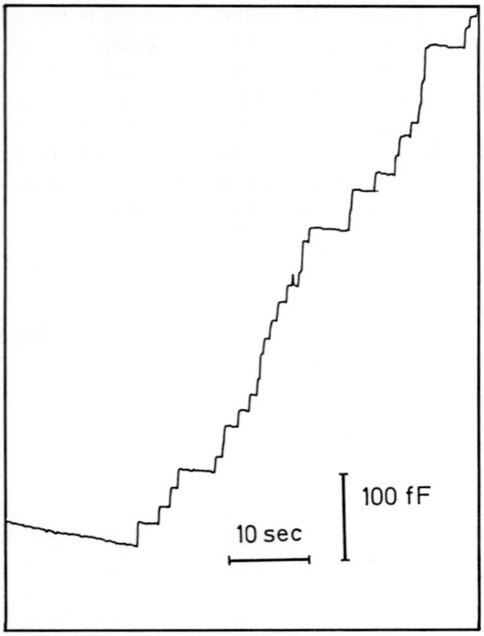

Fig. 5: Discrete steps of capacitance increase during the initial phase of a degranulation (mast cell). Each step represents fusion of a single vesicle.

The secretory process in chromaffin cells is Ca-dependent

Chromaffin cells of the adrenal medulla share many properties with neurones, particularly under cell culture conditions (UNSICKER et al., 1980). They have a set of ion channels (FENWICK et al., 1982 a, b; MARTY and NEHER, 1985) which seems to be typical for excitable membranes (see HILLE, 1984, for an extensive review on ion channels in excitable membranes). With regard to secretion, the presence of a voltage-dependent Ca current with high activation threshold and lacking voltage-dependent inactivation is particularly important. A current with these characteristics has been identified in many neurones and neurosecretory cell types, such as giant synapse of the squid (LLINAS et al., 1981); pituitary cells (HAGIWARA and OHMORI, 1982); rod inner segments (COREY et al., 1984); cochlear hair cells (LEWIS and HUDSPETH, 1983); molluscan giant neurones (ECKERT and CHAD, 1984).

Secretion in chromaffin cells, as monitored by capacitance measurements, appears to be Ca-dependent, conforming in every respect with the expectations of the classical view. The tight seal clamp permits direct proof of the dependency on intracellular Ca-concentration, since cytoplasmic ionic concentrations can be controlled as described above. Fig. 6 illustrates this point. A stationary capacitance can be observed when the Ca concentration is limited to values smaller than 50 nM by addition of a chelator (10 mM EGTA) to the pipette solution. If, however, $[Ca]_i$ is buffered to values between 0.5 μM and 1 μM, the capacitance rises continually after establishment of the tight seal clamp configuration.

With a regimen of weak Ca-buffering to low values of $[Ca]_i$, characteristic capacitive responses can be evoked by depolarizing voltage pulses (NEHER and MARTY, 1982). These responses are strongly correlated with the voltage-dependent Ca current mentioned above. They are absent when Ca current is blocked or after Ca current has ‹washed-out› during prolonged periods in tight-seal clamp conditions. When the amplitude of depolarizing pulses is varied, Ca responses show a maximum at a voltage that coincides with the voltage producing maximal activation of Ca current (CLAPHAM and NEHER, 1984). It can be concluded that $[Ca]_i$ is indeed the most important parameter in the control of secretion in chromaffin cells.

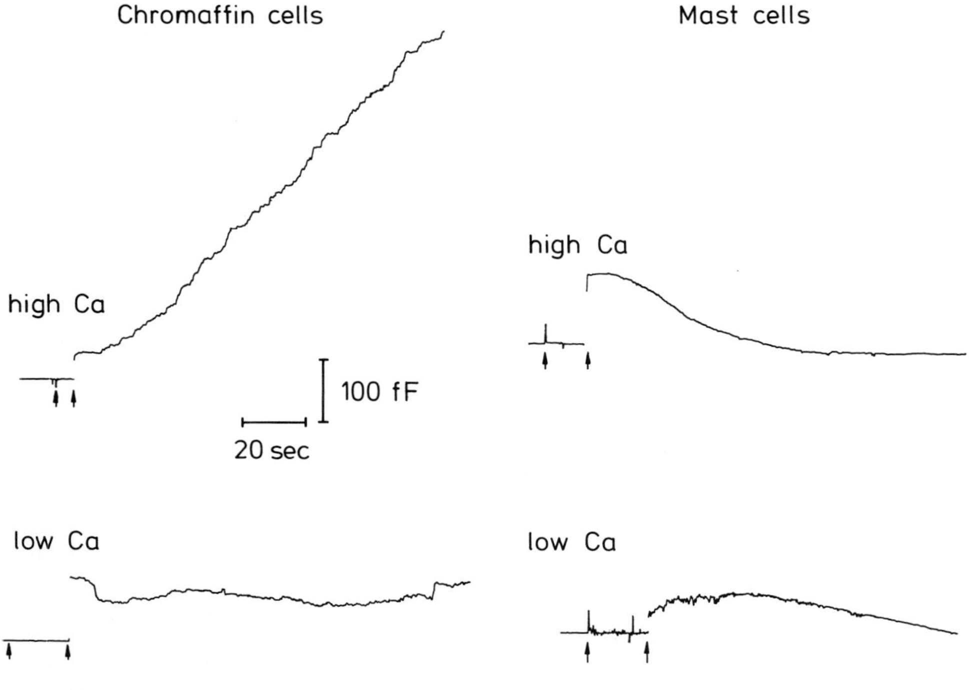

Fig. 6: Comparison between capacitance signals in chromaffin cells (left) and mast cells (right). The pipette solution contained (in mM): 155 K-glutamate; 4 $MgCl_2$, 10 NaOH-HEPES, 0.2 ATP, 10 EGTA. In addition, 8 mM $CaCl_2$ was added and pH subsequently adjusted to 7.2 in the upper two records, buffering [Ca] to approximately 0.6 μM. In the lower two records only 2 mM $CaCl_2$ was added buffering [Ca] to a low value ($\simeq$ 0.04 μm). Capacitance was measured with a lock-in-amplifier at 320 Hz (Neher and Marty, 1982). The membrane potential was clamped to –80 mV in chromaffin cells, in order to minimize contributions of ionic channels to the cell admittance. Mast cells were held either at –40 mV or at 0 mV with similar results. In several experiments on chromaffin cells at high [Ca] capacitance increased by 18 ± 6 % (mean ± S.D.) within 3 to 5 minutes after establishment of the tight-seal clamp configuration. In mast cells capacitance decreased by 1.3 ± 4 %, using the same protocol. Temperature: 24 °C. The first arrow in each trace indicates the time of patch perforation, the second one marks the time when the sinusoidal signal was applied.

Calcium and secretion in mast cells

According to current literature on mast cells, the control of secretion in this cell type should be very similar to the case described above for chromaffin cells. Many recent papers on mast cell secretion start with statements implying that increase in $[Ca]_i$ is a necessary and sufficient stimulus for secretion (SORIMACHI, 1984; GOMPERTS, 1983). It was suggested that dimerisation of IgE receptors by antigen results in the opening of Ca-channels (KANNER and METZGER, 1983; MAZUREK et al., 1984). The patch clamp measurement however does not reveal such channels (LINDAU and FERNANDEZ, 1986). The mast cell seems to be an example of a cell type in which hardly any channels can be observed over a wide voltage range.

The intracellular level of calcium certainly rises in the intact mast cell upon stimulation. This is suggested by flux studies (FOREMAN et al., 1977) as well as by measurements with fluorescent indicator dyes (WHITE et al., 1984). The role of calcium, however, seems to be quite different from that in chromaffin cells. Recent measurements employing the new fluorescent indicator dye fura-2 (GRYNKIEWICZ et al., 1985) showed that elevated $[Ca]_i$ can promote secretion. However, $[Ca]_i$ can also transiently rise to values of several μM without eliciting secretion (NEHER and ALMERS, 1986 a). On the other hand cases could be observed where $[Ca]_i$ stayed below 0.2 μM throughout a full degranulation. Thus, there is no unique relation between $[Ca]_i$ and secretion in mast cells. This points towards another signal responsible for secretion and suggests merely a supplementary role for calcium.

Mast cells lose their ability to respond to stimuli such as antigen or the polyamine compound 48/80 within seconds to minutes after establishment of the tight seal clamp configuration (FERNANDEZ et al., 1984). This is a good example for the ‹washout› of signal mediators described above. In an attempt to identify such mediators the first question again relates to the role of calcium in the dialyzed cell. Variation of $[Ca]_i$ in the pipette in the range 0.1 to 10 μM, contrary to the case of chromaffin cells, did not result in Ca-induced capacitance increase. Fig. 6 shows an example, directly comparing mast cells with chromaffin cells. The same solution, with $[Ca]_i$ buffered to 0.6 μM, which led to rapid capacitance increase in chromaffin cells, resulted in a marked capacitance decrease in mast cells. There are several possible interpretations for the capacitance decrease (ALMERS and NEHER, 1985), but it is most probably not directly related to the secretory process. In any case, there are no discrete step-like changes in capacitance that would be indicative of secretory events. With pipette solutions buffered to low $[Ca]_i$ ($\leq$ 0.05 μM, see lower part of fig. 6) the capacitance was more or less stationary both for chromaffin cells and for mast cells. Looking further for signal mediators in mast cells, we found that GTP-analogues invariably led to degranulation when added to the pipette (FERNANDEZ et al., 1984). This method of stimulating the cell turned out to be independent of $[Ca]_i$ within wide limits.

It seems that degranulation in mast cells under certain conditions is enhanced by elevated $[Ca]_i$. On the other hand, it can proceed independently of $[Ca]_i$, particularly after washout of regulatory cytoplasmic components. One interpretation of these phenomena postulates an analogy to the control of muscle contraction (FERNANDEZ et al., 1984): According to this hypothesis a Ca-dependent repressor (Troponin C for the case of muscle contraction) would prevent secretion in the absence of calcium in the intact cell. This repressor would be washed out in the dialyzed cell such that secretion can proceed without the requirement of elevated calcium. Alternatively the variability of Ca-dependency could derive from the properties of protein kinase C (NISHIZUKA, 1983). This enzyme is dependent on calcium. In the presence of another activator (diacylglycerol), however, the Ca-dependency is shifted into the range of resting $[Ca]_i$. The enzyme could then be permanently activated. There are, indeed, a number of findings that assign an important role to protein kinase C in mast cell secretion (Heiman and Crews, 1985). Diacylglycerol, necessary for activation of protein kinase C, originates from receptor-mediated breakdown of phosphatidylinositol (see review article by Berridge, 1984). Most interestingly, recent results indicate that the IgE-receptor which is activated during mast cell stimulation by antigen may be linked to the lipid-splitting enzyme phospholipase C by means of a GTP-binding protein (Cockcroft and Gomperts, 1985). This might be the basis of the GTP effects mentioned above.

In view of the rapid progress in the biochemical analysis of such interconnections (Joseph, 1985) it can be expected that the initial steps of signal reception and transmission in mast cells will soon emerge in greater detail. From the results presented above, it seems that they will probably not involve the opening of Ca channels in response to IgE receptor activation, but rather the activation of protein kinase C through the phosphatidylinositol cycle and possibly release of calcium from intracellular stores (see Berridge, 1984). It is to be hoped that knowledge about several steps in the stimulus-secretion pathway in mast cells will eventually also lead to a more detailed understanding of the established role of calcium in chromaffin cells and neurones.

Acknowledgement

The records of Fig. 2 were kindly provided by Mr. S. Heinemann. I thank Dr. R. O. Eckert for carefully reading the manuscript.

References

Almers, W.: Gating currents and charge movements in excitable membranes. Rev. Physiol. Biochem. Pharmacol., **82:** 96–190. (1978)

Almers, W. and Neher, E.: Ca^{2+}-induced membrane capacity changes in rat peritoneal mast cells. J. Physiol. **369:** 95 P (1985)

Auerbach, A. and Sachs, F.: Patch clamp studies of single ionic channels. Ann. Rev. Biophys. Bioeng., **13:**269–302. (1984)

Berridge, M. J.: Inositol trisphosphate and diacylglycerol as second messengers. Biochem. J., **220:** 345–360. (1984)

Brandt, B. L., Hagiwara, S., Kidokoro, Y. and Miyazaki, S.: Action potentials in the rat chromaffin cell and effects of acetylcholine. J. Physiol., **263:** 417–439. (1976)

Byerly, L. and Hagiwara, S.: Calcium currents in internally perfused nerve cell bodies of *Limnea stagnalis*. J. Physiol., **322:** 503–528. (1982)

Clapham, D. E. and Neher, E.: Trifluoperazine reduces inward ionic currents and secretion by separate mechanisms in bovine chromaffin cells. J. Physiol., **353:**541–564. (1984)

Cockcroft, S. and Gomperts, B. D.: Role of guanine nucleotide binding protein in the activation of polyphosphoinositide phosphodiesterase. Nature, **314:**534–536. (1985)

Corey, D. P., Dubinsky, J. M. and Schwartz, E. A.: The calcium current in inner segments of rods from the salamander *(Ambystoma tigrinum)* retina. J. Physiol., **354:** 557–575. (1984)

Cushing, H.: Concerning the poisonous effects of pure sodium chloride solution upon the nerve-muscle preparation. Am. J. Physiol., **6:** 77–84. (1901)

Douglas, W. W.: Stimulus-secretion coupling: The concept and clues from chromaffin and other cells. Br. J. Pharmac., **34:**451–474. (1968)

Eckert, R. and Chad, J. E.: Inactivation of Ca channels. Prog. Biophys. Molec. Biol., **44:** 215–267. (1984)

Fenwick, E. M., Marty, A. and Neher, E.: A patch-clamp study of bovine chromaffin cells and of their sensitivity to acetylcholine. J. Physiol., **331**:577–597. (1982 a)

Fenwick, E. M., Marty, A. and Neher, E.: Sodium and calcium channels in bovine chromaffin cells. J. Physiol., **331**:599–635. (1982 b)

Fernandez, J. M., Neher, E. and Gomperts, B. D.: Capacitance measurements reveal stepwise fusion events in degranulating mast cells. Nature, **312**: 453–455. (1984)

Foreman, J. C., Hallett, M. B. and Mongar, J. L.: The relationship between histamine secretion and calcium uptake by mast cells. J. Physiol., **271**: 193–214. (1977)

Gillespie, J. T.: The effect of repetitive stimulation on the passive electrical properties of the presynaptic terminal of the squid giant synapse. Proc. R. Soc. Lond. B, **206**: 293–306. (1979)

Gomperts, B. D.: Involvement of guanine nucleotide-binding protein in the gating of Ca^{2+} by receptors. Nature, **306**: 64–66. (1983)

Grynkiewicz, G., Poenie, M. and Tsien, R. Y.: A new generation of Ca^{2+} indicators with greatly improved fluorescence properties. J. Biol. Chem., **260**:3440–3450. (1985)

Hagiwara, S. and Ohmori, H.: Studies of calcium channels in rat clonal pituitary cells with patch electrode voltage clamp. J. Physiol., **331**:231–252. (1982)

Hamill, O. P.: Potassium and chloride channels in red blood cell In: Single Channel Recording, edited by B. Sakmann and E. Neher, New York: Plenum, pp. 451–471. (1983)

Hamill, O. P., Marty, A., Neher, E., Sakmann, B. and Sigworth, F. J.:Improved patch clamp techniques for high-resolution current recording from cells and cell-free membrane patches. Pfluegers Arch., **391**: 85–100. (1981)

Heiman, A. S. and Crews, F. T.: Characterization of the effects of phorbol esters on rat mast cell secretion. J. Immunol., **134**:548–554. (1985)

Helander, H. F. and Bloom, G. D.: Quantitative analysis of mast cell structure. J. Microscopy, **100**: 315–321. (1974)

Hille, B.: *Ionic channels of excitable membranes,* Sunderland, Mass.: Sinauer. (1984)

Jaffe, L. A., Hagiwara, S. and Kado, R. T.: The time course of cortical vesicle fusion in sea urchin eggs observed as membrane capacitance changes. Dev. Biol., **67**:243–248. (1978)

Joseph, S. N.: Receptor-stimulated phosphoinositide metabolism: A role for GTP-binding proteins? TIBS, **10**: 297–298. (1985)

Kameyama, M., Hofmann, F. and Trautwein, W.: On the mechanism of β-adrenergic regulation of the Ca channel in the guinea-pig heart. Pflügers Arch. **405**: 285–293 (1985)

Kanner, B. I. and Metzger, H.: Crosslinking of the receptors for immunoglobulin E depolarizes the plasma membrane of rat basophilic leukemia cells. Proc. Natl. Acad. Sci. USA, **80**:5744–5748. (1983)

Katz, B.: *The release of neural transmitter substances,* Liverpool: Liverpool University Press. (1969)

Kostyuk, P. G. and Krishtal, O. A.: Separation of sodium and calcium currents in the somatic membrane of molluscan neurones. J. Physiol., **270**: 545–568. (1977)

Lewis, R. S. and Hudspeth, A. L.: Voltage- and ion-dependent conductances in solitary vertebrate hair cells. Nature, **304**: 538–541. (1983)

Lindau, M. and Fernandez, J. M.: A patch clamp study of histamine secreting cells. J. Gen. Physiol. in press (1986)

Llinas, R., Steinberg, I. Z. and Walton, K.: Presynaptic calcium currents in squid giant synapse. Biophys. J., **33**: 289–321. (1981)

Locke, F. S.: Notiz über den Einfluß physiologischer Kochsalzlösung auf die Erregbarkeit von Muskel und Nerv. Zenthl. Physiol., **8**: 166–167. (1894)

Marty, A. and Neher, E.: Tight-seal whole-cell recording. In: Single Channel Recording, edited by B. Sakmann and E. Neher, New York: Plenum, pp. 107–121. (1983)

Marty, A. and Neher E.: Potassium channels in cultured bovine adrenal chromaffin cells. J. Physiol., **367**:117–141. (1985)

Mazurek, N., Schindler, H., Schuerholz, T. H. and Pecht, I.: The cromolyn binding protein constitutes the Ca^{2+} channel of basophils opening upon immunological stimulus, PNAS, **81**:6841–6846. (1984)

Mongar, J. L. and Schild, H. O.: Effect of calcium and pH on the anaphylactic reaction. J. Physiol., **140**:272–284. (1958)

Neher, E. and Almers, W.: Fast Ca-transients in rat peritoneal mast cells are not sufficient to trigger exocytosis. EMBO J., **5**: 51–53 (1986 a)
Neher, E. and Almers, W.: Patch pipettes used for loading small cells with fluorescent indicators dyes. (submitted) (1986 b)
Neher, E. and Marty, A.: Discrete changes of cell membrane capacitance observed under conditions of enhanced secretion in bovine adrenal chromaffin cells. Proc. Natl. Acad. Sci. USA, **79**:6712–6716. (1982)
Neher, E. and Sakmann, B.: Single-channel currents recorded from membrane of denervated frog muscle fibres. Nature, **260**:799–802. (1976)
Neher, E. und Stuehmer, W.: Ionenkanäle zur Signalübermittlung in biologischen Systemen. Phys. Bl. **41**,329–334. (1985)
Nishizuka, Y.: Phospholipid degradation and signal translation for protein phosphorylation. TIBS, **8**: 13–16. (1983)
Rink, T. J., Sanchez, A. and Hallam, T. J.: Diacylglycerol and phorbol ester stimulate secretion without raising cytoplasmic free calcium in human platelets. Nature, **305**: 317–319. (1983)
Shoback, D. M., Thatcher, J., Leombruno, R. and Brown, E. M.: Relationship between parathyroid hormone secretion and cytosolic calcium concentration in dispersed bovine parathyroid cells. Proc. Natl. Acad. Sci. USA, **81**:3113–3117. (1984)
Soejima, M. and Noma, A.: Mode of regulation of the ACh-sensitive K channel by the muscarinic receptor in rabbit atrical cells. Pfluegers Arch., **400**: 424–431. (1984)
Sorimachi, M.: Removal of extracellular Ca stimulates histamine release from rat mast cells by mobilizing a labile cellular source of Ca. Jap. J. Physiol., **34**:919–922. (1984)
Tsien, R. Y., Pozzan, T. and Rink, T. J.: Measuring and manipulating cytosolic Ca^{2+} with trapped indicators. TIBS, **9**: 263–266. (1984)
Unsicker, K., Griesser, G. H., Lindmar, R., Loeffelholz, K. and Wolf, U.: Establishment, characterization and fibre outgrowth of isolated bovine adrenal medullary cells in long-term cultures. Neurosci., **5**:1445–1460. (1980)
White, J. R., Ishizaka, T., Ishizaka, K. and Sha'afi, R. I.: Direct demonstration of increased intracellular concentration of free calcium as measured by quin-2 in stimulated rat peritoneal mast cell. Proc. Natl. Acad. Sci. USA, **81**:3978–3982. (1984)

IV. Session
Cellular processes in vision

Fortschritte der Zoologie, Band 33 · Lüttgau (Hrsg.): Membrane Control
Gustav Fischer Verlag · Stuttgart · New York · 1986

Proteins involved in the control of cyclic GMP phosphodiesterase in retinal rod cells

Hermann Kühn

Institut für Neurobiologie der Kernforschungsanlage Jülich GmbH, Postfach 1913, 5170 Jülich, FRG

Light absorption by rhodopsin in the disk membranes of vertebrate rod cell outer segments (ROS) triggers a chain of events that lead, *via* the activation of an enzyme cascade, to the closure of ion channels in the plasma membrane and, therefore, to hyperpolarization of the rod cell. The present review briefly summarizes our knowledge about the initial part of the light-triggered chain of events, i. e., that part in which photoexcited rhodopsin (R*) directly participates. It will be shown that R* undergoes a series of specific protein–protein interactions with several ROS proteins that are either peripherally membrane-associated or soluble; these interactions first lead to the activation and later on to the deactivation of a phosphodiesterase (PDE) specific for cyclic GMP (cGMP). The results presented here have been obtained with ROS purified from bovine retina, and with purified components from ROS (purified proteins, washed disk membranes).

Results and discussion

Light-induced changes in the rhodopsin molecule

Rhodopsin, the light-sensitive chromoprotein, is the predominant integral membrane protein of the disk membrane. When rhodopsin absorbs a photon of visible light, its chromophore becomes cis-trans isomerized; this leads to a series of protein conformational changes and to the formation of an active form, «photoactivated rhodopsin» (R*). Several lines of evidence (reviewed by Kühn, 1984) indicate that the active photointermediate, R*, is identical with the spectrally defined intermediate metarhodopsin II (380 nm) which, under physiological conditions, is formed within the first millisecond after light absorption and has a lifetime in the range of a few minutes. Light-induced conformational changes occur not only in the hydrophobic, chromophore-binding center of rhodopsin (as revealed by the different absorption spectra of the photointermediates), but also at its hydrophilic surface which is exposed to the cytoplasm (Kühn et al., 1982).

Light-dependent phosphorylation of rhodopsin

Light-activated rhodopsin becomes accessible to a specific protein kinase which, independently of cyclic nucleotides or Ca^{2+}, incorporates up to 9 phosphate groups into serine and threonine residues of the protein (KÜHN and DREYER, 1972; BOWNDS et al., 1972; WILDEN and KÜHN, 1982). ATP is the preferred phosphate donor. Phosphorylation of photolyzed rhodopsin is 50–100 times faster than that of dark-adapted rhodopsin, indicating a highly specific recognition by the kinase of a light-induced conformational change at rhodopsin's cytoplasmic surface. Measured overall phosphorylation rates are slow (taking many minutes) if all of the rhodopsin in a ROS preparation is bleached but can be much faster (taking seconds) if only a small fraction of rhodopsin is bleached (SITARAMAYYA and LIEBMAN, 1983). This seems to be due to the limiting amount of kinase present in ROS. Light-induced phosphorylation of rhodopsin *in vivo* is followed by a slow dephosphorylation in the dark period following illumination (KÜHN, 1974).

Light-induced binding of proteins to rhodopsin

Several ROS proteins that have no affinity to dark-adapted rhodopsin specifically bind to R* (Table 1). The enzyme rhodopsin-kinase and the so-called 48 kDa-protein are two proteins that are soluble in dark-adapted ROS but bind to bleached disk membranes so that they sediment with them (KÜHN, 1978). This light-induced binding is slowly reversed after illumination; it has been used to partially (up to 95 %) purify the 48 kDa-protein (KÜHN, 1978). Both rhodopsin-kinase (Mr 69 000 dalton) and 48 kDa-protein (48 000 dalton) are monomeric proteins.

The third light-dependent protein, namely GTP-binding protein (also termed transducin, G-protein, GTPase) is peripherally membrane-associated at physiological ionic strength but can be readily extracted from dark-adapted disk membranes by lowering the

Table 1: Proteins that undergo light-induced binding to the disk membrane[a]

Name (synonyme)	Native protein[b] (M_r)	Polypeptide (M_r)	Solubility at physiological ionic strength in darkness	Effects of nucleotides
rhodopsin-kinase (opsin-kinase)	69 000	68 000	mostly soluble	ATP increases solubility
48 kDA-protein	48 000	48 000	soluble	ATP and GTP strongly enhance light-induced binding
transducin (G-protein, GTP-binding protein, GTPase)	85 000	40 000 (α) 35 000 (β) 8 000 (γ)	membrane-[c] associated	GTP and analogs dissociate T_α-GTP from R* and $T_{\beta\gamma}$

[a] This table summarizes results from Kühn (1978, 1980, 1984). Either bleached, or unbleached, suspensions of ROS membranes were centrifuged. The clear supernatants were assayed: for rhodopsin kinase activity using kinase-free, illuminated rhodopsin-containing membranes as a substrate; for G-protein by measuring its R* dependent GTPase activity (Kühn, 1980); and for the presence of polypeptides using SDS-PAGE.

[b] Determined from calibrated Sephadex G100 column.

[c] Illumination at physiological ionic strength changes the mode of association of G-protein with the membrane. This is revealed by subsequently treating the illuminated membranes with low ionic strength buffer: the G-protein is readily extractable, at low ionic strength, from dark-dept but not from previously illuminated membranes (see also Fig. 1).

ionic strength below ca. 20 m0sm. Bleaching of rhodopsin changes the mode of binding of transducin so that it can no longer be extracted at low or any other ionic strength (Table 1; KÜHN, 1980). This «light-induced binding» of transducin lasts for many minutes in the absence of GTP.

GTP, and non-hydrolyzable analogs of it (GTPγS, GppNHp), rapidly solubilize transducin from bleached disk membranes. This is due to the exchange of GTP for previously bound GDP on the α-subunit of transducin (FUNG et al., 1981; FUNG, 1983). At low ionic strength, all three subunits (T_α, $T_{\beta\gamma}$) become soluble (KÜHN, 1980); at moderate ionic strength, mainly T_α becomes soluble whereas most of $T_{\beta\gamma}$ remains membrane-associated (KÜHN 1981, 1984). This indicates GTP-induced dissociation of the subunits (Fig. 1). T_α has intrinsic GTPase activity and slowly hydrolyses its bound GTP; the resulting T_α-GDP then reassociates with $T_{\beta\gamma}$ and the membranes.

Binding studies with purified transducin and purified, lipid-free rhodopsin, solubilized in detergent, have shown that transducin indeed binds to rhodopsin specifically upon illumination, and that GTP or GTPγS dissociate the complex between R* and transducin (KÜHN, 1984). This direct molecular interaction between R* and transducin appears to be the primary reaction by which photon absorption is transduced into cellular events in the rod. Binding of transducin to R* enables GDP/GTP exchange on transducin by lowering transducin's affinity for bound nucleotide by a factor of 100 (Bennett and Dupont, 1985); subsequent dissociation of T_α-GTP from the protein complex then restores the high affinity for the bound GTP on T_α.

The effect of nucleotides on the light-induced binding of 48 kDa-protein is opposite to that of transducin: both ATP and GTP (the latter only at high concentrations) *enhance* the binding (Table 1; KÜHN 1980). This effect is due to the phosphorylation of R* by rhodopsin-kinase and ATP (and, to a lesser extent, GTP). It has indeed been shown recently that 48 kDa-protein binds much better to phosphorylated than to unphosphorylated R* (KÜHN et al., 1984).

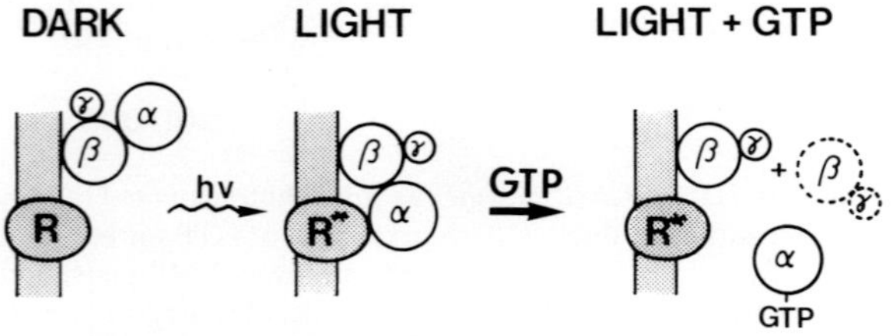

Fig. 1: Light-dependent interactions of transducin (subunits α, β, γ) with the disk membrane at physiological ionic strength. In the dark, transducin is peripherally membrane-associated. Photoactivated rhodopsin (R*) binds transducin (middle), as revealed by centrifugation experiments (Kühn, 1980) and by binding studies with purified rhodopsin in detergent solution (Kühn, 1984). GTP in presence of light (or after illumination) leads to solubilization of the α-subunit in its GTP-binding form (T_α-GTP), which then activates the PDE. Some $T_{\beta\gamma}$ is eluted together with T_α-GTP. GTP in the absence of light has no effect.

Amplified activation of transducin and phosphodiesterase by photoexcited rhodopsin

One R* molecule, during its lifetime, can sequentially interact with several hundred transducin molecules and catalyze the binding of GTP to their T_α subunits. This amplification number (100–500) has been measured by direct binding assays using radiolabeled nucleotides (FUNG and STRYER, 1980; FUNG et al., 1981), as well as by a more indirect light-scattering technique using the saturation behaviour of the «dissociation signal» (KÜHN et al., 1981; VUONG et al., 1984).

The activated subunit T_α-GTP then activates cyclic GMP-phosphodiesterase by interacting with an inhibitory subunit (13 kDa) of the PDE (HURLEY and STRYER, 1982). The affinity of T_α-GTP to the PDE inhibitory subunit seems to be relatively weak; hence, an excess of T_α-GTP is necessary to fully activate the PDE (LIEBMAN et al., 1984). An excess is provided by the natural amounts of proteins present in ROS; the molar ratios of total rhodopsin vs. transducin vs. PDE are approximately 100 : 10 : 1 (BAEHR et al., 1979; KÜHN, 1981).

The fully activated PDE has a turnover number of ca. 2000 sec^{-1} (BAEHR et al., 1979). Absorption of a single photon can, therefore, lead, via the activation of several hundred enzyme molecules, to the turnover of hundreds of thousands of cGMP molecules per second (Fig. 2). Such amplified activation of PDE has first been reported by Yee and LIEBMAN(1978).

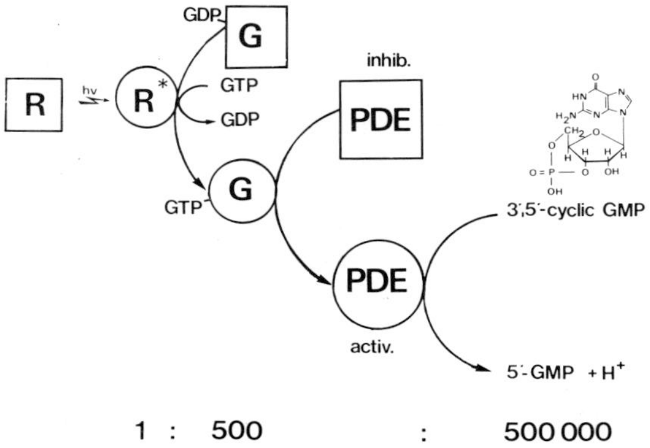

Fig. 2: Scheme of the light-activated cGMP enzyme cascade. Photoactivated rhodopsin (R*) catalyzes, by direct molecular contact with transducin (G), the exchange of GTP for bound GDP on transducin. The active (GTP-binding) form of transducin then activates the cGMP-phosphodiesterase (PDE) by releasing an inhibitory constraint from the PDE. The light signal is amplified in two stages (numbers at bottom): absorption of a single photon can lead to the activation of several hundred enzyme molecules and to the degradation of 500 000 substrate molecules per second.

Deactivation of light-activated phosphodiesterase

The rod cell responds to a light stimulus only transiently and returns to its resting state within a few seconds after a weak flash. If the light-activated PDE enzyme cascade triggers excitation of the rod cell, it should be deactivated in the same time range after a flash. Since there is no evidence of a separate mechanism directly inactivating the PDE, it is assumed that all of the active species of the enzyme cascade (Fig. 2), namely T_α-GTP and R*, must be inactivated to allow PDE deactivation.

T_α-GTP is inactivated by its intrinsic GTPase activity; after GTP hydrolysis, T_α-GDP reassociates with $T_{\beta\gamma}$ on the membrane. In order to prevent R* from further binding $T_{\alpha\beta\gamma}$-GDP and catalyzing GDP/GTP exchange, R* must also be deactivated.

The spontaneous decay of metarhodopsin II occurs in the range of minutes; accordingly, the PDE in isolated ROS suspensions remains active for minutes after flash stimulation. It has been shown, however, that deactivation of PDE can be significantly accelerated by adding ATP, and it has been proposed that ATP exerts its quenching effect *via* phosphorylation of R* (LIEBMAN and PUGH, 1980). According to this hypothesis, phosphorylated R* should no longer be capable of activating GDP/GTP exchange on G-proteins, even though it is spectrally still in the metarhodopsin II state. However, ATP is known to have many effects in the complex ROS system (e. g., HERMOLIN et al., 1982; KAPOOR and CHADER, 1984), so that it is difficult to localize the quenching effect of ATP as being in fact due to phosphorylation of R*.

In order to exclude other reactions of ATP, we have recently investigated the effect of rhodopsin phosphorylation on its capacity to activate PDE by using an ATP-free reconstituted system, consisting of thoroughly washed disk membranes whose rhodopsin had been *previously phosphorylated* and then regenerated will 11-cis retinal. Purified transducin and PDE were added, and PDE activity was measured upon flash illumination of the phosphorylated rhodopsin (WILDEN et al., 1986).

We find that phosphorylated R* is still able to activate tranducin and PDE, although at a reduced rate as compared to unphosphorylated rhodopsin. However, if purified 48 kDa-protein is added to the phosphorylated membranes, it strongly suppresses their light-induced enzyme activating capacity (Fig. 3). The combined effects of rhodopsin phos-

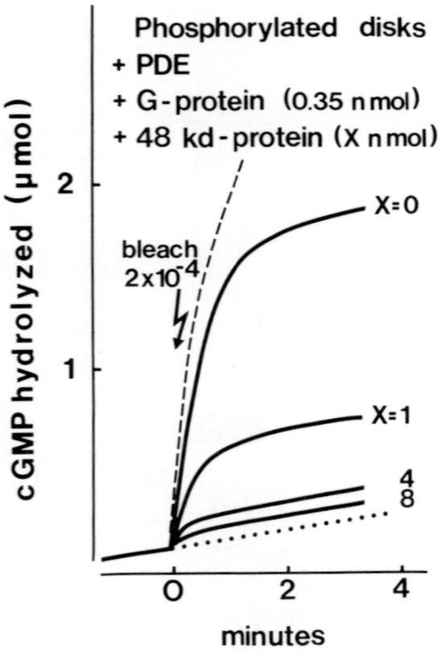

Fig. 3: Suppression by 48 kDa-protein of the PDE-activating capacity of phosphorylated R*. Purified PDE and transducin (G-protein) were reassociated to previously phosphorylated and regenerated disk membranes (solid lines; 5.5 phosphates/average rhodopsin) or, for comparison, to unphosphorylated control membranes (dashed line). Samples contained 3.5 μM rhodopsin, 0.23 μM transducin, 0.012 μM PDE, 100 μM GTP, 2 mM cGMP, and various amounts of 48 kDa-protein as indicated, in a final volume of 1.5 ml. Each reaction was started by a flash bleaching 2×10^{-4} fraction of the rhodopsin. PDE activity was monitored by the H^+ release accompanying cGMP hydrolysis (pH 7.9). The dotted line is an extrapolation of the dark activity. (Courtesy of Dr. U. WILDEN).

phorylation and 48 kDa-protein addition can suppress PDE activation by 98 % (WILDEN et al., 1986). In contrast, 48 kDa-protein added to unphosphorylated control membranes has little effect on their PDE activating capacity. Addition of ATP has little further effect, provided the reassociated preparations are devoid of rhodopsin-kinase activity.

This demonstrates that phosphorylation of R* is a prerequisite, but that yet another factor, the 48 kDa-protein, is required to effectively quench R*'s enzyme activating capacity. It has recently been shown (KÜHN et al., 1984) that 48 kDa-protein binds specifically to phosphorylated R* and thereby competes with transducin for binding. The simplest mechanism to explain the quenching effect of 48 kDa-protein would, therefore, be that 48 kDa-protein binds to the phosphorylated R* and sterically inhibits the capacity of R* to interact with transducin and catalyze GTP binding to transducin.

The 48 kDa-protein is the most abundant soluble protein of ROS; its concentration *in vivo* may approach that of transducin (see PFISTER et al., 1985; DOREY et al., 1982). In Fig. 3, a relatively large excess of 48 kDa-protein over transducin appears to be required to effectively quench PDE activation. This is probably due to the strong (ca. 1000 fold) dilution of the system as compared to the living cell. The soluble 48 kDa-protein, but not the membrane-associated transducin, thereby becomes diluted with regard to rhodopsin. *In vivo*, where both 48 kDa-protein and transducin are present in similarly high concentrations, the competition situation should be much more in favor of the 48 kDa-protein.

Figure 4 schematically summarizes the protein–protein interactions that lead first to

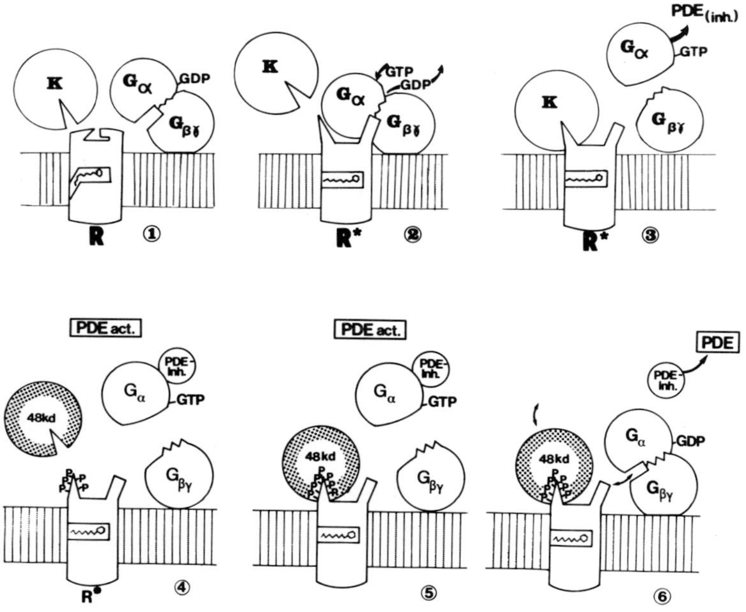

Fig. 4: Scheme of protein–protein interactions at six consecutive stages (numbered 1–6), leading first to light-induced activation and then to deactivation of the PDE enzyme cascade. R, dark-adapted rhodopsin; R*, photoexcited rhodopsin; K, rhodopsin kinase; G_α, $G_{\beta\gamma}$, transducin. For details see text.

activation and later to deactivation of PDE. Photoexcited rhodopsin (R*) exhibits two sites of interaction, one for transducin and one for rhodopsin kinase. Binding of transducin to R* (state 2 in Fig. 4) enables the exchange of GTP for GDP on the T_α subunit, followed by dissociation of T_α-GTP from $T_{\beta\gamma}$ and from R* (state 3). T_α-GTP activates the PDE by binding an inhibitory subunit of the PDE (state 4). One R* can sequentially interact with hundreds of transducin molecules and catalyze their GDP/GTP exchange. The complex R*–$T_{\alpha\beta\gamma}$–GDP (state 2) can be artificially stabilized by omitting GTP from the buffer; under this condition, access of the kinase to R* is sterically blocked (Kühn, 1984). Normally, i. e., in the presence of GTP, the lifetime of the complex R*–$T_{\alpha\beta\gamma}$ is less than a millisecond (Vuong et al., 1984); during the rapid cycles of transducin binding and dissociation, R* is «free» for short periods of time to bind the kinase which then incorporates phosphate groups into R* (states 3 and 4). Since the rod cell contains much more transducin than rhodopsin-kinase (about 100 times more), phosphorylation of R* will lag somewhat behind transducin activation. Phosphorylated R* then is less capable – and when it binds 48 kDa-protein even much less capable – of activating transducin (states 5 and 6). The deactivation of R* by phosphorylation and 48 kDa-protein binding is paralleled by the deactivation of T_α-GTP via GTP hydrolysis and reassociation of T_α-GDP to $T_{\beta\gamma}$ (stage 6). The original dark-adapted state is restored only after subsequent dephosphorylation of opsin, and after regeneration of its chromophore 11-cis retinal (not shown). – It should be mentioned that this scheme still bears some unsolved problems; for instance, measurements of the apparent GTPase activity of transducin suggest a lifetime of ca. 30 sec for the active form T_α-GTP which would be too long for the observed rapid quench of PDE activity; and the rate of R* phosphorylation at low bleaching levels is still controversial (Sitaramayya and Liebman, 1983; Hermolin et al., 1982).

Conclusion

The only function of photo-excited rhodopsin which has been firmly identified is its catalytic (amplifying) role in activating the enzyme cascade that degrades cGMP. It has recently been shown (Fesenko et al., 1985) that cGMP directly enhances the ion permeability of the ROS plasma membrane. Light-triggered hydrolysis of cGMP therefore should lead to closure of the ion channels, thus providing a direct link between photon absorption and the electrophysiological response of the cell. Some of the most prominent proteins are involved in the control of cGMP levels: transducin mediating the activation of PDE by R*, and rhodopsin-kinase together with 48 kDa-protein mediating, with a certain time delay, the deactivation of the system. The activity of the cyclase which synthesizes cGMP seems to be coupled, by an unknown mechanism, to PDE activity, providing an additional control system (Goldberg et al., 1983). In total, however, the biochemistry of vision is certainly more complex than it may look from the simplified schemes given in this review.

Acknowledgements

I thank all my coworkers who have contributed to these results, in particular Dr. U. Wilden and S. W. Hall. I thank E. Wüst and R. Esser for technical assistance, and A. Eckert for typing the manuscript. Part of the work was supported by a grant from SFB 160, Deutsche Forschungsgemeinschaft.

References

Baehr, W., Devlin, M. J., Applebury, M. L.: Isolation and characterization of cGMP phosphodiesterase from bovine rod outer segments. J. Biol. Chem. **254:** 11669–11677. (1979)

Bennett, N., Dupont, Y.: The G-protein of retinal rod outer segments (transducin). Mechanism of interaction with rhodopsin and nucleotides. J. Biol. Chem. **260:** 4156–4168. (1985)

Bownds, D., Dawes, J., Miller, J., Stahlman, M.: Phosphorylation of frog photoreceptor membranes induced by light. Nature **237:** 125–127. (1972)

Dorey, C., Cozette, J., Faure, J. P.: A simple and rapid method for isolation of retinal S-antigen. Ophthalmic Res. **14:** 249–255. (1982)

Fesenko, E. E., Kolesnikov, S. S., Lyubarsky, A. L.: Induction by cyclic GMP of cationic conductance in plasma membrane of retinal rod outer segment. Nature **313:** 310–313. (1985)

Fung, B. K. K.: Characterization of transducin from bovine retinal rod outer segments. Separation and reconstitution of the subunits. J. Biol. Chem. **258:** 10 495–10502. (1983)

Fung, B. K. K., Stryer, L.: Photolyzed rhodopsin catalyzes the exchange of GTP for bound GDP in retinal rod outer segments. Proc. Natl. Acad. Sci. USA **77:** 2500–2504. (1980)

Fung, B. K. K., Hurley, J. B., Stryer, L.: Flow of information in the light-triggered cyclic nucleotide cascade of vision. Proc. Natl. Acad. Sci. USA **78:**152–156. (1981)

Goldberg, N. D., Ames, A., Gander, J. E., Walseth, T. F.: Magnitude of increase in retinal cGMP metabolic flux determined by $^{18}0$ incorporation into nucleotide α-phosphoryls corresponds with intensity of photic stimulation. J. Biol. Chem. **258:** 9213–9219. (1983)

Hermolin, J., Karell, M. A., Hamm, H. E., Bownds, M. D.: Calcium and cyclic GMP regulation of light-sensitive protein phosphorylation in frog photoreceptor membranes. J. Gen. Physiol. **79:** 633–655. (1982)

Hurley, J. B., Stryer, L.: Purification and characterization of the regulatory subunit of the cyclic GMP phosphodiesterase from retinal rod outer segments. J. Biol. Chem. **257:** 11094–11099. (1982)

Kapoor, C. L., Chader, G. J.: Endogenous phosphorylation of retinal photoreceptor outer segment proteins by calcium phospholipid-dependent protein kinase. Biochem. Biophys. Res. Commun. **122:** 1397–1403. (1984)

Kühn, H.: Light-dependent phosphorylation of rhodopsin in living frogs. Nature **250:** 588–590. (1974)

Kühn, H.: Light-regulated binding of rhodopsin kinase and other proteins to cattle photoreceptor membranes. Biochemistry **17:** 4389–4395. (1978)

Kühn, H.: Light- and GTP-regulated interaction of GTPase and other proteins with bovine photoreceptor membranes. Nature **283:** 587–589. (1980)

Kühn, H.: Interactions of rod cell proteins with the disk membrane: Influence of light, ionic strength, and nucleotides. In: Current Topics in Membranes and Transport (W. H. Miller ed.) **15:** 171–201. (1981)

Kühn, H.: Interactions between photoexcited rhodopsin and light-activated enzymes in rods. Progr. Retinal Res. (eds. Osborne, N. N., Chader, G. J., Pergamon Press) **3:** 123–156. (1984)

Kühn, H., Dreyer, W. J.: Light-dependent phosphorylation of rhodopsin by ATP. FEBS Lett. **20:** 1–6. (1972)

Kühn, H., Bennett, N., Michel-Villaz, M., Chabre, M.: Interactions between photoexcited rhodopsin and GTP-binding protein: kinetic and stoichiometric analysis from light-scattering changes. Proc. Natl. Acad. Sci. USA **18:** 6873–6877. (1981)

Kühn, H., Mommertz, O., Hargrave, P. A.: Light-dependent conformational change at rhodopsin's cytoplasmic surface detected by increased susceptibility to proteolysis. Biochim. Biophys. Acta **679:** 95–100. (1982)

Kühn, H., Hall, S. W., Wilden, U.: Light-induced binding of 48 kDa-protein to photoreceptor membranes is enhanced by phosphorylation of rhodopsin. FEBS Lett. **176:** 473–478. (1984)

Liebman, P. A., Pugh, E. N.: ATP mediates rapid reversal of cyclic GMP phosphodiesterase activation in visual receptor membranes. Nature **287:** 734–736. (1980)

Liebman, P. A., Sitaramayya, A., Parkes, J. H., Buzdygon, B.: Mechanism of cGMP control in retinal rod outer segments. TIPS **1984,** 293–296. (1984)

Pfister, C., Chabre, M., Plouet, J., Tuyen, V. V., DeKozak, Y., Faure, J. P., Kühn, H.: Retinal S-antigen identified as the 48 K protein regulating light-dependent phosphodiesterase in rods. Science **228:** 891–893. (1985)
Sitaramayya, A., Liebman, P. A.: Phosphorylation of rhodopsin and quenching of cyclic GMP phosphodiesterase activation by ATP at weak bleaches. J. Biol. Chem. **258:** 12 106–12 109. (1983)
Vuong, T. M., Chabre, M., Stryer, L.: Millisecond activation of transducin in the cyclic nucleotide cascade of vision. Nature **311:** 659–661. (1984)
Wilden, U., Kühn, H.: Light-dependent phosphorylation of rhodopsin: Number of phosphorylation sites. Biochemistry **21:** 3014–3022. (1982)
Wilden, U., Hall, S. W., Kühn, H.: Phosphodiesterase activation by photoexcited rhodopsin is quenched when rhodopsin is phosphorylated and binds 48 kDa-protein. Proc. Natl. Acad. Sci. USA **83:** 1174–1178. (1986)
Yee, R., Liebman, P. A.: Light-activated phosphodiesterase of the rod outer segment. Kinetics and parameters of activation and deactivation. J. Biol. Chem. **253:** 8902–8909. (1978)

Fortschritte der Zoologie, Band 33 · Lüttgau (Hrsg.): Membrane Control
Gustav Fischer Verlag · Stuttgart · New York · 1986

Light-modulated biochemical events in fly photoreceptors

REINHARD PAULSEN and JOACHIM BENTROP

Fakultät für Biologie, Ruhr-Universität Bochum, FRG

In the ciliary photoreceptors of the vertebrate retina, a cascade of enzyme reactions mediates between the primary event, which is the isomerization of the chromophore of rhodopsin by light, and the final event, which is the closing of sodium channels in the photoreceptor's plasma membrane. An important step in this cascade is the interaction of photoactivated rhodopsin with transducin, a particular type of G-protein composed of three subunits (T_α, T_β, T_γ). As a result of this interaction GDP, bound to T_α, is exchanged for GTP. T_α-GTP can then activate a phosphodiesterase which rapidly hydrolyses cyclic GMP. Return of transducin into an inactive state is provided by the intrinsic GTPase activity of T_α (for refs. see STRYER et al., 1981; BOWNDS, 1981; CHABRE, 1985; CHABRE and APPLEBURY, 1986; KÜHN, this volume). Recent electrophysiological findings indicate the possibility that a decrease in the level of cyclic GMP, caused by the light activation of the enzyme cascade, is directly responsible for the closure of sodium channels (FESENKO et al., 1985; YAU and NAKATANI, 1985; YAU et al., this volume).

With the recent progress in the understanding of the phototransduction mechanism of vertebrate photoreceptors, a most interesting problem with evolutionary implications, is the extent to which the photoreceptors of different species share the same biochemical steps of signal transduction and amplification. At the present the mechanism underlying phototransduction in invertebrates is not as adequately understood as it is in the vertebrates. At first sight, certain known differences would suggest dissimilarities in the sequence of reactions mediating between the event of photon absorption and the ensuing generation of a photoreceptor potential in vertebrates and invertebrates. One such difference is that rhodopsin of invertebrates is located in a microvillar photoreceptor membrane. The microvilli possess an ordered substructure and contain elements of a cytoskeleton (SAIBIL, 1982; BLEST et al., 1982). In the microvillar membrane the mobility of rhodopsin seems to be restricted, compared to the high rotational and translational mobility of rhodopsin in the disc membrane of vertebrate rods (GOLDSMITH and WEHNER, 1977; PAULSEN et al., 1983). Another difference lies in the fact that invertebrate rhodopsin is converted by light into a metarhodopsin which is thermally stable, i. e., it does not decay into opsin and retinal, as does vertebrate metarhodopsin. Finally, most invertebrate photoreceptors generate a depolarizing receptor potential while vertebrate photoreceptors hyperpolarize in response to light (for reviews see HAMDORF, 1979; HILLMAN et al., 1983; STIEVE, 1985).

However, early results from cephalopod photoreceptors indicate a transduction mechanism showing similarities to the transducin-phosphodiesterase cascade in vertebrate photoreceptors: squid photoreceptor membranes exhibit light-induced GTPase activity and contain a GTP-binding protein having a sequence partially homologous to the T_α subunit of vertebrate transducin (CALHOON et al., 1980; VANDENBERG and MONTAL, 1984a; SAIBIL and MICHEL-VILLAZ, 1984). Squid rhodopsin and GTP-binding protein also crossreact with vertebrate photoreceptor enzymes (SAIBIL and MICHEL-VILLAZ, 1984). Furthermore, agents known to activate hormone-regulated adenylate cyclase systems (e.g., fluoride, vanadate and certain non-hydrolyzable GTP analogues) produce an excitation when injected into *Limulus* ventral photoreceptors (FEIN and CORSON, 1979; BOLSOVER and BROWN, 1980; 1981; 1982; CORSON et al., 1983) or when otherwise applied to insect photoreceptors (PAYNE, 1982; MINKE and STEPHENSON, 1985). Thus, it has been suggested that the chemically induced excitation may arise from activation of a cyclase system, or at least of a GTP-binding regulatory protein (CORSON and FEIN, 1983). Evidence supporting the role of cyclic GMP in invertebrate phototransduction comes from experiments showing that, in the isolated photoreceptor membranes of the squid, light stimulates the formation of cyclic GMP from GTP (SAIBIL, 1984), and that pressure injections of cyclic GMP into the transduction region of a *Limulus* ventral nerve photoreceptor mimics in some way a light-triggered response (LISMAN, personal communication).

To test the hypothesis that phototransduction in vertebrates and invertebrates is based on a similar signal-amplifying cascade we have performed experiments to identify enzymes and regulatory components of such a cascade in fly photoreceptors. Flies provide a particularly favourable photoreceptor system for studying the molecular basis of phototransduction, mainly because the process can here be probed using mutants which are defective in some aspects of the transduction mechanism. A recent highlight in this respect is the isolation of the gene which in *Drosophila* encodes the opsin of photoreceptors R1–6 (O'TOUSA et al., 1985; ZUKER et al., 1985). One outstanding property of the visual pigment system of fly photoreceptors R1–6 is that light absorption by rhodopsin (P) produces a long-lived metarhodopsin (M) which, due to its absorbance properties, can be reconverted rapidly and completely into rhodopsin by irradiation with red light (HAMDORF et al., 1973; STAVENGA et al., 1973; OSTROY et al., 1974). The particular properties of the visual pigment system of fly photoreceptors allow not only the study of the triggering of enzyme reactions by conversion of rhodopsin into metarhodopsin (P → M), but also to investigate whether the reverse step, i.e. M → P conversion, inhibits or even triggers any enzyme reactions.

Methods

Isolation of photoreceptor membranes

Rhabdomeric membranes were isolated from blowfly retinae (males of *Calliphora erythrocephala*, chalky mutant) under red light, so as to maximize the visual pigment in the rhodopsin state, as described in detail by PAULSEN (1984). A critical step in this isolation procedure is the flotation of rhabdoms on Percoll which has to be carried out in hypoosmotic buffers. As this may lead to a loss of peripheral proteins of the microvillar membrane, we have also carried out experiments using homogenates of whole retinae, or have recombined extracts containing soluble proteins and samples of isolated rhabdoms. In some cases control experiments were carried out using isolated frog rod outer segments (ROS). Purification of ROS was performed by isopycnic centrifugation on Percoll (45 % v/v) in a Hepes-buffered salt solution containing 115 mM NaCl, 2 mM KCl, 2 mM $MgCl_2$, 10 mM Hepes, pH 7.0.

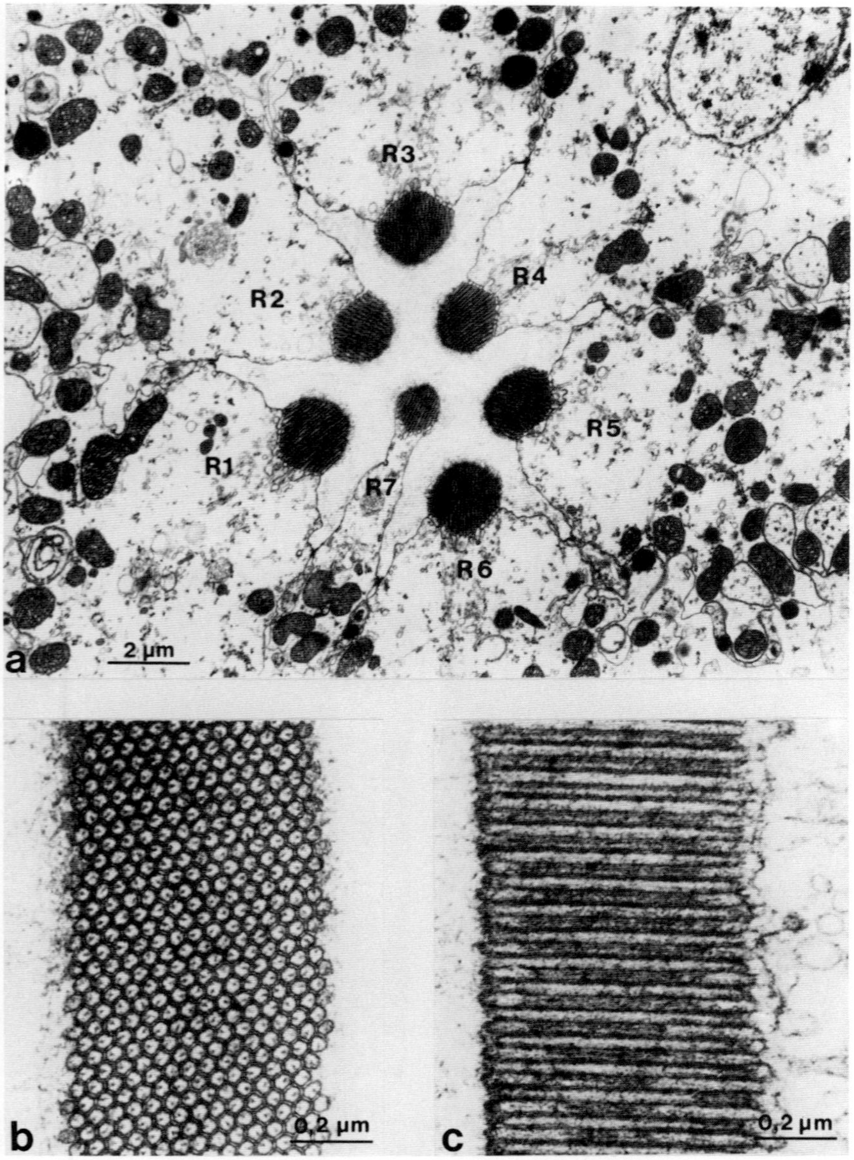

Fig. 1: Blowfly photoreceptor membrane structure. a. Transverse section through an ommatidium to show the typical pattern of seven rhabdomeres formed by six outer photoreceptors (R1–6) and two central photoreceptors (R7 and R8, of which in the distal region of the ommatidium the former is seen). In the «open» rhabdom of muscoid flies, the rhabdomeres are separated by a wide intraommatidial space which contains an interphotoreceptor matrix. b. Transverse section and c. longitudinal section through the microvilli of a rhabdomere. The microvillar structure is stabilized by a cytoskeleton consisting of an axial filament that is linked by side-arms (seen in b as structures with alternating orientation within the microvillar lumen) to the microvillar membrane. Photographs by K. Peters.

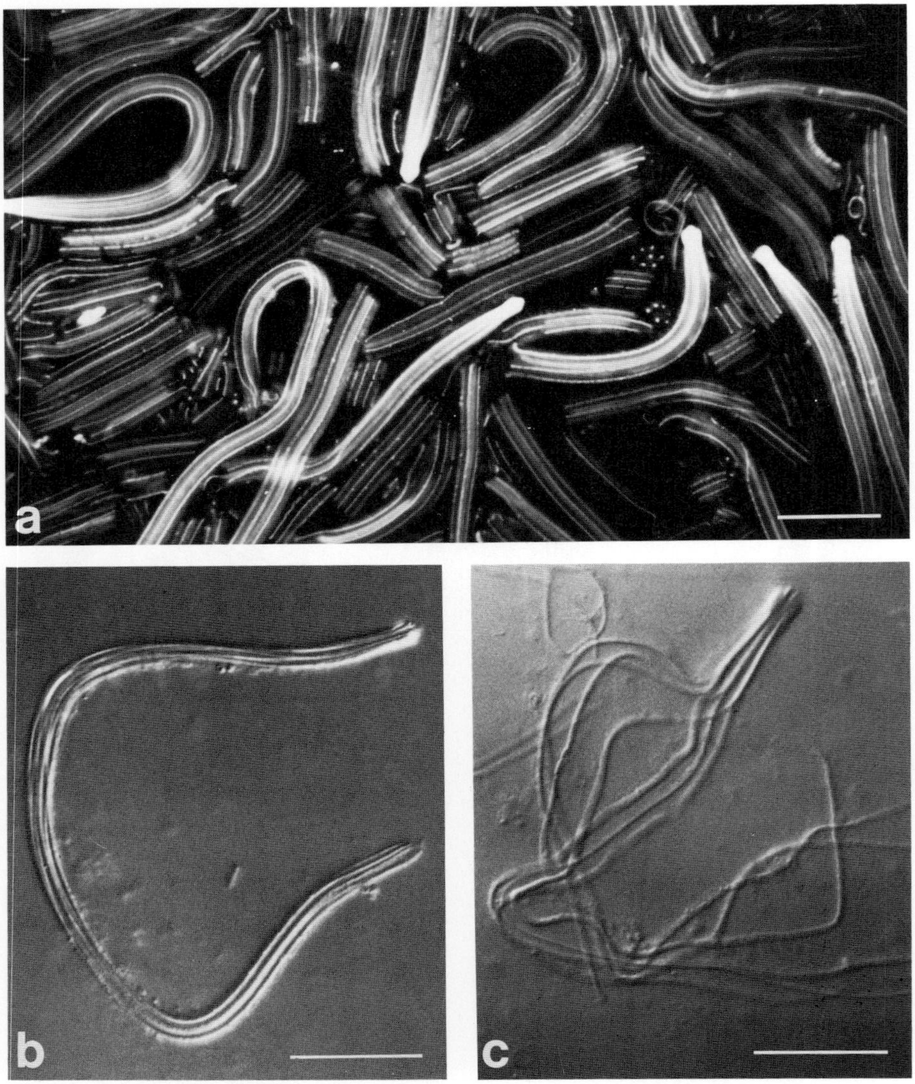

Fig. 2: «Open» rhabdoms isolated from a blowfly ommatidium by flotation on Percoll. a. Suspension of isolated rhabdoms after labeling rhabdomeres with FITC-Con A. Rhabdoms were incubated for 5 min with FITC-Con A (0,5 μg/ml) in lectin-buffer (140 mM NaCl, 1 mM $CaCl_2$, 1 mM $MnCl_2$, 0.05 M Tris/HCl, pH 7.5), washed several times with lectin-buffer, mounted on a slide, and photographed with a Zeiss microscope equipped for epifluorescence with a FITC filter combination. Scale bar, 25 μm. b. Single isolated rhabdom in Hepes-buffered salt solution, pH 6.8 containing 2 mM $CaCl_2$. c. Same rhabdom as in b. after incubation in Hepes buffer containing 5 mM EGTA. The rhabdom structure is distorted due to the dissociation of the interphotoreceptor matrix at low calcium levels. Nomarski differential interference microscopy. Scale bar 25, μm.

Electrophoresis

Sodium dodecylsulphate-polyacrylamide gel electrophoresis (SDS-PAGE) was carried out with the Laemmli buffer system (LAEMMLI, 1970) either on gradient slab gels with 8 to 12 % acrylamide in the separation gel and 4 % acrylamide in the stacking gel, or on gels containing 14 % acrylamide in the separation gel. Gels were stained with coomassie or with silver nitrate according to OAKLEY et al. (1980). Lectin-binding proteins were identified by the peroxidase reaction (HAWKES, 1982) after the proteins were electroblotted onto nitrocellulose paper.

GTPase assay and toxin catalyzed ADP-ribosylation

GTP hydrolytic activity in isolated rhabdoms was measured as the amount of ^{32}P-orthophosphate released from (γ-^{32}P)GTP as described by BAEHR et al. (1982), for determining the GTPase activity of transducin. ADP-ribosylation of proteins was carried out according to the method of ABOOD et al. (1982). The bacterial toxins used to catalyze ADP-ribosylation were cholera toxin (Calbiochem) and pertussis toxin (a gift of Prof. RELYVELD, Institute Pasteur, Paris).

Protein phosphorylation

Light-induced phosphorylation of proteins was performed in a Hepes-buffered salt solution (see above) containing 5 mM (γ-^{32}P)ATP. If not otherwise indicated the reaction was quenched by adding 20 % trichloroacetic acid. The precipitated protein was collected by centrifugation. The pellet was washed twice with 0.01 M Tris/HCl pH 8.0 containing 1 mM EDTA, solubilized in an extraction medium containing 5 % SDS and subjected to SDS-PAGE. The gels were dried onto filter paper and assayed for ^{32}P-incorporation into proteins by autoradiography. For a quantitative determination of phosphate incorporation, protein bands were cut from the gel and the radioactivity of each band was measured by scintillation counting.

Results

1. Protein pattern and spectral properties of isolated rhabdoms

Transverse sections through blowfly retinulae show a typical pattern of seven rhabdomeres. The central rhabdomere is either that of photoreceptor 8 or, as in Fig. 1 a, that of photoreceptor 7 (R7) which lies on top of the rhabdomere formed by photoreceptor 8. The individual rhabdomeres consist of an array of densely packed microvilli (Fig. 1 b and c). Each microvillus contains a cytoskeleton that stabilizes its structure (BLEST et al., 1982). The large extracellular (intraommatidial) space between the rhabdomeres is filled with a matrix. The rhabom, consisting of the eight rhabdomeres and the interphotoreceptor matrix, can be isolated as a whole (PAULSEN, 1984) and has served as the main preparation in the present study.

The protein pattern of isolated rhabdomeres is considerably more complex than that of vertebrate rod outer segments, most likely due to the presence of the interphotoreceptor matrix and components of the microvillar cytoskeleton. Fig. 2 shows a suspension of

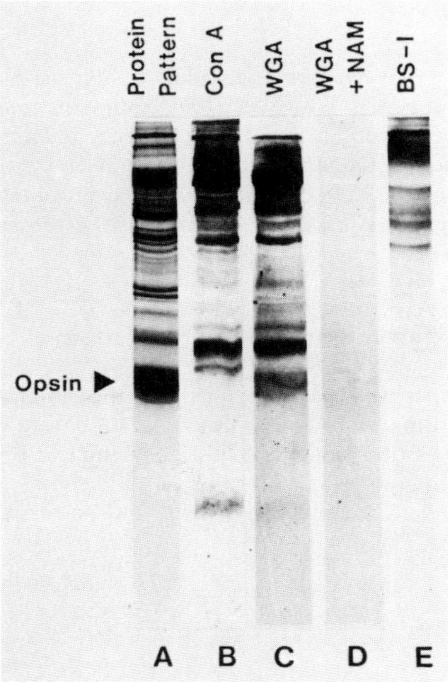

Fig. 3: Electrophoretic pattern and lectin binding properties of proteins extracted from isolated blowfly rhabdoms. Rhabdoms isolated from 500 retinae were extracted first with 5 mM EGTA in Tris/HCl, pH 7.4, to dissociate the interphotoreceptor matrix and to remove soluble proteins from the microvillar membrane. The remaining insoluble material was extracted with 4% digitonin in 0.05 mM phosphate buffer, pH 6.0, to solubilize intrinsic membrane proteins and to enable measurement of the rhodopsin content of the sample. Proteins were separated by SDS-PAGE on (14% acrylamide) slab gels and blotted onto nitrocellulose paper. Blots were prepared for HRP-lectin bindig, using haemoglobin to block non-specific binding sites and 0.5 μg HRP-lectin in 10 ml lectin buffer for labeling glycoproteids. HRP-lectin binding was performed in a buffer containing 50 mM Tris/HCl, pH 7.5, 140 mM NaCl, 2 mM $MnCl_2$, 1 mM $CaCl_2$ and was detected with 4-chloronaphthol in 0.01% H_2O_2.
(A) coomassie stained protein pattern of a digitonin extract containing 10 μg rhodopsin. (B–E) binding of HRP-lectins; (B) HRP-Con A; (C) HRP-WGA; (D) HRP-WGA in the presence of 0.1 M N-acetyl-D-glucosamine (control); (E) HRP-BS-I. Controls for the specifity of Con A and BS-I binding (not shown) were prepared with the appropriate monosaccharides and showed no residual binding. Fly opsin has an affinity for WGA (track C).

isolated rhabdoms after incubation with FITC-labeled concanavalin A (Con A). In particular, the rhabdomeres show a high affinity for Con A, indicating that glycoproteins are present in rhabdomeric membranes. In order to investigate whether opsin, the main membrane protein, is similar to the vertebrate opsin, which is a Con A-binding glycoprotein, binding studies were carried out with lectins of different specificity.

These binding studies revealed a pattern of complex glycoproteins which were extracted, together with rhodopsin, by digitonin. As shown in a more detailed study on glycoproteins of crayfish photoreceptors by de COUET (1984), the opsin band is not

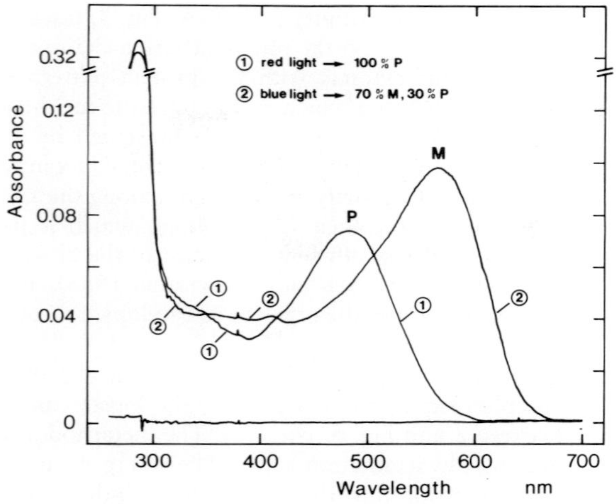

Fig. 4: Absorbance spectrum of visual pigment from blowfly photoreceptors R1–6. Rhabdoms were isolated from 100 blowfly retinae by flotation on Percoll. Components of the interphotoreceptor matrix and soluble proteins were removed by extraction with 2 mM EGTA in 0.05 mM phosphate buffer, pH 6.0. Rhodopsin was extracted with 40 μl of 2% digitonin in 0.05 M phosphate buffer, pH 6.0. Curve 1: absorbance spectrum of the extract from rhabdomeric membranes exposed only to red light. Curve 2: absorbance spectrum of the extract after converting about 70% of rhodopsin into metarhodopsin by irradiation with monochromatic blue light (344 nm) for 30 s, at 8 °C.

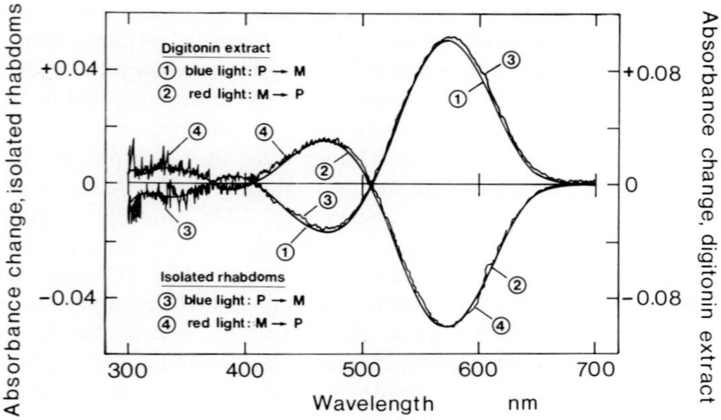

Fig. 5: Difference spectra, recorded to demonstrate the formation of metarhodopsin (M) and its photoreconversion into rhodopsin (P) in a digitonin extract (spectra 1 and 2) and in a suspension of isolated rhabdoms (spectra 3 and 4). Difference spectra were recorded at pH 6.0 and 8 °C. Spectra 1 and 3: 30 s irradiation with blue light (BG 12), to convert P into M. Spectra 2 and 4: 30 s irradiation with red light (RG 644) to convert M into P.

labeled by Con A. It has, however, an affinity for WGA (Fig. 3, track 3) which suggests that N-acetyl-D-glucosamine is present in the oligosaccharide chain(s) of fly opsin.

Spectrophotometry of digitonin extracts with the protein pattern shown in Fig. 3, track 1, yielded an absorbance spectrum which is characteristic for the visual pigment of photoreceptors R1–6 (Fig. 4). According to evidence presented by Vogt (1983), the chromophore of the visual pigment consists of 3-hydroxyretinal, a xanthophyllderivative, and the suggestion has been made to classify this pigment among the xanthopsins (Vogt, 1983;Vogt and Kirschfeld, 1984). Since 11-cis retinal, which is derived from β,β-carotene, has been shown to be a very efficient precursor in the biosynthesis of blowfly visual pigment (Schwemer, 1983; Paulsen and Schwemer, 1983), and to facilitate the discussion, we shall continue to refer to the pigment as rhodopsin throughout the present study.

As shown previously (Hamdorf et al., 1973; Stavenga et al., 1973), irradiation of rhodopsin produces a photoequilibrium between rhodopsin and a thermostable metarhodopsin (Fig. 4, curve 2 and Fig. 5, curve 1). The metarhodopsin can be rapidly photoconverted into rhodopsin by irradiation with red light (Fig. 4, curve 2). Formation of metarhodopsin and its reconversion into rhodopsin can be induced in the same way in isolated rhabdoms (Fig. 5, curve 3 and 4).

2. Evidence for conformational changes in the structure of fly opsin

The mechanism of the light-triggering of the enzyme cascade in vertebrate photoreceptors, as it is understood presently (see Kühn, 1984), illustrates that changes in the structure of opsin at its cytoplasmic surface are an essential prerequisite for the activation of the cascade. One enzyme known to recognize such alterations at the opsin's surface is rhodopsin kinase (Kühn et al., 1973; Miller and Paulsen, 1975; Weller et al., 1975). Thus, light-induced phosphorylation of opsin, observed in cephalopods (Paulsen and Hoppe, 1978; Yoshioka et al., 1981; Vandenberg and Montal, 1984 b) and in flies (Paulsen and Bentrop, 1984; Nichols and Pak, 1985), points to the occurrence of similar changes in the surface structure of invertebrate opsins. Phosphorylation experiments such as shown in Fig. 6, which have been carried out by adding an extract containing soluble proteins from the blowfly retina to a suspension of isolated rhabdoms, indicate that the phosphorylation of blowfly opsin is the result of P → M conversion and is catalyzed by a buffer-soluble kinase. By calculating the number of phosphates bound per mole of metarhodopsin formed, we obtained a maximum value of 4 phosphates (4.03 ± 0.33). Accordingly, fly opsin, like vertebrate and cephalopod opsin (Miller et al., 1977; McDowell and Kühn, 1977; Paulsen and Hoppe, 1978), possesses multiple binding sites for phosphate groups, which become exposed in the metarhodopsin state. The model for the structure of *Drosophila* opsin, as recently proposed by O'Tousa et al. (1985), shows six potential binding sites for phosphate groups to be located near the C-terminus of the opsin molecule (Fig. 7). As in the case of bovine opsin, where it has been shown that under particular conditions seven binding sites near the C-terminal end can be phosphorylated (Wilden and Kühn, 1982), it may be possible to label, under certain conditions, more than four binding sites on fly opsin.

A particularly remarkable result is that M → P conversion initiates the dephosphorylation of opsin. This has already been demonstrated in the isolated retina (Paulsen and Bentrop, 1984) and is confirmed now by the experiments using isolated rhabdoms and a retina extract with soluble proteins to catalyze the dephosphorylation reaction (Fig. 6). This indicates that the conversion of multi-phosphorylated metarhodopsin (M–Pn) into

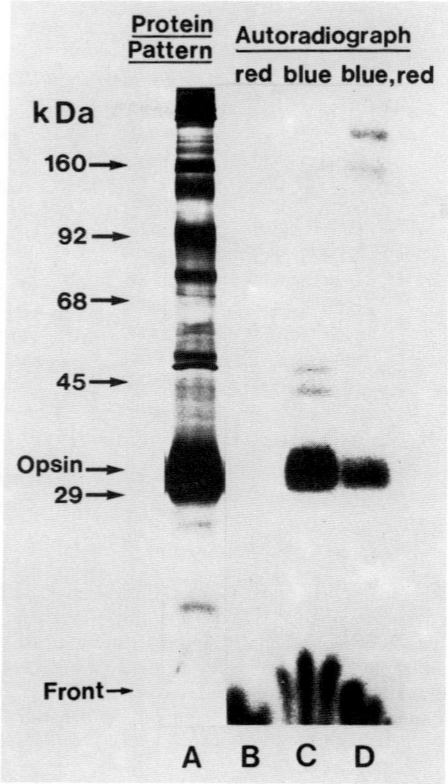

Fig. 6: Light-modulated phosphorylation and dephosphorylation of blowfly opsin in isolated rhabdoms. Rhabdoms were recombined with a soluble extract prepared from a retina homogenate and incubated at 25 °C in a Hepes-buffered salt solution, pH 6.8 containing 5 mM (γ-^{32}P)ATP (3–8 μCi/assay), 1 mM oubain, 5 μM $NaVO_3$. At the end of the incubation period, rhabdoms were washed with ice-cold buffer solution and extracted with 2% digitonin, 0.05 mM Tris/HCl, pH 6.8. The digitonin extract was then subjected to SDS-PAGE. (A) silver stained protein pattern of washed rhabdoms; (B–D) autoradiographs. (B) dark control: ^{32}P-labeling after incubating rhabdoms for 2 min in red light and for 13 min in the dark; (C) light sample: ^{32}P-labeling after incubating rhabdoms for 2 min in blue light and for 13 min in the dark; (D) effect of M→P conversion: rhabdoms were first incubated as in (C), the sample was then irradiated for 2 min with red light and kept in the dark for another 13 min. The autoradiographs show that irradiation with blue light (P→M) initiates opsin phosphorylation. Photoregeneration (M → P) by red light triggers the dephosphorylation of opsin.

multi-phosphorylated rhodopsin (P–Pn) does not only restore the conformation of the opsin pocket surrounding the chromophore, but also induces changes in the conformation of the protein on the cytoplasmic surface. As a result of these changes, rhodopsin can be returned to its non-phosphorylated state, most likely by a protein phosphatase.

3. Evidence for a G-protein in blowfly rhabdoms

If transduction in rhabdomeric photoreceptors is mediated by an enzyme cascade, the enzymes involved might be activated by a G-protein, as has been demonstrated for the

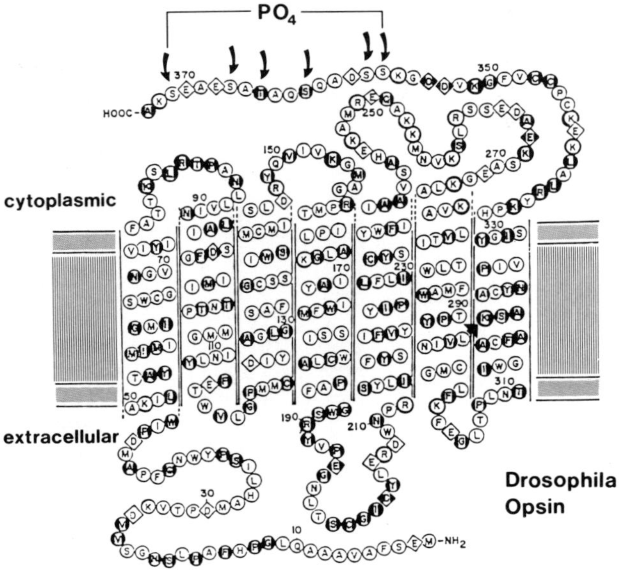

Fig. 7: Predicted structure of *Drosophila* opsin (after O'TOUSA et al., 1985). The opsin has been proposed to contain seven trans-membrane helices. The single arrow at position 319 marks the proposed binding site for 11-cis 3-hydroxyretinal. Curved arrows indicate potential phosphorylation sites located near the C-terminal end. Binding sites for a carbohydrate side chain, which may contain N-acetyl-glucosamine (see Fig. 3), have not yet been identified. Shaded symbols mark positions which are common to *Drosophila* and mammalian opsin (courtesy W. BAEHR).

transducin-activated cGMP-phosphodiesterase of vertebrate photoreceptors. G-proteins may be detected by their intrinsic GTPase activity which is required for their return into an inactive form. Most recent investigations by BLUMENFELD et al. (1985) demonstrate that light activates a GTPase activity in membranes of *Musca* eyes. This GTPase activity can be suppressed to the dark level by photoconverting M to P, however, only if the GTP hydrolysis is measured at 4 °C. We have used isolated rhabdoms to investigate whether a GTPase is associated with the microvillar membrane of the blowfly photoreceptor. In Fig. 8 it is shown that P → M conversion activates a GTP hydrolytic activity in the microvillar photoreceptor membrane. This light effect is observed at low GTP levels (10–50 μM) and is partially reversed by red light (Fig. 8, □). Fig. 8 also reveals that isolated rhabdoms exhibit a high background of a GTP hydrolytic activity which is not light-dependent. GTP hydrolysis in the dark is reduced in the presence of 2 mM ATP and ATPase inhibitors, which suggests that light independent GTP consumption may result from ATPase activities.

As has been already pointed out, a light-stimulated GTPase activity is characteristic for transducin and G-protein of squid photoreceptor membranes. Therefore, the GTPase activity of fly photoreceptor membranes may be used as an indication of the presence of a G-protein. The α-subunits of G-proteins usually have a molecular mass ranging from 39 kDa to 52 kDa. The protein pattern of microvillar membranes shows several bands of this size (Fig. 10). In order to examine whether one of these proteins is the α-subunit of a G-protein, we have attempted to label protein bands by toxin-catalyzed ADP-ribosylation.

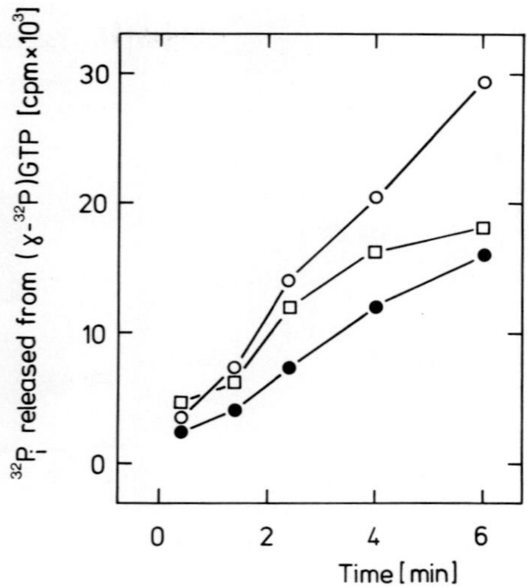

Fig. 8: GTP hydrolytic activity in isolated rhabdoms. GTP hydrolysis was measured as the amount of ^{32}P-orthophosphate released from (γ-^{32}P)GTP. Rhabdoms were incubated at 25 °C in a medium containing 80 mM Hepes pH 7.5, 2 mM $MgCl_2$, 1 mM dithiothreitol, 5 mM creatine phosphate, 30 U/ml creatine phosphokinase and 50 μM (γ-^{32}P)GTP (0.2 μCi/20 μl). At the indicated time aliquots of the reaction mixture were quenched with an ice-cold suspension of 10 % Norite, 10 % trichloroacetic acid, 1 mM H_3PO_4. Radioactivity in the supernatant, obtained after centrifuging samples for 5 min at 13 000 × g, was determined by scintillation counting. (●) Irradiation from 0 to 2 min with red light; (○) irradiation from 0.5 to 2.5 min with blue light (P → M); (□) irradiation from 0.5 to 2.5 min with blue light (P → M) and from 2.5 to 4.5 min with red light (M → P). GTP hydrolytic activity was 0.34 mol P_i per mol of rhodopsin per min in red light and 0.64 mol P_i per mol of rhodopsin per min in blue light.

This method of labeling has been previously used to characterize the α-subunit of transducin and of a G-protein from squid photoreceptor membranes (Abood et al., 1982; Van Dop et al., 1984; Vandenberg and Montal, 1984 a). In the present study, frog ROS were used as a control to demonstrate the reliability of the applied methods. As shown for T_α of bovine ROS (Abood et al., 1982), cholera toxin catalyzes ribosylation of T_α in bleached frog ROS (Fig. 9 a, track F). T_α is also labeled by pertussis toxin (Fig. 9 b, track E). As in bovine ROS (Van Dop et al., 1984), irradiation prevents ADP-ribosylation of T_α by pertussis toxin. Blowfly rhabdoms also contain a protein of about 41 kDa, which is specifically ADP-ribosylated in the presence of cholera toxin (see also Bentrop et al., 1985) and may therefore correspond to the α-subunit of the proposed G-protein. The ribosylated subunit is tightly bound to the microvillar membrane and is not extractable by isotonic and hypotonic buffers. Addition of 2 mM GTP or of the non-hydrolysable GTP-analogue GppNHp (0.05 mM) reduced the dark-light difference in labeling and increased the total amount of incorporated label (not shown). In response to light stimuli, the blowfly 41 kDa subunit of fly G-protein shows a remarkable difference to the 44 kDa subunit of the G-protein associated with squid photoreceptor membranes: its ribosylation is prevented by light (Fig. 9 a, track H) whereas Vandenberg and Montal (1984 a) reported that in squid, light increases the cholera toxin-catalyzed labeling of the 44 kDa

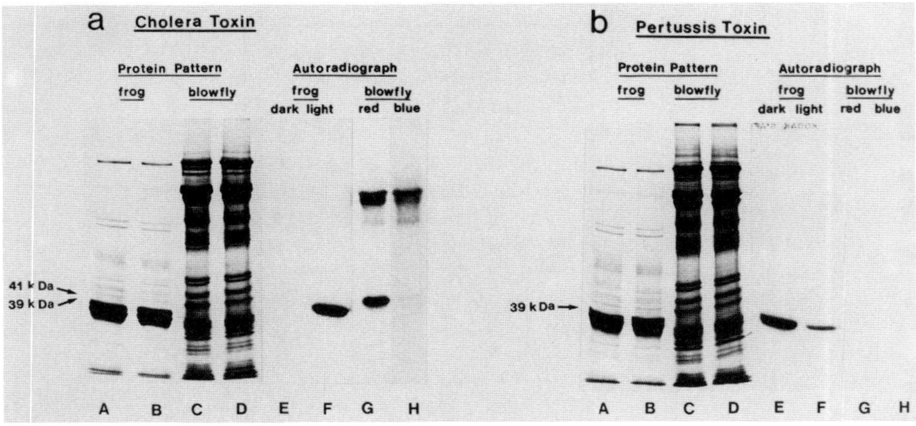

Fig. 9: ADP-ribosylation of proteins in isolated blowfly rhabdoms. Rhabdoms and isolated frog ROS, used as controls, were incubated, according to Abood et al. (1982), for 30 min at 30 °C in a medium containing 100 mM potassium phosphate, pH 7.0, 20 mM thymidine, 20 mM arginine/HCl, 4 mM $MgCl_2$, 100 μg/ml cholera toxin or 193.5 μg/ml pertussis toxin, respectively. Samples containing frog ROS were kept in the dark or bleached by room light as indicated. Samples with isolated rhabdoms were irradiated for 2 min either with red or blue light and then kept in the dark for the remaining incubation period. Membrane-bound proteins were separated by SDS-PAGE on 8–16 % gradient slab gels. Labeling of proteins was detected by autoradiography. a) ADP-ribosylation catalyzed by cholera toxin: (A–D) coomassie stained proteins; (A, B) frog ROS; (C, D), blowfly rhabdoms; (E–H) autoradiographs corresponding to A–D; (E) ROS, dark control; (F) bleached ROS; (G) rhabdoms irradiated only with red light; (H) rhabdoms irradiated with blue light. b) ADP-ribosylation catalyzed by pertussis toxin. (A–D) coomassie stained proteins; (E–H) autoradiographs of tracks A to D.

subunit. Furthermore, unlike T_α, the microvillar 41 kDa polypeptide is not ADP-ribosylated by pertussis toxin (Fig. 9 b, tracks G and H), at least not under conditions which lead to a labeling of T_α in frog ROS. Pertussis toxin does catalyze an ADP-ribosylation of polypeptides (39 and 41 kDa) from homogenates of blowfly retinae and optic lobes (not shown). However, in this case ribosylation was not affected by light. Thus, blowfly retinae apparently contain several G-proteins, at least one of which may have a function in the transduction process.

4. Light-modulated protein phosphorylation and protein binding

As previously reported for cephalopod photoreceptors (Paulsen and Hoppe, 1978; Vandenberg and Montal, 1984 b), we show here that conversion of P → M induces a phosphorylation of fly opsin at multiple binding sites (Fig. 6 and Table 1) which are probably located at the C-terminal opsin end (Fig. 7). Earlier experiments with isolated retinae (Paulsen and Bentrop, 1984) suggested that, in addition to light, calcium may have a function in the regulation of visual pigment phosphorylation. This is supported by phosphorylation experiments using isolated rhabdoms (Table 1). Metarhodopsin phosphorylation, induced by irradiation with blue light, is enhanced in the presence of EGTA, i. e. at low calcium levels; dephosphorylation of phosphorylated rhodopsin, which is

Table 1: Effect of $Ca^{2}+$ on phosphorylation and dephosphorylation of opsin

	irradation sequence	$CaCl_2$ or EGTA added	relative phosphate incorporation into opsin ± S. D.[c]
a	red (dark)	2 mM EGTA	0.1 ± 0.02
	blue (P→M)	2 mM EGTA	1.0 ± 0.03
	red (dark)	2 mM $CaCl_2$	0.08 ± 0.01
	blue (P→M)	2 mM $CaCl_2$	0.23 ± 0.06
b	red (dark)	1 mM EGTA	0.23 ± 0.01
	blue (P→M)	1 mM EGTA	1.0 ± 0.02
	blue (P→M)	1 mM EGTA	
	blue (P→M)	1 mM EGTA	0.8 ± 0.06
	+ red (M→P)	1 mM EGTA	
	blue (P→M)	2 mM $CaCl_2$	0.44 ± 0.01
	+ red (M→P)		

Homogenates of blowfly retinae were incubated as described for phosphorylation of isolated rhabdoms (Fig. 6). Phosphorylation was initiated by irradiating samples with blue light for 2 min. Dephosphorylation was initiated by exposing samples to red light, also for 2 min. In each case irradiation was followed by a 13 min period in the dark. $CaCl_2$ or EGTA were added as indicated. Phosphorylation was terminated by adding ice-cold 10% trichloroacetic acid. Precipitated proteins were separated by SDS-PAGE. Radioactivity in the opsin band was quantified by scintillation counting.
[a], [b] two experiments, [c] maximum phosphate incorporation into opsin in the blue light was 4 moles phosphate per mole of metarhodopsin formed (M–Pn, n = 4)

produced by photoconversion from phosphorylated metarhodopsin through irradiation with red light, is increased at high calcium levels. Inhibition of opsin phosphorylation by calcium has also been observed in ROS membranes (HERMOLIN et al., 1982), and squid photoreceptor membranes (VANDENBERG and MONTAL, 1984 b).

Further phosphorylation experiments were carried out with homogenates of whole retinae to avoid loss of soluble enzymes which inevitably occurs during the purification of rhabdoms. The results suggest that, as in the compound eye of *Drosophila* (MATSUMOTO and PAK, 1984), opsin is not the only protein which undergoes a light-induced phosphorylation. For example, in the experiments described in Fig. 10 we observed, in addition to opsin phosphorylation, a light-dependent labeling of polypeptides with 48 kDa, 68 kDa and 200 kDa (Fig. 10). These polypeptides also seemed to become dephosphorylated after M → P conversion (Fig. 10, track E). However, experiments in which soluble proteins were not removed from the sample by buffer washes prior to SDS-PAGE (see legend to Fig. 10) did not show a noticeable dark – light difference in the phosphorylation of the 48 kDa protein. Therefore, we concluded that the main effect of light is to induce a binding of the 48 kDa protein to the photoreceptor membrane. Such a light-induced binding of proteins has been previously described and analysed by Kühn in bovine ROS (for a summary see KÜHN, 1984 and KÜHN, this volume). The proteins, which were shown to undergo a light-induced binding to ROS membranes, are transducin, rhodopsin kinase, and a 48 kDa protein.

In Fig. 11 it is demonstrated for the first time that in fact P → M conversion triggers a binding of proteins also to microvillar photoreceptor membranes, particularly of a protein with a molecular mass of about 48 kDa (Fig. 11, track B). This protein is released from the

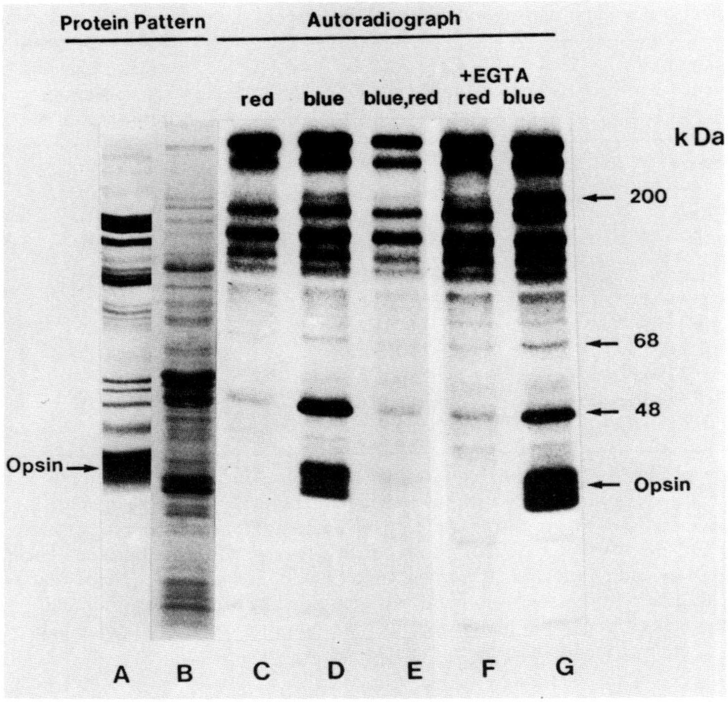

Fig. 10: Light-induced ^{32}P-labeling of membrane-bound proteins in a homogenate of blowfly retinae. A homogenate from blowfly retinae was incubated with $(\gamma\text{-}^{32}P)ATP$ and irradiated as described in the legend of Fig. 9. Reactions were terminated by washing membranes with ice-cold buffer solution. Membranes were collected by centrifugation, solubilized with 5 % SDS and subjected to SDS-PAGE. Coomassie-stained proteins (A) of a digitonin extract from isolated rhabdoms, (B) from a retina homogenate. (C–G) autoradiographs. (C) dark control: incubation for 2 min in red light and for 13 min in the dark. (D) light sample: incubation for 2 min in blue light and for 13 min in the dark. (E) effect of M → P conversion: after incubation as in (C) the sample was irradiated for 2 min with red light and then kept in the dark for 13 min. (F) dark control, low Ca^{2+}: incubation as in (B), 2 mM EGTA added. (G) light sample, low Ca^{2+}: Incubation as in (C), 2 mM EGTA added. In addition to the phosphorylation of opsin, irradiation with blue light induces ^{32}P incorporation into polypeptides of 48 kDa, 68 kDa and 200 kDa (D, G). Irradiation with red light (M → P) reverses this effect (E). Light-induced labeling of the 200 kDa polypeptide is enhanced at low calcium levels (G).

microvillar membrane after M → P conversion (Fig. 11, track E). The concentration of other phosphoproteins (68 kDa, 200 kDa), which may also undergo light-modulated binding to the microvillar membrane, was too low to permit a decision whether light initiated only their phosphorylation or also led to a binding of these proteins to the membrane.

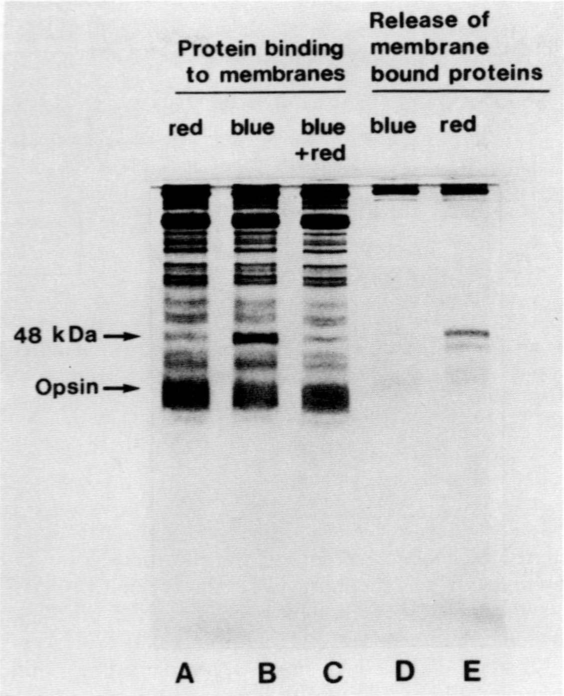

Fig. 11: Light-modulated binding of proteins to blowfly photoreceptor membranes. Rhabdoms from 200 retinae were incubated with soluble proteins (extract of 100 dark adapted retinae) at 20 °C in Hepes-buffered salt solution, pH 6.8, containing 5 mM ATP. Protein binding was initiated by irradiating samples for 1 min with blue light (P → M); release of bound porteins was initiated by irradiating for 1 min with red light (M → P). After irradiation each preparation was left in the dark for 14 min. Protein binding was assayed in 20 μl aliquots of the rhabdom suspension which contained 0.12 μg rhodopsin/μl. After incubation rhabdoms were washed twice with 1 ml of Hepes-buffered salt solution, to remove soluble proteins, and were then subjected to SDS-PAGE. Release of proteins bound in blue light was investigated by incubating washed rhabdoms (aliquots of 50 retinae) in 20 μl of Hepes-buffered salt solution, and irradiating this sample for 1 min with either blue or red light. Microvillar membranes were sedimented by centrifugation, and the proteins released into the supernatant were separated by SDS-PAGE.
(A–C) protein pattern of microvillar membranes; (D–E) protein pattern of supernatants. (A) membranes exposed to red light (dark control); (B) membranes exposed to blue light; (C) membranes as in (B), irradiated additionally with red light; (D) supernatant of membranes treated as in (B); (E) supernatant of membranes treated as in (C). High molecular weight bands in D and E are components extracted from the interphotoreceptor matrix.

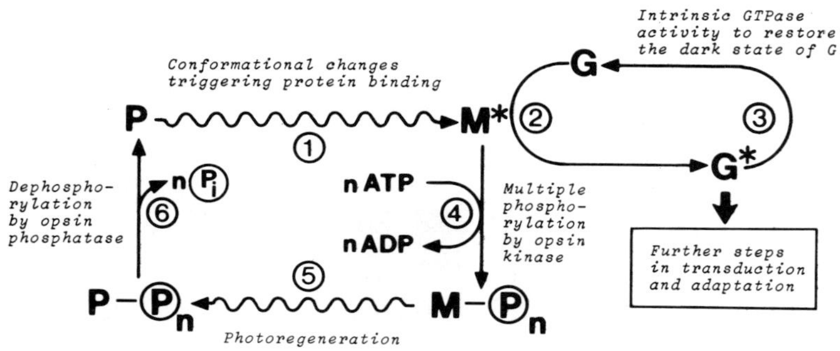

Fig. 12: Scheme summarizing light-modulated biochemical events in fly photoreceptors. P, rhodopsin; M*, activated state of metarhodopsin; M–Pn, P–Pn, multi-phosphorylated states of metarhodopsin and rhodopsin; G, G-protein; G*, activated G-protein.

Conclusions

The light-modulated biochemical events in fly photoreceptors which have been described in the present study are summarized by the scheme depicted in Fig. 12. After absorbing a photon, rhodopsin (P) is thought to be converted, via a number of short-lived intermediates, into a metarhodopsin state M* which actually represents the activated state of rhodopsin (Fig. 12, step 1). This conversion is accompanied by a shift in the absorbance maximum of the pigment (about 480 nm) to longer wavelengths (about 565 nm, Figs. 4 and 5). The red shift is indicative of conformational changes in the vicinity of the chromophore. These changes, resulting from the cis-trans isomerization of the chromophore, are propagated to the cytoplasmic surface of the opsin molecule. As a result metarhodopsin is able to interact with other proteins, in particular with a kinase which phosphorylates the C-terminal end of opsin (Fig. 6). By analogy with the vertebrate transduction mechanism it is assumed that activation of a G-protein and the light-modulated binding of the 48 kDa protein also occur at the cytoplasmic surface of metarhodopsin. As yet, it is not known to what extent the conformational changes initiated by P → M conversion are reversed by M → P conversion. Clearly, the opsin reassumes its structure around the chromophore as the spectral properties of P are restored after M → P conversion (Fig. 4). The release of the 48 kDa protein from the membrane after M → P conversion (Fig. 11) indicates that the corresponding binding sites are not available in the P state.

The next step concerns the interaction of M* with a G-protein (Fig. 12, step 2). ADP-ribosylation of a 41 kDa polypeptide (Fig. 9, see also Bentrop et al., 1985) indicates that at least one G-protein is located in the photoreceptor membrane. This conclusion is further supported by recent studies of BLUMENFELD et al. (1985), which show that, in crude preparations of fly eye membranes, a GTPase activity is induced by P → M conversion and is suppressed by M → P conversion. We assume that, as in vertebrate photoreceptors, hydrolysis of GTP is a mechanism to transfer the G-protein from an activated form G* into an inactive form G (Fig. 12, step 3). The 41 kDa polypeptide of microvillar membranes is specifically ADP-ribosylated by cholera toxin, like the α-subunit of N_s, the stimulatory coupling protein of adenylate cyclase in hormone-sensitive cells and the α-subunit of a G-protein contained in *Limulus* ventral photoreceptors (MALBON et al., 1984). Accordingly, the blowfly G-protein might regulate guanylate or adenylate cyclase activities which are associated with fly photoreceptor membranes (PAULSEN et al., 1984). Another metabolic pathway which may be controlled by the G-protein of the microvillar membrane is the release of polyphosphoinositols from polyphosphoinositides (BROWN et al., 1984; FEIN et al., 1984; BROWN, this volume), especially since blowfly rhabdoms contain the complete set of enzymes required for synthesis and degradation of polyphosphoinositides (ZINKLER et al., 1985).

In order to accomodate repetitive triggering of the transduction mechanism, the enzymatically active M* state must be deactivated to prevent prolonged activation of G. Phosphorylation of opsin is one mechanism proposed to convert active metarhodopsin into a state that does not initiate excitation (LIEBMAN and PUGH, 1980; PAULSEN and BENTROP, 1984; MINKE, 1986). LISMAN (1985) specifically suggests that multiple phosphorylation of opsin is required to reduce the probability of reverse reactions from an inactive, phosphorylated metarhodopsin state into an active, non-phosphorylated one. Opsin phosphorylation induced in isolated retinae (PAULSEN and BENTROP, 1984) and isolated rhabdoms (Fig. 6) demonstrates that in fact fly visual pigment can be shuttled back and forth between multi-phosphorylated and non-phosphorylated states.

Dephosphorylation of the binding sites occurs when metarhodopsin is photoconverted into rhodopsin (Fig. 12, step 5 and step 6). In isolated blowfly retinae, dephosphorylation of photoregenerated, phosphorylated rhodopsin (P–Pn) is a relatively rapid process, with a half-time of less than 20 seconds (PAULSEN and BENTROP, 1984). The state of pigment phosphorylation could, in the simplest case, be determined by the conformation of opsin. For example, P → M conversion may alter rhodopsin into a substrate for opsin (metarhodopsin) kinase, while photoregeneration converts opsin into a substrate for a protein phosphatase. Since P → M conversion also triggers the binding of proteins to the microvillar membrane, e.g. of a 48 kDa phosphoprotein which is present in the retina in excess of other proteins (Fig. 11), the control of the state of pigment phosphorylation may be more complex. KÜHN (KÜHN et al., 1984, KÜHN, this volume) has recently demonstrated that a 48 kDa protein of bovine ROS binds specifically to phosphorylated forms of rhodopsin and that there is a competition between the 48 kDa protein and transducin for binding sites on phosphorylated rhodopsin. Thus, it is possible that dephosphorylation of blowfly metarhodopsin (M–Pn) is prevented by the binding of a «blocking protein», which has a high affinity for phosphorylated forms of metarhodopsin. Dephosphorylation of rhodopsin might then be a result of the low affinity of the «blocking protein» for the P–Pn state, allowing a phosphatase to gain access to the phosphate binding sites. Blowfly 48 kDa protein would be one candidate for such a «blocking function», although at present there is no evidence that blowfly and bovine 48 kDa proteins have identical functions.

The effects of calcium on the dephosphorylation of blowfly rhodopsin (P–Pn) (Table 1) then suggest that dephosphorylation is either catalyzed by a calcium-dependent protein phosphatase, or that the affinity of a blocking protein for phosphorylated pigment forms (M–Pn; P–Pn) is lowered in the presence of high calcium levels. It has been shown for several invertebrate photoreceptors that under light the intracellular calcium concentration increases, and there is convincing evidence that calcium serves as an intracellular transmitter in light adaptation (for refs. see BROWN, 1986; STIEVE, 1985; BROWN and RUBIN, this volume). Thus, the rate of phosphorylation and dephosphorylation, the number of phosphate groups bound in the M–Pn and P–Pn states, and the relation between phosphorylated (M–Pn; P–Pn) and non-phosphorylated pigment forms may change during light adaptation.

As pointed out earlier (PAULSEN and BENTROP, 1984), the phosphorylated pigment states (M–Pn, P–Pn) might correspond to the inactive forms of rhodopsin and metarhodopsin in the «photopigment model» of HAMDORF and RAZMJOO (1977, 1979; RAZMJOO and HAMDORF, 1980). We suggest here that the function of opsin phosphorylation is to transform activated metarhodopsin into a state with altered binding properties for enzyme proteins or regulatory components of the transduction mechanism. The signal-amplifying cascade would then be interrupted and, despite the presence of a thermally stable metarhodopsin, the photoreceptor would remain unexcited. Multiple phosphorylation of metarhodopsin may then be a mechanism to decrease the binding probability of a G-protein or to increase the affinity for a «blocking protein».

In summary, the present study indicates that the early steps of phototransduction in vertebrate and invertebrate photoreceptors are remarkably similar, although there may be differences, for example in the type(s) of G-protein(s) coupling the activated state of metarhodopsin and as yet unknown enzyme reactions. The finding that protein binding to microvillar photoreceptor membranes can be induced and reversed simply by irradiation with different lights, opens up new and promising possibilities for the identification and characterization of enzymes and regulatory components involved in the phototransduction process in invertebrate photoreceptors.

Acknowledgements

This work was supported by the Deutsche Forschungsgemeinschaft (SFB 114, TP B2 and Pa 274/1–3). Mrs. A. DUDZIAK provided valuable technical assistance. The generous gift of pertussis toxin by Prof. E. RELYVELD (Institute Pasteur, Paris) and the helpful suggestions made by Prof. L. STRYER are greatfully acknowledged. The authors wish to thank S. RAZMJOO for his help in the preparation of the manuscript. Part of this work will be submitted by J. B. in fulfillment of requirements for a doctoral degree.

References

Abood, M. E., Hurley, J. B., Pappone, M.-C., Bourne, H. R., Stryer, L.: Functional homology between signal-coupling proteins: cholera toxin inactivates the GTPase activity of transducin. J. Biol. Chem. **257,** 10 540–10 543 (1982).

Baehr, W., Morita, E. A., Swanson, R. J., Applebury, M. L.: Characterization of bovine rod outer segment G-protein. J. Biol. Chem. **257,** 6452–6460 (1982).

Bentrop, J., Peters, K., Paulsen, R.: Lichtregulierte Enzymaktivitäten im Fliegenphotorezeptor: Reversible Sehpigmentphosphorylierung und Aktivierung eines G-Proteins. Verh. Dtsch. Zool. Ges. **78,** 279 (1986).

Blest, A. D., Stowe, S., Eddey, W.: A labil, Ca^{2+}-dependent cytoskeleton in rhabdomeral microvilli of blowflies. Cell Tissue Res. **223,** 553–573 (1982).

Blumenfeld, A., Erusalimsky, J., Heichal, O., Selinger, Z., Minke, B.: Light-activated guanosinetriphosphatase in *Musca* eye membranes resembles the prolonged depolarizing afterpotential in photoreceptor cells. Proc. Natl. Acad. Sci. USA **82,** 7116–7120 (1985).

Bolsover, S. R., Brown, J. E.: Guanosine phosphates and the control of membrane potential in *Limulus* ventral photoreceptors. Biol. Bull. **159,** 480 (1980).

Bolsover, S. R., Brown, J. E.: GTP and GTP analogues mimic some aspects of the light response in *Limulus* ventral photoreceptors. Biophys. J. **33,** 206 a (1981).

Bolsover, S. R., Brown, J. E.: Injection of guanosine and adenosine nucleotides into *Limulus* ventral photoreceptor cells. J. Physiol. **332,** 325–342 (1982).

Bownds, M. D.: Biochemical pathways regulating transduction in frog photoreceptor membranes. In: Current Topics in Membranes and Transport, Vol. **15,** Molecular Mechanism of Photoreceptor

Transduction (W. H. Miller, ed.), pp. 203–214. Academic Press, New York, London, Toronto, Sydney, San Francisco (1981).

Brown, J. E., Rubin, L. J., Ghalayini, A. J., Tarver, A. P., Irvine, R. F., Berridge, M. J., Anderson, R. E.: myo-inositol polyphosphate may be a messenger for visual excitation in *Limulus* photoreceptors. Nature **311**, 160–163 (1984).

Brown, J. E.: Calcium and light-adaptation in invertebrate Photoreceptors. In: The Molecular Mechanism of Photoreception. Dahlem Konferenzen (H. Stieve, ed.), pp. 231–240. Springer Verlag, Berlin, Heidelberg, New York, Tokyo (1986).

Brown, J. E., Rubin, L. J.: Signal transduction: The putative function of inositol triphosphates in *Limulus* photoreceptors. Progr. Zool. **33**, 321–331 (1986).

Calhoon, R., Tsuda, M., Ebrey, T. G.: A light-activated GTPase from octopus photoreceptors. Biochem. Biophys. Res. Commun. **94**, 1452–1457 (1980).

Chabre, M.: Trigger and amplification mechanisms in visual phototransduction. Annual Rev. Biophys. Chem. **14**, 331–361 (1985).

Chabre, M., Applebury, M. L.: Interaction of photoactivated rhodopsin with photoreceptor proteins; the cGMP cascade. In: The Molecular Mechanism of Photoreception. Dahlem Konferenzen (H. Stieve, ed.), pp. 51–66. Springer Verlag, Berlin, Heidelberg, New York, Tokyo (1986).

Corson, D. W. and Fein, A.: Chemical excitation of *Limulus* photoreceptors. I. Phosphatase inhibitors induce discrete-waves production in the dark. J. Gen. Physiol. **82**, 639–657 (1983).

Corson, D. W., Fein, A., Walthall, W. W.: Chemical excitation of *Limulus* photoreceptors. II. Vanadate, GTP-γ-S, and fluoride prolong excitation evoked by dim flashes of light. J. Gen. Physiol. **82**, 659–677 (1983).

De Couet, H. G.: Complex glycoproteins associated with the detergent-resistant membrane matrix of the rhabdomeral microvilli of crayfish photoreceptors. Exp. Eye Res. **39**, 279–298 (1984).

Fein, A., Corson, D. W.: Both photons and fluoride ions excite *Limulus* ventral photoreceptors. Science **204**,77–79 (1979).

Fein, A., Payne, R., Corson, D. W., Berridge, M. J., Irvine, R. F.: Photoreceptor excitation and adaptation by inositol 1,4,5-trisphosphate. Nature **311**,157–160 (1984).

Fesenko, E. E., Kolesnikov, S. S., Lyubarsky, A. L.: Induction by cyclic GMP of cationic conductance in plasma membrane of retinal rod outer segment. Nature **313**, 310–313 (1985).

Goldsmith, T. H., Wehner, R.: Restrictions on rotational and translational diffusion of pigment in the membranes of a rhabdomeric photoreceptor. J. Gen Physiol. **70**, 453–490 (1977).

Hamdorf, K., Paulsen, R., Schwemer, J.: Photoregeneration and sensitivity control of photoreceptors of invertebrates. In: Biochemistry and Physiology of Visual Pigments (Langer, H., ed.), pp. 155–166. Springer Verlag, Berlin, Heidelberg, New York (1973).

Hamdorf, K., Razmjoo, S.: The prolonged depolarizing afterpotential and its contribution to the understanding of photoreceptor function. Biophys. Struct. Mech. **3**, 163–170 (1977).

Hamdorf, K., Razmjoo, S.: Photoconvertible pigment states and excitation in *Calliphora*; the induction and properties of the prolonged depolarizing afterpotential. Biophys. Struct. Mech. **5**, 137–161 (1979).

Hamdorf, K.: The physiology of invertebrate visual pigments. In: Vision in Intervertebrates (Handbook of Sensory Physiology, Vol. VII 6 A) (H. Autrum, ed.), pp. 145–224. Springer Verlag, Berlin, Heidelberg, New York (1979).

Hawkes, R.: Identification of Concanavalin A-binding proteins after sodium dodecyl sulfate electrophoresis and protein blotting. Anal. Biochem. **123**, 142–146 (1982).

Hermolin, J., Karell, M. A., Hamm, H. E., Bownds, M. D.: Calcium and cyclic GMP regulation of light-sensitive protein phosphorylation in frog photoreceptor membranes. J. Gen. Physiol. **78**, 633–655 (1982).

Hillman, P., Hochstein, S., Minke, B.: Transduction in invertebrate photoreceptors: role of pigment bistability. Physiol. Rev. **63**, 668–772 (1983).

Kühn, H.: Interactions between rhodopsin and light-activated enzymes in rods. In: Progress in Retinal Research (N. Osborne, J. Chader, eds.), pp. 123–156. Pergamon Press, Oxford, New York (1984).

Kühn, H., Cook, J. H., Dryer, W. J.: Phosphorylation of rhodopsin in bovine photoreceptor membranes. A dark reaction after illumination. Biochemistry **12**, 2495–2502 (1973).

Kühn, H., Hall, S. W., Wilden, U.: Light-induced binding of 48–kDa protein to photoreceptor membranes is highly enhanced by phosphorylation of rhodopsin. FEBS Lett. **176,** 473–478 (1984).

Kühn, H.: Proteins involved in the control of cyclic GMP phosphodiesterase in retinal rod cells. Progr. Zool. **33,** 287–297 (1986).

Laemmli, U. K.: Cleavage of structural proteins during the assembly of the head of bacteriophage T4. Nature **227,** 680–685 (1970).

Liebman, P. A., Pugh, Jr., E. N.: ATP mediates rapid reversal of cyclic GMP phosphodiesterase activation in visual receptor membranes. Nature **287,** 734–736 (1980).

Lisman, J.: The role of metarhodopsin in the generation of spontaneous quantum bumps in ultraviolet receptors of *Limulus* median eye. J. Gen. Physiol. **85,** 171–187 (1985).

Malbon, C. C., Kaupp, U. B., Brown, J. E.: *Limulus* ventral photoreceptors contain a homologue of the α-subunit of mammalian N_s. FEBS Lett. **172,** 91–94 (1984).

Matsumoto, H., Pak, W. L.: Light-induced phosphorylation of retina-specific polypeptides of *Drosophila* in vivo. Science **223,** 184–186 (1984).

McDowell, J. H., Kühn H.: Light-induced phosphorylation of rhodopsin in cattle photoreceptor membranes: Substrate activation and inactivation. Biochemistry **16,** 4054–4060 (1977).

Miller, J. A., Paulsen, R.: Phosphorylation and dephosphorylation of frog rod outer segment membranes as part of the visual process. J. Biol. Chem. **250,** 4427–4432 (1975).

Minke, B.: Photopigment dependent adaptation in invertebrates – implications for vertebrates. In: The Molecular Mechanism of Photoreception. Dahlem Konferenzen (H. Stieve, ed.), pp. 241–265. Springer Verlag, Berlin, Heidelberg, New York, Tokyo (1986).

Minke, B., Stephenson, R. S.: The characteristics of chemically induced noise in *Musca* photoreceptors. J. Comp. Physiol. A **156,** 339–356 (1985).

Nichols, R., Pak, W. L.: Characterization of *Drosophila melanogaster* rhodopsin. J. Biol. Chem. **260,** 12670–12674 (1985).

Oakley, B. R., Kirsch, D. R., Morris, N. R.: A simplified ultrasensitive silver stain for detecting protein in polyacrylamide gels. Anal. Biochem. **105,** 361–363 (1980).

Ostroy, S. E., Wilson, M., Pak, W. L.: *Drosophila* rhodopsin: photochemistry, extraction and differences in the norp A^{P12} phototransduction mutant. Biochem. Biophys. Res. Commun. **59,**960–966 (1974).

O'Tousa, J. E., Baehr, W., Martin, R. L., Hirsh, J., Pak, W. L., Applebury, M. L.: The *Drosophila nina* E gene encodes an opsin. Cell **40,** 839–850 (1985).

Paulsen, R., Hoppe, I.: Light-activated phosphorylation of cephalopod rhodopsin. FEBS Lett. **96,** 55–58 (1978).

Paulsen, R., Zinkler, D., Delmelle, M.: Architecture and dynamics of microvillar photoreceptor membranes of a cephalopod. Exp. Eye Res. **36,** 47–56 (1983).

Paulsen, R., Schwemer, J.: Biogenesis of blowfly photoreceptor membranes is regulated by 11-cis retinal. Europ. J. Biochem. **137,** 609–614 (1983).

Paulsen, R., Bentrop, J.: Reversible phosphorylation of opsin induced by irradiation of blowfly retinae. J. Comp. Physiol. A **155,** 39–45 (1984).

Paulsen, R., Bentrop, J., Peters, K.: Photochemistry and biochemistry of blowfly photoreceptor membranes. Vision Res. **24,** 1700 (1984).

Paulsen, R.: Spectral characteristics of isolated blowfly rhabdoms. J. Comp. Physiol. A **155,** 47–55 (1984).

Payne, R.: Fluoride blocks an inactivation step of transduction in a locust photoreceptor. J. Physiol. (Lond.) **325,** 261–279 (1982).

Razmjoo, S., Hamdorf, K.: In support of the «photopigment model» of vision in invertebrates. J. Comp. Physiol. A **135,** 209–215 (1980).

Saibil, H. R.: An ordered membrane-cytoskeleton network in squid photoreceptor microvilli. J. Mol. Biol. **158,** 435–456 (1982).

Saibil, H. R.: A light-stimulated increase of cyclic GMP in squid photoreceptors. FEBS Lett. **168,** 213–216 (1984).

Saibil, H. R., Michel-Villaz, M.: Squid rhodopsin and GTP-binding protein crossreact with vertebrate photoreceptor enzymes. Proc. Natl. Acad. Sci. USA **81,** 5111–5115 (1984).

Schwemer, J.: Pathways of visual pigment regeneration in fly photoreceptor cells. Biophys. Struct. Mech. **9,** 287–298 (1983).

Stavenga, D. G., Zantema, A., Kuiper, J. W.: Rhodopsin processes and the function of the pupil mechanism in flies. In: Biochemistry and Physiology of Visual Pigments. (H. Langer, ed.), pp. 175–180. Springer Verlag, Berlin, Heidelberg, New York (1973).

Stieve, H.: Phototransduction in invertebrate visual cells. The present state of research – exemplified and discussed through the *Limulus* photoreceptor cell. In: Neurobiology (R. Gilles, J. Balthazart, eds.), pp. 346–362. Springer Verlag, Berlin, Heidelberg, New York (1985).

Stryer, L., Hurley, J. B., Fung, B. K.-K.: First stage of amplification in the cyclic-nucleotide cascade of vision. In: Current Topics in Membranes and Transport Vol. **15**: Molecular Mechanisms of Photoreceptor Transduction (W. H. Miller, ed.), pp. 93–108. Academic Press, New York, London, Toronto, Sydney, San Francisco (1981).

Vandenberg, C. A., Montal, M.: Light-regulated biochemical events in invertebrate photoreceptors. 1. Light-activated guanosinetriphosphatase, guanine nucleotide binding, and cholera toxin catalyzed labeling of squid photoreceptor membranes. Biochemistry **23**, 2339–2347 (1984 a).

Vandenberg, C. A., Montal, M.: Light-regulated biochemical events in invertebrate photoreceptors. 2. Light-regulated phosphorylation of rhodopsin and phosphoinositides in squid photoreceptor membranes. Biochemistry **23**, 2347–2352 (1984 b).

Van Dop, D., Yamanaka, G., Steinberg, F., Sekura, R. D., Manclark, C. R., Stryer, L., Bourne, H. R.: ADP ribosylation of transducin by pertussis toxin blocks the light-stimulated hydrolysis of GTP and cGMP in retinal photoreceptors. J. Biol. Chem. **259**, 23–26 (1984).

Vogt, K.: Is the fly visual pigment a rhodopsin? Z. Naturforsch. **38 c**, 329–333 (1983).

Vogt, K., Kirschfeld, K.: Chemical identity of the chromophores of fly visual pigment. Naturwiss. **71**, 211–213 (1984).

Weller, M., Virmaux, N., Mandel, P.: Light-stimulated phosphorylation of rhodopsin in the retina: The presence of a protein kinase that is specific for photobleached rhodopsin. Proc. Natl. Acad. Sci. USA **72**, 381–385 (1975).

Wilden, U., Kühn, H.: Light-dependent phosphorylation of rhodopsin: number of phosphorylation sites. Biochemistry **21**, 3014–3022 (1982).

Yau, K.-W., Nakatani, K.: Light-suppressible, cyclic GMP-sensitive conductance in the plasma membrane of a truncated rod outer segment. Nature **317**, 252–255 (1985).

Yau, K.-W., Haynes, L. W., Nakatani, K.: Roles of calcium and cyclic GMP in visual transduction. Progr. Zool. **33**, 343–366 (1986).

Yoshioka, T., Inoue, H., Inomata, K., Hayashi, K. F., Takagi, M. and Takenaka, T.: The parallel study of protein phosphorylation and phosphatidylinositol metabolism in the photoreceptors of squid retina. Proc. Jap. Acad. **57**, Ser. B, 309–313 (1981).

Zinkler, D., Bentrop, J., Paulsen, R.: Phospholipide des Fliegenrhabdoms: Fettsäure- und Phosphoinositolstoffwechsel. Verh. Deutsch. Zool. Ges. **78**, 303 (1985).

Zuker, C. S., Cowman, A. F., Rubin, G. H.: Isolation and structure of a rhodopsin gene from *D. melanogaster*. Cell **40**, 851–858 (1985).

Fortschritte der Zoologie, Band 33 · Lüttgau (Hrsg.): Membrane Control
Gustav Fischer Verlag · Stuttgart · New York · 1986

Signal transduction: The putative participation of inositol trisphosphates in *Limulus* photoreceptors

JOEL E. BROWN and LEONA J. RUBIN

Department of Ophthalmology Washington University School of Medicine, St. Louis, Missouri 63 110, USA

The description of signal transduction as a cascade of reactions has become commonplace in cell biology. Transduction begins with activation of a membrane-bound receptor molecule, is mediated by a cascade of intracellular reactions, and results in a change in activation of membrane-bound effector molecules. The reaction cascade provides (1) amplification of the signal, (2) diffusion of the transduction message through the cytosol of the cell, and (3) possibilities for modulation of the transduction message by parallel reaction cascades or other cellular processes.

Photoreceptor cells offer useful systems for studying such transduction cascades. Signal transduction in a photoreceptor cell begins with the absorption of a photon by a rhodopsin molecule (an integral membrane lipoprotein) and ends with the production of an electrical signal across the plasma membrane of the cell. The intervening mechanisms have been modeled (both biophysically and biochemically) as a cascade of reactions. Biophysical analysis of these models has provided both useful insights and experimental designs for further physiological experiments (see for example, FUORTES and HODGKIN, 1964; BORSELLINO, FUORTES and SMITH, 1965). Moreover, there have been physiological and pharmacological probes that attempted to identify steps in the cascade (see FUORTES, 1965 for an early example).

Amplification of the signal

Signal transduction in a *Limulus* ventral photoreceptor displays the common characteristics of the cascade model. There is a large amplification in the transduction mechanism; the absorption of a single photon in a dark-adapted cell induces an ionic current across the plasma membrane of several nanoamperes for about 100 msec. That is, each effective photon absorption induces the opening of about 10^4 channels, each of which transports about 10^4 charges during its open state (BACIGALUPO and LISMAN, 1983).

Diffusible excitatory message

In response to brief stimuli that cause the absorption of more than a single photon, the amplitude of the light-induced current increases nearly linearly with the number of photons absorbed up to 500–1000 photons. For more than 1000 photons absorbed, the light-induced current begins to saturate (Brown and Coles, 1979). Stated another way, the random activation of rhodopsin molecules across the photoreceptor surface of the cell by each of the first 1000 photons induces an approximately fixed increment of current; however, the activation of the next rhodopsin molecule (at random in the cell) induces a smaller current. That is, each activated rhodopsin molecule signals its excitation to the others such that after the absorption of 1000 photons, the increment of excitatory responses is reduced. The spread of the excitatory influence is dispersed; when 1000 photons have been adsorbed, not more than 1 % of the microvilli in the rhabdom of the cell have adsorbed a single photon (Brown and Coles, 1979). Taken together, the large number of channels opened by the action of a single activated rhodopsin molecule and the disperse excitatory influence of each activated rhodopsin argue that there may be a diffusible message of excitation within the cytosol of the photoreceptor.

Modulation of the excitation cascade

The excitation mechanism may be modulated in several ways. The most obvious is described as «adaptation»; the sensitivity of the excitatory mechanism is modulated by prior illumination. Lisman and Brown (1972 a and b; 1975) proposed that a rise in intracellular calcium ion concentration (Ca_i) was a signal for light-adaptation. There are several lines of evidence consistent with that proposal. Intracellular calcium rises after illumination of a photoreceptor (monitored with aequorin, Brown and Blinks, 1974; monitored with arsenazo III, Brown, Brown and Pinto, 1977; Maaz and Stieve, 1980; Harary and Brown, 1984; monitored with a calcium ion selective electrode, Levy and Fein, 1985). The steady-state level of Ca_i increases as the sensitivity decreases (monotonically) (Levy and Fein, 1985). Iontophoretic injection of Ca^{++} induces a decrease in sensitivity of a normal cell (Brown and Lisman, 1975; Fein and Charlton, 1977) independent of changes of intracellular pH (Bolsover and Brown, 1982). Light-adaptation is local within a cell (Fein and Charlton, 1975; Payne and Fein, 1983); adaptation induced by iontophoretic injection of Ca^{++} is local (Fein and Lisman, 1975); and the light-induced rise in Ca_i is also local within the photoreceptor (Harary and Brown, 1984; Levy and Fein, 1985). In addition, intracellular introduction of calcium sequestering substances tends to prevent light-adaptation (Lisman and Brown, 1975; Brown and Blinks, 1974; Korenbrot et al., 1986).

Calcium ions appear to modulate the transduction cascade in more than one way. As discussed above, a light-induced increase in Ca_i appears to participate in signalling light-adaptation. However, Bolsover and Brown (1985) have reported another action of calcium ions. If calcium ions are removed from the bath around a *Limulus* ventral photoreceptor, and the cell is repetitively stimulated for a prolonged period, the state of responsiveness of the cell becomes changed. This changed state, which we call the «calcium-deprived state», is manifested in several ways. (1) The sensitivity of the cell to dim stimuli is reduced. (2) The shape of the response elicited by prolonged flashes changes from an early large transient that declines to a plateau to a slowly rising response that tends to plateau and then may develop a delayed transient rise. (3) The plot of response amplitude *versus* stimulus intensity is depressed for dim stimuli and rises much more steeply for brighter stimuli (see also: Stieve and Pflaum, 1978). (4) The light-induced increase in Ca_i, as detected by intracellular aequorin, is greatly reduced. The intracellular injection of Ca^{++} into a cell in the calcium-deprived state induces an *increase* in sensitivity, in contrast to the opposite effect observed in normal cells. Moreover, the intracellular injection of

EGTA into a cell in the calcium-deprived state induces a further *decrease* in sensitivity, in contrast to the opposite effect observed in normal cells. BOLSOVER and BROWN (1985) suggested that these findings indicate that calcium ion concentration modulates a step within the excitatory cascade. Thus, when Ca_i is reduced below some optimum value, the amplification provided by that step becomes reduced, and the kinetics of the cascade becomes slower; this condition is manifested in the calcium-deprived state. In this altered state, an increase of Ca_i, provided extrinsically by injection of Ca^{++}, can increase the amplification and kinetics of the light response. An increase of Ca_i provided intrinsically by light-induced release of Ca^{++} from the light-labile intracellular store, can increase the amplification to produce a delayed transient response during a prolonged stimulus. Thus, a light-induced increase in intracellular Ca_i may normally modulate another step in the reaction cascade (in addition to light-adaptation), either within the same path of the cascade or within a parallel cascade of reactions.

Phosphoinositides

Recently, there has been widespread interest in stimulus-induced phosphoinositide metabolism as a component in signal transduction cascades (for recent reviews see: BERRIDGE and IRVINE, 1984; MAJERUS et al., 1984; HOKIN, 1985; MAJERUS et al., 1985). Phosphoinositides are membrane phospholipids in which inositol molecules (that may be multi-phosphorylated) are attached by a phosphodiester linkage to diacylglycerols. Phosphoinositides comprise a small fraction of total membrane phospholipids. Current evidence suggests that the same phospholipase C enzyme is capable of hydrolyzing both phosphatidylinositol (PI) and the phosphatidylinositol polyphosphates (PIP and PIP_2) (for examples, HOFMANN and MAJERUS, 1982; WILSON et al., 1984). In the experiments of HOFMANN and MAJERUS (1982), the selectivity of the enzyme for its several substrates appears to be dependent upon Ca_i; thus PIP and PIP_2 are preferred at low levels of Ca_i, and PI itself is hydrolyzed at high levels of Ca_i.

Stimulus-induced phosphoinositide hydrolysis has been proposed in a variety of cells in which a change in Ca_i apparently participates in the transduction cascade. This proposal was broadly promulgated by MICHELL (1975) and has recently been supported by STREB et al. (1983) in pancreatic acinar cells as well as in a wide variety of other systems (see BERRIDGE and IRVINE, 1984, for review). Specifically, it is proposed that inositol trisphosphate (1,4,5-IP_3) is the cytosolic diffusible messenger molecule that signals the cell to raise its Ca_i.

Inositol polyphosphates in photoreceptors: Electrophysiology

In *Limulus* ventral photoreceptors, it is known that Ca_i participates in the phototransduction cascade. As detailed above, LISMAN and BROWN (1972, a and b, see BROWN, 1977 for a review) proposed that a rise in Ca_i signalled light-adaptation. Because of the work of STREB et al. (1983) that demonstrated an IP_3-induced increase in Ca_i, the participation of phosphoinositide metabolism in the phototransduction cascade was examined (BROWN et al. 1984; FEIN et al., 1984). 1,4,5-IP_3, prepared by Dr. R. F. IRVINE from human red cell ghosts, was pressure-injected into *Limulus* ventral photoreceptors. If the micropipette was positioned inside the rhabdomeric lobe of the photoreceptor, each injection of 1,4,5-IP_3 induced a rapid (and often large) depolarization (Fig. 1). Control injections of salt solu-

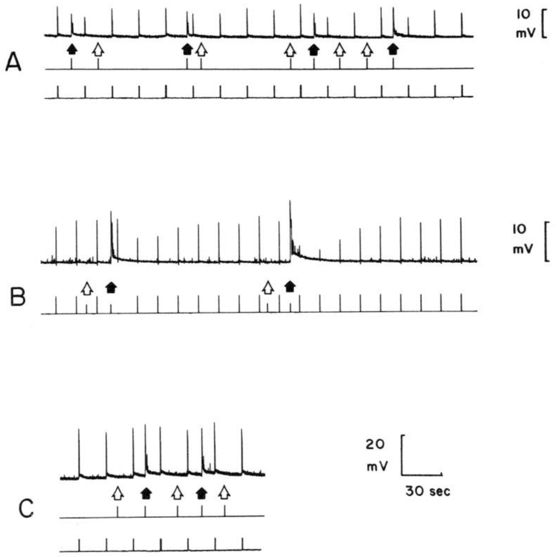

Figure 1: Intracellular injection of 1,4,5-IP_3 into the rhabdomeric lobe of *Limulus* ventral photoreceptors. Each of these cells was impaled with a double-barrel (theta glass) micropipette. One barrel contained 200 mM KCl plus 50 mM HEPES (N-2-hydroxyethylpiperazine-N'-2-ethanesulfonic acid), pH 7.4; injections from this control barrel are indicated by open arrows. The second barrel contained the same solution plus 400 μM 1,4,5-IP_3; injections of 1,4,5-IP_3 are indicated by solid arrows. The upper of each set of traces is a record of membrane voltage. In A and C, the middle trace is a monitor of the pressure injections; the lower trace is a monitor of light stimuli. On the lower trace in B, the pressure injections are indicated by the smaller pulses; the light stimuli are indicated by the larger pulses. Note that in B, the 1,4,5-IP_3 injections were potent enough to adapt the responses to dim illumination.

tions that did not contain 1,4,5-IP_3 were made out of the second barrel of a double-barrel («theta-glass») micropipette, thus insuring that the control injections were made at the same intracellular locus as were the 1,4,5-IP_3 injections. The control injections did not induce depolarizing responses (Fig. 1). Responses mimicking those induced by injection of 1,4,5-IP_3 have been induced by glycerol phosphoinositol-4,5-bisphosphate ($GPIP_2$) (Brown et al., 1984), 4,5-IP_2 and less potently by 1,4-IP_2 (Brown et al., 1984; Fein et al., 1984). The responses were not induced by 2-IP_1, phosphate, myoinositol (Fein et al., 1984), IP_6 (Brown et al., 1984; Fein et al., 1984), or 1-IP_1 (Brown et al., 1984). In addition, injections of 1 : 2(cyclic)-IP_1, 3,4-IP_2 (both kindly provided by Dr. W. Sherman), and 2,3-glycerol diphosphate did not induce the response (Brown and Rubin, unpublished).

The responses induced by injection of 1,4,5-IP_3 mimicked light-responses in several ways. Both induce inward membrane current in cells voltage-clamped to dark, resting voltage. The reversal voltages for both are approximately the same (Brown et al., 1984; Fein et al., 1984), even at different values of extracellular sodium ion concentration (Brown et al., 1984). Injection of 1,4,5-IP_3 adapts the cell's response to light and light adapts the cell's response to injection of 1,4,5-IP_3. Moreover, both light and injection of 1,4,5-IP_3 induce an increase in Ca_i (Brown and Rubin, 1984). All these findings suggest that 1,4,5-IP_3 may be a messenger or modulator molecule in the excitation cascade.

Phosphoinositide metabolism in photoreceptors

A stimulus-induced change in phosphoinositide metabolism that might produce inositol-trisphosphate within photoreceptor cells has been examined biochemically in *Limulus* ventral eyes. In the initial study (Brown et al., 1984), pairs of eyes from individuals were incubated for several hours in darkness in either artificial sea water or *Limulus* serum that contained ^{3}H-inositol. The eyes were then rinsed in artificial sea water; all such manipulations were done in infra-red illumination by use of image converters. One eye of each pair was stimulated by bright light, and both eyes were fixed in chloroform : methanol : HCl (2 : 1 : 0.025). The organic and aqueous phases were separated; the labeled phosphoinositides were analyzed by thin-layer chromatography and the water-soluble inositol phosphates were analyzed by ion exchange chromatography on Dowex 1 resin. The results of these analyses of *Limulus* ventral eyes (Brown et al., 1984) indicated that light decreased the average content of PIP_2 and increased the average content of IP_3. These findings supported the proposal that inositol phosphates participate as messengers or modulators in transduction in *Limulus* photoreceptors.

Phosphoinositide metabolism has also been examined in the retinas of cephalopod molluscs. Yoshioka et al., (1981, 1983) found that continuous illumination decreased the incorporation of $^{32}PO_4$ from ATP into polyphosphoinositides in *Octopus* rhabdomeric membranes and Vandenberg and Montal(1984) found the $^{32}PO_4$ incorporation into polyphosphoinositides was reduced after illumination of rhabdomeric membranes prepared from *Loligo* retinas. More recently, Szuts et al. (1985) reported that illumination increases the content of IP_3 in *Loligo* retinas that had been previously labeled with ^{3}H-inositol in the dark. Szuts et al. (1985) separated IP_3 by ion exchange chromatography on Dowex 1 resin.

1,3,4-IP_3

The isomer of inositol-trisphosphate that is made by living cells often has been assumed to be 1,4,5-IP_3. Irvine et al. (1984) have identified another isomer, 1,3,4-IP_3, in rat salivary glands. This identification of another isomer of IP_3 has been aided by chemical analysis of products separated by high performance liquid chromatography (HPLC) (Irvine et al., 1985). Briefly, the isomers of inositol phosphates can be separated by using Partisil SAX as a stationary phase, and a gradient of ammonium-formate plus phosphate as the mobile phase. This chromatographic system separates the various IP_1's, IP_2's, IP_3's and glycerol–inositol phosphates. In particular, it separates 1,3,4-IP_3 from 1,4,5-IP_3. We have used this chromatography system to analyze the aqueous extracts of *Limulus* ventral eyes (Figure 2). The *Limulus* cells appear to contain both 1,4,5-IP_3 and an IP_3 that has the same chromatographic mobility as 1,3,4-IP_3 (Irvine et al., 1985). Moreover, the material from that putative 1,3,4-IP_3 peak has been oxidized by periodate and then dephosphorylated. The resultant linear sugar was analyzed by paper chromatography (Grado and Ballou, 1961) and electrophoresis (Irvine et al., 1985) and found to be altritol; thus the identification of this linear sugar supports the identification of original material as 1,3,4-IP_3 (Irvine, Brown and Rubin, unpublished results). In addition, we have found that the content of 1,3,4-IP_3 is increased in *Limulus* ventral eyes after illumination proportionately more than is the content of 1,4,5-IP_3 (Irvine et al., 1985).

The synthesis of 1,3,4-IP_3 in living cells has been investigated by Batty et al. (1985) and Irvine et al. (1986). They suggest that this isomer of IP_3 does not arise by the direct

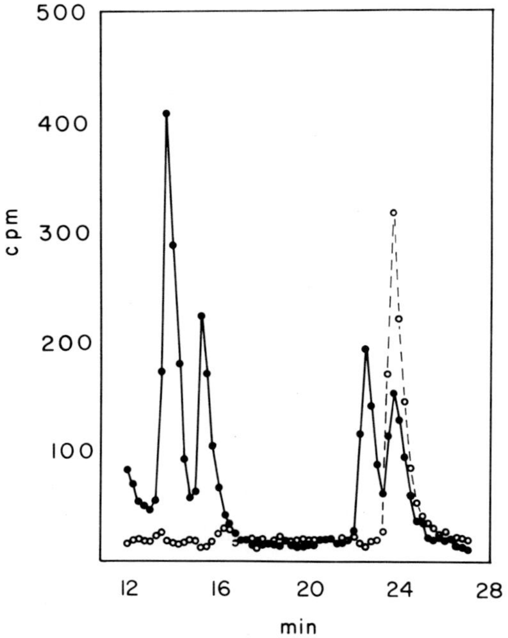

Figure 2: HPLC of inositol polyphosphates from illuminated *Limulus* ventral eyes. 20 eyes were incubated in 5 mCi/ml ^{3}H-inositol in *Limulus* serum for 12 hours in the dark. The eyes were illuminated for 10 sec at 0.01 W/cm^2 and fixed in chloroform : methanol : HCl (2 : 1 : 0.025) at dry ice temperature. The aqueous and organic phases were separated and dried. 10 % of the aqueous phase was chromatographed (according to Irvine, et al., 1985) after addition of ^{32}P labelled 1,4,5-IP_3 made from human red cell ghosts (Downes, et al., 1982). The solid circles are cpm of ^{3}H; the open circles are cpm of ^{32}P. The time is given as minutes after the ammonium formate plus phosphate gradient was begun. The peak that is seen immediately before the 1,4,5-IP_3 peak is that ascribed to 1,3,4-IP_3. The earlier two peaks are ascribed to IP_2 isomers.

hydrolysis of a phosphatidylinositol-3,4-bisphosphate (by analogy with the synthesis of 1,4,5-IP_3 in cells). Rather, they suggest that there is a kinase that phosphorylates 1,4,5-IP_3 to 1,3,4,5-IP_4 (Fig. 3). Then, a 5-phosphomonoesterase cleaves the 1,3,4,5-IP_4 to produce 1,3,4-IP_3. Several lines of evidence support this suggestion. First, there is little, if any, phosphatidylinositol-3,4-bisphosphate in cell membranes. For example, in the phosphoinositides extracted from *Limulus* ventral eyes, any PI-3,4-P_2 must be less than 1 % of PI-4,5-P_2 (by our levels of detection) (Irvine, Brown and Rubin, unpublished data). Second, there are specific 5-phosphomonoesterases that have been found in both red cell ghosts (Downes et al., 1982) and human platelets (Connolly et al., 1985) that cleave the 5-phosphate from the inositol ring; such 5-phosphomonoesterases selective for inositol phosphate substrates are presumably found in many cells. Third, Batty et al. (1985), Heslop et al. (1985) and Irvine et al. (1986) have isolated and identified 1,3,4,5-IP_4 from a variety of animal cells. Fourth, Irvine et al. (1986) have isolated an inositol-kinase from rat brain that phosphorylates 1,4,5-IP_3 at the 3 position, *in vitro*. The resulting IP_4 is hydrolyzed to 1,3,4-IP_3 by the 5-phosphomonoesterase from human red cell ghosts (Batty et al., 1985). Therefore, in addition to a stimulus-induced increase in the cellular content of

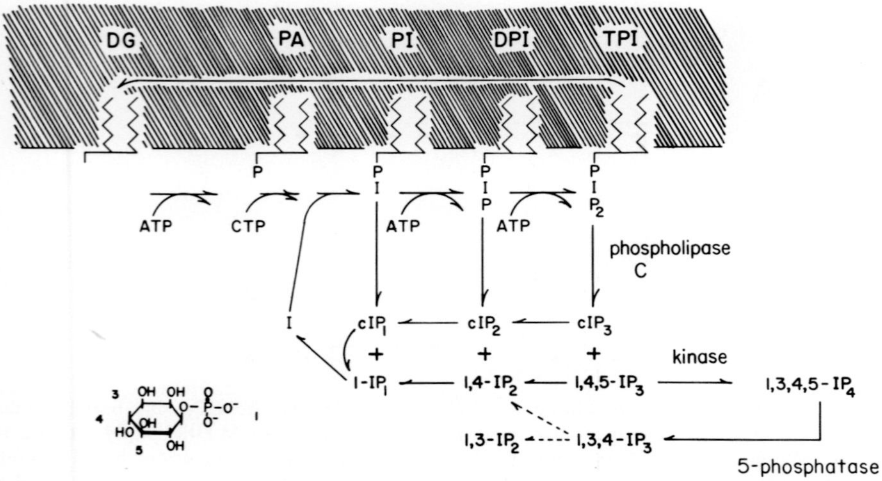

Figure 3: Phosphoinositide metabolism schema. The schematic structure of inositol-l-phosphate is shown on the lower left.

1,4,5-IP_3 that can occur after stimulation of phosphoinositide breakdown in a cell, both 1,3,4,5-IP_4 and 1,3,4-IP_3 may also be formed and may play (as yet undefined) roles in transduction mechanisms.

Cyclic-IP_3

The action of phospholipase C on phosphatidylinositol produces a mixture of inositol-1-phosphate and inositol-1 : 2 (cyclic) phosphate (cIP_1) (Dawson et al., 1971). Moreover, *in vitro* a phospholipase C cleaves phosphatidylinositol-4-phosphate to a mixture of (1,4)-IP_2 plus 1 : 2(cyclic)-4-IP_2, (cIP_2) and phosphatidylinositol-1,4-bisphosphate to a mixture of 1,4,5-IP_3 plus 1 : 2(cyclic)-4,5-IP_3 (cIP_3) (Wilson et al., 1985 a, b). The action of phospholipase C *in vitro* on the polyphosphoinositides can produce cyclic inositol phosphates at yields as high as approximately 50 % of the total inositol phosphates. The cyclic inositol phosphates can be separated from their non-cyclic counterparts by a HPLC system (Wilson et al., 1985 b). Thus, Wilson, Bross and Majerus have been able to manufacture and isolate enough cyclic inositol phosphates for us to be able to test their physiological activities in *Limulus* photoreceptor cells.

When cyclic-IP_3 is pressure-injected into the rhabdomeric lobe of a *Limulus* ventral photoreceptor, the cell rapidly depolarizes. The responses often resemble the summation of many discrete events, and thus resemble the response to a brief flash of light or to the injection of 1,4,5-IP_3 (Wilson et al., 1985 b). Injections of cIP_1 or cIP_2 do not induce such responses. To compare the responses induced by injections of the cyclic and non-cyclic analogues of IP_3, we injected each into the same cell out of the separate barrels of a double-barrel (theta glass) micropipette. We found that not only did both analogues induce inward currents with the cells clamped at dark, resting voltage, but both analogues were capable of inducing a rise in Ca_i, as measured by aequorin (Wilson et al., 1985 b).

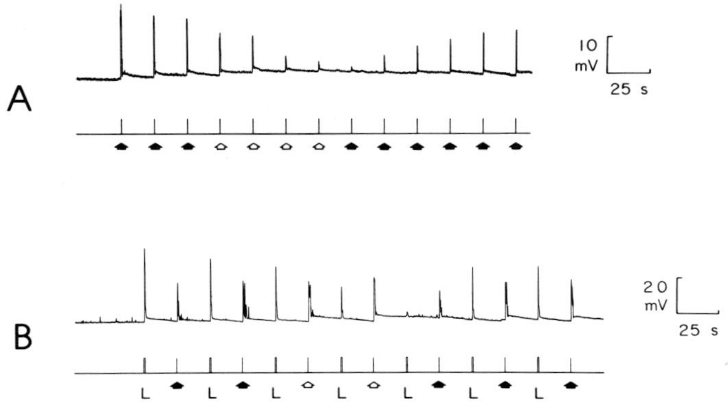

Figure 4: Intracellular injection of inositol-cyclic(1 : 2)-4,5-trisphosphate (cIP_3). One barrel of a double barrel (theta glass) micropipette was filled with 200 mM KCl, 50 mM HEPES (pH 7.4) and 400 μM 1,4,5-IP_3; injections out of this barrel are indicated by open arrows. The second barrel was filled with 200 mM KCl, 50 mM HEPES (pH 7.4) and 400 μM cIP_3; injections out the cIP_3 barrel are indicated by solid arrows. The sizes of injections were monitored by infra-red (940 nm) television (Corson and Fein, 1983); the injections were adjusted to be of approximately equal size within each experiment. A. Injections of cIP_3 do not markedly adapt responses to successive injections of either substance whereas injections of 1,4,5-IP_3 strongly adapt the responses to injections of both substances. B. Same cell. Injections of cIP_3 do not markedly adapt either light responses or injection responses, whereas injections of 1,4,5-IP_3 markedly adapt both. The cell was bathed in sea water in which Ca^{++} was replaced by Mg^{++}.

However, we found that approximately equal size injections of cIP_3 and 1,4,5-IP_3 gave equal size conductance changes when the cIP_3 was at 20 % the concentration of the non-cyclic analogue; that is, cIP_3 is about five times more potent that non-cyclic 1,4,5-IP_3 at inducing a conductance change (Wilson et al., 1985 b). On the other hand, we found that if we made injections of both analogues such that they induced about the same size conductance changes, the cIP_3 injections lead to much less adaptation (of both light responses and injection responses) than did injection of non-cyclic 1,4,5-IP_3. That is, the non-cyclic analogue appeared to be more potent at inducing adaptation (Fig. 4).

Speculative hypothesis

We have found that *Limulus* ventral photoreceptors persist in generating light responses after large amounts of a calcium-buffering substance (EGTA, BAPTA, etc.) have been introduced into the cytosol. Such increases in intracellular buffering capacity tend to prevent adaptation even by bright stimuli. However, light still induces responses, even for dim stimuli, although those responses may become smaller and have altered kinetics (Lisman and Brown, 1975). On the other hand, the responses induced by intracellular injection of IP_3 are blocked by prior injection of calcium-buffering substances (such as EGTA, BAPTA, etc.) (Brown and Rubin, 1984). Thus, we think it unlikely that a light-induced rise in IP_3 concentration is a step in a direct, linear non-branched cascade that mediates excitation.

Because IP_3 analogs do induce increases in Ca_i, and the level of Ca_i modulates the excitatory cascade, we tentatively propose that light acts through a parallel cascade, or a parallel branch from the main-line cascade, to induce an increase in IP_3 that causes an increase in Ca_i; this increase in Ca_i modulates the amplification and kinetics of some step or steps within the main cascade of excitatory reactions.

Conclusion

Illumination of invertebrate photoreceptors stimulates the breakdown of polyphosphoinositides within these cells. Injection of several different inositol-polyphosphates mimics several aspects of the cell's responses to illumination. Taken together, these findings suggest that the metabolism of inositol phosphates may participate as messengers or modulators in one or more reactions within the phototransduction cascade.

Acknowledgement

We thank Drs. R. E. Anderson, T. E. Bross, T. M. Connolly, R. F. Irvine, P. W. Majerus and D. B. Wilson for many helpful discussions. Supported by NIH Grants EY-05166, EY-05168 and the Research to Prevent Blindness Foundation.

References

Bacigalupo, J. and Lisman, J. E.: Single-channel currents activated by light in Limulus ventral photorecptors. Nature. **304**, 268–270 (1983).

Batty, I. R., Nahorski, S. R. and Irvine, R. F.: Rapid formation of inositol(1,3,4,5)tetrakisphosphate following muscarinic receptor stimulation of rat cerebral cortical slices. Biochem J. **232,** 211–215 (1985)

Berridge, M. J. and Irvine, R. F.: Inositol trisphosphate, a novel second messenger in cellular signal transduction. Nature. **312,** 315–321 (1984).

Bolsover, S. R. and Brown, J. E.: Light adaptation of invertebrate photoreceptors: influence of intracellular pH buffering capacity. J Physiol. **330,** 297–305 (1982).

Bolsover, S. R. and Brown, J. E.: Calcium ion, an intracellular messenger of light adaptation, also participates in excitation of Limulus ventral photoreceptor cells. J. Physiol. **364,** 381–393 (1985).

Borsellino, A., Fuortes, M. G. F. and Smith, T. G.: Visual responses in Limulus. Cold Spring Harbor Symp. Quant. Biol. **30,** 429–443 (1965).

Brown, J. E.: Calcium ion, a putative intracellular messenger for light-adaptation in Limulus ventral photoreceptors. Biophys. Struct. Mechanism. **3,** 141–143 (1977).

Brown, J. E. and Blinks, J. R.: Changes in intracellular free calcium concentration during illumination of intervertebrate photoreceptors. Detection with aequorin. J. Gen. Physiol. **64,** 643–665 (1974).

Brown, J. E., Brown, P. K. and Pinto, L. H.: Detection of light-induced changes of intracellular ionized calcium concentration in Limulus ventral photoreceptors using arsenazo III. J. Physiol. **267,** 299–320 (1977).

Brown, J. E. and Coles, J. A.: Saturation of the response to light in Limulus ventral photoreceptor. J Physiol. **296,** 373–392 (1979).

Brown, J. E. and Lisman, J. E.: Intracellular Ca modulates sensitivity and time scale in Limulus ventral photoreceptors. Nature. **258,** 252–254 (1975).

Brown, J. E. and Rubin, L. J.: A direct demonstration that inositol-trisphosphate induces an increase in intracellular calcium in Limulus ventral photoreceptors. Biochem. Biophys. Res. Comm. **125,** 1137–1142 (1984).

Brown, J. E., Rubin, L. J., Ghayalini, A. J., Tarver, A. P., Irvine, R. F., Berridge, M. J. and Anderson, R. E.: Evidence that myo-inositol polyphosphate may be a messenger for visual excitation in Limulus photoreceptors. Nature. **311,** 160–163 (1984).

Connolly, T. M., Bross, T. E. and Majerus, P. W.: Isolation of a phosphomonoesterase from human platelets that specifically hydrolyzes the 5-phosphate of inositol 1,4,5-trisphosphate. J. Biol. Chem. **260,** 7868–7874 (1985).

Corson, D. W. and Fein, A.: Quantitative pressure injection of picoliter volumes into Limulus ventral photoreceptors. Biophys. J. **44,** 299–304 (1983).

Dawson, R. M. C., Freinkel, N., Jungalwala, F. B. and Clarke, N.: The enzymatic formation of myoinositol 1 : 2-cyclic phosphate from phosphatidylinositol. Biochem. J. **122,** 605–607 (1971).

Downes, C. P., Mussat, M. C. and Michell, R. H.: The inositol triphosphate phosphomonoesterase of the human erythrocyte membrane. Biochem. J. **203,** 169–177 (1982).

Fein, A. and Charlton, J. S.: Local adaptation in the ventral photoreceptors of Limulus. J. Gen. Physiol. **66,** 823–836 (1975).

Fein, A. and Charlton, J. S.: A quantitative comparison of the effects of intracellular calcium injection and light adaptation on the photoresponse of Limulus ventral photoreceptors. J. Gen. Physiol. **70,** 591–600 (1977).

Fein, A. and Lisman, J.: Localized desensitization of Limulus photoreceptors produced by light or intracellular calcium ion injection. Science. **187,** 1094–1096 (1975).

Fein, A., Payne, R., Corson, D. W., Berridge, M. J. and Irvine, R. F.: Photoreceptor excitation and adaptation by inositol 1,4,5-trisphosphate. Nature. **311,** 157–160 (1984).

Fuortes, M. G. F.: Visual responses in Limulus eye. Proc. Symp. Info. Proc. Sight Sensory Systems. 37–47 (1965).

Fuortes, M. G. F. and Hodgkin, A. L.: Changes in time scale and sensitivity in the ommatidia of Limulus. J. Physiol. **172,** 239–263 (1964).

Grado, C. and Ballou, C. E.: Myo-inositol phosphates obtained by alkaline hydrolysis of beef brain phosphoinositide. J. Biol. Chem. **236,** 54–60 (1961).

Harary, H. H. and Brown, J. E.: Spatially nonuniform changes in intracellular calcium ion concentrations. Science. **224,** 292–294 (1984).

Heslop, J. P., Irvine, R. F., Tashjian, A. H. and Berridge, M. J.: Inositol tetrakis- and pertakisphosphates in GH_4 cells. J. exp. Biol. **119,** 395–401 (1985).

Hofmann, S. L. and Majerus, P. W.: Modulation of phosphatidylinositol-specific phospholipase C activity by phospholipid interactions, diglycerides, and calcium ions. J. Biol. Chem. **257,** 14359–14364 (1982).

Hokin, L. E.: Receptors and phosphoinositide-generated second messengers. Ann. Rev. Biochem. **54,** 205–235 (1985).

Irvine, R. F., Anggard, E. A., Letcher, A. J. and Downes, C. P.: Metabolism of inositol (1,4,5) trisphosphate and inositol (1,3,4) trisphosphate in rat parotid glands. Biochem. J. **229,** 505–511 (1985).

Irvine, R. F., Letcher, A. J., Heslop, J. P. and Berridge, M. J.: The inositol tris-tetrakisphosphate pathway-demonstration of Ins(1,4,5)P_3-3-kinase activity in animal tissues. Nature **320,** 631–634 (1986).

Irvine, R. F., Letcher, A. J., Lander, D. J. and Downes, C. P.: Inositol trisphosphates in carbachol-stimulated rat parotid glands. Biochem. J. **223,** 237–243 (1984).

Korenbrot, J. I., Brown, J. E., Ochs, D. L., Williams, J. A. and Miller, D. L.: The use of tetracarboxylate fluorescent indicators in the measurement and control of intracellular free calcium ions. In Optical Methods in Cell Physiology, DeWeer, P. and B. M. Salzberg, eds. 347–363 (1986).

Levy, S. and Fein, A.: Relationship between light sensitivity and intracellular free Ca concentration in Limulus ventral photoreceptors. A quantitative study using Ca-selective microelectrodes. J. Gen. Physiol. **85,** 805–842 (1985).

Lisman, J. E. and Brown, J. E.: The effets of intracellular iontophoretic injection of calcium and sodium ions on the light response of Limulus ventral photoreceptors. J. Gen. Physiol. **59,** 701–719 (1972 a).

Lisman, J. E. and Brown, J. E.: The effects of intracellular Ca[2+] on the light response and on light adaptation in Limulus ventral photoreceptors. The Visual System: Neurophysiology, Biophysics and their Clinical Applications. 23–33 (1972 b).

Lisman, J. E. and Brown, J. E.: Effects of intracellular injection of calcium buffers on light adaptation in Limulus ventral photoreceptors. J. Gen. Physiol. **66,** 489–506 (1975).

Maaz, G. and Stieve, H.: The correlation of the receptor potential with the light induced transient increase in intracellular calcium-concentration measured by absorption change of Arsenazo III injected into Limulus ventral nerve photoreceptor cell. Biophys. Struct. Mech. **6,** 191–208 (1980).

Majerus, P. W., Neufeld, E. J. and Wilson, D. B.: Production of phosphoinositide-derived messengers. Cell. **37,** 701–703 (1984).

Majerus, P. W., Wilson, D. B., Connolly, T. M., Bross, T. E. and Neufeld, E. J.: Phosphoinositide turnover provides a link in stimulus-response coupling. Trends Biochem. Sci. **10,** 168–171 (1985).

Michell, R. H.: Inositol phospholipids and cell surface receptor function. Biochim. Biophys. Acta. **415,** 81–147 (1975).

Payne, R. and Fein, A.: Localized adaptation within the rhabdomeral lobe of Limulus ventral photoreceptors. J. Gen. Physiol. **81,** 767–769 (1983).

Stieve, H. and Pflaum, M.: The response height versus stimulus intensity curve of the ventral photoreceptor of Limulus depending on adaptation and external calcium concentration. Vision Res. **18,** 747–749 (1978).

Streb, H., Irvine, R. F., Berridge, M. J. and Schulz, I.: Release of Ca from a nonmitochondrial intracellular store in pancreatic acinar cells by inositol-1,4,5-triphosphate. Nature. **306,** 67–69 (1983).

Szuts, E., Reid, M., Payne, R., Corson, D. W. and Fein, A.: Biochemical and physiological evidence for the involvement of inositol 1,4,5-trisphosphate in visual transduction. Biophys. J. **47,** 202 a (1985).

Vandenberg, C. A. and Montal, M.: Light-regulated biochemical events in invertebrate photoreceptors. 2. Light-regulated phosphorylation of rhodopsin and phosphoinositides in squid photoreceptor membranes. Biochemistry. **23,** 2347–2352 (1984).

Wilson, D. B., Bross, T. E., Hofmann, S. L. and Majerus, P. W.: Hydrolysis of polyphosphoinositides by purified sheep seminal vesicle phospholipase C enzymes. J. Biol. Chem. **259,** 11718–11724 (1984).

Wilson, D. B., Bross, T. E., Sherman, W. R., Berger, R. A. and Majerus, P. W.: Inositol cyclic phosphates are produced by cleavage of phosphatidylphosphoinositols (polyphosphoinositides) with purified sheep seminal vesicle phospholipase C enzymes. Proc. Natl. Acad. Sci. **82,** 4013–4017. (1985 a)

Wilson, D. B., Connolly, T. M., Bross, T. E., Majerus, P. W., Sherman, W. R., Tyler, A. N., Rubin, L. J. and Brown, J. E.: Isolation and characterization of the inositol cyclic phosphate products of polyphosphoinositide cleavage by phospholipase C. J. Biol. Chem. **260,** 13496–13501 (1985 b).

Yoshioka, T., Inoue, H., Inomata, K., Hayashi, F. and Takagi, M.: The parallel study of protein phosphorylation and phosphatidylinositol metabolism in the photoreception of squid retina. Proc. Jap. Acad. **57 B,** 309–313 (1981).

Yoshioka, T., Inoue, H., Takagi, M., Hayashi, F. and Amakawa: The effect of isobutylmethylxanthine on the photoresponse and phosphorylation of phosphatidylinositol in octopus retina. Biochim. Biophys. Acta. **755,** 50–55 (1983).

Fortschritte der Zoologie, Band 33 · Lüttgau (Hrsg.): Membrane Control
Gustav Fischer Verlag · Stuttgart · New York · 1986

Measurement of intracellular calcium levels in vertebrate photoreceptors

P. A. McNaughton, L. Cervetto and B. J. Nunn

Physiological Laboratory, Downing St., Cambridge CB2 3EG, UK

Our view of the events occurring inside a vertebrate photoreceptor following a flash of light has changed considerably in the past year. It was always recognized that an internal transmitter is required to mediate between photoisomerized rhodopsin molecules located in the disc membranes and the closure of light-sensitive channels in the surface membrane of the outer segment. There were two main candidates for this transmitter: calcium ions and cyclic GMP. Support for calcium came from experiments in which calcium ions applied externally (Yoshikami and Hagins, 1973) or injected into the outer segment (Brown, Coles and Pinto, 1977) closed light-sensitive channels. Although these experiments showed that calcium inside the cell suppressed the light-sensitive current, they did not demonstrate that the action was a direct one, nor whether the normal mechanism of channel closure after a light flash occurs by this means. Support for cyclic GMP was based on experiments showing that light caused a drop in the intracellular level of cGMP as a result of the activation of a light-sensitive phosphodiesterase (see review by Stryer, 1986).

The identity of the intracellular transmitter has now been resolved by two different sorts of experiments. Fesenko, Kolesnikov and Lyubarsky (1985) showed that cGMP directly opens channels in excised patches of outer segment surface membrane, and that the properties of these channels appear identical to those of the light-sensitive channel in an intact cell. This result has now been confirmed by other workers (Nakatani and Yau, 1985; Haynes and Yau, 1985). The calcium hypothesis has been disproved by experiments in which a sudden rise in intracellular Ca was found to cause only a slow closure of light-sensitive channels (Hodgkin, McNaughton and Nunn, 1985; see Fig. 3 below) and by others, in which high concentrations of Ca buffers were incorporated into rods and were found to have little effect on the light response (Matthews, Torre and Lamb, 1985).

While calcium is almost certainly not the primary transmitter in the light response, there is nonetheless strong evidence to suggest that intracellular Ca plays a role in the light response. Calcium can suppress light-sensitive channels, probably by an indirect mechanism, and elevations of internal Ca slow the light response (Hodgkin, McNaughton and Nunn, 1986). We do not, in fact, even know for certain whether Ca_i increases or decreases after a flash of light.

To help in resolving these questions we have measured intracellular Ca using the Ca-sensitive photoprotein aequorin. We find that intracellular Ca falls during the light response because the main route for entry of Ca is through the light-sensitive channels themselves. Calcium is pumped out of the cell by a Na: Ca exchange in which three Na^+ ions exchange for each Ca^{++}.

Methods

The methods for recording the light-sensitive current and for changing the solution bathing the outer segment were as described by Hodgkin, McNaughton and Nunn, (1985) and are presented in summary only. Tiger salamanders *(Ambystoma tigrinum)* were decapitated, the eyes enucleated and the retinas isolated. Isolated rods, obtained by mechanical dissociation, were drawn inner-segment first into a tightly-fitting suction pipette connected to a virtual-ground current monitor. The solution bathing the outer segment could be rapidly changed by transferring the rod, held in the suction pipette, across the boundary between two flowing solutions. The current change recorded during this procedure consisted of the light-sensitive current plus a junction current caused by the different mobilities of the ions in the two solutions. The light-sensitive current can be obtained in isolation by repeating the solution change in the presence of a bright light and by subtracting this record from the record obtained in darkness.

The procedure for incorporating aequorin into the outer segment is summarized in Figure 1. A whole-cell recording was obtained from the outer segment by the method of Hamill, Marty, Neher, Sakmann and Sigworth (1981). A fine plastic tube inserted inside the whole-cell pipette as close as possible to the mouth contained approximately 0.1 μl of aequorin, dissolved at 20 mg/ml in the normal pipette filling solution. The aequorin was isolated from the pipette contents by a short buffer zone of filling solution (see Fig. 1, panel 1). Once a successful whole-cell recording had been obtained, the aequorin was ejected from the plastic tube (Fig. 1, panel 2) and about 10 mins was allowed for diffusion into the cell (panel 3). At the end of this period the whole-cell pipette was gently withdrawn; if this is done carefully a long «bridge» of membrane forms (see panel 4), which eventually nips off leaving the rod functioning normally.

An estimate of the time taken for the aequorin to diffuse into the cell was obtained as shown in Fig. 2. In this experiment the aequorin had been prepared in a solution containing 33.5 mM Na, 82.5 mM K instead of the normal 6 mM Na, 110 mM K. The time of injection is shown by the bar above the current trace, with the open bar showing the injection of the «buffer zone» of normal solution and the hatched bar showing the injection of aequorin in elevated Na. The diffusion of Na into the cell caused a reduction of the light-sensitive current which is half complete in about 30 sec. Since the diffusion coefficient of aequorin is 4×10^{-7} cm^2/sec (Baker, Hodgkin and Ridgway, 1971), or about 40 times less than that of Na, half-equilibration of aequorin should take about 20 min. In practice it is difficult to hold a whole-cell recording for this long, and sufficient loading is normally obtained after 5–10 mins.

The light output from the aequorin-loaded rod was collected with a 100 × oil immersion objective and was focused on a photomultiplier tube mounted in place of the eyepieces on a Zeiss IM35 microscope. At the end of the experiment, the total counts in the cell were measured by lysing it in a hypotonic solution containing only 1 mM $CaCl_2$. The rate of disintegration of aequorin could then be calculated and the calcium level determined from the empirical formula, determined from data supplied by Dr. J. Blinks (personal communication), and valid for [Mg] = 1 mM and over the range 1 μM < [Ca] < 25 μM:

$$[Ca] = 4.673 \times 10^{-5}\ (\text{Disintegration rate})^{0.417}$$

Using this method for loading the cell, a total count of up to 4×10^4 has been achieved on lysing the cell, sufficient to detect Ca concentrations down to 1 μM. The total number of aequorin molecules incorporated is about 4×10^6, of the same order of magnitude as the number of phosphodiesterase molecules in the cell.

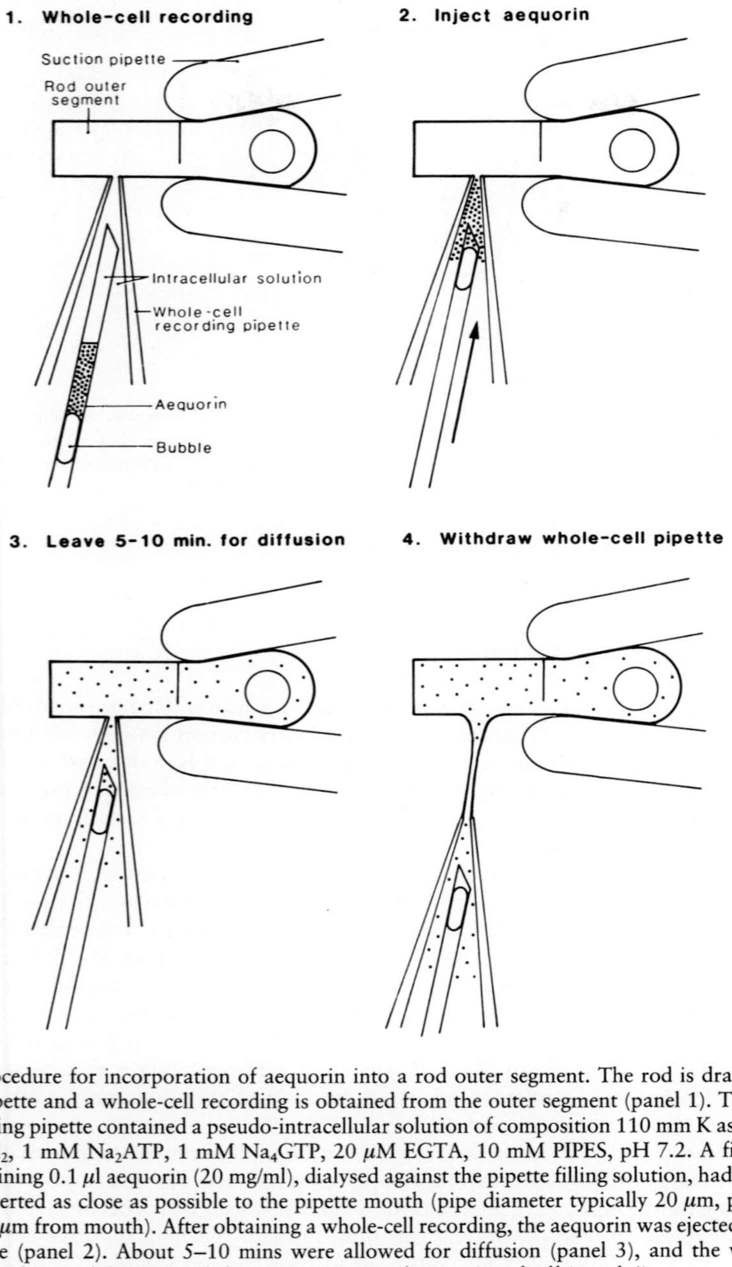

Fig. 1: Procedure for incorporation of aequorin into a rod outer segment. The rod is drawn into a suction pipette and a whole-cell recording is obtained from the outer segment (panel 1). The whole-cell recording pipette contained a pseudo-intracellular solution of composition 110 mm K aspartate, 3 mM $MgCl_2$, 1 mM Na_2ATP, 1 mM Na_4GTP, 20 μM EGTA, 10 mM PIPES, pH 7.2. A fine plastic tube containing 0.1 μl aequorin (20 mg/ml), dialysed against the pipette filling solution, had previously been inserted as close as possible to the pipette mouth (pipe diameter typically 20 μm, positioned about 100 μm from mouth). After obtaining a whole-cell recording, the aequorin was ejected from the plastic pipe (panel 2). About 5–10 mins were allowed for diffusion (panel 3), and the whole-cell pipette was then withdrawn until the connecting membrane nipped off (panel 4).

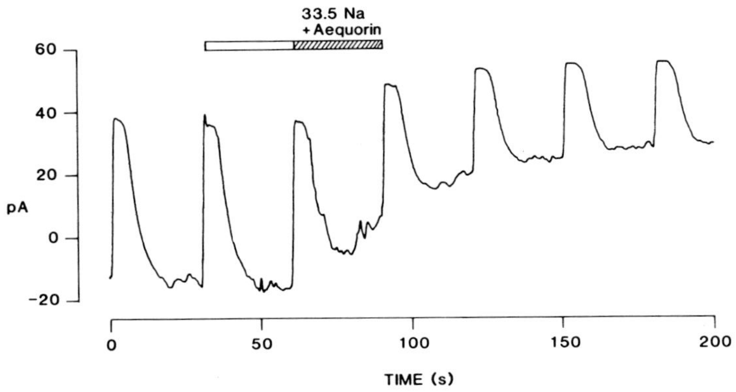

Fig. 2: Whole-cell recording, obtained as shown in Fig. 1, during injection of aequorin dialysed against 33.5 mM Na, 82.5 mM K. Times of ejection of the buffer zone of normal intracellular solution and of the aequorin in elevated Na are shown by the open and hatched bars, respectively. Holding potential –40 mV.

Results

Currents carried by Ca ions

In the first part of this paper we shall review experiments (Hodgkin, McNaughton and Nunn, 1985) showing that calcium ions can carry current through the light-sensitive channel, and that a large increase in $[Ca]_i$ causes only a relatively slow suppression of light-sensitive current. These experiments were performed without the use of aequorin, though later experiments in which aequorin was used to monitor the intracellular calcium level confirm the conclusions.

Figure 3 shows the suppression of light-sensitive current caused by a variety of treatments designed to increase the calcium level inside the cell. In each of these experiments, carried out on the same cell, the solution change was complete in less than 100 msec. Removal of Na causes a decline in light-sensitive current to near zero (Fig. 3 A); the decline is not due to a lower permeability of the membrane to Li, the ion used to substitute for Na, since it occurs on a substantially slower time scale than the solution change rate. In fact, the permeability of the membrane to Li is about 1.1 times that to Na, as is seen by the initial small increase in current. There is now much evidence to show that the suppression of current in experiments of this kind results from a buildup of internal Ca when Na : Ca exchange is prevented by removal of external Na.

Record B shows the effects of replacing all cations in the external medium with Ca. The rod was initially bathed in a medium containing 35 mM Na and 1 μM Ca, and on transferring to isotonic $CaCl_2$, a large inward current is seen which declines to zero in 2–3 sec. This experiment shows that Ca can flow through the light-sensitive channel. The quantity of Ca flowing is 265 pC, sufficient to raise the intracellular Ca by 1.4 mM if distributed throughout an outer segment volume of approximately 10^{-12} l, yet this large Ca load causes a shutoff of light-sensitive current which is not greatly faster than in Fig. 3 A where the quantity of Ca entering is much less. Two conclusions can be drawn from the experiment of Fig. 3 B. First, the experiment is not consistent with a simple version of

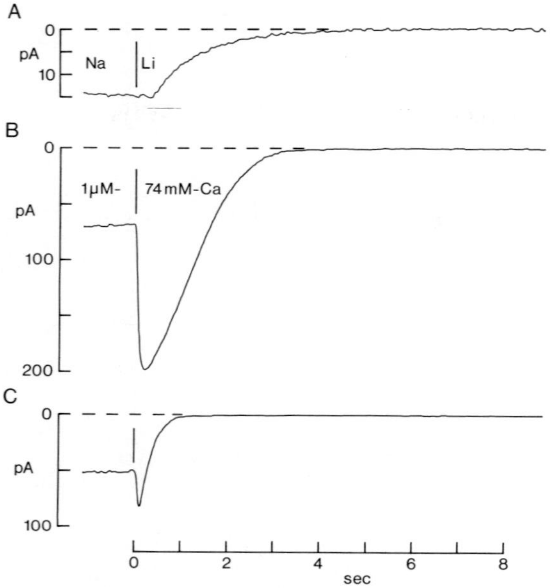

Fig. 3: Panel A: Current recorded by a suction pipette during the change from normal Ringer (110 mM NaCl, 2.5 mM KCl, 1.6 mM $MgCl_2$, 1 mM $CaCl_2$, 10 mM HEPES, 3 mM glucose, pH 7.8) to a Ringer in which all Na was replaced with Li. Solution change complete in 100 ms.
Panel B: Rod initially in 35 mM Na, 1 μM Ca solution; Ca_o raised to 74.3 mM (and Na_o removed) at time zero.
Panel C: Same solution change as in B, in the presence of a dim light (2.4 isomerizations s^{-1}). Modified from HODGKIN et al. (1985).

the Ca hypothesis since under the conditions of the experiment, a bright flash of light is capable of closing channels at least ten times more rapidly and therefore should release the unlikely amount of 14 mM Ca. Second, the rate of closure is not strongly dependent on the Ca concentration in the cell, which implies that Ca ions do not interact directly with channels.

Figure 3 C shows that the rate of closure of channels after an influx of Ca is strongly accelerated by a background light. A similar result can also be obtained if the closure is caused by removal of Na (Fig. 4). In this experiment the rate of closure was observed to be slowed by the application of the phosphodiesterase inhibitor IBMX which inhibits the breakdown of cGMP to GMP, and it is speeded by a background light, which is known to stimulate the rate of cGMP breakdown. An attractive interpretation of these experiments is that the rate of closure of channels on removal of external Na or on elevation of external Ca is a direct measure of the current state of activity of the phosphodiesterase.

There is no direct evidence to show at what point in the light-sensitive pathway Ca acts to suppress light-sensitive channels, but one possibility suggested by HODGKIN, MCNAUGHTON and NUNN (1985) is that calcium may inhibit the guanylate cyclase responsible for synthesizing cGMP from GTP. In this scheme a sudden rise in $[Ca]_i$ would cause a rapid inhibition of the cyclase, and the subsequent closure rate of channels would then reflect the activity of the PDE. The closure rate in this scheme has the required property of being independent of the level of $[Ca]_i$, provided the increase is sufficient to cause a substantial inhibition of the cyclase.

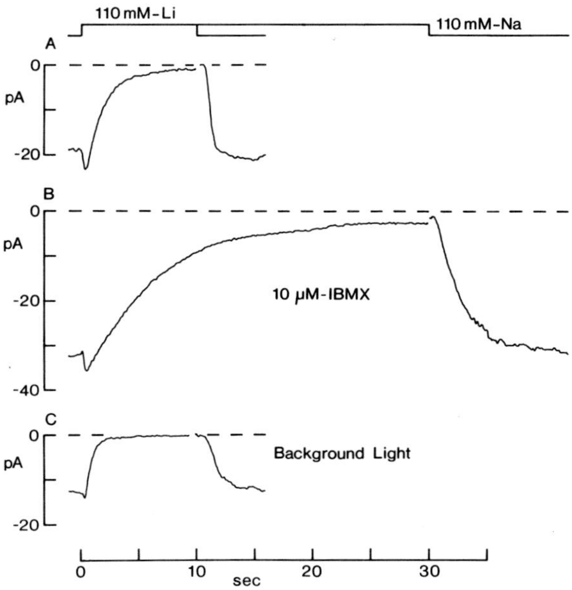

Fig. 4: Effect of IBMX and dim light on the change in light-sensitive current on replacing Na with Li. A, Response to 10 s application of 110 mM Li, in darkness and in the absence of IBMX. B, 30 s application of Li in the presence of 10 μM IBMX throughout. C, repeat of A in dim light (5.4 photoisomerizations s^{-1}). Reprinted with permission from Hodgkin et al. (1985)

Measurement of $[Ca]_i$ using aequorin

In normal Ringer the calcium concentration in a rod outer segment loaded with aequorin is below the limit of detection, determined mainly by the dark noise in the photomultiplier, and no significant change in $[Ca]_i$ can be detected during a flash of light. From the measured aequorin level in the cell an upper limit, at the 95 % confidence level, of 1 μM can be set for the free calcium concentration both in darkness and on the plateau of the light response. However, when the phosphodiesterase inhibitor IBMX is applied the light-sensitive current increases, and a burst of light is recorded from the aequorin-loaded cell (Trace 1 in Fig. 5 B). The light-sensitive current declines again as the light output reaches a peak, probably because the rod detects and responds to the aequorin light emission.

The result shown in Fig. 5, trace 1, is difficult to reconcile with the idea that Ca closes channels, since the application of IBMX causes an increase both in the free Ca concentration and in the light-sensitive current. A more likely explanation is that the light-sensitive channels admit Ca, and that $[Ca]_i$ rises as more channels are opened by the increase in the intracellular concentration of cGMP in the presence of IBMX.

The effect of a flash of light was investigated in Fig. 5, trace 2. The effect of the flash is to cause a decline in $[Ca]_i$ as light-sensitive channels close, with no indication that the flash releases Ca. The small decrease in count rate coincident with the flash is due to the inhibition of counting necessary to prevent the flash photons being recorded by the photo-

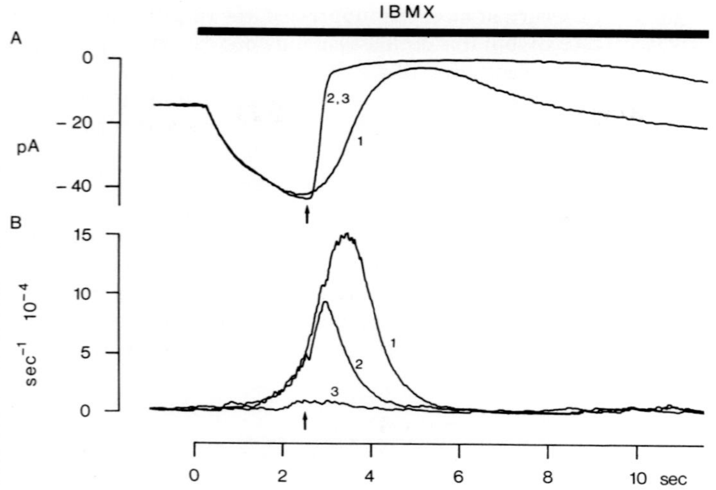

Fig. 5: Simultaneous recordings of light-sensitive current (A) and aequorin light output, expressed as a rate of consumption (B). Duration of exposure to IBMX (500 μM) shown by black bar. Trace 1 in darkness, traces 2 and 3 with a flash (29, 500 Rh*) delivered at the arrow. Aequorin light was recorded either from the outer segment (traces 1 and 2) or from the inner segment (trace 3), and was filtered with a time constant of 0.52 sec. Traces are the average of between 3 and 5 presentations. Reprinted with permission from CERVETTO, MCNAUGHTON and NUNN, 1986.

multiplier; outside this short region the counts are not significantly different with and without the flash. The main effect of the flash is to cause a delayed drop in the count rate due to a drop in $[Ca]_i$ as light-sensitive channels close, as was first proposed on the basic of indirect evidence by BOWNDS (1980) and YAU and NAKATANI (1985).

In trace 3 the aperture which is normally positioned to record counts only from the outer segment was moved over the inner segment; the absence of a large recorded count shows that the light emission recorded in traces 1 and 2 did indeed result from changes in $[Ca]_i$ in the outer segment.

The influx of Ca into an aequorin-loaded cell can be measured by exposing the outer segment to a solution in which all permeant ions have been replaced by Ca, as was done in Fig. 3 B. Fig. 6 shows an experiment of this kind in which IBMX has been added to the external solution to increase the influx of Ca. The initial effect of the solution change is to cause a rapid reduction in current since under these conditions Ca carries less current than Na. There is a subsequent rise in current as cGMP increases, due to the action of IBMX, followed by a complete closure of light-sensitive channels in response to the large aequorin light emission within the cell. The exact origin of these changes in light-sensitive current is in fact not very important in this experiment, since the main purpose is to measure the Ca influx. Trace D in Fig. 6 shows the time course of the integral of the Ca current, beginning at the time of introduction of isotonic Ca. The total Ca entry is 45.6 pC, which corresponds to a rise in total $[Ca]_i$ of 236 μM if distributed over an outer segment volume of 10^{-12} l. The actual rise in free $[Ca]_i$ is about one-tenth of this (Fig. 6 C), although the time course of the rise is similar to the integral of the Ca influx. This experiment shows, therefore, that approximately 90 % of the Ca entering the cell is bound, and that the time course of binding is rapid compared to the time course of the influx.

After the light-sensitive current has been suppressed, the rate of aequorin light emission declines slowly (see Trace B), but this decline is mainly due to consumption of aequorin in the presence of the high concentration of Ca. When consumption is allowed for, the free $[Ca]_i$ is seen to remain approximately constant (Trace C) even in the presence of the 4×10^3-fold gradient for Ca across the cell membrane. We conclude that entry of Ca through the membrane is small when all light-sensitive channels are closed.

On restoration of Na a light-insensitive inward current is recorded, and the free $[Ca]_i$ declines rapidly. This inward current has been attributed to the operation of an electrogenic Na : Ca exchange (Yau and Nakatani, 1984), an interpretation which is borne out by the experiment of Fig. 6 since the time course of the decline in free $[Ca]_i$ (Trace C) is similar to the integral of the «pumping current» (Trace D). The integral of the Ca influx is approximately double the integral of the pumping current, consistent with a 3 Na^+ : 1 Ca^{++} stoichiometry for the exchange pump. The exchange is capable of lowering $[Ca]_i$ at a

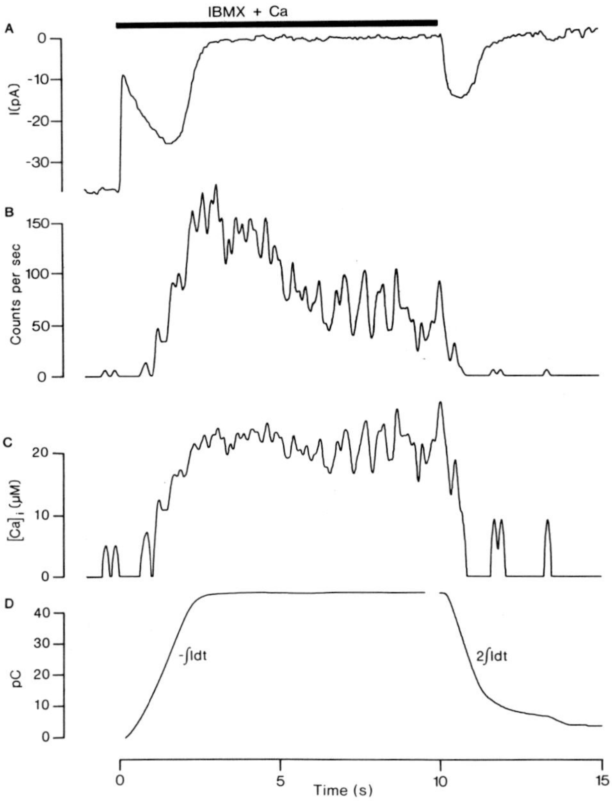

Fig. 6: Exposure of rod outer segment to 77 mM $CaCl_2$, 10 mM HEPES, 500 μM IBMX (duration of exposure shown by black bar). Simultaneous traces of light-sensitive current recorded from the suction pipette (A) and aequorin light output (B). Panel C shows $[Ca]_i$ calculated from B as in methods; panel D shows the integral of the current multiplied by –1 (early part) and 2 (later part). Note the approximate equality of the 2 integrals, consistent with the operation of a 3 Na^+ : 1 Ca^{++} exchange. Unpublished data of Cervetto, McNaughton and Nunn.

rate of 70 μM/s in the experiment of Fig. 6 and, in view of the absence of any decline in $[Ca]_i$ in the absence of Na in this and in other experiments, the Na : Ca exchange appears to be the only significant mechanism of Ca transport in the outer segment membrane.

Conclusions

The experiments described in this paper add to the growing body of evidence to show that Ca is not the internal transmitter in vertebrate photoreceptors. Yet Ca seems to be important to the cell, since the membrane permeability of light-sensitive channels to Ca is high, and since there is a highly active Na : Ca exchange present in the surface membrane. As a consequence the total exchangeable Ca in the cell turns over with a time constant of less than 0.5 sec, well within the time course of the flash response. It remains for future work to determine the role of Ca in the light response, although one likely possibility is that Ca may inhibit the guanylate cyclase responsible for restoring the level of cGMP after a flash (Hodgkin, McNaughton and Nunn, 1985). Since Ca_i drops substantially during the light response, this mechanism would allow a more rapid recovery from a bright flash of light.

We have not been able to detect the resting level of Ca with the methods described in this paper, but an estimate can be obtained as follows. The pumping current on the plateau of the light response declines with a time constant of about 0.5 sec and carries a total charge of about 0.5 pC (Yau and Nakatani, 1985; Cervetto and McNaughton, 1986). If the pump operates as a 3 Na^+ : 1 Ca^{++} exchange, this charge transfer corresponds to a change in total Ca concentration of 5 μM when distributed over an outer segment volume of 1 pl. If 10 % of this Ca is free, as found in the experiment of Fig. 6, then the free Ca in darkness would be 0.5 μM, about one half of our present detection limit of 1 μM. We have assumed here that the Ca concentration in light is small, which seems a likely assumption in view of our demonstration that the main route of Ca entry is via the light-sensitive channel.

Acknowledgement

We thank Professor A. L. Hodgkin and Dr. P. H. Cobbold for helpful advice, and Dr. J. Blinks for a supply of aequorin. Supported by the MRC and by EMBO.

References

Baker, P. F., Hodgkin, A. L. and Ridgway, E. B.: Depolarization and calcium entry in squid giant axons. J. Physiol. **218**, 709–755 (1971).

Bownds, M. D.: Biochemical steps in visual transduction: roles for nucleotides and calcium ions. Photochem. and Photobiol. **32**, 487–490 (1980).

Brown, J. E., Coles, J. A. and Pinto, L. H.: Effects of injection of calcium and EGTA into the outer segment of retinal rods of *Bufo marinus*. J. Physiol. **269**, 707–722 (1977).

Cervetto, L. and McNaughton, P. A.: The effects of phosphodiesterase inhibitors and lanthanum ions on the light-sensitive current of toad retinal rods. J. Physiol. **370**, 91–109 (1986).

Cervetto, L., McNaughton, P. A. and Nunn, B. J.: Aqueorin signals from isolated salamander rods. J. Physiol. **371,** 36 P. (1985).

Fesenko, E. E., Kolesnikov, S. S. and Lyubarsky, A. L.: Induction by cyclic GMP of cationic conductance in plasma membrane of retinal rod outer segment. Nature, **313,**310–313 (1985).

Hamill, O. P., Marty, A., Neher, E., Sakman, B. and Sigworth, F. J.: Improved patch-clamp techniques for high-resolution current recording from cells and cell-free membrane patches. Eur. J. Physiol. **391,** 85–100 (1981).

Haynes, L. and Yau, K.-W.: Cyclic GMP-sensitive conductance in cell free inside-out membrane patches from catfish cone outer segments. J. Physiol. **365,**35 P (1985).

Hodgkin, A. L., McNaughton, P. A. and Nunn, B. J.: The ionic selectivity and calcium dependence of the light-sensitive pathway in toad rods. J. Physiol. **358,**447–468 (1985).

Hodgkin, A. L., McNaughton, P. A. and Nunn, B. J.: Effects of changing Ca before and after light flashes in salamander rods. J. Physiol. **372,** 54 P. (1986).

Matthews, H. R., Torre, V. and Lamb, T. D.: Effects on the photoresponse of calcium buffers and cyclic GMP incorporated into the cytoplasm of retinal rods. Nature, **313,**582–585 (1985).

Nakatani, K. and Yau, K.-W.: cGMP opens the light-sensitive conductance in retinal rods. Biophys. J. **47,**356 a (1985).

Stryer, L.: Cyclic GMP cascade of vision. Ann. Rev. Neurosci. **9,** 87–119 (1986).

Yau, K.-W. and Nakatani, K.: Electrogenic Na : Ca exchange in retinal rod outer segment. Nature, **311,** 661–663 (1984).

Yau, K.-W. and Nakatani, K.: Light-induced reduction of cytoplasmic free calcium in retinal rod outer segment. Nature, **313.** 579–582 (1985).

Yoshikami, S. and Hagins, W. A.: Control of the dark current in vertebrate rods and cones. In: Biochemistry and physiology of visual pigments. Ed. Langer, H. pp. 245–255. New York: Springer-Verlag (1973).

Fortschritte der Zoologie, Band 33 · Lüttgau (Hrsg.): Membrane Control
Gustav Fischer Verlag · Stuttgart · New York · 1986

Roles of calcium and cyclic GMP in visual transduction

K.-W. Yau*, L. W. Haynes* and K. Nakatani*

Department of Physiology and Biophysics, The University of Texas Medical Branch, Galveston, Texas 77550, USA

Retinal photoreceptors – the rods and the cones – respond to light with a graded membrane hyperpolarization. This electrical signal is transmitted to the second-order visual neurons through modulation of transmitter release at the photoreceptors' synaptic terminals. In darkness, the synaptic transmitter is apparently released at a high rate from the photoreceptors; in the light, the membrane hyperpolarization reduces this release in a graded fashion. The effect of light on the second-order neurons can be a hyperpolarization or a depolarization, depending on whether a given synapse from the photoreceptor is sign-preserving or sign-inverting.

In both rods and cones, the way in which light generates the membrane hyperpolarization, that is, the process of visual transduction, seems to be as follows. In darkness, the plasma membrane of the receptor outer segment has a high permeability to Na, resulting in a continuous entry of Na into the outer segment. This steady inward «dark current» depolarizes the cell and maintains the high level of synaptic transmitter release mentioned above. What light does is to reduce this conductance (the «light-sensitive conductance») and hence the inward dark current, leading to a hyperpolarization. The mechanism by which light reduces the light-sensitive conductance has been a subject of intense interest as well as debate for the past fifteen years. Although there is general agreement that an internal diffusible transmitter is involved in communicating between the photon absorption site and the light-sensitive conductance (Baylor and Fuortes, 1970), this transmitter substance has not yet been identified (see Miller, 1981; Stieve, 1986).

One hypothesis is that light increases the concentration of free Ca within the outer segment, and the Ca then binds and blocks the light-sensitive conductance (Yoshikami and Hagins, 1971; Hagins, 1972). This idea has been supported by the finding that a rise in intracellular Ca induced by Ca injection or a Ca ionophore leads to the closure of the light-sensitive conductance, while a fall in internal Ca induced by the injection of a Ca chelator has the opposite effect (Hagins and Yoshikami, 1974; Brown et al., 1977; Oakley and Pinto, 1983; MacLeish et al., 1984). Another piece of supporting evidence is that in the light a Ca efflux occurs from the rod outer segment via a Na–Ca exchange mechanism; this Ca efflux has been interpreted to indicate that in the light free Ca increases in the rod outer segment and it then spills out of the cell (Yoshikami et al., 1980; Gold and Korenbrot, 1980; Schröder and Fain, 1984). The main difficulty with the Ca hypothesis, however, is that there is still no direct evidence for a rise in free Ca

* Present address: Department of Neuroscience, The Johns Hopkins University School of Medicine, 725 North Wolfe Street, Baltimore, Maryland 21205, USA.

concentration within the outer segment in the light. There is also dispute about how much Ca efflux actually occurs during prolonged illumination (Schröder and Fain, 1984; Somlyo and Walz, 1985).

A second hypothesis, at least in rods, is that in darkness the light-sensitive conductance is kept open by a high level of cGMP (guanosine 3′ : 5′-cyclic monophosphate), perhaps via activation of a cGMP-dependent protein kinase, and light closes the conductance by activating a phosphodiesterase which reduces the level of cGMP (Bitensky et al., 1971; Goridis et al., 1974; Woodruff et al., 1977; Yee and Liebman, 1978; Bitensky et al., 1978; see also Hubbell and Bownds, 1979). In parallel with the Ca hypothesis this idea has been progressively gaining experimental support. For example, perfusion of rods with a membrane-permeable cGMP analog or the phosphodiesterase inhibitor IBMX (isobutylmethylxanthine) leads to membrane depolarization and an increase of the light response (Lipton et al., 1977; Capovilla et al., 1982; Waloga, 1983; Cervetto and McNaughton, 1986). Injection of cGMP or cGMP analogs into rods has the same effect (Nicol and Miller, 1978; Miller and Nicol, 1979; Miller, 1982; Waloga, 1983; Kawamura and Murakami, 1983; Lipton, 1983; MacLeish et al., 1984; Pinto and Brown, 1984; Matthews et al., 1985; Cobbs and Pugh, 1985; Zimmermann et al., 1985), while injection of partially purified cGMP-phosphodiesterase mimicks light by causing membrane hyperpolarization (Clack et al., 1983). Furthermore, extensive information has recently been gathered on the biochemical pathway that leads to the reduction of cGMP in the light (for reviews, see Liebman and Pugh, 1981; Kühn, 1984; Stryer, 1986). It is known now that the photoisomerized rhodopsin molecule catalyzes a GDP–GTP exchange at a GTP-binding protein (also called transducin); this GTP-binding protein, once bound to GTP, activates the phosphodiesterase which hydrolyzes cGMP (Fung and Stryer, 1980; Fung et al., 1981; Kühn et al., 1981). A key step in the quenching of the light effect, on the other hand, appears to be the phosphorylation of the photoisomerized rhodopsin, which as a result binds another protein (called the 48 K-protein or S-antigen) and triggers the shut-off of the phosphodiesterase activation (Kühn and Dreyer, 1972; Sitaramayya and Liebman, 1983; Kühn et al., 1984; Pfister et al., 1985). In short, GTP is required for the light-mediated activation of cGMP hydrolysis, and ATP is required for the deactivation or quenching (Yee and Liebman, 1978; Liebman and Pugh, 1980). Despite this rich knowledge, the major problem with the cGMP hypothesis is that the decline in the rod's cGMP content during illumination does not appear to be large enough for this scheme to seem very plausible (Kilbride and Ebrey, 1979; Goldberg et al., 1983).

The debate on the Ca and the cGMP hypotheses continued for many years until it was realized that Ca and cGMP probably both participate in the transduction process. Subsequently, other schemes have been proposed which involve various interactions between Ca and cGMP (Bownds, 1980; Lipton and Dowling, 1981; Sorbi, 1981; Fatt, 1982; George and Hagins, 1983), but these remain largely as conjectures. The crux of the problem therefore lies not so much in a lack of plausible schemes to explain transduction but in the difficulty of selecting the correct one.

This paper outlines some experiments that we have recently done on this problem. Briefly, the results indicate that cGMP is the direct agonist of the light-sensitive conductance, and that the concentration of free Ca in the rod outer segment decreases rather than increases during illumination, implicating a role of Ca in light adaptation rather than excitation. Most of the experiments were performed on rods, but some of the observations were also made in cones. Preliminary descriptions of the results have been published (Yau and Nakatani, 1984 a, b, 1985 a, b; Haynes and Yau, 1985; Nakatani and Yau, 1985, 1986; Yau and Haynes, 1986). Full descriptions of the work will appear in the future.

Methods

Rods from the tropical toad, *Bufo marinus*, and cones from the channel catfish, *Ictalurus punctatus*, were used in the experiments. Single isolated cells were used in both cases, obtained by finely chopping up a piece of retina under Ringer's solution. Two methods of recording were used. The first employed a large suction pipet to record from the entire outer or inner segment of a rod (YAU et al., 1977; BAYLOR et al., 1979; YAU et al., 1980; HODGKIN et al., 1984), and the second employed a patch-pipet to record from an excised, inside-out patch of rod or cone outer segment membrane (see HAMILL et al., 1981; SAKMANN and NEHER, 1983). Most of the technical details can be found in the papers quoted above. The following provides some specific points pertaining to the experiments here.

Ca experiments

These experiments were conducted under infrared light with the help of an IR-image converter. The inner segment of a single, dark-adapted rod was drawn into a suction pipet containing Ringer's solution to record membrane current, while the outer segment was exposed to rapid bath perfusion. Changes in the bath solution took 200–300 msec and were effected by a valve operated pneumatically and with electronic timing so that the solution change could be reproduced exactly many times (NAKATANI and YAU, submitted).

The composition of normal Ringer's was (in mM): 110 Na, 2.5 K, 1.6 Mg, 1.0 Ca, 117.7 Cl, 5 TMA (tetramethylammonium)-HEPES, 5 dextrose, pH 7.6.

Excised-patch experiments

These experiments were conducted in visible light. A patch-pipet containing Ringer's solution was sealed against the tip of a rod or cone outer segment, establishing a gigaseal membrane patch. The bath solution was then switched from Ringer's to a pseudointracellular solution, and a gentle tap on the micromanipulator supporting the pipet yielded an excised, inside-out membrane patch, with its cytoplasmic face exposed to perfusion.

The composition of normal Ringer's was the same as described above, while the pseudointracellular solution contained (in mM): 12.5 NaCl, 100 K Gluconate, 1.6 $MgCl_2$, 0.1 TMA-EGTA, 5 TMA-HEPES, pH 7.0. The retina was incubated for 1 hr in Ringer's solution containing 1 mg/ml hyaluronidase (Sigma Type I–S) prior to chopping.

Truncated rod outer segment experiments

These experiments were conducted under infrared light. A rod outer segment was partially sucked into a regular suction pipet (i. e., same as those used in the Ca experiments) containing Ringer's solution. The inner segment and the basal portion of the outer segment outside the pipet were then removed with a microprobe, leaving an open-ended outer segment envelope whose interior could be dialyzed with a pseudointracellular solution in the bath. The potential difference between the pipet interior and the bath was held at 0 mV (the low leakage resistance between the pipet wall and the outer segment did not permit current measurements at membrane potentials significantly different from zero). The solutions had the same composition as those used in the excised-patch experiments.

Results

Ca experiments on intact rods

These experiments were prompted by a recent observation that the light-sensitive conductance is, counter to previous belief, permeable to both monovalent and divalent cations, including Ca (YAU et al., 1980; HODGKIN et al., 1984; YAU and NAKATANI, 1984 a; HODGKIN et al., 1985). In light of this finding we decided to study the behavior of a large Ca influx into a rod outer segment. The expectation was that if internal Ca indeed blocked the conductance directly, then any sizeable Ca influx through the light-sensitive conductance should shut itself off rapidly because it was a self-inhibitory process. To our surprise, such a rapid shut-off of current was not observed (Fig. 1). In this experiment, the light-sensitive conductance was first increased by perfusing the rod outer segment with a bath Na solution containing low Ca (HODGKIN et al., 1984), and the large inward Ca current was then induced by switching to an isotonic $CaCl_2$ solution. Despite a peak influx of as many as 10^9 Ca ions sec^{-1}, the Ca current decreased relatively slowly (trace a). A similar observation was also described by HODGKIN et al. (1985). This was not expected if the Ca that entered immediately blocked the conductance. In the same experiment, however, the large Ca currents could be rapidly shut off by light (traces b, c and d). Two conclusions can therefore be drawn: firstly, internal Ca is unlikely to block the conductance directly, and secondly light does not shut down the conductance by simply changing the internal Ca concentration. More recent experiments based on the incorporation of Ca buffers into a rod cell have also led to the related conclusion that an elevation of intracellular free Ca is not necessary for the closure of the conductance by light (MATTHEWS et al., 1985).

The experiment of Fig. 1 also provided an estimate for the stoichiometry of the Na–Ca exchange mechanism mentioned in the introduction. After the Ca influx, light was turned on and external Na was restored. As a result, a transient inward current was observed. This current, however, could not be going through the light-sensitive conductance because this was kept closed by the light. The simplest interpretation was that it represented a membrane current associated with electrogenic Na-dependent Ca efflux. This interpretation was reinforced by the findings that: 1) the current disappeared when Li, a cation incapable of driving the Na–Ca exchange, replaced Na externally, 2) the size of the current depended on the transmembrane electrochemical gradients for both Na and Ca, and 3) the total charge transfer due to the current depended only on the Ca load (traces a through d). Assuming that the Ca load was entirely removed by the exchange, the coupling ratio was estimated to be close to 3 Na : 1 Ca (see Fig. 1 legend).

As pointed out in the introduction, a Na-dependent Ca efflux triggered by illumination has been reported by other workers, and this has been taken to be a major piece of supporting evidence for the Ca hypothesis. Since the Na–Ca exchange is electrogenic, this light-induced Ca efflux can be conveniently monitored by measuring the membrane current it generates. Figure 2 shows an experiment to study this Ca efflux. In panel A, the responses of a rod to flashes (traces a, c) and steps (traces b, d) of light are shown. All responses were saturated, but the flash in c and the light step in d were 60–110 times brighter than the corresponding ones in a and b. A striking feature is that all the responses showed at their initial plateau a small secondary climb whose amplitude and time course were independent of the intensity and the duration of illumination. This climb or «transient» disappeared when all external Na around the outer segment was replaced by Li (Fig. 2 B), indicating that it reflected a declining electrogenic Na-dependent Ca efflux. This Na–Ca exchange current (an inward current) had an initial peak of ~ 1.5 pA and declined approximately exponentially, with a time constant of ~ 0.4 sec (Fig. 2 C). In separate

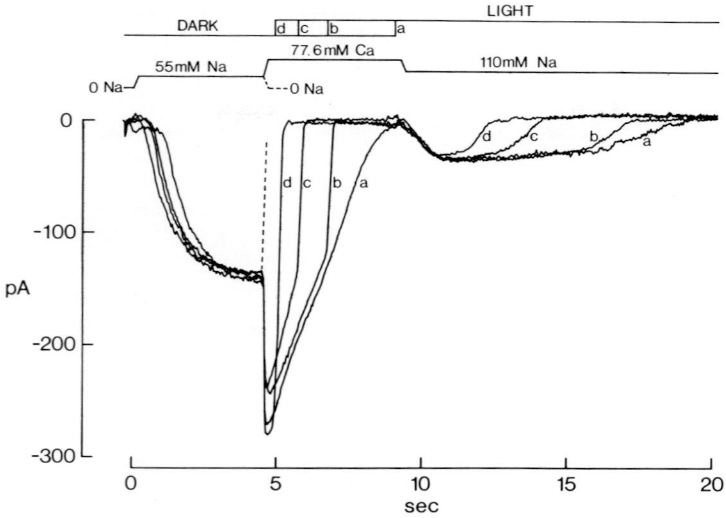

Fig. 1: Ca loading experiment on a single rod outer segment. The degree of Ca loading was controlled by light, which completely shut off the dark Ca influx at various times, as shown by traces a–d. All records were from the same cell. The exchange current was measured as the difference in recorded current on restoring Na, done in light before and after the Ca load. The light-sensitive current in darkness was obtained as the difference between total current recorded in darkness (light-sensitive current plus junction current) and junction current recorded in a repeated run in light. Outward membrane current across the outer segment is plotted upwards on the ordinate scale. The Na solutions, containing ~ 1 μM Ca, had the following composition (in mM): 110 Na or choline in partial or full substitution, 2.5 K, 1.5 Mg, 0.093 Ca, 119.7 Cl, 2 Mg-EGTA, 5 TMA-HEPES, 5 dextrose, pH 7.6. The isotonic Ca solution contained (in mM): 77.6 $CaCl_2$, 5 TMA-HEPES, 5 dextrose, pH 7.6. The broken line indicates the time course of decline of the Na current when 0 Na 110 mM Choline was introduced instead of 77.6 mM Ca. The Ca loads (Q_{load}) were a, 562; b, 404; c, 230; and d, 139 pC, equivalent to ~ 1.7×10^9, 1.2×10^9, 6.9×10^8 and 4.2×10^8 Ca ions respectively. The charge ratios $Q_{load}/Q_{exchange}$ were a, 2.38; b, 2.02; c, 1.87; and d, 2.43 (mean 2.18). This ratio is related to the stoichiometry (n) of the exchange (that is, n Na : 1 Ca) by $Q_{load}/Q_{exchange} = 2/(n-2)$. Hence n was 2.92. From 18 experiments the average value of n was 2.94 ± 0.10 (S.D.). Steady light delivered 300 photons (500 nm) μm^{-2} sec^{-1}, unpolarized; this produced ~ 4.5×10^3 photoisomerizations sec^{-1}, assuming an effective collecting area of 15 μm^2. (Reprinted, with permission, from YAU and NAKATANI, 1984 b.)

experiments we found that intense flashes superposed on a just-saturating steady response failed to produce any further increments in exchange current (Nakatani and Yau, submitted), suggesting that the transient Ca efflux at the onset of illumination was associated with the light-sensitive conductance shutting down rather than with light *per se*.

Since the light-sensitive conductance is permeable to Ca, the transient Ca efflux observed in the light may simply mean that in darkness there is a Ca efflux which balances a steady Ca influx. Light shuts down the influx, and the efflux should therefore become apparent. Consistent with this idea, when the dark Ca influx is stopped by removing external Ca a subsequent light response also lacks the transient; conversely, when the dark Ca influx in Ringer's is increased by the presence of the phosphodiesterase inhibitor IBMX the light response also shows a much larger transient (see YAU and NAKATANI, 1985 a).

Figure 3 shows an experiment to estimate the dark Ca influx under normal conditions.

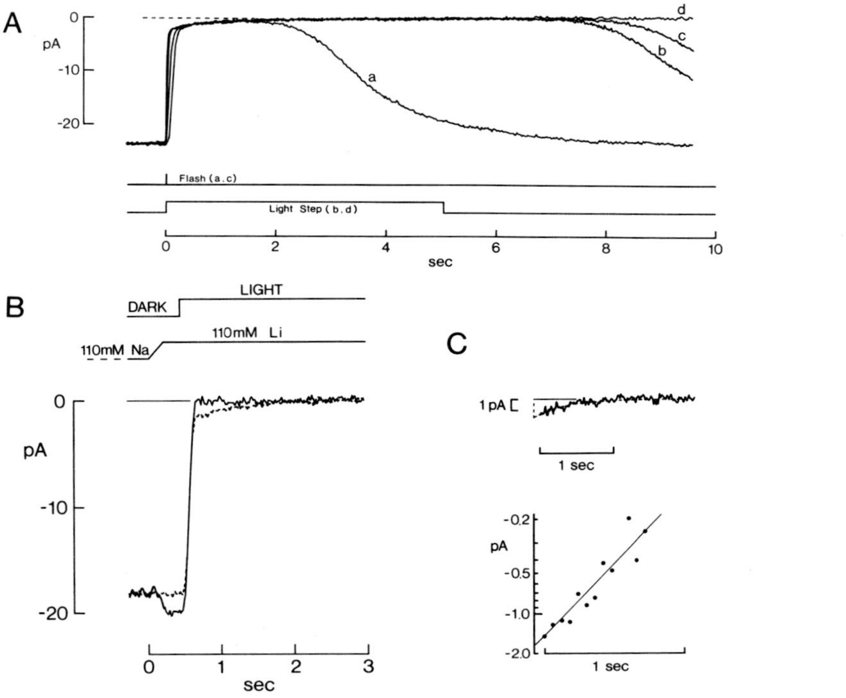

Fig. 2: A, Flash and step responses of a toad rod to light. The outer segment of the cell was inside the recording pipet, which contained normal Ringer's solution. The inner segment was bath-perfused also with Ringer's solution, but this contained in addition 1 mM CsCl to remove the initial hyperpolarizing transient in the voltage response to light (FAIN et al., 1978; TORRE, 1982). We found that in very bright light this transient caused a capacitive current which partially obscured the Na–Ca exchange current at early times of the response plateau. Outward membrane current across the outer segment is plotted upwards. Responses a and c were elicited by flashes (7.6 msec duration), causing $\sim 4.8 \times 10^2$ and 5.4×10^4 photoisomerizations (Rh*). Responses b and d were elicited by light steps (~ 5 sec duration), producing $\sim 8.1 \times 10^3$ and 4.7×10^5 Rh*sec^{-1}. An effective collecting area of 15 μm^2 for the rod outer segment was assumed throughout with unpolarized light. Each response is an average of three sweeps. All recordings were low-pass filtered at 100 Hz, 8 pole; all light stimuli were at 500 nm and unpolarized. Room temperature. B, Substitution of Li for Na around a rod outer segment removes the Na–Ca exchange current transient at the light response plateau. The recording was made with the inner segment of the rod within the suction pipet (containing normal Ringer's solution) and its outer segment perfused. Solid trace, response to a saturating light step in Li. Broken trace, control response (to the same light) in normal Ringer's. The time course of solution change, as indicated by junction currents (HODGKIN et al., 1984), was ~ 200 msec and is shown above the sweeps. The solid trace was obtained from the total recorded current (physiological current plus junction current) measured in a dark/light-step sequence minus the junction current measured in a repeated run in continuous light. Each trace is the mean of three sweeps. The Li solution is identical to normal Ringer's in composition except for equimolar substitution of Li for Na. The saturating light step produced $\sim 2.6 \times 10^4$ Rh*sec^{-1}. The initial increase in inward dark current upon introduction of Li is due to the greater permeability to Li (as compared to Na) of the light-sensitive conductance (YAU and NAKATANI, 1984 a; HODGKIN et al., 1985). C, Upper, difference between control and Li responses. Broken curve, exponential decline with a time constant of 0.39 sec; exponential extrapolation back to the time of 50 % saturated light response gives a peak amplitude of 1.7 pA. Lower, semilogarithmic plot of the same trace (filtered at 25 Hz, 8 pole) at 60-msec intervals. The straight line drawn through the points gives a time constant of 0.39 sec. (Reprinted, with permission, from YAU and NAKATANI, 1985 a).

The dark Ca influx was first trapped within the outer segment by removing external Na and hence stopping the Na–Ca exchange. The amount of trapped Ca was then estimated from the current generated by the reactivated exchange (see Fig. 3 legend). In this way, it was estimated that ~10–15 % of the total normal dark current was carried by Ca, corresponding to an inward Ca current of 2–3 pA. In the steady state such an influx should be extruded completely via the Na–Ca exchanger, which, by virtue of its 3 : 1 stoichiometry, would produce an inward exchange current of 1.0–1.5 pA, a value in rather good agreement with the peak amplitude of the transient (~1.5 pA) observed at the plateau of the light response described earlier.

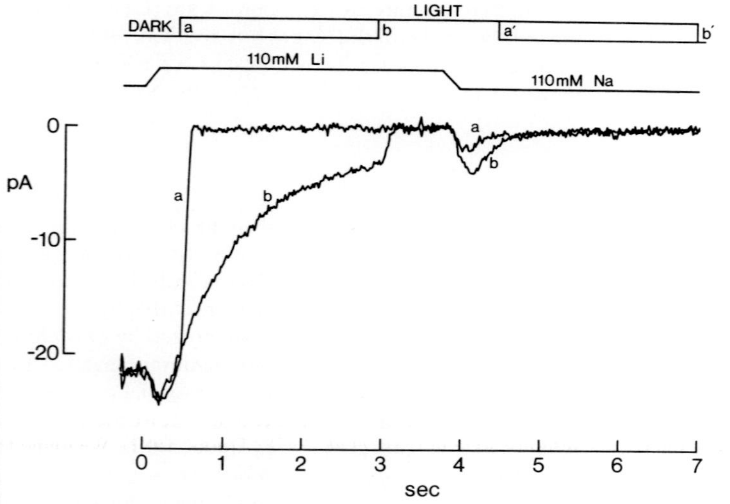

Fig. 3: Estimate of dark Ca influx obtained by trapping the Ca in the rod outer segment with a 0-Na, 110 mM Li solution, followed by reactivated extrusion in Na-Ringer's. The rod inner segment was in the pipet, and the outer segment was perfused. Except for equimolar substitution of Li for Na, the Li solution was otherwise identical to normal Ringer's. Two separate trapping measurements were made on the same cell, and this was controlled by light which shut off the light-sensitive conductance. The longer trapping period (trace b) led to a larger exchange current on readmission of external Na. The difference in total charge influx, ΔQ_{load}, between the two trapping periods (that is, the area between traces a and b during the time in the Li solution) was measured as 19.0 pC. The difference in subsequent charge transfer via the Na–Ca exchanger, ΔQ_{exch} (that is, the area between traces a and b on readmission of Na) was 0.89 pC. The incremental Ca load, ΔQ_{Ca}, is given by $\Delta Q_{exch} \times [2/(n-2)]$, where n is the stoichiometry of the exchange, previously measured to be 3 (see Fig. 1). The fractional Ca influx in the Li-Ringer's, f'_{Ca}, is then given by $f'_{Ca} = \Delta Q_{Ca}/\Delta Q_{load} = 0.094$. As the inward dark current is predominantly carried by Li ions, and since Li is 1.0–1.4 times as permeable as Na (Yau and Nakatani, 1984 a; Hodgkin et al., 1985), the fractional Ca influx in normal Ringer's, f_{Ca}, would be 0.09–0.13. (The higher end of this estimated range is probably more accurate because the estimates for the apparent Li/Na selectivity ratio quoted above were not corrected for any exchange current component in the total dark current in Na-Ringer's; this would lead to a slight underestimate of the Li/Na ratio.) From six experiments, f_{Ca} was measured to be 0.09–0.15. In the light monitor trace (top) a and b indicate turning on, and a′ and b′ indicate turning off, of respective light steps. Steady light in this experiment produced $2.6 \times 10^4 Rh^* sec^{-1}$. (Reprinted, with permission, from Yau and Nakatani, 1985 a.)

A simple picture based on the above experiments is that in darkness Ca steadily enters the rod outer segment at a rather high rate (~ 10^7 ions sec^{-1}), to be balanced by an equal efflux via the Na–Ca exchanger. Bright light completely shuts down the influx; the efflux continues but rapidly declines when the internal free Ca activity falls. Applying this idea to the transient of Fig. 2, it can be calculated that a single photoisomerization causes a net Ca efflux of ~ 10^5 ions (see Yau and Nakatani, 1985 a). This quantity is more than enough to account for the efflux measured in toad retina using an external Ca-sensitive electrode (Gold and Korenbrot, 1980; Miller and Korenbrot, 1984; Gold, 1985). Thus, our results can explain the Ca efflux observed in the light without invoking a rise in internal Ca activity caused by illumination. Furthermore, since the Ca efflux declines immediately after the onset of illumination, the Ca activity should decrease in the outer segment. This conclusion assumes, of course, that light itself does not inhibit the Na–Ca exchanger. This has been verified by showing that the rate of extrusion of any Ca trapped in the outer segment is the same in the light as in the dark (Nakatani and Yau, submitted). Recently, experiments supporting our conclusion of a light-induced Ca decline in rods have been reported by Gold (1986) and Cervetto, McNaughton and Nunn (1986).

Excised-patch experiments on rods

As demonstrated above, internal Ca does not appear to directly block the light-sensitive conductance in rods. Furthermore, the activity of Ca within the rod outer segment seems to decline, rather than increase, during illumination. These results taken together rule out Ca as the internal messenger for phototransduction, and it is therefore natural to think that cGMP is the correct candidate. This conclusion is supported by two kinds of experiments that we have done. The first made use of excised membrane patches from the rod outer segment, and the second consisted in dialyzing the interior of a rod outer segment. In this section the excised-patch experiments are described. The basic idea behind these experiments is to see whether cGMP can activate an ionic conductance in the plasma membrane of the outer segment. An excised, inside-out membrane patch provides a highly simplified preparation in which the cGMP concentration in the bath solution can be made the only variable. Indeed, using such a preparation we found a cGMP-sensitive conductance in the rod membrane with electrical properties very similar to those of the light-sensitive conductance. Our main findings are in agreement with those recently reported by Fesenko et al. (1985).

Figure 4 shows the current-voltage relation (filled circles) for the cGMP-induced current in a rod membrane patch that was exposed to normal Ringer's solution on the extracellular side and pseudointracellular solution (with cGMP) on the cytoplasmic side. The relation shows prominent outward rectification, with a reversal potential near +10 mV. Both the outward rectification and the reversal potential are characteristic of the light-sensitive conductance studied in intact cells (Bader et al., 1979; Baylor and Nunn, 1983; Bodoia and Detwiler, 1985; Zimmerman and Baylor, 1985), suggesting that the two conductances are identical. Associated with the cGMP-induced current there was an increase in current noise, especially at large depolarizations, but no obvious openings and closings of individual channels have been observed. It is rather surprising that cGMP can activate the conductance without the presence of ATP in the solution. This indicates that the cyclic nucleotide acts on the conductance directly rather than via a protein kinase, a usual intermediate in cyclic nucleotide-mediated mechanisms (see Nestler et al., 1984).

The experiment of Figure 4 had 1.6 mM Mg in the pseudointracellular solution. In the presence of this amount of Mg, the cGMP-induced current was not blocked by Ca on the

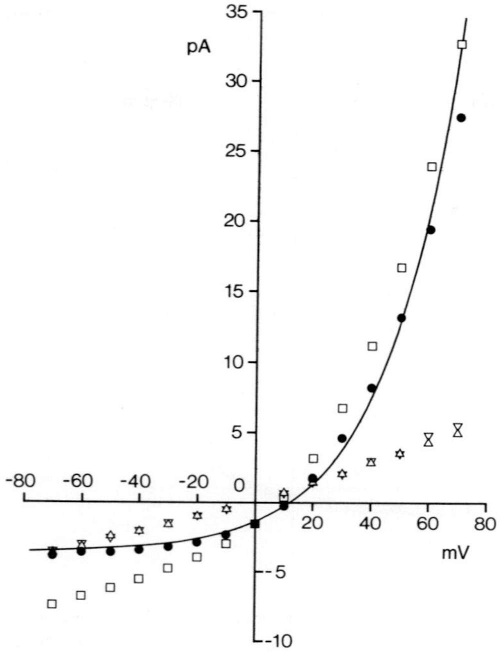

Fig. 4: Current-voltage (I–V) relation of the cGMP-dependent current measured from an excised, inside-out rod membrane patch. Normal Ringer's solution in pipet and pseudointracellular solution in bath (see methods). Each current measurement was made at the end of a 1-sec voltage pulse. △, ▽, I–V relation in control solution before and after the application of cGMP, with resistance of about 15 GΩ; □, I–V relation in the presence of 840 μM cGMP; ●, I–V relation for cGMP-sensitive current, obtained as difference between measurements in the presence and the absence of cGMP. Smooth curve is equation (1) with $V_r = +12$ mV, $V_o = 25$ mV and $\gamma = 0$. (Reprinted, with permission, from Haynes, Nakatani and Yau, in preparation).

cytoplasmic side of the membrane (Fig. 5). This confirmed our previous finding (see above) that internal Ca does not block the conductance directly. When all Mg was removed, the current increased slightly at hyperpolarizing potentials, but at depolarizing potentials it increased by much more; the net result was a considerably steeper outward rectification (Fig. 5; see also Yau and Haynes, 1986). In this case (i. e., the absence of Mg), the addition of Ca to the cytoplasmic side did produce some current blockage at depolarizing potentials, though the effect was less pronounced than with Mg (Fig. 5; see also Yau and Haynes, 1986). Since the membrane potential of a rod is physiologically at –40 mV or more negative (i. e. in the hyperpolarizing range), however, such an intracellular blocking effect of divalent cations on the conductance is unlikely to be involved in the generation of the light response.

In other experiments we omitted divalent cations from both the extracellular and the cytoplasmic sides of a membrane patch and found that the cGMP-induced current recorded under these conditions was generally much larger, especially at hyperpolarizing potentials. At the same time, the current-voltage relation became almost linear rather than showing the characteristic steep outward rectification (Fig. 6; see also Yau and Haynes,

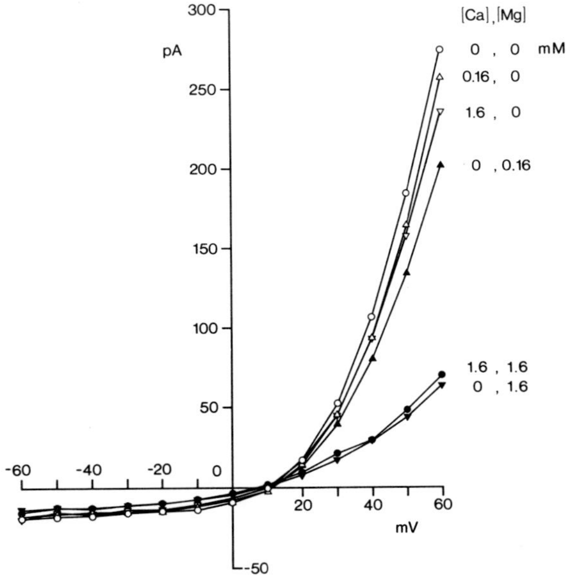

Fig. 5: Divalent cation effects on the relation between cGMP-activated current and voltage in a rod patch. Normal Ringer's solution was present on the extracellular side; pseudointracellular solution (see methods) was present on the cytoplasmic side except for the indicated variations in Ca and Mg concentrations. 1000 μM cGMP. Adjacent points are joined by straight lines. (Reprinted, with permission, from Haynes and Yau, in preparation.)

1986). Thus, divalent cations (both Ca and Mg) seem to block the conductance from the external side as well. Since the steady influx of Na through the light-sensitive conductance in darkness must be continuously pumped out by a Na pump at the inner segment, this blocking action by external divalent cations may have the important function of limiting the Na influx to a level that can be managed by the Na pump. The same blockage or suppression possibly also contributes to the unusually small unit conductance that has been reported for the light-sensitive conductance in the intact rod (Detwiler, et al., 1982; Gray and Attwell, 1985; Bodoia and Detwiler, 1985). At present, we have little information about the mechanism underlying this blocking action. It might represent a fast flickering block, as that observed in other conductances (Nowak et al., 1984; Lansman et al., 1985).

Figure 7 shows the dependence of the cGMP-induced current on cGMP concentration, studied at 0 mV and in the presence of the same solutions as in Fig. 4. The relation was sigmoidal, indicating positive cooperativity of cGMP molecules in opening the conductance. The experiment in Fig. 7 gave a Hill coefficient (n) of 2.2 and a half-saturating cGMP concentration ($K_{1/2}$) of 50 μM. The n and $K_{1/2}$ values obtained from other experiments were 1.8–2.2 and 25–50 μM (at 0 mV) respectively.

The above experiments, while not absolutely conclusive, strongly suggest that cGMP directly activates the light-sensitive conductance.

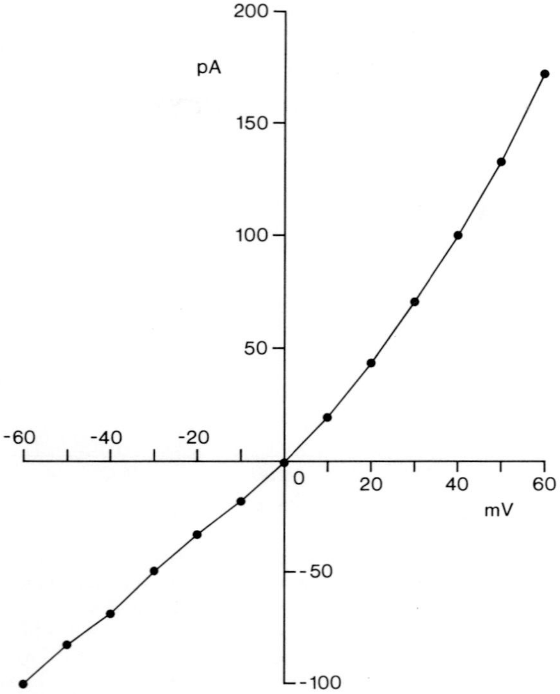

Fig. 6: Current-voltage relation for the cGMP-induced current obtained in the absence of divalent cations on both sides of a rod membrane patch. In this particular experiment, identical solutions (119 mM NaCl, 5 mM Na-HEPES, pH 7.6) were present on both sides of the membrane, which explains why the reversal potential was at 0 mV. 1000 μM cGMP. Adjacent points are connected by straight lines. (Reprinted, with permission, from Haynes and Yau, in preparation.)

Experiments on a truncated, dialyzed rod outer segment

A couple of criticisms may be raised about the excised-patch experiments. The first is that they might not have discriminated completely between the plasma membrane and intracellular disk membranes, which are situated in very close proximity to each other. Indeed, the disk membranes have been thought for several years to contain a cGMP-regulated conductance (Caretta et al., 1979; Caretta and Cavaggioni, 1983; Koch and Kaupp, 1985; Puckett et al., 1985). The cGMP response in an excised patch could therefore have come from disk membrane fragments which became pulled off with the patch. In some excised-patch experiments we observed unusually large cGMP-induced currents which appeared to bear little correlation with the apparent sizes of the patches, perhaps indicating that some patches contained disk membrane fragments which became fused with the plasma membrane to form a convoluted surface of large area (Haynes, Nakatani and Yau, in preparation). The other point is that despite strong circumstantial evidence it remains to be confirmed that the cGMP-induced conductance is light-suppressible.

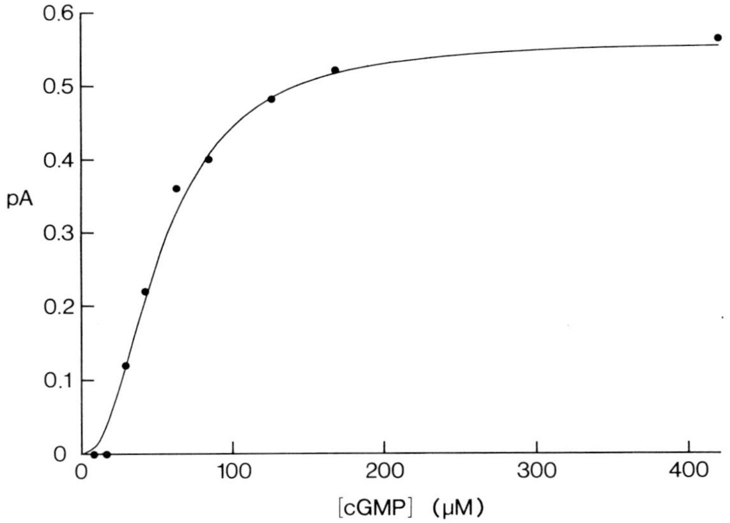

Fig. 7: Dependence of cGMP-sensitive current on cGMP concentration in an excised rod membrane patch. Same conditions as the experiment in Fig. 4. Membrane potential clamped at 0 mV. By sign convention the current should be labelled negative, but only absolute values are shown here. Cyclic GMP concentrations were 8.4, 16.8, 29.4, 42, 63, 84, 126, 168 and 420 μM respectively. Smooth curve fitted to the data is scaled according to the function $f(C) = C^n/[C^n + K_{1/2}{}^n]$ with $K_{1/2} = 50\,\mu M$ and $n = 2.2$, where C is cGMP concentration. (Reprinted, with permission, from HAYNES, NAKATANI and YAU, in preparation.)

To resolve these questions, another kind of experiment was performed, as shown in Fig. 8. Panel A shows a rod with most of the outer segment drawn into a regular suction pipet containing Ringer's solution. A normal light response could be elicited with a flash, indicating that the plasma membrane and the light-sensitive current were still intact. The inner segment and the basal part of the outer segment outside the pipet were then removed with a probe, leaving an open-ended outer segment «envelope» whose interior could be dialyzed with a pseudointracellular solution. The membrane potential was clamped at 0 mV. This preparation resembled an excised-patch experiment, *except here* the plasma membrane was much more well-defined. Furthermore, as will be shown later, the machinery for phototransduction was still intact in this preparation.

As in the excised-patch experiments, cGMP in the dialyzing solution induced a large inward current which was little affected by large changes in Ca concentration (Fig. 8 B). The magnitude of the recorded current induced by a saturating cGMP concentration depended on the length of the outer segment (L) within the recording pipet. In many cases, such as that shown in Fig. 8 C, the dependence was reasonably linear, indicating a uniform current density along most of the outer segment. This linear dependence was similar to that observed previously for the light-sensitive current in intact rods (BAYLOR, LAMB and YAU, 1979). In other experiments the dependence was linear only with short L ($\leqq 25\,\mu m$); with longer L the current density declined progressively, perhaps because cGMP was unable to fully reach and open the conductance at the tip of the outer segment. With short L the longitudinal current density ranged from 4 to 20 pA μm^{-1} at 0 mV. Assuming that

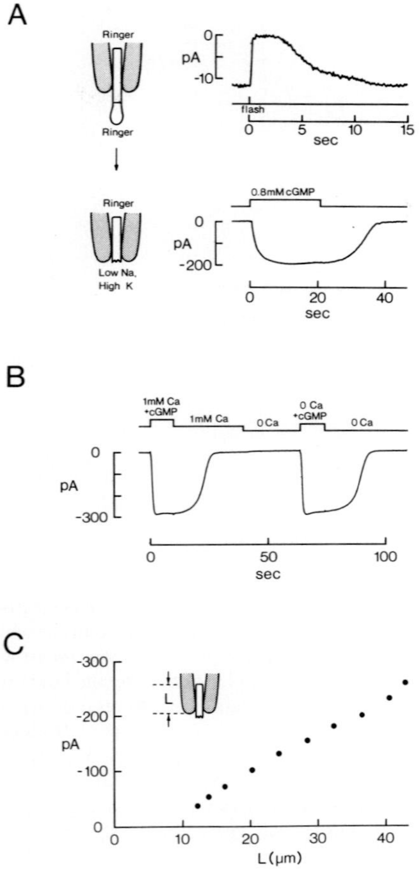

Fig. 8: Cyclic GMP-sensitive current recorded from a dialyzed, open-ended toad rod outer segment. Different outer segments in A–C. A, Demonstration of the method. The length of outer segment within the pipet was 45 μm in both upper and lower panels. The flash delivered ~ 22 photons μm^{-2} (500 nm); diffuse, unpolarized illumination. B, Changing the bath Ca concentration had little effect on the cGMP-sensitive current. The 0-Ca solution was identical in composition to the pseudointracellular solutions described in Methods; the 1 mM Ca solution contained 1 mM $CaCl_2$ and no TMA-EGTA, and was otherwise identical to the pseudointracellular solution. Length of outer segment within the pipette was 42 μm. cGMP concentrations was 0.84 mM. C, Dependence of recorded cGMP-sensitive current on the length of outer segment within the pipette. cGMP concentration was 1.0 mM. Little change in seal resistance was observed throughout the experiment. The slope of the relation gave a current density of ~ 7.0 pA μm^{-1}. The data points did not cross the origin probably because the point of maximal constriction, and hence the initial current-collecting point, of the pipet was some distance behind the tip (see BAYLOR et al., 1979). The cGMP-containing solutions in A–C here and Fig. 9 also contained 100 μM IBMX to inhibit any phosphodiesterase activity. (Reprinted, with permission, from YAU and NAKATANI, 1985 b.)

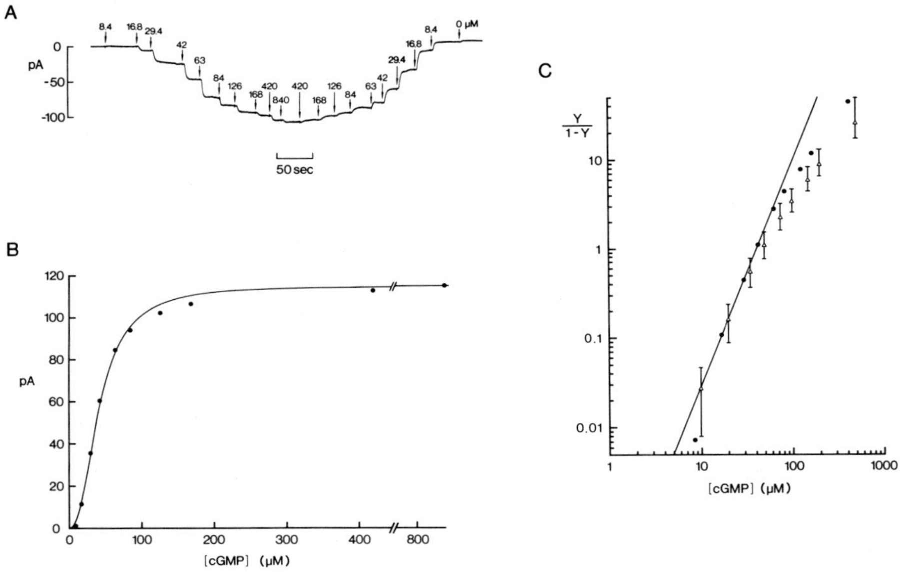

Fig. 9: Dependence of cGMP-sensitive current on cGMP concentration in a dialyzed rod outer segment. A, Acutal recordings. The arrows indicate the time points at which the cGMP concentration was changed. The time taken for a solution change in this experiment was ~ 2 sec. Length of outer segment within the pipet was 19 μm. B, Linear plot of the averaged data from A. Only absolute values of the current are shown. C, Hill plot of the data in A (●), and of averaged results from 12 experiments (△). Error bars indicate standard deviations. Y, Fraction of conductance open. In eight of the 12 experiments, the cGMP concentrations used were 10, 20, 35, 50, 75, 100, 150, 200, 500 and 1000 μM. In the remaining four experiments, the cGMP concentrations were as shown in A. To average over all experiments, the data in the latter four experiments were first interpolated to 10, 20 μM, etc. before grand averaging was done. The smooth curve and the straight line fitted to the solid circles in B and C respectively were drawn according to the function $Y(C) = C^n/[C^n + K^n_{1/2}]$ with $K_{1/2} = 42$ μM and $n = 2.5$, where C is cGMP concentration. (Reprinted, with permission, from Yau and Nakatani, 1985 b.)

healthier preparations showed more cGMP-responsiveness, we consider the top end of this range, 20 pA μm^{-1}, to be a more realistic estimate of the maximally induced current density.

Figure 9 shows the dependence of the current on cGMP concentration. To study this relationship, the outer segment was drawn into the pipet for 25 μm or less to minimize any incompletely dialyzed space within the outer segment. The dose-response relation (Fig. 9 B) was very similar to that described earlier for the excised-patch experiments, indicating that the same conductance was studied in both cases. Figure 9 C shows the Hill plot of collected results from 12 experiments. The Hill coefficient, n, was ~ 2.5 and the half-saturating cGMP concentration, $K_{1/2}$, was ~ 45 μM. In several experiments we have also made measurements in both darkness and light and have observed no light-induced changes in the dose-response relation (but see below). Thus, neither the characteristics of cGMP binding nor the intrinsic conduction properties of the conductance seemed to be influenced by light.

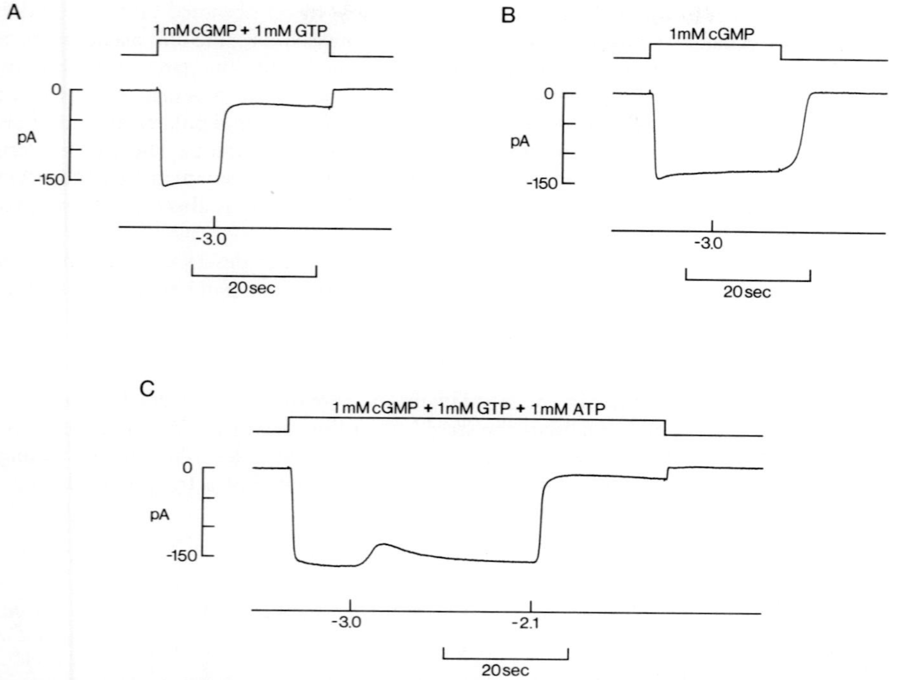

Fig. 10: Effects of GTP and ATP on the cGMP-sensitive current in a dialyzed rod outer segment preparation. Same outer segment for A–C; length of outer segment within the pipette was 25 μm. No IBMX was present in the cGMP-containing solutions. A, In the presence of GTP the cGMP-induced current became light-suppressible. B, The light-sensitivity disappeared on removal of GTP. C, Addition of GTP plus ATP restored the light response, but the sensitivity to light was significantly reduced. The number below each flash monitor indicates the nominal log attenuation of the light intensity. Diffuse unpolarized illumination. The '–3.0' flash delivered ~ 56 photons μm^{-2} (500 nm), which is close to an intensity that would normally just saturate the response in an intact toad rod (cf. Fig. 8 A). The '–2.1' flash delivered ~ 361 photons μm^{-2} (500 nm). (Reprinted, with permission, from YAU and NAKATANI, 1985 b.)

The light-insensitivity of the cGMP-induced current was observed only in the absence of GTP (see, for example, Fig. 10 B). With GTP in the dialyzing solution, the current could be suppressed by light (Fig. 10 A). In the presence of both GTP and ATP, the effectiveness of a light flash was reduced and the suppression also became more transient (Fig. 10 C). Both the requirement for GTP in generating the light response and the quenching effect of ATP are consistent with the known mechanisms underlying light-activated cGMP hydrolysis, as already described in the introduction.

The above results, together with the excised-patch experiments, provide conclusive evidence that the light-sensitive conductance is directly modulated by cGMP.

Excised-patch experiments on cones

We have also applied the excised-patch technique to cones and found a similar cGMP-sensitive conductance in their outer segments. Figure 11 shows the current-voltage relation for this conductance in catfish cones. The relation was again obtained under conditions where normal Ringer's solution was present on the extracellular side and pseudointracellular solution was present on the cytoplasmic side of the membrane patch (see methods). In the experiment of panel A, the reversal potential for the current was near + 15 mV, and the current increased roughly exponentially with voltage in both depolarizing and hyperpolarizing directions. Panel B shows examples from four other patches. These characteristics broadly resemble those of the light-sensitive current in tiger salamander cones (ATTWELL et al., 1982), as expected if the cGMP-sensitive conductance is also the light-sensitive conductance in cones.

It is interesting to note that the same general equation can describe the relations between voltage and cGMP-activated current in both rod and cone patches. This equation is (see JACK et al., 1975):

$$j(V) = \exp[(1-\gamma)(V-V_r)/V_o] - \exp[-\gamma(V-V_r)/V_o] \quad (1)$$

where j(V) is transmembrane current, V is membrane potential, V_r is reversal potential, V_o is a voltage constant which describes the steepness of the current rectification, and γ is a symmetry constant. One interpretation of equation (1) is that it describes current through a membrane conductance with a single energy barrier situated at a fractional distance γ

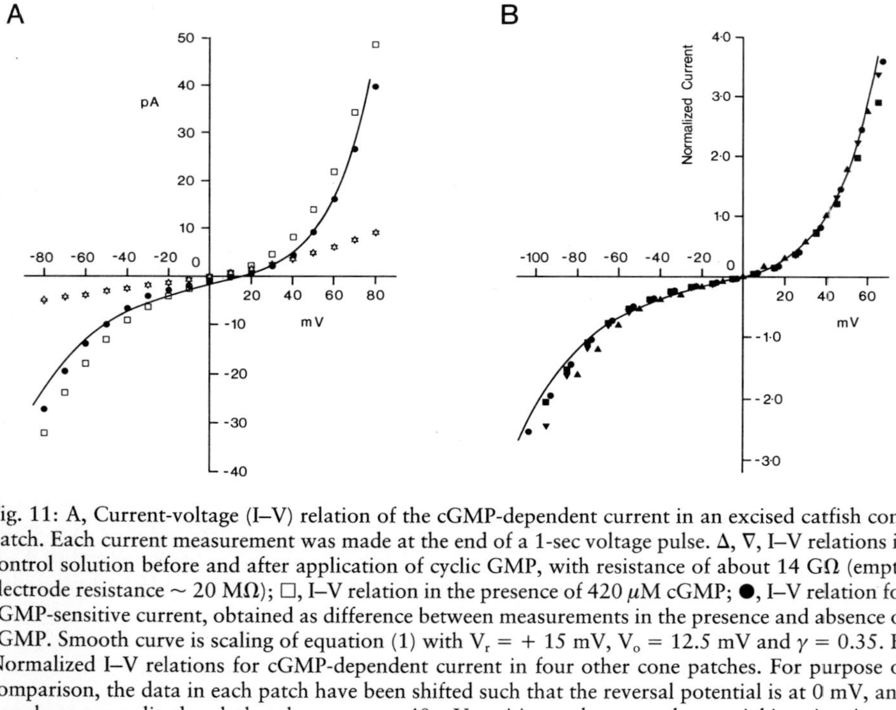

Fig. 11: A, Current-voltage (I–V) relation of the cGMP-dependent current in an excised catfish cone patch. Each current measurement was made at the end of a 1-sec voltage pulse. Δ, ∇, I–V relations in control solution before and after application of cyclic GMP, with resistance of about 14 GΩ (empty electrode resistance ~ 20 MΩ); □, I–V relation in the presence of 420 μM cGMP; ●, I–V relation for cGMP-sensitive current, obtained as difference between measurements in the presence and absence of cGMP. Smooth curve is scaling of equation (1) with V_r = + 15 mV, V_o = 12.5 mV and γ = 0.35. B, Normalized I–V relations for cGMP-dependent current in four other cone patches. For purpose of comparison, the data in each patch have been shifted such that the reversal potential is at 0 mV, and have been normalized such that the current at 40 mV positive to the reversal potential is unity. Actual reversal potentials and currents at 0 mV were: ●, + 13 mV, – 0.8 pA; ▲, + 10 mV, – 0.1 pA; ▼, + 15 mV, – 0.5 pA; ■, + 15 mV, – 1.2 pA. Cyclic GMP concentrations were 420 μM for ●, ▼ and ■, and 840 μM for ▲. Smooth curve is again equation (1) with V_r = 0, V_o = 12.5 mV and γ = 0.35. (Reprinted, with permission, from HAYNES and YAU, 1985.)

(that is, γ varies between 0 and 1) from the extracellular boundary of the membrane (JACK et al., 1975). The current-voltage relation in cone patches could be fitted with $\gamma = 0.35$ and $V_o = 12.5$ mV, while that in rod patches could be fitted with $\gamma \sim 0$ and $V_o = 25$ mV. As already pointed out in reference to Fig. 5, the steepness of rectification (and hence V_o) in rods is affected by divalent cations in that it increases (corresponding to a smaller V_o) with decreasing concentrations of divalent cations on the cytoplasmic side. In the case of cones, the dependence of V_o on divalent cations remains to be examined. (In intact rods, V_o for the light sensitive conductance is between 12.5 and 25 mV. See BADER et al., 1979; BAYLOR and NUNN, 1983; BODOIA and DETWILER, 1985; ZIMMERMAN and BAYLOR, 1985). A difference in γ may suggest that a structural group on the light-sensitive conductance which influences ion permeation is at different locations in rods and cones. The energy-barrier interpretation of the above equation should not be taken too literally because a major determinant of the current-voltage relation is clearly a voltage-dependent block by divalent cations.

The dose-response relation between current and cGMP concentration measured in cone patches is practically the same as in rod patches, with similar values for the Hill coefficient and the half-saturating cGMP concentration (see HAYNES and YAU, 1985). The conductance is also specifically activated by cGMP, and cAMP, for example, is ineffective. There has been some dispute from biochemical studies about whether a cGMP cascade similar to that in rods is present in cones (DEVRIES et al., 1979; BERGER et al., 1980; FARBER et al., 1981; FARBER and BOK, 1985; HURWITZ et al., 1985). The experiments described here, however, indicate that cGMP mediates phototransduction in both kinds of photoreceptors. Recent experiments by others employing the whole-cell recording technique have also arrived at a similar conclusion (COBBS et al., 1985). The similar characteristics of conductance activation by cGMP in rods and cones indicate that the mechanisms underlying the differences in light sensitivity and response kinetics between the two kinds of receptors (BAYLOR and HODGKIN, 1973; DETWILER et al., 1980; SCHNAPF and MCBURNEY, 1980) must reside in earlier stages of the transduction pathway.

Discussion

The experiments described here indicate that cGMP, rather than Ca, is the internal transmitter for phototransduction. The question is, does Ca after all have a role in the transduction process? There is evidence that Ca tends to suppress the level of cGMP in the rod outer segment (COHEN et al., 1978; KILBRIDE, 1980; WOODRUFF and FAIN, 1982), perhaps by inhibiting the guanylate cyclase (KRISHNAN et al., 1978; TROYER et al., 1978; FLEISCHMAN and DENISEVICH, 1979; LOLLEY and RACZ, 1982) or by stimulating the phosphodiesterase (ROBINSON et al., 1980). Since cGMP opens the conductance, a rise in internal Ca should thus shut it down, as indeed observed (HAGINS and YOSHIKAMI, 1974; BROWN et al., 1977; BASTIAN and FAIN, 1982; MACLEISH et al., 1984; HODGKIN et al., 1984; YAU and NAKATANI, 1984 a; HODGKIN et al., 1985). On the other hand, a decrease of free Ca in the light should oppose the effect of light. As such, this negative feedback constitutes a form of light adaptation. Figure 12 summarizes our experimental findings and shows a transduction scheme suggested by the results. This scheme is intended for rods, though most of the features should apply to cones as well. The depicted role of Ca in light adaptation was first hypothesized by BOWNDS (1980), and most recently LAMB et al. (1985) have also obtained some experimental evidence that support this idea.

Although our results indicate that free Ca within the rod outer segment decreases during illumination, this does not necessarily mean that there is no internal Ca release. On the

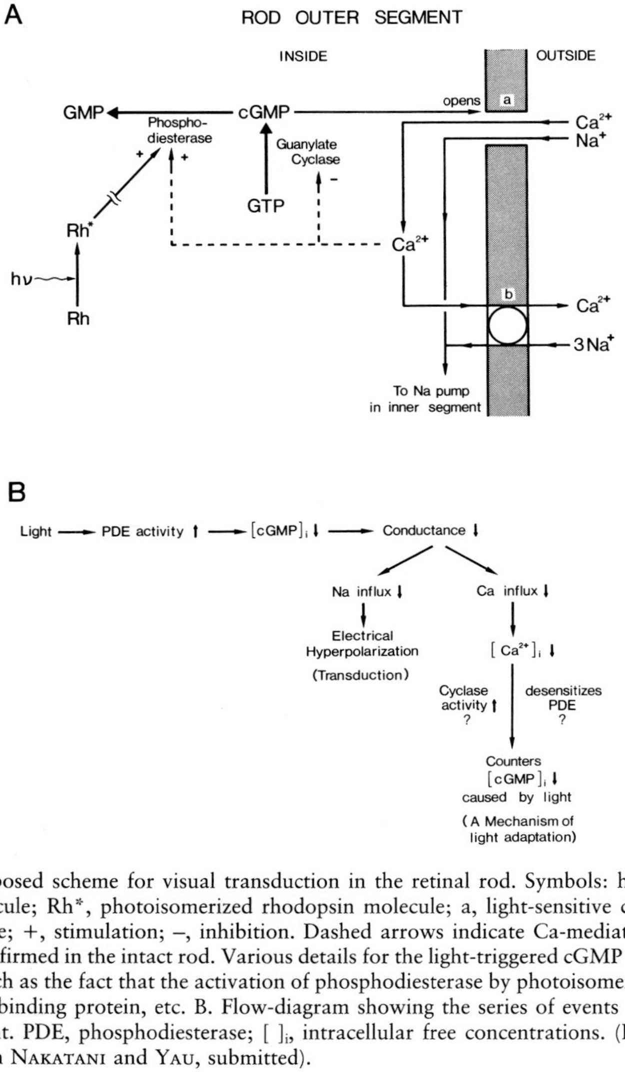

Fig. 12: A. Proposed scheme for visual transduction in the retinal rod. Symbols: hν, photon; Rh, rhodopsin molecule; Rh*, photoisomerized rhodopsin molecule; a, light-sensitive conductance; b, Na–Ca exchange; +, stimulation; –, inhibition. Dashed arrows indicate Ca-mediated actions that remain to be confirmed in the intact rod. Various details for the light-triggered cGMP hydrolysis have been left out, such as the fact that the activation of phosphodiesterase by photoisomerized rhodopsin involves a GTP-binding protein, etc. B. Flow-diagram showing the series of events in transduction triggered by light. PDE, phosphodiesterase; $[\ ]_i$, intracellular free concentrations. (Reprinted, with permission, from Nakatani and Yau, submitted).

other hand, since the Na–Ca exchange activity steadily declines during illumination, the internal Ca release, if it exists, must not be large enough to keep up with the extrusion due to the exchange. From our measurements, the *minimum* amount of Ca extruded in bright light from a toad rod is $\sim 4 \times 10^6$ Ca ions, corresponding to a concentration in the outer segment of $\sim 6\ \mu M$ (see Yau and Nakatani, 1985 a); the real amount extruded is perhaps considerably larger than this lower estimate (see Gold, 1986). Since the free Ca concentration in cells is ordinarily $< 1\ \mu M$, it seems likely that some of the Ca leaving the outer segment in the light are originally bound. Recently, it has been shown (Ghalayini and Anderson, 1984) that light induces in rods a production of inositol-1,4,5 trisphosphate

(IP_3), a substance thought to cause intracellular Ca release (BERRIDGE and IRVINE, 1984). Furthermore, injection of IP_3 into rods leads to a membrane hyperpolarization (WALOGA and ANDERSON, 1985), possibly indicating a triggered release of internal Ca (refer to the previous paragraph on the interaction between Ca and cGMP). Incorporating these findings by others, it seems plausible that in the light IP_3 mediates the release of some bound Ca which are consequently extruded by the Na–Ca exchange. If this is true, there may be an important reason why the cell gets rid of some bound Ca in the light, such as to remove a modulation exerted by Ca on its bound substrate.

One parameter important for understanding the transduction mechanism is the free cGMP concentration in the intact outer segment in darkness. The experiments described above indicate that the maximum current density inducible by cGMP in a toad rod is as high as 20 pA μm^{-1} at 0 mV, equivalent to a current of ~ 1,000 pA for the entire outer segment. Based on the current-voltage relation obtained in excised-patch experiments (see Fig. 4) the current at –40 mV is ~ 2.5 times that at 0 mV. Thus, at –40 mV, the maximally induced dark current in a toad rod should be ~ 2,500 pA, compared with a normal current of ~ 25 pA (see Fig. 2 A). In other words, only ~ 1 % of the conductance is normally open in darkness. From the Hill plot of Fig. 9, this fraction of open conductance corresponds to a free cGMP concentration of ~ 6 μM. Assuming that the total cGMP concentration within the rod outer segment is ~ 60 μM (COHEN et al., 1978; WOODRUFF and BOWNDS, 1979; KILBRIDE and EBREY, 1979; WOODRUFF and FAIN, 1982) and that the cytosolic space is, say, 50 % of the total volume (the rest being occupied by the membranous discs), we estimate that in the dark the free cGMP content constitutes only ~ 5 % of total. This may explain why a significant decline in cGMP content has not been detected in the intact retina in physiological lighting conditions (GOLDBERG et al., 1983). Based on the above estimate, even if all the free cGMP were hydrolysed in the light and the conductance completely shut down, the overall reduction of cGMP content in the outer segment would be only a few per cent. The same is probably true for cones as well (NAKATANI and YAU, 1986).

Acknowledgements

The experiments described here were supported by grants from the U.S. National Eye Institute and the Retina Research Foundation, Houston, Texas. L. W. Haynes was supported in part by a Fight For Sight Inc. (New York) Research Fellowship.

References

Attwell, D., Werblin, F. S. and Wilson, M.: The properties of single cones isolated from the tiger salamander retina. J. Physiol. Lond. **328,** 259–283 (1982).

Bader, C. R., MacLeish, P. R. and Schwartz, E. A.: A voltage-clamp study of the light response in solitary rods of the tiger salamander. J. Physiol. Lond. **296,** 1–26 (1979).

Bastian, B. L. and Fain, G. L.: The effects of sodium replacement on the responses of toad rods. J. Physiol. Lond. **330,** 331–347 (1982).

Baylor, D. A. and Fuortes, M. G. F.: Electrical responses of single cones in the retina of the turtle. J. Physiol. Lond. **207,** 77–92 (1970).

Baylor, D. A. and Hodgkin, A. L.: Detection and resolution of visual stimuli by turtle photoreceptors. J. Physiol. Lond. **234,**163–198 (1973).

Baylor, D. A., Lamb, T. D. and Yau, K.-W.: The membrane current of single rod outer segments. J. Physiol. Lond. **288,** 589–611 (1979).

Baylor, D. A. and Nunn, B. J.: Voltage dependence of the light-sensitive conductance of salamander retinal rods. Biophys. J. **41,** 125 a (1983).
Berger, S. J., DeVries, G. W., Carter, J. G., Schulz, D. W., Passonneau, P. N., Lowry, O. H. and Ferrendelli, J. A.: The distribution of the components of the cyclic GMP cycle in retina. J. Biol. Chem. **255,** 3128–3133 (1980).
Berridge, M. J. and Irvine, R. F.: Inositol trisphosphate, a novel second messenger in cellular signal transduction. Nature **312,** 315–321 (1984).
Bitensky, M. W., Gorman, R. E. and Miller, W. H.: Adenyl cyclase as a link between photon capture and changes in membrane permeability of frog photoreceptors. Proc. Natl. Acad. Sci. U.S.A. **68,** 561–562 (1971).
Bitensky, M. W., Wheeler, G. L., Aloni, B., Ventury, S. and Matuo, Y.: Light- and GTP-activated photoreceptor phosphodiesterase: regulation by a light-activated GTPase and identification of rhodopsin as the phosphodiesterase binding site. Adv. Cyclic Nucleotide Res. **9,** 553–572 (1978).
Bodoia, R. D. and Detwiler, P. B.: Patch clamp recordings of the light-sensitive dark noise in retinal rods from lizard and frog. J. Physiol. Lond. **367,**183–216 (1985).
Bownds, M. D.: Biochemical steps in visual transduction: roles for nucleotides and calcium ions. Photochem. Photobiol. **32,**487–490 (1980).
Brown, J. E., Coles, J. A. and Pinto, L. H.: Effects of injections of calcium and EGTA into the outer segments of retinal rods of *Bufo marinus*. J. Physiol. Lond. **269,** 707–722 (1977).
Capovilla, M., Cervetto, L. and Torre, V.: Antagonism between steady light and phosphodiesterase inhibitors on the kinetics of rod photoresponses. Proc. Natl. Acad. Sci. U.S.A. **79,** 6698–6702 (1982).
Caretta, A. and Cavaggioni, A.: Fast ionic flux activated by cyclic GMP in the membrane of cattle rod outer segments. Eur. J. Biochem. **132,** 1–8 (1983).
Caretta, A., Cavaggioni, A. and Sorbi, R. T.: Cyclic GMP and the permeability of the disks of the frog photoreceptors. J. Physiol. Lond. **295,** 171–178 (1979).
Cervetto, L. and McNaughton, P. A.: The effects of phosphodiesterase inhibitors and lanthanum ions on the light-sensitive current of retinal rods. J. Physiol. Lond. **370,** 91–109 (1986).
Cervetto, L., McNaughton, P. A. and Nunn, B. J.: Aequorin signals from isolated salamander rods. J. Physiol. Lond., in press (1986).
Clack, J. W., Oakley II, B. and Stein, P. J.: Injection of GTP-binding protein or cyclic GMP phosphodiesterase hyperpolarizes retinal rods. Nature **305,** 50–53 (1983).
Cobbs, W. H., Barkdoll III, A. E. and Pugh Jr., E. N.: Cyclic GMP increases photocurrent and light sensitivity of retinal cones. Nature **317,** 64–66 (1985).
Cobbs, W. H. and Pugh Jr., E. N.: Cyclic GMP can increase rod outer segment light-sensitive current 10-fold without delay of excitation. Nature **313,** 585–587 (1985).
Cohen, A. I., Hall, I. A. and Ferrendelli, J. A.: Calcium and cyclic nucleotide regulation in incubated mouse retina. J. gen. Physiol. **71,** 595–612 (1978).
Detwiler, P. B., Conner, J. D. and Bodoia, R. D.: Gigaseal patch clamp recording from outer segments of intact retinal rods. Nature **300,** 59–61 (1982).
Detwiler, P. B., Hodgkin, A. L. and McNaughton, P. A.: Temporal and spatial characteristics of the voltage response of rods in the retina of the snapping turtle. J. Physiol. Lond. **300,** 213–250 (1980).
DeVries, G. W., Cohen, A. I., Lowry, O. H. and Ferrendelli, J. A.: Cyclic nucleotides in the cone-dominant ground squirrel retina. Exp. Eye Res. **29,** 315–321 (1979).
Fain, G. L., Quandt, F. N., Bastian, B. L. and Gerschenfeld, H. M.: Contribution of a caesium-sensitive conductance increase in the rod photoresponse. Nature **272,** 467–469 (1978).
Farber, D. B. and Bok, D.: Light-activated cGMP-phosphodiesterase is absent from cone photoreceptors. Invest. Ophthal. vis Sci. **26 Suppl.,** 334 (1985).
Farber, D. B., Souza, D. W., Chase, D. G. and Lolley, R. N.: Cyclic nucleotides of cone-dominant retinas. Invest. Ophthal. vis. Sci. **20,** 24–31 (1981).
Fatt, P.: An extended Ca^{++}-hypothesis of visual transduction with a role for cyclic GMP. FEBS Letters **149,** 154–166 (1982).
Fesenko, E. E., Kolesnikov, S. S. and Lyubarsky, A. L.: Induction by cyclic GMP of cationic conductance in plasma membrane of retinal rod outer segment. Nature, **313,** 310–313 (1985).

Fleischman, D. and Denisevich, M.: Guanylate cyclase of isolated bovine retinal rod axonemes. Biochemistry **18,** 5060–5066 (1979).

Fung, B. K.-K., Hurley, J. B. and Stryer, L.: Flow of information in the light-triggered cyclic nucleotide cascade of vision. Proc. Natl. Acad. Sci. U.S.A. **78,** 152–156 (1981).

Fung, B. and Stryer, L.: Photolyzed rhodopsin catalyzes the exchange of GTP for bound GDP in retinal rod outer segments. Proc. Natl. Acad. Sci. U.S.A. **77,** 2500–2504 (1980).

George, J. S. and Hagins, W. A.: Control of Ca^{++} in rod outer segment disks by light and cyclic GMP. Nature **303,** 344–348 (1983).

Ghalayini, A. and Anderson, R. E.: Phosphatidylinositol 4,5-bisphosphate: light-mediated breakdown in the vertebrate retina. Biochem. Biophys. Res. Comm. **124,**503–506 (1984).

Gold, G. H.: Plasma membrane Ca fluxes in intact rods are inconsistent with the «Ca hypothesis». Biophys. J. **47,** 356 a (1985).

Gold, G. H.: Plasma membrane calcium fluxes in intact rods are inconsistent with the Ca-hypothesis. Proc. Natl. Acad. Sci. U.S.A. **83,** 1150–1154 (1986).

Gold, G. H. and Korenbrot, J. I.: Light-induced calcium release by intact retinal rods. Proc. Natl. Acad. Sci. U.S.A. **77,** 5557–5561 (1980).

Goldberg, N. D., Ames III, A., Gander, J. E. and Walseth, T. F.: Magnitude of increase in retinal cGMP metabolic flux determined by ^{18}O incorporation into nucleotide α-phosphoryls corresponds with intensity of photic stimulation. J. Biol. Chem. **258,** 9213–9219 (1983).

Goridis, C., Virmaux, N., Cailla, H. L. and Delaage, M. A.: Rapid, light-induced changes of retinal cyclic GMP levels. FEBS Letters **49,** 167–169 (1974).

Gray, P. and Attwell, D.: Kinetics of light-sensitive channels in vertebrate photoreceptors. Proc. R. Soc. **B 223,** 379–388 (1985).

Hagins, W. A.: The visual process: excitatory mechanisms in the primary receptor cells. Ann. Rev. Biophys. Bioeng. **1,** 131–158 (1972).

Hagins, W. A. and Yoshikami, S.: A role for Ca^{++} in excitation of retinal rods and cones. Exp. Eye Res. **18,** 299–305 (1974).

Hamill, O. P., Marty, A., Neher, E., Sakmann, B. and Sigworth, F. J.: Improved patch-clamp techniques for high-resolution current recording from cells and cell-free membrane patches. Pflügers Arch. **391,** 85–100 (1981).

Haynes, L. W. and Yau, K.-W.: Cyclic GMP-sensitive conductance in outer segment membranes of catfish cones. Nature **317,** 61–64 (1985).

Hodgkin, A. L., McNaughton, P. A. and Nunn, B. J.: The ionic selectivity and calcium dependence of the light-sensitive pathway in toad rods. J. Physiol. Lond. **358,** 447–468 (1985).

Hodgkin, A. L., McNaughton, P. A., Nunn, B. J. and Yau, K.-W.: Effects of ion on retinal rods from *Bufo marinus*. J. Physiol. Lond. **350,** 649–680 (1984).

Hubbell, W. L. and Bownds, M. D.: Visual transduction in vertebrate photoreceptors. Ann. Rev. Neurosci. **2,**17–34 (1979).

Hurwitz, R. L., Bunt-Milam, A. H., Chang, M. L. and Beavo, J. A.: cGMP phosphodiesterase in rod and cone outer segments of the retina. J. Biol. Chem. **260,** 568–573 (1985).

Jack, J. J. B., Noble, D. and Tsien, R. W.: *Electric Current Flow in Excitable Cells*. Clarendon, Oxford (1975).

Kawamura, S. and Murakami, M.: Intracellular injection of cyclic-GMP increases sodium conductance in Gecko photoreceptors. Japan. J. Physiol. **33,** 789–800 (1983).

Kilbride, P.: Calcium effects on frog retinal cyclic guanosine 3′ : 5′-monophosphate levels and their light-initiated rate of decay. J. gen. Physiol. **75,** 457–465 (1980).

Kilbride, P. and Ebrey, T. G.: Light-initiated changes of cyclic guanosine monophosphate levels in the frog retina measured with quick-freezing techniques. J. gen. Physiol. **74,** 415–426 (1979).

Koch, K.-W. and Kaupp, U. B.: Cyclic GMP directly regulates a cation conductance in membranes of bovine rods by a cooperative mechanism. J. Biol. Chem. **260,** 6788–6800 (1985).

Krishnan, N., Fletcher, R. T., Chader, G. J. and Krishna, G.: Characterization of guanylate cyclase of rod outer segments of the bovine retina. Biochim. Biophys. Acta. **523,** 506–515 (1978).

Kühn, H.: Interactions between photoexcited rhodopsin and light-activated enzymes in rods. Prog. in Retinal Research **3,** 123–156 (1984).

Kühn, H., Bennett, N., Michel-Villaz, M. and Chabre, M.: Interactions between photoexcited rhodopsin and GTP-binding protein: kinetics and stoichiometric analyses from light-scattering changes. Proc. Natl. Acad. Sci. U.S.A. **78,** 6873–6877 (1981).

Kühn, H. and Dreyer, W. J.: Light-dependent phosphorylation of rhodopsin by ATP. FEBS Letters **20,** 1–6 (1972).

Kühn, H., Hall, S. W. and Wilden, U.: Light-induced binding of 48-kDa protein to photoreceptor membranes is highly enhanced by phosphorylation of rhodopsin. FEBS Letters **176,** 473–478 (1984).

Lamb, T. D., Matthews, H. R. and Torre, V.: Trapped calcium buffer alters the light adaptation properties of rod photoreceptors from *Ambystoma tigrinum*. J. Physiol. Lond. **365,** 37 P. (1985).

Lansman, J. B., Hess, P. and Tsien, R. W.: Direct measurement of entry and exit rates for calcium ions in single calcium channels. Biophys. J. **47,** 67 a (1985).

Liebman, P. A. and Pugh Jr., E. N.: ATP mediates rapid reversal of cyclic GMP phosphodiesterase activation in visual receptor membranes. Nature **287,** 734–736 (1980).

Liebman, P. A. and Pugh Jr., E. N.: Control of rod disk membrane phosphodiesterase and a model for visual transduction. Curr. Top. Memb. Transp. **15,** 157–170 (1981).

Lipton, S. A.: cGMP and EGTA increase the light-sensitive current of retinal rods. Brain Res. **265,** 41–48 (1983).

Lipton, S. A. and Dowling, J. E.: The relation between Ca^{++} and cyclic GMP in rod photoresponse. Curr. Top. Memb. Transp. **15,** 381–392 (1981).

Lipton, S. A., Rasmussen, H. and Dowling, J. E.: Electrical and adaptive properties of rod photoreceptors in *Bufo marinus*. II. Effects of cyclic nucleotides and prostaglandins. J. gen. Physiol. **70,** 771–791 (1977).

Lolley, R. N. and Racz, E.: Calcium modulation of cyclic GMP synthesis in rat visual cells. Vision Res. **22,** 1481–1486 (1982).

MacLeish, P. R., Schwartz, E. A. and Tachibana, M.: Control of the generator current in solitary rods of the *Ambystoma tigrinum* retina. J. Physiol. Lond. **348,** 645–664 (1984).

Matthews, H. R., Torre, V. and Lamb, T. D.: Effects on the photoresponse of calcium buffers and cyclic GMP incorporated into the cytoplasm of retinal rods. Nature **313,** 582–585 (1985).

Miller, D. L. and Korenbrot, J. I.: Simultaneous photocurrent and calcium release measurements from single rod photoreceptors. Biophys. J. **45,** 341 a (1984).

Miller, W. H., ed.: Molecular Mechanisms of Photoreceptor Transduction, Curr. Top. Memb. Transp. Vol. **15,** Academic, New York (1981).

Miller, W. H.: Physiological evidence that light-mediated decrease in cyclic GMP is an intermediary process in retinal rod transduction. J. gen. Physiol. **80,** 103–123 (1982).

Miller, W. H. and Nicol, G. D.: Evidence that cyclic GMP regulates membrane potential in rod photoreceptors. Nature **280,** 64–66 (1979).

Nakatani, K. and Yau, K.-W.: cGMP opens the light-sensitive conductance in retinal rods. Biophys. J. **47,** 356 a (1985).

Nakatani, K. and Yau, K.-W.: Light-suppressible, cyclic GMP-activated current recorded from a dialyzed cone preparation. Invest. Ophthal. vis. Sci. Supp. **27,** 300 (1986).

Nakatani, K. and Yau, K.-W.: Light and dark calcium movements across the plasma membrane of the toad rod outer segment. Submitted.

Nestler, E. J., Walaas, S. I. and Greengard, P.: Neuronal phosphoproteins: physiological and clinical implications. Science **225,** 1357–1364 (1984).

Nicol, G. D. and Miller, W. H.: Cyclic GMP injected into retinal rod outer segments increases latency and amplitude of response to illumination. Proc. Natl. Acad. Sci. U.S.A. **75,** 5217–5220 (1978).

Nowak, L., Bregestovski, P., Ascher, P., Herbert, A. and Prochiantz, A.: Magnesium gates glutamate-activated channels in mouse central neurones. Nature **397,** 462–465 (1984).

Oakley II, B. and Pinto, L. H.: Modulation of membrane conductance in rods of *Bufo marinus* by intracellular calcium ion. J. Physiol. Lond. **339,** 273–298 (1983).

Pfister, C., Chabre, M., Plouet, J., Tuyen, V. V., De Kozak, Y., Faure, J. P. and Kühn, H.: Retinal S antigen identified as the 48 K protein regulating light-dependent phosphodiesterase in rods. Science **228,** 891–893 (1985).

Pinto, L. H. and Brown, J. E.: Pressure injection of 3′, 5′-cyclic GMP into solitary rod photoreceptors of the tiger salamander. Brain Res. **304,** 197–200 (1984).

Puckett, K. L., Rawji, A. J. and Goldin, S. M.: cGMP stimulated calcium release from purified bovine retinal discs. Biophys. J. **47,** 102 a (1985).

Robinson, P. R., Kawamura, S., Abramson, B. and Bownds, M. D.: Control of the cyclic GMP phosphodiesterase of frog photoreceptor membranes. J. gen. Physiol. **76,** 631–645 (1980).

Sakmann, B. and Neher, E. ed.: Single-Channel Recording, Plenum, New York (1983).

Schröder, W. H. and Fain, G. L.: Light-dependent calcium release from photoreceptors measured by laser micro-mass analysis. Nature **309,** 268–270 (1984).

Schnapf, J. L. and McBurney, R. N.: Light-induced changes in membrane current in cone outer segments of tiger salamander and turtle. Nature **287,** 239–241 (1980).

Sitaramayya, A. and Liebman, P. A.: Mechanism of ATP quench of phosphodiesterase activation in rod disc membranes. J. Biol. Chem. **258,** 1205–1209 (1983).

Somlyo, A. P. and Walz, B.: Elemental distribution in *Rana pipiens* retinal rods: quantitative electron probe analysis. J. Physiol. Lond. **358,** 183–195 (1985).

Sorbi, R. T.: Modulation of sodium conductance in photoreceptor membranes by calcium ions and cGMP. Curr. Top. Memb. Transp. **15,** 331–338 (1985).

Stieve, H., ed.: The Molecular Mechanism of Photoreception: Dahlem Konferenzen, Springer, Berlin (1986).

Stryer, L.: Cyclic GMP cascade of vision. Ann. Rev. Neurosci. **9,** in press (1986).

Troyer, E. W., Hall, I. A. and Ferrendelli, J. A.: Guanylate cyclase in CNS: Enzymatic characteristics of soluble and particulate enzymes from mouse cerebellum and retina. J. Neurochem. **31,** 825–833 (1978).

Torre, V.: The contribution of the electrogenic sodium-potassium pump to the electrical activity of toad rods. J. Physiol. Lond. **333,** 315–341 (1982).

Waloga, G.: Effects of calcium and guanosine 3′:5′-cyclic monophosphoric acid on receptor potentials of toad rods. J. Physiol. Lond. **341,** 341–357 (1983).

Waloga, G. and Anderson, R. E.: Effects of inositol-1,4,5-trisphosphate injections into salamander rods. Biochem. Biophys. Res. Comm. **126,** 59–62 (1985).

Woodruff, M. L. and Bownds, M. D.: Amplitude, kinetics and reversibility of a light-induced decrease in guanosine 3′:5′-cyclic monophosphate in frog photoreceptor membranes. J. gen. Physiol. **73,** 629–653 (1979).

Woodruff, M. J., Bownds, M. D., Green, S. H., Morrisey, J. L. and Shedlovsky, A.: Guanosine 3′:5′-cyclic monophosphate and the *in vitro* physiology of frog photoreceptor membranes. J. gen. Physiol. **69,** 667–679 (1977).

Woodruff, M. L. and Fain, G. L.: Ca^{++}-dependent changes in cyclic GMP levels are not correlated with opening and closing of the light-dependent permeability of toad photoreceptors. J. gen. Physiol. **80,** 537–555 (1982).

Yau, K.-W. and Haynes, L. W.: Effect of divalent cations on the macroscopic cGMP-activated current in excised rod membrane patches. Biophys. J. **49,** 33a (1986).

Yau, K.-W., Lamb, T. D. and Baylor, D. A.: Light-induced fluctuations in membrane current of single toad rod outer segments. Nature **269,** 78–80 (1977).

Yau, K.-W., McNaughton, P. A. and Hodgkin, A. L.: Effect of ions on the light-sensitive current in retinal rods. Nature **292,** 502–505 (1980).

Yau, K.-W. and Nakatani, K.: Cation selectivity of light-sensitive conductance in retinal rods. Nature **309,** 352–354 (1984 a)

Yau, K.-W. and Nakatani, K.: Electrogenic Na–Ca exchange in retinal rod outer segment. Nature **311,** 661–663 (1984 b)

Yau, K.-W. and Nakatani, K.: Light-induced reduction of cytoplasmic free calcium in retinal rod outer segment. Nature **313,** 579–582 (1985 a)

Yau K.-W. and Nakatani, K.: Light-suppressible, cyclic GMP-sensitive conductance in the plasma membrane of a truncated rod outer segment. Nature **317,** 252–255 (1985 b).

Yee, R. and Liebman, P. A.: Light-activated phosphodiesterase of the rod outer segment. J. Biol. Chem. **253,** 8902–8909 (1978).

Yoshikami, S., George, J. S. and Hagins, W. A.: Light-induced calcium fluxes from outer segment layer of vertebrate retinas. Nature **286,** 395–398 (1980).

Yoshikami, S. and Hagins, W. A.: Light, calcium and the photocurrent of rods and cones. Abstr. 15th Ann. Meet. Biophys. Soc. TPM-E16.(1971)

Zimmerman, A. L. and Baylor, D. A.: Electrical properties of the light-sensitive conductance of salamander retinal rods. Biophys. J. **47**, 357 a (1985).

Zimmerman, A. L., Yamanaka, G., Eckstein, F., Baylor, D. A. and Stryer, L.: Interaction of hydrolysis-resistant analogs of cyclic GMP with the phosphodiesterase and light-sensitive channel of retinal rod outer segments. Proc. Natl. Acad. Sci. U.S.A. **82**, 8813–8817 (1985).

Fortschritte der Zoologie, Band 33 · Lüttgau (Hrsg.): Membrane Control
Gustav Fischer Verlag · Stuttgart · New York · 1986

An automatic gain control in the *Limulus* photoreceptor

H. Stieve, J. Schnakenberg*, A. Kuhn**, H. Reuss

Institut für Biologie II (Zoologie), Institut für Theoretische Physik D*, RWTH Aachen, 5100 Aachen, FRG, and Institut für Neurobiologie** der KFA Jülich GmbH, FRG

Light adaptation diminishes the light response of the *Limulus* photoreceptor during sustained illumination (Lisman and Brown, 1975 a). We want to show that this desensitization can act fast enough to diminish even the peak amplitude of a receptor current evoked by a flash ($\leqq$ 10 ms) of light, and that it may act as an automatic gain control expanding the intensity range over which the cell can respond with an unsaturated, graded receptor current.

Figure 1 shows single photon-evoked responses of the *Limulus* ventral photoreceptor following very dim light flashes recorded under voltage clamp conditions. The left column shows examples of recordings of the photoreceptor in the dark-adapted state. The bumps vary greatly in size and latency. The right column shows bumps recorded from the same photoreceptor at a slightly light-adapted state. On the average they are smaller and have shorter latencies.

The response to a stronger light stimulus, the «macroscopic light response», is believed to be built up by the summation of many of these single events. Figure 2 shows the comparison of artificially summated bump responses (right) with macroscopic receptor current responses of another cell evoked by a strong flash (left), both in the dark adapted state (upper curves) or in the light-adapted state (lower curves). It can be seen that the time course J(t) of the macroscopic response is considerably faster than that of the artificial bump sum. Hence the time course J(t) of the macroscopic receptor current is not determined solely by the distribution of the bumps following the stimulating flash.

How does the bump sum have to be modulated to result in the measured macroscopic receptor current if we make the following simplifying assumptions?

1. The frequency distribution of the bump latencies is not substantially different for responses to very weak and strong light flashes.
2. The scaling of the bumps following the stronger light flash varies with time during the flash response; the first bumps are not or much less attenuated than the bumps occurring later. In other words the macroscopic receptor current could be described as the summation of the weighted underlying bumps.

The time course of the bump sum may be described as a function $b(\mathrm{t})$. We then postulate a hypothetical attenuation function $a(\mathrm{t})$, which is small initially and increases with time. The bump sum $b(\mathrm{t})$ has to be convoluted with the attenuation function to give receptor currents of realistic shapes, i. e. each value of $b(\mathrm{t})$ is scaled by a corresponding value of $a(\mathrm{t})$. It seemed plausible to test whether the current-time integral of the receptor current, if used as attenuation function $a(\mathrm{t})$, may yield reasonable simulations for macroscopic receptor cur-

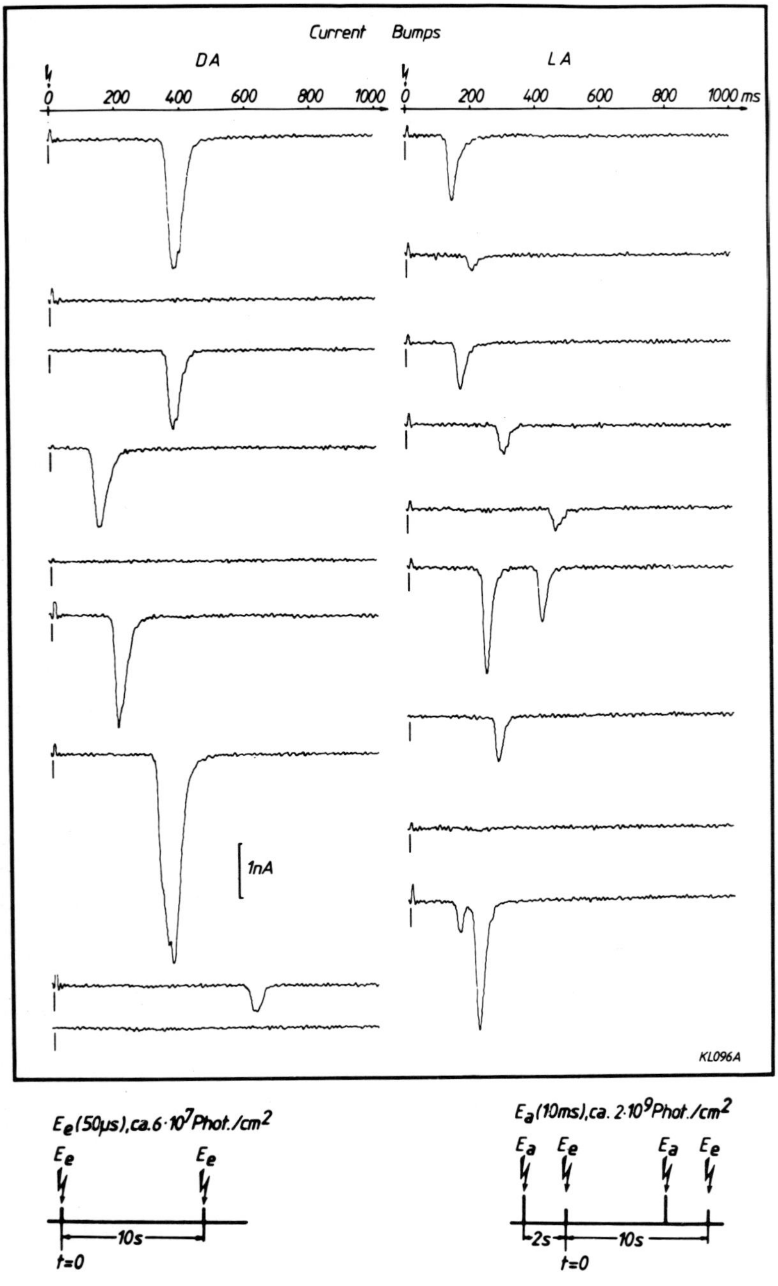

Fig. 1: Current bumps measured from a *Limulus* ventral nerve photoreceptor under voltage clamp conditions. Left column: dark adapted photoreceptor, right column: photoreceptor weakly light adapted by a conditioning, light-adapting flash, two seconds prior to the bump-evoking flash. Bump-evoking flash: 50 μs, ca. 6×10^7 photons cm^{-2}, repetition time 10 s: conditioning, light-adapting illumination: 10 ms, ca. 2×10^9 photons cm^{-2}; both flashes 540 nm, membrane potential clamped to –40 mV; 15 °C. KL 96 A.

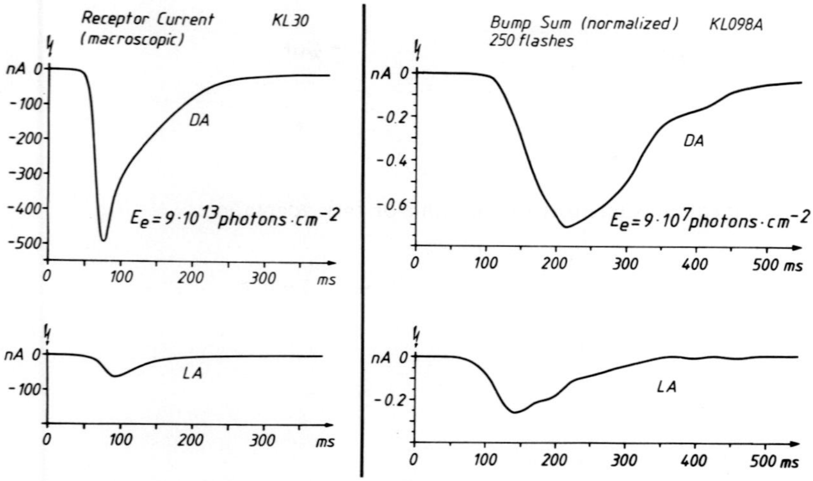

Fig. 2: Comparison of macroscopic receptor current signals evoked by strong stimuli (left) of a dark-adapted or light-adapted photoreceptor cell with the artificial summation of current bump responses to very weak flashes (right) of another cell in the dark- or light-adapted state. Experimental conditions, left side: receptor current evoked by 10 ms flash, ca. 9×10^{13} photons cm^{-2}, membrane potential clamped to –50 mV; record of the light-adapted state: 18 s prior to the receptor current-evoking flash as above, the cell was illuminated for 2 s by a conditioning illumination, intensity ca. 2.3×10^{15} photons cm^{-2}s^{-1}; right: bump-evoking flash, 50 μs, 9×10^{7} photons cm^{-2}, repetition time 10 s, membrane potential clamped to –40 mV; record of the light-adapted state: 2 s prior to the bump-evoking flash the cell was illuminated by a 10 ms conditioning flash (8×10^{9} photons cm^{-2}); 15 °C. The bump-sum was obtained by linear summation in ms steps, starting from the light stimulus. The current of the bump sum is scaled for a single bump response. Kl 30, Kl 98 A.

rents. Figure 3 gives an example. The upper curve shows a normalized bump sum (same as Fig. 2) of the dark adapted photoreceptor and (dotted line) an arbitrary mathematical approximation of the bump sum $b(t)$, which will not be described here in detail since, while giving a reasonable fit for most of the bump sum, it does not give a substantiated description for its initial rise, which is determined by the rare bumps with short latencies recorded in the initial phase of the response (see below).

The central curve shows an example of a hypothetical attenuation function $a(t)$, a modified current-time integral of the receptor current

$$a(t) = 1 + a_o + s \int_{o}^{t-\Delta t} J(t') \cdot dt' \tag{1}$$

where a_o determines the level of preadaptation,

- s is a scaling factor
- Δt the time delay for the action of the attenuation,
- t' the integration variable

The lower curve shows a simulated macroscopic receptor current according to

$$J(t) = \frac{N \cdot b(t)}{a(t)} \tag{2}$$

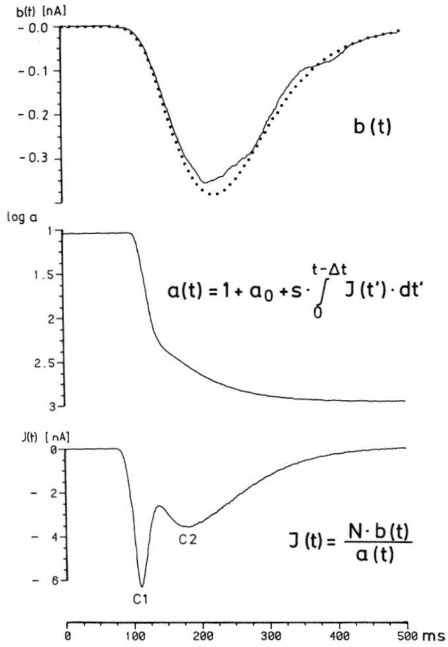

Fig. 3: Simulation of a macroscopic receptor current signal by convoluting the bump sum b(t) with an attenuation function a(t). Top: bump sum achieved by linear summation of 250 bump responses to very dim light flashes (normalized, same data as in Fig. 3). Dotted line: function b(t) approximating the shape of the bump sum. Centre: attenuation function a(t) plotted logarithmically. Example chosen: modified current time integral of receptor current (Equation 1). Bottom: simulated receptor current (Equation 2). In agreement with our experimental observations the components C1 and C2 depend strongly on the state of adaptation. In order to demonstrate the two components pronouncedly a somewhat light-adapted state (a_o = 10, Equation 1) is assumed in the example shown. Scaling factors 0.01 pAs^{-1}, Δt 30 ms.

where N represents the number of bumps evoked by the light flash.

Unexpectedly, convolution of the bump sum with the receptor current-time integral even simulates the two components C1 and C2 of the receptor current previously described by MAAZ et al. (1981). These can be simulated conveniently if the time delay Δt of equation (1) is assumed to be $\geqq$ 5 ms. The two components C1 and C2 have reversal potentials which do not differ significantly. Both in the experiment and in the simulation these two components are very sensitive to variations of the stimulus intensity and of the state of light adaptation.

Figure 4 shows recordings of receptor currents of a *Limulus* ventral nerve photoreceptor cell showing the development of the two components by variation of the dark adaptation time t_{DA}, and Figure 5 the corresponding simulations. In these simulations the bump sum b(t) of a weakly light-adapted cell is used. The bump latency distribution becomes narrower and is shifted to shorter values with light adaptation (STIEVE, 1983 and 1985). For this reason, even better simulations would be achieved by using bump sums b(t) of stronger light-adapted photoreceptors. In the example chosen for simulation the size of the response rises less with increasing dark adaptation in the simulation than in the actual experimental results. (In Fig. 5 the amplitudes of the two largest simulated responses are slightly scaled up for better distinction.)

Figure 6 shows recordings of receptor currents which – by variation of the stimulus intensity – demonstrate the two components C1 and C2. Figure 7 shows the simulated receptor current signals also displaying these components. The simulations demonstrate remarkable similarities. There are, however, important differences to the experimental results: The increase in response size and the shortening of the response latency with increasing stimulus intensity or with time of dark adaptation are too weak in the simulations.

The shortening of the latency (with growing intensity of the light stimulus) in our simulations is solely based on the fact that with higher intensity of the light stimulus bumps with relatively improbable, short latencies become more frequent. Therefore the initial curvature of the approximation of the bump latency distribution or the bump sum $b(t)$ seems to be critical in determining the dependence of the latency of the macroscopic receptor current of the stimulus intensity. The number of bumps recorded to determine the bump sum is relatively small (N = 250); it does not allow to approximate reliably the initial part of the bump sum. If we use approximations with different initial slopes, we can simulate steeper or weaker shortenings of the latency with the stimulus intensity than those experimentally observed.

Figure 8 shows the dependence of the receptor current-time integral of the stimulus intensity in a double logarithmic plot for a dark- and a light-adapted state of the Limulus photoreceptor. The two curves have two sections, a steep, supralinear slope (steeper than 3) which is followed, after a knee, by a weaker, sublinear slope of 0.3–0.5. These curves do not saturate even at relatively high stimulus intensities. Light adaptation causes a shift to higher stimulus intensities. If we calculate (by using equations 1 and 2) how the current-time integral of the simulated receptor current depends on the stimulus intensity we obtain

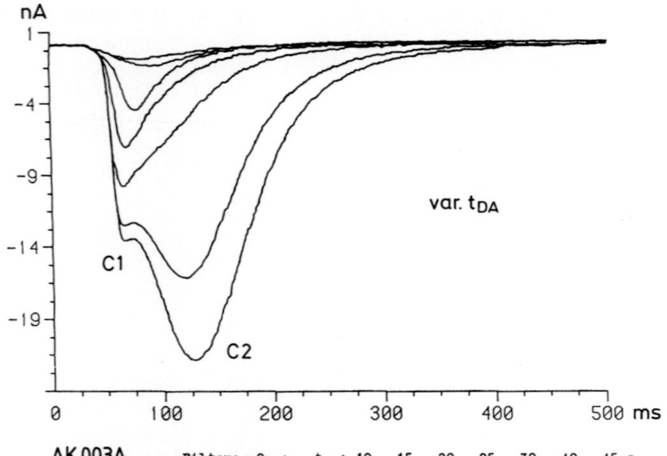

Fig. 4: Macroscopic receptor current, evoked by identical light flashes (2 ms, E = 1.5×10^{15} photons cm^{-2}) at different times t_{DA} after a conditioning, 2 s light adapting illumination (4.34×10^{16} photons cm^{-2}). Clamp voltage U_{cl} –34 mV. Temperature 15 °C.
Dark adaptation time t_{DA} 10, 15, 20, 25, 30, 40, 45 s after light adapting stimulus. As in Fig. 6 the receptor current signals show pronouncedly the development of the two components C1 and C2. AK 3 A.

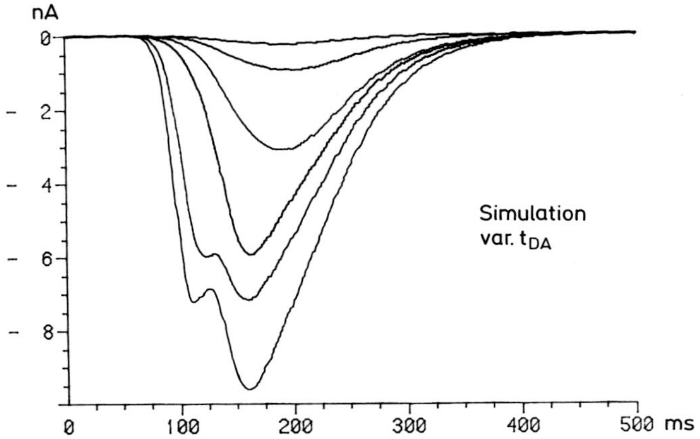

Fig. 5: Simulated receptor current signals for increasing times of dark adaptation, obtained by convoluting the bump sum b(t) with the attenuation function $a(t)$ described above using equation 1 and 2. Preadaptation level a_o (t_{DA}) 3200, 800, 200, 50, 3, 1; scaling factor s 0.01 pAs^{-1}; time delay Δt 20 ms; number of bumps N 1000. For better distinction the current values of the two lowest simulated curves were scaled up by 10 % and 20 %.

(in double logarithmic plot; Figure 9) curves also consisting of two sections, an initial part with slope 1 and, after a knee, a sublinear section with a less steep slope (0.5 in the example plotted). Simulation of light adaptation by changing a_o in equation (1) shifts this curve to higher intensities and the knee to larger responses. When the scaling factor s is enlarged the curve knee is shifted to lower light intensities. With increasing Δt the sublinear curve section becomes less steep, on the condition that Δt is not longer than the rise-

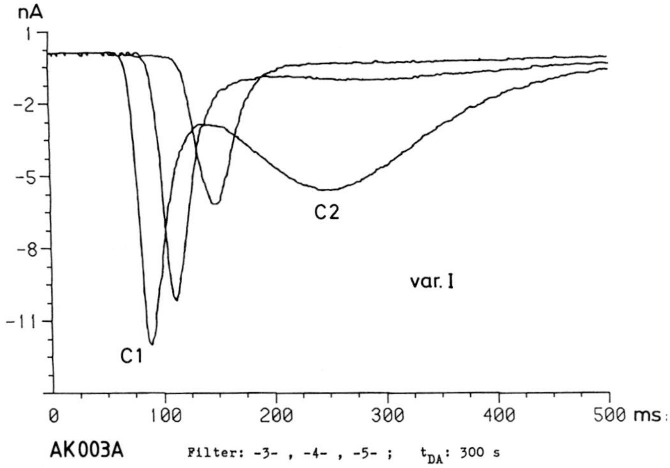

Fig. 6: Macroscopic receptor current signals evoked by 2 ms light flashes recorded at constant state of adaptation, t_{DA} 300 s after a conditioning, 2 s light adapting illumination. Same cell as in Fig. 4, see there for details. Energies $E_o \times 2^{-3}$, $E_o \times 2^{-4}$, $E_o \times 2^{-5}$, E_o 1.5×10^{15} photons cm^{-2}. The signals show the development of the two components C1 and C2. AK 3A.

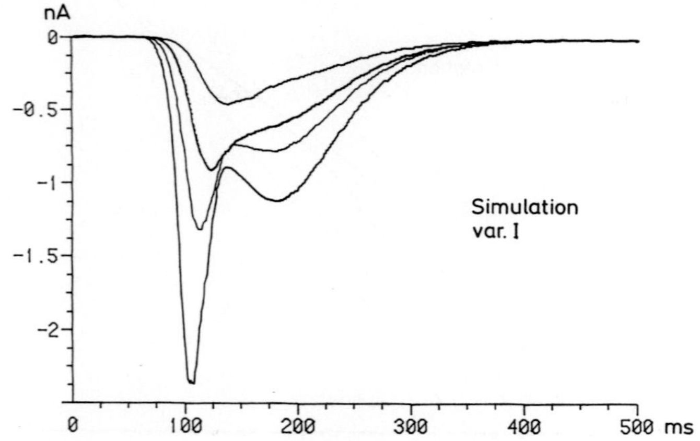

Fig. 7: Simulated receptor current signals for different stimulus intensities (the rise of the simulated response is less steep than that of the experimental record and the latency is less shortened). Simulation conditions a_o 10; s 0.01 pAs^{-1}; Δt 30 ms; N 75, 300, 1250, 5000.

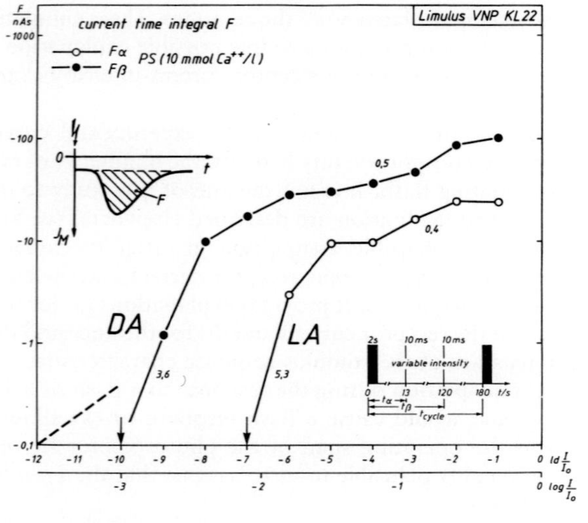

Fig. 8: The dependence of the size F (current-time integral) of the experimentally observed receptor current signal on the intensity of the stimulating flash at two states of adaptation: a) dark adapted (DA), b) moderately light adapted (LA). Double logarithmic plot. The arrows indicate responses smaller than 0.1 nAs. The rise has a supra-linear and a sub-linear region. Light adaptation shifts the curve to higher stimulus intensities (for experimental details see STIEVE, GAUBE, KLOMFASS, in preparation). I_o highest light intensity of 10 ms flash 4 × 10^{16} photons $cm^{-2}s^{-1}$, conditioning 2 s illumination I 2 × 10^{16} photons $cm^{-2}s^{-1}$, 540 nm; 15 °C. (from STIEVE, 1986). KL 22.

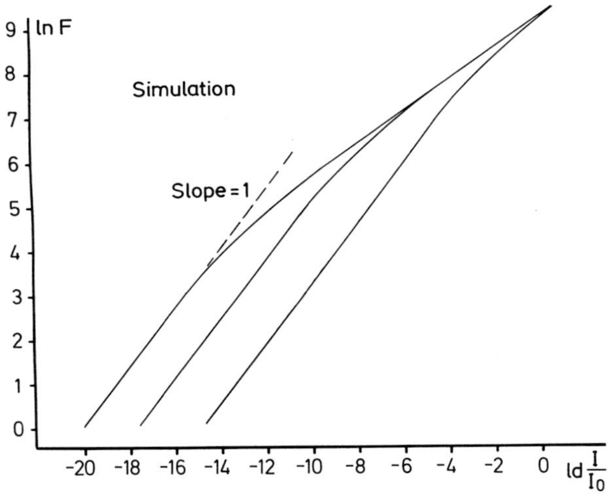

Fig. 9: Intensity dependence of the size F (current-time integral) of the simulated receptor current signal using equation (1) and (2) by variation of N. The stimulus-intensity characteristics has a region with a slope of 1 which leads to a region at higher light-intensities with a slope of 0.5. This sub-linear slope depends on the parameters chosen in equation (1). Conditions of simulation: three states of light adaptation, a_o 10, 100, 1000; s 0.01 pAs^{-1}; Δt 25 ms; N 10^7 (for I_o).

time (peak-amplitude-time minus latency) of the response. These simulations demonstrate that such a feedback attenuation provides a simple possible explanation for the knee and the smaller, sublinear second slope in the receptor current-intensity characteristics of the light response.

The supralinear slope of the first section of the experimental curve (Fig. 8) is not simulated, since we assumed proportionality between the number N of evoked bumps and the intensity of the stimulating flash. It is not the aim of this study to discuss the supralinearity. (Supralinearity and facilitation are described elsewhere, see Stieve, 1986).

The simple and relatively plausible assumption in order to explain the differences between the time course of the macroscopic receptor current and the bump sum unexpectedly has two additional consequences: It provides explanations (a) for the existence of the components C1 and C2 of the receptor current and (b) for the knee and the sublinear slope for higher stimulus intensities of the stimulus-response characteristics.

This type of fast light adaptation during the response to a flash of light could act as an automatic gain control and would cause a flash response to «swallow its own tail». It would serve to expand the operating span of the photoreceptor by opposing response saturation. It seems reasonably plausible to us to assume that the *Limulus* photoreceptor cell is using this mechanism.

The chemical substrate serving as agent of the attenuation function a(t) could be the increase in intracellular calcium ion concentration. The light-induced intracellular calcium increase was originally proposed by Lisman and Brown (1972, 1975 a, b) as a desensitizing intracellular messenger. It was measured by Brown and Blinks (1974), by Brown, Brown and Pinto (1977), Maaz and Stieve (1980), Nagy and Stieve (1983) and Ivens and Stieve (1984). The intracellular calcium increase upon stimulation roughly parallels in its rising phase the current-time integral of the light response and may therefore repre-

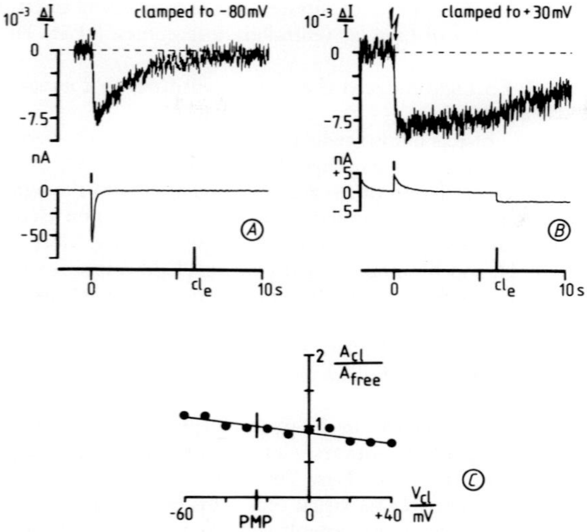

Fig. 10 a–c: The change in intracellular concentration of ionized calcium in the *Limulus* ventral nerve photoreceptor monitored by the calcium indicator Arsenazo III. Arsenazo-signal (upper trace) and receptor current signal (lower trace) of the *Limulus* ventral nerve photoreceptor cell clamped to –80 mV (A) and +30 mV (B) in response to a 10 ms bright stimulus. In each case two signals are averaged. Clamp is switched off at cl_e; 17 °C. The superfusate contained 10 mmol/l Ca^{2+}. The normalized amplitude (A_{cl}/A_{free}) of the Arsenazo signal (C), relative units, is plotted versus the membrane voltage to which the cell is clamped (V_{cl}). By linear extrapolation of the regression line a hypothetical reversal potential of the Arsenazo signal is calculated to be +250 mV. Normalization is obtained by dividing the amplitude of the Arsenazo signal of the clamped cell by the average of the amplitudes of the two Arsenazo signals of the unclamped cell 3 min before, and 3 min after the clamped signal was recorded. PMP: prestimulus membrane potential (from Ivens and Stieve, 1984).

sent the attenuation function *a*(t) (see Figure 10) which determines the attenuation of the bump sum during the first second following the light flash. The molecular mechanism of the gain control is not yet known; one could imagine that calcium controls the amplification by influencing an enzymatic activity.

Supported by the Deutsche Forschungsgemeinschaft, SFB 160

References

Brown, J. E. and Blinks, J. R.: Changes in intracellular free calcium concentration during illumination of invertebrate photoreceptors. J. Gen. Physiol. **64**, 643–665 (1974).

Brown, J. E., Brown, P. K. and Pinto, L. H.: Detection of light-induced changes of intracellular ionized calcium concentration in *Limulus* ventral nerve photoreceptors using Arsenazo III. J. Physiol. **267**, 299–320 (1977).

Ivens, I. and Stieve, H.: Influence of the membrane potential on the intracellular light-induced Ca^{2+}-concentration change of the Limulus ventral photoreceptor monitored by Arsenazo III under voltage clamp conditions. Z. Naturforsch. **39 c**, 939–992 (1984).

Lisman, J. F. and Brown, J. E.: The effects of intracellular iontophoretic injection of calcium and sodium ions on the light response of *Limulus* ventral photoreceptors. J. Gen. Physiol. **59,** 701–719 (1972).
Lisman, J. E. and Brown, J. E.: Light-induced changes of sensitivity in *Limulus* photoreceptors. J. Gen. Physiol. **66,** 473–488 (1975 a).
Lisman, J. E. and Brown, J. E.: Effects of intracellular injection of calcium buffers on light adaptation in *Limulus* ventral photoreceptors. J. Gen. Physiol. **66,** 489–506 (1975 b).
Maaz, G. and Stieve, H.: The correlation of the receptor potential with the light-induced transient increase in intracellular calcium concentration measured by absorption change of Arsenazo III injected into *Limulus* ventral nerve photoreceptor cell. Biophys. Struct. Mech. **6,** 191–208 (1980).
Maaz, G ., Nagy, K., Stieve, H. and Klomfaß, J.: The electrical light response of the *Limulus* ventral nerve photoreceptor, a superposition of distinct components – observable by variation of the state of light adaptation. J. Comp. Physiol. **141,** 303–310 (1981).
Nagy, K. and Stieve, H.: Changes in intracellular calcium concentration in the course of dark adaptation measured by Arsenazo III in the *Limulus* photoreceptor. Biophys. Struct. Mech. **9,** 207–223 (1983).
Stieve, H.: On the transduction mechanism in the photoreceptor cell of an invertebrate studied by single photon responses. Biological Membranes – Information and Energy Transduction in Biological Membranes. Alan List Incorporation, New York (1983).
Stieve, H.: Phototransduction in invertebrate visual cells – the present state of research exemplified and discussed through the *Limulus* photoreceptor cell. Proceeding in Life Sciences. Ed. R. Gilles and J. Balthazar, Berlin, Heidelberg, New York, Tokyo: Springer-Verlag, 346–362 (1985).
Stieve, H.: Bumps, the elementary excitatory responses of invertebrates. Ed. H. Stieve: Molecular mechanism of photoreception. Dahlem Konferenzen. Berlin, Heidelberg, New York, Tokyo: Springer-Verlag, 199–230 (1986).

Fortschritte der Zoologie, Band 33 · Lüttgau (Hrsg.): Membrane Control
Gustav Fischer Verlag · Stuttgart · New York · 1986

Cellular processes in vision – an outlook

Hennig Stieve

Institut für Biologie II, RWTH Aachen, 5100 Aachen, FRG

A prominent characteristic of visual transduction is the controlled amplification of the light response, a graded voltage signal across the cell membrane depending in size upon the strength of the light stimulus. A single photon is sufficient to elicit a light response as large as 400 pC (with an amplitude of about 6 nA). The size of such a light response of a dark-adapted photoreceptor – elicited by the successful absorption of a single photon – corresponds to the opening or closing of ion channels in the order of 1000. This gain can be controlled; light adaptation reduces it by a factor of at least 1000.

There are several conspicuous functional differences between the photoreceptors of vertebrates and those of invertebrates (see the contributions of Kühn and Paulsen, this volume, and Stieve 1977 and 1986), some of which are well established. They include:

1. In invertebrates the visual pigment is converted by light to a thermostable meta-state which is not, or only very slowly, metabolically regenerated.
2. The electrical signal of visual excitation in invertebrates is based upon an increase in membrane conductance as opposed to the conductance decrease in vertebrates, resulting in membrane voltage signals (receptor potentials) of opposite polarity.
3. The rhodopsin molecules have large rotational and translational mobility within the vertebrate photosensory membrane (Cone, 1972). This is in contrast to the invertebrate photoreceptor membrane in which the rhodopsin molecules are virtually immobile.

In spite of these differences, the causal chain leading from absorption of a photon to the elementary light response, the single photon-evoked event, may be schematically characterized as in Figure 1. This transduction chain is at present understood to quite different degrees.

A light-activated rhodopsin molecule starts the response signal generating process by interacting, for a limited period of time, with protein molecules which are peripherally attached to the photosensory membrane (G-protein, rhodopsin kinase, 48 K-protein, see Kühn, this volume). Whether rhodopsin serves other (e. g. transport-)functions is an open question (see Findlay, 1986). The interaction of the activated rhodopsin molecule, sequentially with several G-protein molecules, starts an enzyme cascade, which is already quite clearly characterized for the vertebrate photoreceptor (see Kühn, this volume). The contribution of R. Paulsen indicates that there are many parallels in the invertebrate photoreceptor which will be characterized probably in the near future. For this part of the transduction process our understanding is relatively far advanced to the molecular level. The questions to ask are fairly clear, the methods to solve them available, and especially methods of molecular genetics such as gene cloning are accelerating the progress of our

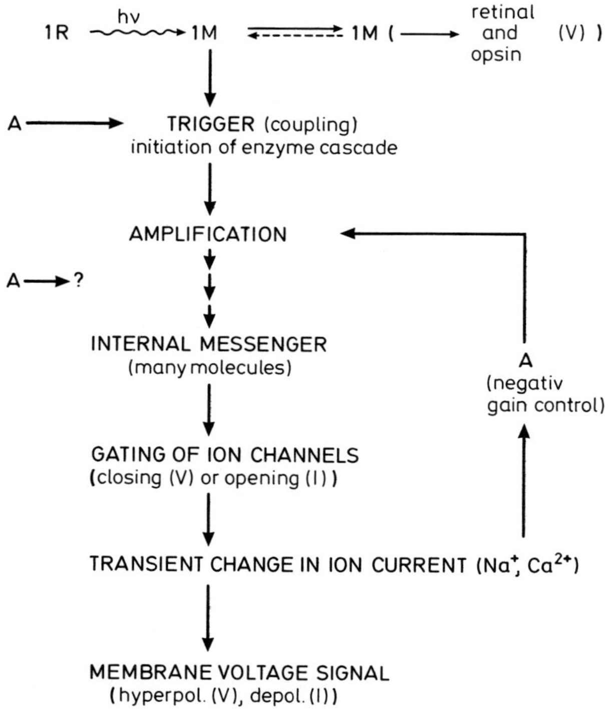

Fig. 1: Flow chart of the processes in visual transduction leading from photon absorption by a rhodopsin molecule to the single photon-evoked event both for vertebrate (V) and invertebrate (I) photoreceptors.
R rhodopsin, M metarhodopsin, M* activated metarhodopsin, Ca_i^{2+} intracellular calcium, A adaptation.

understanding enormously. Here the investigation of invertebrate photoreceptors will prove to be very important. By the combination of gene cloning with the background of knowledge about the genetics of the fruit fly *Drosophila*, it will soon be possible to use *Drosophila* mutants to insert modified rhodopsin as the only visual pigment into photoreceptor cells and test the influence of strategically modified domains of the molecule.

The observed spatial spread of excitation in the photoreceptor cell, involving membrane areas in the order of μm^2, led to the assumption of messenger molecules, internal transmitters. Several kinds of messenger molecules may provide for spatial spread. There is accumulating evidence (see contributions of McNaughton and Yau, both this volume) that cyclic GMP seems to be the terminal messenger, the binding of which causes the opening of the light-modulated ion channels in the vertebrate photoreceptor membrane. The longtime major suspect for this role, the calcium ion, though very important in influencing (modulating) the light response (McNaughton and Yau, both this volume) does not seem to be the transmitter which is the channel-gating agent in the physiological light response.

Not much is known about the nature of the ion channel and about the gating mechanism. Yau(this volume) reports a Hill coefficient of 2.2 which suggests that the binding of more than 2 cGMP molecules is necessary for the opening of a light-activated channel. In invertebrate photoreceptors perhaps cGMP is also the terminal transmitter. The supralinearity observed in the stimulus-response characteristics of *Limulus* (see e. g. STIEVE et al., this volume) may – if it is caused by a binding cooperativity – indicate that even more than 3 terminal transmitter molecules have to be bound for opening of the light-activated channels of *Limulus*.

Inositol polyphosphate IP_3 appears to be an internal messenger in the *Limulus* photoreceptor cell (BROWN, this volume). Its specific role in the transduction process is not yet understood. It does, however, not seem to be in the direct line of the transduction chain and not to be the terminal transmitter.

The molecular processes involved in the generation of the single photon-evoked signals are not yet characterized sufficiently to predict the quantitative time course of the light response. In the macroscopic light response of invertebrates the latency period is not correlated to the size of the single photon-evoked response. This effect is difficult to explain by the molecular processes known, which involve considerable amplification already in the first stages following the light-activation of rhodopsin. Time course and quantity of the concentration change of the terminal transmitter in the photoreceptor cell initiated by weak (physiological) light stimuli are not yet known.

The mechanisms involved in the control of the sensitivity in light-dark adaptation appear to be quite complex. There are several mechanisms controlling the sensitivity in light-dark adaptation. These mechanisms are today better understood for invertebrate photoreceptors than for those of vertebrates:

1. The best known mechanism (in invertebrates), originally discovered by LISMAN and BROWN(1972 and 1975), involves a feed-back loop with the calcium ion concentration responsible for determining the sensitivity. Calcium ions as internal desensitizing, adaptational messengers are also responsible for a spatial spread of adaptation. In the invertebrate photoreceptor the intracellular level of calcium ions probably determines the gain of amplification (Figure 1). There are indications (as pointed out by LAMB 1986; see also YAU and MCNAUGHTON, both this volume) that calcium may serve as sensitivity-modulating, adaptational transmitter also in the vertebrate photoreceptor. Additionally there are other processes regulating the sensitivity in adaptation:
2. A not primarily calcium-controlled desensitation mechanism (Stieve, 1985 and Pugh et al., 1986).
3. A desensitation occurring at very strong rhodopsin bleaches which are accompanied by a so-called ‹prolonged depolarizing afterpotential› (PDA) in invertebrates.
4. The quantum efficiency, i. e. the coupling between rhodopsin reaction and photon response generation, which is also changed in adaptation (Stieve, 1986).

Adaptation in invertebrates may act very fast and this may influence the intensity response characteristics of a photoreceptor even for short light flashes (see STIEVE et al., this volume).

The progress in this field of phototransduction research seems to accelerate at present. The immediate goals of research are the continued pursuit of topics already tackled in the contributions of this volume.

- Further characterization of the process leading from rhodopsin activation via enzyme cascade to the gating of the ion channels (see KÜHN and PAULSEN, this volume).
- Measurement of quantity and time course of the change of internal messengers (including the terminal transmitter) in the photoreceptor cell under physiological conditions (see BROWN and MCNAUGHTON, both this volume).
- Characterization and isolation of the light-modulated ion channel (see YAU, this volume).

– Characterization of the processes and messengers controlling the sensitivity of the photoreceptor cell in the state of light- and dark-adaptation (see BROWN and STIEVE et al., both this volume).

The investigation of these topics will advance more and more to a quantitative and molecular level in the near future, aiming at an understanding of the processes underlying phototransduction in the terms of a quantitative mathematical description.

References

Cone, R. A.: Rotational diffusion of rhodopsin in the visual receptor membrane. Nature New Biol. **236,** 39–43 (1972).

Findlay, J. B. C.: The biosynthetic, functional and evolutionary implications of the structure of rhodopsin. Ed. H. Stieve: Molecular mechanism of photoreceptor. Dahlem-Konferenzen. Berlin, Heidelberg, New York, Tokyo: Springer-Verlag, 11–30 (1986).

Lamb, T. D.: Photoreceptor adaptation – vertebrates. Ed. H. Stieve: The molecular mechanism of photoreception. Dahlem Konferenzen. Berlin, Heidelberg, New York, Tokyo: Springer-Verlag, 267–286 (1986).

Lisman, J. E. and Brown, J. E.: The effects of intracellular iontophoretic injection of calcium and sodium ions on the light response of *Limulus* ventral photoreceptors. J. Gen. Physiol. **59,** 701–719 (1972).

Lisman, J. E. and Brown, J. E.: Effects of intracellular injection of calcium buffers on light adaptation in *Limulus* ventral photoreceptors. J. Gen. Physiol. **66,** 489–506 (1975).

Pugh jr., E. N., Brown, J. E., Hamdorf, K., Hillman, P., Hochstrate, P., Keiper, W. J. M., Kirschfeld, K., Lamb, T. O., Minke, B., Pepperberg, D. R., Schwemer, J. and Shapley, R.: Adaptation – group report. Ed. H. Stieve: The molecular mechanism of photoreception. Dahlem Konferenzen. Berlin, Heidelberg, New York, Tokyo: Springer-Verlag, 467–488 (1986).

Stieve, H.: Thoughts on the comparative biology of photosensory function. Verh. Dtsch. Zool. Ges. S. 1–25 (1977).

Stieve, H.: Phototransduction in invertebrate visual cells – the present state of research exemplified and discussed through the *Limulus* photoreceptor cell. Proceeding in Life Sciences, Ed. Gilles and Balthazar, Berlin, Heidelberg, New York, Tokyo: Springer-Verlag, 346–362 (1985).

Stieve, H.: Introduction. Ed. H. Stieve: The molecular mechanism of photoreception. Dahlem Konferenzen. Berlin, Heidelberg, New York, Tokyo: Springer-Verlag, 1–10 (1986).

V. Session
Active Na and Ca transport and Na-Ca exchange in nerve and muscle

Fortschritte der Zoologie, Band 33 · Lüttgau (Hrsg.): Membrane Control
Gustav Fischer Verlag · Stuttgart · New York · 1986

Dependence of the sodium pump on membrane potential. Introductory remarks

H. Passow

Max-Planck-Institut für Biophysik, 6000 Frankfurt am Main, FRG

Each cycle of the sodium pump leads to the outward movement of 3 Na ions and the inward movement of 2 K ions. Hence, a net outward movement of one positive charge occurs. This gives rise to a current which is associated with a generation of an electrical potential difference. The sodium pump is «electrogenic». The electrogenicity in turn renders the activity of the pump dependent on the electrical potential difference across the membrane.

In the past, the dependence of the activity of the sodium pump on the ionic composition of the media at the 2 membrane surfaces has been studied extensively (see, for example, Glynn and Ellory, 1985). However, comparatively little work has been devoted to the study of the dependence of pump activity on membrane potential. Early attempts to measure the pump activity as a function of potential (e. g. Mullins and Noda, 1963; Isenberg and Trautwein, 1974) were revived only very recently. The papers of Profs. De Weer and Glitsch will provide two representative examples for the type of experiments that are currently being performed in a number of laboratories.

The neglect of the study of potential dependence in the past was to some extent due to technical problems. In most cells the contributions of the electrogenicity of the Na^+–K^+ pump to the total membrane potential is rather small, of the order of a few millivolts or so (e. g. Lederer and Nelson, 1984). It is necessary, therefore, to work with cell species with a high pump activity. However, in such cells the concentration of the intracellular substrates of the pump may change during the time of measurement. As an indirect consequence the activities of channels involved in the mediation of passive ion currents may be affected, and this may obscure the electrogenic effects of the pump. These problems were overcome in different ways.

In our laboratory, Lafaire and Schwarz (1985) chose oocytes of *Xenopus* laevis for their studies. Work by Richter et al. (1984) has shown that the plasma membrane of these oocytes contains sodium pumps at the extraordinary high density of 1000–2000 copies μm^{-2}. The cell volume is so large (1 μl) that in spite of the high pump activity virtually no changes of intracellular Na^+ or K^+ take place during the time required for the measurement of the current voltage relationship. Lafaire and Schwarz (1985) observed a roughly bell shaped potential dependence with a maximum at about +20 mV.

Gadsby et al. (1985) used isolated heart cells whose intracellular composition was clamped by perfusion with solutions of the author's choice. In addition, the passive ion channels were blocked by suitable inhibitors.

Both Lafaire and Schwarz (1985) and Gadsby and associates (1985) used intracellular electrodes to monitor current and potential. Using human red blood cells, which are too small for impalement with microelectrodes, HOFFMAN and LARIS (1984) measured the current flow by means of radiosodium and determined membrane potential by means of fluorescent potential-indicating dyes.

In our institute, FENDLER et al. (1985) introduced an entirely novel technique. Based on Bamberg's earlier work with the light-driven pumps bacteriorhodopsin (BAMBERG et al., 1979) and halorhodopsin (BAMBERG et al., 1984), they attached purified ATPase disks (prepared by the method of JØRGENSEN, 1974) to planar lipid bilayers. The outward-facing surfaces of these disks assume contact with the bilayer while the inward-facing surfaces become exposed to the medium. This preparation can be induced to pump Na^+ and K^+ when ATP is liberated from caged ATP. The capacitative coupling between the ATPase-containing disks and the lipid bilayer allows one to measure the current generated by the pump. This technique revealed immediately that the reaction of the pump observed in the absence of K^+ leads to the generation of a Na^+ current. This is contrary to what was expected on the basis of experimental results obtained with an indirect technique. Although the bilayer technique has not yet been applied extensively, it is clear that in the near future it will become a most important tool for the study of the electrical parameters of electrogenic pumps.

Parallel to the experimental studies quoted, much theoretical work is in progress to correlate the observations on voltage dependence of the pump to the various steps of the pump cycle. Work of LÄUGER and APELL (1986), REYNOLDS et al. (1985) and CHAPMAN (1982) and CHAPMAN et al. (1983) may be mentioned. These authors used the Albers-Post cycle of the sodium pump as a basis for their predictions of the effects of potential. This cycle involves the assumption that the transport protein may occur in two different conformations, E_1 and E_2, each of which may exist in a phosphorylated and a dephosphorylated state. E_1 binds Na^+ and E_2 K^+.

Within the Albers-Post cycle, there are 4 ways in which the potential could be visualised to affect the rate of pumping: 1. by acting as a driving force for the movements of Na^+ and K^+, 2. by modifying the association constants for the binding of substrates and activators, 3. by changing the rates of phosphorylation and dephosphorylation and 4. by shifting the steady state concentrations of the various intermediates of the reaction cycle. The occurence of a maximum indicates that a combination of at least 2 factors is involved. Since Na^+ and K^+ may both exist in occluded forms, it seems plausible to suspect that the rate limiting transport steps are conformational changes of E_1 and E_2 after cation occlusion. This would make it appear unlikely that the potential acts directly as a driving force for the diffusional flow of Na^+ and K^+. It seems more likely that the electrical field shifts the relative concentrations of the various intermediates of the E_1 and E_2 forms (e. g. E_1–P, E_1–P(Na_3), etc.). If the potential gradient would transform most of the intermediates either into the E_1 forms (which include the Na^+ occluding forms) or the E_2 forms (which include the K^+ occluding forms), transport should be slow. When both forms would exist at similar concentrations, the flux should reach a maximum, as observed by LAFAIRE and SCHWARZ (1985).

Effects of the potential as a driving force should become apparent within the time span of a single pump cycle, while the readjustment of the steady state concentrations of the various conformers (i. e. conformational changes of E_1 and E_2 forms) may take a much longer time. A variant of Bamberg's technique that uses capacitative coupling of the pump activity with the total membrane current as determined in the composite of ATPase disks and lipid bilayers (as described above) should become a powerful tool for the determination of such time dependences (FENDLER et al., 1985).

A definitive identification of the potential-sensitive steps requires not only studies with high time resolution. A thorough investigation of the effects of substrates and modifiers of the pump on the steady state current voltage relationship is also needed. DeWeer and his associates have done interesting work along these lines (DeWeer and Geduldig, 1973; DeWeer, 1982; DeWeer and Rakowski, 1984; Rakowski et al., 1985). They studied the effect of potential on the pump under conditions where the pump – instead of pumping Na^+ and K^+ at the expense of ATP hydrolysis – was made to synthesize ATP from ADP and P_i at the expense of downhill movements of Na^+ and K^+. Prof. DeWeer will report on his results.

Electrical studies of the pump, of course, do not only serve to elucidate the molecular mechanism of pumping in terms of a cycle of conformational changes, phophorylations and ion binding. There exists profound physiological interest in an understanding of the factors that control the pump cycle in small cells where electrophysiological events occur under conditions where amongst others, changes of the intracellular and extracellular concentrations take place (see, for example, Glitsch et al., 1982). Prof. Glitsch will report on electrophysiological studies that illustrate the complexities existing in a real system.

References

Bamberg, E., Apell, H. J., Dencher, N., Sperling, W., Stieve, H., Läuger, P.: Photocurrent generated by bacteriorhodopsin on planar lipid bilayer membranes. Biophys. Struct. Mech. **5:** 277–292 (1979).

Bamberg, E., Hegemann, P., Oesterhelt, D.: Reconstitution of the light driven electrogenic ion pump halorhodopsin in black lipid membranes. Biochim. Biophys. Acta **773:** 53–60 (1984).

Chapman, J. B.: Thermodynamics and kinetics of electrogenic pumps. J. Gen. Physiol. **80:** 1 a (1982).

Chapman, J. B., Johnson, E. A., Kootsey, J. M.: Electrical and Biochemical Properties of an Enzyme Model of the Sodium pump. J. Membrane Biol. **74:** 139–153 (1983).

De Weer, P., Geduldig, D.: Electrogenic sodium pump in squid giant axon. Science **179:** 1326–1328 (1973).

DeWeer, P.: Fundamental properties of electrogenic pumps. Theoretical and practical considerations. J. Gen. Physl. **80:** 1 a (1982).

De Weer, P., Rakowski, R. F.: Current generated by backward-running electrogenic Na pump in squid giant axons. Nature **309:** 450–452 (1984).

Fendler, K., Grell, E., Haubs, M., Bamberg, E.: Pump currents generated by the purified Na^+K^+-ATPase from kidney on black lipid membranes. EMBO J. **4:** 3079–3085 (1985)

Gadsby, D. C., Kimura, J., Noma, A.: Voltage dependence of Na/K pump current in isolated heart cells. Nature **315:** 63–65 (1985).

Glitsch, H. G., Pusch, N., Schumacher, Th., Verdonck, F.: An identification of the K-activated Na pump current in sheep Purkinje fibres. Pflügers Arch. **394:** 256–263 (1982).

Glynn, I., Ellory, C. (eds.): The sodium pump. The Company of Biologists Ltd. pp. 765 (1985).

Hoffman, J. F., Laris, P. C.: Membrane electrical parameters of normal human red blood cells. In: Blaustein, M. P., Lieberman, M. (eds.) Electrogenic transport: fundamental principles and physiological implications. Raven, New York: pp. 287–293 (1984).

Isenberg, G., Trautwein, W.: The effect of dihydroouabain and lithium ions on the outward current in cardiac Purkinje fibres: Evidence for electrogenicity of active transport. Pflügers Arch. **350:** 41–54 (1974).

Jørgensen, P. L.: Purification and characterization of $(Na^+ + K^+)$-ATPase Biochim. Biophys. Acta **356:** 36–52 (1974).

Lafaire, A. V., Schwarz, W.: Voltage-dependent, ouabain-sensitive current in the membrane of oocytes of Xenopus laevis. The sodium pump. The Company of Biologists Ltd. pp. 523–525 (1985).

Läuger, P., Apell, H.-J.: A microscopic model for the current voltage behaviour of the Na, K pump. Eur. Biophys. J. **13:** 309–321 (1986).
Lederer, W. J., Nelson, M. T.: Sodium pump stoichiometry determined by simultaneous measurements of sodium efflux and membrane current in Barnacle. J. Physiol. **348:** 665–677 (1984).
Mullins, L. J., Noda, K.: The influence of sodium-free solutions on the membrane potential of frog muscle fibres. J. Gen. Physiol. **47:** 117–132 (1963).
Rakowski, R. F., DeWeer, P., Gadsby, D. C.: Voltage dependence of backward-running Na^+ pump in squid giant axons. The sodium pump. The Company of Biologists Ltd. pp. 511–515 (1985).
Reynolds, J. A., Johnson, E. A., Tanford, C.: Incorporation of membrane potential into theoretical analysis of electrogenic ion pumps. Proc. Natl. Acad. Sci. USA. **82:** 6869–6873 (1985).
Richter, H. P., Jung, D., Passow, H.: Regulatory changes of membrane transport and ouabain binding during progesterone-induced maturation of *Xenopus* oocytes. J. Membrane Biol. **79,** 203–210 (1984).

Fortschritte der Zoologie, Band 33 · Lüttgau (Hrsg.): Membrane Control
Gustav Fischer Verlag · Stuttgart · New York · 1986

The electrogenic sodium pump: thermodynamics and kinetics

Paul De Weer

Washington University, St. Louis, Missouri, USA

An electrogenic pump is a device embedded in the cell membrane, capable of generating an electric current across that membrane, at the expense of chemical energy (for recent reviews see Slayman, 1982, and Blaustein and Lieberman, 1984). In the case of the sodium pump, the current represents the excess of the active sodium transport over the active potassium transport, and the energy source is the hydrolysis of ATP. That is, the sodium pump is a *chemical battery*. Like all such electrochemical devices, it must be characterized by an *electromotive force* (emf) and an *internal resistance*.

Equivalent circuit

Figure 1 gives a schematic representation of a cell membrane in which an electrogenic pump (i. e. a multitude of pump molecules working in parallel) is embedded. The pump's emf, acting against the membrane potential (V_m), drives current over the pump's internal resistance (R_p). The current pathway is closed over the remainder of the membrane, and

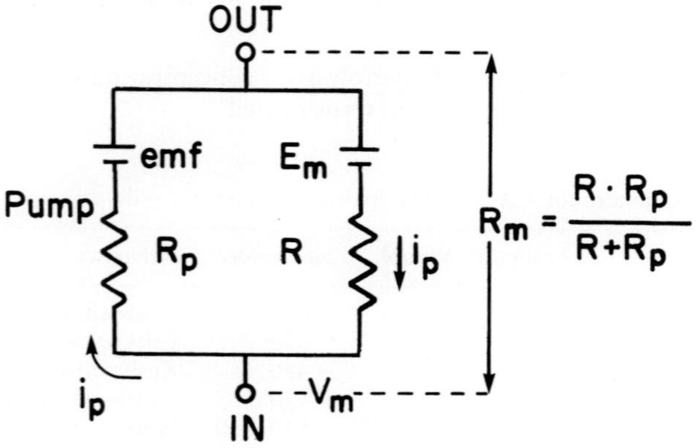

Fig. 1: Equivalent circuit for a membrane with an electrogenic sodium pump. Under physiological conditions, the pump takes positive charges from the inside compartment and delivers them to the outside, thereby hyperpolarizing the membrane. The circuit is closed by an inward current over the remainder of the membrane.

V_m is hyperpolarized beyond the simple diffusion potential (E_m) which would exist in the absence of an electrogenic pump. The pump current (i_p), then, can be said to be driven *either* by the potential drop (emf-V_m) over the pump's internal resistance *or* by the difference between the actual membrane potential and the non-pump diffusion potential, acting over the resistance (R) of the remainder of the membrane:

$$i_p = \frac{\text{emf}-V_m}{R_p} = \frac{V_m-E_m}{R} \tag{1}$$

[Properly speaking, the terms «specific resistance» or «resistivity» and «specific conductance» or «conductivity» (per unit membrane area) should be used, but since there is no danger of misunderstanding, the less ponderous «resistance» and «conductance» will generally be used here.]

Obviously, if the membrane potential V_m were artificially made equal to emf, no pump current would flow; and if V_m were moved beyond emf, the battery would undergo charging, i. e. the pump would run backward. The pump's emf, therefore, is operationally equal to the experimental reversal potential. The figure also shows that the experimentally measured membrane resistance includes the pump's resistance in addition to the conventional (electrodiffusive) components; the total membrane resistance is given by the familiar equation for parallel resistors. How much each contributes to the «black box» cannot be stated without further independent experiments. In most animal cells the electrogenic sodium pump conductance contributes at most a few per cent to the total membrane conductance (ABERCROMBIE and DE WEER, 1978; DE WEER, 1984). In certain plant cells, however, the electrogenic hydrogen pump may constitute the bulk of the total membrane conductance (SPANSWICK, 1972; KEIFER and SPANSWICK, 1978). We will review in turn the emf and the conductance of the sodium pump.

Electromotive force

For a pump driven by ATP, the emf is given by the excess of the free energy of ATP hydrolysis (ΔG_{ATP}) over the reversible concentration work involved in the movement of appropriate amounts of Na and K, divided by the net number of elementary charges translocated:

$$\text{emf} = \frac{\text{free energy (ATP hydrolysis)} - \text{concentration work}}{\text{net charge translocated}} \tag{2}$$

Table I: Published estimates for $-\Delta G$ of ATP hydrolysis in animal cells

Tissue	kcal/mol	kJ/mol	meV/molec	Reference
Squid axon	~14	~58	~610	Caldwell & Shirmer (1965)
Liver mitochondria	~15.4	64	670	Cockrell *et al.* (1966)
Frog muscle	~11	~46	~480	Kushmerick (1969)
Rat liver	~12	~50	~520	Akerboom *et al.* (1978)
Rat heart	12–14	50–58	520–610	Nishiki *et al.* (1978)
Rat muscle	~14	~58	~610	Veech *et al.* (1979)
Frog muscle	~13	~54	~560	Dawson *et al.* (1980)
Rat muscle	~15	~63	~650	Meyer *et al.* (1982)
Rat kidney	~13	~56	~570	Freeman *et al.* (1983)

In Table I are listed a number of published estimates of the free energy of ATP hydrolysis in a variety of animal cells. For convenience, the free energy is expressed in milli-electron Volt per molecule (meV/molec) in addition to the more commonly employed dimensions kcal/mol and kJ/mol. For most cells, the free energy of ATP hydrolysis appears to be in the vicinity of –600 meV per molecule. As for the reversible work of ion concentration, the following gradients are typically found in animal cells:

Ion	Concentration gradient	Work per ion
Na+	≥ 10-fold	≥ 60 meV
K+	~ 30-fold	~ 90 meV

That is to say, a 3 : 2 Na : K pump cycle will require about ≥ 360 meV of reversible ion concentration work. With these numbers the sodium pump's emf or reversal potential can be estimated from equation (2):

$$\text{emf} = \frac{-(\sim 600\ \text{meV}) + (\geq 360\ \text{meV})}{\text{one electronic charge}} = -200 \text{ to } -250\ \text{mV}$$

It should be understood that the theoretical reversal potential can only be computed if the exact stoichiometry of the pump is known or assumed. Conversely, however, an experimentally verified reversal potential would impose definite constraints on possible stoichiometries of the pump. Unfortunately, at least in the case of animal cells, a membrane potential of –200 mV or beyond will be difficult to maintain because of dielectric breakdown of the membrane. Only cells that have their free energy of ATP hydrolysis artificially lowered, or their ion gradients steepened, will likely yield measurable sodium pump reversal potentials.

Pump conductance: chord conductance

The pump's chord conductance (more correctly: specific conductance or conductivity) is simply defined as the proportionality factor relating current (more correctly: current density) to driving force. Typical sodium pump current densities are of the order of ~ 1 $\mu A/cm^2$. As already stated, driving forces (emf-V_m) are 100–200 mV, resulting in typical pump conductances of the order of 5–10 $\mu S/cm^2$. Now animal cell membrane conductances are typically two orders of magnitude larger, or about 1000 $\mu S/cm^2$. Pump conductances in animal cells, therefore, contribute only 1 % or so to the total membrane conductance. From equation (1) and the equivalent circuit diagram in Figure 1 it follows that

$$V_m - E_m = \sim \frac{\text{emf}-V_m}{100} = \text{a few millivolts.}$$

That is, the contribution of the electrogenic sodium pump to the resting potential is generally quite small unless an experimental effort is made to stimulate the pump and/or lower the membrane conductance. In fact, the magnitude of the contribution of an electrogenic sodium pump with a given Na : K pump ratio (r) is under an interesting theoretical constraint in *steady-state* cells. Mullins and Noda (1963) have derived an equation predicting the membrane potential for a steady-state cell potential for a steady-state cell possessing such a pump:

$$V_m = \frac{RT}{F} \ln \frac{r\, P_K\, [K]_o + P_{Na}\, [Na]_o}{r\, P_K\, [K]_i + P_{Na}\, [Na]_i} \qquad (3)$$

(for the simpler case where chloride ions are absent or at equilibrium), where P_K and P_{Na} are permeabilities, the subscripts o and i refer to external and internal media, respectively, and the other symbols have their usual meanings. The contribution of the electrogenic pump to the steady-state membrane potential is obtained by subtracting from equation (3) the familiar GOLDMAN (1943)–HODGKIN-KATZ (1949) equation. ASCHER (quoted by THOMAS, 1972) has pointed out that the *maximum* possible value of this difference equals (RT/F)ln(1/r), or a hyperpolarization of about a dozen millivolts.

It is worth recalling at this point that the chord conductance is a simple operational entity: the proportionality factor between pump current and driving force. A physically more meaningful parameter is the slope or local conductance of the pump, which describes the *dependence* of current on applied voltage, i. e. the current-voltage (I–V) diagram. Early theoretical analyses of the conductance behavior of the sodium pump (see for example, RAPOPORT 1970) used a nonequilibrium thermodynamic approach, which assumes that the velocity of a reaction is proportional to its driving force; in the present case: that the sodium pump current is everywhere proportional to (emf-V_m). For such a model, the slope conductance is constant and equal to the chord conductance. Enzyme-catalyzed reactions, however, generally do not proceed at rates proportional to their driving forces except very near equilibrium (or over narrow ranges), and the sodium pump is no exception. Even for the most elementary enzyme-kinetic schemes, the predicted current-voltage diagram is likely to be complex.

Pump current-voltage diagram: slope conductance

Thermodynamics demands that, if a pump contributes to a cell's resting potential by producing a net current, it in turn be affected by the membrane potential. But concerning the shape of this dependence thermodynamics has nothing to say, except that the direction of the pump current must reverse at V_m = emf. A given pump may, over a given range, be more steeply voltage-dependent (i. e. have a higher slope conductance) than the chord conductance would suggest; or it may be essentially voltage-independent (i. e. behave as a constant-current generator, or so-called «rheogenic» pump); or it may *decrease* its current output even though the driving force is *increased* (displaying, in effect, a domain of «negative conductance»).

To compute from first principles the I–V diagram of an electrogenic pump, one should have available a complete kinetic description of that pump, with suitable rate coefficients for each intermediate step in its reaction cycle as well as the exact voltage sensitivity, if any, of each of these rate coefficients. Needless to say, kinetic information regarding the many intermediate steps of the sodium pump is far too incomplete and/or unsettled to allow such *ab initio* computations with any degree of confidence. On the other hand, the mere ability of a model to predict the «correct» I–V diagram is by no means proof of the model's validity since, as will be shown below, even very elementary models produce I–V curves that are reasonable approximations of the (admittedly limited) existing data. The theoretical analysis of the voltage dependence of carrier-mediated transport kinetics in terms of symmetric Eyring barriers was pioneered by LÄUGER and STARK (1970). An early attempt to incorporate kinetic parameters into a model for the voltage dependence of the electrogenic sodium pump was made by CHAPMAN and JOHNSON (1976). Current-voltage characteristics for specific models of light- and redox-driven electrogenic proton pumps were computed by LÄUGER (1979). A systematic analysis of electrogenic pump models covering various classes of thermodynamic and kinetic constraints was initiated by HAN-

SEN et al. (1981); perhaps the most general treatment is that published by LÄUGER (1984). Other treatments examined specifically either proton pumps (GRADMANN et al., 1982; STEINMETZ and ANDERSEN, 1982) or the sodium/potassium pump (CHAPMAN et al., 1983; DE WEER, 1984; REYNOLDS et al., 1985; LÄUGER and APELL, 1986).

The most disappointing characteristic of these analyses is their relative lack of predictive value. So little is known about the various parameters entering into the overall equation and about the physics of the individual molecular events that great freedom exists in the assignment of numerical values to the multiple kinetic steps and their degree of voltage sensitivity. Current-voltage curves of essentially indistinguishable shapes and forms are generated, within a given class of models by multiple combinations of kinetic parameters, or between disparate models with only minor adjustments of physical characteristics such as the extent of charge displacements during molecular rearrangements or the exact location (e. g. inside or outside the membrane field) of the ion binding sites. The obvious consequence is that an experimental current-voltage curve of a given shape and form reveals relatively little about the detailed kinetics of the underlying mechanism. [At least if the only measured variable is the *net* current or reaction velocity. The constraints imposed by additional information regarding, for example, the rates of one-way forward or backward transport as well as Na/Na and K/K exchange would narrow the field of possible models considerably.] The most satisfying result (in this reviewer's opinion) to emerge so far is that any model, provided it includes two voltage-sensitive steps involving charge movements in opposite directions, can display «negative conductance», i. e. a voltage range where current *decreases* in spite of an increase in driving force (GRADMANN et al., 1982; CHAPMAN et al., 1983; LÄUGER, 1984; REYNOLDS et al., 1985; LÄUGER and APELL, 1986); it appears that the sodium pump displays such behavior. Since the experimental data available so far do not justify the use of elaborate and detailed models, the remainder of this discussion will be held in terms of the most elementary model that displays the requisite properties.

The formidable problem faced by «realistic» modelers is illustrated in Figure 2 which

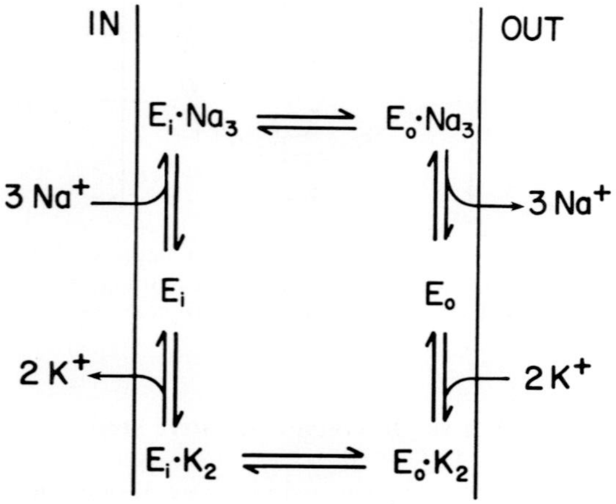

Fig. 2: Simplified scheme for an electrogenic Na : K pump. Three sodium ions are transported from the cell interior to the outside, and two potassium ions transported inward during each clockwise reaction cycle, whose operation is energized by the hydrolysis of ATP. Reactions involving phosphorylation and dephosphorylation of the carrier are not shown.

represents a 3 : 2 Na/K pump model reduced to its barest essentials; the reactions involving binding of ATP and release of ADP and phosphate, which are least likely to be voltage-sensitive, are not included. Yet the model has 12 rate constants (only eleven of them are independent because of the thermodynamic constraint that the reaction velocity must go through zero at reversal potential). Now the likely voltage-sensitive steps are the ion translocation steps (horizontal in Figure 2). For even greater simplicity, all the voltage-insensitive steps can now be lumped with one or both of the translocation steps, leaving an irreducible cycle consisting of only two steps governed by four rate constants, three of them independent (Figure 3). The cycle's velocity, or the current it produces, is given (in arbitrary units) by

$$I_p = \frac{k_1 k_2 - k_{-1} k_{-2}}{k_1 + k_{-1} + k_2 + k_{-2}} \tag{4}$$

Depending on what net charge one chooses to assign to the «empty» carrier, a wide range of possibilities still exists: the number of charges translocated could be, for example, +3 for the sodium step and +2 for the potassium step, or +2 and +1, or +1 and 0, or 0 and –1, etc... In the absence of information regarding the question, only the simplest models are justified. One simple model assigns a net charge of –2 to the carrier so that the sodium translocation step results in a +1 charge translocation and the potassium step is electroneutral and presumed voltage-insensitive, another assigns a single negative charge to the carrier, resulting in sodium and potassium steps translocating +2 and +1 charges, respectively.

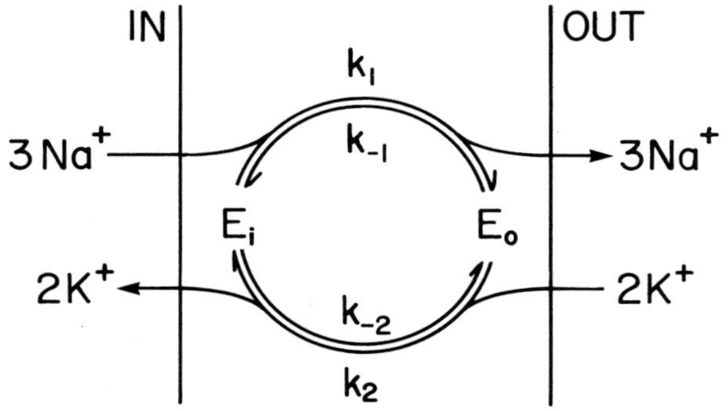

Fig. 3: Further simplification of the reaction cycle shown in Figure 2. Of the four rate coefficients shown, only three are independent, because of the thermodynamic constraint that the net cycling rate (driven by the free energy of hydrolysis of ATP) become zero at reversal potential.

Elementary model with a single voltage-sensitive step

Assume that, in the reaction cycle depicted in Figure 3, only the upper step is voltage sensitive because it is accompanied by a +1 charge translocation. [A simple form of voltage-sensitivity is that popularized by Läuger and Stark (1970) for carrier-mediated fluxes, namely, an Eyring barrier located at the mid-point of the electric field across the membrane.] Two extreme cases can now be envisaged. The first case is represented by curve A in Figure 4 (relevant rate coefficients are listed in Table II): in the absence of a membrane potential, the reaction cycle is limited by the *charge-translocating step* which must cross a high Eyring barrier. An imposed membrane potential will change the rate-limiting barrier height, thereby affecting the overall pumping rate. This extreme case, then, predicts strong voltage sensitivity in the neighborhood of zero membrane potential. The curve (A in Figure 4) also illustrates two experimental problems (De Weer, 1984) that may be encountered in studies of pumps that fall in this category: the relatively shallow approach of the current-voltage curve to the reversal potential will, on the one hand, make it difficult to detect reversal, and on the other, suggest completely fallacious «extrapolated» reversal potentials to the unwary (or impatient) observer.

The other extreme is represented by curve B of Figure 4: in the absence of a membrane potential, the reaction cycle is limited by the *voltage-insensitive step* (see Table II for a set of rate coefficients). Here the pump current will be very little affected by voltage until the membrane is sufficiently hyperpolarized to approach the pump's reversal potential where the current must, of course, vanish by thermodynamic necessity. Models of this second kind can properly be called «rheogenic» because, over limited voltage ranges at least, they behave as constant-current generators.

Published experimental data showing voltage dependence of the sodium pump are still scarce. Figure 5 is taken from Gadsby et al. (1985). These authors reduced the non-pump conductance (see Figure 1) of the membrane of isolated perfused guinea pig cardiac ventricular cells to the point where the pump conductance (defined as cardiotonic steroid-sensitive) constituted a sufficiently large fraction of total conductance that it could be

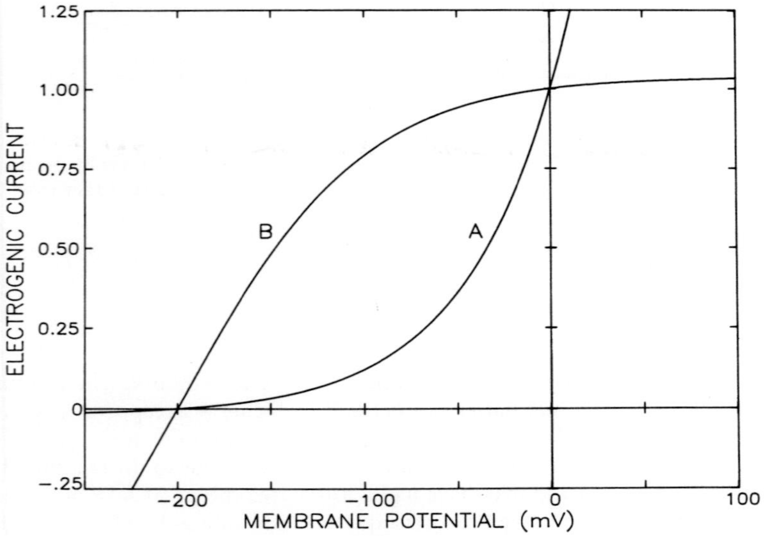

Fig. 4: Current-voltage relationships for two-step electrogenic pump models (Figure 3) where only the sodium-translocating step is voltage dependent. *A*: The voltage-*sensitive* step is rate-limiting. *B*: the voltage-*insensitive* step is rate-limiting («rheogenic» case). The rate coefficients used to generate the curves are tabulated in Table II; they were chosen for computational convenience, not physiological relevance, and are subject only to the constraints that the pump reverse at emf and be reasonably irreversible near resting potential. The hypothetical Eyring barrier for the voltage-sensitive step is assumed to be located at the midpoint of the transmembrane field.

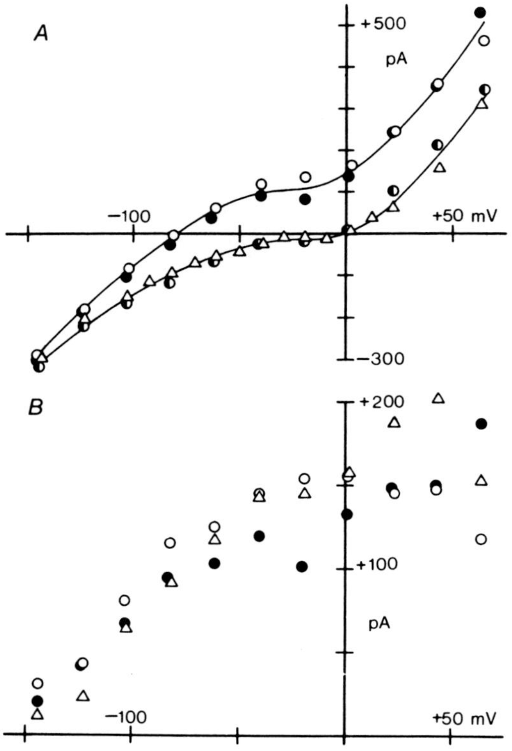

Fig. 5: *A*: Current-voltage relationships in isolated perfused cells from guinea pig cardiac ventricle in the presence (upper curve) and absence (lower curve) of Na/K pumping (defined by the presence and absence of ouabain or by high and low intracellular [Na]). *B*: Difference curve. Taken from Gadsby et al. (1985), with permission.

determined by difference over the range from –140 mV to +60 mV. The resulting curve appears to fit the (rheogenic) pattern of curve B in Figure 4 except for a slightly more positive apparent (extrapolated) «reversal potential». Whether the more positive extrapolated «reversal potential» is a fallacy, as discussed above, or due to the fact that these cells were artificially perfused and may have had a lower free energy of ATP hydrolysis available at the membrane, must await further experiments. Findings by Hasuo and Koketsu (1985) on bullfrog atrial muscle cells and by Glitsch and Krahn (1986) on sheep Purkinje fibers (both presumably powered by «typical» free energies of ATP hydrolysis) also suggest that the sodium pump in these cells displays a «rheogenic» domain at membrane potentials positive to resting and is slowed by hyperpolarization. Fewer data are available to date for the perfused giant axon of the squid, but it appears that the voltage sensitivity of the sodium pump between 0 and –60 mV is somewhat steeper than that in cardiac cells (De Weer et al., 1986).

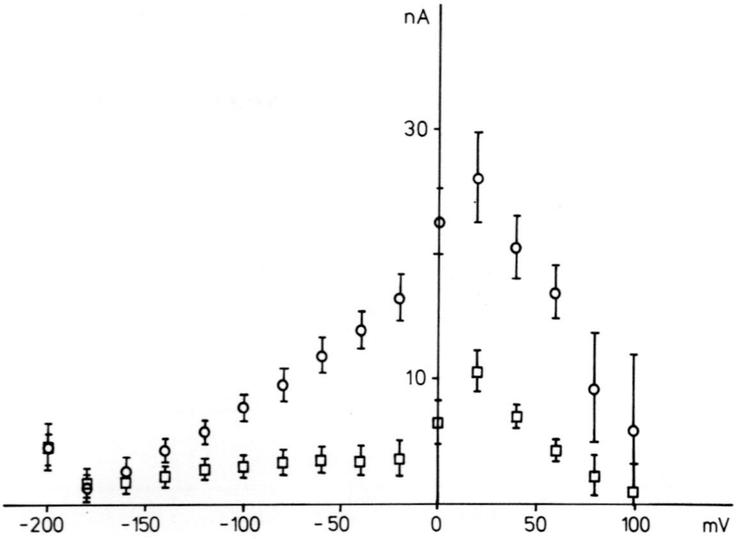

Fig. 6: Current-voltage relationship for the sodium pump of *Xenopus laevis* oocytes with elevated (circles) or normal (squares) intracellular sodium concentration. Note that at voltages positive to +20 mV an increase in driving force results in a *decrease* in current. Taken from LAFAIRE and SCHWARZ (1986), with permission.

Elementary model with two voltage-sensitive steps

Other experimental findings cannot be fit by the simple schemes of Figure 4. For example, LAFAIRE and SCHWARZ (1986), working with *Xenopus* oocytes, found a distinct maximum in the pump current-voltage curve (Figure 6); at potentials positive to +20 mV there lies a domain of *negative conductance*, i. e., where current falls in spite of an increase in driving force. It is possible to interpret (DE WEER, 1984) negative conductance by

Table II: Representative numerical values, in arbitrary units, for the rate coefficients of the 3 : 2 electrogenic Na/K pump model depicted in Figure 3. Membrane potential V'_m is expressed in units of RT/F. These sets of rate coefficients generate, *via* equation (4), the curves of Figures 4 and 7. The values are constrained by the thermodynamic requirement that the pump velocity become zero at reversal potential ($V'_m = -8$ or $V_m \simeq -200$ mV) and by the experimental requirement that the backward/forward ratio at zero membrane potential be ≤ 0.02.

Charge: Na^+ step K^+ step Barrier	+1 0 symmetrical		+2 +1 asymmetrical (9 : 1)
Figure curve	4A	4B	7
Coeff.: k_1	1.04 exp(0.5 V'_m)	57 exp(0.5 V'_m)	1.1 exp(0.2 V'_m)
k_{-1}	1.04 exp(−0.5 V'_m)	0.02 exp(−0.5 V'_m)	0.28 exp(−1.8 V'_m)
k_2	57	1.04	15 exp(−0.9 V'_m)
k_{-2}	0.02	1.04	0.02 exp(0.1 V'_m)

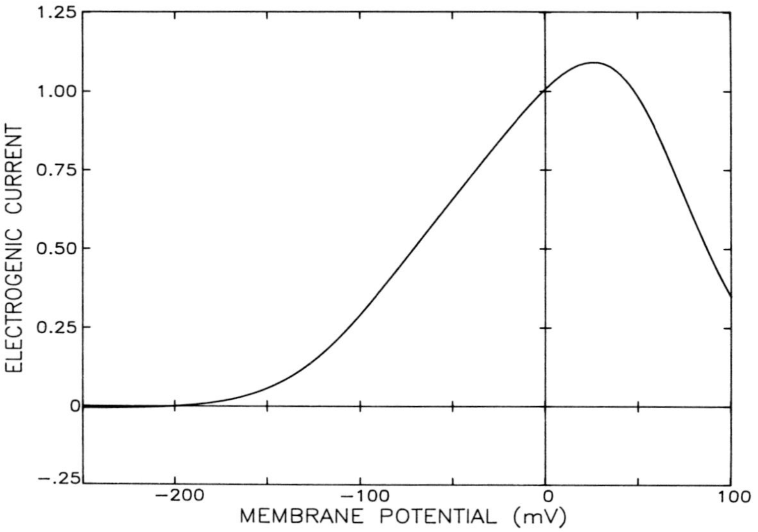

Fig. 7: Current-voltage relationship for two-step electrogenic pump model (Figure 3) where both the sodium- and the potassium-translocating steps (carrying +2 and +1 net charges, respectively) are voltage dependent. The rate coefficients used to generate the curve are listed in Table II (third column). The hypothetical Eyring barriers for both voltage-sensitive steps are assumed to be positioned at 1/10th of the membrane («electrical») thickness from the inner edge.

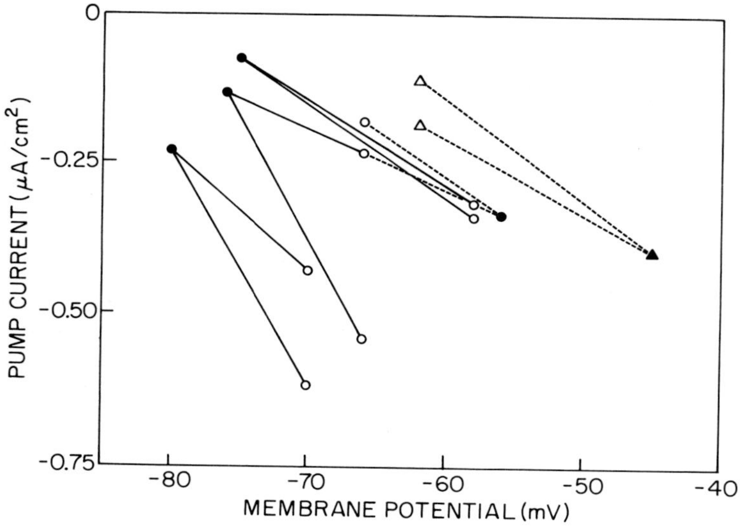

Fig. 8: Effect of membrane potential on reverse sodium pump current in squid giant axon perfused with ADP, P_i and K^+ and exposed to K-free medium. The lines connect sets of bracketing (open symbols) and bracketed (filled symbols) measurements. Solid lines, bracketed test at hyperpolarized potentials; dashed lines, bracketed test at depolarized potential. In every instance, hyperpolarization reduced, and depolarization enhanced, inward pump current. Taken, with permission, from De Weer and Rakowski (1984).

means of a simple model such as the one used to generate the curves of Figure 4 *in series with* a voltage-sensitive «gate» (a «gate» need not be literal, that is, limit the ions' access to the pump; the field could, for example, change the enzyme's conformation such that its turnover rate is reduced). It is more likely, however, that this intriguing behavior betrays the occurrence of a second voltage-sensitive step in the pump cycle in which a charge moves *against* (rather than with) the field (GRADMANN et al., 1982). The third set of rate coefficients listed in Table II was chosen for its ability to generate a curve (Figure 7) that mimics the data published by LAFAIRE and SCHWARZ (1986). The characteristic asymmetry of the I–V curve could only be obtained by assuming asymmetric placement of the Eyring barrier in the transmembrane electric field (in this case, rather near the intracellular edge of the membrane).

Another instance in which negative conductance has been detected in the operation of the sodium pump is when the pump is forced to run backwards in squid giant axons by perfusing them with ADP + phosphate instead of ATP and reversing the ion gradients (DE WEER and RAKOWSKI, 1984; RAKOWSKI et al., 1985). Figure 8 shows that, as the membrane is hyperpolarized, the inward pump current becomes *smaller* even though the driving force is made larger. In addition to providing an example of negative pump conductance, this figure is interesting because it probably represents the first instance in which pump current measurements have been made «on the other side» of reversal potential.

Conclusion

The sodium pump of animal cells has an expected reversal potential of –200 mV or so. Since this is almost certainly beyond dielectric breakdown for animal cell membranes, «native» reversal potentials are unlikely to be measured in the foreseeable future. The shape of the voltage dependence appears to be different for different cells, and for some cells it suggests that there may be at least two voltage-sensitive steps in the pump cycle. The pump, when running backwards, is still electrogenic, and here too it seems safe to conclude that there must be at least two voltage-sensitive steps.

It is clear that even the most elementary of models can generate I–V curves that run the complete gamut from those that remain essentially unaffected by membrane potential (true «rheogenic» pumps) to steeply voltage-sensitive ones that plunge down to very low rates and hover near the baseline (leading to fallacious extrapolated «reversal potentials»), to those that display negative-conductance domains in seeming violation of thermodynamic expectations.

Finally, it is worth recalling that the sodium pump allows many more kinetically relevant measurements than mere current. Analysis of the voltage dependence of, for example, individual one-way Na^+ and K^+ fluxes, K_m's, etc. will yield mechanistic information far beyond the insight gained from just current measurements. Further progress will require experiments, not computers.

Acknowledgements

The author's research is supported by USNIH grant NS11223.

References

Abercrombie, R. F., De Weer, P.: Electric current generated by squid giant axon sodium pump: External K and internal ADP effects. Amer. J. Physiol. **235:** C 63–C 68 (1978).

Akerboom, T. P. M., Bookelman, H., Zuurendonk, P. F., van der Meer, R., Tager, J. M.: Intramitochondrial and extramitochondrial concentrations of adenine nucleotides and inorganic phosphate in isolated hepatocytes from fasted rats. Eur. J. Biochem. **84:** 413–420 (1978).

Blaustein, M. P., Lieberman, M.: Electrogenic Transport: Fundamental Principles and Physiological Implications. Raven Press, New York (1984).

Caldwell, P. C., Shirmer, H.: The free energy available to the sodium pump of squid giant axons and changes in the sodium efflux on removal of the extracellular potassium. J. Physiol. (Lond.) **181:** 25 P (1965).

Chapman, J. B., Johnson, E. A.: Current-voltage relationships for theoretical electrogenic sodium pump models. Proc. Austr. Physiol. Pharmacol. Soc. **7:** 69 P (1976).

Chapman, J. B., Johnson, E. A., Kootsey, J. M.: Electrical and biochemical properties of an enzyme model of the sodium pump. J. Membr. Biol. **74:** 139–153 (1983).

Cockrell, R. S., Harris, E. J., Pressman, B. C.: Energetics of potassium transport in mitochondria induced by valinomycin. Biochemistry **5:** 2326–2335 (1966).

Dawson, J. J., Gadian, D. G., Wilkie, D. R.: Mechanical relaxation rate and metabolism studied in fatiguing muscle by phosphorus nuclear magnetic resonance. J. Physiol. (Lond.) **299:** 465–484 (1980).

De Weer, P.: Electrogenic pumps: theoretical and practical considerations. In: Electrogenic Transport: Fundamental Principles and Physiological Implications (Blaustein, M. P. and Lieberman, M. eds.), pp. 1–15. Raven Press, New York (1984).

De Weer, P., Gadsby, D. C., Rakowski, R. F.: Voltage dependence of Na/K pump-mediated ^{22}Na efflux and current in squid giant axon. J. Physiol. (Lond.) **371:** 144 P. (1986).

De Weer, P., Rakowski, R. F.: Current generated by backward-running electrogenic Na pump in squid giant axons. Nature **309:** 450–452 (1984).

Freeman, D., Bartlett, S., Radda, G., Ross, B.: Energetics of sodium transport in the kidney. Saturation transfer ^{31}P–NMR. Biochim. Biophys. Acta **762:** 325–336 (1983).

Gadsby, D. C., Kimura, J., Noma, A.: Voltage dependence of Na/K pump current in isolated heart cells. Nature **315:** 63–65 (1985).

Glitsch, H. G., Krahn, Th.: The cardiac electrogenic Na pump. Fortschritte der Zoologie **33:** 401–417 (1986).

Goldman, D. E.: Potential, impedance and rectification in membranes. J. Gen. Physiol. **27:** 37–60 (1943).

Gradmann, D., Hansen, U.-P., Slayman, C. L.: Reaction-kinetic analysis of current-voltage relationships for electrogenic pumps in *Neurospora* and *Acetabularia*. In: Electrogenic Ion Pumps. (Current Topics in Membranes and Transport, Vol. 16, Slayman, C. L. ed.), pp. 257–276. Academic Press, New York (1982).

Hansen, U.-P., Gradmann, D., Sanders, D., Slayman, C. L.: Interpretation of current-voltage relationships for «active» ion transport systems: I. Steady-state reaction-kinetic analysis of Class-I mechanisms. J. Membr. Biol. **63:** 165–190 (1981).

Hasuo, H., Koketsu, K.: Potential dependency of the electrogenic Na^+-pump current in bullfrog atrial muscles. Jap. J. Physiol. **35:** 89–100 (1985).

Hodgkin, A. L., Katz, B.: The effect of sodium on the electrical activity of the giant axon of the squid. J. Physiol. (Lond.) **108:** 37–77 (1949).

Keifer, D. W., Spanswick, R. M.: Activity of the electrogenic pump in *Chara corallina* as inferred from measurements of the membrane potential, conductance, and potassium permeability. Plant Physiol. **62:** 653–661 (1978).

Kushmerick, M. J.: Free energy and enthalpy of ATP hydrolysis in the sarcoplasm. Proc. Roy. Soc. Lond. [Biol.] **174:** 348–353 (1969).

Lafaire, A. V., Schwarz, W.: The voltage dependence of the rheogenic Na^+/K^+ ATPase in the membrane of oocytes of *Xenopus laevis*. J. Membr. Biol. **91:** 43–51 (1986).

Läuger, P.: A channel mechanism for electrogenic ion pumps. Biochim. Biophys. Acta **552:** 143–161 (1979).

Läuger, P.: Thermodynamic and kinetic properties of electrogenic ion pumps. Biochim. Biophys. Acta **779:** 307–341 (1984).

Läuger, P., Apell, H.-J.: A microscopic model for the current-voltage behaviour of the Na, K pump. Europ. Biophys. J. **13:** 309–321 (1986).

Läuger, P., Stark, G.: Kinetics of carrier-mediated ion transport across lipid bilayer membranes. Biochim. Biophys. Acta **211:** 458–466 (1970).

Meyer, R. A., Kushmerick, M. J., Brown, T. R.: Application of ^{31}P–NMR spectroscopy to the study of striated muscle metabolism. Amer. J. Physiol. **242:** C1–C11 (1982).

Mullins, L. J., Noda, K.: The influence of sodium-free solutions on the membrane potential of frog muscle fibers. J. Gen. Physiol. **47:** 117–132 (1963).

Nishiki, K., Erecinska, M., Wilson, D. F.: Energy relationships between cytosolic metabolism and mitochondrial respiration in rat heart. Amer. J. Physiol. **234:** C73–C81 (1978).

Rakowski, R. F., De Weer, P., Gadsby, D. C.: Voltage dependence of backward-running Na^+ pump in squid giant axons. In: The Sodium Pump (I. M. Glynn and C. Ellory, editors), pp. 511–515. The Company of Biologists Ltd., Cambridge (1985).

Rapoport, S. I.: The sodium-potassium exchange pump: relation of metabolism to electrical properties of the cell. I. Theory. Biophys. J. **10:** 246–259 (1970).

Reynolds, J. A., Johnson, E. A., Tanford, C.: Incorporation of membrane potential into theoretical analysis of electrogenic pumps. Proc. Natl. Acad. Sci. USA **82:** 6869–6873 (1985).

Slayman, C. L.: Electrogenic Ion Pumps. (Current Topics in Membranes and Transport, vol. 16) Academic Press, New York (1982).

Spanswick, R. M.: Evidence for an electrogenic ion pump in *Nitella translucens*. I. The effects of pH, K^+, Na^+, light and temperature on the membrane potential and resistance. Biochim. Biophys. Acta **288:** 73–89 (1972).

Steinmetz, P. R., Andersen, O. S.: Electrogenic proton transport in epithelial membranes. J. Membr. Biol. **65:** 155–174 (1982).

Thomas, R. C.: Electrogenic sodium pump in nerve and muscle cells. Physiol. Rev. **52,** 563–594 (1972).

Veech, R. L., Lawson, J. W. R., Cornell, N. W., Krebs, H. A.: Cytosolic phosphorylation potential. J. Biol. Chem. **254:** 6538–6547 (1979).

Fortschritte der Zoologie, Band 33 · Lüttgau (Hrsg.): Membrane Control
Gustav Fischer Verlag · Stuttgart · New York · 1986

The cardiac electrogenic Na pump

H. G. GLITSCH* and TH. KRAHN

Institut für Zellphysiologie der Ruhr-Universität Bochum, Postfach 102 148, D-4630 Bochum, FRG

Cardiac cells display rhythmical electrical discharges over a long period of time. The electrical activity tends to dissipate the Na^+ and K^+ gradients across the sarcolemma. Thus a transport mechanism is required which maintains the ionic gradients at rest and restores them following activity. This transport system is a ATP fueled Na–K pump. The pump extrudes Na ions from the cells and takes up K ions into the cells against the respective electrochemical gradient for the two ion species. The active Na and K transport across the cardiac cell membrane is of fundamental significance not only for the electrical excitability but also for many other aspects of cardiac cell activity. During the past, much work has been done in order to elucidate the characteristics of the Na–K pump in heart cells (review: GLITSCH, 1982 a). One interesting attribute of the pump is the ability to generate a current. This property is called the electrogenicity of the Na–K pump. Below we discuss the evidence for the electrogenicity of the cardiac active Na–K transport and some characteristics of the Na pump current in heart cells. For further information the reader is referred to the reviews by GLITSCH (1982 b) and GADSBY (1984).

Evidence for the electrogenicity of the cardiac Na pump

It is crucial for a demonstration of cardiac electrogenic Na pumping to show that the pump induced changes in membrane current or potential are not caused by an electroneutral Na pump via alterations of the Na^+ or K^+ gradient across the cell membrane and/or of the membrane conductance. Though earlier experiments (e. g. PAGE and STORM, 1965; VASSALLE, 1970; GLITSCH, 1972) strongly suggested the existence of an electrogenic Na pump, they could not completely exclude a contribution of such alterations to the observed changes in membrane potential. The control of the membrane potential by the introduction of a voltage clamp technique greatly facilitated the analysis of the cardiac active Na transport. ISENBERG and TRAUTWEIN (1974) were the first to describe the Na pump current of a sheep Purkinje fibre under voltage clamp conditions. Fig. 1 is from their paper. Superfusion of a voltage clamped sheep Purkinje fibre with a Tyrode solution containing 10^{-5} M dihydroouabain (DHO), a specific Na pump inhibitor, shifts the I–V relation of the fibre within 2 min from the control position (open circles) downwards and to the right (Fig. 1 A). The filled circles represent the I–V relation under DHO. Obviously,

* Supported by the Deutsche Forschungsgemeinschaft (SFB 114 ‹Bionach›).

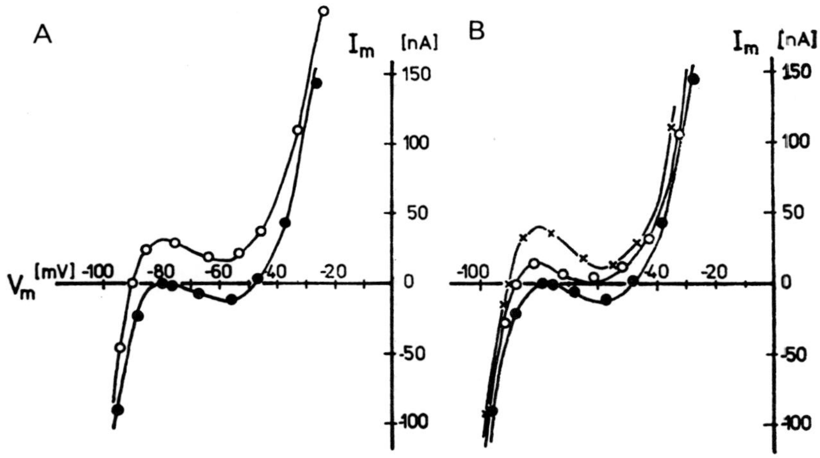

Fig. 1: Effect of DHO on the I–V relation of a sheep Purkinje fibre. The membrane current at the end of a 2.5 s clamp step is plotted versus the clamped membrane potential. A Control I–V curve in Tyrode solution (○) and I–V relation after 2 min in Tyrode solution containing 10^{-5} M DHO (●). B Reversibility of the DHO effect. I–V curves in DHO containing medium (●, from A) and after reapplication of drug free Tyrode solution for 3 min (○) and 10 min (×), respectively. (From ISENBERG and TRAUTWEIN, 1974, with permission.)

inhibition of the Na–K pump blocks an outward current. The amplitude of this current seems to be voltage independent between c. –30 and –90 mV. Since the I–V curve of the DHO treated fibre parallels the control I–V relation in the mentioned potential range, changes in membrane conductance can be excluded. As can be seen from Fig. 1 B, the effect of DHO is easily reversible. After only 3 min in Tyrode solution the I–V curve of the DHO-treated preparation (filled circles) is shifted upwards and to the left (open circles), and after 10 min the I–V relation has reached again the control position. According to the authors, the DHO inhibited outward current is a Na outward current generated by an electrogenic Na pump. The apparent diminution of the pump current at membrane potentials positive to –30 mV is probably due to K accumulation which can occur following blockade of the Na pump. Since under these conditions active K uptake into the cells is blocked, a net K efflux from the cells is observed which can increase the extracellular K concentration ($[K]_o$) at the outside of the cell membrane and might thereby change the membrane conductance. Several experimental procedures were developed to minimize K accumulation and/or its effect on the membrane conductance. These procedures include the use of canine Purkinje fibres which are known to have wide extracellular clefts (GADSBY and CRANEFIELD, 1979 b); application of an unphysiological external cation species to activate the Na–K pump (EISNER and LEDERER, 1980 a) or of Ba ions to suppress the K conductance of the sarcolemma (GLITSCH et al., 1982).

In order to study the Na pump current in detail experiments were carried out under conditions which enhance Na pumping beyond the steady state pump activity of a resting fibre. Continuous measurements of the intracellular Na activity (a^i_{Na}) by means of Na sensitive microelectrodes (THOMAS, 1970) revealed that in fact the inhibition of an outward current by cardiac steroids (such as DHO) reflects a simultaneous inhibition of the cardiac Na–K pump (EISNER et al., 1981 a; GLITSCH et al., 1982). This result is illustrated

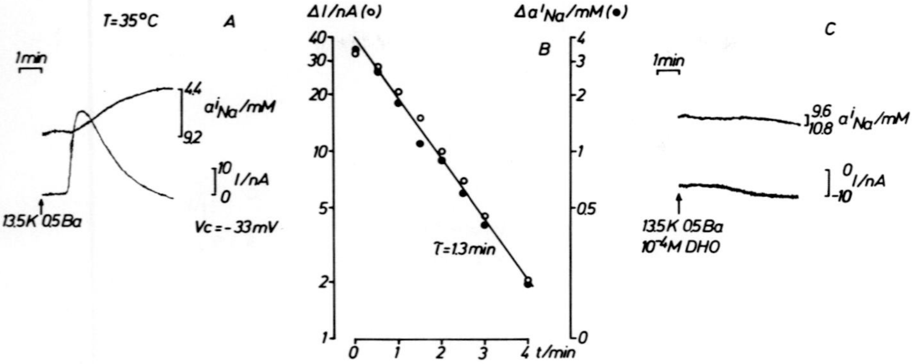

Fig. 2: A Simultaneous measurement of a^i_{Na} (upper curve) and membrane current during enhanced active Na transport in a sheep Purkinje fibre. The Na pump is reactivated by superfusion of the preparation with a K rich, Ba containing solution (arrow) after 15 min in a K free medium. Clamped membrane potential (V_c): –33 mV (also in B and C). B Semilogarithmic plot of the decline of a^i_{Na} (●, right ordinate) and membrane current (○, left ordinate) towards their steady-state values upon reactivation of the Na pump. The transient outward current ΔI represents the transiently increased Na pump current. t = 0 is the time when ΔI reaches its maximum in A. C Blockade of the transient outward current and of the decline in a^i_{Na} by DHO. Same impalement as in A. Upper curve: a^i_{Na}. Lower curve: membrane current. Perfusion with the K rich solution starts at the arrow. (From Glitsch and Pusch, 1984, with permission.)

in Fig. 2. Following 15 min in a K free solution the Na pump of a sheep Purkinje fibre is reactivated in a medium containing 13.5 mM K and 0.5 mM Ba. The cell membrane of the fibre is clamped at –33 mV. Membrane current (lower trace in Fig. 2 A) and a^i_{Na} (upper trace) are measured simultaneously. Application of the K rich solution decreases a^i_{Na} from 9.2 to 4.4 mM and induces an accompanying transient outward current which reaches a peak value of about 30 nA. When during the same impalement in a second run, the K rich bathing fluid contains in addition 10^{-4} M DHO, neither a decrease of a^i_{Na} nor a transient outward current is observed (Fig. 2 C). On the contrary, an increase of a^i_{Na} from 9.6 to 10.8 mM and a small inward shift of the membrane current are recorded. Fig. 2 B reveals that both the transient outward current and the augmented a^i_{Na} in Fig. 2 A decline exponentially with an identical time constant (τ = 1.3 min) towards their respective steady-state levels (Eisner et al., 1981 a; Glitsch et al., 1982). Note that the time constant (τ) of decline in a^i_{Na} or pump current is independent of a^i_{Na} within the range tested. τ is inversely related to the activity of the Na–K pump and will be the smaller the stronger the pump is activated.

Activation of the electrogenic Na pump by external cations

In recent years the activation of the electrogenic Na pump by various extracellular cations was studied in some detail. The effect of various extracellular K concentrations on the decline of a^i_{Na} and the transient outward current of a sheep Purkinje fibre under voltage clamp conditions (–30 mV) is shown in Fig. 3. The experimental procedure is similar to that depicted in Fig. 2 A. Following a period in a K free solution the Na pump of the fibre

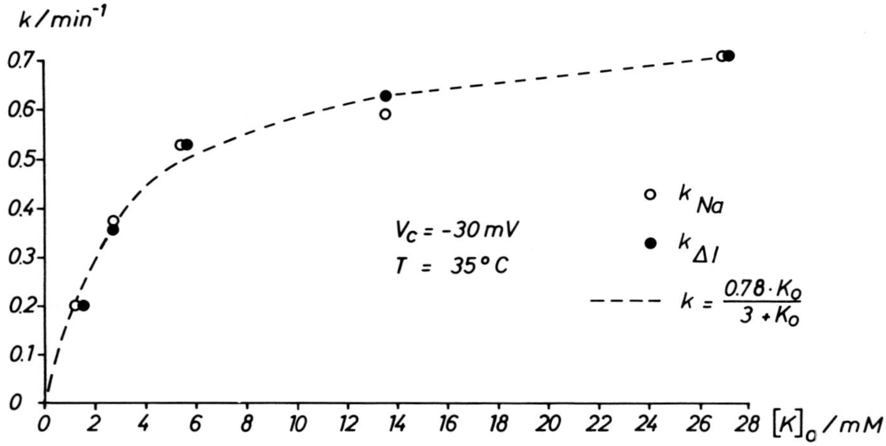

Fig. 3: Rate constant (k) of decline in a^i_{Na} (○) and transient outward current (●) in a sheep Purkinje fibre as a function of the extracellular K concentration. All data from a single impalement. Clamped membrane potential (V_c): –30 mV. The dashed curve is a fit to the data assuming simple Michaelis-Menten kinetics.

is activated in a Ba containing solution with various K concentrations at 35 °C. The rate constant ($k = 1/\tau$) of the decline in a^i_{Na} (open circles) or in transient outward current (filled circles) is plotted versus the K concentration of the bathing fluid. Half maximal activation of the active Na transport occurs at 3 mM K and the maximal rate constant amounts to 0.78 min^{-1}. Corresponding data were obtained by other authors. According to GADSBY (1980) and FALK and COHEN (1984) the electrogenic Na pump in canine Purkinje fibres is half maximally activated at ~ 1 mM K and a similar value is found in guinea pig atria (GLITSCH et al., 1978). EISNER and LEDERER (1980 a, b) reported a half maximal activation of the Na pump current by 6.3 mM Rb or 14.2 mM Cs and noted that 2 mM K, 2 mM Rb, 6 mM Cs, 6 mM NH_4 and 22 mM Li are equipotent with respect to the activation of cardiac electrogenic Na pumping. Tl ions are more potent than K or Rb. The same sequence of potency to activate the pump current and a half maximal activation of the electrogenic Na pump by 5 mM K were observed in rabbit atrio-ventricular node cells by KURACHI et al. (1981). Especially in sheep Purkinje fibres the extracellular K concentration for half maximal activation of the pump current tends to be smaller when studied under steady-state conditions (EISNER et al., 1981 b) suggesting that strong activation of the Na pump may cause K depletion in this preparation (for discussion see GADSBY, 1984). Generally, both the order of potency to activate the active Na transport and the concentration of the various cations for half maximal pump activation resemble closely the values known for the Na, K activated, Mg dependent transport ATPase (for further details see GLITSCH, 1982 a).

Activation of the electrogenic Na pump by intracellular Na

To our knowledge only GADSBY and NAKAO (1986) have studied so far the dependence of the cardiac Na pump current on the intracellular Na concentration ($[Na]_i$) over a wide concentration range. The authors conclude from whole cell recordings on isolated and internally perfused guinea pig ventricular cells that the pump current amplitude is a saturable function of the Na concentration of the pipette solution (and thus of $[Na]_i$). Half maximal pump current activation occurs near 10 mM Na at 0 mV membrane potential. This observation is in line with recent studies on the magnitude of active Na efflux as a function of $[Na]_i$ in canine sarcolemmal vesicles (PHILIPSON and NISHIMOTO, 1983) and sheep Purkinje fibres (GLITSCH et al., 1984). According to these studies cardiac active Na efflux tends to saturate at high $[Na]_i$ and is half maximal at 9 mM Na_i in the vesicular preparation and at 12 mM in Purkinje fibres. The finding of GADSBY and NAKAO (1986) is not in conflict with earlier reports on a linear relation between pump current amplitude and $[Na]_i$ since only a narrow range of $[Na]_i$ was considered previously (e. g. EISNER et al., 1981 a, b; GLITSCH et al., 1982).

Temperature dependence of the electrogenic Na pump

Active Na transport and the generation of the Na pump current require energy which is delivered by ATP splitting. Because of the linkage to a metabolic reaction, the Na pump current is expected to exhibit a marked temperature dependence. The effect of two different temperatures on the intracellular Na activity and the transient outward current of a sheep Purkinje fibre during enhanced Na pumping is shown in Fig. 4. Following 15 min in a K free medium in order to increase $[Na]_i$, the Na pump of the fibre is reactivated in a solution containing 13.5 mM K and 0.5 mM Ba at 21 °C (upper part of the Fig.) and at

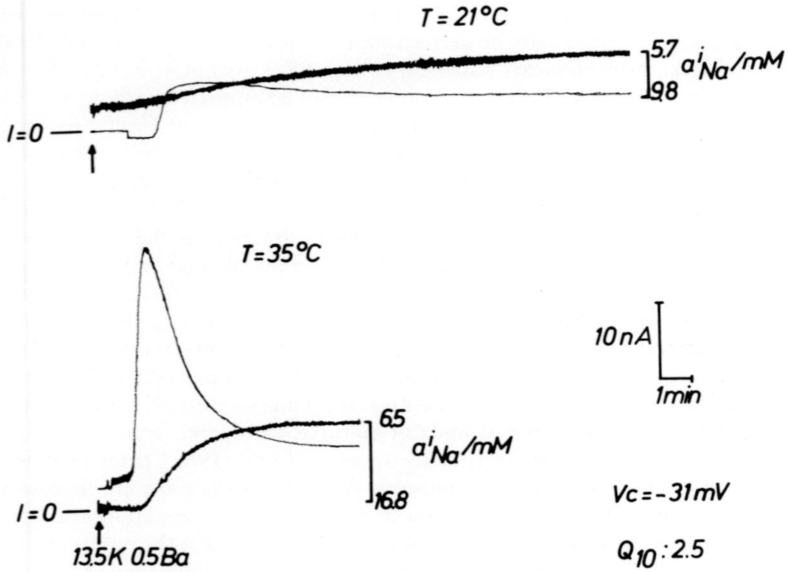

Fig. 4: Effect of temperature on membrane current (thin line) and a^i_{Na} decline during enhanced Na pumping in a sheep Purkinje fibre. All records from a single impalement. The Na pump of the preparation is reactivated by a K rich solution (arrows) after 15 min in a K free medium. Clamped membrane potential (V_c): –31 mV in both panels.

35 °C (lower part). The membrane potential of the preparation is held at –31 mV. The heavy lines indicate a^i_{Na}, the thin lines the membrane current. Obviously, the decline of a^i_{Na} and transient outward current is slowed down at the lower temperature. A Q_{10} of 2.5 can be calculated from the rate constants of a^i_{Na} or pump current decline at both temperatures. Similarly Eisner and Lederer (1980 a) reported on Q_{10} values between 1.6 and 2.3 for the Na pump current transient over a range of temperature, 26–46 °C. A detailed study by Glitsch and Pusch (1984) revealed that the Q_{10} values vary within this range of temperature and amount to only 1.2 between 42 °C and 35 °C. Also the activation energy of the active electrogenic Na transport is not constant between 22 and 42 °C and is calculated to be 3.4 kcal/mol between 42 °C and 35 °C and 15.9 kcal/mol between 35 °C and 22 °C. The variation of the time constant of pump current decline with temperature reflects corresponding changes of the maximal rate constants of active Na transport, whereas the affinity of the Na pump to external K is nearly unchanged.

Electrogenic fraction and coupling ratio

From experiments like that shown in Fig. 2 A it is possible to estimate the fraction of the actively transported Na which constitutes the Na pump outward current (electrogenic fraction). If the electrogenic fraction of the active Na efflux is known, the coupling ratio between active Na efflux and active K influx can be easily derived. In order to estimate the electrogenic fraction, the time integral of the transient outward current (which is thought to represent the transiently increased pump current) is compared with the total amount of Na transported during enhanced Na pumping. The total amount of extruded Na can be calculated from the observed change in a^i_{Na} if the clamped volume of the fibre is known and if the same activity coefficient for Na ions holds in the intra- and extracellular solution. The clamped volume can be derived either from optical (Eisner et al., 1981 a) or electrophysiological measurements (Glitsch et al., 1982). As pointed out by Eisner and his colleagues (1983), the electrogenic fraction can also be estimated without any information about the clamped fibre volume or the Na activity coefficient by comparing a drug induced with a Na pump-evoked shift in a^i_{Na} and membrane current. This estimation requires an assumption about the mechanism of the drug action. So far only Eisner et al. (1981 a, 1983) and Glitsch and coworkers (Glitsch et al., 1982; Glitsch and Pusch, 1984) have published estimations of the electrogenic fraction of the cardiac active Na efflux based on simultaneous measurements of a^i_{Na} and pump current in voltage clamped preparations. From various series of experiments the electrogenic fraction was calculated to be between 26 to 40 % (Eisner et al., 1981 a, 1983) or between 22 and 42 % (Glitsch et al., 1982; Glitsch and Pusch, 1984). A coupling ratio between active Na efflux and active K influx of about 1.3 to 1.7 corresponds to these numbers for the electrogenic fraction. Lieberman et al. (1984) estimated the coupling ratio to be about 1.5 from Na and K flux measurements on polystrands of cultured embryonic chick heart cells. Almost the same number was derived by Daut and Rüdel (1982) from voltage clamp experiments on guinea pig ventricular muscles. All these estimations are necessarily approximate since they are based on – at least in part – debatable assumptions. Therefore, they cannot verify a distinct coupling ratio. What can be said is that the published numbers are in line with a coupling ratio between cardiac active Na efflux and active K influx which is similar to the ratio of 1.5 found in erythrocytes (Post and Jolly, 1957; Garrahan and Glynn, 1967). The coupling ratio of the cardiac Na–K pump is not affected by variations of $[Na]_i$ (Gadsby and Cranefield, 1979 a; Eisner and Lederer, 1980 a; Glitsch and Pusch, 1980), changes of $[K]_o$ (Gadsby, 1980) or by alterations of the external Rb or Cs concentration (EISNER and LEDERER, 1980 a). Similarly, changes in the temperature of the bathing solution between 17 and 42 °C have little effect on the coupling ratio (GLITSCH and PUSCH, 1984). These data suggest a constant electrogenic fraction of the active Na efflux from heart cells under various experimental conditions.

The contribution of the electrogenic Na pump to the cardiac resting potential

The Na pump current contributes to the membrane potential of cells by a current induced voltage drop across the membrane resistance (e. g. ABERCROMBIE and DEWEER, 1978; SPERELAKIS, 1979). Several possibilities to estimate the effect of the electrogenic active Na transport on the resting potential of a sheep Purkinje fibre are shown in Figs. 5 to 7. All records are from the same fibre. When the specific pump inhibitor dihydroouabain (DHO) is applied, the resting potential of the fibre superfused with Tyrode's solution declines immediately from –68 mV to –62 mV (Fig. 5 A).

Simultaneously, the intracellular Na activity increases due to the inhibition of the active Na transport. Following 2 min in the DHO containing bathing fluid the preparation is

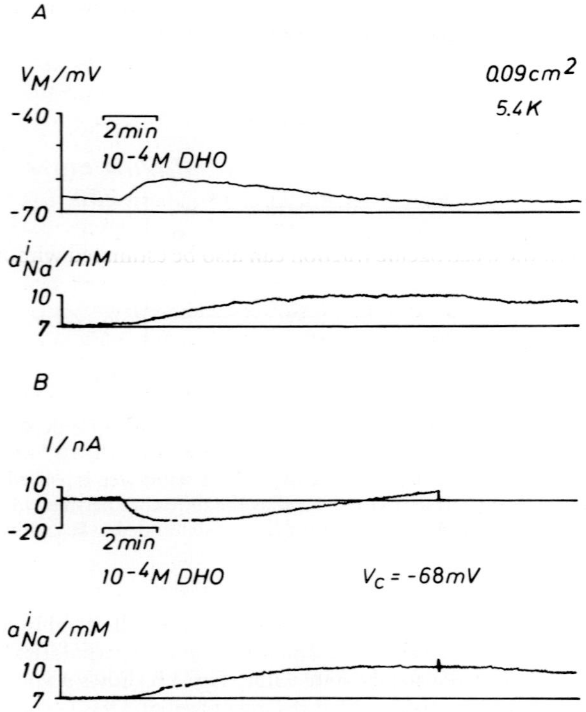

Fig. 5: Effect of DHO on resting potential, membrane current at resting potential and a^i_{Na} in a sheep Purkinje fibre. The period of DHO application is indicated. Data in A and B from a single impalement. A DHO effect on resting potential (upper panel) and a^i_{Na}. B DHO effect on membrane current (upper panel) and a^i_{Na}. The membrane is held at resting potential (–68 mV). Clamped surface: 0.09 cm^2. The dashed part of the curves indicates the period where a I–V curve is recorded.

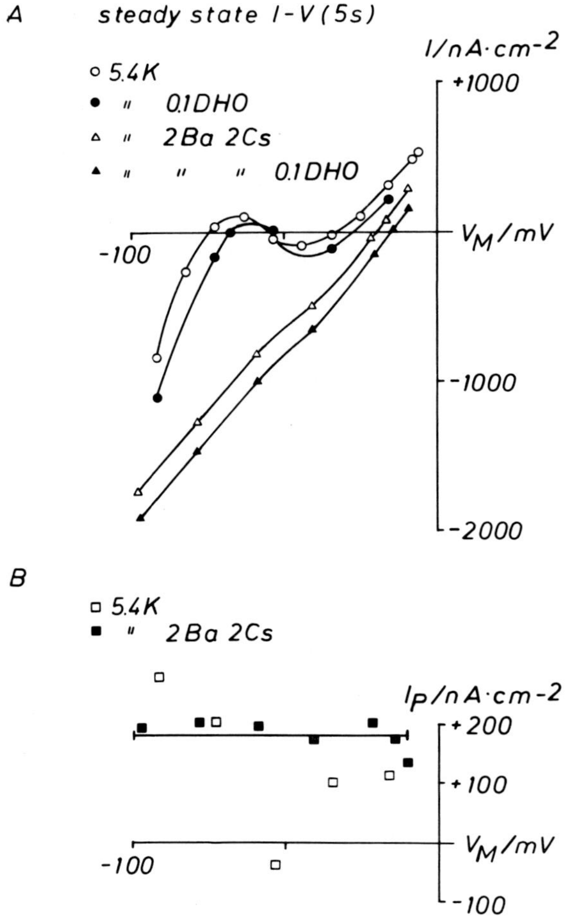

Fig. 6: A I–V relations of a sheep Purkinje fibre bathed in Tyrode solution with (●) or without (○) 10^{-4} M DHO or in a Ba and Cs containing medium with (▲) or without (△) 10^{-4} M DHO. Data from a single impalement. The membrane current at the end of a 5 s clamp step is plotted versus the clamped membrane potential. B Pump current (I_p) estimated as the difference between the two I–V curves in the Tyrode solutions (□; ○ minus ●) or in the Ba and Cs containing media (■; △ minus ▲), respectively.

again superfused with a drug-free Tyrode's solution. The cell membrane repolarizes and reaches the resting potential level after a small transient hyperpolarization. At the same time a^i_{Na} decreases towards the steady state value. Fig. 5 B shows a voltage clamp experiment in which the cell membrane is held at resting potential. DHO causes within 2 min an inward shift of the membrane current by about 19 nA (corresponding to a current density of 211 nA · cm^{-2}). Following wash out of the drug the current is shifted in the outward direction. A transient outward current which corresponds to the small hyperpolarization of the cell membrane observed in Fig. 5 A is recorded. As in Fig. 5 A, DHO increases a^i_{Na} and after switching to a drug-free medium a^i_{Na} declines again towards the resting level.

From measurements of the slope conductance of the I–V curve at resting potential and of the clamped fibre surface (0.09 cm^2) a specific membrane resistance of 28 $k\Omega \cdot cm^2$ is calculated. Multiplication of the DHO inhibited membrane current (211 $nA \cdot cm^{-2}$) with the specific membrane resistance (28 $k\Omega \cdot cm^2$) yields 5.9 mV in accordance with the DHO induced depolarization (6 mV) shown in Fig. 5 A. However, it would be premature to conclude that the pump contributes about 6 mV to the resting potential of the fibre by generating a pump current of ~ 210 $nA \cdot cm^{-2}$, because K accumulation might have affected the measurements in the following way. During inhibition of the pump by DHO, a net K efflux from the fibre occurs since the active component of the K influx is blocked. As a consequence of the net K efflux K ions may accumulate at the outside of the cell membrane. An increase of the extracellular K concentration in turn may cause a depolarization in addition to the depolarization which is evoked by the blockade of the pump current. Furthermore, the augmented external K concentration possibly increases the membrane conductance and may thereby add to the DHO-induced shift of the membrane current in the voltage clamped fibre (Fig. 5 B). Fig. 6 A clearly shows that the I–V relation of the fibre in DHO containing solution (filled circles) is not just shifted in the inward direction in parallel to the control I–V curve (open circles) but intersects the control I–V relation near –50 mV. The difference between both I–V curves is plotted as a function of membrane potential in Fig. 6 B (open squares). The differences is minimal near –50 mV and reaches a maximum at a more negative potential. If a variation of the extracellular K concentration were to contribute to the difference current, a similar dependence of the current on membrane potential would be expected. A K accumulation at the outside of the cell membrane at potentials positive to the K equilibrium potential (E_K) tends to shift the I–V curve of the fibre in the DHO containing medium in the outward direction. This shift diminishes the difference current. At potentials negative to E_K, a shift of the I–V curve in

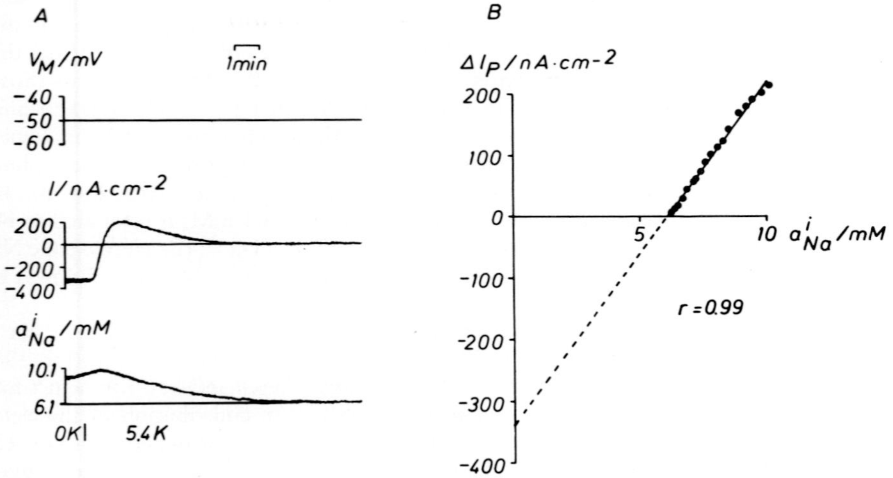

Fig. 7: A Membrane current (middle panel) and a^i_{Na} (lower panel) during enhanced Na pumping of a sheep Purkinje fibre. The cell membrane is held at –50 mV (upper panel). After 15 min in a K free medium the Na pump of the preparation is reactivated in Tyrode solution. B Plot of the amplitude of the transient outward current (ΔI_p) versus a^i_{Na}. Data from A. The dashed line intersects the ordinate at –340 $nA \cdot cm^{-2}$.

the inward direction is expected since K depletion should be reduced due to the inhibitory DHO action on the K influx. As a consequence an apparent increase of the difference current is often observed. In order to minimize the effects of alterations of $[K]_o$ on the difference current, the I–V curves of the fibre were measured in a 2 mM Ba and 2 mM Cs containing solution with (filled triangles) or without (open triangles) DHO (Fig. 6 A). Ba ions are known to suppress the background K conductance g_{K1} of cardiac Purkinje fibres (DIFRANCESCO, 1981). CsCl was added in order to inhibit the pacemaker current (ISENBERG, 1976; DIFRANCESCO, 1981), which is carried in part by K ions (DIFRANCESCO, 1981). The reduction of the net K flux by both ion species diminishes the variation of $[K]_o$. Furthermore the I–V curve of a fibre superfused with a solution containing Ba and Cs is nearly insensitive to changes of the extracellular K concentration (see Fig. 8 C). As can be seen from Fig. 6 A, the I–V curve of the fibre bathed in a Ba and Cs containing medium with DHO (filled triangles) is shifted into the inward direction in parallel with the curve obtained in the solution without DHO (open triangles). Thus, the diminution of changes in $[K]_o$ reveals a DHO-inhibited difference current which in this fibre shows little voltage dependence between –10 and –100 mV. This difference current is thought to be the Na pump current. It is represented by the filled squares in Fig. 6 B and amounts to 180 nA · cm^{-2} in the voltage range tested. A pump current of 180 nA · cm^{-2} causes a voltage drop of 5 mV across a specific membrane resistance of 28 kΩ · cm^2. Thus, the contribution of the electrogenic Na pump to the resting potential of the fibre is estimated to be 5 mV and the pump current density at resting potential is about 180 nA · cm^{-2}. Another way to estimate the pump current, first described by EISNER et al. (1981 a), is shown in Fig. 7. Following 15 min in a K free medium the Na pump of the fibre is reactivated in Tyrode's solution containing 5.4 mM K. The cell membrane is clamped at –50 mV. The membrane current and the intracellular Na activity are measured simultaneously (Fig. 7 A). The amplitude of the transient outward current as a function of a^i_{Na} during the reactivation of the Na pump is plotted in Fig. 7 B. The dashed regression line intersects the current axis at about 340 nA · cm^{-2}, suggesting a pump current density in the steady state (a^i_{Na} : 6.1 mM) of the same magnitude. It seems likely that this method overestimates the pump current density in the steady state. The reason is that the relation between active Na efflux and a^i_{Na} below the steady state value of a^i_{Na} bends towards smaller values for the Na efflux than those expected from a linear extrapolation (PHILIPSON and NISHIMOTO, 1983; GLITSCH and PUSCH, 1984). Thus the ‹true› pump current density in the steady state is probably lower than 340 nA · cm^{-2}. This estimation is further based on the assumption that the coupling ratio between active Na efflux and active K influx remains constant even at low a^i_{Na}. In summary, the pump current density of the resting fibre (a^i_{Na} : 6.1 mM) is estimated to be smaller than 340 nA · cm^{-2} and most probably about 180 nA · cm^{-2}. The electrogenic Na pump contributes 5 mV to the resting potential of the preparation (–68 mV in 5.4 mM K Tyrode solution).

Earlier estimations of the steady state pump current density yielded 320 nA · cm^{-2} (ISENBERG and TRAUTWEIN, 1974), 150 nA · cm^{-2} (EISNER et al., 1981 a) and 100 to 200 nA · cm^{-2} (GLITSCH and PUSCH, 1984) for sheep Purkinje fibres and 810 nA · cm^{-2} for guinea pig ventricular muscle (DAUT and RÜDEL, 1982). The contribution of the electrogenic active Na transport to the resting potential was previously estimated to be 6 to 13 mV for sheep Purkinje fibres (EISNER et al., 1981 a) and 6.4 mV for guinea pig ventricular muscle (DAUT and RÜDEL, 1982; 3 mM K Tyrode solution). According to DEITMER and ELLIS (1978) the resting potential of a sheep Purkinje fibre drops rapidly by 5 mV upon application of 10^{-5} M strophanthidin or ouabain. GADSBY and CRANEFIELD (1979 b) mentioned a rapid depolarization of 9 mV caused by acetylstrophanthidin at the *lower* resting potential level of canine Purkinje fibres. A smaller depolarization of only 3.4 mV was found in A–V node cells of the rabbit heart (KURACHI et al., 1981). Thus, it seems reasonable to conclude that c. 5 to 10 % of the resting potential in cardiac preparations are produced by the electrogenic Na pump.

The dependence of the Na pump current on membrane potential

The active Na transport extrudes Na ions from and takes up K ions into the cell against their respective electrochemical gradients. The energy required is delivered by ATP splitting. In theory it seems possible to increase the electrochemical gradients by manipulation of the chemical gradients or the membrane potential until the free energy available from ATP hydrolysis is no longer sufficient to fuel the active Na–K transport in the physiological direction. Under these conditions the Na–K pump may stop or even reverse the direction of the pumped fluxes. The membrane potential at which the electrochemical gradients of the Na and K ions across the cell membrane just equal the energy delivered by ATP hydrolysis is called the reversal potential of the electrogenic Na pump. It is estimated to be c. –250 mV, under the assumption that $[Na]_i$ is ten times lower and the internal K concentration is 30 times higher than the corresponding extracellular concentrations (DE WEER, 1984). In line with these considerations one would expect a reduction of the active Na efflux and thus (assuming a constant electrogenic fraction) a diminution of the Na pump current at more negative potentials. However, previous studies failed to detect a marked potential dependence of the pump current in cardiac Purkinje fibres. As described above, ISENBERG and TRAUTWEIN (1974) found a pump current of constant amplitude at membrane potentials between –30 and –90 mV in sheep Purkinje fibres. Their observation was confirmed and extended by EISNER and LEDERER (1980 a) who reported that the Na pump current of a sheep Purkinje fibre bathed in a Rb containing medium displays little voltage dependence within a range of membrane potentials from –5 to –80 mV. Similarly the authors showed the pump current of a fibre superfused with a solution containing Cs to be unchanged upon alterations of the membrane potential between –16 and –74 mV. Furthermore, GADSBY (1984) inferred from the experiment depicted in Fig. 9 that in canine Purkinje fibres too the pump current is barely affected by changes in the membrane potential between c. –20 and –70 mV. GLITSCH et al. (1982) studied the amplitude of the pump current as a function of membrane potential in sheep Purkinje fibres bathed in a Ba containing Tyrode solution and found little voltage dependence in the potential range between –30 and –100 mV. A diminution of the current amplitude was occasionally observed at clamp potentials of –100 to –120 mV. In recent experiments we were able to demonstrate more clearly a voltage dependence of the pump current in sheep Purkinje fibres. One example is given in Fig. 8. The steady state I–V curves of a fibre bathed in Ba and Cs containing solution with (filled squares) and without (open squares) 10^{-4} M DHO are shown in Fig. 8 A. The difference between both curves is plotted in Fig. 8 B. It represents the Na pump current of the fibre. In contrast to Fig. 6 B where the pump current of the fibre bathed in the medium containing Ba and Cs is voltage insensitive up to –100 mV the pump current of the preparation studied here displays a voltage dependence. The current decreases markedly at potentials negative to –50 mV and reaches a very small value at –110 mV. The decrease of the pump current at potentials negative to E_K (–90 mV) is certainly *not* due to K depletion. K depletion should be smaller in the medium containing DHO than in the drug-free solution since DHO blocks the active K influx. As a consequence, the extracellular K concentration should increase and should shift the I–V curve into the inward direction compared to the I–V relation obtained in the drug free

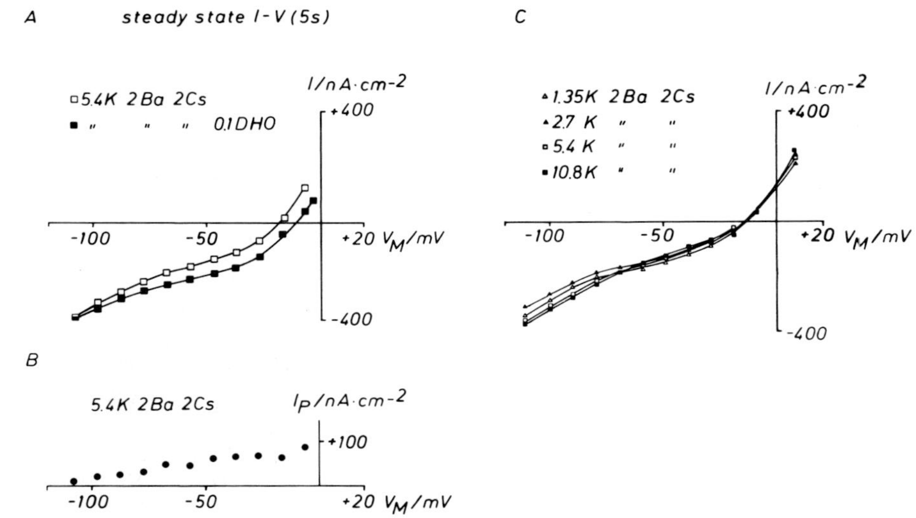

Fig. 8: A I–V relations of a sheep Purkinje fibre bathed in Ba and Cs containing solution with (■) or without (□) 10^{-4} M DHO. The membrane current at the end of a 5 s clamp step is plotted versus the clamped membrane potential. B Voltage dependence of the Na pump current (I_p). I_p is estimated as the difference between the I–V curves shown in A. C I–V relations of the preparation in Ba and Cs containing media with various K concentrations. The membrane current at the end of a 5 s clamp step is plotted versus the clamped membrane potential.

solution. This shift should *augment* the difference current between both I–V curves and thus the apparent pump current. Furthermore, Fig. 8 C demonstrates that the I–V relation of the fibre is little affected by changes of the extracellular K concentration between 1.35 mM K and 10.8 mM K under our experimental conditions. Similar results of experiments carried out on 10 sheep Purkinje fibres indicated that the pump current amplitude is barely affected by the membrane potential between +10 and –70 mV. This observation confirms the earlier findings cited above. However, the amplitude of the pump current decreased significantly at membrane potentials negative to –70 mV. The amplitude of the current measured at –110 mV amounted to 70 % of the amplitude at –50 mV. The intracellular Na activity remained constant at 6.5 mM. Thus, the voltage dependence of the pump current in sheep Purkinje fibres is apparent only at potentials negative to the resting potential in normal Tyrode solution (5.4 mM K). A comparable voltage dependence of the pump current in bullfrog atria bathed in 2 mM K Ringer solution was recently described by Hasuo and Koketsu (1985). They found a nearly constant amplitude of the pump current at membrane potentials between –50 and –90 mV. The pump current declined at more negative potentials and reached at –110 mV about 50 % of the amplitude observed at –50 mV. Possible effects of a K depletion due to enhanced K pumping or of changes in a^i_{Na} were not excluded. Gadsby and his colleagues (1985) succeeded in measuring the voltage dependence of the strongly activated Na pump current in isolated ventricular cells of the guinea pig heart in a range of membrane potentials between +60 and –140 mV. They found a maximal amplitude of the pump current near 0 mV. The pump current declined steadily at more negative membrane potentials. The zero-current potential was estimated to be near –155 mV. It is not yet clear whether the differences of the pump

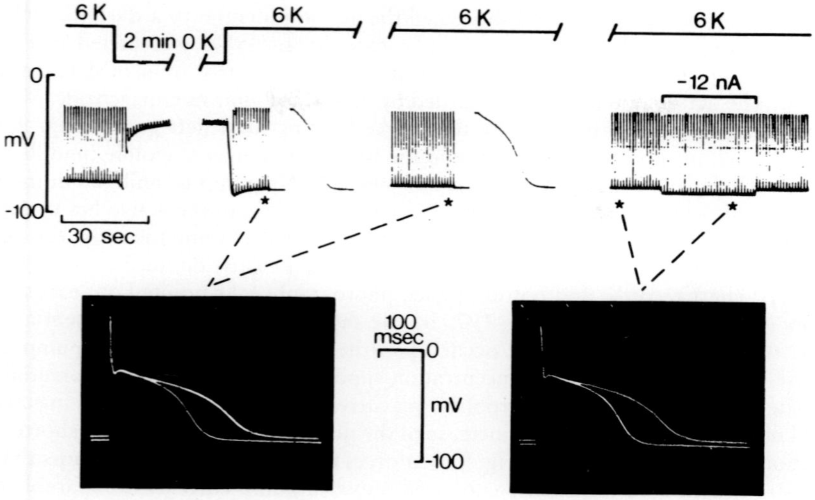

Fig. 9: Hyperpolarization and action potential shortening caused either by enhanced Na pumping (left part of the Fig.) or by intracellular injection of a constant current (right part) in a canine Purkinje fibre. The preparation is driven at 1 Hz in Tyrode solution containing 6 mM K. Application of a K free medium for 2 min and omission of three sections of record of duration 90 s, 10 min, and 3 min are indicated by the top line. Action potential upstrokes are attenuated by the pen recorder. The two high-speed chart records (time calibration now represents 500 ms) show the transient shortening of the action potential duration during enhanced Na pumping. The asterisks mark when the action potentials superimposed in the bottom panel were displayed on the storage oscilloscope. (From Gadsby and Cranefield, 1982, with permission.)

current-voltage relations are caused by undetected changes of the extracellular activator cation concentration in the multicellular preparations, by differences in the metabolic state, or by the unphysiological ionic gradients across the sarcolemma of the perfused single cells. The physiological shape of the pump current-voltage curve is of considerable interest since it may point to the number of voltage dependent partial reactions in the mechanism of ion translocation performed by the Na pump (cf. Chapman, 1984; De Weer, 1984).

Effect of the electrogenic Na pump on action potential

As mentioned above the contribution of the electrogenic active Na transport to the cardiac membrane potential depends on both the amplitude of the pump current and the magnitude of the membrane resistance. Fig. 1 shows that the membrane resistance of a cardiac Purkinje fibre is appreciably higher at membrane potentials which are characteristic for the plateau of the cardiac action potential than at diastolic potentials. Thus for a constant pump current one would expect a larger contribution of the Na pump to the membrane potential at the plateau of an action potential than to the diastolic potential. In fact Isenberg and Trautwein (1974) observed a marked prolongation and an incomplete repolarization of the action potential of sheep Purkinje fibres following inhibition of the electrogenic Na pump by 10^{-5} M DHO. Vice versa stimulation of the Na pump during the recovery from the cardiac steroid shortened the action potential to a duration below the control. A similar finding by GADSBY and CRANEFIELD (1982) is depicted in Fig. 9. A canine Purkinje fibre is electrically driven at 1 Hz in a K free or 6 mM K containing solution. The action potentials are recorded by an intracellular microelectrode. When the K containing medium is replaced by the K free bathing fluid (left part of Fig. 9, upper panel), the cell membrane depolarizes and the fibre is no longer excitable (middle panel). The intracellular Na concentration increases since the Na pump is inhibited in the K free solution. Following reapplication of the K containing medium the active Na transport is reactivated and the active Na efflux is transiently enhanced. Simultaneously, the diastolic potential is increased and the action potential duration is clearly diminished (middle panel, high speed chart records, and bottom panel, photographs). As pointed out earlier by the authors (GADSBY and CRANEFIELD, 1979 b), the shortening of the action potential cannot be due to K depletion that might occur upon the reactivation of the Na pump since a decrease of the extracellular K concentration should *lengthen* the action potential duration. The fact that a constant hyperpolarizing current which is intracellularly injected by a second microelectrode mimics the increase of the diastolic potential, and the shortening of the action potential (right part of Fig. 9) reinforces the conclusion of the authors that both effects are caused by a transiently enhanced outward pump current. Comparable results were obtained by BOYETT and FEDIDA (1984) from a study of the rate dependent changes in the electrical activity of dog cardiac Purkinje fibres. Following a change to a higher stimulus frequency the action potential shortens, the rate of repolarization of the action potential and the maximum diastolic potential increase whereas the amplitude of the pacemaker potential decreases. According to the authors, the slowly developing alterations of these parameters are most probably due to an increase of the Na pump current. In conclusion, the Na pump modulates the action potential duration, the rate of repolarization, the maximum diastolic potential and the amplitude of the pacemaker potential in cardiac Purkinje fibres.

Effect of electrogenic Na pumping on cardiac pacemaker activity

When the discharge frequency of a spontaneously active Purkinje fibre is enhanced by external stimulation, the maximum diastolic potential increases to more negative potentials. Following cessation of the stimulus train the diastolic depolarization is flat and the pacemaker activity slowly reaches its original frequency often after a complete standstill of the fibre. VASSALLE (1970) was the first to study this overdrive suppression in detail. He pointed out that the overdrive increases the intracellular Na concentration and thereby the activity of the electrogenic Na pump. The augmented pump current hyperpolarizes the cell membrane and slows down the pacemaker frequency. Observations by other authors confirmed Vassalle's concept (review: VASSALLE, 1982). Overdrive suppression is probably an important mechanism *in vivo* for the inhibition of latent pacemakers. The dominant pacemaker in the sinoatrial node is thought to suppress other pacemakers by virtue of its higher discharge frequency. If this overdrive suppression is removed by a block in the conducting system, a latent pacemaker will escape from the suppression and will generate an ectopic impulse. The concept of overdrive suppression implies that the electrogenic Na pump might generally modify cardiac pacemaker activity. In fact, the discharge frequency of the sinoatrial node (NOMA and IRISAWA, 1974) and the AV node (KURACHI et al., 1981) of the rabbit heart decreases when the active electrogenic Na transport is enhanced. Similarly, a transient increase of the Na pump current inhibits or even blocks the pacemaker activity of canine Purkinje fibres at the low and the high level of resting potential (GADSBY and CRANEFIELD, 1979 b). The same mechanism is obviously involved in the spontaneous cessation of triggered repetitive discharges of cells in the canine coronary sinus (WIT et al., 1981) and in the suppression of a burst-like pacemaker activity in rabbit Purkinje fibres (VERDONCK et al., 1982). Thus, there is ample evidence for a modification of cardiac pacemaker activity by the electrogenic Na pump.

The physiological significance of electrogenic Na pumping in the heart

The Na pump current is an outward current and therefore tends to hyperpolarize the cell membrane of cardiac cells. The current counteracts the depolarizing effect of the Na influx and contributes to the maintenance of the resting potential and its restoration following activity. At first sight, the contribution of the electrogenic Na pump to the cardiac resting potential of about 5 to 6 mV seems negligible. However, in view of the steady-state inactivation-voltage curve for the fast Na inward current (cf. CARMELIET and VEREECKE, 1979), it is clear that variations of the resting potential by a few millivolts have a profound effect on the amplitude of the fast Na inward current which governs the rate of rise of the action potential in most cardiac cells. The rate of rise of the action potential is a determinant of the conduction velocity and therefore of the physiological spread of excitation. The effect of the Na pump current on the action potential duration is also important for the spread of excitation. An increase of the heart rate activates the electrogenic Na pump via an enhanced Na influx and an augmented intracellular Na concentration. The increased Na pump (outward) current shortens the action potential duration and reduces thereby the refractory period. The reduced refractory period is a prerequisite for an unimpaired impulse conduction at high pacemaker frequencies. The pump current does not only affect the impulse propagation but also the impulse generation. As outlined above, the pump current inhibits or even transiently blocks cardiac pacemaker activity. One mechanism involved seems to be a reduction of the membrane resistance at the resting potential level. This reduction is due to the pump current evoked shift of the I–V relation in the outward direction (comp. Fig. 1). Thus, a given pacemaker current will cause a smaller pacemaker potential when the active Na transport is enhanced. The inhibitory effect of the pump current on cardiac pacemaker activity is the basis of the physiological overdrive suppression of latent pacemakers by the dominant sinoatrial node (VASSALLE, 1970). In conclusion, the Na pump current contributes to the cardiac resting and action potential and modulates the generation and the conduction of electrical impulses in the heart. Thus, there is little doubt that the pump current is of physiological significance for cardiac cells.

References

Abercrombie, R. F., De Weer, P.: Electric current generated by squid giant axon sodium pump: external K and internal ADP effects. Am. J. Physiol. **235**: C 63–C 68 (1978).

Boyett, M. R., Fedida, D.: Changes in the electrical activity of dog cardiac Purkinje fibres at high heart rates. J. Physiol. (Lond) **350**, 361–391 (1984).

Carmeliet, E., Vereecke, J.: Electrogenesis of the action potential and automaticity. In: Handbook of Physiology. The Cardiovascular System I: The Heart (Berne, R. M., Sperelakis, N., Geiger, S., eds.), pp. 269–334. Am. Physiol. Soc. Bethesda, Maryland (1979).

Chapman, B. J.: Thermodynamics and kinetics of electrogenic pumps. In: Electrogenic Transport: Fundamental Principles and Physiological Implications (Blaustein, M. P., Lieberman, M., eds.), pp. 17–32. Raven Press, New York (1984).

Daut, J., Rüdel, R.: The electrogenic sodium pump in guinea-pig ventricular muscle: inhibition of pump current by cardiac glycosides. J. Physiol. (Lond) **330**, 243–264 (1982).

Deitmer, J. W., Ellis, D.: The intracellular sodium activity of cardiac Purkinje fibres during inhibition and re-activation of the Na–K pump. J. Physiol. (Lond) **284**, 241–259 (1978).

De Weer, P.: Electrogenic pumps: theoretical and practical considerations. In: Electrogenic Transport: Fundamental Principles and Physiological Implications (Blaustein, M. P., Lieberman, M., eds.), pp. 1–15. Raven Press, New York (1984).

DiFrancesco. D.: A new interpretation of the pace-maker current in calf Purkinje fibres. J. Physiol. (Lond) **314**, 359–376 (1981).

Eisner, D. A., Lederer, W. J.: Characterization of the electrogenic sodium pump in cardiac Purkinje fibres. J. Physiol. (Lond) **303**, 441–474 (1980 a).

Eisner, D. A., Lederer, W. J.: The relationship between sodium pump activity and twitch tension in cardiac Purkinje fibres. J. Physiol. (Lond) **303**, 475–494 (1980 b).

Eisner, D. A., Lederer, W. J., Vaughan-Jones, R. D.: The dependence of sodium pumping and tension on intracellular sodium activity in voltage-clamped sheep Purkinje fibres. J. Physiol. (Lond) **317**, 163–187 (1981 a).

Eisner, D. A.. Lederer, W. J., Vaughan-Jones, R. D.: The effects of rubidium ions and membrane potential on the intracellular sodium activity of sheep Purkinje fibres. J. Physiol. (Lond) **317**, 189–205(1981 b).

Eisner, D. A., Lederer, W. J., Sheu, S.-S.: The role of intracellular sodium activity in the anti-arrhythmic action of local anaesthetics in sheep Purkinje fibres. J. Physiol. (Lond) **340**, 239–257 (1983).

Falk, R. T., Cohen, I. S.: Membrane current following activity in canine cardiac Purkinje fibers. J. Gen. Physiol. **83**, 771–799 (1984).

Gadsby, D. C.: Activation of electrogenic Na^+/K^+ exchange by extracellular K^+ in canine cardiac Purkinje fibers. Proc. Natl. Acad. Sci. USA **77**, 4035–4039 (1980).

Gadsby, D. C.: The Na/K pump of cardiac cells. Ann. Rev. Biophys. Bioeng. **13**, 373–398 (1984).

Gadsby, D. C., Cranefield, P. F.: Direct measurement of changes in sodium pump current in canine cardiac Purkinje fibers. Proc. Natl. Acad. Sci. USA **76**, 1783–1787 (1979 a).

Gadsby, D. C., Cranefield, P. F.: Electrogenic sodium extrusion in cardiac Purkinje fibers. J. Gen. Physiol. **73**, 819–837 (1979 b).

Gadsby, D. C., Cranefield, P. F.: Effects of electrogenic sodium extrusion on the membrane potential of cardiac Purkinje fibers. In: Normal and Abnormal Conduction in the Heart (Paes de Carvalho, A., Hoffman. B. F., Lieberman, M., eds.), pp. 225–247. Futura Mount Kisco, N. Y. (1982).

Gadsby, D. C., Nakao, M.: Dependence of Na/K pump current on intracellular [Na] in isolated cells from guinea-pig ventricle. J. Physiol. (Lond) **371**, 201 P. (1986).

Gadsby, D. C., Kimura, J., Noma, A.: Voltage dependence of Na/K pump current in isolated heart cells. Nature **315**, 63–65 (1985).

Garrahan, P. J., Glynn, I. M.: The stoichiometry of the sodium pump. J. Physiol. (Lond) **192**, 217–235 (1967).

Glitsch, H. G.: Activation of the electrogenic sodium pump in guinea-pig auricles by internal sodium ions. J. Physiol. (Lond) **220**, 565–582 (1972).

Glitsch, H. G.: Characteristics of active sodium transport in intact cardiac cells. In: Excitation and Neural Control of the Heart (Levy, M. N., Vassalle, M., eds.), pp. 37–58. Am. Physiol. Soc. Bethesda, Maryland (1982 a).

Glitsch, H. G.: Electrogenic Na pumping in the heart. Ann. Rev. Physiol. **44**, 389–400 (1982 b).

Glitsch, H. G., Pusch, H.: Correlation between changes in membrane potential and intracellular Na activity during K activated response in sheep Purkinje fibres. Pflügers Arch. **384**, 189–191 (1980).

Glitsch, H. G., Pusch, H.: On the temperature dependence of the Na pump in sheep Purkinje fibres. Pflügers Arch. **402**, 109–115 (1984).

Glitsch, H. G., Grabowski, W., Thielen, J.: Activation of the electrogenic sodium pump in guinea-pig atria by external potassium ions. J. Physiol. (Lond) **276**, 515–524 (1978).

Glitsch, H. G., Pusch, H., Schumacher, T.: Dihydroouabain-sensitive Na efflux at low intracellular Na activity in sheep Purkinje fibres. Pflügers Arch. **400**, Suppl., R5 (1984).

Glitsch, H. G., Pusch, H., Schumacher, Th., Verdonck, F.: An identification of the K activated Na pump current in sheep Purkinje fibres. Pflügers Arch. **394**, 256–263 (1982).

Hasuo, H., Koketsu, K.: Potential dependency of the electrogenic Na^+-pump current in bullfrog atrial muscles. Jap. J. Physiol. **35**, 89–100 (1985).

Isenberg, G.: Cardiac Purkinje fibers: cesium as a tool to block inward rectifying potassium currents. Pflügers Arch. **365**, 99–106 (1976).

Isenberg, G., Trautwein, W.: The effect of dihydro-ouabain and lithium-ions on the outward current in cardiac Purkinje fibers. Pflügers Arch. **350**, 41–54 (1974).

Kurachi, Y., Noma, A., Irisawa, H.: Electrogenic sodium pump in rabbit atrio-ventricular node cell. Pflügers Arch. **391**, 261–266 (1981).

Lieberman, M., Horres, C. R., Jacob, R., Murphy, E., Piwnica-Worms, D., Wheeler, D. M.: Physiologic criteria for electrogenic transport in tissue-cultured heart cells. In: Electrogenic Transport: Fundamental Principles and Physiological Implications. (Blaustein, M. P., Lieberman, M., eds.), pp. 181–191. Raven Press, New York (1984).

Noma, A., Irisawa, H.: Electrogenic sodium pump in rabbit sinoatrial node cell. Pflügers Arch. **351**, 177–182 (1974).

Page, E., Storm, S. R.: Cat heart muscle *in vitro*. VIII. Active transport of sodium in papillary muscles. J. Gen. Physiol. **48**, 957–972 (1965).

Philipson, K. D., Nishimoto, A. Y.: ATP-dependent Na^+ transport in cardiac sarcolemmal vesicles. Biochim. Biophys. Acta **733**, 133–141 (1983).

Post, R. L., Jolly, P. C.: The linkage of sodium, potassium, and ammonium active transport across the human erythrocyte membrane. Biochim. Biophys. Acta **25**, 118–128 (1957).

Sperelakis, N.: Origin of the cardiac resting potential. In: Handbook of Physiology. The Cardiovascular System I: The Heart (Berne, R. M., Sperelakis, N., Geiger, S., eds.), pp. 187–267. Am. Physiol. Soc. Bethesda, Maryland (1979).

Thomas, R. C.: New design for sodium-sensitive glass micro-electrode. J. Physiol. (Lond) **210**, 82–83 P (1970).

Vassalle, M.: Electrogenic suppression of automaticity in sheep and dog Purkinje fibers. Circ. Res. **27**, 361–377 (1970).

Vassalle, M.: The role of the electrogenic sodium pump in controlling excitability in nerve and cardiac fibers. In: Current Topics in Membranes and Transport Vol. **16** (Slayman, C. L. ed.), pp. 467–483. Academic Press, New York (1982).

Verdonck, F., Glitsch, H. G.. Pusch, H.: Importance of electrogenic sodium extrusion for suppression of spontaneous rhythmic activity in rabbit Purkyne fibres. Arch. Int. Physiol. Biochim. **90**, 36–37 P. (1982).

Wit, A. L., Cranefield, P. F., Gadsby, D. C.: Electrogenic sodium extrusion can stop triggered activity in the canine coronary sinus. Circ. Res. **49**, 1029–1042 (1981).

Fortschritte der Zoologie, Band 33 · Lüttgau (Hrsg.): Membrane Control
Gustav Fischer Verlag · Stuttgart · New York · 1986

The energetics of the Na, K-pump in cardiac muscle

J. DAUT

Physiologisches Institut der Technischen Universität München, Biedersteiner Straße 29, D-8000 München 40, FRG

In cardiac muscle the determinants of cellular energy expenditure are of particular interest because the heart operates essentially aerobically, i. e. its function depends critically on the ratio between demand and supply of oxygen. Simultaneous measurements of oxygen consumption and heat production have shown that the energy equivalent of oxygen is about 20 J/ml O_2 (COULSON, 1976; CHAPMAN et al., 1982) which is in agreement with classical biochemical predictions. This means that the rate of oxygen consumption under steady state conditions can be calculated directly from the heat produced in a cardiac preparation which is not doing any external work.

The classical studies of the energetics of muscular contraction were based on a subdivision of the total energy expenditure into various components attributable to functional parameters such as developed tension, external work, electrical excitation and basal metabolism (e. g. MOMMAERTS, 1969). More recently it has been tried to separate energy expenditure into the components attributable to different enzymes such as the myofibrillar myosin ATPase, the sarcoreticular Ca-ATPase and the sarcolemmal Na, K-ATPase (GIBBS and CHAPMAN, 1979; CHAPMAN, 1983). This enzymatic compartmentalization of energy flux may greatly improve our understanding of the interdependence of the various molecular and cellular processes which finally lead to the transformation of chemical energy into mechanical work.

The resting metabolism of cardiac muscle is four to five times higher than that of skeletal muscle (GIBBS, 1978). The contribution of cardiac resting (or tension-independent) metabolism to the total metabolism of the beating heart in vivo has been estimated to be 20–25 % in various species including guinea-pig and man (Loiselle and Gibbs 1979). However, the contribution of the various ATPases to the resting energy expenditure of cardiac muscle is still far from clear (GIBBS, 1982; CHAPMAN, 1983).

In the present paper, an estimate of the contribution of the Na, K-ATPase to the energy expenditure of guinea-pig ventricular muscle will be derived from electrophysiological measurements of the turnover rate and of the electrochemical work of the pump. The turnover rate of the myocardial Na, K-ATPase can be calculated from the density of the electrogenic pump current and the surface/volume ratio of the cells, which have been measured previously (DAUT, 1982 a; DAUT and RÜDEL, 1982). These measurements have now been complemented under the same experimental conditions, by a study of the transmembrane gradients of Na and K using ion-sensitive micro-electrodes. Together with recent estimates of the free energy of ATP hydrolysis in intact cells (see VEECH et al., 1979; MAYER et al., 1982; DAWSON, 1983; DEWEER, 1984, 1985), these data permit calculation of the following parameters: (1) the electrochemical work, (2) the thermodynamic efficiency, (3) the reversal potential, (4) the turnover rate, (5) the power, (6) the heat production of the Na, K-pump in quiescent cardiac muscle. It will be concluded that the thermodynamic efficiency of the Na, K-pump and the heat production (energy expenditure) of the Na, K-pump are much higher than was assumed previously (Tanford, 1981; Gibbs and Chapman, 1979; Gibbs, 1982).

Methods

The intracellular activities of Na and K were recorded with ion-sensitive micro-electrodes in guinea-pig ventricular muscle. Strands of papillary or trabecular muscle of 100–500 μm diameter were dissected from either ventricle. The solutions, the recording chamber and the electronic apparatus were as described previously (Daut, 1982 a; Daut and Rüdel, 1982). The standard Tyrode solution contained (mM): NaCl, 117; KCl, 3; $CaCl_2$, 2; $MgSO_4$, 1; Na pyruvate, 2; $NaHCO_3$, 26.2; NaH_2PO_4, 1.67; glucose, 10. It was gassed with 95 % O_2 and 5 % CO_2, the pH was 7.4. The K concentration was varied by replacing part of the NaCl by equimolar amounts of KCl. The temperature was 35–37 °C and was held constant within 0.3 °C during an individual experiment.

All results are reported as mean values ± standard deviation. The number of preparations from which the data were obtained (n) is given in parenthesis.

Na-sensitive micro-electrodes were fabricated from borosilicate glass pipettes of 1.5 mm diameter. When filled with 3 M KCl the electrodes had resistances of about 5 MΩ. The micro-electrodes were silanized in the conventional way (see Thomas, 1978) and back-filled with the liquid ion-exchanger ETH 227 (Steiner et al., 1979), which was a gift from Prof. W. Simon, Zürich. The reference solution in the pipette was 150 mM NaCl.

The calibration procedure was similar to that of Dagostino and Lee (1982). The calibration was carried out in the recording chamber at 35–37 °C before and after the experiment. Calibrating solutions contained various Na and K concentrations to give a total concentration of [Na] + [K] of 150 mM. In addition, all calibrating solutions contained 1×10^{-5} M $CaCl_2$ and 2 mM $MgCl_2$. The Nicolski equation was used to correct for the Ca and K selectivity coefficients ($k_{Na,Ca}$ and $k_{Na;K}$) of the Na sensitive micro-electrodes (see Lee, 1981). The values of $k_{Na,Ca}$ and $k_{Na,K}$ were estimated individually for each microelectrode. The average k_{NaCa} was 0.7 (range 0.2–1.6). The values of $k_{Na,K}$ ranged between 0.008 and 0.02.

The intracellular Na activity of guinea-pig papillary muscle preparations was studied by simultaneous impalement with a Na-selective micro-electrode and a convential KCl-filled micro-electrode. Na sensitive electrodes had resistances between 10^{10} and 10^{11} Ω. Electrodes of lower resistance were less noisy but gave less consistent results because they tended to damage the cells during impalement (see Taylor and Thomas, 1984). Usually the potential measured after withdrawal of the electrode from the cell agreed within 2 mV with the potential measured before the impalement. Also, the calibration curves made before and after the experiments usually agreed within 2–3 mV. When there were such small differences, the average value was taken to calculate a^i_{Na}. When the differences were larger the results had to be discarded.

K sensitive micro-electrodes were made with the Corning liquid ion exchanger 477 317, which was a gift from Prof. H. D. Lux. They were fabricated in the same way as the Na-sensitive micro-electrodes. They had resistance of 5×10^8 to 5×10^9 Ω. The calibrating solutions were also as described above.

The Na selectivity coefficient of these electrodes ($k_{K,Na}$) ranged between 0.015 and 0.03. No correction for a^i_{Ca} was introduced because with the high values of a^i_K measured $k_{K,Ca}$ is probably irrelevant.

Results

The aim of the experiments reported here was to calculate the work, the thermodynamic efficiency and the power of the Na, K-pump in cardiac ventricular muscle. In trying to determine these parameters, it is essential to measure the intracellular activities of Na and K (a^i_{Na} and a^i_K), the membrane potential (E_m) and the density of the electrogenic pump current (I_p) in the steady state under exactly the same experimental conditions. In particular, it is important to use the same external K concentration, because a^i_{Na} depends on external K (ELLIS, 1977; EISNER et al., 1981; SHEU and FOZZARD, 1982).

In Tyrode solution containing 3 mM K, the intracellular Na activity in quiescent guinea-pig ventricular muscle was 7.1 ± 2.0 mM (n = 10). The intracelluar K activity was found to be 108 ± 7 mM (n = 12) under the same conditions. This agrees well with the value of a^i_K extrapolated from the relation between E_m and E_K obtained in the same preparations.

The values of the Na and K equilibrium potentials (E_{Na} and E_K) calculated from the results reported here are +73 mV and –103 mV, respectively. The average membrane potential (E_m) measured in 3 mM $[K]_o$ in the steady state was –94 mV (DAUT, 1982 a). From these figures the work of the Na, K-pump per mol ATP can be calculated. The molar electrochemical work, W(J/mol), of the active transport of an ion across a cell membrane equals the sum of osmotic work plus electrical work (see e. g. SPERELAKIS, 1979):

$$(1) \qquad W = RT \ln (a^o/a^i) + zF \cdot E_m,$$

where a^i and a^o are the intra- and extracellular activities and z is the charge of the transported ion. Thus the electrochemical work of the outward transport of Na can be defined as

$$(2) \qquad W_{Na} = -RT \ln (a^o_{Na}/a^i_{Na}) + F\, E_m = F\,(-E_{Na} + E_m),$$

and the electrochemical work of the inward transport of K can be defined as

$$(3) \qquad W_K = +RT \ln (a^o_K/a^i_K) - F\, E_m = F\,(E_K - E_m).$$

Since the stoichiometry of the Na, K-ATPase has been found to be close to 3 Na : 2 K : 1 ATP in various tissues including heart (see e. g. EISNER et al., 1981; DAUT and RÜDEL, 1982), the electrochemical work performed by the Na, K-pump during hydrolysis of 1 mol ATP (W_p) equals ($3\,W_{Na} + 2\,W_K$) and can be written as

$$(4) \qquad W_p = F\,(-3\,E_{Na} + 2\,E_K + E_m).$$

The value of W_P calculated from the measured parameters is 50.2 kJ/mol. This figure can be used to calculate the thermodynamic efficiency (see GIBBS, 1974, 1982) of the Na, K-pump (ε) which is defined as

$$(5) \qquad \varepsilon = W_p/\Delta G_{ATP},$$

where ΔG_{ATP} is the free energy of hydrolysis of ATP in the quiescent cardiac cell. The free energy of ATP hydrolysis has recently been investigated in various preparations (see VEECH et al., 1979; MEYER et al., 1982; DAWSON, 1983; DEWEER, 1984, 1985). It is probably close to the standard chemical potential of intracellular ATP (see TANFORD, 1982), which depends on the aqueous intracellular concentrations of ATP, ADP and P_i.

Since the estimates of free cytosolic ADP concentration have dramatically decreased in recent years (see MEYER et al., 1982), the most recent estimates of ΔG_{ATP} tend to be higher than previous ones. For the present investigation, ΔG_{ATP} in quiescent guinea-pig heart was assumed to be −60 kJ/mol, i. e. similar to the highest values found in other nerve and muscle cells (see DEWEER 1984, 1985; KAMMERMEIER et al., 1982). This yields a value of 0.84 for ε.

The plausibility of the assumed ΔG_{ATP} may be checked by considering the reversal potential (E_r) of the Na, K-pump. From the excess free energy available from ATP hydrolysis ($\Delta G_{ATP}-W_p$), the electromotive force of the Na, K-pump (i. e. the difference between E_m and E_r) may be calculated (see also Abercrombie and DEWEER, 1978; DEWEER, 1984) using the equation

(6) $$E_r - E_m = (\Delta G_{ATP} - W_p)/F.$$

Combining equations (4) and (6) yields

(7) $$E_r = 3\ E_{Na} - 2\ E_K + \Delta G_{ATP}/F$$

(see CHAPMAN and JOHNSON, 1978 and TANFORD, 1981). The calculated reversal potential of the Na, K-pump in quiescent guinea-pig ventricular muscle is –195 mV in 3 mM $[K]_o$. In two experiments a^i_{Na} was measured after reducing $[K]_o$ from 3 to 1 mM. The average E_m in 1 mM $[K]_o$ was –118 mV. The steady-state a^i_{Na} rose to 9 resp. 10 mM. Thus a reversal potential of the Na, K-pump of –164 mV is obtained in 1 mM $[K]_o$, which is only 40–50 mV negative to the steady-state resting potential. This corroborates the assumption that ΔG_{ATP} in quiescent guinea-pig ventricular muscle may be as high as in other nerve and muscle cells.

The turnover rate of ATP per gram tissue per second (N_{ATP}) can be calculated from the measured electrogenic pump current (DAUT and RÜDEL, 1981, 1982) using the equation

(8) $$N_{ATP} = I_p/F \cdot s/v \cdot 1/b = I_g/F$$

where I_p is the density of the electrogenic pump current (A/cm^2), s/v is the cellular surface/volume ratio (cm^{-1}), b is the specific gravity of the myocardium (g/cm^3) and I_g is the pump current per gram tissue (A/g). The parameter that was actually measured in a previous paper (DAUT and RÜDEL, 1982) was the pump current per volume, which was 5.8 mA/cm^3. Therefore, if one assumes a specific gravity of cardiac tissue of about 1.05 g/cm^3, a value of 5.5 mA/g is obtained for I_g without any assumptions about specific membrane capacity or surface/volume ratio. This corresponds to a N_{ATP} of 57 nM ATP per gram per second. Multiplying N_{ATP} with W_p (eqns. (4) and (8)) gives then the power of the Na, K-pump per gram tissue, which is simply

(9) $$P = (-3\ E_{Na} + 2\ E_K + E_m)\ I_g.$$

The power of the Na, K-pump in resting guinea-pig myocardium calculated from eq. (9) is 3.0 mW/g.

Discussion

The most serious problem when using the liquid ion exchanger ETH 227 is the Ca-sensitivity of the Na-sensitive micro-electrodes. The Ca activity seen by the micro-elec-

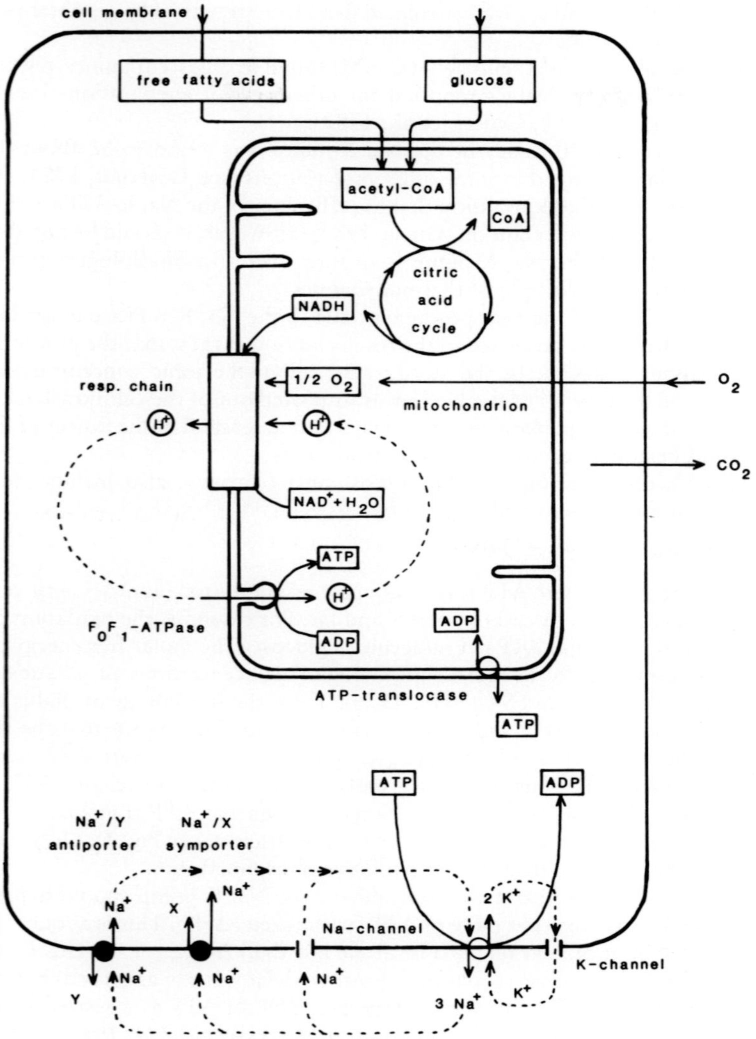

Fig. 1: Schematic diagram of some of the metabolic pathways contributing to aerobic ATP synthesis.

trode changes by a factor of about 10 000 during impalement of a quiescent cardiac cell (MARBAN et al., 1980; SHEU and FOZZARD, 1982) and this produces an electrode potential of unknown magnitude. This is usually accounted for by calculating from the Na, Ca selectivity coefficient the apparent a^{o}_{Na} produced by a^{o}_{Ca} (which is in the order of 40–250 mM) and the apparent a^{i}_{Na} produced by a^{i}_{Ca} (which is in the order of 0.3–7.0 mM, SHEU and FOZZARD, 1982; BERS and ELLIS, 1982). In contrast, in the present experiments only the potential jump due to the difference between the Ca activity of the calibrating solution

($a^c_{Ca} \approx 0.32 \times 10^{-5}$ M) and a^i_{Ca} was calculated from the estimate of $k_{Na,Ca}$ obtained for each individual micro-electrode.

The values of a^i_{Na} (7.1 mM) and a^i_K (108 mM) found in quiescent guinea-pig ventricular muscle are similar to the values reported for other cardiac preparations (see e.g. LEE, 1981; GLITSCH et al., 1981; COHEN et al., 1982).

The thermodynamic efficiency of the Na, K-pump was found to be about 0.84. This contrasts with data obtained in some other preparations (see TANFORD, 1981, 1983), but is in a agreement with the expectation that the efficiency of the Na, K-ATPase should tend towards 1 in the course of evolution (GIBBS, 1982). However, it should be noted that ε can never quite reach 1 if the Na, K-pump is to turn over at a physiologically useful rate, because of the second principle of thermodynamics.

How can we calculate the heat production due to the Na, K-ATPase in resting cardiac muscle? The calculations presented in the results section suggest that the power of the Na, K-pump is about 3 mW/g. In the steady state all of the ionic concentrations remain constant, i. e. on average all of the Na ions transported out of the cell flow back passively and no external work is performed. This means that at least all of the power of the Na, K-pump should be converted to heat in the steady state.

The heat liberated during ATP hydrolysis must of course also include the entropy change $T\Delta S$ of the reaction and is given by

(10) $$\Delta H_{ATP} = \Delta G_{ATP} + T\Delta S_{ATP}.$$

However, in the steady state ATP is continuously resynthesized (and ΔH_{ATP} is restored) at the expense of oxidation of carbohydrates and fat. For example, the oxidation of glucose yields 38 (or 36) molecules ATP per molecule of glucose. The molar free energy of glucose oxidation is about −2790 kJ/mol at physiological concentrations of all substrates and products (MONTGOMERY and SWENSON, 1976). Thus, the free energy available for synthesis of 1 mol ATP from ADP and P_i is only about 73 kJ. This means that the thermodynamic efficiency of ATP synthesis ($\Delta G_{ATP}/(\Delta G_{glucose} : 38)$) is about 0.82 (assuming a ΔG_{ATP} of −60 kJ/mol). This includes glycolysis, the respiratory chain, ATP synthesis through the F_0F_1-ATPase, ATP/ADP-exchange through the ATP translocase, etc. All of these processes must therefore be energetically very efficient (see Fig. 1). Only 18 % of the free energy is degraded to heat during oxidative phosphorylation.

In the steady state the heat production due to the Na, K-pump should depend on the enthalpy change of glucose per mole of ATP synthesized (ΔH_p). This is about −72 kJ/mol ATP, i. e. the amount of heat released is a little less than $\Delta G_{glucose} : 38$. This is so because the entropy change of glucose oxidation is positive (heat is being absorbed) but very small compared to $\Delta G_{glucose}$. The enthalpy change per mole of ATP synthesized is nearly the same for oxidation of either carbohydrates or fat (CHAPMAN, 1974; 1983; CHAPMAN and GIBBS, 1974). Thus, the rate of heat production due to the activity of the Na, K-ATPase (Q) should be given by the equation

(11) $$Q = \Delta H_p \cdot N_{ATP} = P \cdot \Delta H_p/W_p.$$

From the data presented above, the rate of heat production due to the Na, K-pump is calculated to be 4.3 mW/g.

Myothermic measurements suggest that the resting heat rate in mammalian ventricular muscle is between 7 and 12 mW/g (LOISELLE and GIBBS, 1979). For guinea-pig ventricular muscle an estimate of 12 mW/g at 37 °C was given by LOISELLE and GIBBS (1979, their table 3). This implies that the Na, K-pump may contribute about 30–40 % to the resting heat production of guinea-pig ventricular muscle. Previous estimates, which were based on measurements with radioactively labelled Na (LANGER, 1967), suggested that the contribution of the Na, K-pump to the basal metabolism of mammalian cardiac muscle can only account for 7–10 % of the observed resting heat rate (GIBBS and CHAPMAN, 1979; LOISELLE and GIBBS, 1983). The main reason for this discrepancy is that the rate constant of the exchange of intracellular Na may have been markedly underestimated in the radioactive tracer studies (see DAUT, 1982 b, 1986). In this context it is interesting to note that reduction of extracellular Na, which reduces the turnover rate of the Na, K-pump (DAUT, 1983), also markedly reduces the oxygen consumption of the resting heart (LOCHNER and DUDZIAK, 1965).

The energy consumption of the Na, K-pump increases with the Na-load imposed in the cells, i. e. with stimulation frequency (COHEN et al., 1982). GIBBS and CHAPMAN (1979) estimate an energy expenditure of active Na transport of 1–2 mJ/g per beat. This means that at physiological frequencies of guinea-pig heart (280 min^{-1}) the energy expenditure of the Na, K-pump may be about twice as large as at rest and may contribute 10–20 % to the active myocardial metabolism (comp. LOISELLE and GIBBS, 1979, Table 3; ELZINGA and WESTERHOF, 1980). If the rate of Na, K-exchange in the human heart is similar to that found in guinea-pig heart, the myocardial Na, K-ATPase may require about 3 ml O_2/min in the arrested human heart (≈ 1 W) and 4–5 ml O_2/min in the healthy human subject at rest.

Acknowledgements

I thank Prof. J. DUDEL for help and advice and for reading the manuscript. The assistance of Mrs. E. BLOB and Ms. S. HARTMANN is gratefully acknowledged. The liquid ion exchanger ETH 227 was a generous gift of Prof. W. SIMON, Zürich. Supported by the Deutsche Forschungsgemeinschaft.

References

Abercrombie, R. F., DeWeer, P.: Electric current generated by squid axon sodium pump: external K and internal ADP effects. Am. J. Physiol. **235**: C 63–C 68 (1978).

Bers, D. M., Ellis, D.: Intracellular calcium and sodium activity in sheep heart Purkinje fibres. Effect of changes of external sodium and intracellular pH. Pflügers Arch. **393**: 171–178 (1982).

Chapman, J. B.: Energy sources of cardiac contraction. Advanc. Cardiol. **12**: 128–138 (1974).

Chapman, J. B.: Heat production. In: Drake-Holland A. J. and Noble M. I. M. (eds.) Cardiac Metabolism. Wiley, New York p. 239–256 (1983).

Chapman, J. B., Gibbs, C. L.: The effect of metabolic substrate on mechanical activity and heat production in papillary muscle. Cardiovasc. Res. **8**: 656–667 (1974).

Chapman, J. B., Johnson, E. A.: The reversal potential for an electrogenic sodium pump. A method for determining the free energy of ATP breakdown? J. gen. Physiol. **72**: 403–408 (1978).

Chapman, J. B., Gibbs, C. L., Loiselle, D. S.: Myothermic, polarographic and fluorometric data from mammalian muscles. Correlations and an approach to biochemical synthesis. Fedn. Proc. **41**: 176–184 (1982).

Cohen, C. J., Fozzard, H. A., Sheu, S.: Increase in intracellular sodium ion activity during stimulation in mammalian cardiac muscle. Circ. Res. **50**: 651–662 (1982).

Coulson, R. L.: Energetics of isovolumic contractions of the isolated rabbit heart. J. Physiol. **260**: 45–53 (1976).

Dagostino, M. and Lee, C. O.: Neutral carrier Na^+- and Ca^{2+}-selective microelectrodes for intracellular application. Biophys. J. **40**: 199–207 (1982).

Daut, J.: The passive electrical properties of guinea-pig ventricular muscle as examined with a voltage-clamp technique. J. Physiol. **330:** 221–242 (1982 a).

Daut, J.: The role of intracellular sodium ions in the regulation of cardiac contractility. J. mol. cell Cardiol. **14:** 189–192 (1982 b).

Daut, J.: Inhibition of the sodium pump in guinea-pig ventricular muscle by dihydro-ouabain: effects of external potassium and sodium. J. Physiol. **339:** 643–662 (1983).

Daut, J.: Cardiac glycosides and intracellular calcium in mammalian cardiac muscle. In: Intracellular Calcium Regulation (ed. Bader, H., Gietzen, K. et al.), Manchester Univ. Press, Manchester U.K. (1986).

Daut, J., Rüdel, R.: Cardiac glycoside binding to the Na/R-ATPase in the intact myocardial cell: electrophysiological measurements of chemical kinetics. J. molec. cell Cardiol. **13:** 777–782 (1981).

Daut, J., Rüdel, R.: The electrogenic sodium pump in guinea-pig ventricular muscle: inhibition of pump current by cardiac glycosides. J. Physiol. **330:** 243–264 (1982).

Dawson, M. J.: in: Cardiac Metabolism (ed. Drake-Holland A. and Noble, M. I. M.), Wiley, Chichester (1983).

DeWeer, P.: Electrogenic pumps: theoretical and practical considerations. In: Blaustein, M. P. and Lieberman, M. (eds.) Electrogenetic Transport – Fundamental Principles and Physiological Implications. Raven Press, New York (1984).

DeWeer, P.: Cellular sodium–potassium transport. In: The Kidney: Physiology and Pathophysiology (ed. Seldin, D. W. and Giebisch, G.) pp. 31–48. Raven Press, New York (1985).

Eisner, D. A., Lederer, W. J., Vaughan-Jones, R. D.: The dependence of sodium pumping and tension on intracellular sodium ion activity in voltage-clamped sheep Purkinje fibres. J. Physiol. **327:** 163–187 (1981).

Ellis, D.: The effects of external cations and ouabain on the intracellular sodium activity in sheep heart Purkinje fibres. J. Physiol. **273:** 211–240 (1977).

Elzinga, G., Westerhof, N.: Pump function of the feline left heart: changes with heart rate and its bearing on the energy balance. Cardiovasc. Res. **14:** 81–92 (1980).

Gibbs, C. L.: Cardiac energetics. In: Langer, G. A. and Brady, A. J. (eds.) The Mammalian Myocardium. Wiley, New York, p. 105–133 (1974).

Gibbs, C. L.: Cardiac energetics. Physiol. Rev. **58:** 174–254 (1978).

Gibbs, C. L.: Modification of the physiological determinants of cardiac energy expenditure by pharmacological agents. Pharmacol. Therap. **18:** 133–159 (1982).

Gibbs, C. L., Chapman, J. B.: Cardiac energetics. In: Berne, R. M. (ed.) Handbook of Physiology, Section 2. The cardiovascular system, Vol. I. American Physiological Society, Bethesda, p. 775–804 (1979).

Glitsch, H. G., Kampmann, W., Pusch, H.: Activation of active Na transport in sheep Purkinje fibres by external K or Rb ions. Pflügers Arch. **391:** 28–34 (1981).

Kammermeier, H., Schmidt, P., Jüngling, E.: Free energy change of ATP-hydrolysis: a causal factor of early hypoxic failure of the myocardium? J. mol. cell Cardiol. **14:** 267–277 (1982).

Langer, G. A.: Sodium exchange in dog ventricular muscle. Relation to frequency of contration and its possible role in the control of myocardial contractility. J. gen. Physiol. **50:** 1221–1239 (1967).

Lee, C. O.: Ionic activities in cardiac muscle cells and application of ion-selective microelectrodes. Am. J. Physiol. **10:** H 459–H 478 (1981).

Lochner, W., Dudziak, R.: Stillstandsumsatz und Ruheumsatz des Herzens. Pflügers Arch. **285:** 169–177 (1965).

Loiselle, D. S., Gibbs, C. L.: Species differences in cardiac energetics. Am. J. Physiol. **237:** H 90–H 98 (1979).

Loiselle, D. S., Gibbs, C. L.: Factors affecting the metabolism of resting rabbit papillary muscle. Pflügers Arch. **396:** 285–291 (1983).

Marban, E., Rink, T. J., Tsien, R. W., Tsien, R. Y.: Free calcium in heart muscle at rest and during contraction measured with Ca^{2+}-sensitive microelectrodes. Nature **286:** 845–850 (1980).

Meyer, R. A., Kushmerick, M. J., Brown, T. R.: Application of ^{31}P-NMR spectroscopy to the study of striated muscle metabolism. Am. J. Physiol. **242:** C 1–C 11 (1982).

Mommaerts, W. F. H. M.: Energetics of muscular contraction. Physiol. Rev. **49:** 427–508 (1969).
Montgomery, R. and Swenson, C. A.: Quantitative Problems in Biochemical Sciences (2nd edition), Freeman, W. H., San Francisco (1970).
Sheu, S. S., Fozzard, H.: Transmembrane Na^+ and Ca^{2+} electrochemical gradients in cardiac muscle and their relationship to force development. J. gen. Physiol. **80:** 325–351 (1982).
Sperelakis, N.: Origin of the cardiac resting potential. In: Berne, R. M. (ed.) Handbook of Physiology, Section 2. The cardiovascular system, Vol. I. American Physiological Society. Bethesda, p. 187–268 (1979).
Steiner, R. A., Oehme, M., Ammann, D., Simon, W.: Neutral carrier sodium ion-selective microelectrode for intracellular studies. Anal. Chem. **51:** 351–353 (1979).
Tanford, C.: Equilibrium state of ATP-driven ion pumps in relation to physiological ion concentration gradients. J. gen. Physiol. **77:** 223–229 (1981).
Tanford, C.: Mechanism of active transport – free energy dissipation and free e nergy transduction. Proc. natn. Acad. Sci. USA **79:** 6527–6531 (1982).
Tanford, C.: Mechanism of free energy coupling in active transport. Ann. Rev. Biochem. 52, 379–409 (1983).
Taylor, P. S. and Thomas, R. C.: Effect of leakage on micro-electrode measurements in intracellular sodium activity in crab muscle fibres. J. Physiol. **352:** 539–550 (1984).
Thomas, R. C.: Ion-sensitive micro-electrodes. Academic Press, New York and London (1978).
Veech, R. L., Lawson, J. W. R., Cornell, N. W., Krebs, H. A.: Cytosolic phosphorylation potential. J. Biol. Chem. **254:** 6538–6547 (1979).

Fortschritte der Zoologie, Band 33 · Lüttgau (Hrsg.): Membrane Control
Gustav Fischer Verlag · Stuttgart · New York · 1986

Membrane potential modulates the rate of the Na^+/K^+ pump and not the number of pumping molecules

W. Schwarz and A. V. Lafaire

Max-Planck-Institut für Biophysik, D-6000 Frankfurt/M-71, FRG

Under physiological conditions the Na^+/K^+-ATPase maintains the electrochemical gradients for Na^+ and K^+ by pumping per pump cycle three Na ions out of the cell but only two K ions into the cell. This imbalance of ion transfer leads to an outwardly directed net movement of cations. Hence, stimulation of the Na^+/K^+-ATPase results in a hyperpolarizing contribution to the membrane potential. Conversely, the rate of transport of the Na^+/K^+ pump should depend on membrane potential, but the question has been raised whether this potential dependence plays a detectable role within the physiological range. In several investigations the potential dependence has only been studied for a limited potential range and no clear decision was possible. Recently, voltage dependence of the current generated by the pump has clearly been demonstrated for a potential range of more than 200 mV in heart cells (Gadsby et al., 1985) and in oocytes of *Xenopus laevis* (Lafaire and Schwarz, 1984); according to these experiments, the pump current increases with depolarization and leads to saturation or even to a maximum at positive membrane potentials.

In a recent publication it was reported that repetitive stimulation of nerve bundles leads to stimulation-dependent activation of the Na^+/K^+-pump and stimulation-dependent ouabain binding (Maximov and Kols, 1985). This was interpreted by a stimulation-dependent number of active molecules of the Na^+/K^+-ATPase in a manner that increasing rate of stimulation up to 10 or 100 Hz (depending on the preparation) increases the number of pumping molecules that are sensitive to ouabain. Since increasing rate of stimulation produces an increased averaged time of depolarized membrane potential, we asked the question whether the voltage dependence of the pump current as seen in voltage-clamp experiments is indeed due to a voltage dependence of the rate of transport of the pumping molecules or whether the number of pumping molecules is modulated.

The answer to this question would be of extreme importance for the interpretation of current-voltage relations of the Na^+/K^+-ATPase in terms of possible reaction schemes. In this contribution, we performed measurements of ouabain binding, of membrane potential and of the current generated by the Na^+/K^+-ATPase to answer this question.

Methods

Prophase-arrested, full grown oocytes of the clawed toad *Xenopus laevis* were obtained and voltage-clamped as described previously (Jung et al., 1984). The bath solution contained (in mmol/l) 88 NaCl, 0.41 $CaCl_2$, 0.33 $Ca(NO_3)_2$, 0.82 $MgSO_4$, 2.4 $NaHCO_3$, 3

KCl; the pH was buffered to 7.6 by 5 mmol/l N-2-hydroxyl-ethylpiperazin-N'-ethansulfonic acid. The experiments were performed on oocytes that had been preincubated in K^+-free medium for several hours. This treatment reversibly blocks the Na^+/K^+ pump and leads to an increase of intracellular Na^+. Under these conditions of elevated intracellular Na^+ and of the 3 mmol/l K^+ in the bath solution the pump is maximally stimulated (Lafaire and Schwarz, 1986). The experiments described in the following have exclusively been performed under these optimized conditions.

For the determination of ouabain binding, three oocytes that had been exposed under voltage-clamp conditions to 3 μmol/l ^{3}H-ouabain (from Amersham) were washed in ouabain-free and K^+-free bath solution and were collected in a vial for scintillation counting.

Results

The current generated by the Na^+/K^+-ATPase can be determined as the difference of total membrane current with stimulated and inhibited Na^+/K^+-ATPase. For inhibition of the Na^+/K^+-ATPase, we used 10 μmol/l ouabain or dihydroouabain (DHO) which was added to the bath solution. Application of the inhibitors depolarizes the membrane potential because the hyperpolarizing contribution of the Na^+/K^+-ATPase ceases. Figure 1 A demonstrates the complete reversibility of inhibition of the Na^+/K^+ pump by DHO. The effect of ouabain, on the other hand, is only partially reversible (Fig. 2), and even after allowing recovery in ouabain-free solution for 50 min, the membrane potential asymptotically regains only 50 % of its original level. The time course of this partial recovery from inhibition by ouabain is similar to the time course of full recovery from inhibition by DHO. The binding of ouabain to the oocytes was usually assumed to be nearly irreversible (Richter et al., 1984). The partial reversibility in our experiments is probably due to the elevated K^+ concentration in the bath solution. If oocytes that have bound ^{3}H-ouabain were washed in K^+-free medium, no release of ouabain was detected even after 6 hours of incubation (Beckers, pers. communication).

To determine the voltage dependence of the current generated by the Na^+/K^+-ATPase, current-voltage curves were determined under the conditions of stimulated activity of the Na^+/K^+-ATPase and with the pump inhibited. Figure 1 B shows the voltage dependencies of total membrane current obtained under the conditions indicated in Figure 1 A. The voltage dependence of the difference current which represents the current generated by the Na^+/K^+ pump is shown in Figure 1 C. Its characteristics are that the pump current increases with increasing depolarization and shows a maximum at about +20 mV (see also Lafaire and Schwarz, 1984, 1985, 1986).

We now wanted to answer the question whether the depolarization increases the number of active pump molecules or the rate of transport of the pumping molecules. For this reason, we blocked the operating pump molecules and tried to determine whether depolarization in the absence of excessive ouabain can lead to an additional electrogenic contribution to the membrane potential. The result is shown in Figure 3 A. In this experiment, 10 μmol/l ouabain was applied for 10 min to completely inhibit the Na^+/K^+ pump while the membrane potential is clamped to its resting level of –85 mV. After removal of the excessive ouabain from the bath solution, the voltage clamp is turned off. The membrane potential now depolarizes to –52 mV because of the inhibited electrogenic Na^+/K^+-ATPase. Since the inhibition by ouabain is partially reversible, the membrane potential partially hyperpolarizes. If ouabain is once more applied when the membrane potential is at about –60 mV, the potential again depolarizes to the level of –52 mV. This demons-

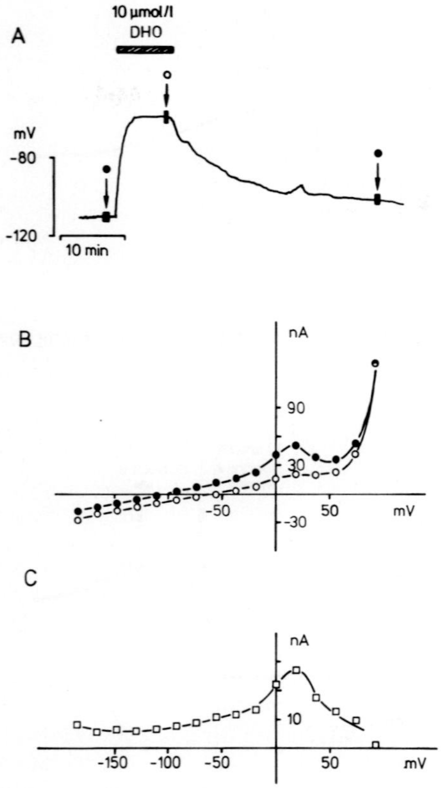

Fig. 1: (a) Reversible depolarization of the membrane resting potential by 10 μmol/l DHO in the bath solution (Exp. IV 20 D, E, F).
(b) Dependence of the steady-state membrane current on the amplitude of test pulses applied from the resting potential under the conditions indicated in (a).
(c) Voltage dependence of the current generated by the Na^+/K^+-ATPase determined as the difference of the currents shown in (b).

trates that the depolarization from –85 mV has not activated further electrogenic pump molecules that can be inhibited by ouabain. In addition to these potential measurements, we recorded current-voltage curves (Fig. 3 B) under the conditions indicated in Figure 3 A. The difference between curve I and III represents the current of the pump molecules that were active at –85 mV; these molecules are inhibited by the first application of ouabain. Pump molecules that could have been activated by the depolarization are inhibited by the second application of ouabain. On the other hand, the difference between curve I and II represents the current produced by the pump molecules that were active at –85 mV minus the current produced by those molecules that have possibly been activated by the depolarization or stimulation. The two difference curves (I–III and I–II) are plotted in Figure 3 C. They coincide and hence indicate that neither the depolarization nor the stimulation by the voltage-clamp pulses activate further pump molecules.

To further support the assumption that the rate of transport of the pump molecules is

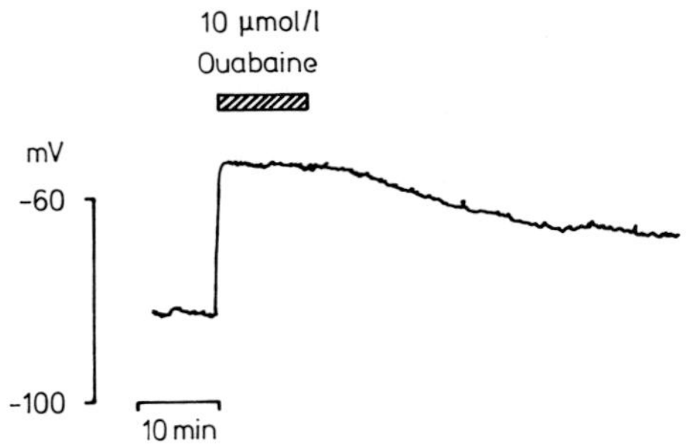

Fig. 2: Partial reversibility of the depolarization of the membrane resting potential after application of 10 μmol/l ouabain (Exp. 061 185).

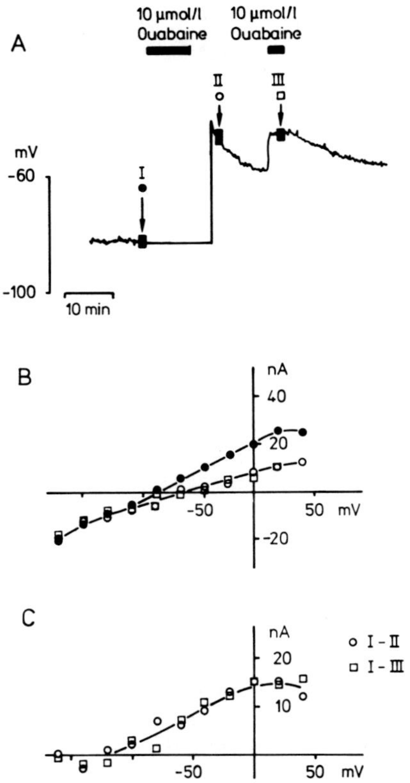

Fig. 3: (a) Depolarization of the membrane potential by repeated application of 10 μmol/l ouabain under voltage clamp and after the voltage clamp is turned off (Exp. 111 185).
(b) Dependence of the steady-state membrane current on the amplitude of test pulses applied from the resting potential under the conditions indicated in (a).
(c) Voltage dependence of the current sensitive to ouabain determined as the difference of the currents shown in (b).

modulated by the membrane potential rather than the number of active pump molecules, we tried to determine whether stimulation to +20 mV increases the number of active pump molecules that can bind ouabain. We, therefore, measured the binding of ^{3}H-ouabaine to the oocytes under the following conditions: First, the membrane potential was clamped to the resting potential (–60 to –70 mV) while 3 μmol/l ^{3}H-ouabain was applied for 5 min. Under these conditions, we obtained an average of bound ouabain of 9.1 ± 1.1 (n = 10) fmol/oocyte. And second, oocytes were exposed to ^{3}H-ouabain while potential pulses to +20 mV were applied from the holding potential of –60 to –70 mV for 5 min. The pulses had the same duration of 500 ms as for the determination of the current-voltage curves and were applied every 2 s. Under these conditions, the amount of bound ouabain was 9.5 ± 0.4 (n = 15) fmol/oocyte and hence nearly identical to the value obtained without stimulation.

Discussion

The transport of Na^+ and K^+ by the Na^+/K^+-ATPase can be regulated by alteration of the number of transporting molecules of the ATPase (see KARIN and COOK, 1983) or by alteration of the rate of a fixed number of ATPase molecules in the membrane; the latter involves alterations of pump activity e. g. by the substrate concentrations (for review see DEWEER, 1985). The voltage dependence of the current generated by the Na^+/K^+-ATPase has also been interpreted in terms of alterations of transport activity (see e. g. LÄUGER and APELL, 1986, DEWEER, this volume). Changes of the number of transporting molecules is a slow process that can be expected to depend e. g. on biosynthesis or degradation of the enzyme. Hence, modulation of the number of molecules during voltage-clamp pulses seems unlikely. On the other hand, the observations by MAXIMOV and KOLS (1985) suggest changes in the number of ^{3}H-ouabain-binding sites during rhythmic exitation; increasing rate of stimulation up to 10 or 100 Hz increases the number of ouabain-binding sites, higher frequencies are inhibitory. This dependence on the frequency of stimulation resembles our observations of voltage-dependent pump current in the oocytes with the maximum at +20 mV.

If the increase of pump current at +20 mV were due to an increase in the number of ouabain binding sites, the amount of specifically bound ^{3}H-ouabain should approximately be doubled (compare Fig. 1 C, 3 C). But we found that the voltage-clamp pulses that produce maximum pump current do not affect the number of binding sites for ouabain in the oocytes in contrast to the high stimulation rates in nerve bundles. In addition, if all Na^+/K^+-ATPase molecules are inhibited by ouabain at the resting potential of –85 mV, depolarization does not lead to activation of further enzyme molecules. Inhibition of such molecules by additional ouabain should produce further depolarization, but we were not able to detect such further depolarization (Fig. 3 A). Neither, the depolarization to –50 mV nor the voltage-clamp pulses can stimulate an additional current that is sensitive to ouabain, as is demonstrated by Figure 3 C.

The results presented above demonstrate quite convincingly that the changes of pump current by the membrane potential were due to alterations of the activity of the individual enzyme molecules.

Acknowledgement

We thank Dr. H. PASSOW for his comments on the manuscript.

References

DeWeer, P. (1985): Cellular sodium-potassium transport. In: The Kidney: Physiology and Pathophysiology (eds. Seldin, D. W. and Giebisch, G.) Raven Press, New York.

Gadsby, D. C., Kimura, J., Noma, A. (1985): Voltage dependence of the Na/K pump current in isolated heart cells. Nature **315:** 63–65.

Jung, D., Lafaire, A. V., Schwarz, W. (1984): Inhibition of Na-alanine cotransport in oocytes of *Xenopus laevis* during meiotic maturation is voltage-regulated. Pflügers Arch. **402:** 39–41.

Karin, N. J., Cook, J. S. (1983): Regulation of Na, K-ATPase by its biosynthesis and turnover. Curr. Top. Membr. Transp. **19:** 713–751.

Lafaire, A. V., Schwarz, W. (1984): The electrogenic Na/K-ATPase in the membrane of *Xenopus laevis* oocytes. Pflügers Arch. **400: (Suppl.):** R 26.

Lafaire, A. V., Schwarz, W. (1985): Voltage-dependent, ouabain-sensitive current in the membrane of oocytes of *Xenopus laevis*. In: The sodium pump pp. 523–525 (eds. Glynn and Ellory) The Company of Biologists Ltd., Cambridge.

Lafaire, A. V., Schwarz, W. (1986): The voltage dependence of the reogenic Na^+/K^+-ATPase in the membrane of oocytes of *Xenopus laevis*. J. Membrane Biol. **91:** 43–51.

Läuger, P., Apell, H.-J. (1986): A microscopic model for the current-voltage behaviour of the Na, K pump. European Biophys. Journal **13:** 209–321.

Maximov, G. V., Kols, O. R. (1985): Mechanism of activation of Na, K-ATPase in nerve fibres during rhythmic excitation. Gen. Physiol. Biophys. **4:** 279–285.

Richter, H.-P., Jung, D., Passow, H. (1984): Regulatory changes of membrane transport and ouabain binding during progesterone-induced maturation of *Xenopus* oocytes. J. Membrane Biol. **79:** 203–210.

Fortschritte der Zoologie, Band 33 · Lüttgau (Hrsg.): Membrane Control
Gustav Fischer Verlag · Stuttgart · New York · 1986

The human red blood cell calcium pump

H. J. SCHATZMANN

Dept. of Veterinary Pharmacology, University of Bern, Switzerland

It stands to reason that the low free cytosolic Ca^{2+} concentration of $\sim 10^{-7}$ M found in all animal cells must be the consequence of Ca^{2+} extruding mechanisms at the surface membrane and cannot be explained by Ca^{2+} accumulating organelles within the cell, however effective these may be in removing rapidly Ca^{2+} loads that occur discontinuously. These extrusion mechanisms are the Na^+–Ca^{2+}-exchange system (REUTER, 1982) and the ATP-driven Ca^{2+}-pump (SCHATZMANN, 1983). When the available information on different cells is scrutinized one gains the impression that the pump is the more universal solution nature has contrived for Ca^{2+} extrusion (MARTONOSI, 1983; SCHATZMANN, 1985) and the question may be asked why some, if not all, cells sport two different means to what seems the same end.

The surface membrane Ca-pump has reasonably well been studied in red cells, the obvious reason being that these are very nearly a natural preparation of pure surface membranes. However, there is no doubt that very many complete cells do have it, too. For cardiac muscle (TRUMBLE et al., 1980; CARONI and CARAFOLI, 1980, 1981; LAMERS and STINIS, 1981) and smooth muscle (MOREL et al., 1981; WUYTACK et al., 1981, 1983) it is well documented. In skeletal muscle its demonstration seems fraught with difficulties. As in other cells, there is a considerable Ca^{2+}-influx, particularly during excitation and the pump and/or the Na^+–Ca^{2+}-exchange system obviously cope with this Ca^{2+} entry. The transverse tubular membrane extrudes in an ATP-dependent manner Ca^{2+} against the existing gradient (BRANDT et al., 1980; HIDALGO et al., 1986), but the underlying (Ca^{2+} + Mg^{2+})-ATPase seems difficult to track down (MARTONOSI, 1983; SABBADINI and OKAMOTO, 1983). In addition, the problem seems quite real as how to explain that the surface membrane pump, if it exists, does not compete with that of the sarcoplasmic reticulum, thus rapidly depleting the whole muscle fibre of its Ca^{2+} and, therefore, jeopardizing the well known self-sufficiency of striated muscle with respect to Ca^{2+}. How is it that even a quick muscle can twitch in Ca^{2+}-free solution for half an hour?

1. The red cell Ca-pump

The surface membrane Ca-pump has been reviewed several times in recent years with due emphasis on findings made on erythrocytes (SCHATZMANN, 1982, 1983, 1985; CARAFOLI and ZURINI, 1982; PENNISTON, 1983; AL-JOBORE et al., 1984; REGA and GARAHAN, 1986). In the latter it can be studied in intact cells, resealed cells, inside-out vesicles made artificially from the cell membranes or, if one is content to look only at the enzymic function which is Ca^{2+} + Mg^{2+}-dependent ATP hydrolysis, also in isolated disrupted membranes. The protein has been obtained in highly pure form coated with phospholipids (Carafoli and Niggli, 1981; Niggli et al., 1979; Gietzen et al., 1980) and so far the experiments on the purified preparation vastly confirm what was originally found in the intact system. The purified protein is very labile, but despite the fact that a high percentage of non-functional pumps are present in the preparation it was possible to demonstrate that the protein, upon incorporation into liposomes, indeed does transport Ca^{2+} against the gradient (Carafoli and Niggli, 1981; Gietzen et al., 1980; Haaker and Racker, 1979; Stieger, 1982). It is similar in performance to the sarcoplasmic reticulum (SR) Ca-pump, but not identical with it. The most salient property not shared by the SR is the susceptibility to calmodulin (see below).

1.1. Properties

The monomeric mol. weight of the protein is ~ 140 000. In the native membrane it behaves as a functional dimer (Cavieres, 1984; Minocherhomjee et al., 1983; Hymel et al., 1985). There is precious little of it in the membrane: It amounts to only about 0.1–0.2 % of the membrane proteins which constitute in turn about 0.5 % of the cell weight.

In the presence of calmodulin the properties of the red cell protein are briefly as follows. The pump transports, apparently, the equivalent of the passive Ca^{2+} influx which is some 50 μmoles/l cell · h, and it does so at a Ca_i^{2+} concentration of $\leqq 3 \cdot 10^{-8}$ M (Lew et al., 1982) and thus against a gradient of ~ 40 000 (Ca^{2+} concentration in blood plasma 1.3 mM). For this only a minor fraction of its capacity is used: at saturating $[Ca^{2+}]_i$ ($\geqq 10\ \mu M$) the rate is 10–20 mmoles/l cell · h. This corresponds to a turnover of some thousands per minute. The affinity for Ca^{2+} is high on the inside ($K_{Ca_i} \leqq 1\ \mu M$, which rises with decreasing pH) and low on the outside of the membrane ($K_{Ca_o} \sim 10$ mM) (Kratje et al., 1985). There is good evidence that more than one Ca^{2+} ion is involved in the performance (Ferreira and Lew, 1976) (the Hill coefficient found by different authors is $1 < n < 2$ (Scharff, 1978; Schatzmann and Roelofsen, 1977)). This does, however, not mean that two g-atoms of Ca^{2+} ions are transported per cycle (per 1 mole of ATP hydrolysed). Direct measurements of the stoichiometry at or near level flow resulted in a ratio of 1 Ca^{2+} : 1 ATP (Schatzmann and Roelofsen, 1977). In point of fact, a stoichiometry of 2 Ca^{2+} : 1 ATP is thermodynamically impossible, if one accepts for $[Ca^{2+}]_i$ the figure of $3 \cdot 10^{-8}$ M (Lew et al., 1982), particularly in view of the maximal efficiency being somewhere near 50% (Wüthrich, unpublished).

The system hydrolyzes ATP in most experiments at the rate of Ca^{2+} transport (1 Ca : 1 ATP). There are two sites for ATP. The enzymic site proper has a K_{m_1} of 2–3 μM. With this site alone the system operates at about one tenth of the rate at high ATP concentrations. In addition there is a «regulatory» site with a K_{m_2} of 100–300 μM whose occupancy steps up the maximal rate (Richards et al., 1978).

An important point is the requirement for Mg^{2+} ions. In our experiments K_{Mg} was ~ 15 μM (Schatzmann, 1982). This must not be confused with the possible requirement for Mg–ATP rather than free ATP at either ATP site (the high affinity site certainly also admits free ATP or even Ca–ATP since phosphorylation proceeds to similar levels with an without Mg^{2+}). In cases of a Ca-pump allegedly not requiring Mg^{2+} one must suspect, unless demonstrated otherwise, that the affinity for Mg^{2+} is so high that Mg^{2+} impurities of the preparation (by «bound» Mg^{2+}) suffice to give optimal performance, as is true e. g. in hepatocyte membranes (Lotersztajn et al., 1981; Pecker and Lotersztajn, 1985).

The specificity for metal ions is high: the only other divalent cation transported is Sr^{2+}. The recent finding by SIMONS (1984) that red cells are able to extrude lead from their interior and that this transport is inhibited by Ca^{2+} opens up the possibility that Pb^{2+} is also accepted by the Ca-pump.

It is quite certain that the system does not exchange Ca^{2+} for another cation (in particular Na^+, K^+ and Mg^{2+} can be ruled out). Nor does Ca^{2+} pass the system as an ion pair (e. g. with Cl^-) (ROSSI and SCHATZMANN, 1982). Yet there is fairly good evidence that an exchange for protons takes place, i. e. that the mobile Ca^{2+} site returns in protonated form to the interior side of the membrane (SMALLWOOD et al., 1983). The evidence is that after blockade of the anion transporter in band III with DIDS (4,4′-diisothiocyano-2,2′ disulfonic acid stilbene), anions that pass the membrane in undissociated form (acetate) stimulate Ca^{2+} transport, whereas those that pass in ionized form (like thiocyanate) do not. The former are able to dissipate a proton gradient (created by the Ca-pump), whereas the latter will short-circuit a potential gradient. The experiments are, however, not sufficient to allow a decision as to whether the pump really is electroneutral, which would require 2 H^+ for 1 Ca^{2+} transported. In accord with the Ca^{2+} – n H^+ exchange hypothesis there is some sort of antagonism between Ca^{2+} and H^+ at the external surface (where Ca^{2+} is inhibitory in the 10 mM range) and apparently competitive antagonism at the internal surface of the membrane (where Ca^{2+} is stimulating in the 0.1–10 μM range) (LUTERBACHER, unpublished). However, the kinetics at the internal surface are complicated in that Ca^{2+} is more cooperative at high pH than at low pH (LUTERBACHER, unpublished), as was also observed in the SR Ca-pump.

1.2. The reaction cycle

The reaction cycle is remarkably similar to that of the sarcoplasmic reticulum Ca-pump and the Na–K-pump. Much as in the latter two systems, ATP hydrolysis proceeds under transient phosphorylation of the protein and the phosphoprotein exists in two different consecutive conformations (E_1, E_2) (see fig. 1). The phosphoryl bond is at an acyl group (it is acid stable and can be decomposed by hydroxylamine). Phosphorylation requires Ca^{2+} only. The E_1–P → E_2–P conformational change is accelerated by Mg^{2+} ions and dephosphorylation of E_2–P is greatly accelerated by high (> 100 μM) ATP (GARRAHAN and REGA, 1978) possibly as Mg–ATP. Thus all the observations on ligands made on th overall reaction find a plausible explanation in the study of partial reactions. It is not decided yet whether the $E_1 \rightarrow E_2$ reaction also requires Mg^{2+}. At any rate, the fact that Mg^{2+} accelerates phosphorylation, without altering the steady state amount of phosphoprotein very much, makes it probable that reaction II (fig. 1) is not the only step influenced by Mg^{2+} (LAROCCA et al., 1981). The scheme of fig. 1 simplifies matters: It does not show that there is ATP binding before formation of the covalent phosphate bond, that Ca^{2+} and ATP are likely to bind in random sequence, and that very probably an ionic P-bond is formed before phosphate leaves the system (at the inside of the membrane). In addition it is quite possible that there are more conformational forms than E_1 and E_2, but it seems fastidious at the present time to refuse the idea that Ca^{2+} is translocated across the membrane during the reaction $E_1P \rightarrow E_2P$.

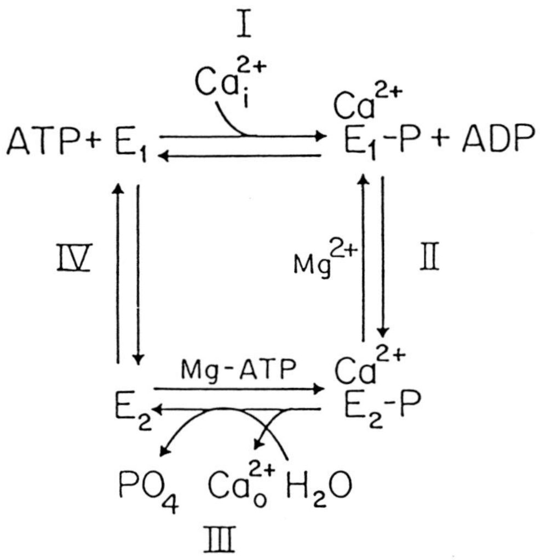

Fig. 1: Reaction cycle of the Ca-pump. The cycle starts at the upper left-hand corner and runs in clockwise direction. E_1 and E_2 designate two conformations of the protein, E_1–P and E_2–P are phosphorylated forms of the protein. Ca^{2+} is translocated across the membrane during reaction II. Reaction II requires Mg^{2+}, reaction III high concentration of ATP (or MgATP). Alkali cations accelerate a step beyond phosphorylation.

1.3. The action of calmodulin

Calmodulin, the soluble intracellular protein of 16700 mol. weight with four metal binding sites that mediates a host of Ca^{2+} actions within all cells, also stimulates the surface membrane Ca-pump (GOPINATH and VINCENZI, 1977; JARRETT and PENNISTON, 1977). When several of the metal binding sites are occupied by Ca^{2+} calmodulin binds to the pump and thereby increases the Ca^{2+} affinity of the transport site by a factor of ~ 30 (FODER and SCHARFF, 1981; SCHARFF and FODER, 1982) and K_{m_2} for ATP by a factor of ~ 70 (ROSSI et al., 1985) and increases the maximal rate somewhat. With the information that the Ca^{2+} binding sites on calmodulin have a K_{Ca} ~ 1 μM, that there is 3–5 μM calmodulin in the human red cell and that Ca-calmodulin binds at a concentration for half saturation in the nanomolar range to the pump, it can be calculated that under physiological conditions ($[Ca^{2+}]_i < 0.1$ μM, $[Mg^{2+}]_i = 0.4$ mM) the calmodulin pump complex is dissociated (FODER and SCHARFF, 1981; SCHARFF and FODER, 1982). Since association of the complex is a rather slow process (SCHARFF and FODER, 1982), this has the interesting consequence that the cell responds in a hysteretic manner to an abrupt increase in Ca^{2+} permeability: The internal Ca^{2+} concentration overshoots before reaching the new steady state value (SCHARFF et al., 1983; FERREIRA and LEW, 1976). For transient increases of Ca^{2+} permeability, which occur in excitable cells, this means that the calmodulin mechanism prolongs Ca^{2+} signals which may be important for cell activating processes that have a time course being slow compared to the Ca^{2+} extrusion rate of the calmodulin associated Ca-pump.

MUALLEM and KARLISH(1980) have shown that calmodulin accelerates phosphorylation without increasing the steady state amount of the phosphoprotein. Experiments with the purified protein in the presence of Mg^{2+} show that calmodulin brings about a moderate increase (by ~ 30 %) of the steady state phosphorylation (LUTERBACHER, 1982). All this is compatible with the assumption that calmodulin accelerates the $E_1 \rightarrow E_2$ transition.

An interesting observation is that controlled tryptic digestion dispenses with the need for calmodulin: The Ca^{2+} affinity in the trypsinized preparation without calmodulin is as high as in the native preparation with calmodulin (NIGGLI et al., 1981; SARKADI et al., 1980; STIEGER and SCHATZMANN, 1981). Since SARKADI et al. (1980) have shown that the trypsinized enzyme no longer binds calmodulin, it seems likely that the C-terminal 10 kD part of the pump molecule (SARKADI et al., 1986) hinders the access of Ca^{2+} to the transport site and that calmodulin binding is able to attenuate this hindrance. The action of calmodulin is also mimicked by acidic phospholipids like phosphatidylserine instead of phosphatidylcholine.

2. General aspects

2.1. The problem of Ca^{2+} buffering with EGTA

A curious observation which awaits elucidation is that EGTA, 2,2′-ethylenedioxybis[ethyliminodi(acetic acid)], widely used to buffer Ca^{2+} concentrations, seems to increase the affinity of the Ca-pump for Ca^{2+} by a factor of 50–100 (SARKADI et al., 1979). There are three different ways of explaining this phenomenon: 1. The pump might accept the Ca-EGTA-complex instead of free Ca^{2+}. Considering the chemical potential of Ca^{2+} in CaEGTA this seems rather absurd. 2. EGTA might, by its chemical nature, influence the pump protein in the observed way. 3. EGTA might serve as a carrier for Ca^{2+}, translocating interior Ca^{2+} from the bulk fluid of the cell into a confined water space adjacent to the Ca^{2+} site on the protein. If the supposed barrier is relatively impermeable for positively charged particles the Ca^{2+} concentration in the underlying pocket might be considerably less than in the bulk fluid and could reach the latter if the uncharged Ca-EGTA complex is able to cross the barrier. This amounts to saying that the Ca^{2+} concentration which is seen by the Ca^{2+} accepting site on the pump is not what one adds to the membrane preparation. The fact that this behaviour was not observed in frozen-thawed membranes is in favour of explanation (3). If explanation (1) or (2) is correct, the observation should be a serious warning against conclusions drawn from very many experiments in biology in which Ca^{2+} was buffered with EGTA.

2.2. Interaction of Ca^{2+}-pump and Na^+–Ca^{2+}-exchange

The foregoing discussion shows that the Ca-pump is perfectly able to keep $[Ca^{2+}]_i$ at the required low value. Why is it then that some animal cells (like nerve, muscle or intestinal epithelium, but unlike human red cells) in addition are equipped with the Na^+–Ca^{2+}-exchange system which normally also removes Ca^{2+} from the cell sap? There are three answers to the question: 1. The exchange system has (e. g. in nerve) a lower affinity for Ca^{2+} than the pump but a tenfold higher maximal rate. It seems suited, therefore, to pump large amounts of Ca^{2+} at elevated internal concentration, which might be useful in strenuous nerve activity or, in the intestine, at high 1,25-dihydroxy-vitamin-D levels. 2. Should the 2 H^+ : 1 Ca^{2+} stoichiometry prove correct the pump is independent of the membrane potential whereas the exchange system is not, because of the 1 Ca^{2+} : 3 Na^+ stoichiometry. 3. The exchange is a coupling link between the Na–K-pump and the Ca-pump. If the

Na–K-pump fails, Na^+ can be removed from the cell by the energy supply from the Ca-pump and vice-versa. Dog red blood cells provide a good example for the Ca-pump taking care of Na-extrusion. They are devoid of a Na–K-pump but display a Ca-pump and the Na^+Ca^{2+}-exchange system which, even under normal conditions, cooperate in preventing the cells' Na-content and thereby their volume from going beyond bounds (Parker, 1977, 1978, 1979; Parker et al., 1975). This is a peculiar way of a cell's avoiding swelling and eventually bursting.

References

Al-Jobore, A., Minocherhomjee, A. M., Villalobo, A., Roufogalis, B. D. (1984): Active calcium transport in normal and abnormal human erythrocytes. In: Erythrocyte Membranes 3. Alan R. Liss Inc., New York, pp. 243–292.

Brandt, N. R., Caswell, A. H., Brunschwig, J. P. (1980): A energized Ca^{2+}-pump in isolated transverse tubules of skeletal muscle. J. Biol. Chem. **255,** 6290–6298.

Carafoli, E., Niggli, V. (1981): Purification and reconstitution of the calcium–magnesium adenosine–triphosphatase of the erythrocyte membrane. Ann. N. Y. Acad. Sci. **358,**159–168.

Carafoli, E., Zurini, M. (1982): The Ca^{2+} pumping ATPase of plasma membranes. Reconstitution and properties. Biochim. Biophys. Acta **683,** 279–301.

Caroni, P., Carafoli, E. (1980): An ATP-dependent Ca-pumping system in dog heart sarcolemma. Nature **283,** 765–767.

Caroni, P., Carafoli, E. (1981): The calcium pumping ATPase of heart sarcolemma. J. Biol. Chem. **256,**3267–3270.

Cavieres, J. D. (1984): Calmodulin and the target size of the (Ca^{2+} + Mg^{2+})-ATPase of human red cell ghosts. Biochim. Biophys. Acta **771,** 241–246.

Ferreira, H. G., Lew, V. L. (1976): Use of ionophore A 23 187 to measure cytoplasmic Ca buffering and activation of the Ca-pump by internal calcium. Nature **259,**47–49.

Foder, B., Scharff, O. (1981): Decrease of apparent calmodulin affinity of erythrocyte (Ca^{2+} + Mg^{2+})-ATPase at low Ca^{2+} concentration. Biochim. Biophys. Acta **649,** 367–376.

Garrahan, P. J., Rega, A. F. (1978): Activation of partial reactions of the Ca^{2+}-ATPase from human red cells by Mg^{2+} and ATP. Biochim. Biophys. Acta **513,** 59–65.

Gietzen, K., Tejcka, M., Wolf, H. U. (1980): Calmodulin affinity chromatography yields a functional purified erythrocyte (Ca^{2+} + Mg^{2+})-dependent ATPase. Biochem. J. **189,** 81–88.

Gopinath, R. M., Vincenzi, F. F. (1977): Phosphodiesterase protein activator mimics red blood cell cytoplasmic activator of (Ca^{2+} + Mg^{2+})-ATPase. Biochem. Biophys. Res. Comm. **77,** 1203–1209.

Haaker, H., Racker, E. (1979): Purification and reconstitution of Ca^{2+}-ATPase from plasma membrane of pig erythrocytes. J. Biol. Chem. **254,** 6598–6602.

Hidalgo, C., Gonzales, M. E., Garcia, A. M. (1986): Calcium transport in transverse tubuls isolated from rabbit skeletal muscle. Biochim. Biophys. Acta **854,** 279–286.

Hymel, L., Nielsen, M., Gietzen, K. (1985): Target size of human erythrocyte membrane Ca^{2+}-ATPase and Mg^{2+}-ATPase activities in the presence and absence of calmodulin. Biochim. Biophys. Acta **815,** 461–467.

Jarrett, H. W., Penniston, J. T. (1977): Partial purification of the (Ca^{2+} + Mg^{2+})-ATPase activator from human erythrocytes. Its similarity to the activator of 3′ : 5′-cyclic nucleotide phosphodiesterase. Biochem. Biophys. Res. Comm. **77,** 1210–1216.

Kratje, R. B., Garrahan, P. J., Rega, A. F. (1985): Two modes of inhibition of the Ca^{2+} pump in red cells by Ca^{2+}. Biochim. Biophys. Acta **816,** 365–378.

Lamers, J. M. J., Stinis, J. T. (1981): An electrogenic Na^+/Ca^{2+} antiporter in addition to the Ca^{2+}-pump in cardiac sarcolemma. Biochim. Biophys. Acta **640,** 521–534.

Larocca, J. N., Rega, A. F., Garrahan, P. J. (1981): Phosphorylation and dephosphorylation of the Ca^{2+}-pump of human red cells in the presence of monovalent cations. Biochim. Biophys. Acta **645,** 10–16.

Lew, V. L., Tsien, R. Y., Miner, C., Bookchin, R. M. (1982): Physiological (Ca_i^{2+}) level and pump-leak in intact red cells measured using incorporated Ca chelator. Nature **298**,478–481.

Lotersztajn, F., Hanoune, J., Pecker, F. (1981): A high affinity calcium-stimulated magnesium-dependent ATPase in rat liver plasma membranes. J. Biol. Chem. **256**, 11 209–11 215.

Luterbacher, S. (1982): Die Teilreaktionen der ATP-Spaltung durch das isolierte Protein der Ca^{2+}-Pumpe aus der Erythrocytenmembran. Thesis, University of Bern.

Martonosi, A. (1983): The regulation of cytoplasmic Ca^{2+} concentration in muscle and non-muscle cells. In: Muscle and Non-muscle Moltility, Vol. 1, pp. 233–357. Academic Press, London.

Minocherhomjee, A. M., Beauregard, G., Potier, M., Roufogalis, B. D. (1983): The molecular weight of the Ca^{2+}-transport ATPase of the human red blood cell determined by radiation inactivation. Biochem. Biophys. Res. Comm. **116**,895–900.

Morel, N., Wibo, M., Godfraind, T. (1981): A calmodulin stimulated Ca^{2+}-pump in rat aorta plasma membrane. Biochim. Biophys. Acta **644**, 82–88.

Muallem, S., Karlish, S. J. D. (1980): Regulatory interaction between calmodulin and ATP on the red blood cell Ca^{2+}-pump. Biochim. Biophys. Acta **597**,631–636.

Niggli, V., Adunyah, E. S., Carafoli, E. (1981): Acid phospholipids, unsaturated fatty acids and limited proteolysis mimic the effect of calmodulin on the purified erythrocyte Ca^{2+}-ATPase. J. Biol. Chem. **256**, 8588–8592.

Niggli, V., Penniston, J. T., Carafoli, E. (1979): Purification of the (Ca^{2+} + Mg^{2+})-ATPase from human erythrocyte membranes using a calmodulin affinity column. J. Biol. Chem. **254**, 9955–9958.

Parker, J. C. (1977): Interdependence of calcium and sodium movements in dog red blood cells. Fed. Proc. **36**,271.

Parker, J. C. (1978): Sodium and calcium movements in dog red blood cells. J. gen. Physiol. **71**, 1–17.

Parker, J. C. (1979): Active and passive calcium movements in dog red blood cells and resealed ghosts. Am. J. Physiol. **237**, C 10–C 16.

Parker, J. C., Gitelman, H. J., Glosson, P. S., Leonard, D. L. (1975): Role of calcium in volume regulation by dog red blood cells. J. Gen. Physiol. **65**, 84–96.

Pecker, F., Lotersztajn, S. (1985): Fe^{2+} and other divalent metal ions uncouple Ca^{2+} transport from (Ca^{2+} + Mg^{2+})-ATPase in rat liver plasma membranes. J. Biol. Chem. **260**, 731–735.

Penniston, J. T. (1983): Plasma membrane Ca^{2+}-ATPase as active Ca^{2+}-pumps. In: Calcium and Cell Functions Vol. IV, pp. 99–149. Academic Press, London.

Rega, A. F., Garrahan, P. J. (1986): The Ca^{2+}-pump of plasma membranes. CRC-Press Boca Raton, Florida.

Reuter, H. (1982): Na–Ca countertransport in cardiac muscle. In: Membranes and Transport (Martonosi, A., ed.), Vol. 1, pp. 623–631. Plenum Press, New York.

Richards, D. F., Rega, A. F., Garrahan, P. J. (1978): Two classes of site for ATP in the Ca^{2+}-ATPase from human red cell membranes. Biochim. Biophys. Acta **511**, 194–201.

Rossi, J. P. F. C., Rega, A. F., Garrahan, P. J. (1985): Compound 48/80 and calmodulin modify the interaction of ATP with the (Ca^{2+} + Mg^{2+})-ATPase of red cell membranes. Biochim. Biophys. Acta **816**,379–386.

Rossi, J. P. F. C., Schatzmann, H. J. (1982): Is the red cell calcium pump electrogenic? J. Physiol. **327**,1–15.

Sabbadini, R. A., Okamoto, V. R. (1983): The distribution of ATPase activities in purified transverse tubular membranes. Arch. Biochem. Biophys. **223**, 107–119.

Sarkadi, B., Enyedi, A., Gardos, G. (1980): Molecular properties of the red cell calcium pump I/II. Cell Calcium **1**, 287–310.

Sarkadi, B., Enyedi, A., Földes-Papp, Z., Gardos, G. (1986): Molecular characterisation of the in situ red cell membrane calcium pumps by limited proteolysis: J. Biol. Chem. **261**, 9552–9557.

Sarkadi, B., Schubert, A., Gardos, G. (1979): Effects of Ca-EGTA buffers on active calcium transport in inside-out red cell membrane vesicles. Experientia **35**, 1045–1047.

Scharff, O. (1978): Stimulating effect of monovalent cations on activator-dissociated and activator-associated states of Ca^{2+}-ATPase in human erythrocytes. Biochim. Biophys. Acta **512**, 309–317.

Scharff, O., Foder, B. (1982): Rate constants for calmodulin binding to Ca^{2+}-ATPase in erythrocyte membranes. Biochim. Biophys. Acta **691**,133–143.

Scharff, O., Foder, B., Skibsted, U. (1983): Hysteretic activation of the Ca^{2+}-pump revealed by calcium transients in human red cells. Biochim. Biophys. Acta **730**, 295–305.
Schatzmann, H. J. (1982): The plasma membrane calcium pump of erythrocytes and other animal cells. In: Membrane Transport of Calcium (Carafoli, E., ed.), pp. 41–108. Academic Press, London.
Schatzmann, H. J. (1983): The red cell calcium pump. Ann. Rev. Physiol. **45**, 303–312.
Schatzmann, H. J. (1985): Calcium extrusion across the plasma membrane by the calcium pump and the Ca^{2+}–Na^{+} exchange system. In: Calcium and Cell Physiology (Marmé, D., ed.), pp. 18–52. Springer, Berlin.
Schatzmann, H. J., Roelofsen, B. (1977): Characteristics of the Ca-pump in human red blood cells. In: Biochemistry of Membrane Transport (Semenza, G., Carafoli, E., eds.), pp. 389–400. Springer, Berlin.
Simons, T. J. B. (1984): Active transport of lead by human blood red cells. FEBS lett. **172**, 250–254.
Smallwood, J. I., Waisman, D. M., Lafreniere, D., Rasmussen, H. (1983): Evidence that the erythrocyte calcium pump catalyzes a $Ca^{2+} : nH^{+}$ exchange. J. Biol. Chem. **258**, 11 092–11 097.
Stieger, J. (1982): Characterisierung und Reconstitution der isolierten Ca^{2+}-Pumpe aus der Erythrocytenmembran. Thesis, University of Bern.
Stieger, J., Schatzmann, H. J. (1981): Metal requirement of the isolated red cell calcium pump ATPase after elimination of calmodulin dependance by trypsin attack. Cell Calcium **2**, 601–616.
Trumble, W. R., Sutko, J. L., Reeves, J. P. (1980): ATP-dependent calcium transport in cardiac sarcolemmal membrane vesicles. Life Sci. **27**, 207–214.
Wuytack, F., de Schutter, G., Casteels, R. (1981): Partial purification of (Ca^{2+} + Mg^{2+})-dependent ATPase from pig smooth muscle and reconstitution of an ATP-dependent Ca^{2+} transporting system. Biochem. J. **198**,265–271.
Wuytack, F., de Schutter, G., Verbist, J., Casteels, R. (1983): Antibodies to the calmodulin binding Ca^{2+} transport ATPase from smooth muscle. FEBS lett. **154**,191–195.

Fortschritte der Zoologie, Band 33 · Lüttgau (Hrsg.): Membrane Control
Gustav Fischer Verlag · Stuttgart · New York · 1986

Na–Ca exchange in cardiac muscle

D. A. Eisner and M. Valdeolmillos

Department of Physiology, University College London, Gower St, London WC1E 6BT, UK

Much work has shown that the Na–Ca exchange is one of the major mechanisms responsible for the control of the intracellular calcium concentration ($[Ca^{2+}]_i$). An enormous amount of work has therefore been devoted to studying this exchange system. However, there are still a large number of unanswered questions. In this paper we will consider some of these points. Rather than trying to cover all aspects of this subject, we will concentrate on three related aspects. (i) The stoichiometry of the exchange: in other words, the number of Na ions which exchange for each Ca ion. (ii) The effects of membrane potential on the exchange and (iii) the electric current which may be generated by the exchange.

The stoichiometry of the exchange

It has long been realised that the stoichiometry of the Na–Ca exchange has great importance for the regulation of $[Ca^{2+}]_i$ (Blaustein and Hodgkin, 1969). This is because the energy required for the Na–Ca exchange to be able to expel a Ca ion from the cell must be provided by the Na ions which enter. Therefore, the more Na ions that enter, the greater the gradient against which Ca can be pumped.

Specifically, the work required to pump one mole of Ca out of the cell ($\Delta\mu_{Ca}$) is given by:

$$\Delta\mu_{Ca} = R.T.\ln\,[Ca^{2+}]_o/[Ca^{2+}]_i - 2.F.E_m$$

Similarly, the work available from each Na^+ entering the cell ($\Delta\mu_{Na}$) is given by:

$$\Delta\mu_{Na} = R.T.\ln\,[Na^+]_o/[Na^+]_i - F.E_m$$

Under resting conditions ($E_m = -90$ mV; $Ca_i = 100$ nM; $Ca_o = 1$ mM., $Na_i = 10$ mM; $Na_o = 145$ mM) one obtains:

$$\Delta\mu_{Ca} = 41\ kJ \cdot mol^{-1} \text{ and } \Delta\mu_{Na} = 15\ kJ \cdot mol^{-1}$$

Therefore, if the exchange is to be responsible for pumping Ca ions out of the cell, then it must exchange at least three Na per Ca^{2+}. Alternatively, if less than three Na exchange per Ca, then something other than the Na–Ca exchange must be pumping Ca out of the cell.

This argument has been appreciated for many years (Blaustein and Hodgkin, 1969). In cardiac muscle, it is possible to make a similar sort of argument, to show that no *more* than three Na ions can exchange per Ca (EISNER and LEDERER, 1985). The evidence for this comes from experiments such as that of Fig. 1. This figure, which is taken from the work of DEITMER and ELLIS (1978 b), shows the effects on $[Na^+]_i$ of inhibiting the Na–K pump with the cardiotonic steroid strophanthidin. This manoeuvre increases $[Na^+]_i$ from 6 mM activity to about 20 mM. Even the subsequent addition of 0.5 mM ouabain does not produce a further increase of $[Na^+]_i$. Deitmer and Ellis concluded that something other then the Na–K pump must be responsible for the regulation of $[Na^+]_i$. They presented much evidence to suggest that, under these conditions, when the Na–K pump is inhibited, $[Na^+]_i$ is kept low by the Na–Ca exchange operating in a mode in which Ca entry fuels net Na extrusion (DEITMER and ELLIS, 1978 a). This hypothesis requires two conditions to be satisfied. First, something must remove the Ca which enters: either it must be sequestered inside the cell or it must be pumped out by a Ca-ATPase. Secondly, there must be enough energy available from the Ca entering to expel Na. Obviously, the more Na ions that exchange per Ca, the harder it is for Ca to expel Na.

SHEU and FOZZARD (1982) measured $[Na^+]_i$ and $[Ca^{2+}]_i$ under such conditions. They found values of $[Na^+]_i$, $[Ca^{2+}]_i$, $[Na]_o$, $[Ca]_o$ of 33 mM, 1.5 μM, 151 mM, 1.8 mM and E_m of –69 mV. This gives a value of 32 kJ · mol^{-1} for $\Delta\mu_{Ca}$ and of 10 kJ · mol^{-1} for $\Delta\mu_{Na}$. Therefore, only if $n \leqslant 3$ can the Na–Ca exchange be responsible for the extrusion of Na. If $n = 4$, then there is not enough energy in the Ca gradient to expel 4 Na ions.

The above has then shown the importance of the value of *n* for the control of Na and Ca. The various methods used to measure this value have been reviewed (EISNER and LEDERER, 1985). The first data on this subject were provided by flux measurements in squid and then in myxicola (BAKER et al., 1969; SJODIN and ABERCROMBIE, 1978). The squid data are consistent with between 2 and 5 Na ions exchanging per Ca, and those from myxicola are in agreement. These isotopic flux studies are difficult to interpret for two reasons. (i) There is no specific inhibitor of Na–Ca exchange; (ii) One must allow for problems of self-exchange (i. e. Ca–Ca exchange). It is worth pointing out that the best evidence for the stoichiometry of the Na–K pump comes not from isotopic fluxes which (GARRAHAN and GLYNN, 1967) require much correction but from measurement of net ionic movements.

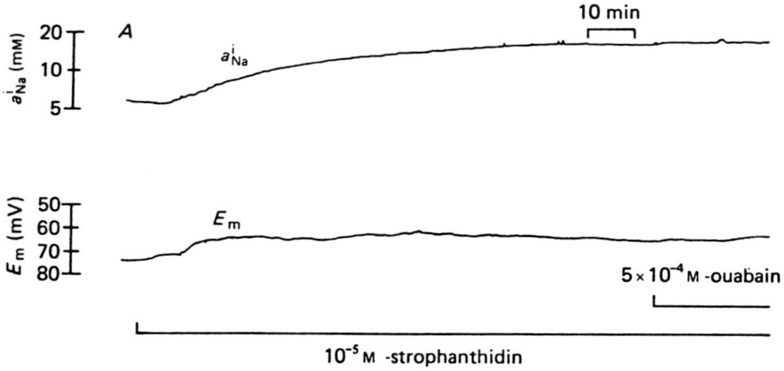

Fig. 1: The effects of inhibition of the Na–K pump on intracellular Na in sheep cardiac Purkinje fibres. In this experiment the intracellular Na activity (a^i_{Na}) was measured with a Na-sensitive microelectrode traces show: top, a^i_{Na}; bottom, membrane potential. Strophanthidin (10 μM) and ouabain (500 μM) were added for the periods shown. Taken from DEITMER and ELLIS (1978 b).

In cardiac muscle, because of the complications of the multicellular preparations generally used, until recently there were little data available on the stoichiometry. However, the introduction of preparations consisting of vesicles made out of cardiac sarcolemma has changed this. The stoichiometry has been measured by comparing fluxes of Na and Ca, and a value of about 3 Na per Ca has been obtained (PITTS, 1979; WAKABAYASHI and GOSHIMA, 1981).

A rather different method to obtain the stoichiometry of Na : Ca exchange was used by REEVES and HALE (1984) and is illustrated in Fig. 2. They incubated sarcolemmal vesicles in media with various Na concentrations in order to vary the transmembrane Na gradient. The Ca concentration was the same on both sides of the vesicles. A membrane potential could be imposed across the vesicle membrane using the valinomycin technique. Depending on the value of Na, the vesicles either gained or lost Na. At a certain level of Na there was no change of Ca content. This balance point reflects the fact that the effects of the Na gradient are being offset by those of membrane potential. It can be seen that, as the membrane potential is changed, then equilibrium is reached at a different level of Na. From this balance one can calculate the stoichiometry. A value of 3 : 1 was obtained.

If the stoichiometry is 3 : 1 then, as discussed above, there is enough energy in the Na gradient to expel Ca ions. One must then consider whether, at physiological $[Ca^{2+}]_i$, the exchange is sufficiently activated to produce a significant Ca efflux. For example, in the squid axon it has been suggested that, at physiological $[Ca^{2+}]_i$, most of the Ca efflux is on

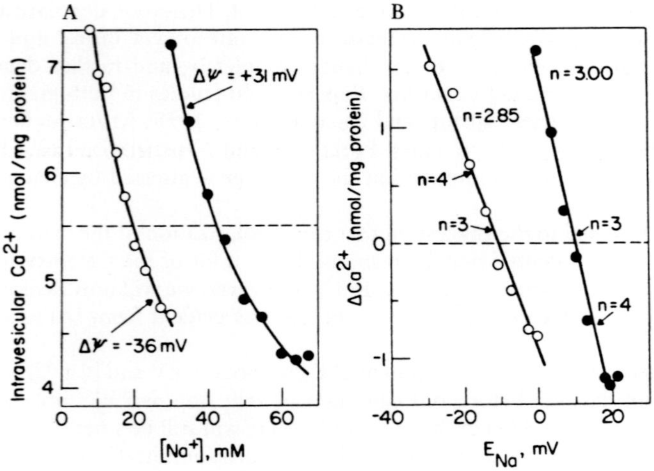

Fig. 2: Determination of the stoichiometry of Na–Ca exchange in cardiac sarcolemmal vesicles. Cardiac sarcolemmal vesicles containing 0.1 mM $^{45}CaCl_2$, 30 mM NaCl, 20 mM KCl and 110 mM LiCl, treated with valinomycin were put into solutions containing 0.1 mM $^{45}CaCl_2$ and the $[Na^+]$ indicated. $[K^+]_o$ was adjusted to give calculated membrane potentials of either −36 mV (○) or +31 mV (●). *A.* Measurement of vesicular Ca content as a function of $[Na^+]_o$. The points show the Ca content of the vesicles 2 sec after adding them to the incubation solution. The dotted line shows the Ca content of vesicles suspended in a medium identical to their contents. *B.* Change of Ca content as a function of E_{Na}. The arrows show the theoretical values of E_{Na} at which there would have been no net Ca flux for the stoichiometry indicated. It can be seen that n = 3 is nearest to the experimental values. Taken from REEVES and HALE (1984).

the Ca-ATPase rather than Na–Ca exchange (DIPOLO and BEAUGE, 1979). In cardiac muscle such a comparison is more difficult since the flux produced by a Ca-ATPase has never been shown in intact cardiac preparations. Comparative measurements are therefore only available in sarcolemmal vesicle preparations. CARAFOLI (1985) gives values for the kinetic parameters of both systems. The Ca-ATPase has a V_{max} 30 to 60 times less than that of the Na–Ca exchange and a K_m 4 to 40 times less. Depending on which of these values one takes will determine whether, at physiological $[Ca^{2+}]_i$, the Na–Ca exchange or the Ca-ATPase is contributing most of the Ca efflux. It should be noted, however, that taking the values which maximize the Ca-ATPase and minimise the Na–Ca exchange, one concludes that the two are equally important. Taking any other values would increase the contribution from the Na–Ca exchange. A further complication of this calculation is produced by the fact that the affinity of the Na–Ca exchange for $[Ca^{2+}]_i$ can be regulated by conditions which are thought to phosphorylate the Na–Ca exchange. Phosphorylation of the exchanger increases the apparent affinity for $[Ca^{2+}]_i$ (CARONI and CARAFOLI, 1983). Therefore the present, tentative conclusion must be that in cardiac muscle one cannot assess the extent to which the Na–Ca exchange contributes to the regulation of resting $[Ca^{2+}]_i$.

The effects of membrane potential on the exchange

In the previous section, we have shown that the Na–Ca exchange exchanges about 3 Na ions per Ca ion. It is therefore likely that the exchange will be sensitive to membrane potential. Specifically, if at rest it is taking 3 Na ions into the cell and expelling 1 Ca, then it is producing a net influx of positive charge into the cell. Therefore, depolarization of the cell (making it more positive) will decrease the net rate of Na influx and Ca efflux. Sufficient depolarization will stop the exchange completely, and further depolarization will reverse it an produce a net Ca influx. Experimental studies in both giant axons and cardiac sarcolemmal vesicles (SJODIN and ABERCROMBIE, 1978; MULLINS and BRINLEY, 1975; BAKER and MCNAUGHTON, 1976; PHILIPSON and NISHIMOTO, 1980; BARTSCHAT and LINDENMAYER, 1980) have shown that the exchange is affected by changes of membrane potential.

These results have led to the suggestion that the depolarization of the membrane potential during the action potential may be responsible for a lot of the Ca entry into the cell (MULLINS, 1979, 1981; BARRY and SMITH, 1982). However, we will now demonstrate that this is not likely to be the case. A similar conclusion is evident from DIFRANCESCO and NOBLE (1984).

At the plateau of the cardiac action potential E_m is about 0 mV and $[Ca^{2+}]_i$ is elevated to 5 μM. On the same basis as before, one can calculate that $\Delta\mu_{Na}$ is 7 kJ · mol^{-1} and $\Delta\mu_{Ca}$ is 14 kJ · mol^{-1}. Therefore, if 3 Na exchange per Ca, there will still be a net Na influx and Ca efflux. The important point is that although the depolarization itself would have reversed the direction of Na–Ca exchange, the release of Ca ions from the s. r. increases $[Ca^{2+}]_i$ sufficiently to allow there to be still a net Ca efflux. In conclusion then it is probable that, even during the action potential plateau, the exchange carries Ca ions out of the cell.

We will now consider more general aspects of the effects of membrane potential on Na–Ca exchange. Most discussions go along the lines of the thermodynamic approach just presented. However, we will now demonstrate that the effects of membrane potential may be much more complicated. Fig. 3 A shows a simple model for Na–Ca exchange. For simplicity a circulating carrier model has been used although, as discussed previously (EISNER and LEDERER, 1985), the general conclusions do not require this assumption. We assume that the carrier can cross the membrane only when it has either one

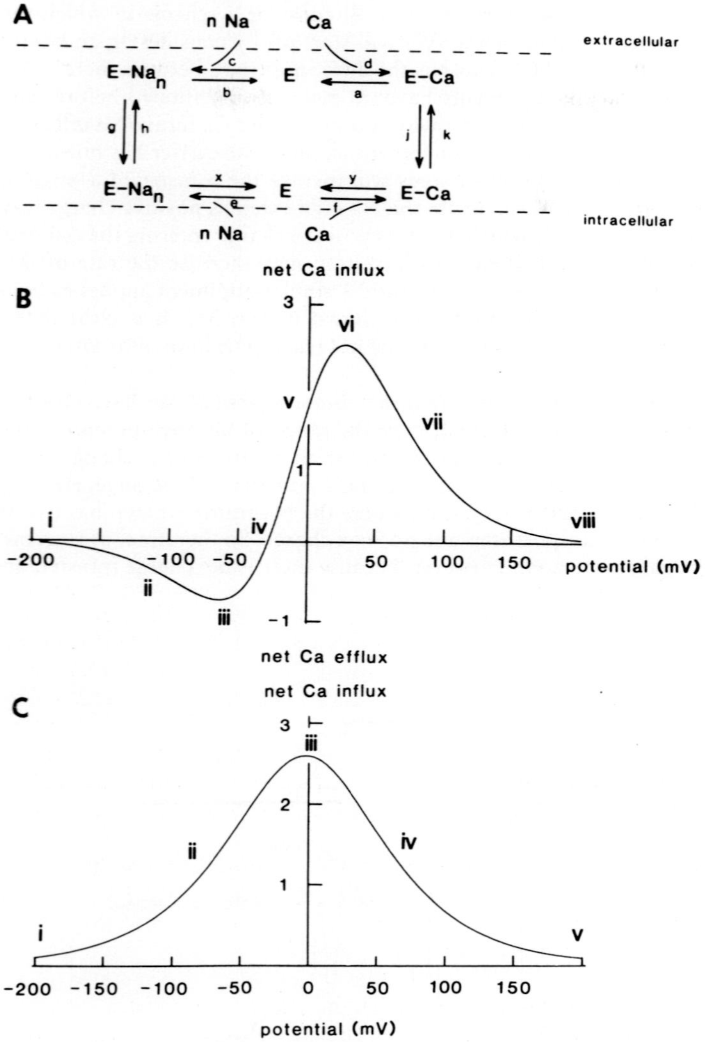

Fig. 3: Theoretical aspects of the effects of membrane potential on Na–Ca exchange. *A*. Model. The Na–Ca exchange is represented as a circulating carrier which can cross the membrane when it has either n Na^+ or 1 Ca^{2+} bound. *B*. Predictions of the model for a 3 Na/1 Ca exchange. *C*. Predictions for a 2 Na/1 Ca exchange. For further details see EISNER and LEDERER (1985) from where this figure is taken.

Ca or n Na ions bound. The effects of membrane potential on this model will depend on various factors. First the number of Na ions exchanging per Ca. Second the charge on the unloaded carrier. The situation is simple if the carrier has a charge of either n or 2. In this case then either the Na or Ca-loaded forms respectively will have no net charge. Therefore, only the Ca or the Na transport step need be sensitive to membrane potential. However, in general this will not be the case and we will consider a scheme in which the unloaded carrier has one net negative charge. We will start off by considering an electroneutral (2 Na/1 Ca) exchange (Fig. 3 C). This has the advantage that, because there is no net charge transfer, thermodynamic arguments have no place. As mentioned before, under cellular conditions such an exchange must always produce a net Ca influx/Na efflux. This will be the case irrespective of the membrane potential. Since the carrier has one negative charge, both the Na and the Ca transport steps will involve the transfer of a single net positive charge. Depolarization will accelerate the Na efflux step as positive charge leaves the cell. However, the Ca entry step which involves positive charge entering the cell will be slowed down. Therefore, although some depolarization may increase the rate of the exchange, further depolarization will decrease the rate. A similar argument applies to hyperpolarization. A graph of the predicted effects is shown in Fig. 3 C. It is clear that at extreme potentials the flux goes to zero because the net reaction is limited by either the Na or the Ca transport step.

The above argument has shown that membrane potential can have effects on an electroneutral Na–Ca exchange. Indeed, over the range of negative potentials the effects of depolarization are those generally predicted for an electrogenic exchange. The next question to consider is what the effects of membrane potential will be on an electrogenic 3 Na/ Ca exchange. We now have a situation where the Na-transport step has two net positive charges and the Ca-transport step one positive charge. So therefore, at extreme potentials the flux will again go to zero. However, because there is net charge transfer, at intermedi-

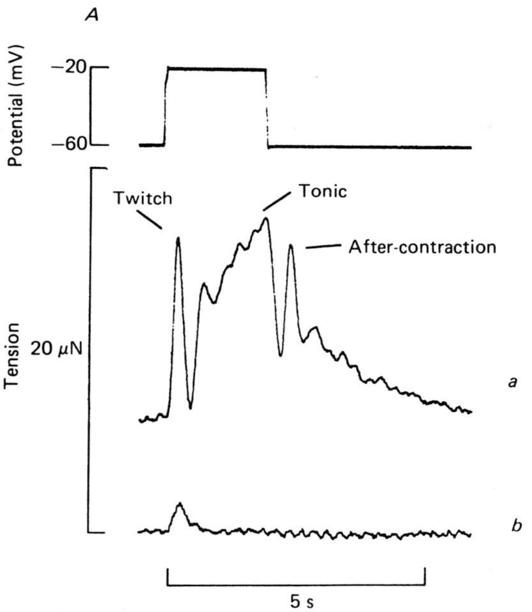

Fig. 4: The effects of elevating $[Na^+]_i$ on tension recorded from a sheep cardiac Purkinje fibre. The top trace shows a depolarizing voltage-clamp pulse. The two lower records show the tension responses produced by this depolarization. *b* is a control record (a^i_{Na} = 9.4 mM) and *a* was obtained after inhibiting the Na–K pump (a^i_{Na} = 23.4 mM). Taken from EISNER et al. (1983)

ate potentials, the exchange will reverse. The effects are summarized in Fig. 3 B. One can see that there is a potential with zero net flux. Here the electrochemical gradients balance. Depolarization from this point produces net Ca influx and Na efflux which is accompanied by net efflux of positive charge and is, therefore, facilitated by depolarization. Depolarization will accelerate the Na efflux step. However, it also slows down the Ca entry step and eventually the flux goes to zero. A similar argument applies to hyperpolarization. A further point is that the decrease of Ca entry with extreme depolarization is the sort of behaviour normally attributed to Ca channels. The Ca influx through a Ca channel increases with moderate depolarization as the number of open channels is increased but eventually declines as the electrochemical driving force decreases. This is similar to that shown in Fig. 3 B.

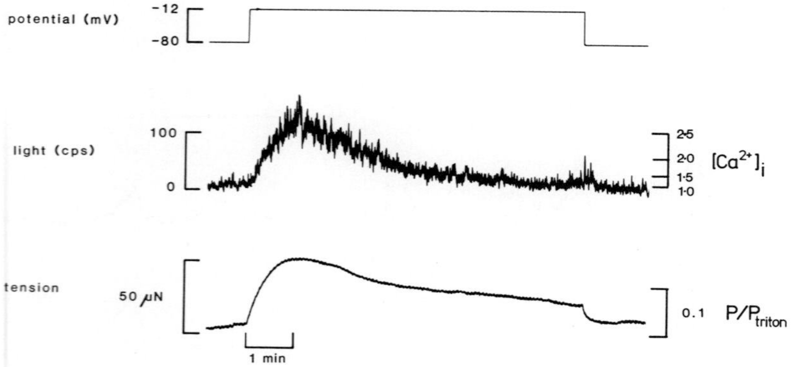

Fig. 5: The effects of prolonged depolarization on $[Ca^{2+}]_i$ and tension in a voltage-clamped sheep cardiac Purkinje fibre. Traces show: top, membrane potential; middle, aequorin light emission (a function of $[Ca^{2+}]_i$); bottom, tension. The preparation had been exposed to strophanthidin (10 μM) for 45 min in order to inhibit the Na–K pump and to ryanodine (1 μM) for 20 min in order to abolish the twitch component of tension. Taken from EISNER and VALDEOLMILLOS (1985 a).

We will now turn to experimental studies of the effects of membrane potential in intact cardiac preparations. Fig. 4 shows the effects of depolarizing a cardiac Purkinje fibre with a voltage-clamp pulse. Record b shows that, under control conditions, depolarization produces a phasic twitch. The other trace shows the effects of depolarization after elevating $[Na^+]_i$ by Na–K pump inhibition. As well as an increase of twitch tension there is a component of tonic tension which is maintained throughout the depolarizing pulse. This component of tonic tension is very sensitive to $[Na^+]_i$ (EISNER et al., 1983). The tonic component of tension differs from the twitch in several important respects. (i) Unlike the twitch, it is not inhibited by blockers of s. r. function (CHAPMAN and TUNSTALL, 1981; EISNER and VALDEOLMILLOS, 1985 b; SUTKO and KENYON, 1983). (ii) Again, unlike the twitch, it is not inhibited by blockers of the Ca channel (CHAPMAN and TUNSTALL, 1981; EISNER et al., 1984). Therefore, the tonic component of tension is Ca-dependent but does not appear to result from the Ca current. This and the great sensitivity to $[Na^+]_i$ have led to the suggestion that this component of tonic tension results from Ca entry into the cell on Na–Ca exchange.

Now tension is a very indirect indicator of $[Ca^{2+}]_i$ and in the experiment shown in Fig. 5 we have measured Ca itself using the photoprotein aequorin. Ryanodine had previously been added in order to inhibit the twitch component of tension. Depolarization produced an increase of both $[Ca^{2+}]_i$ and tension. However, as the depolarization was prolonged, both tension and $[Ca^{2+}]_i$ decayed spontaneously. This spontaneous decay of tension is investigated in more detail in the experiment of Fig. 6. This experiment was performed on a ferret papillary muscle and membrane potential was changed by altering the extracellular potassium concentration. Depolarization produced an increase of both $[Ca^{2+}]_i$ and tension which then spontaneously decayed. The preparation was then repolarized for about 2 min. Subsequent depolarization had essentially no effect on either $[Ca^{2+}]_i$ or tension. However, the preparation was then repolarized for a longer period (10 min) and depolarization now produced a transient increase of both $[Ca^{2+}]_i$ and tension similar to the control.

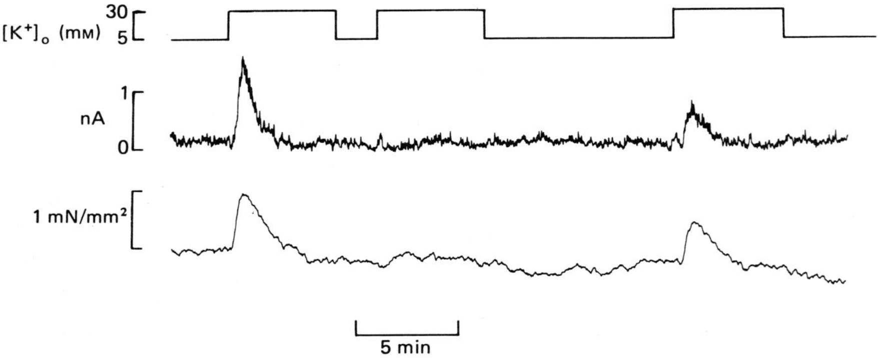

Fig. 6: Kinetics of the decay and recovery of tonic tension and $[Ca^{2+}]_i$ in a ferret papillary muscle. Traces show: top, aequorin light; bottom, tension. The preparation was depolarized by elevating $[K^+]_o$ for the periods shown above the record. Taken from Allen et al. (1984).

The two previous figures have shown that depolarization produces only a transient increase of tension. An explanation for the secondary decay of $[Ca^{2+}]_i$ and tension is provided by the experiment of Fig. 7. $[Na^+]_i$ was measured along with tension. Again prolonged depolarization produced an increase of tension which then slowly decayed. This decay of tension was accompanied by a fall of $[Na^+]_i$. Both the initial rise and subsequent fall of $[Ca^{2+}]_i$ and also the fall of $[Na^+]_i$ can be explained by a Na–Ca exchange. This is illustrated by the model shown in Fig. 8. Fig. 8 A shows the model. We assume that the Na–K pump is inhibited and that, as mentioned before, $[Na^+]_i$ is now regulated by the balance between an inward leak of Na ions and extrusion on a Na–Ca exchange. The resulting net influx of Ca ions through the Na–Ca exchange must be balanced by some process removing Ca ions. At present we cannot distinguish between intracellular sequestration or pumping out of the cell. However, for the purposes of the present model all that matters is that some process removes these Ca ions from the cytoplasm. The results of the model are shown in Fig. 8 B. Depolarization will increase Ca entry on Na–Ca exchange. This will produce an increase of $[Ca^{2+}]_i$ until the Ca extrusion by the other mechanism

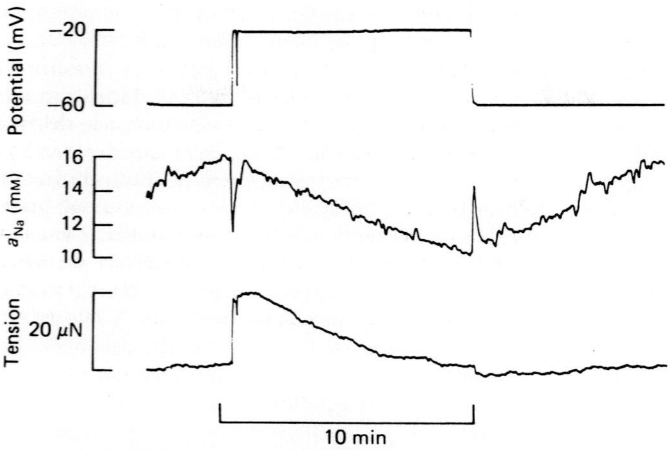

Fig. 7: The effects of membrane potential on intracellular Na activity a^i_{Na} in a voltage-clamped sheep cardiac Purkinje fibre. Traces show: top, membrane potential; middle, a^i_{Na}; bottom, tension. The solution was K-free in order to inhibit the Na–K pump. Taken from EISNER et al. (1982).

increases to balance the influx and, at this point, a temporary steady-state will be reached. However, the depolarization will have increased Na extrusion by the Na–Ca exchange to a level greater than the passive influx of Na and, therefore, $[Na^+]_i$ will decrease. This will decrease Ca influx on Na–Ca exchange and the removal process will decrease $[Ca^{2+}]_i$. Therefore, the model can account for the slow fall of both $[Ca^{2+}]_i$ and $[Na^+]_i$.

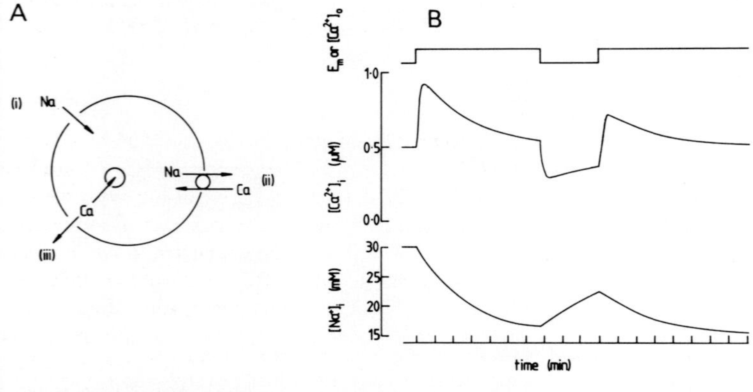

Fig. 8: Simulation of the effects of membrane potential on a^i_{Na} and $[Ca^{2+}]_i$. *A*. Diagram of the model. The Na–K pump is assumed to be completely inhibited. $[Na^+]_i$ is determined by the balance between a passive influx of Na and extrusion on the Na–Ca exchange. The resulting net influx of Ca ions through the Na–Ca exchange is balanced by some other process which removes Ca ions from the cytoplasm. *B*. Predicted effects of depolarization. For further details see EISNER, ALLEN and ORCHARD (1985) from where this figure is taken.

Electrogenic currents produced by Na–Ca exchange

As discussed above, there is evidence that the Na–Ca exchange transports more than 2 Na per cycle and will therefore generate an electric current. Much attention has been devoted to looking for such a current, particularly in cardiac muscle. Most of this work can be summarized by saying that the search for this current is bedevilled by the fact that when the activity of the Na–Ca exchange is altered, then the intracellular concentrations of Ca and Na change. These changes of intracellular concentration will affect membrane currents and it is very difficult to separate these effects of membrane current from those directly due to the Na–Ca exchange. Another problem is, however, produced by the fact that it is uncertain what properties are to be expected from the Na–Ca exchange. In most experiments the effects of elevating $[Ca^{2+}]_i$ have been investigated. It is generally assumed that this will increase Ca efflux and decrease Ca influx on the exchange thus increasing inward current. This is illustrated in Fig. 9 A. which shows the current produced by the model of Fig. 3. The current is zero at the equilibrium position for the Na–Ca exchange and is shifted in the positive direction by an increase of $[Ca^{2+}]_i$. At all other potentials there is less inward/more outward current. However, we must now consider whether this is an appropriate model for the Na–Ca exchange. In particular, it assumes that the effects of $[Ca^{2+}]_i$ can be expressed simply as a product/reactant. There is experimental evidence which suggests that this model is too simple. In particular, DIPOLO (1979) and more recently DIPOLO, ROJAS and BEAUGE (1982) have shown that increasing $[Ca^{2+}]_i$ can increase the $[Na^+]_i$-dependent Ca influx. While there is no obvious explanation for this, it will greatly complicate the effects of changing $[Ca^{2+}]_i$ or membrane potential on the exchange. The result of such an effect is shown in Fig. 9 B. Here an increase of $[Ca^{2+}]_i$ shifts the zero flux potential by the same amount as in Fig. 9 A: this must be the case as the position of this point is determined entirely by thermodynamic considerations and is independent of the mechanism of the exchange. However, in this model, in order to take account of the effects of changing $[Ca^{2+}]_i$, we also assume that increasing $[Ca^{2+}]_i$ increases the flux at all potentials. In other words, an increase of $[Ca^{2+}]_i$ has a catalytic action on the

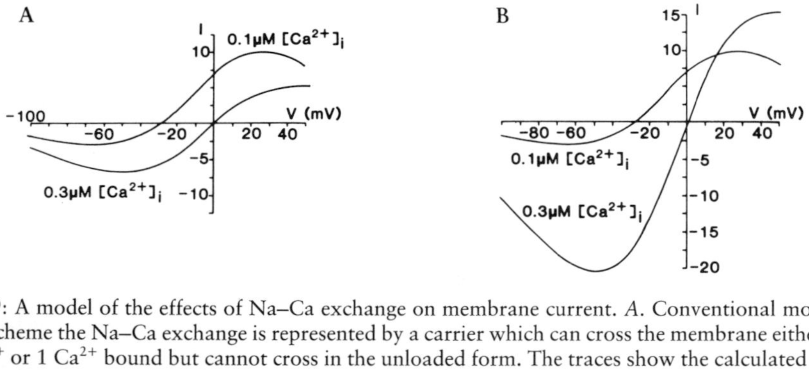

Fig. 9: A model of the effects of Na–Ca exchange on membrane current. *A*. Conventional model. In this scheme the Na–Ca exchange is represented by a carrier which can cross the membrane either with 3 Na^+ or 1 Ca^{2+} bound but cannot cross in the unloaded form. The traces show the calculated effects of membrane potential on the current produced by a 3 Na^+/1 Ca^{2+} Na–Ca exchange. The two curves were calculated at 0.1 and 0.3 μM $[Ca^{2+}]_i$. Positive current denotes net Na efflux/Ca influx while negative current is net Ca efflux/Na influx. *B*. The predictions of a more complicated model. The model is similar to that in A except that, elevating $[Ca^{2+}]_i$ increases the fluxes in both directions. For further details see EISNER and LEDERER, 1985.

exchange. The result of this is then to give two curves which intersect: the direction of the effect of increasing $[Ca^{2+}]_i$ on current depends on the membrane potential. This possibility contrasts strongly with what is normally expected from a Na–Ca exchange. In particular, there will be a potential at which changes of $[Ca^{2+}]_i$ have no effect on membrane current. In an experimental record this might appear to be the reversal potential of a Ca-activated conductance.

We mentioned above some of the problems in looking for the electrogenic Na–Ca exchange current. The problems of intracellular ionic concentration changes have been overcome recently in cardiac muscle by Kimura et al. (1986) who worked on single cells injected with EGTA to control $[Ca^{2+}]_i$. They found a current which appears to be Na–Ca exchange. The only other convincing example of what is probably an electrogenic Na–Ca exchange comes from work on isolated photoreceptors (Yau and Nakatani, 1984). These workers loaded photoreceptors with Ca ions by exposing them in the dark to a high Ca solution. They then illuminated them in order to switch off the light sensitive conductance. The subsequent addition of high external Na produced an inward current which decayed away. It is this current which was attributed to Na–Ca exchange. In support of this contention it was inhibited by La and the amount of charge pumped increased with the degree of Na-loading.

Conclusions

It is now clear that Na–Ca exchange is electrogenic and can generate a significant membrane current. Further work is, however, required to characterize this current and its dependence on intracellular and extracellular ionic concentrations. This will provide a better understanding of the contribution of this current to the normal action potential.

The effects of membrane potential on the exchange also deserve further study, both for the information this may give about the control of $[Ca^{2+}]_i$ and also for the light it may shed on the mechanism of the exchange.

References

Allen, D. G., Eisner, D. A. and Orchard, C. H. (1984): Factors affecting free intracellular calcium concentration in quiescent ferret ventricular muscle. Journal of Physiology **350**, 615–630.

Baker, P. F., Blaustein, M. P., Hodgkin, A. L. and Steinhardt, R. A. (1969): The influence of calcium on sodium efflux in squid axons. Journal of Physiology **200**, 431–458.

Baker, P. F. and McNaughton, P. A. (1976): The effect of membrane potential on the calcium transport systems in squid axon. J. Physiol. **260**, 24 P.

Barry, W. H. and Smith, T. W. (1982): Mechanisms of transmembrane calcium movement in cultured chick embryo ventricular cells. Journal of Physiology **325**, 243–260.

Bartschat, D. K. and Lindenmayer, G. E. (1980): Calcium movements promoted by vesicles in a highly enriched sarcolemma preparation from canine ventricle. Journal of Biological Chemistry **255**, 9626–9634.

Blaustein, M. P. and Hodgkin, A. L. (1969): The effect of cyanide on the efflux of calcium from squid axons. Journal of Physiology **200**, 497–528.

Carafoli, E. (1985): The homeostasis of calcium in heart cells. J. mol. cell. Cardiol. **17**, 203–212.

Caroni, P. and Carafoli, E. (1983): The regulation of the Na^+–Ca^{2+} exchanger of heart sarcolemma. Eur. J. Biochem. **132**, 451–460.

Chapman, R. A. and Tunstall, J. (1981): The tension-depolarization relationship of frog atrial trabeculae as determined by potassium contractures. J. Physiol. **310,** 97–115.
Deitmer, J. W. and Ellis, D. (1978 a): Changes in the intracellular sodium activity of sheep heart Purkinje fibres produced by calcium and other divalent cations. Journal of Physiology **227,** 437–453.
Deitmer, J. W. and Ellis, D. (1978 b): The intracellular sodium activity of cardiac Purkinje fibres during inhibition and re-activation of the Na–K pump. Journal of Physiology **284,**241–259.
DiFrancesco, D. and Noble, D. (1985): A model of cardiac electrical activity incorporating ionic pumps and concentration changes. Phil. Trans. R. Soc. Lond. **B 307,** 353–398.
DiPolo, R. (1979): Calcium influx in internally dialyzed squid gaint axons. J. gen. Physiol. **73,** 91–113.
DiPolo, R. and Beauge, L. A. (1979): Physiological role of ATP-driven calcium pump in squid axons. Nature **278,** 271–273.
DiPolo, R., Rojas, H. and Beauge, L. (1982): Ca entry at rest and during prolonged depolarization in dialyzed squid axons. Cell Calcium **3,** 19–41.
Eisner, D. A., Allen, D. G. and Orchard, C. H. (1985): The regulation of resting calcium concentration in cardiac muscle. In *Control and manipulation of calcium movement* pp. 65–86 (ed. Parrat, J. R.) Raven press: London
Eisner, D. A. and Lederer, W. J. (1985): Na–Ca exchange: stoichiometry and electrogenicity. Am. J. Physiol. **248,** C 189–202.
Eisner, D. A., Lederer, W. J. and Vaughan-Jones, R. D. (1982): A fall of intracellular Na activity accompanies the decay of tonic tension during prolonged depolarization in sheep cardiac muscle. J. Physiol. **328,** 21–22 P.
Eisner, D. A., Lederer, W. J. and Vaughan-Jones, R. D. (1983): The control of tonic tension by membrane potential and intracellular Na activity in the sheep cardiac Purkinje fibre. Journal of Physiology **335,** 723–743.
Eisner, D. A., Lederer, W. J. and Vaughan-Jones, R. D. (1984): The quantitative relationship between twitch tension and intracellular sodium activity in sheep cardiac Purkinje fibres. J. Physiol. **355,**251–266.
Eisner, D. A. and Vadeolmillos, M. (1985 a): Relaxation of tonic tension and $[Ca^{2+}]_i$ in voltage-clamped sheep cardiac Purkinje fibres. J. Physiol. **360,** 61 P.
Eisner, D. A. and Valdeolmillos, M. (1985 b): The mechanism of the increase of tonic tension produced by caffeine in sheep cardiac Purkinje fibres. Journal of Physiology **364,**313–326.
Eisner, D. A. and Valdeolmillos, M. (1986): Measurement of intracellular calcium during the development and spontaneous relaxation of tonic tension in sheep cardiac Purkinje fibres. J. Physiol. **375,** 269–281.
Garrahan, P. and Glynn, I. M. (1967): The stoichiometry of the sodium pump. Journal of Physiology **192,** 217–235.
Kimura, J., Noma, A. and Irisawa, H. (1986): Na-Ca exchange current in mammalian heart cells. Nature, Lond. **319,** 596–597.
Mullins, L. J. (1979): The generation of electric currents in cardiac fibers by Na/Ca exchange. Am. J. Physiol. **236,** C 103–C 110.
Mullins, L. J. (1981): *Ion transport in heart* Raven: New York. 136 pp.
Mullins, L. J. and Brinley, F. J. (1975): Sensitivity of calcium efflux from squid axons to changes in membrane potential. Journal of General Physiology **65,** 135–152.
Philipson, K. D. and Nishimoto, A. Y. (1980): Na^+–Ca^{2+} exchange is affected by membrane potential in cardiac sarcolemmal vesicles. Journal. biol. Chem. **255,** 6880–6882.
Pitts, B. J. R. (1979): Stoichiometry of sodium–calcium exchange in cardiac sarcolemmal vesicles. J. biol. Chem. **254,** 6232–6235.
Reeves, J. P. and Hale, C. C. (1984): The stoichiometry of the cardiac sodium–calcium exchange system. Journal of Biological Chemistry **259,** 7733–7739.
Sheu, S.-S. and Fozzard, H. A. (1982): Transmembrane Na^+ and Ca^{2+} electrochemical gradients in cardiac muscle and their relationship to force development. J. gen. Physiol. **80,** 325–351.
Sjodin, R. A. and Abercrombie, R. F. (1978): The influence of external cations and membrane potential on Ca-activated Na eflux in *Myxicola* giant axons. J. gen. Physiol. **71,** 453–466.

Sutko, J. L. and Kenyon, J. L. (1983): Ryanodine modification of cardiac muscle responses to potassium-free solutions. Evidence for inhibition of sarcoplasmic reticulum calcium release. J. gen. Physiol. **82,** 385–404.
Wakabayashi, S. and Goshima, K. (1981 a): Kinetic studies on sodium-dependent calcium uptake by myocardial cells and neuroblastoma cells in culture. Biochim. Biophys. Acta **642,** 158–172.
Yau, K.-W. and Nakatani, K. (1984): Electrogenic Na–Ca exchange in retinal rod outer segments. Nature London **311,** 661–663.

Subject index